They Came From Babel

S. A. Cranfill

Biblical History of the Americas Series - Volume I

The Write House, Ltd.
Publishers of Educational and Creative Christian Materials
Reno, Nevada

They Came From Babel
Volume I of the Biblical History of the Americas Series

© **1994 by The Write House, Ltd.**
Published by:
The Write House, Ltd.
Grande Suite
108 Roff Way
Reno, Nevada 89501

All rights reserved.
No part of this book may be reproduced in any form or by any electronic or mechanical means including information storage and retrieval systems without permission in writing from the publisher, except for brief quotes used for reference purposes in reviews or research materials, and as provided by USA copyright law.

Address inquiries to:
New Works Distribution Center
P.O. Box 637
Rockwall, TX 75087-0637

Any Scriptures marked NIV are taken from *The Holy Bible: New International Version* used by PC Study Bible software by Biblesoft™

Printed and bound in the United States of America.

First Printing 1994

Biblical History of the Americas Series
ISBN 0-9639202-0-0

They Came From Babel, Vol. I of Series
ISBN 0-9639202-1-9

CONTENTS

Introduction: Whose New World Is This? ... i

Chapter 1
How Do We Examine History Through Biblical Glasses? ... 1

Chapter 2
Ancient American Man: Do We Know His Age, Origin, and IQ? ... 21

Chapter 3
Ancient American Geography: How Did God Create the New World? ... 40

Chapter 4
After the Flood: Restarting Civilization in a New World ... 55

Chapter 5
The Renewal of Rebellion and the Birth of Paganism ... 68

Chapter 6
The First Antichrist: Nimrod and the New World Order ... 81

Chapter 7
The Legacy of Nimrod & Semiramis: The Mystery System ... 93

Chapter 8
Why Astronomy is the Telescope to Find the Ancient World ... 109

Chapter 9
Sifting for Truth Through a Variety of Scholarly Views ... 142

Chapter 10
Ancient Technology for Worldwide Dispersal ... 161

Chapter 11
Ancient World Maps *Before* the Ice Caps ... 196

Chapter 12
Ancient Ocean Vessels and Global Navigation ... 214

Index ... 241

Biblical History of the Americas Series - Volume I

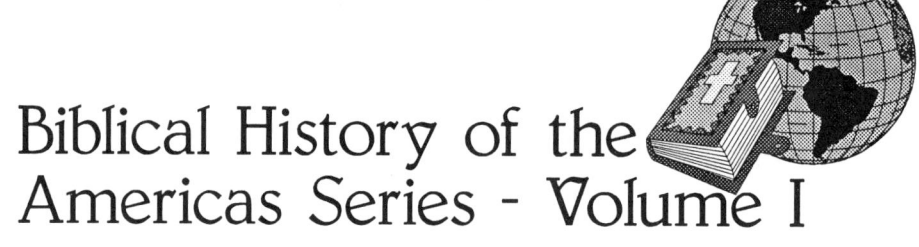

A *unique*, biblical approach to the history of the Americas...

using the Bible, Christian sources, and secular sources to examine the story of the Western Hemisphere in the light of God's Plan of the Ages and the spiritual warfare that has raged since the fall of Lucifer.

Volume I

They Came From Babel is Volume I, introducing you to an ancient world you won't find in standard history books, and to man as he was created by God – intellectually and physically superior, but faced with coming millennia of degeneration under the curse of sin in a fallen world. Volume I establishes the ranging foundation necessary for ...

Volume II is still in progress due to unforeseen circumstances.

Volume II

They Crossed the Oceans is scheduled to appear in **mid-1994** as Volume II, tracing the dispersion of the Egyptians, Phoenicians, Scandinavians, Hebrews, Asians, and Europeans who became the "Indians" of the Americas. Our history on these continents is much longer and much grander than is taught by the traditionalists, and *far* more sophisticated than that taught by the evolutionists.

Coming Volumes...

Future volumes will continue our story through the European contest over the New World, the birth of the United States as The Great Experiment, and our subsequent march into today's New World Order as we approach what seems to be the culmination of God's Plan and the climax of the spiritual warfare that must be resolved by the return of the victorious Lamb.

The **uniqueness of our approach** lies in the fact that:
1) we take a biblical approach
2) we examine a broad spectrum of subjects that, when brought together, cast new light on old facts
3) we demonstrate that evolutionist, traditional, and even occultic sources contain truths that unintentionally support and illuminate the conservative, literal-biblical point of view.

This book is written for

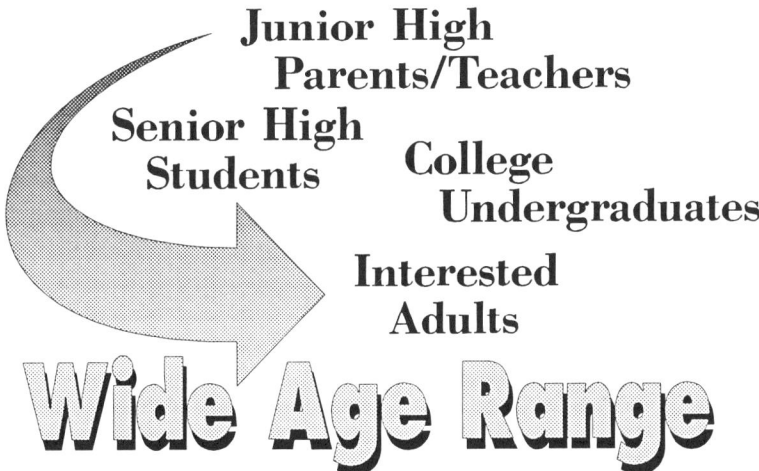

Upper Elementary Parents/Teachers

Junior High Parents/Teachers

Senior High Students

College Undergraduates

Interested Adults

Wide Age Range

General Reading for Adults
who are interested in history and a deeper, biblical perspective of God's Plan

Home Schoolers
in upper grades looking for challenging studies

Home School Parents or Teachers
for their own education and for material which they can retool for their younger students

Christian schools
as a text or as outside reading

Christian Colleges and Universities
as outside reading or research material for undergraduate studies

Church Bible Studies or Sunday Schools
for adults or senior high groups

Biblical Glasses – The Ancient Mystery System – Creationist Science – Biblical Chronology – The Old and New Gods – Archaeoastronomy – Diffusion vs. Autochthony – Worship of the Pre-Flood World – Shem vs. Nimrod – Ancient World Maps – Ancient Global Navigation – History of World Climate – Understanding Secular Scholarly Views – How to Be a Berean in Your Search for Truth

Question

Whose New World Is This?

When the crew of the wave-battered Mayflower finally saw land in November of 1620, the small group of exhausted English voyagers on board had mixed emotions. Their terrible, two-month ordeal by sea was finally over, but they were in the wrong place. From both published charts and some personal experience, the crew readily recognized the shore of Cape Cod, a good distance north and east of the Hudson River valley where the "Pilgrim" Puritans were supposed to settle.

According to their agreement with their British landlords, the Virginia Company, the now-famous Pilgrims had a patent (legal document) for land in a place the British claimed as Virginia and the Dutch claimed as New Netherlands. (The place was present-day New York State.) How different our history would be had they settled there, we will never know.

They tried to sail south to reach the Hudson River but strong winds and dangerous waters frightened them back to Massachusetts where, the next day, the crew managed to round the rocky shoals of Cape Cod's "fist" and find safe harbor within the protection of the Cape's outstretched arm. Later they would realize that God had provided them the calmest winter the

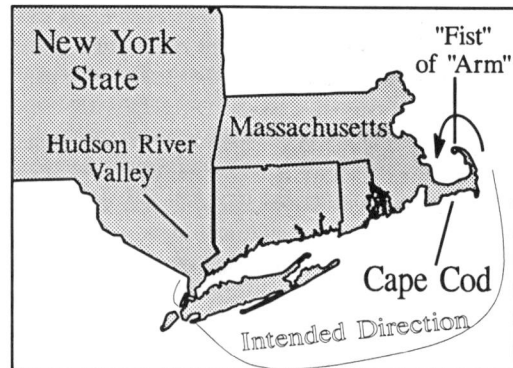

area would see for many a year.

The weary Pilgrims had no reasonable choice before them but to settle as soon as possible in the best place they could find. After three weeks of exploration, a crew member guided the search party across Cape Cod Bay to Plymouth Bay, which the seaman knew from a previous trip. The spot was picked, but they still had a problem. They had no "legal claim" to the land. They were out of the jurisdiction of the Virginia Company's charter. However, they were also out of options, so they proceeded with their settlement and sent news to England in the spring by way of the returning Mayflower that a new patent was needed. Meanwhile, they drew up and signed the Mayflower Compact to constitute civil authority and order "for the general good of the Colony," therefore establishing government by consent of the governed before they ever went ashore to settle in the "New World."

But upon what could the English base any "legal claim" to this land? In 1496, British King Henry VII commissioned Venetian (Italian) navigator John Cabot to find a western trade route to Asia. The following year, on June 24, 1497, Cabot went ashore in northern North America (probably Newfoundland), thrust a British flag in the ground, and claimed "the new isle" for the king. That was that!

Of course, Cabot, who thought he had reached Asia, sailed on the wake of fellow Italian Christopher Columbus who had voyaged to the Bahamas and the Caribbean under the flag of the monarchs (king and queen) of Spain. The Portuguese sailed further to the south and claimed Brazil (South America), in 1500 with the accidental arrival of Pedro Cabral. Ambitious French fishermen are recorded as working the waters of the Grand Banks (off Newfoundland) as early as 1504 but they were not "officially" part owners of New World real estate until

that were already occupied? Europeans of the 15th Century had originally set out to find a sea route to the Middle East and Asia to obtain exotic trade goods and earn large profits. By the time Balboa's exploration of Panama in 1513 succeeded in finding the fabled "other sea," (the Pacific), the Europeans were convinced of what Columbus had begun to suspect in 1498—that they had bumped into another continent which lay between them and Asia. Columbus and others after him believed that this continent, this New World, was unknown to the ancients, a "fourth part of the world," unmentioned in the Bible. (The prevailing European belief was that, after the Great Flood, Noah's three sons, Japheth, Shem, and Ham, populated three continents, Europe, Asia, and Africa.) Now that they had found it, why should these "advanced and cultured" Europeans waste a perfectly good New World on backward and barbaric tribes of "Indians"?

Even Pilgrim leader William Bradford, a godly man, described the natives and the land of New England as wild and savage. He explained that the Pilgrims chose to pursue a land grant in "some of those vast and unpeopled countries of America," because they were "fruitful and fit for habitation, being devoid of all civil inhabitants, where there are only savage and brutish men which range up and down, little otherwise than the wild beasts of the same." [William T. Davis (ed.), *Bradford's History Of Plymouth Plantation, 1606-1646.* New York: Barnes & Noble, Inc., 1959, pp. 46-7]

On the other hand, there was also the acknowledgment that the American inhabitants were indeed human beings, Pope Julius II officially declaring them so in 1512, thus recognizing the natives as fellow descendants of Adam and Eve. Columbus wrote to the Spanish King in 1493 that the "Indians" were not monsters but quite informative. He found the Caribbean Arawaks to be peaceful cloth and pottery makers who were useful as guides because they learned Spanish so quickly. As the natives were not black and thus not from Africa, it was decided that they looked and acted like the barbarous tribes of Asia and so must have originated there.

another hired Italian, Giovanni da Verrazzano, explored present-day New York Bay and the mouth of the Hudson River in 1524 under the flag of French King Francis I. The Dutch finally joined the ranks of European "claimers" by way of an Englishman named Henry Hudson who, as an employee of the Dutch East India Company, explored New York Bay and what came to be known as the Hudson (not Verrazzano) River in 1609. (Verrazzano eventually got a bridge named after him.)

If these were the claimers, who were the claimees? People were already living in all these places, from Newfoundland to the Caribbean to South America. Columbus called these people "Indians" because he thought he had reached the Indies (Asia or India). The Spanish took land from the natives by force. The Dutch bought land from the natives. The French traded, negotiated, lived, and formed alliances with the natives. The English alternately traded, negotiated, and fought with the natives.

In choosing Plymouth, the Pilgrims "just happened" to settle in an area devoid of native claimants due to a terrible pestilence of 1617 (measles? European Black Plague?) which greatly weakened the Massachuset tribe and wiped out all but one member of the Patuxet tribe (Squanto, who had been kidnapped and taken to England). Thus, the Pilgrims were not trespassers on an active tribe's territory and were soon able to form a lifesaving friendship and formal alliance with the Wampanoag tribe.

So, why should all these "good Christian nations" battle over "newly discovered" lands

Certainly, European civilization, even in

1492, did see itself as far in advance of the existing native cultures of America in politics, science, technology, education, arts, and daily life. The Spaniards were able to awe and overpower even the exceptional, highly developed civilizations of the Aztec, Maya, and Inca. [However, in Volume II of this series, we shall see that widespread American legends of "returning white men" (or gods) protected the arriving Spaniards from attack.] Obvious evidence of knowledge, talent, and achievement among the various Indian tribes was apparently overwhelmed by their blatant idolatry and comparative crudity and literary ignorance. Though occasionally fascinated by certain Amerindians, Europeans in general felt quite superior to them and thus justified in claiming and colonizing their "discovery."

This New World offered fresh opportunities to European nations that were involved in an ever-intensifying political, economic, and religious contest. They all wanted new outlets for trade as well as raw materials and raw wealth (gold). Some countries were overcrowded. The Catholics wanted to contain the Protestants and the Protestants wanted to block the Catholics. Some European groups were genuinely interested in taking Christianity to a pagan land while escaping persecution in their own.

However, what the Europeans didn't know as they proceeded with their initial explorations and settlements was that a variety of *ancient, stone, astronomical observatories* already dotted New England, the Midwest, and the Southwest as far as California. They had no idea that ample evidence lay in the Great Lakes region of an industrious, *copper-mining society* that had traded with Scandinavian mariners some 18 or 19 centuries before Christ. They didn't realize that areas like Virginia and Ohio were covered with *ancient furnaces for smelting iron*, and that inscriptions would be discovered from Canada to South America in ancient Irish, Phoenician, Egyptian, Norse, Libyan, Iberian, and even Hebrew. ***The "New" World was an old neighborhood to the ancients!***

So, why didn't the 15th- and 16th-Century, Christian Europeans know all this? Why had so much been forgotten and lost? What had happened to the obviously skilled and knowledgeable societies and navigators of the past? Why did so many of their descendants appear "savage and brutish"? Why were the relatively advanced Aztec, Mayan, and Inca civilizations stymied in their development several hundred years behind the Europeans?

Just whose New World was this, anyway?

Whose New World Is This?

Chapter 1
How Do We Examine History Through Biblical Glasses?

Realizing That All History is Biblical

The Bible says that the Lord God Jehovah has done whatever He pleased in the heavens, in the Earth, and in the seas and all deep places (Ps. 135:6), that the Lord God Almighty is King of all the Earth and reigns over the heathen as well as the righteous. Daniel the prophet states, by way of a "born-again" Nebuchadnezzar, that the same Lord God is the King of the heavens, that all His works are truth, and that He is doing His will among the forces of the heavens and those who dwell on Earth and no one has the power to question Him (Dan. 4:35-37). Daniel also informs us that the God of the heavens changes times and seasons and removes and raises up kings (Dan. 2:21). Hannah, the mother of the prophet Samuel, testifies that the Lord Jehovah both kills and keeps alive, makes poor and makes rich, brings low and lifts up (I Sam. 2:6). The Apostle Paul makes it clear that all authorities are appointed by God (Rom. 13:1), while John the Apostle records that the Lord made all things for His own pleasure (Rev. 4:11).

Of course, anyone truly familiar with the Bible knows that these are just a meager sprinkling of the verses attesting to the sovereignty, authority, and primacy of the One-but-Triune God (Father, Son, and Holy Spirit). There are only two categories of existence: 1) that which is not created, and 2) that which is created. God stands alone in the first category. Everything else falls into the second, all made by the first. So, God made it all, owns it all, and runs it all. And, according to Col. 1:17 and Heb. 1:3, He literally holds it all together, we humans having defined "it" as the sum total of all matter and energy.

What in the world does this have to do with history, especially American history? Everything. The modern world in general would have us all believe that God is an outsider, an observer, at best an occasional intervener, and perhaps merely the product of overactive imaginations. *God says different.*

The logical conclusion to be drawn from the above verses, and indeed, from the entire Bible, is that God created this whole show for a purpose and that He is running the whole show according to His plan. If each sparrow and each hair of our heads is noticed and numbered (Matt. 10:29-30), then each person and each event, no matter how minor or minuscule, is important and part of the vast, spiritual scheme.

If we do not view and analyze the history of creation and mankind within that spiritual scheme, then we misinterpret history and, like the non-Bible-believer, haven't the slightest idea what is really going on.

Writing A Prescription for Biblical Glasses

So, how do we take a biblical approach to the study of American history? The uniqueness – and truthfulness – of our approach will be determined by the *truths, laws, and premises* that we apply to the events of history and from which we draw logical conclusions.

We can reason logically using *inductive reasoning* (specific to general), or *deductive reasoning* (general to specific). For example, an evolutionist observes a river slowly eroding a piece of land. From that specific observation, he inductively concludes that the Grand Canyon was formed by erosion and, because the process is so slow, it must have taken millions of years. Therefore, everything we observe on Earth was formed by the slow, geologic processes we observe today and so the Earth must be millions or even billions of years old. (About 4.5 billion years is the general consensus.) His mistake is that he ignores all the evidence of catastrophic change. He uses good logic to draw a faulty conclusion.

Deductive reasoning begins with a general statement or premise. A *syllogism* consists of a major premise, a minor premise, and a conclusion. For example:

Major premise: God created everything that exists.
Minor premise: Man exists.
Conclusion: Therefore, God created man.

If we begin with truth, logical reasoning leads us to further truth. Let's look at another example:

Major premise: Everything that swims in the sea is a fish.
Minor premise: Whales swim in the sea.
Conclusion: Therefore, a whale is a fish.
(Wrong! A whale is a mammal!)

Here we see that, no matter how logically you reason, if you begin with a faulty premise, your conclusion will be faulty. *In order to pursue truth, we must begin with absolute truth.*

Therefore, the Bible gives us an edge. We know the *basic rules of the game.* In fact, we even know the game plan and the outcome of the game, as well as the Coach (the Father), the Quarterback (the Son), and the Sports Announcer (the Holy Spirit). We who believe the Bible definitely have the edge!

What are our limitations? First, the Bible gives no specifics on the entire Western Hemisphere. The Bible does give us general truths (and some possible references) which can be applied to American history, but nothing specific. Second, like everyone else, we weren't there when it happened, and the longer ago it happened, the more we are removed from the people, the events, and the culture of the times. Third, for specifics on the Americas, we have to rely solely on what others have recorded for us and on any physical evidence that remains. Even current history, for which we are present and accounted, is often difficult to fully interpret because of the *deceitfulness of mankind.* Our sources (other than the Bible) are human, and they may, intentionally or unintentionally, lie, misinterpret, forget, or misrepresent. They may be diabolical, lazy, inept, or misinformed. So, all things considered, we do the best we can, using the Bible first, and then other sources which we think are reasonable with some truth to be gleaned.

Four Basic Approaches to History

Let's examine four basic approaches to the interpretation of history:

I. The biblical approach
II. The humanistic approach
III. The special-interest-group approach
IV. The occult/cultic approach.

The second one is by far the dominant and most popular, embraced by professionals and taught by public schools, universities, and research foundations. Unless you have been particularly sheltered, the humanistic approach is what you are taught in school, what you read in books and newspapers, and what you hear everyday in the media. The third and fourth categories usually bear some relation to the second. The first stands alone and is hated and ridiculed by most of the world.

[**NOTE:** In this series, we have decided to follow the lead of the astronomers and **capitalize Earth, Sun, and Moon** when referring to our own planet and the two heavenly bodies given to us by God to mark time and seasons. We believe that this is also consistent with biblical teaching that Earth is absolutely unique in the Universe, as well as the fact that these are the proper names of these bodies.]

I
The Biblical Approach

The following are basic premises of one who approaches history from a biblical point of view which embraces the literal interpretation and divine inspiration of the Scriptures.

1) Absolute Truth: *The Bible is a Reliable Source*

The Bible is not only a reliable, but an *infallible* (meaning absolutely no mistakes) source of knowledge concerning theology, history, physics, astronomy, health, philosophy, geology, biology or whatever area it happens to address. It is reliable not only in what it has recorded, but also in what it *predicts*. There are many excellent studies on every aspect of the general subject of the Bible's accuracy, most of which are designed for the lay (non-professional or non-scholar) reader. Consider Josh McDowell's two-volume work called *Evidence That Demands A Verdict*, Dr. S.I. McMillen's *None of These Diseases*, Henry Morris's *Genesis Flood, Scientific Creationism*, and *Many Infallible Proofs*, Dr. Carl Baugh's *Dinosaur!* and *Panorama of Creation*, lawyer Frank Morison's *Who Moved the Stone?*, Dr. Charles Ryrie's *Basic Theology*, and Dr. W.H. Griffith Thomas's *How We Got Our Bible*, just to name a few.

2) Divine Plan: *History is the Plan of a Sovereign Creator*

Sixteenth-Century playwright William Shakespeare began a famous speech in *As You Like It* with the words, "All the world's a stage, And all the men and women merely players." (AYLI, II.vii.139) Actually, this is true, except that the playwright is God. So, we must remember that **American history is part of an orderly plan** of known, earthly history that proceeds from Adam and Eve to the Second Coming of Christ and the Millennium, or to the latter-day glory and kingdom, depending on your prophetical viewpoint. See the accompanying box for a brief explanation of millennial and *a*millennial points of view.

The existence of a plan indicates that the

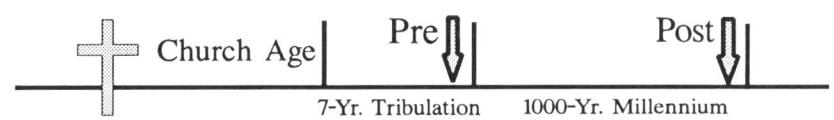

End-Times Terminology

Millennium: a period of 1,000 years described in Rev. 20:1-7 in which *Jesus Christ* will reign on Earth (assisted by the *bodily* redeemed Church) over the spiritually redeemed, remaining portion of Israel and certain gentile nations or individuals (Matt. 25:31-34) while Satan is bound. Certain scholars such as Dr. Carl Baugh believe that the pre-Flood canopy system will be restored, especially considering verses like Isa. 65:18-25, 11:6-10, 2:1-4, Acts 3:21. The Millennium is the earthly Messianic Kingdom promised to Abraham (Gen. 12:1-4, 14:15-16, 15:7-21, 17:1-19) and to David (II Sam. 7:8-16, 23:5; Ps. 89).

Premillennialist: one who believes that the Second Coming (Second Advent) of Christ occurs *before* the Millennium.

Postmillennialist: one who believes that the Second Coming of Christ occurs at the end of, or after, the Millennium which is a period of reign on Earth by the unresurrected Church.

Amillennialist: one who believes that there is no earthly, 1,000-year rule.

Dispensationalist: one who is premillennial, who believes that Christ alone (and not the Church) brings in the Kingdom, that the Kingdom is the earthly, 1,000-year reign of Christ, and that the Kingdom promises made to Israel were literal and will be fulfilled on Earth. The dispensationalist recognizes that the nation of Israel and the Church are two separate entities, and that the Church does not supplant or replace Israel. The Church is *raptured* (resurrected) to heaven (I Thess. 4:13-18, I Cor. 15:51-57) before the 7-year Tribulation. At the end of the Tribulation (Daniel's 70th Week of Dan. 9, Rev. 4-19), Christ comes back to Earth, accompanied by His Church, wins the Battle of Armageddon, and rules on Earth for 1,000 years. After that comes another battle, the resurrection of the unsaved, the Great White Throne judgment, and then the new heavens and new Earth (Rev. 20, 21).

This series recognizes a dispensational outline of history, though it is certainly not necessary to hold a dispensational view to study and benefit from this series. No matter what your "end-times" viewpoint, it would be an excellent exercise to compare the differing beliefs. Dr. Charles Ryrie's *Basic Theology* gives an easy-to-read explanation of all viewpoints, though he is dispensational. Your own church or Christian school should have denominational literature on their specific beliefs.

planner has a purpose or purposes and an end result to accomplish. **What does God want to accomplish through history?** We know that God is reconciling all things in heaven and Earth to Himself through Christ (Col. 1:20, Eph. 1:10). We know (if we are dispensational) that He called out Israel as a special nation to whom He made promises, and we must look to see those promises fulfilled (Micah 7:20). We also know that, at Pentecost (50 days after the resurrection), God revealed the great mystery of the Church, which consists of both Jewish and gentile believers.

The most documented and powerful portion of American history falls into the last 2,000 years (and particularly the last 500 years) during which God has been calling out and preparing His Church to be the Bride of Christ as well as co-rulers with Christ in His coming Kingdom.

What the Church does on Earth and what happens to the Church is of supreme importance because the Apostle Paul tells us that the Church is on Earth to demonstrate God's wisdom to the spiritual beings of the Universe (Eph. 3:10). We *are* on a stage and the whole Universe is watching!

What we must remember is that God's purposes apply directly to all of world history and, thus, to American history.

3) Spiritual Warfare: *History Reflects Satan's Attempt to Foil the Plan*

We must realize that all of earthly history, including American history, is part of the **massive, spiritual battle** that is being played out, according to God's plan, throughout the Universe. It so happens that we here on Earth, especially Jews and Christians, are leading players on center stage. The great battle is between God the Creator and Lucifer (Satan), the created spiritual being, and includes all of the other created spiritual and human beings who choose one side or the other.

The **major theme of earthly history** from Adam and Eve to the stable in Bethlehem is God's creation and preservation of the line which will produce the promised Savior (Gen. 3:15), and Satan's continuous attempts to destroy the line and prevent the birth of the Child. Once the Child is born, Satan tries to discredit and then to destroy Christ, but the cross of Calvary is revealed as the place of Jesus Christ's victory over sin, death, and Satan. If the "princes of this age," meaning Satan and the fallen angels, had known the meaning of the cross and Christ's resurrection, they would *not* have crucified Christ (I Cor. 2:7-8). After the cross, Satan turns to the destruction of Israel, the destruction of the Church, and the prevention of Christ's return to Earth as King, and those are Satan's goals from Pentecost to his final judgment when he is thrown by God into the Lake of Fire.

4) Catastrophism: *The Universe Operates Under Certain Laws and Processes but Its History is Punctuated with Eras, Catastrophes, and Miracles*

We humans have discovered that God instituted certain physical laws and processes that govern His physical creation, such as the law of gravity and the laws of motion. Uniform laws and their resulting processes are those that have always been in effect and which remain in effect today, at least as far as we know.

However, things on Earth have not always been as they are today. A number of drastic changes and disruptions have occurred in the natural processes of the heavens and the Earth due to catastrophic judgments, their aftereffects, and certain miracles. Some processes have changed, some have been disrupted, and some new laws have been introduced.

Eras

When God laid out His plan for the ages, He *defined certain eras with vastly differing physical characteristics,* which means that we humans cannot determine the age of fossils, rocks, artifacts, or the Earth based on physical processes we observe today.

ERA 1: ORIGINAL CREATION We believe that there is enough evidence to argue that the "heavens and the Earth" were originally home to vast angelic realms and that Earth, at the center of the Universe, was the privileged domain of the highest of all angels, Lucifer, the "day star," the anointed cherub that covers. (Ez. 28, Isa. 14)

Gen. 1:1 indicates the original creation of the heavens and the Earth. We know from Heb. 12:22 and Rev. 5:11 that God created an *innumerable company of spirit beings* who shouted for joy when God laid the foundations of the Earth (Job 38:4-7).

We know from Eph. 3:10, 6:12, Col. 1:16-

17, Ps. 89:5-7, Jude 9, Rev. 12:7, and Dan. 10:10-20 (and other verses) that the spirit beings we call **angels** were created in a **hierarchy of power and responsibilities**. Thrones and dominions, princes and chief princes, imply powerful beings that rule kingdoms of other beings. Thrones, kingdoms, and armies require a place to rule and duties to be carried out. Where do these kingdoms exist and where are these thrones located? Did the Universe -- the original "heavens" -- provide locations for these angelic realms? [Every reference to "heaven" or "heavens" in Genesis, Ezekiel, and Isaiah is the *plural*, all-inclusive, unspecific Hebrew word *shamayim*. New Testament writers use the Greek word *ouranos* in the same way, to refer to the sky in which the birds fly, the space in which the planets and stars move, and the place in which God's throne sits in a heavenly temple.]

The **angels** are sometimes called **stars** or connected with stars, as in Lucifer, the "day star," or Jud. 5:20, Job 38:7, Isa. 14:13, Rev. 1:20, and especially Rev. 12:4. The Bible also refers to *them that dwell in heaven.* (Rev. 12:12, 13:6) The archangel Michael and his angels fight a war in heaven against Satan and his angels. The latter are defeated and thrown out of heaven and to the Earth. These references seem to connect the angels with the "heavens" (Universe) that contain the stars and planets, including Earth.

Or, is the *"***third heaven***"* Paul briefly mentions in II Cor. 12:2, as some explain, a "spiritual abode" of angelic kingdoms as well as God's throne, with the "first heaven" being Earth's atmosphere and the "second heaven" being the physical Universe? Or is the third heaven the abode only of God's throne and temple, that which we see portrayed in Job, Isaiah, Ezekiel, and Revelation? (See Rev. 14:17, 15:5, 16:17)

Is there such thing as "spiritual space" as opposed to "physical space"? Apparently there is "spiritual matter" and "physical matter," because there are **spiritual bodies and physical bodies** (I Cor. 15). Angels are **spirit** beings but they are creatures and so have bodies which allow them only to be one place at one time. The Bible does indicate that spiritual bodies are capable of certain transformations (Jesus changed His appearance often during His 40 days of post-resurrection ministry). Jesus could materialize in a room and yet eat food like a man. The disciples watched as He ascended into heaven in His spiritual body. Angels, in their spiritual bodies, travel through the Universe from God's throne to Earth and, though they must be able to attain speeds beyond our comprehension, their journeys take time. (Dan. 10) Adam possessed a perfect, uncursed **physical** body which was apparently capable of unending existence, but did not have the above-stated powers of spirit beings. We just do not know what is involved in "glorification."

In Isa. 14:13, Satan (Lucifer) stated that he would *ascend* to heaven (from the Earth?), to the mountain of congregation (where the angels congregated before God?) in the "sides of the north." God condescends to the limitations of His creatures, giving them a location at which they may appear before Him, as the angels do in Job 1 and the souls of unbelieving men do in Rev. 20:11-15. At the same time, God is truly spirit, with no bodily limitations, and says that He fills heaven and Earth, and that heaven is His throne and Earth His footstool. (Jer. 23:24, Isa. 66:1, Mt. 5:35, Acts 7:49) Once again, the Bible is not specific as to what all "heaven" entails.

We know that angels are **created beings** which means they have a **beginning**. They are "immortal" in the sense that they have **no end**, but this only at the grace and pleasure of God. Thus, like us, they are creatures of TIME. *Only God is eternal*, meaning that He has **no beginning and no end**, and that not by anyone else's pleasure but by His very essence and nature. (Charnock, Existence, I, 279-280, 291) *Time must have begun at the moment of God's first creative act, and it must continue forever* because creatures can never be "ever present" with no past or future and without succession (one event after another) as is only God. (Charnock, Existence, I, 287-8)

Lucifer (Satan) was created as the "high priest" of all the created, spiritual beings in the Universe. He is called "the anointed cherub that covereth." (Ezek. 28:14, KJV) Lucifer had *sanctuaries* and was in the presence of God. According to Dr. Donald Grey Barnhouse, "he received the worship of the Universe beneath him and offered it to the Creator above him," (Barnhouse, Invisible, 28) much as a trusted servant receives messages and gifts and passes them on to the king. Ezekiel 28 also indicates that, as he was in charge of all worship, Lucifer was also in charge of all music.

It seems that the strongest evidence for linking angelic realms with the physical Universe is Satan's (Lucifer's) connection with the Earth both before and after his sin and fall. **Lucifer** apparently had his own special dominion and it seems to have been **Earth**. Isn't it intriguing that, in the sweeping statement of creation in Gen. 1:1, *Earth is the only body individually identified?* God says that Lucifer, the highest of all created beings, dwelled in **Eden, the garden of God**. "The Eden pictured by Ezekiel is not the Eden in which Adam walked," explains Barnhouse, "for that Eden was described as a garden of trees and vegetable growth. This Eden in Ezekiel is a place of rare mineral beauty." (Barnhouse, Invisible, 25) Dr. Barnhouse compares the original Eden of Ezek. 28 with the New Jerusalem of Rev. 21, stating that the "jeweled city of the past is to be replaced by the jeweled city of the future." (Barnhouse, Invisible, 25)

God also states (Ezek. 28) that Lucifer walked up and down in the midst of the stones of fire. Was that on Earth or before God's heavenly throne? The same sentence reveals that God set Satan upon **the holy mountain of God**. The Bible makes it very clear that God's holy mountain is Mount Zion, meaning **Jerusalem**. Kingdom references in Isa. 11:9, 56:7, 57:13, and 65:11,25 connect God's holy mountain with Christ's rule in the Millennium while Isa. 27:13, II Pet. 1:18, Isa. 66:20, and Joel 2:1, 3:17 all specifically identify God's holy mountain with Zion and Jerusalem. It is most intriguing that, as revealed in Gen. 2:8, "God planted a garden eastward in Eden" and put Adam in it. *Eden was already a place, before Adam was created!* And, east of what? (His holy mountain?) Jerusalem was certainly not there at that time, though the mysterious "type of Christ" and the Earth's first priest, Melchizedek, appeared in "Salem" to bless Abraham in Gen. 14:18.

We know from Isa. 14:9-17 and Ezek. 28:11-19 that **Lucifer sinned and became Satan**. From Rev. 12:4, we learn that he convinced one-third of the spirit beings to follow him in rebellion against God. God said that He would throw Satan out of heaven to the Earth to be humiliated before the kings of the Earth. In Matt. 4, Satan offers Christ the kingdoms of the world as if they were his to offer, while in John 12:31, 14:30, and 16:11, Christ calls Satan the "prince of this world." The Apostle Paul names Satan as the "god of this world," (II Cor. 4:4) the "prince of the power of the air," (Eph. 2:2) and "the ruler of darkness of this world." (Eph. 6:12) All of these are references to Earth. *Why would Satan be made the prince of this world after he sinned unless he was the prince of this world before he sinned?*

We are told in Isa. 45:18, Ps. 18:30, 147:4, 148:3, Job 26:13 and Job 38 that the *original* creation of the heavens and Earth was a wonderful, good, and perfect result. The angels were present and shouted for joy when Earth was created. (Job 38:7) However, **Lucifer's** (Satan's) **sin** and the resulting angelic rebellion (one-third of the angelic beings, Rev. 12:4) **brought judgment upon Earth and, eventually, the Universe**. In Gen. 1:2, because *Satan defiled his sanctuaries*, we find an Earth without form and void, dark and covered with water, not with precious stones. God must have changed or destroyed the former Garden of God in Eden.

What effects this **initial era of Earth's existence** has on our present-day scientific findings, we cannot say. We can be sure, though, that *Earth and the Universe were drastically different during this time.* The foundation and development of all these angelic activities, hierarchies, and relationships required locations and time. How much time passed before the focus of events shifted to man, we do not know.

ERA 2: PERFECT MAN IN EDEN A new **Earth** was formed and inhabited by a *new, unique, spirit/soul/physical creature* called **man**. A new garden was planted in Eden. The Earth was covered with a **canopy** and a special atmosphere to protect the newly created **physical creatures** whose bodies, though immune from deterioration and capable of never-ending existence, were **unfit for exposure to the Universe**. The spiritual bodies of Lucifer and the angelic beings were perfectly at home anywhere in the Universe and not bound by certain physical laws and so, had never needed a protective atmosphere.

It is interesting that in Gen. 1 and 2, the Hebrew word *bara* is only used in **Gen. 1:1** and for the **creation of animals and man**. It means creation in the absolute sense and is used only with God as its subject. All other acts of "creation" described in Gen. 1 & 2, including light and the stars, etc., employ the word *asah* which means to form (or reform), fashion, or make in the broadest sense of accomplishment. The word used for creating **woman** is *banaw* which is closer to *bara* and means literally to build. It is not used anywhere else in Genesis. (See Strong's Concordance)

Man is unique in creation, different from the spirit beings. Any **UFOs** that are real are merely **manifestations of spirit beings**, most likely evil spirit beings, and beliefs in other humans or physical, human-type creatures on other planets result solely from **evolutionary beliefs**. Jesus Christ is certainly not going from world to world, dying over and over again for various groups of humans, humanoids, or some evolved product of a self-organizing and self-creating Universe. The thought that, just because the Universe is so massive, this scenario must be going on elsewhere is totally erroneous and unbiblical. (See also Levitt and Weldon, *UFOs: What on Earth is Happening?*, Harvest Press)

Thus, we have a **"gap"** between Gen. 1:1 and 1:2. What is *terribly regrettable* is that Christians anxious to *accommodate new evolutionary theories and faulty "scientific discoveries"* grasped this basic truth and destroyed it with their own "Gap Theory," saying that there were plants, animals and even some sort of men before Gen. 1:2, and that the fossils, the dinosaurs, and the long geologic ages are explained by this gap. Even Dr. Barnhouse, a theological and intellectual giant, gave lip service to such ideas. Because of this, fine scientists like Dr. Henry Morris and even Dr. Carl Baugh and others **totally reject any "Gap Theories"** and begin with the entire Universe at Gen. 1:1 and 1:2, giving no time for the establishment of the incredibly huge, complex, and powerful spirit world, and no time for Lucifer (Satan) to lead worship before his sin, battle, fall, and resulting temptation of man in the new Eden. (Barnhouse, Invisible; Ryrie, Basic Theology, chapters on angels and Satan)

Sin and death were not present in the reformed Earth and its new Garden of Eden. The **Second Law of Thermodynamics**, a law of gradual disintegration or degradation, did not exist or was not in effect. The Earth was surrounded by the new **crystalline water canopy** which created a greenhouse on Earth and kept harmful radiation from affecting the new physical creatures. Weather was quite different from today because it **never rained**. The climate was **subtropical from pole to pole**, atmospheric pressure was approximately twice as high with a higher oxygen ratio, and sunlight was diffused by the canopy such that it was **never totally dark**. Man and animal were **vegetarian**. Indeed, **man and animal communicated**, as indicated by Eve's conversation with the serpent and Adam's relationship with the animals. It was paradise indeed! (Gen. 1-3; See Chapter 3 for documented details on pre-Flood world)

CHANGING ERAS OF GOD'S PLAN
which destroy the assumptions of humanist uniformitarians

Era 1: Original Creation

Era 2: Perfect Man in Eden

Era 3: Fallen Pre-Flood World

Era 4: Post-Flood World

Era 5: After Babel

Era 6: The Tribulation

Era 7: The Millennium

Era 8: New Heavens & Earth

ERA 3: FALLEN PRE-FLOOD WORLD
Then Adam sinned. We do not know if the judgment of the entire creation (Universe, other than the unfallen angels) occurred at Satan's sin or at Adam's sin. We do know that, with man's disobedience, the judgment spoken of by Paul in Rom. 8:19-22 now applied to man, to animal, and to Earth as well as to Satan, his angels, and the physical Universe.

This **curse** brought the Second Law of Thermodynamics into force, a law that has a degenerating effect on energy and physical order. Everyone and everything would now inescapably run down, wear out, rust, decay, and fall apart. Childbirth would now involve pain, and work would bring frustration as well as fruit. Paradise now had thorns and thistles. Animals had to be slain to **atone for sin**, a newly introduced spiritual law.

Man would still live some 900 years but **physical death** was his inevitable end. Adam died spiritually in the day (24-hour day) that he sinned, and he died physically within the first "day" (1,000 years, II Pet. 3:8) of God's plan for man. (Gen. 2, 3; See Chap. 2)

This introduction of decay and death where there was none before certainly prevents any *"scientific dating"* by radioactive decay methods beyond a few thousand years. We shall soon see that other catastrophic events further restrict and skew any radiometric dating results based on observations of current atomic decay rates.

Astronomers and astrophysicists tells us that our Universe is full of exploding stars, novas, dying suns, asteroid debris, and even "black holes." (See Chap. 8) Through modern technology, we have seen pictures of inhospitable planets and moons covered with massive volcanoes, huge craters, giant crevices, and hot, poisonous gases. Space probes have measured amazing extremes of heat and cold, ice and desert, but nothing approaching the delicate, intricate, life-preserving balance of elements we have on Earth. These are the *"dastardly results" of judgment* explains Dr. Emil Gaverluk, Christian writer and science lecturer. "The **stars** may have been beautiful worlds but now they are nothing but **gaseous giants**, raw energy burning brightly in the blackness of space." (Gaverluk, Rapture, 164) Just as both Dr. Gaverluk and Dr. Barnhouse write, **an invisible spiritual war rages!** The features of our own Moon, Venus, Mars, Mercury and the other planets certainly scream "Judgment!" and not perfect creation.

We Christians see a cursed Universe under judgment and subjected to the throes of angelic war. Humanist scientists see a Universe that is developing and evolving, forming and reforming, the ongoing results of natural processes. ***This should caution us in our acceptance of the teachings of modern science concerning our Universe!*** (See Chap. 8)

ERA 4: POST-FLOOD WORLD Then God judged the entire world with what we call the **Flood**. The crust of the Earth erupted with fountains of water and molten rock. The **canopy was broken up** and fell to Earth for 40 days and nights. Man's world was now bathed in cosmic radiation and man's **life span began to decrease**. *This particular effect of the Flood guarantees that radiometric dating based on current rates of decay is totally unreliable for dates older than a couple of thousand years before Christ.*

The global greenhouse effect of the canopy is witnessed to by the huge **mammoths** and other animals which have been found within the Arctic circle, buried and frozen with *grass and buttercups still in their mouths and stomachs*, so well preserved in the tundra that *modern men have fed the mammoths' flesh to their sled dogs!* The face of the Earth and its weather patterns changed drastically. Even though preserved by Noah on the Ark, baby dinosaurs could not grow to their former gargantuan size in the new environment and so eventually died out or developed into much smaller representatives of their family tree. Both man and animal were now **carnivorous** and the **fear of man** came upon every animal. (Gen. 7-9; see Chapters 3 & 4 for documented details on the Flood and post-Flood world)

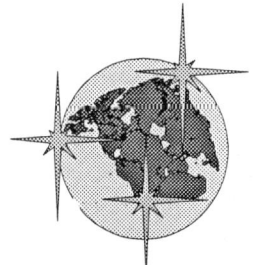

Original Creation

**Man in Eden
Fallen Pre-Flood**

Post-Flood

After Babel

ERA 5: AFTER BABEL A most significant change in Earth's geography came about as an effect of the Tower of Babel judgment. The land mass that was ripped apart by the power of the Flood separated into continents (see Chap. 3) and the world was divided by God into nations and mankind was scattered, against his collective will, across the face of the Earth. We do not know if this separation was somewhat gradual or catastrophically quick, only that the Earth was divided (canaled by water) in the days of Peleg. Actually, portions of the land mass may very well have sunk, literally canaling the land into continents. How much volcanic and mountain-building activity occurred at this point, we do not know, though most creationists believe that aftereffects of the Flood continued for quite some time.

ERA 6: THE TRIBULATION The Bible prophesies a **future era of only seven years** that is generally known as the **Tribulation** during the last part of which the Earth will be subject to a series of amazing miracles and judgments wrought by God (Isa. 24; Rev. 4-19).

ERA 7: THE MILLENNIUM We also know from the Bible that in another future era, the **Millennium** or the **Kingdom Age**, man's life span will again be long, animals and man will again be vegetarians, and man and animal will live in peace enforced by the presence of the ruling Christ. (Isa. 11 & 65, Rev. 20) These passages seem to indicate that God will *restore the Earth to the physical characteristics that prevailed before the Flood.*

> The illustrations below are intended to SHOW CHANGE. We can only guess the shape of the original land mass and we have no idea what it will look like in the Millennium or New Earth. *(See pgs. 40, 42, 80)*

ERA 8: NEW HEAVENS & EARTH The **final era** revealed to us in the Bible is called the new heavens and the new Earth (Rev. 21), which will come into being after the Millennium. The apostle Peter explains that the heavens will pass away with a great noise, that the elements will melt with intense heat, literally "dissolving" the heavens and the Earth. Exactly what laws and processes will be in effect then, we don't know. (II Pet. 3:10-13)

It is actually quite amusing that Peter predicted the **"scoffers" of the "last days,"** who would question the return of Jesus Christ and who would say (as does every good **evolutionist**), "For since the fathers fell asleep, *all things continue as they were from the beginning of the creation.*" These people, says Peter, are obviously and willfully ignorant, because God tells us that the heavens were of old, and the Flood destroyed the **"world that then was,"** leaving us with the **"heavens and Earth which are now,"** which are preserved by God (man cannot destroy them) for the future fiery judgment mentioned above. **(II Pet. 3:3-8)**

This gives us a **minimum of eight eras** of earthly history which exhibit different physical characteristics and processes. *And that means that we cannot make assumptions about the past based on physical processes we observe today!*

Catastrophes

Catastrophic judgments change, disrupt, or affect the Earth's physical processes. As we have already seen, the curses that followed Satan's sin and man's sin, as well as the Flood, were **catastrophes that brought about drastic changes**. The aftereffects of the Flood included continued volcanic activity and all manner of geologic instability. The judgment at the **Tower of Babel** led to the separation or **"canaling with water"** of the original land mass into continents.

Tribulation

Millennium

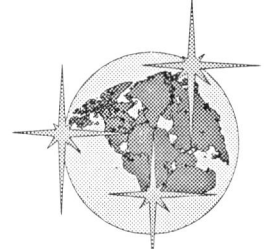
New Heavens & Earth

History Through Biblical Glasses

The fiery judgment of **Sodom and Gomorrah** certainly affected the amount of radioactive carbon in the atmosphere, a further reason that **radiometric dating** used by evolutionists is **unreliable**.

We have already shown that the Earth, our Moon, the planets, indeed the whole Universe, show the scars and results of catastrophic events. Both **Mars** and our **Moon** are severely pocked with craters, while Mars is also ripped by a 3,000-mile-long, four-mile-deep canyon. On Earth, the *very existence of fossils demands one or more catastrophic events for their existence.* Numerous, massive, animal graveyards span the Earth, preserved in frozen tundra, tar pits, and layers of rock. Cover your yard with dead animals and see how many fossils you get. Only a quick-acting catastrophe which covers bodies with mud or rock in such a way that they are preserved from decay will create fossils. *The evidence of catastrophic judgment is everywhere!*

Miracles

The miraculous (divinely supernatural) **judgments on Egypt** may have had more than a local effect, considering the **evidence for general catastrophe** in the region from the Indus Valley to the mid-Mediterranean about the time the Exodus took place. (This will be discussed in later chapters.)

The miracle of **Joshua's famous "Long Day"** brought both the Sun and Moon to a halt in the midst of the sky for "about a whole day." (Joshua 10:13-14). That puts at least one small disruption into astronomical extrapolations into the past. Did the **Sun "stand still"** because God *stopped the Earth's rotation?* (Every good humanist "knows" that the Earth orbits the Sun.) Or did the *Earth flip its poles* (turn upside down) as has been suggested by a number of scientists? That would merely *reverse* the Sun's movement, not bring it to a halt. Either maneuver would certainly wreak havoc on the inhabitants of Earth without divine suspension of most of the laws of physics. *Or did God do exactly as the Bible says and stop both the Sun and Moon because both bodies orbit around a stationary Earth?* According to Dr. Jonathan F. Henry, Dr. Gerardus Bouw, and astrophysicist Fred Hoyle, **either model of the solar system (and Universe) is valid -- heliocentric or geocentric -- and neither one can be proved beyond doubt!** (Henry, Geocentrism, 21, 26; Bouw, Geocentrism lecture, Feb. 12, 1990; see Chap. 8)

Some seven centuries after Joshua, **King Hezekiah** of Judah asked for a sign from God, Who then brought the *Sun backward ten degrees* (40 minutes). This happened in the same year and about the same time that God miraculously destroyed 185,000 Assyrians in Sennacherib's army, about 701 B.C. (II Kings 19:35-37 and 20:1-11). Once again, heavenly motions were divinely disrupted. At some point, possibly at the time of the Exodus, Earth's **360-day year changed to the present 365¼-day year**, meaning that, this time, heavenly motions were altered on an on-going basis. Could this event have involved a close fly-by of Mars or Venus which affected the orbital relationship of the Earth and Sun, as suggested by some scientists? (See Chap. 8) Ancient cosmology worldwide tempts us to consider the heavenly histories of Mars and Venus in particular as these planets were closely tracked, worshipped and feared on every continent.

The point is that *once again, we cannot draw conclusions about the past by observing current physical processes.* Why is this important? *Because reconstructing the past on the basis of the present is the foundation of the so-called "science" embraced by every evolutionist!*

5) Fallen Man: *Man Has a Sin Nature and is Basically Sinful*

The Bible tells us that man commits sins. (Rom. 3:23) We observe this every day. However, it also teaches that **man's very nature is sinful** as a result of Adam's sin (Rom. 5:12, 6:6; Eph. 4:22; Jer. 17:9; Eze. 18:31). That is why we must literally be **"born again"** (John 3), and why a **virgin birth** was necessary for Jesus Christ to avoid the sin nature which is, because of Adam's disobedience, passed down through the human male. It is also why humans talk about their faults and say things like, "I'm only human." The president of the nation's largest independent mortgage bank was quoted in the *Wall Street Journal* on April 5, 1991 (pg. 1, col. 1) as saying, "'Human beings are basically rotten. If you give them an opportunity to screw up, they will.'" (See Ryrie's *Basic Theology* for a study of the human sin nature.)

Even **pagans** have a **concept of sin and atonement**, as exhibited by the Aztecs of Mexico and every culture in the history of Earth. However, **modern humans** prefer to believe that they are **basically good** while *one of the major tenets of evolutionist thought is that man is getting better every day.*

6) Time Line: *History Occurs in Time Which is Absolute and Sequential with a Beginning*

Though it is a bit beyond our ability to comprehend, we conclude from the Bible (and from common sense) that, since *God does not need either space or time for His existence, then space and time must somehow be creations of God.* We have already decided that time must have come into being (begun) at God's first creative act. Thus, time has a beginning and has not always existed on its own. **Only God is infinite**, and so must exist "outside" of time, while all creatures and created things must exist within time.

Time is also absolute. This means that **events are real and not imagined** and take place at specific, unique, unrepeatable points of time that occur in a continuous, sequential manner, one after another. That is why we speak of "time lines." Every created being or thing, whether spiritual or physical, can only be at one place at one time. Only God is omnipresent and "fills heaven and Earth."

Harold S. Slusher, a Ph.D. in physics at the University of Texas - El Paso, explains that, according to classical physics, time is absolute, one-dimensional, irreversible, and independent of any material thing or body. It flows at a constant rate and is the same everywhere and under all conditions. (Barnes, Space, 7-8)

God commanded man to measure time by the Sun, Moon, and stars (Gen. 1:14), not by atomic clocks based on the revolutions of electrons around a nucleus. It is interesting that, while on an autumn, 1989 lecture trip, Rev. Walter Lang noticed an item in the Denver papers relating the discovery that star time is far more accurate than atomic time. (Lang, Astronomy, 70)

We may say that **"history repeats itself,"** but we only mean that people tend to make the same mistakes and that human nature since the Fall has not changed. We do not mean that there are *predetermined cycles of time that repeat themselves*. **Hinduism is cyclical** in thought. In fact, Hindus believe that death is merely the transmigration of the soul to another bodily form (man or animal) to begin another cycle of life. This **reincarnation** is an "endless" cycle and the "heaven" of the Hindu is to break the cycle. The *modern concept of evolution actually comes from Hinduism.*

The Christian, however, believes that physical death occurs once for each person (unless they are instantly physically transformed in the Rapture or like Enoch or Elijah), that each body is eventually **resurrected**, and that each soul (and its resurrected body) goes either to eternal life with God or eternal punishment. The Christian believes that **matter (the Creation) is quite real** and is not a figment of our imagination or perception, that everything we see and feel is truly there, and that there is only *one version of reality and truth.*

The belief in recurring ages of specific lengths is common in pagan thought, including that of the Maya and Aztec cultures of Mesoamerica. It is also found in New Age writings. One of the major foundations for this is the ancients' obsession with the **precession of the equinoxes** which marks ages of roughly 2,000 years defined by the progressive occurrence of the vernal equinox within the "jurisdiction" of a particular sign of the Zodiac. A complete cycle is estimated to take about 26,000 years, at which point time would "start over again." (see Chap. 8)

7) Devolution: *Created Perfect, the Universe and Man Are Now Subject to Devolution*

The **First Law of Thermodynamics** is a law of *conservation*, saying that matter is neither created nor destroyed. The **Second Law of Thermodynamics** is a law of *degeneration*, saying that the Universe is basically going downhill, that in every transfer of heat, less and less energy is capable of "work."

British theoretical physicist Dr. Paul Davies agrees that, according to the Second Law, the Universe grows more disordered every day in a "sort of gradual but inexorable descent into chaos." He points to examples of decay, age, erosion, and depletion. However, he points out that the law applies to the *total system.* "The concentration of order in one region of the Universe is always paid for by increasing disorder somewhere else," he notes. *Entropy* is a mathematical quantity used to measure disorder. The logical conclusions drawn from the Second Law is that the Universe 1) must have had a beginning, and 2) "will eventually die, wallowing, as it were, in its own entropy," reaching "thermodynamic equilibrium" or "heat death." (Davies, God, 10-11)

These *scientific observations fit the biblical account perfectly*, as we know that once God finished creating the Universe out of nothing, that was it. No more creation, no absolute destruction. Only God can do that. We humans can certainly do some drastic rearranging of matter. We even think that we have "changed matter into energy" with nuclear explosions, though we are certainly not very successful at turning energy into matter. But the matter is still there, whatever its form. [Whether or not this is true, we cannot say, because classical physics, as presented by Thomas Barnes and others, shows that *mass and energy are not equivalent* and do not have the same units. Einstein's famous equation $E=mc^2$ merely describes a *functional relationship between mass and energy*. It is a useful equation, but incomplete. (Barnes, Space, 95, 104-6, 138; note Davies, God, 162, to see that humanists believe the equation *does* state that energy and mass are indeed equivalent)]

In addition, everything dies, or rusts, or decays. No machine is 100% efficient. That is the Second Law in action, effective on Earth since the Fall of man. Logic also tells us that if we reverse the Second Law, or "wind it backwards," we reach a point in time when everything was perfect with no decay present. (Hence, special creation!)

This means that, in this Universe, things *in general* do not self-organize from **simple to complex**, evolving into ever-higher life forms, but rather the general direction of creation is a decline from **complex to simple**. We are *devolving*. We are degenerating. We humans (and animals) today are mere shadows of the physical and mental specimens who existed in Adam's time, or even Noah's time. Both man and Universe are under the **curse of Genesis 3**. (Rom. 8:20-23) In terms of energy, the Universe is running down and burning out. *The Second Law is evidence of the curse and a manifestation of the curse. It does not necessarily embody the entire curse.* Besides chronicling the curse and its cause, the Bible (Dan. 12:4) also prophesies the **technical revolution** of the past few centuries that has allowed mankind to offset, though only to some degree, the law of degeneration.

It is amazing that some leading theoreticians of the "new physics" have managed to outmaneuver the laws of thermodynamics with theories of negative entropy, self-organization, effect without cause, order out of disorder, an expanding Universe, and the creation of matter out of empty space by gravity! (Davies, God, 50-2, 164-176, 214-17) Beware! *Today's mathematicians and physicists can theorize their way out of and around any "airtight," common-sense argument.* So don't expect to win any debates with theoretical physicists or mathematicians about the biblical world view. The latest development of the bizarre theories of relativity and quantum physics is **chaos theory** which mistakes complexity for chaos. This theory finds order in disorder and disorder in order. The Universe is defined by randomness and dissipation, governed by some sort of self-direction. (Gleick, Chaos, 299-300, 307-8, 314; see Chap. 8)

II
The Modern Humanist Approach

The humanist has an *optimistic view of man*, believing that man is basically good, improvable, and capable of achieving self-fulfillment. The humanist believes in the *potential greatness of man by man's own efforts*. Humanists believe that, to a point, **man is in control**. However, the humanist acknowledges that man is at the "mercy" of **powerful, random forces** of the Universe. The humanist also tends to replace God with the Universe. Well-known author **Dr. Carl Sagan** writes in his book *Cosmos* that the "'Cosmos is all that is or ever was or ever will be." He adds that "'[i]f we must worship a power greater than ourselves, does it not make sense to revere the Sun and stars?'" (Gaverluk, Rapture, 166, quoting from p. 243 of *Cosmos*) Of course, this is mere **paganism**, and God warned the Israelites against it, saying "And when you look up to the sky and see the Sun, the Moon and the stars — all the heavenly array — do not be enticed into bowing down to them and worshipping things the LORD your God has apportioned to all the nations under heaven." (Deut. 4:19, NIV)

The Bible has a *realistic view of man*,

knowing that man is basically sinful, selfish, and incapable of achieving self-fulfillment. The Christian believes in the **potential greatness** of a humble man spiritually reborn, indwelt and **empowered by God**. The Christian also acknowledges that **God is in control** of both man and the Universe.

Humanism is **nontheistic (secular)**, meaning it centers on man and what is physically "natural," either subordinating or completely dismissing the "supernatural." Some humanists are *atheists*, meaning they don't believe in God (or gods); some are *agnostics*, meaning they believe they have no proof that there is a God; and some believe in a supreme being or "force" of their own definition. There is a growing group of **church members who are in between true Christianity and humanism.** For example, they accept certain teachings of the Bible but dismiss anything supernatural as myth or spiritual symbolism. There are also church members who believe that evolution as taught by the humanists is actually God's method of creation. They are called *theistic evolutionists.*

Psalms 14:1 and 53:1 indicate that there were foolish individuals a thousand years before Christ who said in their hearts that there was no God. However, these same people probably worshiped pagan gods. The Greek philosophers acknowledged the divine in some form as did the Greek intellectuals of Paul's day (Acts 17) who worshipped pagan deities and erected an altar "To the Unknown God." **Throughout history, man has been a religious being, even while denying the true God.** The secular humanist movement did not solidify until the late Middle Ages, partly as a reaction to the medieval mind set that put all its hopes in eternity, dismissing life on Earth as meaningless drudgery. [This is an understandable attitude considering the Black Death of the 14th Century and its aftermath destroyed nearly 50% of Europe's population from about 1350 to 1400. (Tuchman, Distant, 124)] Humanism gave rise to the Renaissance which exalted the abilities of man and put all its hopes in life on Earth (an amazing attitude, considering the above).

> **Humanism**
> *"Science has so radically reoriented our society that the biblical perspective of the world now seems largely irrelevant."* -- Davies

These are the basic premises of one who approaches history as a humanist:

1) Relative "Truth": *The Bible is Only Partially Reliable and Heavily Mythical*

The Bible may be correct in some of its history but the Bible is not scientific, Jesus Christ was just a man, and anything miraculous is myth. Truth is not absolute. What was true yesterday may not be true today. (Truth changes with the times.) What is true for one person may not be true for another. Morality is determined by man as an individual or man as "the State." Truth is whatever you "perceive" it to be. In a democracy, truth and morality is determined by the majority. In socialism or communism (elitism), the elites determine truth and morality. In a republic (supposedly), truth is determined by law. Once again, the question is, "the law of God, or the law of man?" The humanist believes that the Bible has no place in modern education or anything that affects the public.

As explained by Dr. Paul Davies in *God and the New Physics*, "Science and religion represent two great systems of human thought." Davies explains that science, through technology, has so radically altered our lives that religion is no longer seen as effective in dealing with today's personal and social problems. "If the Church is largely ignored today it is not because science has finally won its age-old battle with religion, but because it has so radically reoriented our society that the biblical perspective of the world now seems largely irrelevant." (Davies, God, 2) The main purpose of this series is to demonstrate that *only the biblical perspective is relevant!*

2) Random Events: *History is the Result of Random Forces as Shaped by the Will and Power of Man*

There is no plan. There is no Planner. Events are random. In other words, everything is accidental – it just happens. Man must exercise what control he can over these powerful forces.

Quantum physics teaches that the atomic world is random and thus chaotic. Individual quantum events have no direct cause. In quan-

	BIBLICAL WORLD VIEW	MODERN HUMANIST	NEW AGE/OCCULTIC
GOD	Eternal Personal Creator	Self-Generating Universe	Initiated Man/ Oneness/Satan
TRUTH	Absolute	Relative	Esoteric
MAN	Created	Evolved	Quantum Leaps
MAN'S NATURE	Consequentially Evil	Intrinsically Good	Potentially Divine
PHYSICAL UNIVERSE	Catastrophism	Uniformism	Cyclical Catastrophism
TIME	Absolute	Relative	Cyclical
BIBLE	Divine Revelation	Unreliable Mythology	Jewish/Christian Scriptures
JESUS CHRIST	Creator God	Good Teacher	Adept/Master

tum theory, reality is not concrete but consists of ghost images until an image is brought into being (reality) only by a conscious observer (which could theoretically be a computer). (Davies, God, 100-18) Classical physics rejects quantum theory. (Barnes, Space, 131) Chaos theory rests on the cracked cornerstones of humanism and quantum theory.

3) Natural Conflict: *There is No Spiritual Battle, Only Earthly Conflict*

Try telling a humanist that the reason the abortion conflict is so intense is the fact that it is a battle in an even greater spiritual war. The humanist will tell you that there are no spiritual beings who affect life on Earth. However, he might say that there are natural beings throughout the Universe who have evolved into higher life forms than man, and he may or may not believe that these beings affect life on Earth. The potential exists, says the UFO-believing humanist, for either conflict or cooperation with these other "products" of the Universe.

4) Uniformitarianism: *The Universe Operates Under Certain Uniform Laws and Processes From Which We Can Draw Conclusions About Earth's History*

This means that physical processes have always operated about the same as they do today so that we can, for example, determine the age of rocks, bones, pottery, and animal fossils based on current processes of radioactive decay. Because we have seen relatively steady advancement in knowledge and technology over the past five or six hundred years, humanists conclude that the random universal processes have always worked to produce more and more complex forms of matter and life, and that things generally go from simple to complex, disorder to order. Humanists extrapolate the past from the present.

5) Human Potential: *Man Has a Human Nature Which Is Basically Good*

Man is a product of nature, a "child of the Universe." Anything bad about man is caused by his environment or education. If given two choices, man will always make the better choice (as taught most dogmatically in this writer's 1970 college sociology class). Man has the potential for greatness and for great good. Many believe that man is poised for a "quantum leap" in his evolution into a higher order of creature. The New Age movement, which is merely Eastern or Hindu paganism married to secular humanism and packaged for the Western mind, has brought out the "religious" aspect of humanism. Instead of merely a good nature, man now possesses the nature of a god, the *"god within you."*

6) Timewarp: *Time is a Relative, Possibly Infinite, Reversible Spatial Dimension*

There are most likely humanists who hold a more classical view of time as absolute, finite, and linear, but the world in general has accepted as fact the hypothetical definitions of **Einsteinian relativity**. It is frightening to discover how much of this bizarreness *all* of us have swallowed without question!

According to Einstein's *special theory of relativity* of 1905, time is part of a **four-dimensional space-time continuum** in which both space and time are *elastic*. One stretches when the other shrinks. Time is relative to each observer depending on motion. A timewarp increases as the **speed of light** is approached. As an observer goes faster, time goes slower. The speed of light seems to be Einstein's only absolute. If the speed of light is broken, says his theory, time turns inside out. The key word for relativistic time is *dynamical*, a word you will find repeated often in quantum and chaos theory. (Davies, God, 119-124)

Relativists measure time with atomic clocks, not by the mechanics of the heavenly bodies as God commanded. According to Einstein's *general theory of relativity*, time (atomic clocks) runs faster in space where **gravity** is weaker. Is that really *time* running faster or just the effects of mass on mass? [By the way, scientists *know* a lot less about atomic structure than they have led us to believe.] God states that *He* controls His appointed timekeepers. (Ps. 104:19, Job 38:32, Jer. 31:35) He also controls each and every molecule and atom, but He did not appoint them as timekeepers.

Einstein generalized his special theory, explains Davies, "to include the effects of gravity, ... not as a force, but a distortion of spacetime geometry." The result was "curved space." (Davies, God, 121) Dr. Jonathan Henry states that "Einstein developed the concept of curved (non-Euclidean) space in part to avoid the conclusion that the Universe must be finite. But there is no genuine scientific evidence that space is curved." (Henry, Geocentrism, 35) Walter van der Kamp maintains that Einstein developed his space-time continuum at least partly in order to support the unproven Copernican theory that the Earth orbits the Sun, even though Einstein admitted that "here on Earth experiments with light, electricity and magnetism, suggest us to be at rest in space." (Van der Kamp, How Long, 104)

Quoting Burniston Brown, Dr. Barnes accuses Einstein of double-mindedness and inconsistency regarding the point of whether or not the Einsteinian hypothetical alterations in time and space are real or merely apparent to a particular observer. "Einstein," writes Barnes, "never really wrote a definitive treatment of relativity." (Barnes, Space, 84)

We have long known that humanistic biological and geological science is nothing more than a house of cards. It appears that the same is true for what most of us have accepted as the "objective" sciences of higher mathematics, astronomy, and physics. Much more cooperative research needs to be done among creationists in these areas.

Depending on the New Age orientation of the individual, a humanist may or may not incorporate the ancient, mystical belief that time is cyclical.

7) Evolution: *An Infinite and Random Universe Produced Man Through the Evolutionary Process*

The Universe and everything in it is evolving according to random processes from simpler to ever-more-complex organisms. Man, therefore, is nothing more than a random product of a random Universe. Currently the most complex organism, man is evolving into a higher life form. Man is improvable and educable and, being on the top of the evolutionary chain, possesses unlimited potential.

Dr. Paul Davies, a brilliant writer with an intimidating but invitingly friendly command of his field of theoretical physics, blindly upholds **the typical dogma of humanism**. Incredible complexity does not demand a designer, he states. Biological and geological "evidence" adequately explain the "extraordinary characteristics of biological organisms." Evolution by mutation and natural selection is now accepted by virtually all scientists and theologians, he continues. The "basic principles and mechanisms of evolution are no longer seriously in doubt," he further assures us. Scientists now talk of a self-organizing Universe in which even "space and time could have sprung into existence spontaneously" thanks to the quantum theory. (Davies, God, 165-6, 215)

These beliefs, of course, have *profound implications for man's identity, value and purpose.* Why shouldn't we abort babies (fetuses) if we are nothing but animals? Why should we restrict our sexual behavior if we are nothing but animals? Why shouldn't we "eliminate" (euthanize) people who have outlived their usefulness or who are damaged beyond repair to an "acceptable quality of life" if we are nothing but animals? Only the fittest and best must survive for the good of the whole. In **humanism** and **socialism**, *the good of the **whole** always prevails over the good of the **individual** (except for the elitists who are in control).*

III
The "Interest-Group" Approach

The Russian communists are a good example of a **political group** with specific interests in how history is written. Until the late 1980s, the Communist State controlled the writing and publishing of all Russian history books and all newspapers. Facts were changed or left out, creating a "history" which distorts and suppresses truth, exalting the Communist State as the "worker's paradise" and conveniently ignoring the imprisonment, torture, and murder of millions and millions of people. Only God knows how much of ancient, medieval, and modern history has been doctored to make individuals, governments, or peoples look their best.

Religious cults have rewritten history to fit their beliefs. The Mormons are a leading example of this. Grounded heavily in the ancient Mystery religions, **Mormonism** is the legacy of an American named Joseph Smith who, most probably, received direct instructions from the Satanic spirit world. That "Smith was a **Master Mason**, there is indisputable evidence," states *A Masonic Digest* by Col. H.H.H. Clark. A "renegade," Smith borrowed much from the Masons to establish Mormonism. His oath-breaking revelations of certain Masonic secrets were probably the cause of his assassination. (Clark, Masonic, 4-6) This cult teaches that, in the 1820s, Joseph Smith was led by the angel Moroni to unEarth golden plates buried in New York State that contained the "whole Gospel." The plates revealed the *"true history"* **of America** and claimed that Jesus Christ had visited His "other sheep" there following His resurrection. The plates mysteriously disappeared.

Mormons basically teach that God is man and men are gods, and that men ("intelligences") have no beginning or end. Jesus and Satan (actually brothers) each offered a plan for Earth. The plan of Jesus was accepted while the plan of Satan was rejected. Damnation is merely salvation without exaltation. (Richards, Marvelous, Chaps. 6, 7, 19-22) In certain of its teachings, Mormonism is very moral and very family oriented, but it is not Christianity in any form. In fact, Dave Hunt quotes John Taylor, the third Mormon president, as saying "that Christianity was 'hatched in hell' and 'a perfect pack of nonsense.'" (Hunt, Seduction, 67-8) However, the Mormon teaching that an ancient civilization came to Central America after the Tower of Babel is closer to the truth than that taught in "traditional" textbooks.

There is still much controversy over the assassination of John Kennedy, the war in Vietnam, and the Iran-Contra scandal, to mention just a few examples. *There are always powerful political, economic, social, and religious groups who want to shape history to fit their own purposes.* There has even been recent talk in the midst of a growing **neo-Nazi** movement of rewriting European history, eliminating any reference to the **Holocaust** which neo-Nazis and anti-Semites say "never happened."

The May 15, 1993 international edition of *The Jerusalem Post* reports the undercover mission of Yaron Svoray, a Jewish journalist who infiltrated the neo-Nazi network in Germany from October 1992 to April 1993. He discovered that the movement has been "profoundly underestimated" by the German government and that neo-Nazism extends "deeply into the German middle and educated classes." These groups draw inspiration from the children and widows of WWII Nazi leaders and plan the rise of the Fourth Reich. (Hitler's government was the Third Reich.) Svoray's "cover" was checked out by the **Institute for Historical Review**, "America's pre-eminent, quasi-academic institution of **Holocaust denial**." During his dangerous assignment, Svoray was astounded at "sitting here in Germany in 1993, in the same beerhall, after 40 years of 're-education,' hearing the same garbage about the Jews, about conspiracies, *about how the Holocaust never happened*." (*Jerusalem Post*, May 15, 1993, 14-15) *The Chosen People* magazine issue of March 1993 notes rising anti-Semitism in Germany, Sweden, Italy, Russia, France, and the United States.

In its May 8, 1993 international edition, *The Jerusalem Post* addresses the problem of "disinformation" regarding the **Israeli--Palestinian conflict**. The *Post* accuses a Palestinian publication, recommended by the United States Information Agency, of **rewriting history** "to make the Arabs the sole 'indigenous inhabitants' [of present-day Israel] and victims, rather than the initiators of injustice, terrorism and war." The Palestinians usurp history, states the columnist, by denying Jewish historical rights in the land. (*Jerusalem Post*, May 8, 1993, 13)

The fact that powerful people have always guided history behind the scenes to whatever extent they were able is only common sense. There is ample evidence available which reveals **various concerted efforts** over the centuries by some of the western world's most powerful and wealthiest families, by political figures, or by idealistic individuals to exercise **significant political and financial control** over nations or even the world.

In his massive history *Tragedy and Hope*, famed Georgetown University professor Carroll Quigley describes "an international Anglophile network" called the Round Table Groups which have "no aversion to cooperating with the Communists, or any other groups, and frequently [do] so." Professor Quigley explains that he was allowed, for two years in the 1960s, to examine the papers and secret records of this network. He sympathizes with most, but not all, of these elitists' policies, disagreeing chiefly with the fact that the network wishes to remain unknown. The "relationship between the financial circles of London and those of the eastern United States," writes Quigley, "reflects one of the most powerful influences in twentieth-century American and world history." (Quigley, Tragedy, 950, 956) *The point is that our "establishment" history books certainly do not reveal the plans, plots, or maneuvers of these powerful individuals.*

Think how our history books would read if all the secret papers of the world's governments, banks, the FBI, CIA, NSA, KGB, MI5 & 6, the Mossad, etc. were released in total without censorship!

IV
The Occultic Approach

A *cult* is a group with usually one exalted leader and a group of devoted followers, united by certain beliefs or practices. The *occult* refers to that part of the spiritual world that follows Satan and not God. Some, but not all, cults are occultic.

We could truly say that anything not Jewish or Christian is occultic because anything not of God is of Satan. However, in this case, we generally refer to groups having active connections to the Satanic spiritual world, such as Hinduism and related pagan religions, the Theosophical Society, the Satanic Church, covens of witches and Satan worshippers practicing "white magic" or "black magic," and the Tara Center, to name a few.

The worldwide human movement that follows Satan, dating from Cain, is today called the **New Age Movement**. According to lawyer and author Constance Cumbey, New Agers trace their modern roots to the **Theosophical Society** created by Helena Petrovna Blavatsky in 1875, though "New Age-ism" is easily identified in the history and doctrines of the **Masons**. The Masons trace their own origins back through Adam Weishaupt's Illuminati of 1776, the Crusaders of medieval Europe, Hiram Abif of Solomon's Temple, Egypt's Great Pyramid, and all the way back to Tubal-cain, the craftsman of Gen. 4. (Clark, Masonic, 9, 24-5, 38-9, 52; Brooke, When, 250)

The New Age movement is a modern, westernized version of Eastern mysticism and the ancient **Mystery religion** which gave birth to all idolatry. *Actually, the New Age Movement is a marriage between Eastern spiritual mysticism and Western secular humanism.* The secular humanists dominated the movement from the 1500s to the mid-1970s. Then humanism became dominated by the spiritual New Agers.

To read about the *New Age from their own point of view*, look for books by Marilyn Ferguson, Benjamin Creme, David Spangler, and particularly the series by Alice Bailey and the writings of Blavatsky. Most book stores have entire sections on the New Age. To read critiques of the *New Age by Christian writers*, look for Constance Cumbey, Dave Hunt, Tal Brooke, Caryl Matrisciana, Johanna Michaelsen, and Martin and Diedre Bobgan, to mention some of the best. Prominent national figures like lawyer Phyllis Schlafly (Eagle Forum) deal with the New Age movement in the arenas of education and politics.

Many people involved in various forms of meditation, mind control, relaxation training, astrology, certain environmental causes, and certain educational movements do not realize that they are part of the occult. Even Jewish and Christian congregations have been infiltrated and affected. In its loosely networked form, the New Age Movement has considerable influence on the recording of history and the news that is reported to the public by the media.

New Agers believe that we are approaching a New Age, an enlightened age called the **Age of Aquarius**, and that properly enlightened people are taking a **quantum leap** in their evolutionary development to become gods. **Man is god.**

Though we have separated these approaches to history, they are often overlapped or combined in various ways to satisfy individual viewpoints.

Sifting for Truth in Secular Sources

Most of the sources we use to study American history are what we call *secular* (not religious) sources, meaning they are written by people who do not take the biblical approach outlined above, but generally take the modern, humanist, evolutionist approach.

Sadly, this usually involves a *political* as well as a *philosophical* bias. For example, most history textbooks written in the 20th Century have:
1) a *socialist* bias, promoting big government and the good of the group at the expense of the individual. Actually, socialism, fascism, communism, absolute monarchism, czarism, are all various forms of *elitism*. Powerful or all-powerful elites rule the masses by force, intimidation, and/or manipulation. The idea is to make the masses *dependent upon the governing powers*. People tend to support, and not bite, the hand that feeds them.
2) a *Keynesian* bias, believing that the government should control and stimulate the economy through deficit financing (debt), and centralized fiscal stimuli and planning, with the goal of creating and maintaining full employment. Lord John Maynard Keynes (1883-1946) was a British economist and intellectual.
3) a *power* bias, (usually hidden) supporting the organized effort of specific groups of the country's and world's elites to exercise significant financial, social, and political control over the governments and peoples of the world.
4) an *anti-Christian* bias, opposing the theology and morality of the Bible and the Judeo-Christian ethic, as well as ignoring, downplaying, or twisting the record of Christian influence in historical events. Though the Bible and the Judeo-Christian ethic form the foundation of Western civilization, their ultimate rejection is the expected result of the spiritual warfare that has raged since Lucifer sinned.

Since the 1970s, the humanist movement has become increasingly New Age and an increasing number of the **secular scientists** have moved, as author Dave Hunt says, from **physics to metaphysics**, suddenly embracing the supernatural. (Hunt, Seduction, Chap. 7) This shift has taken place in the political and economic realm as well. A growing number of government and military officials are New Agers, and an amazing number of Wall Street analysts use astrology and chaos theory to predict the financial markets.

Does that mean we reject everything the humanists and New Agers say? No, not at all. It means we **approach these sources critically**, using what seems to check out as truth and rejecting what we know is false. As they are knowledgeable of the spirit world and pagan traditions, New-Age sources can often provide clues of truth in piecing together ancient history. Several schools of **"maverick" evolutionists** also provide us with tremendous evidence to support what we know to be biblical truth. Many of the sources used in this series are written by

Christians, but the majority of the sources we use are secular.

Cleaning Your Slate And Being A *Berean*

Thus, we need to approach the study of history from a biblical point of view, but also with as clean a slate as we can manage, conscious of the humanist, special-interest-group, and New Age biases we have all absorbed from public-school textbooks, humanist teachers and professors, government officials, and the media.

In fact, in every aspect of life, we should be *Bereans*. When Paul and Silas went from Thessalonica to Berea, they found that the Berean Jews received the preaching of the Word with **minds open and eager for the truth** (Acts 17:10-12). However, the Bereans studied their own copies of the Scripture in order to **test for themselves** everything Paul and Silas taught, measuring it against the Scripture. That's the way we should approach teaching of any kind, including this book and the sources cited in this book.

You will never go wrong **pursuing the truth**. So, pursue it ... *and be a Berean!*

BIBLIOGRAPHY

Barnes, Thomas G., *Space Medium, The Key to Unified Physics*. El Paso: Geo/Space Research Foundation, 1986. [P.O. Box 13560, El Paso, TX 79913, or Genesis Institute, 7232 Morgan Ave. S., Richfield, MN 55423]

Barnhouse, Donald Grey, *The Invisible War*. Grand Rapids: Zondervan Publishing (Ministry Resources Library), 1965.

Bouw, Gerardus D., Videotape of presentation on Geocentricity, Bloomington, MN, Feb. 12, 1990. [Available from Genesis Institute]

Brooke, Tal, *When the World Will Be As One*. Eugene, OR: Harvest House Publishers, 1989.

Charnock, Stephen, *Discourses Upon the Existence and Attributes of God*, Vol I. Grand Rapids: Baker Book House, 1987.

Clark, Col. H.H.H., *A Masonic Digest*. Winston-Salem: Hunter Publishing Co., 1984.

Cumbey, Constance, *The Hidden Dangers of the Rainbow*. Shreveport, La.: Huntington House, Inc., 1983.

Davies, Paul, *God and the New Physics*. New York: Touchstone, 1983.

Floyd, Marlene, "The Rising Tide of Anti-Semitism," *The Chosen People*, Vol. XCIX, No. 7, March 1993, pp. 6-8, 11. [Chosen People Ministries, 1300 Cross Beam Dr., Charlotte, NC 28217-2834]

Gaverluk, Emil, *The Rapture Before the Russian Invasion of Israel*. Oregon: Solid Rock Books, 1988. [Available from Solid Rock Books, Inc., 979 Young Street, Ste. E, Woodburn, OR 97071]

Gleick, James, *Chaos*. New York: Penguin Books, 1987.

Henry, Jonathan F., "Geocentrism and Heliocentrism," *Proceedings of the Second Conference on Absolutes*, Minneapolis, MN, July 28-29, 1992, pp. 21-38. [Assoc. for Biblical Astronomy, 4527 Wetzel Ave., Cleveland, OH 44109; Genesis Institute (under Barnes)]

Hunt, Dave and McMahon, T.A., *The Seduction of Christianity*. Oregon: Harvest House Publishers, 1985.

Jerusalem Post International Edition, No. 1696, week ending May 8, 1993, "The US Disinformation Agency," (Lyonson), 13.

Jerusalem Post International Edition, No. 1697, week ending May 15, 1993, "A look inside the vipers' nest," 14-15.

Lang, Walter, "Astronomy in the Book of Job," *Proceedings of the Second Conference on Absolutes*, Minneapolis, MN, July 28-29, 1992, pp. 67-74. [see Henry above]

Quigley, Carroll, *Tragedy and Hope*. New York: The Macmillan Co., 1966.

Richards, LeGrand, *A Marvelous Work and a Wonder*. Salt Lake City: Deseret Book Co., 1976.

Ryrie, Charles C., *Basic Theology*. Wheaton: Victor Books, 1986.

Tuchman, Barbara, *A Distant Mirror*. New York: Alfred A. Knopf, 1978.

When God wanted to speak to us, he gave us something to read.

PROJECTS

Humanism: analyze textbooks, newspaper and magazine articles, and television shows for humanist beliefs and for statements which derive from an evolutionist viewpoint. Learn to identify humanism wherever you see or hear it.

Contrast the statements you find with the biblical point of view. Be sure and find Bible verses to support your conclusions.

New Age: read up on the New Age Movement using books by the authors recommended in this chapter. Then do the same sort of analyses suggested above.

Visit a general bookstore and find the section marked "New Age". (There will be one.) Skim the book titles and notice some of the authors. Also look at the magazine section and notice the publications specifically for the occult.

Theology: read up on prophecy and decide what position you think the Bible teaches. Your church library or a Christian bookstore can help you with research material.

Current Events: look for mention in newspapers and television news of the growing *Neo-Nazi* movement (also called "skinheads") in both Europe and the U.S. Look for statements concerning the Holocaust and the question of rewriting history.

WRITING NOTES

Serial Commas, or the Enumerative Series: In college, this writer was taught to punctuate a series in this manner: *a, b and c*; or, *a, b, c and d*; or, *a, b, c or d*. Notice that there is no comma before the conjunction (and, or, and but are conjunctions) which joins the first part of the series to the last member. Journalistic publications, particularly newspapers, drop the serial comma because of **space**. In columned publications where space is limited and also valuable (advertising dollars), and paper expensive, every comma counts. In addition, there is a relatively modern school of thought that believes in eliminating unnecessary punctuation wherever possible. The question is whether the serial comma before the conjunction is, or is not, necessary for clear communication. According to the Wilson Follett guide to *Modern American Usage*, this subject "is argued with more heat than is called forth by any other rhetorical problem except the split infinitive." (p. 397)

Throughout college, graduate school, and some 15 years of a writing career, this author vigorously argued the above case, that the comma before the conjunction was unneeded and merely a detriment to flow. (Note the comma after "graduate school.") Obviously there has been a change. While working for a political research firm, producing books that contained a tremendous amount of facts and figures, this writer began to run into situations in which the serial comma was indeed vital for clarity.

For example, consider the following sentence: *The landing of the Pilgrims at Plymouth was due to a delayed departure, the resulting winds which altered their course and divine providence.* We have a nice, rhythmical, three-point parallelism with "delayed departure," "resulting winds," and "divine providence." But, do the winds alter both their course *and* divine providence? Or is providence the third member of the series? Only the serial comma makes it certain. It is best, then, to consistently practice its use when space is not a major consideration, as shown in both *Modern American Usage* and *The Chicago Manual of Style* (p. 143) Even the *Associated Press Stylebook* for journalists recommends the comma before the conjunction in all but simple series such as "blue, white and green."(p. 269)

Note, on the preceding page, the paragraph on Keynesian bias, listed as "number 2." There is a comma after "financing," but no comma after "stimuli." By making it a rule to always use the serial comma, the omission in this case readily indicates that "centralized" is intended to modify both "stimuli" and "planning." Note also the series directly under "Being A Berean." The serial comma after "officials" helps to show that "humanist" modifies both "teachers" and "professors," while "the media" is a separate item.

The Associated Press *Stylebook and Libel Manual*, edited by Norm Goldstein. New York: Addison-Wesley Publishing Co., 1992.
The Chicago Manual of Style, 13th Ed. Chicago: Univ. of Chicago Press, 1982.
Wilson Follett *Modern American Usage*, edited by Jacques Barzun. New York: Hill & Wang, 1966.

Chapter 2
Ancient American Man: Do We Know His Age, Origin, and IQ?

The Age of Earth and Man

When did America begin and who were the first Americans?

How far back do we have to go to find the answers to these questions? To Columbus in 1492? Obviously farther than that. To the Vikings around A.D. 1000? Keep going. To somewhere between 70,000 and 38,000 B.C.? That's where the humanists/evolutionists would have you go.

The accepted theory (taught as fact) is that "prehistoric" Asian (Mongoloid) hunters followed herds of game across the Bering Strait between Siberia (Russia) and Alaska on a **"bridge" of land** that was created by massive glaciers that lowered the sea level. The bridge came and went with successive ice ages and so, over tens of thousands of years, waves of migration thus populated the entire Western Hemisphere (McKern, 16). Does this mean that Russia has first claim on the Americas? Should we give it all back to them?

Some evolutionists believe that creatures evolved into man in the Americas just as they did elsewhere in the world. Thus, they believe that there was more than one **"cradle of civilization."** The traditional cradle has been Mesopotamia, though many evolutionists now point to Africa or even the Indus River Valley in Pakistan. Those who believe that the Americas were also a cradle explain away the extraordinary links between European, Asian, and American cultures as "parallel evolution."

However, a Biblical approach to determining the age, origin, and IQ of Mr. and Mrs. Ancient America leads us to a different time and a specific individual — *the time of the Flood, and Noah!* First, we need to *establish a time line of history, based on biblical and scientific evidence.*

Science Defies Evolutionist Dating

The **evolutionists' recipe for life** on Earth has been demonstrated to be **mathematically impossible** numerous times because it requires an incomprehensible number of happy accidents. For example, a simple organism of only 100 parts can be linked in 10^{158} ways, or the number "1" followed by 158 zeros. There is only one chance out of all those ways that it will link up correctly. Now multiply that by the complexity of one cell and then by the 10 billion integrated cells in the cerebral cortex of one human brain! This is why evolutionists' magic ingredient is *time*, the idea being that in millions and billions of years, anything and everything can, and did, happen, resulting in the delicately complex and orderly world we know today. However, a little further calculation shows that "even 30 billion years" is not enough time for "the chance evolution of the simplest living molecule." (Morris, Sci. Cre., 60, 69, 131)

Geochronologists (scientists who study the age of the Earth) use over 80 different methods

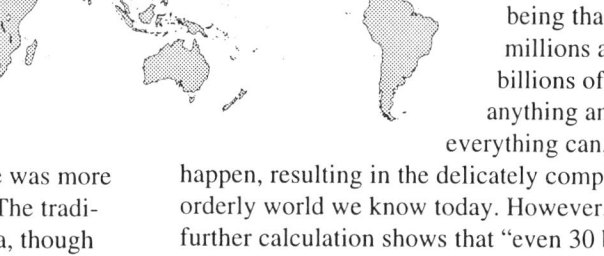

of measurement, the majority of which indicate a relatively young Earth ("only" 500 million years to as few as 4,000 years), with at least nine or ten methods in the 4,000- to 10,000-year category. Thus, the evolutionist claim that the Earth is around *five billion years old* defies the science of geochronology. In fact, used together, **the methods of geochronology point to an age of less than 10,000 years.** (McLean, 24-32; Blick, Correlation, 31-41; Blick, Special, 19-28)

A recent, intriguing study by two Australian mathematicians demonstrates, using a large body of experimental data, that the **velocity of light** is not a constant, but has **decayed over time**. In terms of a graph, the decay seems to have been quick and steady for a long time ("a virtually linear drop"). The rate of decay then "underwent an oscillation, with its last maximum being near 1200 A.D." The rate slowed (the graph line begins to curve from a vertical drop to an increasingly horizontal movement) and now it is not known "whether the trend will drop to zero rate of change, taper off slowly, or perhaps reverse and become an increase." Setterfield and Norman estimate that, *at the time of Creation, the speed of light was 10.6 million times faster than it is now!* They also estimate that one million "atomic years" (light is produced by atomic processes) equal two "orbital" years (Earth/Sun orbit). From this, they calculate **Creation** to have taken place **about 5792** B.C. (Setterfield/Norman, Atomic, 51; Setterfield, Geological, 2, 5, 8) Once again, geochronology and physics experiments support a Creation date much closer to 4000 B.C. than to 5 Billion B.C. [See Chapter 8 for further discussion of Setterfield's and Norman's work.]

Population statistics are of particular interest. The evolutionist claims that man has been around for one to three million years. A human population growing at a rate of only 1/2% per year (our present growth rate is 2%), over just one million years, would result in more than 10^{2100} people on the Earth today, which is absurd. Ten to the 2100th power means 1 with 2100 zeros behind it, a totally impossible number! *Today's world population is far better explained using a time period of about 4,000 to 5,000 years.* (Morris, Sci. Cre., 167-9)

Biblical Genealogies

The **narrative and the genealogies** of the Bible indicate that the world is **about 6,000 years old**, dating from Adam, or from Genesis 1:2. [See Chap. 1] Some scholars (including Dr. Henry Morris) point out that biblical genealogies leave gaps for various reasons and that **"begot"** or "son of" can mean a father or a great-grandfather, and in certain cases, this is true. The verse Ezra 7:1 says that Ezra was the son of Seraiah, the chief priest executed by Babylonian King Nebuchadnezzar. (II Kings 52:18-21)

However, I Chron. 6 says that Seraiah begot Jehozadak who was taken as part of the 70-year Babylonian captivity. Considering the time period, Ezra was probably Jehozadak's son and thus Seraiah's grandson. This is only a "gap" of one generation and is "filled in" by I Chron. 6. The Ezra 7 genealogy continues through verse five to show Ezra descended from Aaron, though it leaves a large gap in verse 3 from Azariah to Meraioth. This gap is also filled in by I Chron. 6. In another case, Christ's genealogy in Matthew 1:8 says "Joram begot Uzziah." By looking at I Chron. 3:11-12 and II Kings 15:1 & 13, we see that the line actually includes Joram, Ahaziah, Joash, Amaziah, and then Azariah who is also called Uzziah. Uzziah is really the great-great-grandson of Joram. But, once again, the "gap" is filled in elsewhere.

The pre-Flood **genealogy of Adam** in Genesis 5 is very specific, giving ages for each person. The same list of names is repeated in Luke 3 and in I Chron. 1. In addition, Enoch is listed as number seven, counting Adam, and Jude 14 refers to him as "the seventh from Adam." With these **numerical specifics**, there is no reason to believe that this is not a *tight, father-to-son genealogy*. However, even a number of conservative scholars say that there are gaps in the Genesis genealogies. Perhaps these Bible scholars are relying on historical dating systems that assume a creation date of about 10,000 years ago and on Egyptian chronologies heavily influenced by humanist/evolutionist dating methods. Hebrew scholar Dr. Allen Ross writes, "Some have argued that the names in the genealogical lists in chapters 5 and 11 are contrived," selected for symmetry, "but this view cannot be substantiated by consistent exegesis." (Ross, BKC I, 45)

In their famous and foundational work, *The Genesis Flood*, Dr. Whitcomb and Dr. Morris align themselves with those who argue that the Genesis chronologies are symmetrical and not exact in their generations. They cannot believe that the Flood, the Tower of Babel, and the birth of Abraham could all have occurred within 400 to 500 years, so they date the Flood at 3,000 to 5,000 years before Abraham (Abram).

For example, they believe that Shem and other patriarchs could not have been alive when Abram was born and so there must be more time involved than the Bible allows. One of their reasons for taking this position is Joshua's statement that the Jews' ancestors, specifically Abram's father **Terah**, worshipped other gods. Perhaps Drs. Whitcomb and Morris believe that as long as Shem was alive, there could be no paganism, or that Semites would not fall so *quickly* into paganism?

We argue first of all that Shem personally fought the idolatry of Nimrod. [See Chaps. 6 & 7) We add that idolatry was a problem with the Jews throughout history, that Terah wandered from his Shemite (Semite) relatives into the Hamite civilization, and that the patriarchs lived elsewhere in an age when communications were much more limited than they are today. Also, according to "the traditions which have lingered in the common talk of the unchanging East," **Abram** (Abraham) was opposed to his father's idol worship, destroying idols and refusing to bow to the sacred fire of the Chaldeans. (Meyer, Abraham, 12) According to 1st-Century Jewish historian Josephus, Abram was a skilled astronomer who believed that one God was the Creator of the Universe, arousing the Chaldeans to the point that Abram's life was in danger. (Josephus, Antiquities, I.VII) Abram's brother Nahor, however, continued in idolatry as demonstrated by his grandson Laban in Gen. 31:19.

We have considered these and the few other objections listed in *The Genesis Flood* which argue for several thousand years more time between Creation and the Flood and Abraham, and we are not convinced to accept the arguments. (Morris, Gen. Flood, 474-489) It is interesting that, in a later book called *Many Infallible Proofs*, Dr. Morris points out that Dr. William F. Albright, one of the "two greatest authorities on biblical archaeology," deems the **Table of Nations** in Gen. 10 to be a **document of astonishing accuracy**. Then Dr. Morris continues on the same page to reiterate his position "that quite possibly there *are* gaps in the genealogies of Genesis 11, the formulas for which are similar to those of Genesis 5." (Morris, Proofs, 301, 313) We do recommend that the reader review the material and weigh the evidence on both sides. For the purposes of this book, however, we conclude that we can literally **count the years from Adam to Noah and his sons**.

The list of **Shem's descendants** in Genesis 11 also gives specific ages, with an average of only 30 years between all but the first and last of the father-son pairs. Dr. Ross agrees that these verses "seem to present a tight chronology." (Ross, BKC I, 45) This list is also repeated in I Chron. 1 and Luke 3. However, in verse 36, Luke adds one person, **Cainan**, to the list. It could have been an accidental repeat of "who was the son of Cainan" in verse 37. More likely is Matthew Henry's explanation that the addition occurred through Luke's use of the Greek **Septuagint** translation of the New Testament. (Luke the physician is assumed by some to have been a Greek-speaking gentile who became a Jewish proselyte.) The Septuagint incorporated a number of errors, says Matthew Henry, including the addition of Cainan to this genealogy (Henry, 618). It is also possible that the name was never listed in the original, perfect manuscript of Luke.

So, once again, there is evidence to believe that we can **count the years from Shem to Abraham**. [Note that Acts 7:4 and Gen. 12:4 confirm that Abraham left Haran *when his father was dead* and Abraham was 75 years old. Terah died at the age of 205, according to Gen. 11:32. That means Terah was 130 when Abraham was born. Looking at Gen. 11:26, Terah probably fathered Haran at 70, then Nahor, and then Abraham at 130.] Further, we know that we can **count the years down to Jacob's 12 sons**, including Judah. From Gen. 38:29, we know that Perez was the son of Judah. The genealogy from Perez to David, given in Ruth 4:18-22, also appears from other references, such as I Chron. 2, to be a father-to-son chronology. [It is also reasonable to believe, in spite of certain authorities, that Rahab was indeed the wife of Salmon, the mother of Boaz, as stated in Matt. 1:5. See

Matthew Henry's Commentary, Vol. 2, I Chron. 2, p. 841.]

The point is that possible gaps are not large enough or numerous enough to disturb the 6,000-year estimate, and that the Bible gives us a strong guideline, with specific age lengths as far down as Joseph, from which we can closely estimate the passage of time.

The Ussher Chronology

Realizing this, an Irish church leader and distinguished scholar named **James Ussher** devised his famous work, *The Chronology on the Old and New Testament,* in A.D. 1650. He determined that the creation of Adam took place 4,000 years before the birth of Christ. Archbishop Ussher "had access to many ancient church manuscripts which were tragically lost in the burning of early Irish churches during the savage Irish wars...." (Jeffrey, Armageddon, 179) Most likely after researching the date of Herod the Great's reign, he decided that **Christ's birth** was actually in **4 B.C.** and set the date of the Genesis **creation at 4004** B.C. He then predicted that the Millennial Kingdom would commence in A.D. 1997 (Jeffrey, Armageddon, 179)

Though Dr. Henry Morris states that Ussher's date for the Flood of 2348 B.C. "is of course much more recent than even most conservative Bible archaeologists believe is possible," Dr. Morris also says that the "much-maligned Ussher chronology...may have been discarded too quickly." He acknowledges Archbishop Ussher as an outstanding scholar of the Old Testament and secular history, who "no doubt knew much more about ancient chronology than do most of those who ridicule him today." (Morris, Proofs, 313, 290)

In an anti-evolution argument concerning **population statistics**, Dr. Morris uses a formula to derive the time it took to produce the Earth's 1970's population, arriving at a figure of 4,300 years, which, he says, "is the Ussher date for the Flood, when the present population got its start, according to the Bible. All known population data fit these factors very well, indicating the Biblical record of population origins is very reasonable and conservative." (Morris, Proofs, 296)

Six Days and 6,000 Years

So, geochronology points to less than 10,000 years and the Bible to about 6,000 years as the age of the Earth as we know it. It is also interesting to note that **Jewish tradition**, recorded in the *Talmud* (Sanhedrin 97:a), "says that the age of man will be 6,000 years: 2,000 of chaos, 2,000 of the Law, and 2,000 of Messiah. If this is true, then Messiah should have come about 2,000 years ago, for we know the Law was given approximately 4,000 years ago." (Crenshaw, Chosen People, 4) Our "approximate" dating systems with which we are working show "about" 2,000 years from Adam to Abraham and about 2,000 years from Abraham to Christ.

Of course, God works "to the very day" as indicated in Ex. 12:41. *For His own reasons, He has left out just enough information to keep us a little hazy on some exact dates.* **Jewish teacher Esther Jungreis** *illustrates* this point with the blasphemous feast of **Belshazzar** (Dan. 5). She explains that the last of the Babylonian kings thought the prophesied **70 years of Babylonian captivity** had run their course and that, since the Jews were still under Belshazzar's captivity, the Jewish God was dead, Jewish prophecy false, and the Jews' existence as a nation finally ended forever. Thus, Belshazzar (and Satan) celebrated in drunken idolatry by defiling the Temple vessels stolen and stored by Nebuchadnezzar. *But Belshazzar did not know exactly from which date to count. There was some confusion over the matter.* God spoke by way of the famous handwriting on the wall, which Daniel interpreted. Then, that very night, God led the Medes and Persians to conquer the Babylonians and

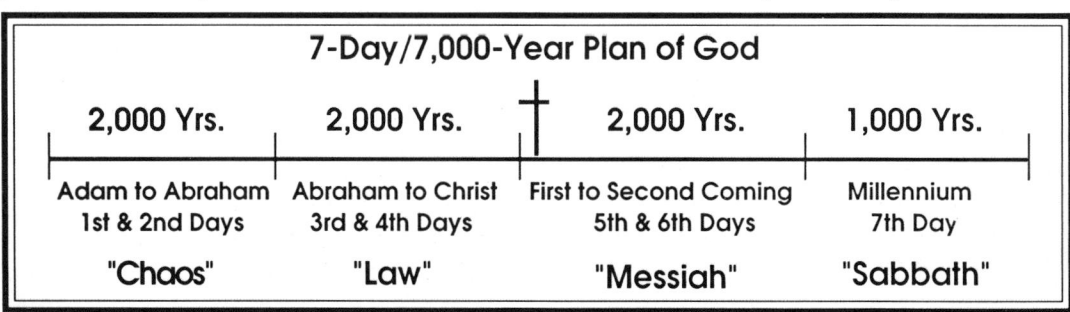

slay Belshazzar. Darius the Mede took over, probably under the overall reign of Cyrus the Persian in whose first year the 70 years did indeed end (Ezra 1) when Cyrus allowed any willing Jew to return to Jerusalem to rebuild the Temple. (From teachings of Esther Jungreis, Hineni Ministries [*traditional Jewish,* not Messianic], New York City)

There is much Scriptural evidence and strong Jewish tradition to support the belief in a six-day/6,000-year history of man. And if it is indeed true, it would follow that we should be able to predict the "end of the six days" (marked by the end of the Tribulation) and the "beginning of the seventh day" (the Millennium). However, historians may be off in their calendar dates, especially since there have been so many different calendars and calendar changes throughout history, by so many nations. *Once again, God keeps certain things just a little fuzzy.*

It is getting close to 2,000 years since Jesus Christ was born, and many dispensational Bible scholars believe that prophetic Scripture and current events indicate that the time is right for a soon-to-occur Rapture and seven-year Tribulation climaxed by the Second Coming of Christ and His 1,000-year earthly reign (the dispensational outlook, see Chap. 1).

A Scripture verse central to this teaching is **II Peter 3:8**, which says "that one day is with the Lord as a thousand years, and a thousand years as one day." Jewish tradition connects this verse (and Ps. 90:4) with the **six-day work and one-day Sabbath rest of Creation**, saying that this specific time period of 24-hour days also doubles as a symbol for 6,000 years of human-ruled history and 1,000 years of divine rule. This idea is also applied to **Hosea 6:2** which says that the Lord will revive the Jewish nation after two days (2,000 years after the Jews rejected Christ) and raise the nation up to live in His sight in the third day (the 1,000-year Millennium.)

It is also interesting to note that, in John 11, Jesus waited two days (2,000 years?) before going to resurrect **Lazarus** who had lain dead for four days (total of 4,000 years of Jewish and pre-Jewish history). In Matthew 16:28 and 17:1, Jesus talks of His coming and Kingdom, then waits six days (6,000 years of human history?) to demonstrate the **Transfiguration**. (Every number in the Bible has a meaning and purpose.)

Joseph Good points out that six steps led to Solomon's throne, the six steps representing the 6,000 years of human history leading to the Davidic throne of Christ and the "7th-day" reign of 1,000 years. The first two chapters of John record the events of seven days. The first is mentioned in John 1:19. Verses 29 and 35 specify the second and third days. On the *fourth* day (4,000 years), Messiah takes "a trip" into Galilee, then is not mentioned again until the seventh day (three days later, John 2:1) when He attends a *wedding*, His first demonstrated miracle. The wedding of Christ to His bride (the Church) takes place at the beginning (or immediately before the beginning) of the "7th day," the 1,000-year reign of "Sabbath rest."

Joseph Good also explains the coronation of **Joash** as Judah's rightful king, after six years of delay, as a reference to Christ's earthly reign after 6,000 years (II Kings 11:3). The story of **Absalom's** 7-year rebellion against David is symbolic of the Antichrist who arises during the Tribulation, right before the "7th day." Many other "types and shadows" and rabbinical teachings illustrate the 7-day/7,000-year plan of God. (Good, Rosh HaShanah, 59-79)

Thus, certain Jewish and Christian teachings underscore the genealogical/historical records of the Bible to reinforce the conclusion that the Earth is approximately 6,000 years old, giving us 4,000 years of human history before the birth of Christ. [For New Age/occult beliefs concerning "ages" of about 2,000 years and the significance of A.D. 2000, see Chap. 8.]

The Birth of Christ

If we accept the teaching that God planned 6,000 years of human history plus a "Sabbath" of 1,000 years, then our key reference to determine the date of Creation is the date of the birth of Christ. We have noted that the chronology of Archbishop Ussher begins with Creation at 4004 B.C. because of a 4 B.C. date for Christ's birth. This 5/4 B.C. date is the one espoused by many (if not most) prominent, conservative scholars.

Many factors are considered, but the dates of **Herod the Great's reign and death** are the most crucial. [See Matt. 2] The Jewish historian **Josephus** records that Herod was appointed "King of the Jews" by Mark Antony and Augustus Caesar "on the 184th Olympiad" and that Herod's reign lasted 37 years, at which point

Herod died. (Josephus, Ant., XIV.xiv.5; XVII.viii.1) The *traditional* year for the **1st Olympiad** is 776 B.C. (Kagan, Hellenic, 462) The Romans continued the Greek method of keeping time by Olympiads (every four years). Thus, if the traditional date is correct and there were no disruptions over 736 years, the 184th Olympiad would have begun in 40 B.C. Though 40 - 37 = 3 B.C., Herod's 37th year could actually have been during 4 B.C. Josephus also states that Herod reigned 34 years from the 185th Olympiad (36 B.C.) when he actually conquered Jerusalem. (Josephus, Ant., XIV.xvi.4) Though this should give us a date of 3 or 2 B.C., it is explained to support a date of 4 B.C. However, **Olympiads were periods of four years**, and *so a reference to the 184th could mean anytime from 40 to 37 B.C., while the 185th would refer to anytime from 36 to 33 B.C.*

Thus, it is possible that Herod was appointed in 38 B.C. and conquered Jerusalem in 35 B.C. Josephus states that Herod began his project to **rebuild and enlarge the Temple** in the **18th year** of his reign. (Josephus, Ant., XV.xi.1) Counting from 35 B.C. as the first year of his actual reign, the 18th year would be during **18 B.C.** (17 B.C. would begin the 19th year.) *Forty-six years later, Jesus observed the Feast of Passover at Jerusalem.* After chasing the money-changers from the Temple (that Herod built), Jesus said to the Jewish religious leaders, "Destroy this temple, and in three days I will raise it up." The Jewish leaders thought He meant **Herod's Temple** which they exclaimed had been **46 years "in building."** (John 2:19-20, Scofield KJV) Forty-six years after 18 B.C. would place this event in the spring of A.D. 29, exactly when we believe Christ observed His first Passover, after **beginning His ministry** in the **fall of A.D. 28** (Jeffrey, Armageddon, 229)

Luke 3 explains that it was in the **15th year** of the **reign of Tiberius Caesar** that the ministry of Jesus began with His baptism by John the Baptist. Tiberius was crowned Roman Emperor on August 19, A.D. 14. The 15th year of his reign began on August 19, A.D. 28. If Christ was indeed born in the **fall of 1 B.C.**, Jesus would have been 29 years old in the fall of A.D. 28 (at that time, Jewish babies were dated from *conception* and were considered to be one year old at birth) and so would have begun **His 30th year** at that time. Luke 3:23 states that "Jesus himself began to be about thirty years of age...." (Scofield, KJV; Jeffrey, Armageddon, 228; Good, Rosh HaShanah, 169)

Joseph Good gives a detailed explanation of why Christ was born in the fall during the **Feast of Tabernacles** *(Sukkot)* in the month of **Tishri 15-21**. Aside from John 1:14 which says that "the Word was made flesh and tabernacled among us," he uses the **priestly cycles** set up by King David to determine the approximate birth date of **John the Baptist** to be during **Passover** *(Pesach)*, when the Jews look for **Elijah** to appear. (Matt. 11:12-14; 17:10-12) According to Luke 1, Jesus would have been born **six months** later in the fall. Jesus was born in a **stable** which is called a *"sukkah."* The word "Sukkot" (tabernacles or booths) is the plural of sukkah. People would takes months to come to and from Bethlehem to register for the census of Luke 2:1, but there would be no room at any inn during the fall feasts. At this time, it was still warm enough for shepherds to keep their flocks out all night. (Good, Rosh HaShanah, 57, 165-173; Jeffrey, Armageddon, 225-7)

The Jewish Feasts
(Lev. 23)
Spring Feasts -- March/April/May
Messiah's First Coming

Nisan 14   Passover
Slaying of Passover lamb in Egypt and the Crucifixion of Christ.

Nisan 15-21   Unleavened Bread
Meal on Passover night of lamb and unleavened bread in Egypt, a week of eating unleavened bread, and the burial of Christ after Crucifixion.

Sunday   Firstfruits
after Nisan 15-21 Sabbath
Crossing of the Red Sea in Egypt, offering of firstfruits of barley harvest, and the Resurrection of Christ.

50 Days   Pentecost/Weeks
After Firstfruits
Giving of the Law on Sinai, giving of the Holy Spirit to the Church

If Christ was born in 1 B.C., then Herod could not have died in 4 B.C. However, Josephus notes an **eclipse of the moon** during Herod's **terrible illness** in the last year or two of his reign. Astronomers chronicle an eclipse on **March 12/13, 4 B.C.** (Josephus, Ant., XVII.vi.4) It is said by some that Herod died between that eclipse and the following Passover in April. Others say Herod died before the Passover a year later. (See Whiston's note, Josephus, 368)

What now? It so happens that the eclipse of 4 B.C. was of low degree and took place between 2 and 4 a.m. A *total* **lunar eclipse** occurred on **Jan. 9, 1 B.C.** (Ozanne, First, 147-50; Jeffrey, Armageddon, 226) Herod's illness lasted for some time after the eclipse. The Jewish wise men from Babylonia arrived about the time of Christ's birth. The male Jewish children that Herod killed were actually one year old and under (remember the birth date?). Joseph hid Mary and Jesus in Egypt for about a month, then returned upon news of Herod's death, in time to dedicate Jesus at the Temple 40 days after His birth. Josephus indicates that a lot of events take place before the Passover of the next year. (Josephus, Ant., XVII.viii & ix; Good, Rosh HaShanah, 165-173)

The only real problem with Josephus is the reference that **Herod's son Philip** reigned 37 years after his father, dying in the 20th year of Tiberius Caesar's reign (A.D. 33) That would push Herod's death back to about 4 B.C. However, in light of all of the Scriptural evidence, we must conclude that the number 37 was wrong or miscopied, or that there is some other explanation. (Josephus, Ant., XVIII.iv.6)

Thus, we believe that Christ was born in the fall of 1 B.C., during Sukkot (Tabernacles), that His ministry began in the fall of A.D. 28, during the fall feasts, and that the Rapture of the Church and the Second Coming and beginning of the Millennium will all occur during various of the three fall feasts of Rosh HaShanah, Yom Kippur, and Sukkot. (See Joseph Good's *Rosh HaShanah and the Messianic Kingdom to Come* as well as books by Zola Levitt)

We find additional evidence for this position in the prophecy of Daniel 9:20-27. In his book *The Coming Prince*, **Sir Robert Anderson** calculated the time from **March 14, 445 B.C.**, when Artaxerxes issued the decree "to restore and to build Jerusalem," (Dan. 9:25; Neh. 2:1-6) until **April 6, A.D. 32**, when Messiah would be "cut off," as 173,880 days. Daniel's prophecy states that this time would equal 7 weeks (of years) plus 62 weeks (of years), or a total of 69 weeks of years of 360 days each. (Prophecy is counted in the original 360-day years that we find used for the Genesis Flood and for the Tribulation referenced in Revelation 11 & 12.) By multiplying 69 x 7 = 483, then multiplying by 360, we get 173,880 days!

From the fall of A.D. 28 to **April 6, A.D. 32** is a period of about 3½ years, the length of Christ's ministry. In A.D. 32, Nisan (Aviv) 10 (April 6) fell on Sunday when Christ rode into Jerusalem. As the sacrificial Lamb, He was examined for four days and slain on Nisan (Aviv) 14 which, *in that year*, fell on a **Thursday**. By tracing a detailed account of the Exodus and the original Passover, and explaining the "high Sabbaths," Joseph Good demonstrates that Messiah was truly crucified on a Thursday. (Good, Rosh HaShanah, 18-29; Jeffrey, Armageddon, 26-33, 229-30) Christ ate the Passover meal on Wednesday night (Thursday, Nisan 14, began on

---

The Jewish Feasts
(Lev. 23)
Fall Feasts -- September/October
Messiah's Second Coming

Tishri 1   Rosh HaShanah
The Feast of Trumpets is associated with the original New Year, Creation, repentance, the destruction of the Temple, crowning and wedding of Messiah, Day of Judgement (start of Tribulation, start of Millennium, and resurrection of the dead (the Rapture?)

Tishri 10   Yom Kippur/Day of Atonement
Day of Judgement (end of Tribulation), Day of Redemption for Israel, Second Coming of Christ

Tishri 15-21   Sukkot/Tabernacles
Wandering in the wilderness, birth of Messiah, the 1,000-year Messianic Kingdom, dedication of the Temple

Wednesday night at 6 p.m.), then was crucified from 9 a.m. to 3 p.m. on Thursday. He was taken down and buried in time for the feast of Unleavened Bread which began at 6 p.m. (Good, Rosh HaShanah, 34-9)

Other Dating Methods

We have already noted that Australian mathematician **Barry Setterfield** has estimated the date of **Creation**, using measurements based on the **decay of the velocity of light**, to be about **5792 B.C.** We are certainly not qualified to assess the ramifications of this research in relation to the physical laws of the Universe. It is intriguing to us that, at the same time, there are prominent Creationist scientists with doctorates in physics whose writings expose the fallacies of Einsteinian relativity and Quantum theory and, in turn, explain physical phenomena using **Classical, cause-and-effect physics** centered on electromagnetism. [This work will be explored further as this series continues.]

In addition to his work in physics and mathematics, Setterfield has also presented his own research in biblical chronology. His work is interesting and educational (and worth reading), even though we must disagree with much of it. *By coordinating dates based on his atomic-decay curve with dates based on orbital mechanics (solar days and years), he structures his biblical chronology to fit the **accepted evolutionist chronology**.* Though a Bible-believing Christian, he accepts the evolutionist teachings that have been totally debunked by other Creationists. He presents a detailed case for the elongated chronologies of the **Septuagint Text** while we base our findings on the conservative **Masoretic Text**. [That is a whole other study in itself.] He argues for a longer chronology than what we propose.

Setterfield and others also employ various versions of what is referred to as the **Principle of Omission**. This means that God omitted from the biblical chronology certain **"wasted" years** of unbelief when the pre-Flood people or Israelites turned away from Him, or omitted from chronologies names of those who rebelled against Him, or omitted names of some born during the sojourn in Egypt. There are supposedly 93 **"missing" years** of divine judgment in the period of the book of Judges. Paul's use of "about 450 years" in **Acts 13:20** seems to refer directly to the time that judges ruled Israel. This would mean that there were 573 years between the Exodus and the foundation of Solomon's Temple, instead of the 480 years specified in I Kings 6:1. The extra 93 years are supposedly accounted for by periods of oppression listed in Judges which add up to 93. However, the actual number is 111. (Setterfield, Chronology, 22; Lindsey, BKC-I, 375; Henry, Commentary, Vol VI, 165-6)

Young's Literal Translation is enlightening on this subject of Acts 13:20. It reads "And after these things, about four hundred and fifty years, He gave judges -- till Samuel the prophet...." Dr. C.G. Ozanne and Dr. Stanley Toussaint agree that Paul is referring to the 400 years of oppression by Egypt, 40 years in the wilderness, and "about" 10 years during the conquest of Canaan, or "these things" which happened before the judges. (Ozanne, First, 30-33; Toussaint, BKC-II, 390) *In this series, we have generally rejected the schemes of omission.*

Among chronologists, you will also find a plethora of "counting" methods which involve the **numerics** of 7, 70, 490, 2520, etc. *We are strong believers in the fact that Hebrew and Greek are both numerical languages, that the original manuscripts of the Bible are divinely constructed in complex numerical patterns, and that every number in the Bible has a significant meaning.* However, there seems to be an endless variety of ways for us humans to devise **periods of time** involving divine numbers so that it is often difficult to assess their validity. Ozanne

---

Daniel's 70 Weeks of Years (490 Yrs.) in Dan. 9:20-27

69 Weeks of 7 Years Each = 483 yrs. x 360 days = 173,880 days

| Mar. 14, 445 B.C. | April 6, A.D. 32 |
| Decree to Rebuild Jerusalem | Messiah is cut off |

Daniel's 70th Week of 7 Years is the *Tribulation*

makes certain *chronological assumptions* based on biblically meaningful numbers, as do many others. Some or many of these may indeed be valid. But numbers can be pushed to prove our own preconceptions (and all of us humans are subject to preconceptions) so that we must be careful in considering these various proposals. Some rather intriguing calculations of time periods, prophecies, and historical events are featured in Grant Jeffrey's *Armageddon*. [See also E. W. Bullinger's *Number in Scripture* and Jerry Lucas's *Theomatics*.]

The brief chronological "exercise" pursued in this book should demonstrate that the disagreements over dates among most major, conservative Bible scholars concern differences of only a few days or a few years. We admit in this book to being heavily influenced by our own long-held leanings toward a Thursday crucifixion and by the teachings regarding the Jewish feasts so ably explained in Joseph Good's *Rosh HaShanah and the Messianic Kingdom to Come* and in Grant Jeffrey's *Armageddon*.

However, we strongly recommend a close reading of Dr. J. Dwight Pentecost's *The Words and Works of Jesus Christ* and Dr. Harold Hoehner's *Chronological Aspects of the Life of Christ*. Dr. Hoehner (quoted by Dr. Pentecost) explains and critiques the Wednesday, Thursday, and Friday crucifixion days, preferring the Friday view. He also holds to A.D. 33 as the year of Christ's death. Dr. Pentecost's book includes extensive quotes from Dr. Hoehner's work and documents detailed discussions of the dates of Herod's reign and death and the Roman census.

A serious study of chronology also demands careful consideration of the work of Eugene Faulstich, an electronics engineer and founder of the Chronology-History Research Institute. Since 1975, Faulstich and his group have used computer programs, astronomical tables, biblical numerical patterns, and historical research (including the Hebrew, Egyptian, and Roman calendars) to produce what they believe to be the exact days and dates of biblical history. The work is astounding in both amount and detail, and the message is biblical as it exalts the Scriptures as the Word of God (though it does ascribe Joshua's Long Day to a solar eclipse.) Faulstich's group believes that the Earth is basically 6,000 years old, as he gives a 4001 B.C. date for Creation and states that the age of the Universe is 5,992 years as of A.D. 1992. In fact, they compute that the fourth day of Creation, on which they say the Sun, Moon, and planets were created, began at 6 p.m. on Tuesday, March 21 (Gregorian calendar), 4001 B.C., which they indicate as a vernal equinox. Faulstich's group connects many events to solstices and equinoxes. They hold to a Friday crucifixion on April 5, A.D. 30 and compute Christ's birth as Sunday, May 14, 6 B.C. (Gregorian), an interesting connection to the birth of Israel on May 14, 1948. (Faulstich, Computer, 2-4, 6-13)

And so the scholarly debate continues, including the absolute precision of astronomical tables extrapolated backwards over long periods of time. The chronology featured in this book is intended only to serve as a workable reference tool based on the sources we have quoted.

As for future prophetical events, there are many views as to when Daniel's 70th Week and/or the Millennium will begin, whether before, at, or after the year 2000 – or at all! We are certainly *not* trying to be date setters, but we are indeed amazed at long-expected world developments occurring at an ever-accelerating pace.

Counting Back From Solomon

Probably the most commonly used and widely accepted chronology among today's prominent conservative Bible scholars is based on the research of Edwin R. Thiele in *The Mysterious Numbers of the Hebrew Kings*. Thiele's work "established" to the satisfaction of many scholars that the **beginning of Solomon's reign was 971 B.C.** (In the 1600s, Ussher dated it at 1015 B.C. Some secular sources date it in the 960s or 950s B.C. There is still controversy among both secular and biblical scholars.) The verse **I Kings 6:1** (most Bibles use the Hebrew or Masoretic text) states that Solomon began to build the Temple in the fourth year of his reign, which was also **480 years** after the Exodus from Egypt. Dr. Allen Ross counts that year as 966 B.C. [Thiele interprets "in the fourth year of Solomon's reign" to mean 967 B.C., thus adding one year to Dr. Ross's calculations.] **Counting backward,** Ross adds 480 years to calculate the date of the **Exodus as 1446 B.C.**

Ussher dated the Exodus at **1491 B.C.** because he believed that the **430 years** of **Egyptian bondage** referred to in Ex. 12:34 and Gal. 3:17 began when Abraham left Haran, 215 years before Jacob entered Egypt. Those who agree with Ussher (many do and many don't) also usually agree that the 400 years of oppression prophesied in Gen. 15:13 began, not actually in Egypt, but with the weaning of Isaac in Gen. 21:8-13. Ishmael, who was half Egyptian, mocked Isaac and God told Abraham to heed Sarah's wishes and cast out the illegitimate son. This is thought to have happened when Isaac was five years old and Abraham was 105, or 30 years after the original giving of the covenant. Dr. Ross and many other conservatives who rely on Thiele's work believe that the 430 years in Egypt began with God's reaffirmation of the covenant to Jacob as the Jews entered Egypt and that the oppression started with a new pharaoh 30 years later. (Ross, BKC I, 89, 96-7; Hannah, BKC I, 104-5, 129; Constable, BKC I, 499)

Thus, in many sources you will see these dates, counting backward from Solomon, as "standard and accepted": 931 for the divided Kingdom, 971 for Solomon's reign, 1446 (or 1447) for the Exodus, and 1876 to enter Egypt. Continuing to count back using conservative numbers, this gives a date of 2166 for Abraham's birth, 2518 for the Flood, and 4174 for Creation. *The main point is that this is only 173 years off a 4001 B.C. Creation date.*

Our Own Dating System

In this series, we have decided to present our own conclusions drawn from a wide range of chronological studies, not because we think we have made all the right decisions, but because we do think that *chronology is a valuable study in the accuracy of Scripture.* After weighing the evidence, we have decided that, at this point, the **7,000-year plan of God** is a reasonable assumption, that Christ was most likely born in **1 B.C.** and that Creation should then be dated from **4001 B.C.**

We first decided to give Israel a full **430 years in Egypt**, but realized that this did not fit with the dates and the prophecies related to the captivities, the return of the remnant to rebuild the Temple, the order to rebuild Jerusalem, and particularly the time specified by Daniel unto the crucifixion of Messiah. It simply didn't allow enough time for the years of the divided kingdom. The only other option was to push back dates in the other direction, accepting a date for Creation in the range of 4174 B.C.

Other considerations in dealing with the 430-year time period are the statement God made to Abraham in Gen. 15:16 that the Israelites would return to Canaan "in the **fourth generation**," and the **genealogy of Levi**. According to Exodus 6 and Num. 26:57-9, Moses and Aaron were the sons of Amram, the son of Kohath, the son of Levi, the son of Jacob. Kohath accompanied his father Levi into Egypt (Gen. 46), so that part of the genealogy is tight. Amram was the father (not forefather) of Moses, so that part of the genealogy is tight. Moses is the fourth from Levi, which agrees with God's statement. If the Israelites were actually in Egypt for a full 430 years, there would have to be a "gap" in the genealogy and the only possibility is between Kohath and Amram. However, Amram married his father's sister who was born to Levi in Egypt (Num. 26:59). That doesn't seem to allow for much of a gap, if any at all. This argument is upheld by Dr. Ozanne, who also supports Ussher's belief that **only 215 years** passed between Jacob's arrival and his descendants' exit. Ozanne claims that this shorter time period was adequate to produce the large number of Israelites led out by Moses, due to their still-long lifespans (137 years for Levi and Amram, Ex. 6), polygamy, and God-given fertility. (Ozanne, First, 20-23)

It is also interesting that it is exactly 215 years from Abraham's entrance into Canaan when he was 75 to Jacob's entrance into Egypt. Of course, **215 + 215 = 430**. Thus, we decided to bow to the recognized scholarship of Archbishop Ussher (and others) and **count the 430 years from Abraham's call.**

Does Anyone Really Know What Day This Is?

The question arises, *"If ancient man was as intelligent and superior as this series proposes, and was so meticulous in tracking the movements of the heavens and keeping calendars, why do we not know exactly how many days have passed since Creation and Adam?"* We should, but E.W. Bullinger attributes this problem to the **sin nature of man**. "Notwithstanding the fact that God gave to man these heavenly timekeepers," writes Bullinger, "he [man] has so misused the gift (as he has every other gift which God has ever given him) that he cannot tell you now what year it really is!" Bullinger continues

Biblical Chronology

B.C.	Biblical	E.Y. (Earth Year)	E.Y. (Earth Year)	Chronology	B.C.
4001	Creation	1	2187	Eber dies	1814
3071	Adam dies	930	2259	Joseph born	1742
3014	Enoch raptured	987	2276	Joseph sold/Egypt	1725
2945	Noah born	1056	2296	Famine begins	1705
2345	FLOOD	1656	2298	Jacob enters Egypt	1703
2343	Arpachshad born	1658	2369	Joseph dies	1632
2244	Peleg born	1757	2433	Moses born	1568
2174?	TOWER OF BABEL?	1827?	2513	EXODUS	1488
2123	Terah born	1878	2553	Moses dies	1448
2005	Peleg dies	1996	2555?	Joshua's Long Day?	1446?
1995	Noah dies	2006	2950	David crowned king	1051
1993	ABRAHAM born	2008	2990	Solomon is king	1011
1984?	Nimrod executed?	2017?	2993	Solomon starts Temple (480 yrs to Ex.)	1008
1918	Abraham leaves Haran (Covenant given)	2083	3030	Divided Kingdom	971
1907	Ishmael born	2094	3396	Babylonian Captivity (Temple burned 586)	605
1894?	Sodom/Gomorrah?	2107?	3466	End of Captivity/ Cyrus (rebuild Temple)	535
1893	ISAAC born	2108	3556	Artaxerxes' decree	445
1888	Isaac mocked at weaning (Affliction)	2113	4000	BIRTH OF CHRIST	1
1843	SHEM dies	2158	4032	PALM SUNDAY	A.D. 32
1833	JACOB born	2168	5993?	Daniel's 70th Week? *(Note: today's calendar may be off 1 or more years.)*	1993?
1818	ABRAHAM dies	2183	6000?	Millennium?	2000?

Ancient American Man

to say that "No subject is in more hopeless confusion, made worse by those who desire the dates to fit in with their theories of numbers, instead of with the facts of history." (Bullinger, Number, 3-4)

The most important conclusions that we hope you draw from this study are these:
1) the **Bible** provides a far more **reasonable** explanation for science and history than any humanistic, evolutionist scheme;
2) the **genealogies** of the Bible seem to be quite tight and **accurate** and fit rather well into the findings of other conservative, historical research;
3) due perhaps both to human sin and divine plan, there is **just enough confusion** to prevent anyone from compiling an "infallible" chronology and thus predicting specific dates for certain future events; *we do not know if this is really the 1993rd year after the birth of Christ -- we may be off one, two, or more years.*
4) on the other hand, the weight of Scriptural evidence encourages us to make close "guesstimates" and heightens our anticipation of **events soon to come;**
5) though we have not in this series detailed the **Jewish feasts** and their meanings, an understanding of these feasts and many Jewish teachings is vital to your interpretation of the Scripture and a study which should be pursued through men such as Zola Levitt and Joseph Good;
6) that **God has a plan** of which He is in absolute control, that the Scripture reveals a complex design of mathematical intricacy and beauty, and that God seems to accomplish His purposes "to the very day," whether or not we are able, with our information, to count those very days.

The IQ of Ancient Man

We have established a timeframe of about 4,000 years of human history before Christ, as opposed to billions and billions or millions or tens of thousands of years. This certainly changes the context in which we view man, especially compared to the pervasive concepts of the evolutionists. Now, to determine the intellectual abilities and technological level of those who first settled the Americas, we must develop an **intellectual profile of ancient man before and after the Flood.**

Our inclination is to ask how "advanced" or how "developed" was human civilization right before and after the Flood, rather than how knowledgeable was man. Why? Because the humanists have taught us to think of man as developing **from an amoeba to a monkey to cave man to modern man**, always advancing from *lower to higher*, physically and intellectually. We Christians may dismiss the monkey, but we still tend to think "lower to higher" because we focus on tracing the development of modern technology from the Middle Ages (about A.D. 900) to the present. It's hard not to think of everything as "lower to higher" when we see the progression of horse-and-buggy to supersonic jet. *However, we are amazingly ignorant of the knowledge and technical abilities of the ancients.*

Human civilization right after the Flood consisted of one family of eight people, headed by Noah. The former civilization was destroyed and the Earth radically changed. These eight people had only what was left on the boat plus their own knowledge and abilities, and that was all in the way of human resources. How much divine guidance or evil angelic guidance they may have received, we do not know. So the question is really, *"What did Noah know?"*

What Did Noah Know?

To answer that question, we need an idea of what civilization was like *before* the Flood, and the best source for that is the first six chapters of Genesis. Let's begin with Gen. 1:26 and list our observations of the very first humans:

1) IMAGE OF GOD: man was created, not evolved, and set apart and above all other physical creations; this implies that man, from the very beginning, was rational and moral, with a personality.

2) DOMINION: man was given, from the

very beginning, dominion (authority to rule) over all other physical creatures. (Remember angelic beings are spiritual creatures.) So, man not only had the authority to rule, but the intellectual ability and knowledge to control and subdue the physical creation.

3) LIVING SOUL: man had a physical body made from the same elements as the Earth, but his true self was an indestructible spiritual being. Man exists forever in spiritual form, whether it be in heaven or hell. Doctrinally and intellectually, it is difficult for us to dinstinguish between soul and spirit, though we try. According to Scripture, the reason we need to be "born again," to have fellowship with God is the fact that we are born spiritually dead because of Adam's sin. The day Adam sinned, he died spiritually. He died physically later, though at some point we assume he was "born again" by faith, as was Abraham. Thus, we could conclude that an unbeliever has only a soul and no spirit. But, this same unbeliever will be bodily resurrected and sentenced to an everlasting punishment. Thus, the unbeliever must have an eternal spiritual aspect, even though that spirit is not "born again" to God.

This implies an ability to communicate and interact with spiritual beings.

4) GARDENER (AND BOTANIST?): Adam immediately had the knowledge and ability to manage the Garden of Eden, a massive undertaking.

5) COMMANDMENTS: demonstrates that Adam was an intelligent being with a moral nature, capable of entering into a contract with God.

6) ZOOLOGIST: Adam had the intellect and memory to distinguish and name every beast and every bird on the face of the Earth. Dr. Carl Baugh points out that God paraded all of the cattle, fowl, and beasts before Adam to *see* what Adam would call them. (Gen. 2:19) He did not tell Adam what to call them. (Baugh, Panorama, 22-23; lecture, Dallas, TX, 7/25/92)

7) LANGUAGE: Adam had a fully developed language through which he could communicate with God, with other humans, and possibly with the animals, seeing that Eve showed no distress at having a conversation with an animal, and Adam reviewed all of the animals in search of a companion (Gen. 2:20). Josephus, the 1st-Century Jewish historian, records the ancient belief that, before the Fall, "all the living creatures had one language," so that communication between Eve and the serpent, "which then lived together with Adam and his wife," was quite normal. (Josephus, Ant., I.i.4.) There is no mention of writing before the Flood in the Bible; however, it is not denied. Could any cuneiform tablet or petroglyph date from before the Flood? Did Noah carry any written records on the Ark? Once again, Josephus notes that those who lived before the Flood "noted down, with great accuracy, both the births and deaths of illustrious men." (Josephus, Ant., I.iii.3.)

8) UNDERSTANDING OF HUMAN RELATIONSHIPS: Adam immediately understood Eve's purpose and role, and prophesied about parents, something which he had not experienced.

9) ANALYSIS AND CHOICE: Both Adam and Eve had the ability to analyze a situation, weigh the pros and cons, and choose a course of action. In their sin, they aspired to the wisdom of God promised them by Satan, if not equality with God. (Read Gen. 3 very carefully.)

10) OCCUPATIONS: Adam was also a teacher, instructing his sons in farming and ranching which were the immediate occupations of the first humans born on Earth. He also instructed his sons in spiritual matters such as blood sacrifice to atone for sin.

11) RELIGION/SPIRITUALITY: the very first men had an understanding of sin, blood sacrifice (grace/Abel), bloodless offerings (works/Cain), proper and improper giving, guilt, judgment, mercy, and forgiveness.

12) TECHNOLOGY: Cain, who is recorded as the first human born on Earth, went to the east and immediately built a *CITY*. The seventh generation from Cain fathered the nomadic shepherd culture, musicians, and metal craftsmen who worked in ***BRONZE*** and ***IRON***. This is particularly important because archaeology and most published histories are based on the "lower-to-higher" **Three-Age System** which says the *Stone Age (before 3500 B.C.)* came first, then the *Bronze Age (c. 3500 B.C. - 1000 B.C.)*, and then the *Iron Age (c. 1000 B.C. - A.D. 100)*, using commonly accepted European dates (Webster's New World Dictionary). The Bible says that man worked in both bronze and iron before the Flood, only a few hundred years after Creation and perhaps earlier. In addition, **Noah,**

with only his three sons to help, constructed an **Ark** the size of a **modern ocean liner**, using wood and "pitch," meaning bitumen (tar or asphalt). Some kind of tar must have occurred naturally, as petroleum deposits would be formed by the catastrophe of the Flood.

13) PASSAGE OF TIME: ages were recorded by years and farming was done by seasons. Even in the climate-controlled, pre-Flood environment, there must have been "seasons" and growing times (Gen. 1:14). Pre-Flood man must have already had the **predecessor of the *360-day* Jewish calendar** as the beginning of the Flood is recorded in Gen. 7:11 as the 600th year of Noah's life in the 17th day of the second month of the year. Flood events continue to be dated by the day of the month.

14) ANGELIC INTERACTION: This is a controversial point on which the reader will find respected conservatives divided. Gen. 6 says that "sons of God" (used in the Old Testament for angels) physically interacted with female descendants of Cain (the evil line of men) to produce giants (*"Rapha"* or *"Rephaim"*) who were **half angel and half man**. Of course, the angels involved were fallen angels and followers of Satan (*"Nephilim"* or "fallen ones").

Some Bible scholars say that the "sons of God" in this case were the **sons of Seth** who married **daughters of Cain**. Still others say that fallen angels influenced or even indwelt rebellious **sons of Cain** who took many wives for themselves and became fearsome leaders. Their main arguement against the literal "half angel/half man" interpretation is **Matt. 22:30** which says that men shall not marry following the resurrection but will be "like the angels in heaven." However, Dr. S. Lewis Johnson points out that this reference only indicates that angels do not normally marry. It does not preclude them from losing "their first estate" and leaving "their own habitation" (Jude 6) and mixing physically with the daughters of men. (Johnson, tape series on Matthew, Believers Chapel, Dallas, TX)

William Whiston, the 17th/18th-Century mathematician, theologian, and translator of the works of Josephus, notes the belief that the fallen angels were fathers to the giants was "the constant **opinion of antiquity**." (Josephus, Ant., I.iii.1, note) Also to be considered is the widespread and persistent **pagan "mythologies"** of the half-god/half man beings, found not only in Greece but all over the world, including the Americas. A man who was half angel would not be half divine (as only God is divine), but would certainly be supernaturally superior to a normal physical man. The **occult** recognizes beings they call incubus (male demons) and succubus (demons in female form) who mate with humans. (Drury, Dict. of Myst., 129, 246)

In His written Word, the Lord God (who is a master of understatement and reserve, to say the least), says these men were **"mighty" and famous**, with reputations that were widely celebrated. They were very probably Satan's attempt to **pollute all of mankind** in order to prevent the birth of the promised "Seed" or Christ. This evil pollution thus forced God to utterly destroy the Earth, saving only Noah who was "perfect in his generations" (Gen. 6:9), or unpolluted by the evil angels. In addition, Gen. 6:4 says that there were giants in the Earth in those days and "also after that," leading certain scholars to note the **giants in Canaan** at the time of Joshua, and their descendants, Goliath's family, who later were killed by David. Could this possible second attempt at pollution be a reason (besides idolatry) that cities like Jericho (Joshua 6) were "accursed" and had to be destroyed, to every man, woman, child, and animal?

If the literal interpretation is indeed the true one and pre-Flood mankind included half-breed beings that were **half demonic angel and half human**, then the very first men were capable of *intellectual and social interaction with intellectually superior supernatural beings.* Actually, the fact that this interaction occurred is evidenced, whether or not such half-breeds were physically reproduced. Adam and his specific line through Seth to Noah remained pure and possessed knowledge given by God. Those who **interacted with the fallen angels** received knowledge from that superior, supernatural source, in addition to the knowledge they had from God through Adam.

We have already referenced (Chap. 1) one book by Emil Gaverluk, M.Div., Ph.D., Ed.D. A writer, science lecturer, and conservative Christian, Dr. Gaverluk wrote another book (now out of print) titled *Did Genesis Man Conquer Space 5,000 Years Ago?* In both works, he presents evidence gathered by NASA's Viking Orbiter showing **ruins on the surface of Mars** that include huge pyramids (maybe one-half mile high), water courses, agricultural terraces, a mile-wide face carved out of a mountain, and a naturally occurring laser beam 40 miles above the surface with power equivalent to 1,000 nuclear reactors. Dr. Gaverluk believes that the **antediluvians** (pre-Flood man), perhaps in concert with their demonic-angel contacts, **traveled to Mars** and *used lasers to carve the spectacular structures* mentioned above, including pyramids that would serve as giant capacitors to tap into the electromagnetic field of Mars in order to store an electric charge.

The huge laser 40 miles above the surface, that is said by NASA to occur naturally, could have been used, explains Dr. Gaverluk, to produce water from ice in space and hydrogen/oxygen for a new atmosphere. This space program was part of **Satan's plan to restore the solar system and colonize the Universe**. However, the program was frustrated, concludes Gaverluk, when God forced the antedeluvian giants to return to Earth to face the judgment of the Flood. (Gaverluk, Rapture, ii, 227, 272-274)

The question arises, are the structural remains found on Mars **ruins of one of the angelic kingdoms** of the pre-human, pre-Gen. 1:2 Universe? The main objection that comes to mind is the fact that the **sphinx-like face** and the **pyramidal structures** are like those of Egypt, and are both *pagan* and *human* in character and concept. Why would spirit beings in a totally spiritual Universe, subject to God, carve a massive human face? It would

MYSTERIOUS STRUCTURES ON MARS

In the summer of 1976, **NASA's Viking I** spacecraft established an orbit around the planet Mars. In July, it captured and relayed the image of what looked to be a massive human face, carved out of a "knob" (large hill), but the single frame was viewed and dismissed without further analysis as a trick of light and shadow. Several years later, Vincent DiPietro and Gregory Molenar, two engineers working at NASA's Goddard Space Flight Center, found another very recognizable image of the face, taken 35 orbits later, proving that the image was not merely a fleeting trick of light and shadow.

The **Face** is about 1.55 miles long, 1.25 miles wide, and 1,312 feet high. If a building story was 10 feet, the Face would be some 131 stories tall. It has eyes below bilaterally crossed lines, a ridgelike nose, a mouth with a fine structure that some have called teeth, and some sort of headpiece or helmet with regularly spaced lateral stripes. These same features appear in both images, 35 orbits apart. The right side of the Face is either degraded or was never completed, though it also shows an eye and part of the mouth.

Near the Face is a group of pyramidal structures called the **City** which includes a trapezoidal formation nicknamed the **Fortress** which "appears to include several wall-like sections including two straight sides enclosing an inner space." (Carlotto, Martian, 7-9, 20, 23) Nearby is another large, five-sided pyramid which appears to be damaged. Called the **D&M Pyramid**, this object displays hexagonal symmetry, pentagonal symmetry, and a **Golden Section** (*phi* or 1.618) Vortex. [See Chapter 10 on the Great Pyramid.] This was discovered in 1988 by a formerly skeptical cartographer named Erol Torun of the U.S. Defense Mapping Agency who, attempting to disprove these geometrical characteristics, discovered that this pyramid may indeed have a **mathematical message**, just as the **Great Pyramid** in Egypt.

These and several other enigmatic structures or objects in the Cydonia region of the northern hemisphere of Mars demonstrate a construction layout and **geometrical relationships** strongly reminiscent of astronomical complexes in Egypt, Mexico, and Central America, according to Richard Hoagland and Erol Torun. Of course, these researchers have no other explanation than extraterrestrial life (ETs). Because of elevations, surface contours, and signs of water channels, some conjecture that the **Cydonia complex** lies near the shoreline of an ancient ocean. There *(cont'd.)*

> are also several other intriguing formations in other regions, specifically the Crater Pyramid, the Radial Complex, and the Runway, which demonstrate artificial or "man-made" (angel-made?) characteristics. (Carlotto, Martian, 7, 11, 29, 109-11)
>
> **Dr. Mark J. Carlotto** has spent five years analyzing the Viking I images of Mars using advanced computer systems. Dr. Carlotto is an expert in digital image processing, pattern recognition, and perspective transformation, among other subjects, with a Ph.D. in Electrical Engineering from Carnegie-Mellon University. At the time of his research, from 1985 to 1990, he was (and may still be) employed by a high-tech firm in the Boston area. After his **3-D analysis** of the Face, Carlotto concluded that the "features are present in the underlying topography and do seem to reflect recognizably facial characteristics over a wide range of illumination conditions and perspectives." (Carlotto, Martian, 33)
>
> He also applied a mathematical method to the Cydonia complex known as *fractal modeling*. **Natural** objects are fractal, meaning that they exhibit similar, repetitive patterns. **Artificial** structures are *non*-fractal. This method can be used to identify military tanks or vehicles, for example, in an aerial photo. Carlotto concluded that preliminary results "suggest that the Face and other nearby objects in Cydonia do share objectively measurable qualities that set them apart from the surrounding terrain." Basically, the Cydonia formations "lack the kind of structure that is characteristic of naturally shaped landforms." Or, in other words, these tests show that these objects are artificial formations. (Carlotto, Martian, 48-52)

seem that these structures are the work of fallen angels, after Satan's sin and God's judgment upon the Universe. Perhaps Mars was the location of an angelic domain and these angels were indeed trying to restore it.

Of course, then, the question follows, why should angels carve something so **human in character**? This does seem to point us back to Dr. Gaverluk's mind-blowing hypothesis, that **pre-Flood giants** were involved in building an outpost in the solar system, with a massive face that was perhaps a beacon recognizable to other fallen spirit beings. Also, scientists generally agree that Mars shows evidence of *dry river beds, former stream channels, flood plains, and perhaps an ancient ocean*. Carbonates and sulfates have been found which are "provocative evidence" for a Martian atmosphere (conducive to water formation) that no longer exists. (*Science News*, 1987, 173; Carlotto, Martian, 11)

This domain of fallen angel (and possibly pre-Flood giant) may not have been judged as we see it now until the time of the Flood. God may have **devastated Mars** then, throwing the planet into a new orbit which affected the Earth at certain times or intervals until perhaps 1500 to 1200 B.C. or even the 700s B.C. See Chapter 8 on the heavens for a discussion of mankind's **worship and fear of Mars**, the red planet of war, and the very **careful observations** made of its movements (**Venus** also) by ancient astronomers in the Middle East and in the Americas. At least nine meteorites found in India, Antarctica, France, Egypt, Brazil, Nigeria, and the state of Indiana show characteristics which indicate Mars as their origin. (*Newsweek*, 1983, 73; *Earth Science*, 1983, 20-1)

So, **Noah** knew about cities, bronze, iron, music, farming, ranching, shipbuilding, timekeeping, legal contracts, and spiritual issues. He possessed a highly developed language and the ability to follow instructions and build according to plans. He was genetically far superior to 20th-Century man, as were his long-lived ancestors, and lived to be 950 years old, 20 years longer than Adam. Noah knew, personally, all of the chosen line of patriarchs except Adam, Seth, and Enoch, while Noah's father, Lamech, knew them all. Noah's father was alive when Adam died and when Enoch was raptured. According to the biblical and scientific **"higher to lower"** principle, both Adam and Noah were intellectually superior as well. Modern man makes up for his degeneration through **technology**, prophesied by **Daniel 12:4** which says that knowledge would increase in the end times.

In his book *Panorama of Creation*, Dr. Carl E. Baugh includes a chapter called "Superior Man from the Beginning" in which he lists, in scientific terms, **56 superior characteristics** possessed by pre-Flood man. With this foundation, we can proceed to include **secular sources** as well as the Bible to discover more about the knowledge and capabilities available to the men who repopulated the post-Flood world. *We will discover that these men were masters of advanced mathematics, astronomy, architecture, construction, boat building, world geography, navigation, colonization, manufacturing, and trade.*

There is also the evidence of *trepanned* skulls that demonstrate *ancient surgical skill and medical knowledge.* **Trepanation** is the surgical removal of portions of human skull for the purpose, say Peruvian natives, of curing headaches, neuralgia, vertigo, etc. A trepanned skull found in West Germany is dated by evolutionists at 3000 B.C. (in other words, it's ancient), and other such skulls have been found in Europe, Asia, Africa, North and South America, and throughout the South Pacific. Certain skulls show that those individuals *survived as many as five operations!* (McKern, Exploring, 43-48)

The Origin of the First Americans

We have made some basic determinations about the age and IQ of ancient man, and thus, about his post-Flood ancestors who would settle the Americas. In later chapters, and particularly in Volume II of this series, we will study the various national and cultural origins, over several thousand years, of Mr. and Mrs. Ancient America.

Obviously, according to **biblical evidence**, all men have a single origin within a time period that stretches only a few thousand years. We have already seen some, and we will see much more, **secular evidence** that supports the *diffusionist* view of creationists — that mankind diffused over the entire Earth from a single location.

BIBLIOGRAPHY

Baugh, Carl E., *Panorama of Creation*. Oklahoma City: Southwest Radio Church, 1989. [Creation Evidences Museum, P.O. Box 309, Glen Rose, TX 76043, (817) 897-3200]

Blick, Edward, *Special Creation vs. Evolution*. Oklahoma City: Southwest Radio Church, 1981.

Blick, Edward, *Correlation of the Bible and Science*. Oklahoma City: Southwest Radio Church, 1988.

Bullinger, E.W., *Number in Scripture*. Grand Rapids: Kregel Publications, 1967.

Carlotto, Mark J., *The Martian Enigmas, A Closer Look*. Berkeley: North Atlantic Books, 1991.

Constable, Thomas L., "I Kings," *The Bible Knowledge Commentary*, Old Testament (Vol. I). Wheaton: Victor Books, 1985.

Crenshaw, Winn, "Letter to a Skeptic, Part II," *The Chosen People*. Charlotte, N.C.: Chosen People Ministries, Vol. XCVIII, No. 3, Nov. 1991.

Drury, Nevill, *Dictionary of Mysticism and the Occult*. San Francisco: Harper & Row, 1985.

Faulstich, Eugene W., *A Computer Demonstration About God's Existence* (I) and *The Messiah of Israel & Signs from Heaven* (II). Spencer, Iowa: Chronology-History Research Institute, 1992 [P.O. Box 3043, Spencer, IA, 51301, or contact Walter Lang, The Genesis Institute, 7232 Morgan Ave., Richfield, MN, 55423, (612) 861-5288)]

Faulstich, Eugene W., *History, Harmony & the Hebrew Kings*. Spencer, Iowa: Chronology Books, 1986.

Gaverluk, *Rapture*, Bib. Chap. 1, p. 19.

Good, Joseph, *Rosh HaShanah and the Messianic Kingdom to Come*. Port Arthur, Texas: Hatikva Ministries, 1991. [P.O. Box 3125, Port Arthur, TX, 77643-3125, (409) 724-7601)]

Hannah, John D., "Exodus," *The Bible Knowledge Commentary*, Old Testament (Vol. I). Wheaton: Victor Books, 1985.

Henry, Matthew, "Luke," *A Commentary on the Whole Bible*. New Jersey: Fleming H. Revell Co., Vol. V of six; "Acts," Vol. VI.

Jeffrey, Grant R., *Armageddon*. (Toronto: Frontier Research Publications, 1988.

Josephus, [see *Whiston*] References given in Book, Chapter, Section, such as I.iv.3.

Kagan, Donald (revised), *Botsford and Robinson's Hellenic History*. New York: The Macmillan Company, 1969.

Lindsey, F. Duane, "Judges," *The Bible Knowledge Commentary*, Old Testament (Vol. I). Wheaton: Victor Books, 1985.

McKern, Sharon S., *Exploring the Unknown,*

Mysteries in American Archaeology. New York: Praeger Publishers, 1972

McLean, G.S., and Oakland, Roger, and McLean, Larry, *The Early Earth*. Oklahoma City: Southwest Radio Church, 1987. [For publications and daily radio broadcasts, contact Southwest Radio Church, P.O. Box 1144, Oklahoma City, OK 73101, (800) 652-1144. Also, FGBI Productions, Box 579, Eston, Saskatchewan, CANADA, S0L 1A0, (306) 962-4755]

Meyer, F.B., *Abraham*. Fort Washington, Pennsylvania: Christian Literature Crusade, 1985.

Morris, Henry M., *Many Infallible Proofs*. San Diego: Creation-Life Publishers (CLP), 1974.

Morris, Henry M., (ed.), *Scientific Creationism*. San Diego: Creation-Life Publishers, 1974.

Ozanne, C.G., *The First 7000 Years*. New York: Exposition Press, 1970.

Ross, Allen P., "Genesis," *The Bible Knowledge Commentary, Old Testament (Vol. I)*. Wheaton: Victor Books, 1985.

"Rocks from Moon & Mars?" *Earth Science*, 36:20-1, Spring, 1983.

"Scientists Hail a Visitor from Mars," *Newsweek*, 101:73, March 28, 1983.

Scofield, C.I. (ed.), *The New Scofield Reference Bible*, King James Version. New York: Oxford University Press, 1967.

Setterfield, Barry, and Norman, Trevor, *The Atomic Constants, Light, and Time*. Menlo Park, California: Stanford Research Institute International, Aug. 1987 (Technical Report). [Walter Lang, Genesis Institute, listed under Faulstich]

Setterfield, Barry, *Geological Time and Scriptural Chronology*, 1991. Barry Setterfield, Box 318, Blackwood, S.A., 5051, Australia.

"Signs of old Mars: Written in the dust," *Science News*, 135: 173, March 18, 1987.

"The Man on the Planet Mars: Who Dunnit?" *Newsweek*, 112:64, July 25, 1988. (with photo of face)

Thiele, Edwin R., *The Mysterious Numbers of the Hebrew Kings*. Grand Rapids: William B. Eerdmans Publishing Co., 1965.

Toussaint, Stanley, "Acts," *The Bible Knowledge Commentary, New Testament (Vol. II)*. Wheaton: Victor Books, 1985.

Webster's New World Dictionary of the American Language, Second College Edition. Cleveland: William Collins + World Publishing Co., Inc., 1976.

Whiston, William (translator), "Antiquities of the Jews," ***Josephus**, Complete Works*. Grand Rapids: Kregel Publications, 1960.

Whitcomb, John C., Jr., and Morris, Henry M., *The Genesis Flood*. Presbyterian and Reformed Publishing Co.: 1961.

PROJECTS

Creationism: We have only touched on the amount of evidence available to support the creationist point of view. Read as many books as you can on this subject. Contact organizations such as Southwest Radio Church and the Creation Evidences Museum (see Bibliography) for further information. Several of the books referenced in this chapter list organizations such as the Institute for Creation Research founded by Dr. Henry Morris.

If you live in or nearby Texas, or plan a vacation, visit the Creation Evidences Museum in Glen Rose and see the dinosaur and human prints for yourself. Call ahead for special seminars and digs in which you can participate. Creation Evidences Museum, (817) 897-3200.

Genealogies: Make your own chart of the genealogies in Genesis 5 and 11. Pay special attention to such verses as Gen. 7:6,11,24; 8:13; 11:10,26,32; 12:4; 17:1,17,21-25; 21:5; 23:1; 25:7,20,26; 26:34; 35:28; 37:2; 41:46; 47:9,28; Ex. 12:41; Acts 7:4.

Mars: Try to find Carlotto's book on Mars. The digitally enhanced pictures are fascinating. The library may also have the Viking Orbiter photos. Look for 35A72 and 70A13. Look up the magazine articles referenced here and also check the *Reader's Guide* for other articles. Your librarian will help you.

Trepanation: Look for trepanned skulls in museums. Find books or articles on the subject in the library. Once again, ask your librarian if you are not familiar with basic research tools. They love to help you learn how to use the library.

Evolution: Look in the encyclopedia and make a list of the basic "ages" and their dates. If you have not already studied it, it will amaze you. Also look for the Geologic Column. It is only theoretical (though it is foundational teaching for evolutionists) because an example of it cannot be found in reality. Fossils are dated by strata and strata are dated by fossils. That's called convoluted thinking.

Bible: Research the origins and reliability of the Bible. There are *many* good books on this subject. Josh McDowell's *Evidence That Demands A Verdict* in two volumes is an excellent source (Chapters 1 through 4 in Vol. 1), as is W. H. Griffith Thomas's *How We Got Our Bible*. Check your local Christian book store.

WRITING NOTES

Parallelism and Rhythm: In Chapter 1, we talked about serial commas. Have you ever noticed that most series are in threes? It falls well on our ears. It's a good rhythm. Perhaps it's also another connection to the Trinity which seems to run throughout every aspect of the universe, including our very souls.

When you write, see that your structures are parallel. This contributes both to rhythm and clarity. For example, consider this sentence: *When I was young and bursting with optimism, my most propulsive desires were to go to college, to travel the world, and to achieve recognition as a writer.* Each member of the series is constructed as an infinitive. What if the sentence read: *to go* to college, *traveling* the world, and *involved* a successful writing career. Yuch! The three different verb forms (infinitive, gerund, past tense) strung together sound terrible (destroy the *rhythm*) and cloud the meaning (destroy the *clarity*). Verbs, phrases, and clauses should have the same basic construction.

All elements that are linked (coordinates) should be parallel. When Shakespeare composed Marc Antony's famous speech, he did *not* write "Friends, people of Rome, and fellow citizens," but, instead, "Friends, Romans, and countrymen...." (*Julius Caesar*, III.II.75-80) You can find an excellent discussion of parallelism in *Prose Style for the Modern Writer* by Robert Miles and Marc Bertonasco (New Jersey: Prentice-Hall, Inc., 1977, pp. 76-7, 151-161).

An effective way to examine the rhythm and clarity of your writing is to **read it aloud**. Then, let it sit for an hour, or a day, or a week, and read it aloud again. You will find that your perspective has sharpened! Also, when you read aloud, remember that a **comma** denotes a **pause** that is intended to enhance the rhythm and clarity of the sentence. Reading your work aloud will help you determine whether or not a comma is necessary or extraneous.

Plurals and Possessives: Rules for these two word forms are many and complex. In some cases, authorities disagree! Let's look at a few of the usages we encounter in this series.

Dates, years, and numbers are common on our pages. Some experts prefer to add *'s* to numbers or years to make them plural. We have decided to follow the guidelines agreed on by *The Associated Press Stylebook and Libel Manual* and *The Chicago Manual of Style*. Thus, we say "in the 1920s" or "the 900s B.C." The *s* is easily distinguishable from the numbers in this typeface, and the presence or absence of the apostrophe clearly indicates plural or possessive. When we write "the 1920's rebelliousness" or "the 1500's race to discovery," it is obvious that the apostrophe denotes possession.

In the case of letters, such as "x's and y's" or "Ph.D.'s," we use the apostrophe to make a plural in order to avoid confusion. *Clarity* is the overriding determinant.

The possessives of *proper names* generally require the *'s*, such as Burns's poems, Marx's theories, Paul's letters, Dickens's novels, and James's books. However, *classical names* are usually given only the apostrophe, such as Jesus' works, Moses' words, Artaxerxes' decree, and Ramses' tomb.

Plurals of names ending in *s* are usually formed with an *es*, such as Rosses, Charleses, and Stephenses. Their possessives would only get an apostrophe (Rosses', Charleses') as an *'s* would look funny and require another *"ez"* sound.

Read back over all of the above examples and pronounce them aloud. Note that an *'s* usually calls forth an "ez" sound, especially if it follows an *s* or a *z*. The apostrophe originated as a mark of omission for a missing *e*. You will find in most cases that the decision to add an apostrophe with or without the *s* is guided by these questions: Is it clear? How does it look? How does it *sound*? Does the "ez" sound natural to your ear? Are there too many "ezes" in a row? The answers to these questions should clear up some confusion.

Chapter 3
Ancient American Geography: How Did God Create the New World?

Before the Flood

We have raised the question of the origin of the first Americans. But what about America itself? From where did the American continents come? Were they there from the beginning just as they are now? What effects did the Flood have on the Americas, and how did those results affect those who became the first Americans?

Some of the answers to these questions will become apparent as we continue our study through this and the next volume in this series. Here, we will begin with the continents.

One Land Mass

Evidence points to the fact that the continents once formed a central land mass. Our first and guiding source, the Bible, indicates that, before the Flood, all the **animals** were on the same land mass because God brought all of them to Adam to be named (Gen. 2:19-20). The creation account in Gen. 1:9-10 states that God **gathered the waters** under heaven (or under the "firmament," vs. 8) into *one* place so that dry land would appear. God called the dry part "Earth" and the gathered waters He called "Seas," using a Hebrew word, according to *Strong's Concordance*, that refers to roaring. The same word is used many times in the Bible for all or some part of the ocean and is translated more often in the singular than the plural, meaning that "Seas" in Gen. 1:10 could just as easily read "Sea." According to II Peter 3:5-6, the Earth "that then was...stood out of the water and in the water."

So, it would seem that the Earth was originally one land mass with an ocean gathered in one place. (The new heaven and new Earth described in Rev. 21:1 will have *no sea*.) In addition, the biblical description of the **rivers** running out of the **Garden of Eden** seems to indicate a geography quite different from what we see today in the Middle East (Gen. 2:10-14). First-Century Jewish historian, Josephus, derived his Edenic geography from writers more ancient than he, saying that the river watering the garden "ran round about the whole Earth," something possible only with a central land mass. He names the "other" two rivers as the Nile and the Ganges, an ancient tradition which defies the modern map. (Josephus, Ant., I.i.3.)

The idea of one original land mass has captured the interest of a growing number of **secular** (non-Bible-believing) **scientists** in the fields of geophysics and physical geography, climatology, and even biology. Austrian geologist **Eduard Suess** was first credited in the early 1900s with the observation that South America, Africa, India, Australia, and Antarctica had significant geologic and biologic similarities. He concluded that they were once the supercontinent of **"Gondwanaland,"** parts of which sunk and are now covered by the southern oceans. [Secular scientists have also called the

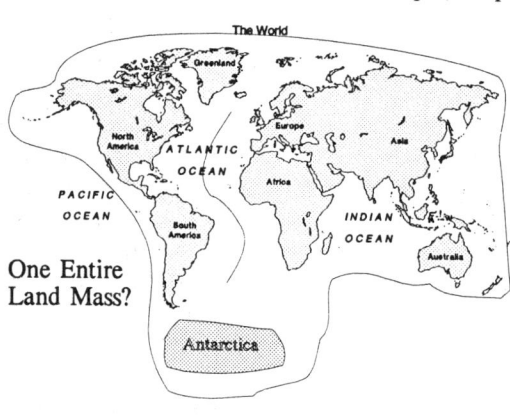

Was "Pangaea" actually the entire land mass before it was canaled by water? The "Atlantic" (and other ocean bottoms) may have sunk, leaving the present Mid-Atlantic Range.

original land mass **"Pangaea."**] In the 1920s, German meteorologist **Alfred Wegener** expanded on the idea of an original land mass by introducing the theory of **"continental drift."** He observed that North and South America fit like jigsaw-puzzle pieces into western Europe and Africa, and suggested that, for some unknown reason, the land mass broke up and formed continents which slowly (over vast amounts of time) drifted into their present positions.

Obviously, the slow-drift part of the theory is evolutionist in approach. A good evolutionist is a **uniformist**, believing that the processes we observe today are the same processes which have always existed and which formed, in a natural manner, over billions of years, the Earth and the universe. However, these scientists were now partially delving into **catastrophism** for explanations of present phenomena, as pointed out in 1961 by creationists Morris and Whitcomb in *The Genesis Flood*. They note that the continental drift "theory of course bears quite hard on the uniformist concept, and so is rejected by most geologists." As an example, they quote evolutionist Ernst J. Opik's 1957 book on ice ages which asserts that the positions of the continents have proved to be essentially the same for the past 100 million years. (Morris, Gen. Flood, 246)

But, after 1960, the deviation from strict uniformist thought caught on, as reported in a textbook edited by Dr. Morris in 1974. By the 1970s, most geologists had become committed to drift-centered concepts, discarding "the older explanations, which they once dogmatically accepted as certainties...." (Morris, Sci. Cre., 128) In 1984, *National Geographic* reported that the Crustal Dynamics Project at NASA's Goddard Space Flight Center near Washington, D.C. was using lasers to track continental drift, which they defined as continents rafting "across Earth's hot, plastic interior on stiff plates of planetary crust," thus colliding and creating Earthquakes, volcanoes, and mountain ranges. (Boraiko, Nat'l. Geog., 343) So, what was initially a subject for ridicule is now the field of **global plate tectonics** and "widely accepted as a geological truth." (McLean, Early Earth, 70, writing in 1987)

The point is that the majority of evolutionist scientists abandoned strict uniformist dogmas to embrace a theory based on initial observations which prompted the belief that the Earth was once one land mass. (See "The One Land Mass," Sec. I-7 in McLean's *The Bible — Key to Understanding The Early Earth*.) Creationist **Dr. Henry Morris** may not have held the belief in the one land mass at the time he co-authored *The Genesis Flood*, as evidenced by the remark that "we must look to the land bridges as the principal means of animal distribution around the world." (Morris, Gen. Flood, 85)

Or, he believed that the land mass separated during the Flood, requiring the animals to use land bridges to repopulate the whole Earth. A book edited by him in 1974 states that the cataclysmic Flood model alone offers the energy necessary for continental division and relocation. "It is plausible that it may have occurred," says the book, "along with continued tectonic and volcanic activity, as another aftereffect of the great Flood." (Morris, Sci. Cre., 128) Referring to the land bridges, there is compelling evidence from ancient cartography (maps), changes in sea level, and human tradition to indicate that some *possibly large* **land bridges** *did indeed exist for perhaps a good while after the Babel dispersion.* Before the major portions of polar ice formed, the area of the Aleutian Islands of Alaska may have been a large land area, and Indonesia may well have provided a solid block of land from Asia to Australia.

Baugh's *Panorama of Creation* and McLean's *Early Earth* are two creationist books which proceed on the basis that there was indeed an original, single land mass. Unlike the evolutionists, these creationists point to God's relatively quick and violent judgements of the Flood and the **Tower of Babel** as the agents of continental division. Both of these books present the scenario that the land mass ripped apart during the Flood, but was not divided by God until the Babel judgement, during the days of **Peleg** (Gen. 10:25). Peleg's name means **"canaled by water."** McLean and his fellow authors also argue that the initial separation did not immediately result in our present-day arrangement, but that *later judgements and catastrophes continued the process until Earth's geography stabilized, perhaps as late as the 700s B.C.* (Baugh, Panorama, 81-2, 94; McLean, Early, 71)

One of the phenomena that the continental drift proponents have tried to explain is the worldwide findings of tropical and subtropical **plant and animal life fossils**. Animal fossils of all climate types are found together in massive graveyards. Antarctic ice reveals petrified trees. Buried under frozen tundra and Arctic snow are the fossil imprints of giant palm leaves. Evolutionist Hugh A. Brown points to the remains of mammoths, mastodons, and dinosaurs that are found "at widely scattered areas of the Earth, at many different latitudes, and in successive Earth formations," showing that "their habitations extended over widely scattered and now separated land areas." This indicates, concluded Brown, that these animals **"roamed freely over a connected land area, in a warm climate...."** (Brown, Cataclysms, 23)

Another theory offered to explain this climatological phenomenon is the wandering of the Earth's poles, or **"spin-axis shifts."** There are arguments from *some* in both camps, evolutionist and creationist, that the Earth has tilted or even rolled over one or more times and (according to some on the creationist side) may have done so at the time of the Flood, Joshua's Long Day, and the 701 B.C. destruction of the Assyrians. There is also compelling evidence to believe that it *hasn't*. This will be considered further as we progress through our catastrophic history. However, the best explanation for the ample evidence of a mild worldwide climate seems to be the canopied-Earth system.

The Canopied Earth System

The creation model presented by Dr. Carl Baugh in *Panorama of Creation* shows the pre-Flood Earth as a large "egg" with a solid granite crust varying in depth from six to 16 miles, covering massive reservoirs of water ("the fountains of the great deep," Gen. 7:11). The "skin" of the crust, or the topography, had only "gentle, sloping elevations." The inside of the Earth was a perfectly balanced nuclear reactor. (Baugh, Panorama, 66-7, 78, 81, 94)

The creation account in Gen. 1:6-10 indicates the canopied Earth with the **water canopy** above the "firmament" which God called "Heaven," and the water below the firmament. [*Panorama of Creation* gives the best and most easily read scientific explanation of the canopy.]

II Peter 3:4-7 records that there were the heavens "of old" and the Earth "that then was," and then the heavens and Earth "which are now," giving us solid biblical evidence that the Earth and the heavens (which would include the firmament) before the Flood were significantly different from the Earth and the heavens that emerged from the Flood. The **climate** was mild and uniform from pole to pole. There were no weather changes or storms as we have today. There were growing seasons (sowing and reaping) and there was a regular, 24-hour, night-and-day cycle, but never total darkness. (See *Panorama of Creation*) The canopy provided more oxygen, a heavier **atmosphere**, and most significant, **a radiation shield**. Instead of an atmosphere 21 miles high as we have today, an atmospheric "heat sink" indicates that the Earth had an 11-mile-high atmosphere capped by the "firmament" of **crystalline hydrogen**. This firmament was like a transparent sheet of metal, formed by the compression of water in cryogenic (super cold) temperatures, with crystalline ice on either side of the metallic sheet. The Earth's magnetic field levitated or held up this superconductive canopy. What is truly interesting is that the Hebrew word for firmament is *raqiya*, which is derived from a word meaning to compress, stretch, or pound out, or overlay with thin sheets of metal. (Strong's; Baugh, Panorama, 47-9) This firmament created nearly two atmospheres of pressure (instead of one) with an oxygen

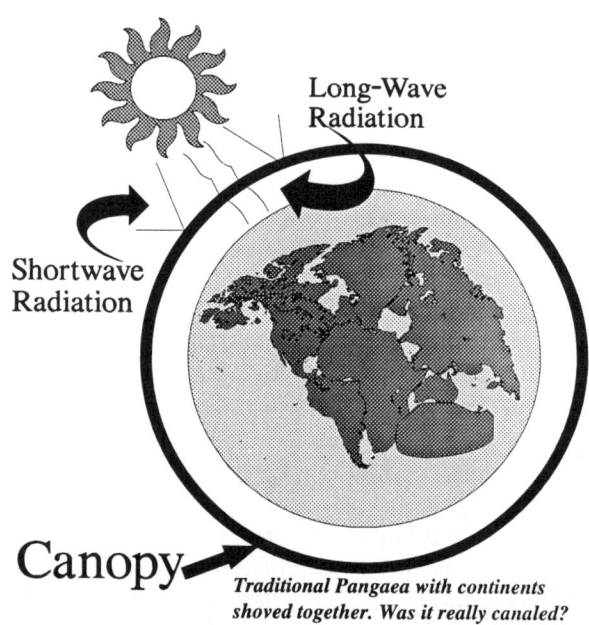

Traditional Pangaea with continents shoved together. Was it really canaled?

content of 30% instead of today's 19% to 21%. (Baugh lecture, 7/25/92)

Biblical evidence for the canopy and the uniform climate includes the length of man's life, the description of the "waters" and the "firmament" (Gen. 1:6-8), the fact that men and animals were all vegetarian (Gen. 1:29-30), the fact that it did not rain (Gen. 2:5-6), the description in Gen. 7 of the process of the Flood judgement, and the subsequent introduction of meat eating and the shortening of man's life span. **Scientific evidence** exists as well, most dramatically in the lush vegetation and animal carcasses buried all over the Earth, particularly within the Arctic Circle (surrounding the North Pole). An interesting picture taken in Antarctica (continent of the South Pole) has this caption in the *Encyclopædia Britannica*: "Petrified log found in the Horlick Mountains, indicative of a milder climate and proof that higher forms of plant life once existed." (EB, 1972, 2:4C) This unintentional support for the Creation Model comes from a humanistic publication that teaches evolution from A to Z.

Physical evidence that the atmosphere at one time (before the Flood) was certainly different exists at the Creation Evidences Museum at Glen Rose, Texas. A **wooden handled hammer** with an iron head was excavated from sandstone there in 1934. The sandstone contains seashell fossils. What is inexplicable is the fact that the hammer head is 96.6% iron, 2.6% chlorine, and .74% sulphur with no silicon or carbon present, a combination impossible to achieve today as there is no known process to alloy iron and chlorine without silicon. There is no carbon present but the hammer head is amazingly similar to steel and highly resistant to corrosion. The hammer had to be crafted in a very different environment. (Creation Disc. Digest, Winter 1992, 7)

Men and Dinosaurs

The Paluxy River bed in the area of **Glen Rose, Texas,** has long been known for its **dinosaur tracks**. However, in 1910, local resident Charlie Moss became the first to find **fossilized human footprints** among the large, three-toed indentations. Other prints were found over the years and verified as human in the 1940s by geologist Dr. Clifford Burdick. Documentation was added later by Dr. Cecil Daugherty and Dr. John Morris.

In 1982, archaeologist and anthropologist **Dr. Carl Baugh** and Australian archaeologist Dr. Clifford Wilson began excavations in the area. They began to find human prints among, and even under, dinosaur prints buried beneath thick layers of limestone which they removed with jackhammers and, later, a backhoe. These discoveries electrified creationists and infuriated evolutionists! Dr. Baugh was ridiculed on national television as a bumbler and a faker. Evolutionists do not take kindly to those who dare to challenge their monopoly viewpoint.

Dr. Baugh has continued his excavations, always meticulously conducted and documented (usually videotaped) with various expert witnesses present. The general public is invited to join special summer digs and this author was an eyewitness to the uncovering of dinosaur and human prints, in close proximity to one another. Fakery was absolutely out of the question.

Dr. Baugh's teams have uncovered a number of 16-inch-long human prints. Nearby, an over-7-foot-long, female human skeleton was found some years ago by another anthropologist about 12 miles from Glen Rose. Dr. Baugh has also found a "probable" series of saber-toothed tiger tracks, a dinosaur tail drag, a human-hand imprint, two dinosaur skeletons, various dinosaur and human prints in long, left-right series, and a human tooth. All finds have been extensively tested. He has established the Creation Evidences Museum in Glen Rose to exhibit many of these finds.

According to Dr. Clifford Wilson, there are also dinosaur and human prints together in Australia. A report in *Moscow News*, No. 24, 1983, p. 10, tells of some 1,500 dinosaur prints discovered in Asia in Southeast Turkmenia by the Turkmenia Institute of Geology. Among the dinosaur tracks are human prints. Human prints among dinosaur tracks prove that humans and dinosaurs coexisted.

The fossilized tracks seem to indicate that both humans and beasts were running from the rising waters of the Flood, and that the strata preserving the tracks were formed sequentially and rather quickly by the silt carried in by the Flood action. Tracks were made in a soft, fresh, newly laid limestone layer which partially dried and then was quickly covered by another layer. Geological analysis confirmed that the Paluxy strata containing the tracks were hardened like modern concrete within 24 hours of deposition under hydraulic pressure, between "great cataclysmic tidal impacts." It should also be noted that the tracks and strata at Glen Rose challenge the theoretical **Geological Column** (that exists nowhere) of the evolutionists. (Baugh, Dinosaur, 20-22, 27-9, 44, 46, 112, 125-6, 139, 142, 144-8; Baker, Dinosaurs, 111-115)

During and After The Flood

The Canopied Earth System Explodes

Dr. Baugh continues to explain that the Flood was a **massive thermonuclear explosion**, much like an egg blowing up in a microwave. The land mass literally came apart at the seams and the new pieces or continents pushed against each other and were heaved upward by the breaking up of the "fountains of the great deep." However, says Baugh, the new pieces of land were *not yet separated*, but merely **ripped** at the seams. (Baugh, Panorama, 81, 82)

All of this **cataclysmic action**, plus the incredible hydraulic effects of the flood waters formed by the destroyed canopy and other water, formed many of the catastrophic marks we call mountain ranges and gorges and canyons and cliffs, etc. Also formed, in rapid manner, were

layers of coal, sandstone, sediment, limestone, shale, volcanic ash, lava, and various kinds of rock, as well as oil deposits. (Morris, Scientific, 101-110) Original geologic strata were tossed about in chunks or crushed together. So much for the evolutionists' nicely ordered, slowly formed, **geological column**, a real-world example of which is impossible to find. (McLean, Early Earth, 146)

As part of the cataclysmic judgement of the Flood, the **axis** of the Earth may have been moved (or begun a move) to what appears today to be a **23½° tilt**, further contributing to the change of climate and perhaps the eventual formation of ice at the poles and the "deep freeze" of so many plants and animals. Or, if some biblical geocentrists are indeed correct (even geocentrists don't all agree), Earth's axis remained in its original position while the universe (and/or Sun, or solar system) underwent an alteration in its revolutionary path. (See Chap. 8)

It is very interesting that we have dated the Flood at **2345 B.C.** while, before he died, the government astronomer of South Australia, George F. Dodwell, "compiled 66 ancient observations of the Obliquity of the Ecliptic that reveal[s] a significant change in the [E]arth's axis tilt in 2345 B.C." (Setterfield, Geological, 16) The *ecliptic* is the path that we observe the Sun and planets taking over the course of the year "through" the 12 constellations of the zodiac. (Gallant, Constellations, 174, 192) Dodwell included astronomical notations of medieval Europeans and Arabs, ancient Greeks, Chinese and Hindus, and ancient Egyptians, with

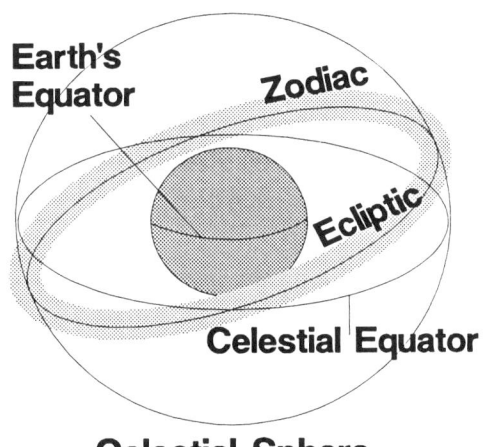

Celestial Sphere

two observations recorded at Karnak (Egypt) in 1570 B.C. and 2045 B.C. Australian mathematical scientist Barry Setterfield believes that Dodwell's research indeed demonstrates an "obvious change in axis tilt occurred in 2345 B.C." and that this is confirmed by "worldwide geological, archaeological and climatic data" collated by an American researcher, Dr. M.M. Mandelkehr.

However, Setterfield believes the Flood occurred earlier in 3536 B.C. (with Creation at 5792 B.C.) and that the 2345 date represents "a chain of continuing disasters that disrupted civilizations worldwide," followed by Sodom and Gomorrah and the rift of the Jordan River Valley in 2205 B.C. (Setterfield, Geological, 11, 16)

Obviously we disagree with Setterfield on dates and events (Setterfield matches his physical, mathematical, and biblical findings to the accepted evolutionary framework), but it is intriguing that research shows such a disruption in celestial movements in the same year we believe the Flood erupted. *Remember, no one can prove **exactly what moved**, only that observable celestial positions and paths show that the relationship between the Earth and certain heavenly bodies changed, and apparently continued to change over a period of time.* (See Chap. 8)

Our **ice caps** are still actually quite a mystery, and Dr. Immanuel Velikovsky's writings maintain that a vast amount of *heat*, not cold, is necessary to form ice on land. [See this chapter's section on Ice.] It is commonly accepted that it is our angled axis that gives us our **seasonal extremes** today, tilting us toward or away from the sun as the Earth makes its yearly journey. However, geocentrists have other explanations for the same phenomenon. (See Chap. 8)

The suddenness and power of the initial explosions which triggered the Flood are illustrated by the remains of **giant animals** who have been found **frozen in place** with food in their mouths and stomachs. Among the millions of mammoths buried in Siberia and Alaska are almost intact carcasses of those huge creatures that were feeding on buttercups and grasses and were buried along with camels, sheep, rhinos, bison, horses, and lions. Most of the massive burial grounds show animals torn apart and entangled, the obvious victims of a swift catastrophe. (McLean, Early Earth, 179, 180) One of the mysteries is that a number of these animals were frozen quickly enough to preserve their flesh, but the Earth remained warm enough to prevent the formation of the ice caps for perhaps hundreds of years. (See Chap. 11)

The same type of **burial ground** in Sioux County, Nebraska, includes a six-foot-high swine and a clawed horse-like animal. Some 100 mastodons are buried in Big Bone Lick, Kentucky, while mastodons are preserved in standing positions in San Pedro Valley, California. There are whale skeletons in Michigan and a "modern-type" human skeleton buried under the remains of an extinct vulture in the La Brea Tar Pits of Los Angeles, California. In China, scientists have identified human skeletal remains as European, Melanesian, and Eskimo types mixed together with animals which, today, **represent every climate on Earth.** This is also true of the variety of animals, including a saber-toothed tiger, found at La Brea. (Velikovsky, Earth, 46, 61-68) The Love Bone Bed near Gainesville, Florida, reveals saltwater (and extinct) sharks, whales, and manatees along with freshwater gar, alligators, and turtles. Mixed in are snakes, rodents, raccoons, wolves, a saber-toothed cat, an ele-phant, a tapir, two kinds of rhinos, seven kinds of horses, a llama, and three kinds of camels. (McLean, Early Earth, 156-7)

Large numbers of top-heavy, armored dinosaurs have been found fossilized in upside-down positions, obviously victims of a great catastrophe. The recently discovered (late 70s, early 80s) Egg Mountain, Montana, site revealed the tomb of an estimated 10,000 dinosaurs. Other **mass burial sites** include Como Bluffs and Bone Cabin Quarry in Wyoming; Cleveland Lloyd Quarry and Dinosaur National Monument in Utah; Ghost Ranch near Albuquerque, New Mexico; the Red Deer River Valley in Alberta, Canada; two separate beds at Trossingen, Germany; the Gobi Desert in Mongolia; and a place called Tendaguru in eastern Africa. (Baker, Dinosaurs, 131-147)

The list of these finds goes on and on and the extraordinary extent of **subtropical vegetation** buried and remarkably preserved throughout the **Arctic Circle** is widely documented, as is the presence of fossil leaves, petrified logs, and coal in the **Antarctic**. *All of this evidence certainly strengthens our conclusion that all of these animals, plants, and humans were: 1) together on one land mass, 2) inhabitants of a mild, uniform climate, and 3) destroyed suddenly and violently.*

Why do we not find the same such massive graveyards of **humans**? There are certain sites as the one in China mentioned above. But, as the canopy and the Earth's crust began to explode, man would have been more able than the animals to flee to higher ground and less likely to get caught in sediment flows. In addition, there were probably a whole lot more animals than there were humans. As people were overtaken and drowned by the rising water, their bodies would tend to float for a few days, then sink, after much of the sediment had already settled. Thus, their bodies would decay and not fossilize. (Baker, Dinosaurs, 103) The Bible states that the **sea** will *give up the dead who are in it* at the time of the great white throne judgement. (Rev. 20:13)

Mountain Formation

Mountains are first mentioned in Gen. 7:20 when the Flood waters were 15 cubits deep (about 22.5 feet). Much of the initial explosive action had already occurred by this time. *Were these mountains newly formed or part of the original, pre-Flood landscape?*

Dr. Carl Baugh asserts that the Earth's **original, gently sloping elevations** were turned mountainous by the Flood. (Baugh, Pan. Cre., 94) Dr. Henry Morris seems to support less of a contrast, saying that the Flood caused mountains to rise to heights never before attained (Morris, Gen. Flood, 77) because, before the Flood, there were no "rugged mountains." (Morris, Many Inf., 314) However, he also states that, before the Flood, there were no substantial differences from region to region in land densities or elevations. The "mountains" were relatively low and the "oceans" were relatively shallow. (Morris, Gen. Flood, 268) *The point here is that both Baugh and Morris see the Flood as the major agent of mountain building.* Morris also emphasizes that the Flood was followed by continued uplifting and other catastrophic effects for centuries. (Morris, Gen. Flood, 313, 315)

It is interesting that such a drastic change as mountain formation is so subtly mentioned and practically brushed over in the Bible. However, most of the amazing and catastrophic events recorded in the Bible are described in tantalizingly little, if any, detail. Enoch's rapture is casually mentioned in one verse. All of biblical pre-Flood history rates a mere six chapters. Joshua's long day and Hezekiah's reversal of the sundial are briefly referenced. The Holy Spirit is certainly the Master of understatement, and maddeningly so for us curious humans when it concerns these astounding events.

What is quite interesting is that a number of

evolutionist scientists have unwittingly contributed additional evidence to the creationist Flood Model with their observations of Earth's mountains. In an August 1949 *Scientific Monthly* article, E.H. Colbert admitted that when dinosaurs walked the Earth, the climate was universally what we might call subtropical. He concluded from the evidence he saw that animals freely roamed the entire land area and pointed out that this would preclude the existence of any physical or climatic barriers such as high mountains. (Morris, Gen. Flood, 243)

Another interesting observation by evolutionists is that **Earth's mountains are very young** by evolutionary standards and that much of the uplift seems to have been formed since the appearance of man. The Yale glacial geologist, Richard Foster Flint, writes in his findings that the Earth's greatest mountain chain, the **Himalayas**, as well as most of the world's mountain chains, formed or "uplifted" in the "recent" Pliocene and Pleistocene (appearance of man) eras, meaning that the mountains are young and all formed about the same time. (Morris, Scientific, 126, and Gen. Flood, 128) Dr. Immanuel Velikovsky cites evidence from a number of writers that the Himalayas are not only the highest but the **youngest mountains on Earth**, rising to their present height in the age of modern, historical man.

Velikovsky also notes that **North America's Sierras** are believed to be **younger than man**, and quotes explorer Bailey Willis as saying that the great Asian mountain chains "challenge credulity by their extreme youth." (Velikovsky, Earth, 72-3, 78, 151) Once again, the key phrase here is *"in the age of, or younger than, man."* To an evolutionist, that means sometime within the Pleistocene Epoch (began about two million years ago) of the Cenozoic Era (began about 65-70 million years ago). Creationists then translate that as sometime after Adam was created, only thousands and not millions of years ago.

One of the most interesting pieces of evidence that links the Flood and mountains is the list of what is found at the tops of Earth's mountains. In his book *Cataclysms of the Earth*, Hugh Brown states that **sea shells and marine-life specimens** have been found in the **highest elevations** in mountains all over the world (94), while Dr. Velikovsky records that marine skeletons have been found at the top of Mt.

Everest, the Earth's highest mountain. *Obviously, these mountains were at one time either 1) part of the ocean floor and then uplifted, 2) flooded by ocean and then uplifted, or 3) uplifted and then covered by ocean water.* Whichever happened (maybe even a combination of the three possibilities), the marine animals would have to have been covered quickly by mud or some type of deposit that would preserve the remains as fossils.

Velikovsky also writes that **human artifacts** have been found in the Alps at **altitudes too high to support human habitation**, a fact he finds "baffling." (Velikovsky, Earth, 72-74) Are these pre-Flood artifacts? Would post-Flood people, with plenty of unsettled, subtropical land available, migrate to the tops of the highest mountains to attempt to live in a new and inhospitable terrain and climate? *The only other explanation would be that mountains were formed or further elevated during catastrophes that occurred centuries after the Flood.* Keep these observations in mind as you consider evidence for later disruptions in human history.

The great stone city of **Tiahuanaco**, 25 miles from **Lake Titicaca** near the top of the **Andes Mountains** in Peru, South America, raises many questions. The lake is the largest in South America (110 miles long) and the highest navigable lake in the world, sitting at 12½ thousand feet above sea level. The people who built the city were highly skilled stone masons, like those of Egypt, and lived **long before the Inca** civilization. The remains of their farming terraces reach as high as 15,000 to 18,000 feet above sea level, at the line where snow now stays on the ground all year round. The brackishness (somewhat salty) of the lakes and the presence of salt beds is also confusing. (Velikovsky, Earth, 81-85)

There is evidence that this mysterious mountain city once supported a large, sophisticated population who managed to move stones weighing 200,000 pounds or more from quarries 60 to 200 miles away. Indian tradition maintains that the city was originally built by **giants**, a story common to other cultures in areas with megalithic structures. Another "legend" of ancient palaces in the lake led to the discovery of high, mud-covered walls, paved paths, and curious stone structures hidden by the waters of Titicaca. Was this great city and its amazing stones originally the work of giant, pre-Flood peoples before the mountains were formed? Or the work of incredibly ingenious engineers hundreds of years after the Flood? Why would people work so hard to build so much in such challenging terrain? Why would agricultural terraces be at such altitudes? *Is it possible that the great city was constructed before the Flood, elevated and damaged by the Flood, then reconstructed and even expanded by a series of post-Flood migrants, mainly for religious rites?*

The Earth is ringed by two long lines of mountain ranges. The **Alpine-Himalayan Cycle** lies in an east-west direction, while the **Circum-Pacific Cycle** stretches in a north-south direction. Dr. Emil Gaverluk says that the spin of the Earth, generating centrifugal force, would have thrown out the first ring of mountains, probably the east-west line. *A spin-axis shift (a tilting of the Earth's poles) that would lay the Earth on its side would have to occur to throw out the other ring,* and this would have to coincide with a major catastrophe. (Gaverluk, Rapture, 76) Of course, this reasoning stands only if the Earth indeed does spin. *We see the evidence of so many catastrophic happenings and yet we modern, sophisticated humans are inadequate to put the whole jigsaw puzzle back together.* God says that His ways are past finding out. (Rom. 11:33)

Since the Flood was the first, and worst, of Earth's physical catastrophes after the creation of man (even though the Curse went into effect after the Edenic judgement), *it seems sensible to ascribe initial mountain formation to the catastrophe of the Flood.*

Ocean Formation and Changes in Sea and Lake Levels

There is evidence of land sand on the bottom of the Atlantic Ocean. (Velikovsky, Earth, 100-101) In fact, according to Dr. Morris, much of the present ocean floor was **once dry land**, indicating that while some land heaved upward, other land sunk to great depths. Dr. Morris and certain other creationists point out through Psalm 104:6-9 that God had to create a place for the vast amount of water that came from the canopy and from the "great deep." Thus, *there must have been much more land area before the Flood than there is now.* The "sea" was much smaller and shallower and the sea level much lower. The long, sloping continental shelves may indicate the pre-Flood sea level.

Famous American landmarks like the **Grand Canyon** and the **Royal Gorge** were probably wholly or in part the results of the heaving and sinking action that formed the mountains and the oceans. Perhaps verse 8 of Psalm 104 indicates the formation of massive gorges and canyons as raging rivers of water cut through soft, freshly laid sedimentary layers, flowing from the uplifted mountains into the new sunken basins. **Deep undersea canyons**, many of which are connected with present-day rivers like New York's Hudson, must also have been carved above water by powerful runoff through soft sediment and then submerged to form part of the new ocean basin. (Morris, Gen. Flood, 121-6, 153-4, 325-6; McLean, Early Earth, 82) *This evidence may also point to the fact that God "canaled the Earth with water" after the Babel judgement, rather than actually pushing continental pieces around.*

Raised beaches or marine terraces (former water lines) exist around all the world's sea coasts and around many present lakes. Raised beaches and corals in Chile (South America), Hawaii, and the New Hebrides Islands (South Pacific) are found at 1,200 to 1,300 feet above sea level. (Velikovsky, Earth, 85, 181) Terraces around all of the continents show the upheaval of the land combined with the recession of Flood waters into newly created basins of great depths. Some of this activity may also have occurred during one or more later aftereffects or separate judgements, perhaps around 1500 to 1200 B.C. *There is evidence to believe that the polar ice did not begin to form until the 1500s B.C.*

The same type of evidence traces the extent and recession of **ancient, massive lakes**, indicating trapped Flood water that evaporated over time in the new and harsher climatic conditions. A massive body of water called Lake

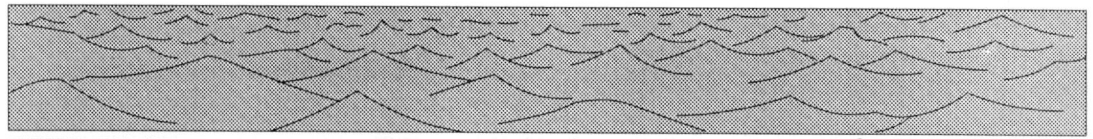

Agassiz once covered an area in central Canada larger than the present Great Lakes. It lapped over into North Dakota and Minnesota. The region is now important for wheat growing. The Great Salt Lake of Utah is one of the remnants of what is called Lake Bonneville, which apparently covered much of the north and western part of Utah and parts of Idaho and Nevada, totaling about 20,000 square miles, with a depth of over 1,000 feet. What is called Lake Lahontan covered about 8,400 square miles in Nevada, Oregon, and California. At least 68 former lakes have been discovered in the western United States, now the most arid part of the country. California's Death Valley desert was once what is called Lake Manley, which probably connected with Lake Tahoe to the north. *Lakes all around the world were much higher and most (perhaps all) large deserts were formerly large lakes.* (Morris, Gen. Flood, 313-24; EB, 1972, 18:46-7; Tallcott, 65-7)

So, a great portion of the world's surface, particularly the Western United States, is drastically different today than it was for the period following the Flood. *We can only guess how long it took for these lakes to shrink or disappear, leaving farm land in some cases and desert sands in others.*

Ice – A Slippery Subject

Arguments over Noah's Flood as the major cause of Earth's catastrophic features waxed and waned through the 1600s and 1700s, though most naturalists of the early-to-mid-1800s generally attributed these features to the Flood. Then a German forestry professor named Bernhardi and a young, Swiss naturalist named **Louis Agassiz** introduced the idea that *glaciers* were the cause of certain deposits of soil, rocks, and boulders as well as scratches and grooves on bedrock and boulders and specific types of hills and depressions. Agassiz went on to teach at Harvard, but it took three decades for the majority of scientists in Europe and America to agree that ice and not water was the cause of the deposits and markings.

Humanistic geology now calls its Pleistocene Epoch the Glacial Epoch or the **Great Ice Age**, when great sheets of ice allegedly covered large areas of the continents. Supposedly, the first ice age began about 1½ million years ago. Four ice ages came and went, each lasting a few hundred thousand years, until the last ice sheet left North America some 10,000 to 7,000 years ago. (EB, 1972, 18:43-52; Tallcott, 77-9)

In *The Genesis Flood*, Drs. Morris and Whitcomb do not aggressively fight the ice-age theory, allowing that one (and not four) glacial period of continental ice coverage could have followed the Flood. However, they assert that there is only **circumstantial evidence** for the ice-age theory and that all of the evidence is much **better explained in terms of "catastrophic diluvial action"** (meaning the Flood). They also note that Sir Henry Howorth, president of the Archaeological Institute of Great Britain in the late 1800s and a non-believer in the Genesis account, wrote extensively to demonstrate the scientific inadequacy of the glacial theory and the high probability that a great flood from the north formed the so-called glacial deposits. Here was a secularist refuting the ice-age theory. However, Howorth's mass of evidence was ignored and his criticisms of the ice-age theory remain unanswered. (Morris, Gen. Flood, 143, 290-3, 300-1)

Dr. Velikovsky makes some interesting statements regarding the alleged ice sheets. He apparently agrees with most geologists that the oceans would have dropped 300 to 400 feet during glacial periods. However, referring to the opinion of British physicist John Tyndall, Velikovsky says that a **great amount of *heat, not cold,*** is necessary to transport that much ocean water to the polar regions in the form of snow to form ice on land. "Even if the sun disappeared and the Earth lost its heat to cosmic space," says Velikovsky, "there would be no Ice Age: the oceans and all the water would freeze, but there would be no ice formation on land." (Velikovsky, Earth, 131-2)

This statement completely **disagrees with ice-age theorists** who connect cooling temperatures with glacial formation and warming periods with glacial melt

Ancient American Geography

or "interglacial ages." (EB, 1972, 18:48) A catastrophist, Velikovsky believes the only explanation for the great heat necessary to form glacial ice sheets across continents would be a **"celestial confrontation"** such as a close encounter between Earth and a comet. He also notes that Louis Agassiz found **"glacial markings"** in equatorial Brazil, Argentina, India, Africa, and New Zealand, as well as North America and Europe. In Africa, the markings showed the ice moving in the "wrong direction," from the equator toward the south, and in India, the "ice" moved uphill. (Velikovsky, Earth, 40). Of course, we would attribute these markings to the Flood.

What we do have, of course, are **two ice caps** – one on **Greenland** and one over the continent of **Antarctica** (the South Pole) – which constitute 98% of the glacier ice that covers 10.4% of the world's modern land area. Ice is supposed to have covered at least 28% of the Earth's land area at the height of the Great Ice Age. (EB, 1972, 18:44, 51) Antarctica has a higher average elevation than any other continent, which is interesting considering that it is weighed down by 90% of the world's ice. Its ice sheet averages 6,600 to 8,200 feet thick with one measurement at 14,000 feet thick (over 2½ miles!). The western region may actually be several "islands" if the ice were removed. About 2,200 square miles of Antarctica are mysteriously free of ice. These "dry valleys" feature snow-free ground and unfrozen lakes. (EB, 1972, 2:4, 4A; Tallcott, 100)

The **Arctic Circle** drawn around the North Pole at 66°33' N latitude defines the area in which at least one day a year the sun never rises and one day a year the sun never sets. There is no land at the North Pole itself – only pack ice floating in the Arctic Ocean – and 3/5 of the Arctic is outside the zone of permanent ice. The circle takes in the northernmost parts of Canada, Alaska, Russia, and Scandinavia. Most of Greenland is within the Arctic Circle while Iceland lies just to the south of it. Almost 85% of Greenland is covered by an ice sheet as thick as 6,700 feet. The center of the ice cap has been measured as extending more than 1,000 feet below sea level, which suggests that **Greenland may not be a single island.** (This point will be very important later.)

Ice, in the form of small glaciers and large plateau ice caps, covers only 11.5% of **Iceland** where records show that ice has waxed and waned since the A.D. 900s. Whereas *Antarctic* ice is in **equilibrium** (not growing or shrinking), the 20th Century has shown *Arctic and Icelandic* ice to be *receding*. The Arctic Ocean's pack ice is thinner, sheep are again grazing in southern Greenland, and Atlantic cod are now thriving north of the 70th parallel which runs through the middle of Greenland. Mountain glaciers in Alaska and the American Northwest have retreated this century, one as much as 62 miles, though a few began to show some amazing growth spurts about 1945. (Tallcott, 18, 112; EB, 1972, 10:896; 11:1036; 2:331-3, 341)

The so-called "ozone hole" is supposed to be over the South Pole, not the North, but Antarctic ice shows no evidence of melting while Arctic ice indicates warming. *Does this mean that ice formation on Earth is not connected (as Velikovsky maintained) with any supposed warming or cooling of Earth's atmosphere?*

We conclude from our research that all of the Earth's ice formed as an *eventual* result of the Flood, and some might conclude that it formed immediately at the time of the Flood. However, as we study the repopulation of the Earth, we will examine evidence that shows all of these areas may have remained free of ice for a lengthy period after the Flood, *showing Earth's "Little Ice Age" to be very limited and very recent in nature.*

Meteorites and Cosmic Catastrophe

Probably since the Flood, pieces of iron or stone fallen from the sky, ranging from dust to 90 tons in size, have been collected by man for worship, curiosity, science, or, in the case of iron, for smelting. We know from II Peter 3:5-7 that the "heavens" that are now are not the "heavens of old" which existed before the Flood. The most obvious change was the "firmament called Heaven" (Gen. 1) or Earth's pre-Flood canopy which blew up as part of the judgement.

But other things may have changed in our solar system and galaxy, and God may have used **other planets, comets, and meteors** as causal agents or participants in the judgement. Dr. Velikovsky questions the fact that **meteoritic dust** is so sparse today that it can hardly be measured on mountain snow, *but it makes up a substantial portion of oceanic sediment.* (Velikovsky, Earth, 102) It would seem that the windows of heaven possibly rained a significant shower of meteors as well, with the Flood waters carrying off the dust which then settled on the newly sunken ocean floors. (Or could part of this occurred at Babel?)

Velikovsky notes that there are an estimated half million **elliptical craters**, all parallel in orientation from northwest to southeast with elevated rims on the southeast, that are found from **New Jersey to Florida**, and believes they could have been formed by a closely passing comet breaking into meteors. A large number of meteorites have been found in the Southeastern states. There are 28 fields of sharp, burned, broken stones and craters in Arabia, and a number of craters in **Australia**. (Velikovsky, Earth, 96-100) Of course, there is the incredible meteor crater in **Arizona** which is 4,000 feet across and 600 feet deep with a rim 200 feet high. (EB., 1972, 15:271, 274) Eskimos made weapons from meteoric iron found on Disko Island (Greenland), and a 90-ton iron meteorite was found at Cape York, **Greenland**.

Were any of these celestial collisions associated with the Flood or with later catastrophic judgements? A great portion of human legends and writings, as well as mysterious physical evidence, points to the fact that the heavenly bodies, at God's command, have played a significant role in human history. We will examine much of this evidence as we attempt to reconstruct the repopulation of planet Earth and the settlement and development of the Americas.

BIBLIOGRAPHY

Baker, Mace, *Dinosaurs*. Redding, CA: New Century Books, 1991. [If your Christian bookstore can't find it, contact Creation Evidences Museum or Southwest Radio Church (See Bib., Chap. 2)]

Baugh, Carl, *Dinosaur, Scientific Evidence That Dinosaurs and Men Walked Together*. Orange, CA: Promise Publishing, Inc., 1987. [Contact Creation Evidences Museum or Southwest Radio Church]

Baugh, Carl, *Panorama of Creation*, Bib. Chap. 2, p. 37.

Boraiko, Allen A., "Lasers: A Splendid Light," *National Geographic*, Mar. 1984, 335-363.

Brown, Hugh Auchincloss, *Cataclysms of the Earth*. New York: Twayne Publishers, Inc., 1967.

Creation Discovery Digest, edited by Dennis Petersen. South Lake Tahoe, CA: Creation Resource Foundation, Winter 1992. [2100 Eloise Ave., S. Lake Tahoe, CA 96150]

Encyclopaedia Britannica (EB). Chicago: William Benton, 1972.

Gaverluk, Emil, *Rapture*, Bib. Chap. 1, p. 19.

Gallant, Roy A., *The Constellations*. New York: Four Winds Press, 1991.

Josephus, (see Whiston) Bib. Chap. 2, p. 37-8.

McLean, *Early Earth*, Bib. Chap. 2, p. 38.

Morris, Henry, *Genesis Flood*, (see **Whitcomb**) Bib. Chap. 2, p.38.

Morris, Henry, *Many Infallible Proofs*, Bib. Chap. 2, p. 38.

Morris, Henry, *Scientific Creationism*, Bib. Chap. 2, p. 38.

Setterfield, Barry, *Geological Time and Scriptural Chronology*. Rev. ed. Aug. 4, 1991. [Genesis Institute (see Bib., Chap. 1) or Setterfield, Box 318, Blackwood, S.A., 5051, Australia]

Strong's Exhaustive Concordance of the Bible, Abingdon Press, 1970.

Tallcot, Emogene, *Glacier Tracks*. New York: Lothrop, Lee & Shepard Co., mid-60s? (no date given)

Velikovsky, Immanuel, *Earth in Upheaval*. Garden City, NY: Doubleday & Co., Inc., 1955.

PROJECTS

Debates/Essays: A debate is an excellent classroom project. If you are a home schooler, perhaps you know other home schoolers with whom you can organize debates. The topic of creation vs. evolution is plausible but broad. Consider debating the existence of UFOs and the nature of UFOs from a humanist and a biblical point of view. What about the existence of cavemen, yea or nay? You will get ideas for lots of debate topics as you study this series. Writing essays allows you to debate yourself.

Climate Trends from the Flood to the Present

B.C.

Generally Warm - Wet to Dry Transition

2345 FLOOD—totally New World, new atmosphere, new geography, Earth's axis (or ecliptic) tilted at 23½°, large flood lakes, new mountains and instability with earthquakes/volcanoes

2200s ? Wet-to-dry transition in Northeast Africa actually dated about 2500 by a climatology expert from Texas A&M University (an evolutionist) who believes this transition lasted only decades to centuries. (Thomas J. Crowley, Letters to Editor, NYT, 7/18/92)

2174? BABEL—New Geography, continents driven apart or canaled by water, worldwide dispersion. People dwelling in GREEN SAHARA which was not desert but teeming with wildlife, water, plant life.

2100s-2000s? GREAT PYRAMID—area was *not desert then*. When the Sphinx was dug out later, sand would immediately refill the area between the paws. Obviously sand was not there when the Sphinx was constructed. (Tompkins, GP, 142; see Chap. 10)
BABYLON—Old Ur said to be *watered, forested, green*. Today the area has no metal, stone, forests, or water, just sand. (Heyerdahl, Tigris, 129)

2100-2000?? EGYPT--Minister of Pharoah Mentuhotep ordered to send ship to Punt; an 8-day trip w/ 3000 men across land *between Thebes* (on the Upper Nile) *and the Red Sea*. The area there had *no water* but the minister dug 12 wells to provide water for his army. (Casson, Mariners, 10; see Chap. 12)

1910s PALESTINE--**Famine** drove Abraham to Egypt. Intermittent regional famines.

1894? SODOM &GOMORRAH. Until this judgement, the area was the *beautiful rich Jordan River Valley* that Lot saw in Gen. 13:10, but not enough grass west of there to support all the herds of both Lot and Abraham. By the time of Joshua (1440s B.C.?), the area was desolate.

1950s EGYPT--Tale of Sinuhe about the time of Sosostris I (Senusert I) — *desert or dry land in Sinai* perhaps between Egypt and Palestine.

ANCIENT MAPS show Antarctica, Greenland, Iceland, with no ice!! (see Chaps. 10 & 11)

1703 **Famine** throughout Middle East and Egypt (Jacob enters Egypt).

1750 **Weather change?**--Casson says Persian Gulf *trade died out* mysteriously sometime after this date. It came back only about 1,000 yrs later (700s BC). Trade, he says, shifted west toward Mediterranean. (Casson, Mariners, 9)

1700s **Woden-lithi's** trading voyage from Norway to American Great Lakes. The whole Earth must have had a *much milder climate* than 1000 yrs later because of the **outdoor astronomical calendar site** Woden-lithi constructed at what is now Peterborough, Ontario. The area was probably then plains rather than forest because those establishing calendar dates from the astronomical rock alignments had to be able to see the horizon. There was no terrible cold or snow to disrupt site then. (Fell, Bronze, 125; see Chap. 8 and Vol. II)

1500s?, before? Fell says that at the "peak of the Bronze Age," there was a *warming and melting trend.* Fell dates the "Bronze Age" in North America at about 2000-800 B.C. (Fell, Bronze, 288) [Remember, Stone Age, Bronze Age, Iron Age, are evolutionist, "lower-to-higher"

Page 52 — Chapter 3

Catastrophe? Ice Formation? — **Cooling**

1500s progressions, while we know from the Bible that man worked in both bronze and iron before the Flood.] International Geological Congress 1910—**Climatic plunge**, especially in northern Europe. European lake dwellings wiped out in Scandanavia, Germany, Switzerland, and Italy. Included earthquakes. The ocean level dropped.

1488 EXODUS—Sinai desert, but Canaan described as land of milk and honey. Giants dwelt there. Period of GREAT MEDITERRANEAN & MID-EAST DESTRUCTION and DISRUPTION.

1446? Joshua's LONG DAY when the Sun and Moon stood still for almost a full day.

1200s/1100s? Ruth, during time of the Book of Judges. Naomi and family go east into Moab because of *famine* in Palestine.

800s COOLING about this time. Climate (snow) *forced North Americans south and/or inside*, to partially buried **stone astronomical chambers** rather than outdoor stone circles for calendar regulation. Fell (an evolutionist!) says that it was at end of "Bronze Age" when *northern polar icecap came into being*. Gives this as **one reason ancient Europeans "forgot" about America.** (Fell, Bronze, 33,125) MAPS that possibly show some glaciers in Europe (Great Britain, Scandinavia)—could they be from this time? (see Chaps. 10 & 11)

1000?-700 "Klimasturz" in Scandinavia at end of "Bronze Age." *Catastrophic decline in climate* which came on suddenly. Climatological instability. (Velikovsky, Earth, 173-4)

700s **Climatic plunge** in the 700s-680s. Climatic disturbances in California show up in the Great Sequoia trees. European lake dwellings in Scandinavia, Switzerland, Germany, Italy again wiped out by flood. (Velikovsky, Earth, 173-8; Intl. Geological Congress 1910)

Short Warm

700s-500s Rhone Glacier in Alps started to MELT in midst of a cooling period. (Velikovsky, Earth, 201) Climate/ice relationship??

Before 500 Short warming here? Connected with Rhone glacier above? (Tallcott, Glacier, 82)

Cooling

500 Cooling—glaciers advance. (Tallcott, 82; see Chap. 3)

500-400 *Much colder* in Britain/North Europe. (EB, 1972, 1:370B) Berosus reported to visit Ark site about 475 B.C. and said *Ark visible "on glacier."*

330 Voyage of Pytheas to THULE. Further north, the SEA TURNED SOLID. Was told that the night was only 2-3 hours long. This shows how far north he was and that **ice** had certainly formed by this time. (Landstrom, 34)

Warmer

27 *Warming*—glaciers retreat. (Tallcott, Glaciers, 82)

PARTIAL GREENLAND ICE SHEET on Ptolemaic Map of the North. Could it be from this time? Or later after 1200 AD? (see Chaps. 10 & 11)

A.D.

Cooling

400-1600? Cooling?—glaciers advance (just regional? probably off and on). (Tallcott, Glacier, 82) *General warming trend* recognized by most as taking place in 700s or 900s to 1300s.

500s Oxhide curraghs designed for COLD WATER in North Atlantic Would not work in tropical water. (Brendan, Nat'l. Geog., 777; see Chap. 12) Irish Saint Brendan saw iceberg?

536 Volcano cloud so thick, it obscured shadows at noon. Caused starvation in some parts of China, according to Chinese and Mesopotamian historians. (McMaster, Reaper, 7/9/91, 10)

Warmer

900s-1300s WARMING—Ice restricted in Iceland. (EB, 1972, 2:341)

700 Onset of Viking voyages, conquests, expansion. Climate got warmer, **opened northern route to America**, *northern icecap melted back*, polar

---

Ancient American Geography   Page 53

A.D.

Warm but Cooling

	seas opened. (Fell, Bronze, 33, 289)
1075	**Grapes in Vinland**, the Viking name for Newfoundland. (Morison, Euro. N, 51-2; see Chap. 12) Wines from Vinland became world famous. (Mallery, 111; see Chaps. 10 & 11)
1000s	North Atlantic—ice reported only twice in this century. (Mallery, 157)
1100s	North Atlantic—ice reported three times. (Mallery, 157)
pre-1400s	Perhaps even long before this in North America, **"medicine wheels"** of large circles of stones layed out for astronomical alignments, calendar regulation. Mostly in Wyoming, Montana, and Canada. Canadian Trail Ridge Road rock solstice alignments are in a "high, cold, inhospitable place." (Krupp, In Search, 163) *Probably warmer in these areas when these astronomical "wheels" were constructed.*
1200s-1300s	North Atlantic—ice moved south, winters colder and longer. Up to 1200 A.D., grain grown in *northern* Iceland. (Mallery, 157)

Colder

post 1200	EUROPE--began COOLING—vineyards of William Conqueror's England died. Normans (French) went to south Europe for vines. No vineyards now in England. **Deserted routes to America**—cut off America from Europe. (Fell, Bronze, 289; see Chap. ???)
1400s-1750	**COOLING--Ice advanced, cooling in Iceland.** (EB, 1972, 2:341)
1400s	Drop in summer temperature in Greenland. (Morison, Euro. N, 61) Grain no longer gown in *southern* Iceland. Earthquakes, volcanoes, tidal waves in Iceland, North Atlantic area. *Greenland cut off from Europe* by ice for 100 yrs. (Mallery, 157)
1502	Cantino Map shows East Greenland with ice. (Morison, Euro. N, 69)
1600-1850?	Much COOLER—rapid glacial advance, farmlands covered, villages threatened in Europe. (Tallcott, Glacier, 82)
1750?	**Minor WARM.** (EB, 1972, 2:341)
Early 1800s	Rhone glacier advanced into the valley, shown in painting.

Warmer

	(Tallcott, Glacier, 81)
? to 1850	**COOLING.** (EB, 1972, 2:341)
1850?-1940	*Warming*—glaciers retreat; warm weather over whole world. (Tallcott, Glacier, 82) Turkish government soldiers said to have found and entered *exposed Ark* in 1883.
1885	Icebergs, *field ice* off **Newfoundland**. (Morison, Euro. N, 171)
1890-1970s	**WARMING—ice retreat in Iceland, noticeable general Arctic warming.** (EB, 1972, 2:341) Very warm summer in 1902 in Turkey *fully exposed Ark*. In 1916 or 1917, Russian soldiers under Czar claimed to have found and measured Ark.
1920s	*Polar ice retreat* in **Greenland** revealed long-forgotten western settlements. (Fell, Saga, 342-3)
1940-1960s	*Cooler—glaciers advance.* Tallcott says world's average temperature went down (Tallcott, Glacier, 82) but *does not jive with rest of evidence*. Shows complications.
1945-1960	**General Arctic WARMING.** 12% less area covered by ice over 15 yrs. and ice is 40% thinner. Codfish migrated north from New England to Labrador for cooler waters and Canadian crop line moved 50 to 100 miles north.([Tallcott, Glacier, 80)
1960s	Rhone glacier retreated between the two mountains, out of the valley. (Tallcott, Glacier, 81)
1980s-90s	*Ark* covered in ice and snow on Ararat.

ANTARCTIC MYSTERY—over 2 miles of ice in one place, but some large areas and some lakes not frozen!!! (Tallcott, Glacier, 100)

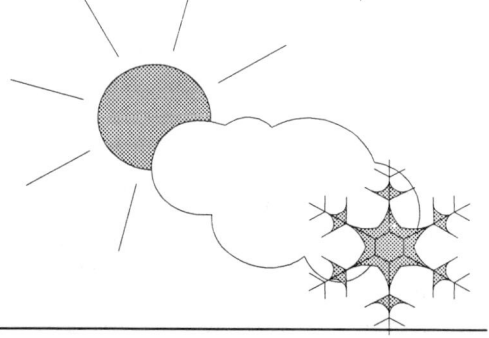

Chapter 4
After the Flood: Restarting Civilization in a New World

Starting the World Over Again

Every person and every animal (other than sea life) on earth today is descended from those people and animals who walked or flew off the ark. (Gen. 8:15-19, 9:19) Is that possible? According to biologist Dr. Kenneth Ebel, each family of creatures on Earth today has a single pair of ancestors. (Ark documentary, 2/20/93) In addition, at least one research team which compared the genes of modern people has linked every person alive today to "a fully human common ancestor" called "Eve." (*World Press Review* [Economist], Nov. 1988, 54) Thus, post-Flood history began with all men and all animals in the same vicinity.

Based on our prior research, we have placed the date of the Flood at **2345 B.C.** According to Gen. 8:4, **Noah's Ark** landed on **"the mountains of Ararat,"** in the 7th month of that same year. Noah and his family did not emerge until the end of the second month of 2346 B.C. (Gen. 8:13-14) The biblical account strongly suggests that they were not resting in ice or snow and that the climate at that time, even on Ararat, was not yet severe. Remember the subtropical climate from which they came. It is also possible that Ararat thrust upward one or more times in the centuries following Noah's landing.

Today, Ararat is a rugged, treeless mountain that is nearly 17,000 feet high. Ice and snow is now permanent all year from about the 14,000-foot level on up. Surrounded by Russia, Turkey, Iran, and Iraq, it lies in a politically explosive region. The area has also remained geologically unstable, beset by storms, avalanches, and earthquakes. An incredibly tremendous earthquake in June 1840 destroyed the mountain village of Aghuri and the St. Jacob Monastery (guardian of Ark relics at 7,000 ft.), creating the awesome Aghuri Gorge which is deeper than the Grand Canyon. At some point, an earthquake and/or avalanche split the Ark into two pieces, both of which are now covered with ice and snow. Exceptionally warm summers, like the one of 1902, expose the Ark to view. (Ark documentary, 2/20/93; Blick, Creation, 4)

"Ararat" is the Hebrew equivalent of the later Babylonian name for the area. The mountains have two major peaks, Great and Little Ararat, which are joined by a "saddle" and are believed to be the product of one or more extinct volcanoes, though neither has a crater. Formed totally of volcanic rock and covered with lava, these mountains were probably a newly uplifted, quickly cooled volcano(es). Geologist and geophysicist Grant Richards has identified on Ararat a specific type of lava that is an underwater formation. Salt crystals found at the 14,000-foot level of the mountain also indicate that Ararat was formed during the Flood. (EB, 1972,

2:210; Ark documentary, 2/20/93) [Volcanoes were not part of the pre-Flood world. See Chap. 3, Mountain Formation.]

The **Armenians** believe themselves to be direct descendants of the post-Flood first family and maintain that the Ark was long visible on the slope of Great Ararat, though God prevented anyone from actually reaching the remains. They point to the village of Aghuri as the place where Noah built his altar and planted his vineyard. A Persian (Iranian) tradition also refers to Ararat as Noah's mountain, the beginning of the "New World." (EB, 1972, 2:210) One Armenian story relates that the Ark, now guarded by angels, was visited periodically by Noah's early descendants and that some evil descendants of Ham planned, for some reason, to destroy the Ark. To prevent this, explains the story, God sent a mighty storm to bury the Ark in ice. (Blick, Creation, 4)

We will see in the course of our research that more and more scientists are recognizing that "traditions" and "mythologies" are often quite reliable in their observations, though not often in their explanations.

Citing "all the writers of barbarian histories," particularly Berosus the Chaldean and Nicolaus of Damascus, the 1st-Century Jewish historian, Josephus, affirms that the Ark landed on the "top of a certain mountain in Armenia." (Josephus, Antiquities, I.iii.5,6.) Berosus is recorded to have visited Ararat about 475 B.C. He apparently wrote that the Ark was quite easy to discern upon the glacier. (Ark documentary, 2/20/93)

So, Noah and his immediate family alighted onto a brand new, volcanic mountain, into a devastated, drastically changed, environment. It must have been something akin to landing on Mars. They had never seen the sun without the canopy. They had never seen volcanoes and mountain ranges. This was a totally different world!

Our sovereign, all-knowing God may very well have originally programmed **man's genetic code** to be able to **adapt to the major physical changes** of the new atmosphere. Noah was such an incredible physical specimen (especially by our standards) that he lived to be 950, or 20 years longer than Adam, despite the new exposure to radiation and the lower levels of oxygen and atmospheric pressure. The second generation, Noah's sons, lost about 300 years off their **life span**, as we know that Shem lived to be 600. The next three generations had life spans in the 400s while the next five died in their 200s. From Abraham to Moses, the major Jewish leaders, if not the rest of the Earth's population, lived into their lower or upper 100s. Then life spans began to drop to the 70s and lower.

The full extent of the know-how, abilities, progress, and possessions of the ancient world was confined to **eight people and the baggage of one big boat**. "It is no wonder," writes Dr. Henry Morris, "that they were forced for some little time to make use of **stone and wooden implements**...." Dr. Morris goes on to say that it would also be quite natural for families to live in **caves** until man-made shelter could be erected. Noah's **tent**, whether made from animal hides, animal hair, or plant material, took time to construct. Did they bring a loom with them on the Ark? **Daily survival** would be the dominant concern. It certainly seems logical that this new beginning in a flood devastated world would explain some of the "Stone Age" remains discovered by modern archaeologists. (Morris, Many, 304)

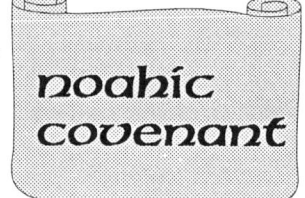

Still in direct contact with God, Noah and his sons received certain **divine explanations, instructions, and promises** that are recorded in **Gen. 9 (Noahic Covenant)**. They were told to reproduce abundantly and **"fill" the Earth**, the exact same command given to Adam and Eve in Gen.1:28. (Though the KJV says "replenish," *Strong's Concordance* indicates the Hebrew word is better rendered "fill.") This would indicate, that despite the Curse, God blessed their childbearing and women were able to have many babies, successfully, without hospitals or operating rooms (signs of man's and Earth's degeneration, offset to some degree by modern technology). They were advised of their *new, adversarial relationship with the animal kingdom* and instructed to **eat meat**. Could it be that this new source of protein was necessary for strength in a new and increasingly hostile environment, an environment that would no longer support the lush vegetation of pre-Flood days?

Capital punishment at the hand of man,

and therefore human government, was established (Gen. 6). We know that before the Flood, the descendants of Seth called upon the name of the Lord and brought proper sacrifices to God to cover their sin. We know that Cain's descendants built a civilization that, though advanced, was murderous and evil and polluted by Satan's fallen angels. However, there is no mention of any kind of **human government** or human system of law until after the Flood. God also promised never again to destroy the Earth by flood and made the **rainbow** the token of the covenant. The appearance of a rainbow was not possible before the Earth's canopy disintegrated. It is strictly a phenomenon of the "New World." God's **sacrificial system** of clean and unclean animals, the shedding of substitutionary blood, the significance of the smell of smoke from burned offerings, and the ritual of the altar, was continued, as shown by Noah's sacrifice in Gen. 8:20.

Dinosaurs After the Flood

God must also have programmed the animals for **adaptation**, but only up to a point. We know that the gargantuan animals of the past no longer exist, but there is evidence that they survived for a while after the Flood. The book of Job in the Old Testament refers to two mysterious animals called "behemoth" and "leviathan."

It is generally agreed that **Job** was a patriarch, meaning that he lived before or during the time of Abraham, certainly before Moses (no mention of Mosaic Law). Job lived 140 years after his sickness, and Jewish tradition says that his later years were twice the sum of his former years, which means that he was about 70 when the events recorded in the Book of Job occurred. If Job then lived to be about 210, he may have lived 150 or so years before Abraham, when men still lived to their 200s, which we would date roughly between 2200-2000 B.C.

However, many individual and family names mentioned in Job are the same as the names of grandchildren or other early descendants of **Abraham**, when men still lived to be 150 to 180. Job had huge herds of livestock, as did Abraham, and probably lived in Edom (southern Jordan or northern Arabia). If this is so, we could then date Job sometime between 1900-1600 B.C. On the other hand, the names of Abraham's descendants mentioned in Job may have come from Shemites who lived a little before Abraham or during his early years, and so Job may very well date between 2200-2000 B.C. Of Job, God says that there was "none like him" on Earth (Job 1:8), which is quite a statement for the days of Noah, Shem, and Abraham.

In Job 40:15-24, Job is ordered to "behold" what must be a contemporary creature called *"behemoth"*, which is really the Hebrew plural for beast, used not only to emphasize the greatness of this vegetarian animal, but also as a *generic* term for God's huge, **swamp- or river-dwelling dinosaurs**. (Baugh, Dinosaur, 88; Baker, Dinosaurs, 24) God compares its tail to the mighty Lebanon cedar and its bones to bars of iron, and then says that behemoth is the "first" or the "chief" (KJV) of the ways of God, an amazing statement. The phrase "ways of God" is used in Job 26:14 to indicate God's acts of creation. *Young's Literal Translation* renders verse 23 as "Lo, a flood oppresseth," saying that the unafraid behemoth does not hurry to avoid a flash flood of the Jordan, though the river rises up to the animal's mouth, once again indicating the animal's great size and strength. As far back as the A.D. 1600s, this animal was debated as an elephant or, more often, a hippopotamus, but commentators really have to stretch to explain away most of the descriptive details.

Creationist Dr. Carl Baugh maintains that no living animal, only some type of dinosaur, fits the description of the behemoth given in Job. What we once knew as the reconstructed **"Brontosaurus,"** but is now known generally as a *"Sauropod,"* has been suggested as the behemoth, possibly a *Brachiosaurus* or *Apatosaurus*. (Baker, Dinosaurs, 16-28) Dr. Baugh relates an October 1980 United Press International report that natives of the **African Congo** described a 15-to-30-foot creature with three-clawed feet as big as frying pans. When shown pictures of elephants or buffalo they did not respond, but when shown a Brontosaurus (or Sauropod) drawing, they

called it **"mokele-mbembe."** The African creatures were said to be vegetarian and submerged themselves in deep pools or underwater caves. A type of dinosaur surviving in the African jungle (as many reports have indicated over the past 200 years) might still be large, but certainly much smaller than its mighty ancestors, due to the change in atmosphere. (Baugh, Dinosaur, 88-91, 103, 120)

God's lengthy description of *"leviathan"* in Job 41:1-34, when taken literally, sounds like nothing other than the **"mythological" fire-breathing, snake-like sea dragon** that adorns maps and legends throughout the Far East, Middle East, Africa, and Europe. Mace Baker quotes Chinese evolutionist Dong Zhiming who writes that the "interpretation of dinosaurs as dragons goes back more than two thousand years in Chinese culture." (Baker, Dinosaurs, 8)

The leviathan Job knew was a real creature and common wisdom was that no wise man aroused the animal, according to Job 41:10 and 3:8. (The phrase "raise up their mourning" in the KJV literally reads "rouse leviathan.") Leviathan was **untameable** and could not be caught by conventional means. Barbed irons and fish spears were useless against him. His mouth was full of **"terrible teeth"** and he was covered with an **airtight armor of scales**. **Fire** came from his mouth and **smoke** from his nostrils and his breath would set coals on fire. He was strong and fierce and frightening, even to the mighty. Swords, spears, javelins, and arrows were useless against him and he left claw prints in the mud (vs. 30). His great thrashings could make the sea "boil" and he must have made quite a wake when he swam (vs. 32). As God called behemoth (the land dinosaur) one of His major creations, He declared leviathan (the sea dragon) to be fearless and **without equal** (vs. 33-4).

How could this description possibly be stretched to fit a crocodile?! Theistic evolutionist Dr. Hugh Ross believes that this was a metaphorical description, depicting the fierceness of a **crocodile** as seen by man. (TBN TV network interview, aired in 1992) But Dr. Carl Baugh asserts that it was indeed one of God's great **"terrible lizards"** that lived for a time after the Flood. (Baugh, Dinosaur, 36, 73, 77-82, 88-91, 102-3) *Thus, the virtually worldwide and amazingly consistent "mythology" of the dragon is in fact the result of **reliable observations** woven into a variety of **fanciful explanations**.* As with the worldwide Flood "legend" or "myth," the dragon legend has a common and factual origin in antiquity.

Leviathan is also referred to in Psalm 74:13-14, where it says God broke the heads of the dragons (or serpents) in the water when he divided the **Red Sea**, breaking the head of leviathan and giving its meat to the people as food. In Psalm 104:26, it says that God made leviathan to play in the ocean.

And in Isaiah 27:1, leviathan the sea monster is connected with **Satan the crooked serpent**, just as the serpent animal was connected with Satan himself in the curse of Genesis 3. This verse indicates the spiritual symbolism of evil and sin connected with the dragon or snake, symbolism originated by God but perverted and developed by the pagan world in concert with demonic spirits.

Dragon of myth inspired by the real leviathan and Satan

The dinosaurs that came off the ark or survived in the ocean would find the **new environment hostile to their great size**, which needed giant vegetation and a generous amount of pressurized oxygen. Note that Baker effectively argues that dinosaurs were **cold-blooded reptiles** (one reason they depended on the pre-Flood atmosphere), and not warm-blooded mammals. Evolutionists want this changed to establish dinosaurs as the ancestors of birds. (Baker, Dinosaurs, 24-5, 185-194)

Many dinosaurs eventually became **extinct**, some perhaps quickly, while others **"devolved"** into much smaller versions of their magnificent ancestors. A fossilized **pterodactyl** found in West Texas has a wingspan of 52 feet! Fossilized **dragonflies** show wingspans of 36 inches! These huge wingspreads could no longer be supported by the new, thin atmosphere and so these may have been among the early victims of the "New World." (Baugh, Panorama, 58-9)

The **body** of a surviving descendant of a **Plesiosaurus** was snagged and pulled aboard a Japanese fishing trawler off the coast of New Zealand in April **1977**. A photograph of the still-meaty, two-ton, 32-foot-long carcass was taken and appears in *Newsweek* magazine that year. Japanese marine biologists suggested that the creature was a Plesiosaurus, an observation easy to make from the photo. Regrettably, the scientists were not able to examine the carcass because the fishermen threw it back into the sea. They were afraid the fatty fluids oozing from its flesh would spoil their catch of fish. (*Newsweek*, Aug. 1, 1977, 90:77)

Of course, the hunt for the famous **Loch Ness monster of Scotland** continues. The first recorded sighting of "Nessie" was in A.D. 565 by Saint Columba and there have been regular sightings ever since, with two in 1992. The **most recent and comprehensive survey** of the loch used high-tech sonar to scour the waters and found that the lake was much deeper than expected at 846 feet. The scientists found no deepwater valleys or caves, but they did find "strange metal lumps, resembling stepping stones, spaced out for several miles along the lake bed." After tracking for a month, they also picked up and followed a **large, unidentified object** for two minutes. "'It wasn't a shoal of fish, because there aren't any there, and it definitely wasn't a technical fault with the sonar,'" stated Bob Manson. "'Quite frankly,'" he added, "'we don't know what it was.'" (Reuter UK News Clip, Oct. 28, 1992)

What about **adaptation in diet** and the **change of relationship between man and animal**? The Bible clearly shows that man became a meat eater after the Flood. Before the Flood (and after the Fall), animals were used for sacrifices, clothing, farming, perhaps traveling, and probably milk. After the Flood, according to the Noahic Covenant in Gen. 9, man no longer had a cooperative relationship with animals and could now use animals for food. Animals would now be afraid of man and some would be dangerous to man.

Many animals became carnivorous. What about the dinosaur remains that show the terrible rows of teeth such as the reconstructed **Tyrannosaurus Rex**? Wasn't he always a meat eater? Dr. Henry Morris believes that the Fall and the resulting Curse of Gen. 3, which introduced death into the world (rather than the covenant of Gen. 9), was the point at which "changes took place in the animal kingdom which led to the production of fangs and claws and the gradual development of carnivorous appetites." (Morris, Many, 239; Gen. Flood, 461-5) However, Dr. Baugh believes that the serrated teeth of Tyrannosaurus Rex were **"better designed for eating canes than for eating meat,"** though the dinosaur may have been part of the "cleanup crew" that ate dead animal bodies after the Fall. Though Rex probably preferred a herbivorous diet, he "would act as a scavenger when gases of decomposition suggested the right response in his preprogrammed brain." (Baugh, Dinosaur, 81, 122) Baker agrees that serrated teeth more likely indicated an omnivorous animal, especially since, today, "we note that few, if any, carnivorous animals have serrated teeth. (Baker, Dinosaurs, 14, 34-8)

Thus, Dr. Baugh believes that animals were not carnivorous hunters and killers until Gen. 9, after the Flood. Perhaps teeth and claws evident today were part of the original animals but were used for other purposes than killing and eating flesh. Admittedly, though, it is difficult to imagine the jaws of a Great White Shark as the mouth of a vegetarian! However, God's control over His animal world is, more often than not, beyond human understanding. For example, the **Antarctic seal**, an air-breathing mammal, can dive to depths of more than a quarter mile (which would crush a human), swim there for some 30 minutes, then come straight to the surface without developing nitrogen bubbles, called the "bends" or decompression sickness. (Tallcott, Glacier, 119)

Besides the Bible and human tradition, there is **physical evidence** to believe that **giants like the mammoth and mastodon survived on the Ark and lived for a time after the Flood.** The elephant-like **mammoth** apparently had a hairy coat, curved tusks as long as 12 feet, and a height of 11 to 13 feet at the shoulder. The **mastodon** is distinguished by scientists as having had shorter, straighter tusks, a flat head, and molars of a different structure. (Tallcott, Glacier, 90; Webster's) These ancient elephants roamed all over North America, along with such companions as wooly rhinos, giant sloths and beavers, massive bison with a horn spread of six feet, saber-toothed cats the size of a lion, camels, zebra, reindeer, moose, tapirs, and horses.

The interesting thing is that mammoth, mastodon, and giant bison remains have all been found, from **Alaska to Mexico**, with **man-made spear points in their rib sections**, indicating they died as a result of spears or arrows, possibly finished off with large stones which have also been found among the remains. In at least one case in Mexico, **stone knives and scrapers** were discovered close to the find. (Johnson, Men and Elephants, 215-6; Velikovsky, Earth, 3; Tallcott, Glacier, 84-5) *The obvious conclusion is that men all over North America were hunting and killing these animals.* If so, we know from Gen. 9 that this must have been *after* the Flood, as men did not hunt and kill animals for food before that time. Before the Flood, men only killed domestic animals for sacrifices and clothing.

We can also presume that these particular incidents took place in **North America** after the Tower of Babel judgement, after the newly changed land mass was divided by God, and man was dispersed across the face of the world. *This tells us that the Americas were settled before the mammoths became extinct.* When we judge the "primitiveness" of these hunts, we must remember that man had never hunted before, that there must have been hardships in dispersement and separation from the Middle Eastern civilization, as well as in starting over once again, and that it must have taken a great deal of cunning and organization to quickly develop these weapons, learn how to use them, and trap and kill such a mighty animal.

Thus, we can conclude that the giant animals of pre-Flood days remained with man in a new, adversarial relationship after the Flood, after the Babel judgement, and became extinct or devolved into smaller and smaller varieties over the next 1,000 or even 1,500 years. We will consider this subject further in Volume II of this series when we examine the American Indian legends about the mammoth and other large animals.

Seeds of Rebellion

Noah immediately began to **farm** to raise food for survival. He may well have been a farmer before he became a carpenter for 100

Man did not hunt until after the Flood

years. There is no specific mention of Noah carrying **farming implements** or **tools** on the Ark, but it is certainly logical to assume that he did. We also know that he was familiar with bronze and iron. However, his family's immediate needs were limited to eight people, and to work with metal to make more tools or implements meant looking for and locating veins of ore in a drastically changed landscape. How soon they accomplished that, we can only guess, but they **may have used stone for implements in the meantime**. (If we consider the hammer found at Glen Rose, Texas, made from the "impossible" alloy of iron and chlorine with no silicon, we realize that they would have also had to learn how metals behaved in the new environment.)

Genesis records that Noah planted a **vineyard**, then drank the wine and became **drunk**. It has been suggested that perhaps grape juice did not ferment into alcohol in the pre-Flood world and that drunkenness was a new and unexpected experience for Noah. Or perhaps the effect of alcohol on the brain was greater in the new environment. If indeed alcohol use and abuse had been part of pre-Flood life (it is not mentioned before this incident), Noah was certainly not known for abuse as he "walked with God habitually." (Gen. 6:9, *Young's Literal*) Obviously, Noah knew about vines and grapes and making a special beverage from grapes. However, for some reason, whether or not he knew what to expect, Noah drank enough to get himself fall-down, mindbending, clothes-discarding drunk. Perhaps he merely overheated from the alcohol and threw off his clothes because he was hot. Though he may have been hot, he was soon out cold, but he at least had the good sense to confine this behavior to his tent.

The problem is that we Westerners have a difficult time understanding this incident. Why was Ham's discovery of his father worthy of the curse that followed? Was it Ham's boasting? Was Noah humiliated? Did something else happen? Dr. Allen Ross explains that **Ham** demonstrates a mind set **inclined toward power and immorality** in general, (Ross, 41) an observation which naturally raises a question concerning Ham's character and why he was chosen to live and help populate the "New World."

We know from the Bible and history that **Noah and Shem were godly men**, particularly blessed of God, but it would seem that Ham was not of the same character. **Ham's progeny** through Cush would introduce idolatry into the world, while his progeny through Canaan would carry a curse from God. His progeny through Mizraim would promote idolatry and would enslave the Jews for some 400 years.

However, God pronounced a **general blessing on Noah and all three sons** (9:1) and established His covenant with Noah and all three sons and their future sons (9:8-9). All three sons obeyed their father in the building of the Ark, and all three remained **physically unsullied** by the evil angels and evil people of the pre-Flood world. Perhaps Ham was **spiritually sullied**. Ham and the other seven survivors, though saved from physical death, **retained their fallen human natures**. Each must come to the Lord through belief and sacrifice. Ham does not give the impression of a true believer. Further questioning leads us to such basic human puzzlements as, "Why did God allow evil to continue in the world?" which can only find their answers in the sovereignty, righteousness, and holiness of an all-knowing and all-powerful God. *Satan had tried to destroy the line of Christ, but God, through righteous judgement, had preserved it. The Plan marches on!*

Ham was obviously **disrespectful** of his father, defying what would come to be a widely recognized system of **Eastern family traditions**. Ham may also have been trying to **undermine his father's authority** and **assert himself over his brothers**, hence the **curse** which made Ham's son Canaan the lowest of servants to the descendants of both brothers. That Noah, even though sound asleep, knew what had happened and that Ham was the guilty party (vs. 24) must mean that Shem and Japheth told Noah what happened.

Dr. Ross points out that the phrase used in verse 22, that Ham "saw" his father's nakedness, means exactly that, and is *not* the same as the phrase "to uncover" someone's nakedness, which is used by Moses in Lev. 18 to describe the sexual sins of Egypt (Mizraim) and Canaan, both sons of Ham. (Ross, 41) *If indeed a correct analysis, this means that Ham did not commit a sexual sin, but that his rebellious attitude bore such sinful fruit in his descendants.* [It would certainly seem that most of the proscriptions in Lev. 18 regarding sexual relationships were in effect from the beginning, except the one regarding **brothers and sisters** and half-sisters. Though practiced as late as Abraham, such **marriages** were no longer necessary by the time of Moses as the population had greatly increased. Also, they were no longer advisable as the **gene pool** became increasingly burdened over time with the defects of the Curse.]

Another interesting note concerning **Noah's vineyard** was reported in a British newspaper called the *Morning Herald* on Oct. 26, **1855**. The story, from **Italy**, was about the near destruction of the vineyards of Tuscany due to a plant disease. Tuscany is a region of Italy, the chief city of which is Florence. The **Roman Catholic Archbishop of Florence** contrived to save the vineyards and the region's winemaking industry by having the people repeat **prayers, not to God, but to** the "'Most holy patriarch **Noah** who didst employ thyself in thy long career in cultivating the vine, and gratifying the human race with that precious beverage....'" The Archbishop's prayers stated that the blight was obviously punishment for the Italians' sins and entreated Noah to prostrate himself before the throne of God and beg mercy for the Tuscany vines as the Tuscans promised to repent of their sins with the aid of divine grace. An *indulgence* of forty days was promised to all who would devoutly recite the prayers to Noah. (Hislop, third note, 245) [An indulgence is remission of punishment still due for a sin--Webster's] *Whether or not Noah continued to cultivate* *grapevines, we see how paganism employed the story of the incident.*

What is interesting is that the emphasis of the entire incident, beginning beforehand in Gen. 9:18, is on *Canaan*, not Ham, which, of course, raises the question: **"Why curse Canaan and not Ham?"** The puzzling emphasis on Canaan is partially explained by Dr. J. Vernon McGee, and by 17th-Century commentator Matthew Henry, as Moses' demonstration to the 12 Jewish tribes that Canaanites were cursed by God and would easily be run out of the **promised land** if the Jews would obey God, cross the Jordan, and fight. Moses most likely penned Genesis through Deuteronomy while leading Israel through the wilderness on the way to the land of Canaan.

The significance of the entire passage lies in Noah's *prophecy* of **post-Flood world history**, specifically aimed at the **future nation of Israel**. Noah states that **Shem** and his descendants will be specially blessed by God. *Young's Literal Translation* renders Gen. 9:26 as "Blessed of Jehovah my God is Shem,...." The Jewish nation, and thus the line of David and Jesus Christ, would come from Shem through Arpachshad. The Jews, uniquely chosen by God, would give the Scripture and the Church to the world, and will survive to receive the fulfillment of the covenants and the Kingdom promises.

Noah also says that **Japheth** and his descendants will be "enlarged." *Strong's Concordance* shows that Japheth's very name is derived from this Hebrew word which can mean "to open up," "to make roomy," or "to expand." This is generally interpreted to mean that Japhethites were enlarged in tribes and territory, but also, perhaps, ego. (*Young's Literal* says "God doth give *beauty* to Japheth,...") The Hebrew word in question is translated "enlarged" in the KJV only in this one verse. It is translated as verbal flattery in Ps. 78:36 and Prov. 20:19, but most often as "deceive" or "deceived." Elsewhere, in I Kings 22 (the lying spirit sent to Ahab) and Prov. 25:15, it is translated as "persuade" or "persuaded," and in Hosea 2:14 as "allure." Some believe that God "persuaded" Japheth when Paul successfully planted the Church among Eurasian and European gentiles.

Noah adds that Japheth will also **"dwell in the tents of Shem."** Arthur Pink argues that this refers to the "grafting in" of the gentiles (Rom. 11). "The kingdom of God was to be established in Shem," states Pink, "but Japheth should be received into its community." (Pink, 93) Another scholar believes it indicates that Europeans and other Westerners would derive much of their civilization from the Semites. (Pict. Dic., 783) Dr. Ross contends that it merely meant peaceful relations between neighboring Japhethites and the conquering nation of Israel. (Ross, 42) However, this changed over 1,000 years after Joshua, when Greece and then Rome conquered Israel, and the scattered Jews have since **"dwelled in the tents of Japheth,"** in alternating prosperity and persecution, throughout Europe, Russia, and the Americas. Today, there are more Jewish people living in the United States than in any other country, including modern Israel.

It does certainly seem that God has blessed His chosen people, the Jews, with amazing gifts in the fields of commerce and finance, though we also see that the benefits of hard work and a seemingly natural business acumen abound among Asians also. Both the Jews and the Asians have shown the ability to succeed through adversity. Whether or not it is true that the majority of real estate mortgages in Western Civilization are held by Jewish people ("Japheth shall dwell in the tents of Shem"), this belief has, sadly, added fuel to the flames of **anti-Semitism**. [Remember who wants to destroy Israel? Satan!]

According to Gen. 10 (called the Table of Nations), **Ham** had four sons. **Cush** is associated with Ethiopia, **Mizraim** with Egypt, **Put** with Libya, and **Canaan** with the land of Canaan (Israel), giving Canaan a peculiar relationship to Israel. In response to the incident in question, Noah begins his prophecy with a curse upon Canaan. Both the Bible and archaeology reveal that the **Canaanites** practiced a sexually centered and grossly **perverted religion** so abominable that God ordered their **complete annihilation**, animals and all, at the hands of the Israelites. (Josh. 6:21; Deut. 7:2-3)

Israel's failure to destroy and even to remove the Canaanites led to their own downfall (Judges 1; 2:10-15; 3:5-7). Noah explains that the curse will make Canaanites the lowest of servants to Shem, a prediction that Joshua fulfills with the Gibeonites (Josh. 9:23). However, this is only after the Jews had spent some 400 years

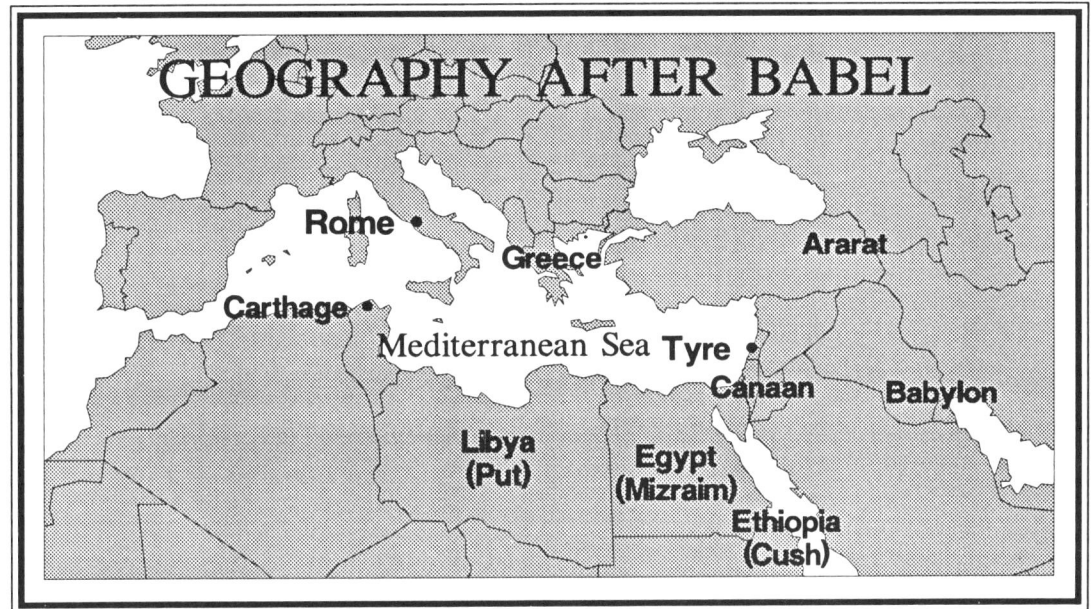

as slaves to descendants of another of Ham's sons, Mizraim of Egypt. Perhaps the fulfillment of the curse is in the fact that the Canaanites eventually disappear into history, succumbing in part to Israel, and later to Japheth, when Greece destroys Tyre, and Rome defeats Carthage. (Phoenicians were considered Canaanites, and Tyre and Carthage were Phoenician cities. Greeks and Romans were generally Japhethites.)

The Americas in the Bible?

It is interesting, in the general scheme of world history and the **great kingdoms** of the world, that, of the three brothers, **Ham** is the **first to be given prominence**, as it is his progeny who establish Babylon and Egypt. World prominence is then shifted to **Shem** through Israel under David and Solomon, and then to **Japheth** through Greece and Rome. It is also interesting that the focus of world power remains in the Middle East and Near East until *Rome and Christianity thrust the Western World into the forefront.* Only in the 20th Century does the East rise again to play a major role in world politics. The **Bible generally ignores the Far East** until the end times of Revelation when the "kings of the East" march westward to do battle at Armageddon. Concerned with redemptive history, the **Bible also generally ignores the Western Hemisphere and the Pacific Islands.**

However, the Bible does make reference to the American continents. The key words are **"coastlands"** and **"isles,"** depending on whether your translation is, for example, King James, Scofield King James, New American Standard, or New International. The Scriptures refer to "the kings of the coastlands (coasts or isles) across the sea," (Jer. 25:22) "distant coastlands," (Jer. 31:10; Isa. 66:19) and "Ships of the western coastlands," (Dan. 11:30). "The islands have seen it and fear; the ends of the earth tremble," says Isaiah 41:5. "Sing to the Lord a new song, his praise from the ends of the earth, you who go down to the sea, and all that is in it, you islands, and all who live in them." (Isa. 42:10 NIV)

Dr. J. Vernon **McGee** teaches that **"continents"** is often a better translation for "isles" or "coasts," such as in Isa. 51:5 where he states that "the isles" are "all the continents which are inhabited by the human family." The "isles afar off" in Jer. 31:10 Dr. McGee says refers to the isles (continents) of the earth, all around the world. But, in Dan. 11:18, "the isles" refers to Greece and all the Greek islands. (McGee, Thru the Bible, 307, 403, 597)

Professor Cyrus **Gordon** cites the Greek **Theopompus of Chios** of about 380 B.C. who wrote *Meropis*, a work in which he talked about "Meropids" on an enormous continent beyond Africa and the islands of the ocean. The people built cities and lived exotic life styles, with gold and silver in such abundance that the precious metals were worth less to them than iron. Gordon explains that "Old Mediterranean people used the term 'Island' to mean any land mass

Restarting Civilization in a New World

that can be reached by sea — even huge continents — as is natural for mariners who, on reaching some shore, cannot tell whether they have come to a large island or a whole continent." (Gordon, Before, 38, 193) **Aristotle, Diodorus Siculus, and Strabo** all used the term "island" to refer to a "vast land" or a continent. Strabo wrote that, since the sea is found everywhere, the whole world is an island. (Gordon, Before, 38-41) In referring to verses in Ezekiel, Dr. Charles H. **Dyer** states that "'coastlands,' already mentioned several times by Ezekiel..., imply the farthest reaches of the known world." (Dyer, BKC I, 1301)

What is most disconcerting to Americans is that the Bible has **no obvious, specific, prophetic reference** to the United States, the premier country of modern history in wealth, power, and accomplishments — perhaps of all history in the realm of technological achievements and influence over the entire globe. Many scholars argue for symbolic references. Both the U.S. and Great Britain are **extensions of Rome**. As the British Empire was symbolized by a lion, some see references to a mother lion and **"the young lions"** (Ezek. 38:13) as meaning Britain with the U.S., Canada, Australia, and New Zealand. The merchants of Tarshish in Ezekiel 38, they say, refer to Mediterraneans and Europeans, including England. (Church, Guardians, 220, 237) Some also see the U.S. as a **modern-day Babylon**, and there are, indeed, many parallels. Dr. S. Franklin Logsdon, former pastor of Moody Memorial Church in Chicago, has written a book entitled, *Is the U.S.A. in Prophecy?* However, there are others like Dr. Charles Dyer who believe that the **rebuilding of the original Babylon** will be successfully completed, shifting the world's focus from the West back to the East. (Church, Guardians, 166, 238-246; Gaverluk, Rapture, 92-109; Dyer, Babylon)

A major problem for Americans is **perspective**, in that we are inclined to see our nation as the defining moment of history, the apex of human ascension, and the now-permanent world leader. This author personally remembers what a shock it was for a college professor to remind the students of an upperclass Latin American History course that no country or kingdom lasts forever, that **all nations and empires come and go**, ascend and decline. Rest assured that the Babylonians and especially the Romans were terribly shocked when their worlds were turned upside down. To a Roman, the entire "known world" was the Roman Empire. The saying was that "all roads lead to Rome." Consider Luke 2:1 in which it says that "all the world shall be taxed," meaning the Roman Empire. Rome was sacked in A.D. 455 and the empire officially fell in A.D. 476.

A New Civilization

Despite Noah's incredibly long life of **950 years**, second only to Methuselah's of 969 years, **Noah had only three children**. We know this from Gen. 9:19, which tells us that the *entire Earth was overspread by the three sons of Noah*. The Table of Nations in Gen. 10 outlines the division of mankind into **nations with borders established by God**, according to their families and the languages God gave them. Note that the action is done by God, to the nations, and only after Babel. The nations did not divide themselves.

Though greatly altered, the **land was still one mass before Babel**. Noah probably remained in the area of Ararat. Shem may also have lived his life in this region north of the Euphrates and Tigris Rivers. The "whole Earth" had **only one language**, possibly a forerunner of Chaldee (Babylonian language from the time of Daniel), or Hebrew. Abraham spoke ancient Babylonian and so probably continued to speak it in Canaan, leading Alexander Hislop to conclude that, "at that period, Chaldee and Hebrew were substantially the same." (Hislop, ix) The Old Testament section of *Strong's Concordance* is titled as a "Hebrew and Chaldee Dictionary". *Thus, a form of **Hebrew** may have been the original language.*

For the next probably 200 years, the sons of Noah and their descendants multiplied in number, struggled against the new elements, and worked to reestablish a civilization. They apparently stayed in the same vicinity, even as they began to multiply. Everything they knew would be taught by Noah and his three sons. The **government was patriarchal**, meaning that the oldest male was the ruler of the family or tribe and the priest of the household and of the people. In the ancient language of Greece, *pater* meant "father" and *archein* meant "to rule." Thus, patriarchy is the rule of the fathers.

The **animals probably began to migrate**, seeking climatic regions and altitudes that best suited them. As the animals now feared humans, man may have had to **redomesticate** cattle, sheep, goats, camels and other beasts of burden. Man would also have to learn the advantages certain animals would develop as they adapted to specific climates (*e.g.,* camels in the desert), as these climates themselves developed. **Newly "wild" and newly carnivorous** animals may have migrated away from the human population.

Marsupials, pouched animals such as kangaroos, koalas, wombats, etc., are now unique to **Australia**. However, fossils show that they lived in Europe and the Western Hemisphere prior to the Flood. Either their kind were trapped on Australia as it broke away, or was cut off, from the land mass following the Tower of Babel, or they thrived in Australia and died out elsewhere. From Bible books of the Judges, Samuel, and Kings, we find that **lions inhabited Palestine** for centuries, though no lions have lived there for well over 2,000 years and no lion fossils are found there.

Horses lived in North and South America before the Flood, but apparently had not migrated into the area when the Western Hemisphere broke away (or was cut off from Europe and Africa) after Babel. Horses thrived once again in the Americas when they returned by way of Spanish boats in the 1500s. The **oldest known sculpture of a domesticated horse** was recently discovered in northern **Syria** and dated about 2300 B.C. The clay figure is 5" long and 3" high, but "exquisite in detail." This discovery has forced evolutionist scholars to revise their thinking about the earliest domestication of the horse back about 500 years. The sculpture was found in the ruins of an ancient Euphrates River site about 200 miles northeast of Damascus, Syria. This city was already an **important trading center**, replete with one-handled storage jars that seem to be connected to Cyprus, so the site and the horse would actually date **after the Babel judgement**. A number of model **chariots** were also found, indicating the very early use of the horse and chariot. (*New York Times,* 1/3/93)

A strong indication that the world still had a **single land mass before Babel** is found in Gen. 11:1-2 where it says that the **"whole Earth" had one language and pronunciation** (*Young's Literal*) and **"they" journeyed from the east**. (You have wondered who are the "they" who are always cited as doing this or saying that? Here are the original "they"!) The majority of people, *ex*cluding Noah, Shem, and close descendants who followed their godly teachings, migrated "from the east," which probably meant they moved toward, and crossed into, the large, alluvial plain of the rivers Tigris and Euphrates (though, remember, the geography had not yet "modernized").

This mass of people had found an area that became known as **Shinar**, legendary for its fertility. The Greek historian Herodotus (400s B.C.) would later write of 200-fold yields of grain produced there. (Pict. Dict., 787) Was this the original location of the **Garden of Eden**? Adam was run out of the Garden (Gen. 3:24), which was then guarded "at the east" to protect fallen man from the tree of life. At some point, the tree of life was taken to heaven (Rev. 22:2,14). Was the Garden destroyed and the tree taken at the time of the Flood? Is the buried Garden one of the major reasons for the vast **petroleum** deposits of the Middle East?

BIBLIOGRAPHY

Baker, Mace, *Dinosaurs*, Bib. Chap. 3, p. 51.
Baugh, Carl, *Dinosaur*, Bib. Chap. 3, p. 51.
Baugh, Carl, *Panorama*, Bib. Chap. 2, p. 37.
Blick, Edward F., *Creation and Noah's Ark*. Oklahoma City: Southwest Radio Church, 1986. [Southwest Radio Church, Box 1144, Oklahoma City, OK 73101; 405/235-5396]
Dyer, Charles H., "Ezekiel," *The Bible Knowledge Commentary, Old Testament* (I). Wheaton: Victor Books, 1985.
Encyclopædia Britannica, Bib. Chap. 3, p. 51.
Gordon, Cyrus H., *Before Columbus, Links Between the Old World and Ancient America*. New York: Crown Publishers, Inc., 1971.
Henry, Matthew, Commentary, Bib. Chap. 2, p. 37.
Hislop, Alexander, *The Two Babylons*. New Jersey: Loizeaux Brothers, 1959. [First published by Rev. Hislop in Scotland in the 1850s. An extensively researched, scholarly work by a theologian and linguist.]
Johnson, Ludwell H., "Men and Elephants in America," *The Scientific Monthly*, October 1952, pp. 215-221.

Josephus, *Antiquities*, Bib. Chap. 2, p. 37-8.

McGee, J. Vernon, *Thru the Bible* (5 Volumes). Pasadena, Calif.: Thru the Bible Radio, 1982.

Morris, Henry, *Genesis Flood*, Bib. Chap. 2, p. 38. (see **Whitcomb**)

Morris, Henry, *Many Infallible Proofs*, Bib. Chap. 2, p. 38.

Newsweek, "South Pacific Nessie?" 90:77, Aug. 1, 1977. [with photo of plesiosaurus]

Pink, Arthur W., *The Divine Covenants*. Grand Rapids: Baker Book House, 1973.

Ross, Allen P., "Genesis," *The Bible Knowledge Commentary*, Vol. I, Bib. Chap. 2, p. 38.

Sellier, Charles E., and **Balsiger**, David W., *The Incredible Discovery of Noah's Ark*, CBS television documentary, aired February 20, 1993. [also a book]

Strong's Exhaustive Concordance, Bib. Chap. 3, p. 51.

Tallcott, Emogene, *Glacier Tracks*, Bib. Chap. 3, p. 51.

Velikovsky, Immanuel, *Earth in Upheaval*, Bib. Chap. 3, p. 51.

World Press Review, "The Mother of Us All," from *The Economist*, November 1988, p. 54-5.

Young's Literal Translation of the Holy Bible, Revised Edition, Baker Book House.

Zondervan Pictorial Bible Dictionary, Nashville: The Southwestern Company, 1972.

PROJECTS

Essay Topics: Compose an essay on the subject of capital punishment. Is it indeed biblical? Should a Christian support **capital punishment**? Examine the arguments of those against capital punishment. Refer to Gen. 9.

Another very timely topic involves submission to authority, particularly the authority of **human government**. The legalization of abortion in this country has raised the question of **civil disobedience** among Christians, as did the question of slavery before the Civil War. Does the Bible give Christians the grounds to defy the government over abortion? At what point does a Christian actively defy the government? Draft a thesis statement -- take a stand on an issue -- and argue your point, supporting your thesis with relevant evidence. Refer to Rom. 13 and Heb. 13 as well as to Acts.

For a **creative essay**, pretend you are Noah or a member of his family getting off the Ark, seeing the "New World" for the first time. Use descriptive devices such as metaphors, similes, and personification. Choose adjectives that are vivid and specific. Use parallel construction. Avoid ineffective cliches. However, if a well-known cliche does the best job of communicating your point, then use it. *Don't be a slave to rules for the sake of rules. Know the rules. Break the rule when you have a reason to break it.*

What would you do if you, your family, and close relatives (if there aren't any close relatives, invent some) had to restart civilization from the beginning as Noah did? Draw up a plan.

WRITING NOTES

Enliven (breathe life into) your writing with figurative language. Employ figures of speech to improve communication and engage the imagination of your reader. ***Personification*** is a figure of speech. To "employ" a figure of speech is to treat it as if it were a person, capable of being employed. Anytime you give an inanimate object the *attribute of a person*, you *personify* it. "The landscape screams catastrophe!" Attributing the landscape with the ability to scream is personification.

Similes and ***metaphors*** are comparisons. A simile compares one thing to another in a direct manner by using such words as "like" or "as." Refer to page 56 where we compare Noah's departure from the Ark to landing on Mars, or page 59 where Loch Ness researchers compare strange metal lumps to stepping stones. Neither statement uses "like" or "as," but "something akin to" and "resembling." However, each statement essentially says "This is like that." "Insurance is like a wager. The insurance company bets that you will live longer, while you bet that you will die sooner." That is a simile.

A metaphor compares two things *implicitly* rather than *explicitly*. Refer to page 55 where Great and Little Ararat are said to be joined by a "saddle." The formation that joins them is not actually a saddle, but it looks like one. Refer to page 57, then turn to Job 40 and 41. The behemoth "eats grass as an ox." That is a simile. But of leviathan, God asks, "Who can strip off his outer armor? Who can come within his double mail?" (ASV) God is comparing the scales of leviathan to a man's armor. In a metaphor, scales *are* armor, they are not "like" armor. See how many figures of speech you can identify in Job, the Psalms, and throughout the Bible.

Refer to page 58 where we report that a theistic evolutionist believes that the entire description of leviathan is *metaphorical*, essentially saying that "leviathan is really like a crocodile" and the "fanciful" comparisons of Job are exaggerations (exaggeration is called *hyperbole*) to depict man's fear of the crocodile.

An **allusion** refers "to something other than the primary subject," explain the authors of *Prose Style for the Modern Writer*. (p. 199; see Chap. 2, p. 32) Usually the allusion is a prominent figure or quote. *Classical allusion* refers to something or someone in classical (Greek, Roman) literature, including biblical references. "Even Job would have given up by now," alludes to the patience of Job. The bizarre Vietnam movie called *Apocalypse Now* refers to the book of Revelation, a prophetic message of divine judgement and triumph to the Christian, but a picture of bizarre and violent destruction to the unbeliever. If you have the "sword of Damocles" hanging over your head, you are in immediate danger, just as the mythological ancient Greek courtier whose king sat him down at a feast beneath a sword suspended by a single hair.

Writers often allude to *classic,* as well as classical, literature such as Shakespeare. If a man is a Romeo, he's an ardent lover, but if he's a Shylock, he's a merciless businessman. Shakespeare's *Romeo and Juliet* is a story of "star-crossed" lovers, while his *Merchant of Venice,* in which Shylock threatens to exact a "pound of flesh" as a loan repayment, reflects the prejudices and hatreds that developed over the centuries between too many European Jews and Christians.

A good liberal arts education should provide you with a broad, general knowledge of classic literature such as the Bible, ancient mythology and epic poetry (like Homer's *Iliad* and the *Odyssey*), and Shakespeare, just to name the most well-known examples. Without these familiarities, you will be hampered in both your understanding and enjoyment of much of your reading, including many magazine and newspaper articles, as well as novels, short stories, histories, and biographies.

Chapter 5
The Renewal of Rebellion and the Birth of Paganism

Leaders of Rebellion

Whom did they follow, if they were not following Noah or Shem? Knowing from Gen. 11 and from ancient historians what would happen, we conclude that they most probably followed **Cush**, the son of Ham. Just as before the Flood, when God had dealt with a small minority of believers descended from Seth and a vast majority of unbelievers descended from Cain, so it was after the Flood, that a **small minority** would follow the **godly** leading of Noah and his son Shem, while the **vast majority** followed leaders who **rebelled** against God. And so, from Adam down to the present day, God has always dealt with a remnant of true believers, while the vast majority of people have gone their own way. This is ever the case, even in the history of God's chosen Jewish nation.

The Old Question of Race and the Three Sons

We have already noted the flaws in Ham's character from the incident with Noah in Gen. 9. The name **Ham**, according to *Strong's Concordance*, means to be hot or warm or to inflame oneself. Hislop translates it as **"the hot or burning one,"** or even "the burnt one." (Hislop, 25) This meaning led to a widely taught belief that Ham must have possessed the physical characteristics of the Negroid or black race and so is the father of that race, while Japheth is the father of the loosely designated "white race," and Shem the father of the Jews and other Middle Easterners.

There is obviously some truth to this generalization. Jews are indeed Semites. Ham's son Cush is associated with Ethiopians known for their black skin. Japhethites fathered many Caucasoid Europeans. However, the **Table of Nations** of Gen. 10 is concerned about *nations*, not races. Isolation of some peoples over time developed certain distinctive physical characteristics while intermarriage among others blended physical features. Actually, **Ham** was the father of a *variety of peoples*, including Mesopotamians, Arabians, North Africans (including Egyptians), and Near Eastern Mediterranean Canaanites. Japheth fathered both Asians and Europeans, while Shem fathered Mesopotamians, Arabians, and Asians. **Ham's name** probably refers directly to his spiritual characteristics and to the resulting idolatry of his racially varied progeny. He was inflamed with rebellion and pride and so was **spiritually charred**.

It does so happen that there are three broad, physical categories of humanity that have been identified by **anthropologists**, categories which are still generally referenced in anthropological discussions. The groups are called **Caucasoid** (European, North African, Near Eastern, South Asian), **Negroid** (much of Africa, Melanesia, New Guinea), and **Mongoloid** (Asian, Eskimo, North American Indian). *Exactly what Shem, Ham, and Japheth looked like, we don't know.*

However,

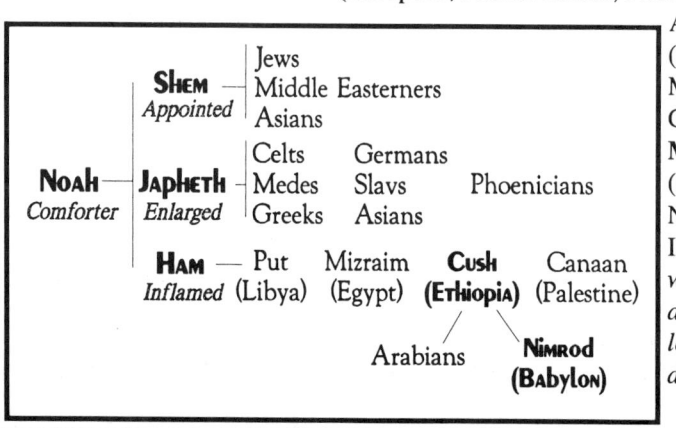

both evolutionists and creationists agree that **"segregation into small groups** is necessary in either model (creation or evolution) if distinctive characteristics are to emerge and become stabilized in each group." (Morris, Sci. Cre., 181) Creationist Dr. Henry Morris points out that *as long as men remained together in one large group with free gene flow, physical distinctions would tend to offset each other,* resulting in a "fairly constant set of dominant characteristics." The stereotypical "black man," "white man," "red man," "yellow man," "brown man," had to develop from previously recessive genes, *after people scattered and were concentrated in separate groups,* **after** the Tower of **Babel** judgement. The **potential** for all of these characteristics was obviously **provided by God.** (Morris, Sci. Cre., 181-2)

Racial prejudice is certainly not biblical or godly. God determines, through the genetics He controls, the physical characteristics of each one of us, for His own purposes. The fact that Ham's name refers to a "blackened" or "burnt" character (hot pride), and that two of the first leaders of rebellion (Cush and Nimrod) are Ham's descendants and are associated with Negroid characteristics, is no more of a comment on black people than the fact that Stalin, Hitler, and Mussolini were Caucasoid (white) and that Mao Tse-tung was Mongoloid (Oriental). *Through the history of Ethiopia, God demonstrates His attitude toward a nation begot by a rebel, blackened in appearance, but bent toward God.*

One of Ham's sons, **Cush**, is strongly associated with **Ethiopia**. Cush fled Shinar to this area as a **result of Babel** and founded this nation. Most of the **sons of Cush** are the fathers of modern-day, **brown-skinned** Middle Easterners living in and around Arabia (Gen. 10:7-8). However, **Ethiopian Cushites** have been known for their **black skin** since before the time of Moses, and the very term "Cushite" is usually translated as "Ethiopian." A proverbial saying in Jer. 13:23 asks, "Can the Ethiopian (actual word is Cushite) change his skin or the leopard his spots?"

God used Cush to father several nations or peoples. Why did God allow the Ethiopian (Cushite) people to be "blackened" with Cush's name? Were they rebellious against God like Cush? Quite the contrary.

First of all, **Moses** married an Ethiopian woman. (Num. 12:1) Later in time, Israel's **King Solomon** and Ethiopia's **Queen of Sheba** (both world famous then and today) had a **son** named *Prince Menelik I.* This is documented in the *Ethiopian Royal Chronicles.* Because of Menelik (half Jewish) and because of the Queen's great respect for Solomon and for God (I Kgs. 10), a large segment of Ethiopian descendants carried Jewish royal blood and adopted the Jewish religion. Modern-day Ethiopian **Emperor Haile Selassie**, murdered by Communists in 1975, called himself the

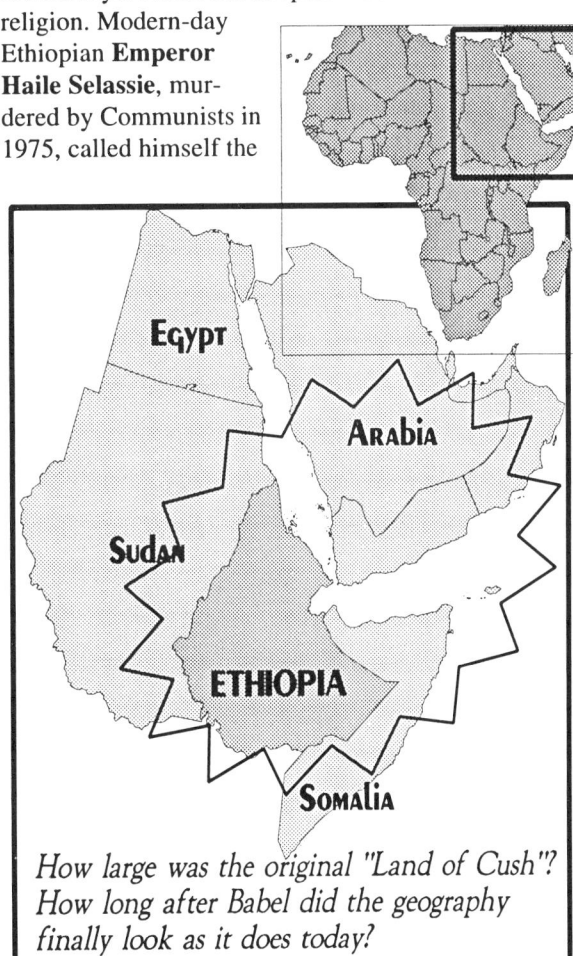

How large was the original "Land of Cush"? How long after Babel did the geography finally look as it does today?

"Lion of Judah" because he was descended from the son of King Solomon and the Queen of Sheba. The Ethiopian tongue, *Amharic*, is a Semitic language, and Menelik's Jewish descendants dominated the ruling class of Ethiopia throughout most of their history. In 1991, the *Jerusalem Post* pictured **Ethiopia's Black Jews** (called "Falashas") who were rescued from the Communists and brought to Israel by a secretly planned airlift. The pictures show people whose skin ranges from very black to jet black.

The **Apostle Philip's** 1st-Century A.D.

conversion of the **Ethiopian Jewish royal eunuch**, treasurer to Queen Candace, (Acts 8:26-39) resulted in a strong Ethiopian **Christian** community called the **Coptic Church**. *Thus, even though Cush was a rebel leader, God has bestowed prominence and grace upon a large segment of black Ethiopians throughout history.* There is even evidence to believe that the **Ark of the Covenant** may be hidden in Ethiopia, though there is also evidence that it may be hidden beneath the Temple site in Jerusalem. (Jeffrey, Armageddon, 113-123)

Certain ancient records and drawings portray **Nimrod**, the rebellious son of Cush, as **Negroid** in features and skin color. (Hislop, 43-4) Once again, Nimrod's physical features had nothing to do with his moral character. But his physical features do tie him closely to Cush, and the relationship between Cush and Nimrod, as we shall soon see, was important enough to be immortalized in mythologies around the world. If Nimrod was indeed physically Negroid, that means that *the world's first king and conqueror was a black man*. As we will document in the next chapter, in purely *human* terms, Nimrod was one of history's greatest and mightiest men!

Leadership of Cush

We know from the Bible that Cush was the **first-named son of Ham** and the **father** (some say ancestor) **of Nimrod**. How do we know that he was the leader of "they" who journeyed from the east and found Shinar? One of Nimrod's prominent pagan Babylonian names was **Ninus**, and Ninus was considered to be the son of **Bel**, who is recorded as the founder of Babylon. Baal in Babylon was "Lord," but Bel was *"The Confounder."* Though the Greek name "Belus" represented both Baal and Bel, the two titles were distinct from one another. Jer. 50:2 pronounces judgement on Babylon, saying that "Bel is confounded" (or ashamed). This is a play on words, saying that "The Confounder is confounded." (Hislop, 24-7) **Ba-bel** is translated as "confusion," taken from the word "ba-lal" which means to mix. (*Strong's*) As **Ninus was Nimrod**, the son, **Bel would have been Cush**, the father. *Cush actually led the migration to Shinar and founded Babylon and led the building of the Tower of Babel.* Nimrod would not take over leadership (and his father's titles) until after the Tower judgement.

Ancient Roman historian **Gregorius Turonensis** apparently attributes much to Cush that was more often attributed by others to Nimrod, but, by doing so, confirms that Cush was generally considered to be the original leader of the rebellion, and thus the migration. Nineteenth-Century Scottish pastor and linguist **Alexander Hislop** states that Cush's leadership is "amply confirmed from other sources." (Hislop, 25)

Hislop also demonstrates that the two-faced god, **Janus**, with two faces pointing in opposite directions, was originally connected with Cush. Janus was called "Chaos" by the ancients, and thus was the "god of confusion." In Chaldee, the name of Cush was also Khus which, in pronunciation, became Khawos or **Khaos**. Janus also had a **club**. The Chaldee name for a club is derived from a word that means "to break in pieces" or "to scatter abroad." (**Vulcan** and his hammer are the same as Janus and his club.) (Hislop, 25-8) **Cush**, *then, as the original Janus, was the leader who was responsible for the confounding of languages, the breaking in pieces of the continents, and the scattering of the ungodly majority of the human race.* The Hebrew word used in Gen. 11:8 for "scattered" also means to "break in pieces." (*Strong's*) The two-faced Janus also came to represent the old Cush and the young Cush (Nimrod).

Hislop's documentation of Cush's leadership continues with the definition of the name **Hermes**. Hermes was originally Egyptian, then Greek, and was the same as the Roman **Mercury** and the Babylonian **Nebo**. He was considered the author of pagan religious rites and the **interpreter of the gods**. According to a Roman work called the *Fabulae*, men lived for many ages under the government of Jehovah, with no laws or cities and with one common language. But then Mercury (or Hermes) interpreted the words of men and divided the nations. At that

CUSH	NIMROD
Bel *(The Confounder)*	Ninus *(son of Bel)*
Chaos	
Hermes *(son of Ham)*	
Old Janus	Young Janus

point, says the legend, discord began. [Hislop attributes the *Fabulae* to the 1st-Century Roman scholar Hyginus, but others say the *Fabulae* was written by another Roman in the 2nd Century. (Hislop, 25-6; E.B., 1972, 11:983)]

The Chaldee word for interpret was "peresh," but was pronounced by ancient Egyptians, Greeks, and even Chaldees the same as "peres," which means **"to divide."** Thus, Mercury or Hermes was actually the "divider" of the languages of men. In Egyptian and Chaldee, Her and Ham were equivalent. In Egyptian, Ra-mes means "the son of Ra" and Thoth-mes means "the son of Thoth." Thus, **Her-mes** was the **"son of Ham,"** or Cush. *Therefore, Cush was seen as the divider of the languages of men, causing the division into nations, the breaking apart of the continents, and the beginning of discord.* Further interesting is the fact that the term *"hermeneutics"* is the science of interpretation and is used by seminaries as the name for the study of Biblical exegesis. (*Webster's New World Dict.*)

Why did the majority of men migrate to the east with Cush? As the population grew, it makes sense that men would spread out further and further. More land would be needed for planting and grazing. But the spiritual nature and actions of "the whole Earth" in Gen. 11 strongly suggests the conclusion that the vast majority of Noah's descendants **chaffed under** the **godly leadership** of Noah and Shem and looked instead to the proud and ambitious Cush. Moses tells us that these people were determined to stay together and were afraid of being scattered over the face of all the Earth.

Why were they afraid? Probably everyone of these people knew Noah and his family personally. (The Tower of Babel period was only five generations removed from the Flood and Noah lived for 350 years after the Flood.) They had all certainly heard Noah and Shem teach. Everything they knew had been taught them by Noah's family. There is no record of God directly addressing anyone during this period but Noah and his sons. However, through Noah, these people knew all about God, Adam and Eve, Satan, the Fall, the previous age of rebellion, the Flood, and the Ark. They knew how to worship God, as Noah was essentially the high priest. They were one patriarchal community under the rules of God's Noahic Covenant (Gen. 9) and the guidance of Noah, with no cities or human codes of law. They had been told by God in Gen. 9:1 to "fill" (same Hebrew word used for "fill" and "replenish") the Earth, but they feared and tried to disobey the command. Why?

Influence of Ham

Ham and his wife lived in the world before the Flood. Obviously, **Ham told his sons** all about the incredible **pre-Flood** environment and the sons could see the difference for themselves. They could see the evidence of judgement all around them. They knew the struggles of restarting a civilization from scratch, while all the time they heard **grand stories** about the marvelous civilization that had thrived in the pre-Flood world. That world, though full of rebellion and subject to the Curse, had been a comparative paradise of giant plants, animals, and men who lived to be over 900 years old. It had cities, culture, and commerce. It was populated by mighty men—**heroes**—men who gained great fame both before and after the Flood. We have noted that **Ham was "the hot one,"** inflamed with pride, spiritually charred. *Was he also inflamed over the fact that God had destroyed his wondrous world?*

The Bible itself tells us in Gen. 6 about the "mighty men," the children of the sons of God and the daughters of men. We have noted that the term "sons of God" in the Old Testament always referred to angels. The word translated "giants" is **Nephil(im)**, which means bully, tyrant, or giant, and is derived from a word which means to fall, throw down, overthrow, or be a fugitive. These giants were *the fallen ones*, thrown out of heaven, formerly powerful but overthrown by God, and now fugitives from heaven. (The sons of Cain were not overthrown until the Flood, and, though fugitives from God, were not fugitives on an Earth totally dominated by their own kind. Also, they were no more "fallen" than every other human. Only Satan's angels were "the fallen ones," thus distinguished from the "unfallen angels.") Their children were half angel (not divine) and half man. Thus, the **pagan "mythology"** of the **half-god, half-man heroes** was based on these mighty men, men of renown, physical/spiritual half-breeds. A 9th/8th-Century B.C. Greek work called the *Catalogues of Women*, perhaps falsely attributed in part to the poet Hesiod, tells of women who united with gods to produce heroes and thus became the ancestresses of nobility. (E.B., 1972, 11:461)

The first listed **definition of "hero"** in Webster's *New World Dictionary* is from "myth and legend" and describes "a man of great strength and courage, favored by the gods and in part descended from them, often regarded as a **half-god** and worshipped after his death." (Webster's, New World, 1976) During their lifetimes before the Flood (900-year lifetimes), the giants, or heroes, would not have been considered "men of old," and so their renown, or fame, had to spread *after* the Flood, and this had to be done by Noah's family, who had known these mighty men personally.

The **sons of Ham** would be most active in developing the **post-Flood mythology** which glorified the **pre-Flood and post-Flood heroes**, so it seems perfectly reasonable to assume that *Ham was the main one responsible for spreading the tales of the mighty men of old.* Ham had also witnessed the interaction of the fallen angels and mankind and knew the power those angels retained, despite their defeat. Though the specific angels who fathered children with women were chained by God, awaiting judgement, (Jude 6; II Pet. 2:4) the rest of Satan's angels, his demonic forces, were anxious to **restore their spiritual traffic** with men, and Ham's sons were the ones who would first promote this demonic traffic.

Later, the **sons of Japheth**, the Greeks and the Romans, would perpetuate paganism while the **sons of Shem** would continually be ensnared by it. [Gen. 6 says that there were **giants "also after that,"** and we read about giants in Deut. 2 & 3 and in Joshua and the two books of Samuel. These giants were targeted by God for destruction. They must have been conceived in the same way, indicating that some angels continued the practice, though they were apparently limited in their activities. Dr. Gaverluk describes this as ancient **"experimentations in biogenesis"** and points to the modern-day fascination with biogenetics and with UFOs and aliens and crossbreeding with aliens, *e.g.* the first and second *Star Trek* series. (Gaverluk, Rapture, 271)]

Knowing what he knew, knowing God Himself, how could Ham have propagated the knowledge and attitudes that resulted in the birth of paganism? Such is the strength of the rebellious human nature—to stare truth in the face, to talk directly with God, to be saved from worldwide judgement, to witness the results of rebellion, to enjoy the blessings of God, and then to reject God and go one's own way. *Each of us has that very same nature, and yet we think we can make and keep decisions regarding our own salvation. Only the Holy Spirit can overthrow that nature and save us in spite of ourselves!*

If we estimate that there were about 200 years between the Flood and the Tower of Babel, then we can further guess that the population had **multiplied for 100-plus years** when they elected to follow Cush and began their journeying from the east to the **land of Shinar**. (Remember, Cush was born into a series of generations whose lives spanned some 400 years.) Hislop argues that the name Shinar was derived from "shené" which means *"to repeat,"* and from "naar" which means *"childhood."* To repeat childhood is to be *"born again"* or regenerated. Shinar, then, may have referred to the **"land of the Regenerator,"** referring, of course, not to Jesus Christ, but *to the one who would become the pagan savior.* (Hislop, 4th note, 137)

Paganism & Worship of the Pre-Flood World

Inflamed by Ham, rallied by Cush, the majority of Noah's descendants chafed under the godly leadership of Noah and delighted in the stories of the heroes and the comparable paradise of the pre-Flood world. Much later, in the 800s/700s B.C., the Greek poet **Hesiod** wrote of a **"Heroic Age"** or "Golden Age" populated with a worldwide race of demigods who were more just and virtuous than the degenerated men of his own "iron age." This preoccupation with the pre-Flood world, destroyed by water, most probably gave birth to the legend of **Atlantis**, a perverted recollection furthered by the writings of **Plato** in the 300s B.C. (Gordon, Before, 196, 43)

The persistent and pervasive **pagan doctrine of demigods** derives from the half-breeds produced by the evil angels and the daughters of Cain before the Flood. (We do not know for certain whether or not some of the descendants of Seth also chose to rebel against God and follow Satan.) The post-Flood world, aside from the remnant that followed the godly leading of Noah and Shem, wanted to revive and emulate their pre-Flood ancestors' relationship with the evil but powerful members of the **spirit world**. Then, as now and always, **Satan** promised knowledge, power, possessions, and immortality with no godly restraints, something which is irresistible to the unregenerate human nature.

For a time, he delivers certain material and miraculous rewards or powers, but these are ultimately followed by **total destruction**. This is why serious, Satanic, spiritual involvement so often leads to homicide and suicide. In her book, *The Beautiful Side of Evil*, Johanna Michaelsen explains how the "velvet claws" of Satan allowed her to participate in truly miraculous, demonic healings, until the veil of **demonic deception** was lifted and she saw the permanent evil behind the temporary beauty. A counterfeit "Jesus Christ," one of the *"avatars"* or "manifestations of deity," was her spirit guide until she found true regeneration in the real Jesus Christ. (Michaelsen, Beautiful, 138-9)

The Occult and the Old New Age

The modern pagan movement called the **New Age**, which is sweeping the world in the 20th Century, perpetuates the Babylonian obsession with the pre-Flood world and the legends of Atlantis. New Age prophetess **Alice Bailey** dictated for a demon called the Tibetan for 25 years, beginning in 1919, and these writings refer to an evolution of racial types or **root races** that began even before Atlantis. The first named is called the **Lemurian** race, Lemuria being a supposed lost continent either in the Indian or Pacific Ocean. Lemurians were the "third root race," and represented the *"physical plane consciousness of humanity,"* which is, of course, a lower stage of evolution. The Lemurians were supposedly destroyed by some sort of cataclysm. (Bailey, Education, 54, 71; Dict. of Myst., 150, 226)

Next came the famous and fabled **Atlantean** race, the "fourth root race," who represented the *astral plane of human consciousness and emotional dominance*. "In Atlantean times, the idea that predominated was basically **sensory religious idealism** or **mysticism**, expressing itself in terms of approach to a felt but unseen deity, an expression of the way of feeling," says the Tibetan through Bailey. Religion and life after death were the Atlantean's total focus and reason for existence. It is from the Atlanteans that modern history inherits the concepts of "animism, spiritualism, lower psychism and feeling. The sense of God, the sense of immortality, the sense of subtler inner relationships, the sense of worship and the undue sensitivity of modern man is our outstanding inheritance from the civilisations which existed upon old Atlantis," writes Bailey. This was all inherited "when history as we now have it arose (from the time of the flood, whenever that might have been)...." Thus, the New Agers teach that Atlantis existed before the Flood and that they were very "religious." (Bailey, Education, 39-42)

They also say that the **New Age movement** is as old as Atlantis, revived after the Flood, and spread across the world at the time of the founding of Babylon. According to Christian writer Constance Cumbey, the New Age Secret Doctrine "glorifies the pre-Flood world, a world that, according to both the Bible and the Secret Doctrine, was alive with demonic contact and psycho/spiritual power." [A written work entitled *The Secret Doctrine* was authored in the late 1800s by **Theosophist Helena Petrovna Blavatsky**.] Cumbey suggests that *Atlantis most likely refers to the pre-Flood world.* (Cumbey, Hidden, 93, 101-2)

Lemurian Race	*Physical Plane*
Atlantean Race	*Astral Plane*
Aryan Race	*Mental Plane*
Aquarian Race	*State of Consciousness!*

The **Aryans** are the "fifth root race," or modern man from the Flood to the present. Aryans represent the *plane of human mental knowledge*. According to Bailey's writings, the Atlanteans and Aryans are both too extreme and must be merged into the **middle path**, resulting in a new race called the New Age or **Aquarian** race. This new racial type will be "more *a state of consciousness* than a physical form,....a state of mind more than a peculiarly designed body." [Does that sound scary and demonic?] This new race will have intuitive understanding and control of energy and will bring humanity to the enlightened level of the **willing sacrifice of the individual to the group**, moving from "selfish desire into group love." (Bailey, Education, 41-2, 71, 119) Basically, that means if you're an outsider, you're dead.

Sacrificing the individual for the group is the basis of everything in the agenda of New Age socialists, and particularly the **Clinton "co-presidency"** of Bill and Hillary Clinton. *Listen carefully for this philosophy.* It's everywhere. It forms the philosophical foundation for big, elitist government paid for with excessive taxation ("from those according to their means to those according to their needs") as well as abortion, euthanasia, zero-population growth, and other shocking methods of social engineering. Yes, the Clintons and their cronies are New Age to the core.

The **Aryan** race was also used by **Hitler** as part of the Nazi movement, the Aryans being the blond, blue-eyed Germanic superhumans who should rule the world. The *Secret Doctrine* also teaches that the Aryans were the **master race** of the seven Atlantean races, educated by "God-men" and highly developed through a **quantum leap in evolution** "to give them the necessary faculties to live in a post-diluvian world." Magical and psychic powers were sacrificed to gain superior mental powers. The intellectually superior Aryans now had to be guided by **spiritual "masters"** through the process of **initiation** in order to maintain their former spiritual power. (Cumbey, Hidden Dangers, 102-3) Every **occultic** group in history has required *progressive initiations into secret doctrines*. In this way, groups like the Mormons and Masons reveal their occultic origins.

These occult doctrines thinly mask the underlying truth revealed in the Bible of the demonically active pre-Flood world, the judgement of the Flood, and the development of post-Flood paganism. The legends of Atlantis were embellished over time and took a number of forms.

Noah in Mythology

We know that Noah outlived Peleg by 10 years, **dying** (by our calculations) in **1995 B.C.** If indeed the Tower of Babel judgement occurred when Peleg was about 70 years old, or about 2174 B.C., then Noah would have lived some 180 years after the dispersion, dying only 11 years before Nimrod is said to have been executed, and two years before the birth of Abraham.

That Noah and his **amazing deliverance** were soon **celebrated** in all manner of tradition, legend, and myth, is only natural for the mind and nature of man. The Mesopotamians would maintain a tradition that the **level of science** was much higher at the beginning of civilization, referring most likely to both the pre-Flood world and the "New World" immediately following the Flood. Writing in about the year 280 B.C., a Babylonian priest named **Berossus** describes a **half-man, half-fish god** called *Oannes* who supposedly came from the Red Sea (actually the Persian Gulf, which was called the Red Sea by the ancients) and who "civilized" mankind, teaching them the arts, sciences, politics, and religion. This legend spoke of **Noah**, who came from the "sea" and taught his descendants the knowledge he brought from the pre-Flood world. However, Oannes would also come to represent Nimrod who "enlightened" mankind with the knowledge of pagan worship, war, and empire building. (Gordon, Before, 53, 76; Hislop, 243-4; see next chapter) Nimrod is also credited by certain ancient historians with the establishment of the sciences of magic and astronomy/astrology. (Hislop, 67)

E-anush was the Chaldean form of Oannes, meaning "the man," or even "the fallen man." This, of course, referred to **Adam**, the first father of the human race, as **Noah** was the second father of the human race. (Hislop, 271-3) Another symbol of this **dual representation of Adam and Noah** is *Capricorn*, the goat-horned fish of the zodiac. The goat-horned god *Pan* was the head of the *Satyrs*, or "hidden ones." Adam, the fallen man who hid himself, was represented in **Pan**. Thus, **Capricorn**, the goat-horned fish,

ADAM	**NOAH**
Old Janus	Vishnu
E-anush	New Janus
Pan (goat)	Oannes
	Dagon (fish)
Capricorn (goat/fish)	

again represents Adam, the first father (goat), and Noah, the second father (fish). (Hislop, 310-11)

Also closely related to Oannes was the name *Janus*, the god of two faces, one old and one young. Another name for **Janus** was *Diphues* which means **"twice born."** Noah was born into the "Old World" and "reborn" into the "New World." The legends of Janus include his being the *father of the world* as well as the *inventor of ships*. This identification with the great patriarch Noah gave the later pagan mysteries a **mantle of respectability**. Janus also represented Cush, the father, and Nimrod, the son, as well as Adam, the first father, and Noah, the second father. (Hislop, 134-5; 26-7) In addition, Janus was connected with *Dagon*, the fish god, once again a reference to Noah. The Roman Catholic Pope wears the **mitre of Dagon**. A side view of the Pope's mitre reveals the outline of the mouth of a fish. (Hislop, 214-15)

According to Hislop, the "whole mythology of Greece and Rome, as well as Asia, is full of the history and deeds of Noah, which it is impossible to misunderstand." (Hislop, 135) Even India's god *Vishnu* is supposed to have miraculously saved one righteous family from a flood that drowned the entire Earth. **Vishnu** is the Sanskrit version of the Chaldee *Ish-nuh*, which means "the man (ish) Noah (nuh)," or the "man of rest." (Hislop, 135) We shall also find Noah celebrated in the mythologies of Europe, the Americas, and the South Pacific. *This shows us that the ancients certainly knew the truth about Noah and the judgement of the Flood, that Noah did indeed father, teach, and lead the first generations of the "New World," and that Noah commanded respect, even from the rebellious majority.*

Getting God Off Their Backs

Noah's descendants knew who **God** was and knew that He was the Creator. But, to them, He was also the **destroyer of the heroes and the paradise**. Despite God's promise in the Noahic Covenant never again to destroy the world by **flood**, and His new reminder of that promise, the rainbow, the **fear of such destruction** would always haunt the lore of pagan peoples. In fact, Josephus attributes one of the most ancient and pervasive traditions, that the world would be destroyed one time by fire and another time by water, originally to a prediction made by Adam. (Josephus, I.iii.3.) Adam may well have voiced the prophecy, as Enoch prophesied about the return of Christ with His saints. (Jude 14) We find the same two judgements in II Pet. 3. The **Flood** brought about a new heavens and Earth (vs. 7), as will the purifying judgement of **fire** which will produce the new heavens and Earth following the Millennium (Rev. 21). Even though the Flood had already occurred, the **double prophecy** *would weave its way tenaciously into the pagan beliefs that spread around the world.*

The **Polynesian sky fable** (found also among North American tribes and probably elsewhere) is a degenerated version of the story of the people who followed Cush. An ancient tradition of the South Sea islanders, the story says that the heavens were originally so close to the Earth that men could not stand up and walk but had to crawl. This **oppression by the heavens** was a great evil, but the people were delivered from it by a **hero** who, in four progressive stages, lifted the heavens to their present height. This great benefactor of mankind was deified and worshipped as the **"Elevator of the heavens."** (Hislop, 52-3)

The **Chewkee** tribe on the *American Gulf Coast* teach that the Sun was once too close and too hot and was lifted seven times. The **Kaska** tribe in *British Columbia, Canada*, also say that the sky was too close to the Earth a very long time ago, but the Sun stopped and grew smaller, apparently solving the problem. (The details about the Sun may also involve the later phenomenon of Joshua's Long Day in Josh. 10.) The **Snohomish** tribe of *Puget Sound* in Washington State relate a very ancient time when all the animals were still human beings, when the sky was so low that people could not stand up. It was necessary for all the people of the world to come together and push the sky up with poles. They agreed that the signal to push would be the word *"Yahu."* (Yes. This is the quote.) With several pushes, they succeeded in lifting the sky. (Velikovsky, Worlds, 189-90)

These fables from Polynesia and North

America are obviously related to the well-known Greek legend of the **Titan** (giant) called **Atlas** who held the heavens upon his shoulders. (He was later shown as holding the world on his shoulders, to promote maps or "atlases.") Atlas, we shall see, is none other than **Nimrod** who, in modern vernacular, *"got God off the back of mankind."* (See next chapter.)

As is so often repeated in Judges, man wishes to do what is right in his own eyes. The natural man (I Cor. 2) wants **freedom *from* God**. The godly rule of the patriarchs and the fear of heavenly judgement was oppressive. *The people wanted deliverance from God and freedom to pursue the wisdom of the demonic forces and the promises of human achievement.*

The Tower of Babel

In the spirit of Cain, the group decided to build a **city**. However, they also determined to erect a great **tower** that would reach to the heavens. Obviously, they had the knowledge and abilities to do these things. As had Noah, they used bitumen for **mortar** and, probably using ovens, they made **bricks**. Most authorities assume they used the Sun, but the words "burn them thoroughly" in Gen. 11:3 as well as their abilities and access to knowledge suggest a more sophisticated approach. Dr. Charles Dyer writes that the people in that region "use **kiln-fired bricks** for added strength. The builders of Babel used kiln-fired bricks because they wanted their project to last."(Dyer, Rise, 52)

Professor Cyrus Gordon of Brandeis University notes the strong Mesopotamian tradition that the **level of science** was much higher at the beginning of civilization. (Gordon, Before, 76) So, this was *not* the "Stone Age." There are remains of a massive **ziggurat** at Ur, still showing the long staircases that ascended the artificial mountain. The remains or sites of some two dozen other ziggurats have been found—temple towers in a **stepped pyramid** construction that are supposed to illustrate the original Tower of Babel. (Pict. Dict., 913; Pritchard, Ancient, photo 188) [We will also explore later the fact that the stepped pyramids of Mexico and Guatemala are Babylonian and not Egyptian in origin.]

The ziggurats are probably copies of the tower effort, but the original **Tower of Babel** must have been **superior and special** for several reasons: **1)** these people were not "primitive" but were intelligent and capable, with 200- to 400-year life spans, the knowledge of the ancients, and instruction from superior angelic beings; **2)** God came down to see the accomplishment of the people's "dream" (see *Young's Literal*) and said that, *now*, they could not be restrained from doing anything they determined to do; **3)** this tower received attention that no other ziggurat or pyramid ever received.

What was the intention and potential of these people that they moved God to such statements and action? Some say the height of the Tower was to defy God's ability to drown them. Josephus writes that **Nimrod**, co-conspirator with his father Cush, proclaimed his intention to seek **revenge against God** (imagine that!) if God so dared again to **drown the world**, and that Nimrod "would build a tower too high for the waters to be able to reach!" and "would avenge himself on God for destroying their forefathers!" (Josephus, I.iv.2) Josephus explains that they used bitumen (asphalt found in a natural state that Noah used on the Ark) in order to make the Tower waterproof. If finished, would the Tower have been big enough to hold them all? Josephus comments that such actions were essentially insane, (Josephus, I.iv.3) and they certainly do not seem very feasible or intelligent. However, this tradition was strong enough to survive in the annals of the ancients, to be researched and recorded by Josephus in the 1st-Century A.D.

Dr. Ross writes that the Tower was an expression of **human pride** and a center for **pagan worship**. The word *babili* means "the gate of God," and later Babylonian records regard **Babylon** as a heavenly city built by the **gods**. (Ross, BKC I, 44-5; Pritchard, Ancient, 31-8) Does this mean that the fallen angels ("gods") had a role in building the Tower?

Others, including Dr. Gaverluk, contend that the Tower was a device intended to reestablish **communication with the demonic world** of fallen angels. In fact, recalling Jer. 51:53 which says, "Though Babylon should mount up to heaven, and though she should fortify the height of her strength," Dr. Gaverluk states that the Tower was intended to be a **launching tower** for a spacecraft. These first Babylonians wanted to colonize the planets, he says, duplicating the attempt of the antediluvian (pre-Flood) giants, which is demonstrated by the massive carved face and pyramids on Mars discovered by NASA's Viking Orbiter. (Gaverluk, Rapture, 229-30, 236, 171, 272-3; see Chap. 2) Dr. Gaverluk believes that it is *Satan's dream to colonize the universe.* (Gaverluk, Rapture, 232)

Josephus quotes "The Sibyl," (a sibyl was a Greek prophetess) as saying the people "built a high tower, as if they would thereby ascend up to heaven;...." (Josephus, I.iv.3) They did actively seek **immortality**, though on their own terms. Did they really believe that they could build a tower that would physically lift them **to heaven** and immortality? Did they really believe that such a tower could physically lift them **to the planets**? Were they insane? Or, are these traditions degenerated to the point that they hide the true intelligence and potential capabilities of Noah's immediate descendants? *It is difficult, if not impossible, to delineate between pure human reasoning and the insane, convoluted thinking that comes from Satan.*

Someone had to construct the **face and pyramids on Mars** photographed by NASA. If the antediluvian half-breeds were not taken to Mars by the fallen angels, perhaps Mars was a base for the fallen angels who themselves built the truly immense structures. If the Tower was not a launching tower, perhaps it was intended to be a **communications tower**. Dr. Gaverluk quotes a scientist from a prominent California high-tech corporation as saying that if the 13-acre base of the Great Pyramid in Egypt (Cheops) were constructed on a thin layer of gold, silver, or copper, with a metallic or crystal feedhorn at the top, the pyramid would then be a **giant capacitor** capable of tapping into the electromagnetic field of the Earth and acting as a **giant radioscope** more powerful than any in existence today. (Gaverluk, Rapture, 273) The incredibly huge and mysterious drawings on the Nazca plain in South America and the similar chalk carvings in Great Britain can be effectively viewed only from the air. How were they accomplished? Were they signs, markers, or messages for the fallen angels? [These will be further discussed later.]

It would seem that man was certainly up to more than a little idle idol worship. God says the equivalent of, "now, they can accomplish anything that they are capable of imagining." Does this mean "now that they are totally **united** in purpose and task," or "now that they have established communication and an **alliance** with the fallen angels," or both? They wanted to make a *name* for themselves, "lest they be scattered abroad upon the face of the whole Earth." Did this refer to establishing a **reputation** among the spiritual principalities and powers of the universe? *Did they truly believe that Satan and the fallen angels were capable of preventing their dispersion? Or did they believe that their own power was sufficient to defy God successfully?*

The Babel Judgement

Whatever their true beliefs, God provided the answer on all counts. He "confused" their **language**, giving them a number of languages and pronunciations so that they could not understand one another. Then He saw to it that they were **scattered** upon the face of *all* the Earth. Note that the action was done *by God, to them.*

This was the point at which God now **broke apart the continents**. We derive this from Gen. 10:25, where it names **Peleg** as one of the two sons of Eber, and says that it was in the *days of Peleg that the Earth was divided*. The name Peleg means to be split or *divided as by canals of water.*

This was an action of judgement and may have been **physically spectacular**. We don't know if God immediately moved the continents to their present positions or employed more gradual means. Dr. Baugh and others believe that forces unleashed by God pushed the newly ripped pieces of land apart in a relatively rapid fashion for a few hundred years until the continental drift slowed considerably to produce the kind of minor movements studied today by experts in **plate tectonics**. (Baker, Dinosaurs, 128; Baugh, Panorama, 81-2) Perhaps part (or all) of the process was a genuine **canaling by water** as God created great trenches through which the ocean rushed to create new *"islands"* of land. (See Chap. 3, p. 47)

Josephus writes that **colonies of men** went out everywhere, led by God to their appointed places. "There were some also," he continues, "who passed **over the sea in ships**, and inhabited the islands...." (Josephus, I.v.) Notice that

Josephus had no trouble with the thought that "early man" was successfully seafaring. Josephus had far superior access to ancient records than any modern historian.

Peleg, a great-great-grandson of Shem through Arpachshad, was born (according to our calculations) in 2244 B.C., lived to be 239 years old, and died in 2005 B.C. Let's suppose he was 70 years old when the great division took place. That would date the **Tower of Babel judgement at 2174 B.C.** With this assumption, there would have been about 170 years between the Flood and Babel, and about 190 years between Babel and the traditional date for the execution of Nimrod. (see next chapter)

Both Josephus and Hislop refer to the traditions that God (or the gods) **toppled the Tower** with great storms of **wind**. (Josephus, I.iv.3; Hislop, 55) Wind is also symbolic of the Holy Spirit. Some of the traditions say that Nimrod perished in the ruins, but we know that Nimrod accomplished much after the division of men into nations. Hislop also says that the Tower stood long after Nimrod's day, but the evidence he refers to may be the discovery of ziggurat remains. Ziggurats were temple towers of the Babylonians and Assyrians, built like stepped pyramids. The actual Tower of Babel may have been merely the first ziggurat. However, considering our discussion above, it *may have been unique and perhaps was destroyed by God*. The Bible only says that the people "ceased building the city." (Gen. 11:8)

A book released in 1990 called *Europe is Rising!* has a poster on its cover showing a stylized version of the Tower of Babel **painting** by Flemish (Belgian) artist **Pieter Bruegel** the Elder in the A.D. **1500s**. Bruegel was originally inspired by the remains of the Colosseum in Rome. The modern-day poster was created by the **Council of Europe in Brussels, Belgium**, part of the **European Economic Community** (EEC), and shows Bruegel's tower with a high-rise-construction crane. This indicates, says the book, that "the Common Market alliance in 1992 will complete the building of a one-world order whose top will reach to Heaven." The poster is titled, "Europe: Many tongues, one voice." (Hutchings, Europe, cover caption; Atlas, 11) The 1992 EEC goals were not met, but the effort to unite Europe continues. *Man's "dream" of the tower and one-world unity has never been lost.*

As mankind scattered, **Mizraim**, one of the sons of Ham, founded **Egypt**, his very name referring to Egypt, as the name of Cush refers to Ethiopia. According to Greek historians and general consensus, **Menes** was the first king of Egypt. He is reputed to have built embankments that *diverted the course of the Nile River* and caused it to run in the center of the valley. Where before was water, he built the city of **Memphis**. Diodorus Siculus, Herodotus, and Plutarch each say that all of ancient Egypt, except for Thebes in what is now Upper Egypt, was *once under water*, a virtual sea. Before Egypt could be settled, the **Nile** had to be tamed. In fact, the ancients called the Nile by a name that meant "ocean" or "sea." Hislop denies that Mizraim is a plural word indicating both Upper and Lower Egypt. He demonstrates instead that the Hebrew **"Mizraim,"** without the points (vowel marks), is **"Metzr-im,"** or "Metsr-yam," which means *"encloser or embanker of the sea."* Thus, Hislop concludes that Ham's son *Mizraim was the historical Menes.* (Hislop, 292-4)

Conventional history identifies Menes as the "Fighter," the first to unify (not settle) Upper and Lower Egypt, and dates him between 3500 and 3000 B.C. *Egyptian history is very difficult to sort out because it has been terribly distorted in length and complexity.* Hislop refers to **Herodotus** who " vouches for the fact that **at one time there were no fewer than twelve contemporaneous kings in Egypt**," (they all ruled at the same time), kings who were listed successively by others. (Hislop, 292) Much of ancient historical dating is referenced to the long and flawed line of Egyptian dynasties, thus compounding the errors. *Remember this when referring to conventional histories and even to many Christian chronologies.*

While **Mizraim** founded Egypt, **Cush** fled

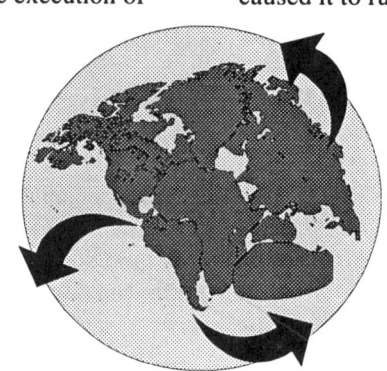

Continents break apart? Canaled by water?

to what became Ethiopia. **Put** (or Phut) settled Libya (the vast area west of Egypt) while **Canaan** led a colony to the area of modern-day Lebanon and Israel (Palestine). All four were **sons of Ham**. However, **Nimrod**, the grandson of Ham and "the son of Chus," as Josephus calls him, "stayed and tyrannised at Babylon,...." (Josephus, I.iv.2)

Faulty Traditional Outline of Egyptian History
Based on Writings of Manetho, Egyptian Priest, 200's B.C.

The generally accepted, traditional outline of Egyptian history begins about **5000** B.C. with the **Predynastic Period**, not (of course) forgetting the "millions" of years of evolving human and near-human existence that preceded. Remember that the term *"history"* is used to refer to that portion of man's existence which is **recorded** or documented in some fashion. Since evolutionists believe that spoken and written language had to evolve, they refer to everything prior to a recorded past as *"prehistory."*

We have presented evidence to support the belief that post-Flood history began in the 2300's B.C. We date the *end* of the **Flood** at **2344** B.C. According to anthropologist Ralph Linton, as quoted by Dr. Henry Morris, the oldest known date in Chinese history comes from China's *Book of History*. It is a dated astronomical reference interpreted to be 2250 B.C. (Morris, Gen. Flood, 396) We have also referenced linguistic evidence from Alexander Hislop that Mizraim of Gen. 10 was indeed the legendary King Menes. Traditionalists say that Menes "united" an already settled Egypt. **The Bible says that Mizraim (Menes)** *founded* **Egypt after the Tower of Babel in the 2200's to 2100's B.C.**

Obviously the accepted Egyptian time line and our biblical time line are in serious conflict. We mistrust Manetho's dynasty list because 1) it is oriented toward evolutionary beliefs, 2) it is based on fragmentary evidence of a dynasty list compiled centuries after the fact by an Egyptian priest who may very well have intended to "glorify" his country's history, 3) Herodotus tells us that there was a period when at least 12 and possibly more kings ruled at the same time in Egypt, kings who were listed *successively* by other historians, and 4) it conflicts with a conservative biblical time line.

You will find that all evolutionists and many Christian writers follow Manetho's chronology. Be a Berean, do your own research, and decide for yourself whether or not much of ancient history is corrupted by faulty assumptions drawn from an inaccurate and misleading list.

5000- 3100	**Prehistoric and Predynastic Period**
3100-2686	**Protodynastic Period** 1st & 2nd Dynasties
2686-2181	**Old Kingdom** 3rd to 6th Dynasties *Imhotep, Cheops, Chephren*
2181-2040	**1st Intermediate Period** 7th to 10th Dynasties
2133-1603	**Middle Kingdom** 11th to 14th Dynasties *Menuhoteps, Sesostris*
1720-1567	**2nd Intermediate Period** 15th to 17th Dynasties *Hyksos*
1567-525	**New Empire** 18th to 26th Dynasties *Amenhoteps, Thutmoses, Hatshepsut, Ramses*
525-332	**Persian Domination, (then Greeks)**

(Ency. Brit., 1972, 8:31-9; Walvoord & Zuck, Bible Knowledge Commentary I, 105)

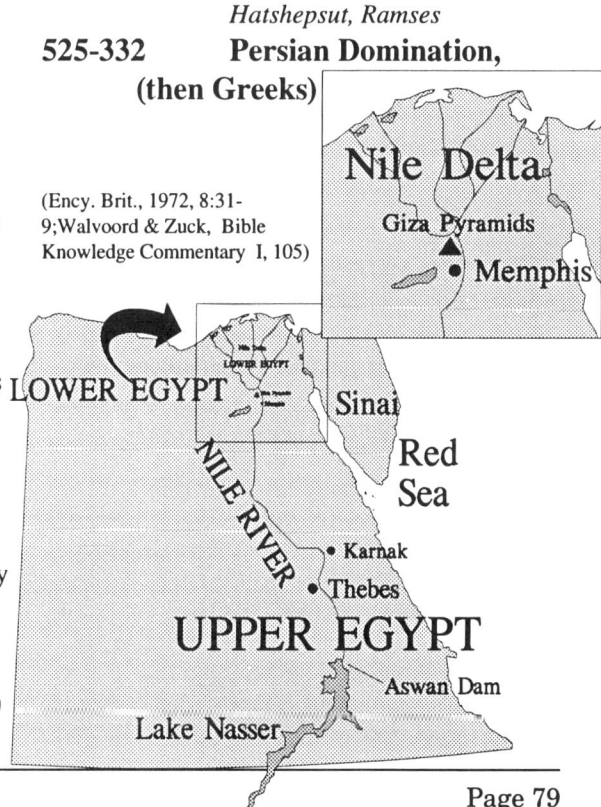

Rebellion and Paganism

BIBLIOGRAPHY

Atlas of the Bible, Pleasantville, N.Y.: The Reader's Digest Assoc., Inc., 1981.

Bailey, Alice A., *Education in the New Age*. New York: Lucis Publishing Company, 1954.

Baker, Mace, *Dinosaurs*, Bib. Chap. 3, p. 51.

Baugh, Carl, *Panorama*, Bib. Chap. 2, p. 37.

Bible Knowledge Commentary, Vol. 1 (Walvoord & Zuck, Dallas Theological Seminary), Bib. Chap. 2, p. 38 (see **Ross**)

Cumbey, Constance, *The Hidden Dangers*, Bib. Chap. 1, p. 19.

Drury, Nevill, *Dictionary of Mysticism*, Bib. Chap. 2, p. 37.

Dyer, Charles H., *The Rise of Babylon*. Wheaton: Tyndale House Publishers, Inc., 1991.

Encyclopaedia Britannica (EB), Bib. Chap. 3, p. 51.

Gaverluk, Emil, *Rapture*, Bib. Chap. 1, p. 19.

Gordon, Cyrus H., *Before Columbus*, Bib. Chap. 4, p. 65.

Hislop, Alexander, *The Two Babylons*, Bib. Chap. 4, p. 65.

Hutchings, Noah W. (ed.), *Europe is Rising!* Oklahoma City: Hearthstone Publishing, 1990.

Jeffrey, Grant R., *Armageddon*, Bib. Chap. 2, p. 37.

Josephus, "Antiquities," (see Whiston) Bib. Chap. 2, p. 37-8.

Michaelsen, Johanna, *The Beautiful Side of Evil*. Eugene, OR: Harvest House Publishers, 1982.

Morris, Henry, *Genesis Flood*, (see **Whitcomb**), Bib. Chap. 2, p. 38.

Morris, Henry, *Scientific Creationism*, Bib. Chap. 2, p. 38.

Pritchard, James B. (ed.), *The Ancient Near East*. Princeton: Princeton University Press, 1958.

Ross, Allen P., "Genesis," *The Bible Knowledge Commentary*, Vol. I, Bib. Chap. 2, p. 38.

Strong's Exhaustive Concordance of the Bible, Bib. Chap 3, p. 51.

Velikovsky, Immanuel, *Worlds in Collision*. New York: Doubleday & Co., Inc., 1950.

Young's Literal Translation of the Bible, Bib. Chap. 4, p. 66.

Zondervan Pictorial Bible Dictionary, Bib. Chap. 4, p. 66.

PROJECTS

NEW AGE: If you really want to get some idea of how the evil spirit world thinks, do some reading in one or more of Alice Bailey's books. If you can't find them in the library, you can usually find the whole series of small paperbacks in the New Age or Occult section of your local book store. Remember that these are literally dictated by a demon called the Tibetan and merely transcribed by Alice Bailey. Her series is considered to be the "Bible" of the New Age. She was preceded by Theosophist Helena Petrovna Blavatsky whose laborious work called *The Secret Doctrine* you will probably find near Bailey's books. Notice the strange way that the thoughts are composed and the oft-mentioned idea that the thoughts "may or may not be true." Once you read part of a Bailey book, you will be able to identify the same "occultic style" of thought in other New Age writings.

HITLER: Try your hand at researching Hitler's background and his strong connections with the occult. You will find him mentioned, or at least referred to, in Bailey's works and other occultic writings. You may also find relevant material in certain biographies of Hitler.

MODERN EUROPE -- REVIVED ROMAN EMPIRE?: Note newspaper and magazine articles concerning Europe's ongoing attempt to put together a single, unified, economic and political union. Check newspapers such as *The Wall Street Journal*, *The New York Times*, and London's *Financial Times*. Some aspect of this topic is in the news almost everyday and springs straight from Bible prophecy about the revived Roman Empire of the last days. (Dan. 2; Rev. 13 & 17)

NOTE: In his excellent and massive (540 pgs.) work called *Job and Science*, Rev. Walter Lang references findings that resulted from studies of the 1964 Alaskan earthquake and 1969 exploratory drillings by the research ship *Glomar*. Scientists discovered that **mantle rock** under the **oceans** is only one or two miles thick while the mantle rock under **each of the seven continents** is about *300 miles thick*. (see Job 38:6) This pushes us further toward the *"canaling"* of **Pangaea** rather than massive continental shifts. [Lang, *Job & Science*, p. 442-3. Richfield, MN: Genesis Institute, 1992. (7232 Morgan Ave. S., 55423)]

Chapter 6
The First Antichrist: Nimrod and the New World Order

The Rise of Nimrod

In Gen. 10, the **Table of Nations**, the Bible gives special attention to **Nimrod**, a son of Cush with a wide-ranging reputation as "the mighty hunter before the Lord." When the mind-boggling events of the first 11 chapters of Genesis are sketched for us in such sparse detail, the type of emphasis given to Nimrod should clue us to give particular notice to this individual.

The *Young's Literal* translation gives us a better understanding of verses 10-12: "And the first part of his kingdom is **Babel**, and Erech, and Accad, and Calneh, in the land of **Shinar**; from that land he hath gone out to **Asshur** (or "to Assyria," or "gone out strengthened"), and buildeth **Nineveh**, even the broad places of the city, and Calah, and Resen, between Nineveh and Calah; it is the great city." So, God allowed the defiant Nimrod to remain at Babylon with a significant number of followers, while the rest of the population was divided and dispersed by God according to their families and the language He gave each of them.

The name Nimrod means *"subduer or tamer of the leopard"* (Nimr=leopard and rad=subdue). The history of India shows the use of leopards as hunting companions, as dogs are so often used today. Through a maze of mythology, Alexander Hislop demonstrates that Nimrod was also the *tamer of the horse* and a great **archer**, celebrated by Babylonian temples and coinage as the bow-carrying **Centaur**, half man and half horse. (Hislop, 41-44) This same character, glorifying Nimrod, also appears in the zodiac as **Sagittarius**. (For an explanation of the zodiac, see Chap. 8)

As man dispersed into the post-Flood world, the **newly adversarial relationship** with the **animals** became a problem. We have already seen that mammoths and even dinosaurs remained in some sizable form until the days of Job. Many animals were now carnivorous and **hunting** was something man had to learn after the Flood. Hislop refers to Ex. 23:29-30, in which God promises Israel that He will drive the Canaanite nations out before them, but only gradually so that *the beasts of the field will not multiply against them.* If this was still a problem in the days of the Exodus, imagine what a danger it was at the time of the Tower of Babel and the great dispersion. But Nimrod became the **mightiest of hunters**, ridding his area of wild beasts and "monsters," and thus rose in reputa-

---

The Bible and archaeology both indicate that God must have stabilized the geography of the Middle East very soon after the Babel judgement, considering it was not long before Nimrod established Babylon on the Euphrates River, and Asshur and Nineveh on the Tigris River. Note that even evolutionist archaeologists outline an ancient Persian Gulf coastline much different than today.

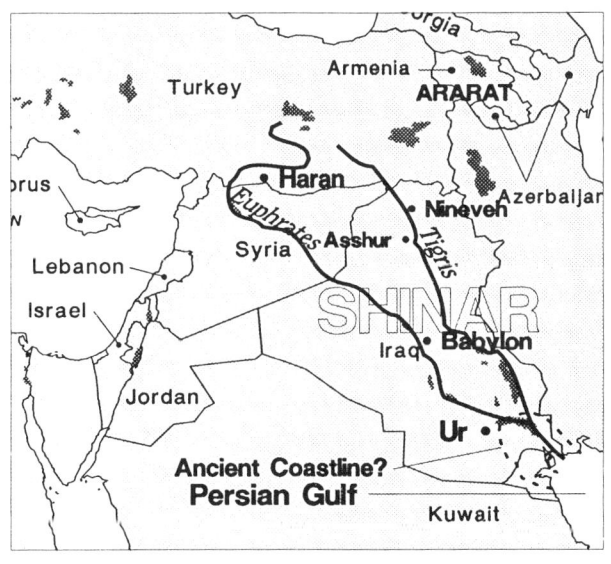

tion as a great **benefactor of mankind.** (Hislop 51)

Again through ancient traditions, Hislop shows Nimrod to be regarded as the first man (after the Flood) to **gather people into communities.** He is also glorified as the first man to **build fortifications** to protect the people. He shares that honor with his wife, **Semiramis**, who is credited with surrounding Babylon with a brick wall. Semiramis was later deified as **Diana of Ephesus** and as the Roman **Cybele**, both of whom are represented with **fortified towers** on their heads. In addition, the ancient historian Megasthenes records that Belus (or Bel) surrounded Babylon with a wall. We know that Cush was Bel, but Cush left Babel unfinished. Nimrod inherited his father's titles, including that of Bel or Belus. (Hislop, 51, 30-1)

Thus, Nimrod became a *physical* deliverer and protector of the people who remained in the area of Shinar. He delivered them from wild beasts, brought them into cities, and protected them with walls and towers. Why would they need walls and towers for safety from animals? Walls do indeed keep out wild animals; however, **fortifications and towers** are for only one purpose—**defense against** aggressive, or revengeful, **humans**.

We know from ancient traditions that Nimrod was the first mortal to defy the patriarchal system and set himself up as a **king**. He is identified with the legendary **Phoroneus** who, according to the Greeks, was the *"first of mortals that reigned."* Nimrod is later deified as the bloody god, **Moloch**, called "horrid king" by Milton in *Paradise Lost*. The name Moloch signifies "king." **Bacchus** is another of his later deifications, and Bacchus is "celebrated as the first who wore a crown." (Hislop, 51, 150-1, 185)

In the process of becoming the world's first king, Nimrod introduced **war** to mankind. One of his myriad identities in ancient history is that of **Ninus**, a word derived from the Hebrew "niyn," which means "a son." Ninus is considered to be the son of Bel, or Belus, who we know was Cush. (We will also see later that Ninus, or Nimrod, would be celebrated as *both the husband and son of Semiramis*, so that, under his inherited title as Belus, Ninus himself becomes his own son.) According to Justin, a Roman historian of the A.D. 200s, Ninus was king of the Assyrians and "'the first who carried on war against his neighbors,'" **conquering every nation from Assyria to Libya**, "'as they were yet unacquainted with the arts of war.'" (Hislop, 22-3) Diodorus Siculus, the 1st-Century B.C. Greek historian, corroborates this account, identifying Ninus as the first Assyrian king, and adding that Ninus armed, trained, and conditioned a large group of valorous young men to be **hunters and warriors**. (Hislop, 23) The 2nd-Century Greek historian, Apollodorus, states that "'Ninus is Nimrod.'" (Hislop, 40)

From Gen. 10:8-12, we see that the *beginning* of Nimrod's *kingdom* was **Babylonia** (or Accadia, or Akkadia). Growing stronger and

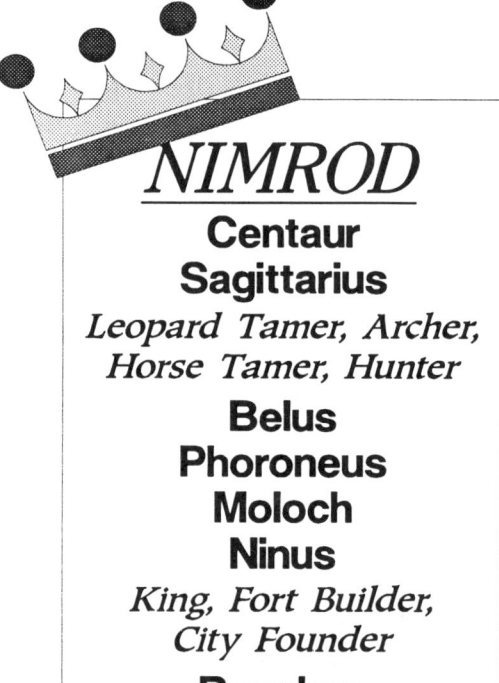

NIMROD

Centaur
Sagittarius
Leopard Tamer, Archer, Horse Tamer, Hunter

Belus
Phoroneus
Moloch
Ninus
King, Fort Builder, City Founder

Bacchus
Tammuz
Lamented One

more powerful, Nimrod (Ninus) expanded his kingdom into **Assyria**, where he built a number of cities, including **Nineveh**. "Niyn" means "son," and "navah" means "habitation." Thus, Nin-neveh was the "habitation of the son" or *"the habitation of Ninus."* Nimrod was "the son" of Cush, the original leader of Babel, but his title would receive its true importance from another source. If the Greek historians are correct,

Nimrod **subjected even the lands of his father and uncles** (Ethiopia, Egypt, Libya, Palestine) to his rule. Justin the Roman writes that Ninus conquered all the people of the East, "'as far as Lybia.'" (Hislop, 23-5, 40; Strong's)

We have seen that Nimrod was the "father" of hunting, archery, horsemanship, fortified cities, war, and monarchical government. He was the *physical* deliverer, protector, and hero of the people. However, we shall see that Nimrod would also become their *spiritual* leader, deliverer, and savior as well. Nimrod would be the **"father" of paganism and idolatry**. Many Bible commentators say that "the mighty hunter before the Lord" was also a hunter of men's **souls**. *We cannot overestimate the role of Nimrod in the entire history of the world.*

The Mother of Paganism

Neither can we overestimate the importance of Nimrod's partner in the spiritual corruption of mankind—**his wife, Semiramis**. According to ancient tradition, Semiramis was a woman of great beauty, the embodiment of female perfection. She was a married woman of humble origin when Nimrod was smitten by her charms and took her as his own wife. An ancient, revered Babylonian sculpture pictured a "'*quiver-bearing Semiramis*" riding to the chase with her bow, accompanied by her husband, Ninus (Nimrod, the mighty hunter before the Lord). She would have many children, due to her **licentiousness**. (Hislop, 40, 58, 69, 75, 298)

Semiramis, like all ancients, knew the prophecy of **Gen. 3:15**, given by God to Satan at the time of man's fall, that the **seed of the woman** would bruise the head of the serpent, after the serpent bruised the heel of the woman's seed. All ancients understood that "seed" stood for child and that this normally referred to the seed of a man. The seed of a *woman* signaled a most unusual event, a **virgin birth**, requiring no man. The promise of a virgin giving birth to a savior who would conquer the serpent was **lore known to all of the ancients**. Semiramis would turn this prophecy to her advantage after the death of her famous husband, and would become the true initiator and **"mother" of the secret rites** of the occult. *Thus, Semiramis would have an equally important role in shaping world history.*

Shem vs. Nimrod

Noah's son **Shem**, who was born 98 years before the Flood, would live to be **600 years old**, dying, according to our calculations, in 1843 B.C., 152 years after the death of Noah, and ten years after the marriage of Isaac and Rebekah. (Gen. 11:11, 25:20) When Noah cursed Canaan, the son of Ham, he blessed Shem, and Shem was to be the **father of the Jewish nation**, through his son **Arpachshad**. Of the genealogies of the sons of Noah, only Shem's is recorded in detail, by name and year, as it meticulously traces the ancestry of **Abraham**.

Shem, as Seth before him, fathered the **godly line**, the line of the **promised Messiah**. As implied by the Scripture and evidenced by tradition, Shem carried on his father's godly leadership over the minority who remained faithful to the Truth. *Because of the exercise of this godly authority, Shem would become the "devil" of the pagan world.*

While Nimrod set himself up as the king of his newly conquered empire, as well as the physical protector and savior of the Babylonians and Assyrians, he also **led the people into rebellion** against God, into an apostasy, says Hislop, that "appears to have been **open and public**." (Hislop, 62) According to the evidence, though "they knew God, they glorified him not

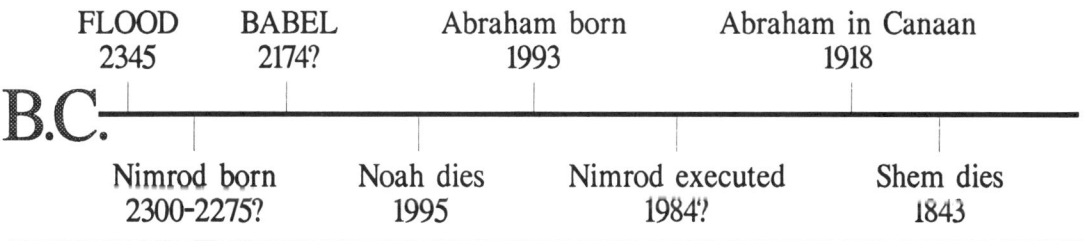

B.C.	A.D.
3rd Century, 2nd Century, 1st Century	1st Century, 2nd Century, 3rd Century
300 250 200 150 100 50 1	1 50 100 150 200 250 300
200s 100s 10s	10s 100s 200s

Remember that "1st-Century B.C." refers to the years 1 through 99 "Before Christ" while the "2nd-Century A.D." refers to the years 100 through 199 "Anno Domini" (in the year of the Lord).

as God, neither were thankful, but became vain in their imaginations, and their foolish heart was darkened." (Rom. 1:21, KJV) Nimrod, the mighty giant, was chosen over God as the one who would provide knowledge, material gain, godhood, and the way to earn eternal life. (Remember, the Satanic promise, "you will not die, your eyes will be opened, you will be as God, knowing good and evil" in Gen. 3?) *Nimrod was probably taught by his father Cush to be the **liaison** between the **evil spirit world** and the people of the "New World."*

Old "Gods" and New "Gods"

The rather well-known Babylonian creation epic, called the *Enuma Elish*, features a **battle** between the new, **young gods** and the **old gods**. This theme refers to the pagan **Cush and Nimrod** and their followers who fought against the godly patriarchs, **Noah and Shem** and their descendants. *Tiamat* was the goddess of the sea and the personification of evil and chaos. Obviously, this represented the judgement of the Flood and, perhaps, the Holy Spirit. Tiamat was also a **serpent/dragon**. The serpent was originally connected with Satan and sin and Gen. 3:15. The serpent would take on many roles and identities as paganism developed over the centuries, but, as in most paganism, in this case the *good became evil and the evil became good*. The good judgement (and hence, the Judge Himself) became the evil dragon, while the evil rebel (Nimrod) became the serpent/dragon slayer (the Messiah) of Gen. 3:15.

Apsu was one of the three old gods, as was Tiamat. *Marduk* was the newly elected king of the young gods (Nimrod). Marduk slayed the dragon Tiamat and cut her body into two pieces which became the sky and the constellations. The constellation **Draco the Dragon** is Tiamat. Marduk became the dragon slayer and the inventor of the pagan constellations (see Chap. 8), as well as a sun god. This same battle between the old and young gods is seen in **Greek mythology**. The young gods were led by **Zeus** who fought against the "evil" **Giants** (the patriarchs). (Pritchard, Ancient, 31-9; Dict. of Myst., 172, 256; Gallant, 34-7)

Baal, meaning "Lord," became the one creator god and was apparently *represented* by the **sun**. Actually, **Nimrod replaced God with Satan** and **Nimrod** made himself the **high priest of Baal**. Later, after his execution, Nimrod himself was deified as Baal and even later, *the sun would become the actual deity rather than the symbol of deity.*

Evil becomes Good and Good becomes Evil

Irrationality of Man

We have noted before that the **people feared God** and His judgements and **looked to Nimrod** to liberate them from God's covenant rule, which was administered by the patriarchs. Nimrod was the **Atlas** who lifted the heavens off their shoulders. *Nimrod was able to*

Page 84   Chapter 6

do this because man's fallen nature 1) flees responsibility, and 2) wants control. This statement could be criticized as contradictory, and indeed it is; however, man's fallen nature is related to Satan's fallen nature and *neither Satan nor the natural man makes sense.* The fallen nature is irrational, or "depraved," or, in actuality, **insane.** Even born-again Christians have to fight the presence of this insane nature. (Rom. 7)

1) People do not naturally want to take responsibility for their actions. They want pleasure without the price. We see that clearly demonstrated today in the 1990s in the pro-abortion movement. In America in the 1960s, it was evident in the choice to live together without getting married, or the cry for "free sex." *Ultimately, the natural man wants "heaven" without the holy presence of God.* As Hislop puts it, "men will readily rally around any one [sic] who can give the least appearance of plausibility to any doctrine which will teach that they can be assured of happiness and heaven at last, though their hearts and natures are unchanged, and though they live without God in the world." (Hislop, 52)

So, they rallied around the mighty hunter, the warrior, the king, Nimrod. They were willing to give up their true liberties under the patriarchal system and subject themselves to King Nimrod in turn for *physical security, physical pleasures, and the promise of spiritual regeneration without a change in their nature or actions.* As Hislop explains, "men were led to believe that a real spiritual change of heart was unnecessary, and that so far as change was needful, they could be regenerated by mere external means." (Hislop, 55) Nimrod also introduced them to *hedonism.* Once again, Hislop concludes from the abundant evidence of history and tradition that Nimrod "led mankind to seek their chief good in sensual enjoyment, and showed them how they might enjoy the pleasures of sin, without any fear of the wrath of a holy God. In his [Nimrod] various expeditions he was always accompanied by troops of women; and by music and song, and games and revelries, and everything that could please the natural heart, he commended himself to the good graces of mankind." (Hislop, 55)

We see the same basic mentality throughout history in people who seek the security of a

LIFE SPANS AFTER THE FLOOD		
SHEM	**600 yrs.**	**HAM**
begat		*begat*
Arpachshad	**438 yrs.**	**Cush**
begat		*begat*
Shelah	**433 yrs.**	**Nimrod**
begat		
Eber	**464 yrs.**	
begat		
Peleg	**239 yrs.**	
begat		
Reu	**239 yrs.**	
begat		
Serug	**230 yrs.**	
begat		
Nahor	**148 yrs.**	
begat		
Terah	**205 yrs.**	
begat		
Abraham	**175 yrs.**	

dictator or monarch or big, socialist, government bureaucracy. Many people conditioned under Communist rule would rather have a low-paying but guaranteed job that requires little effort, individuality, or ambition, rather than the opportunity to succeed or fail on their own merits. Recent (1992-3) stories in newspapers like *The Wall Street Journal* have more than adequately documented such cases in "liberated" Russia.

Many people under modern-day America's ever-growing welfare state would rather take handouts from the government than cope with the risks, rewards, and responsibilities of the marketplace. More and more people are willing to give up liberties and even property if the government will just take care of them, or if the government will establish order over a fearful outbreak of crime or anarchy. Witness the first example as people send "contributions" to the Clinton government to reduce the deficit and approve higher taxes ("sacrifice") for universal health care. Witness the second example as Americans accept gun control, a marked currency, and ever-more-liberal government search-and-seizure tactics in the name of fighting drug dealers, rioters, and counterfeiters.

2) At the same time, people want control. The fact that God is in control always maddens the fallen nature of man. The human being wants to be "captain of his fate" and "master of his destiny," making his own decisions and getting what he thinks he deserves. That is why, though man flees responsibility, he wants to *earn* his way to heaven and to "create" God in man's own image. Thus, all paganism — every unbiblical religion to be found in the world — is based on **"works,"** or certain rules which allow a person to merit some sort of salvation or heavenly reward. Only true, biblical Christianity is based on pure **grace** (the unmerited favor of God), which saves the totally depraved sinner by the merit and work of Christ alone. Christianity is not humanistic religion in which man seeks God on man's terms. It is God seeking man on God's terms. This is confusing and difficult, even to Christians, something which once again shows the strength of our sin nature. Paul deals with the subject of "law and grace" in the book of *Galatians*, and we still see the struggle in many churches today as people try to earn their salvation.

Cutting the cords of heaven

We need to remember that those post-Flood people who rebelled against God still had an innate sense of sin and a **need to be "cleansed"** in some way. Every **man-made religion** on Earth has provided man a set of rules and certain actions which, if properly performed, **purchase the desired cleansing** from the acknowledged god or gods. The **exception** to be carefully noted is the **Jewish system of the Old Testament**. Their Law and the intricate system of sacrifice was given by the true God and was based on faith in His promises, even though the Law included an elaborate system of "works" to be performed. Abraham and all Old Testament saints were **saved by faith** (Rom. 4; Heb. 11), obediently performing the repetitious sacrifices which illustrated and looked forward to the "once-for-all" sacrifice performed by God Himself.

The pagans illustrated the relationship of **heaven and Earth** by using a **rope** or ropes that bound the two together and/or provided their "god" access to both. In southern **Peru**, on the hills above the Bay of Pisco about 100 miles from the famous and mysterious drawings on the plains of Nazca, is another massive drawing some 820 feet long of a **figure with a rope**. Historian R. A. Jairazbhoy equates the figure with the **Egyptian Coffin Text** which speaks of the great hidden one who had guide ropes to ascend and descend to and from heaven. (Nimrod was also known as the "hidden one.")

Quetzalcoatl, the feathered serpent of Mexico, is also shown descending from a tear in the sky on a rope. (Jairazbhoy, Ancient Egyptians, 89-90)

In the **Polynesian** story of the low heavens, which were successfully lifted in stages by a hero, the heavens and Earth were said to be bound together with **ropes** or cords. In the story, the cords were cut by the wings of **dragonflies**, the origin of which is probably the Babylonian **winged serpent**, also found in Mexico as the feathered serpent. The Babylonian history by Berossus, a Chaldean priest of Bel in Babylon in the 300s B.C., records that Bel or Belus (Nimrod) "dispelled the primeval darkness," separated heaven from Earth, and "orderly arranged the world." (Hislop, 54) Thus, Nimrod was the hero or "giant" who cut the cords of heaven and established a **NEW WORLD ORDER**, something which world leaders are trying to reachieve as we approach the year A.D. 2000.

So, this is why **Psalm 2** says that the nations rage and the people imagine vanity, that the kings of Earth station themselves and the princes take counsel together against the Lord and His anointed (the Messiah). "Let us draw off Their **cords**," they say, "and cast from us Their thick bands." (Psalm 2:1-3, KJV and *Young's Literal*) Their were no "nations" before the Flood, though the people certainly raged and rebelled.

However, since the Flood and the formation of nations after the Tower of Babel, the nations have done nothing but rage for almost 4,000 years. Thank God that He laughs at the rebels and mocks them, and that He promises to set His King upon His holy hill of Zion. He will give all the nations to Christ for His inheritance and Christ shall break them with a rod of iron. *But we who serve the Lord with fear and put our trust in Him, rejoice with trembling because we are blessed by Him. (Psalm 2:4-12, KJV)*

Execution of Nimrod

Because of Nimrod's terrible apostasy, **Shem**, through the power of the Holy Spirit, struck a godly fear into the civil and religious **judiciary of Egypt**, convincing those judges to bring **Nimrod to trial** for his abominable crimes. According to Egyptian law, a lower tribunal of 30 judges had the power of life and death over the accused, and they condemned Nimrod to death. The higher tribunal of 42 judges decided whether or not the condemned was to be allowed a burial. In this case, the decision was "no." (Hislop, 63-4, 179)

Nimrod was **legally executed** (not murdered) and then **cut into fourteen pieces**, each one being delivered to a city in the empire, that all the people might fear the deeds and doom of Nimrod. What a way to hold a revival! This occurred, according to Syncellus, *when Abraham was about nine years old*, or about 1984 B.C. (or, according to Eusebius, in the time of Abraham). (Hislop, 6, 179)

We find this **same terrible custom** practiced twice in the **Bible**. The first instance occurred toward the end of the time of the **judges** in Israel. Lodging for the night in a city belonging to the tribe of Benjamin, a Levite encountered a Sodom-and-Gomorrah type of situation that ended in the brutal death of his concubine. He announced the terrible deed to the nation by cutting the woman into 12 pieces and sending one to each of the 12 tribes. This led to a civil war with the tribe of Benjamin, and graphically illustrated the depths of spiritual and moral degradation in the land of Israel. (Judges 19-21) The second instance involved the young **King Saul**, Israel's first human king, who cut up two oxen and sent the pieces to all of the communities in Israel, threatening the people with similar destruction of their own oxen if they did not rally to fight the Ammonites. (I Sam. 11) Such an act is obviously meant to be a *terrible and graphic warning against sin.*

Mythologies and customs from around the world, but strongest in the Middle East, give us ample indication of what happened following Nimrod's execution. After the initial fear dissipated and the apostates regained some of their power and confidence, Nimrod's strong-willed widow, **Semiramis**, searched for every piece of the body and apparently had each piece buried wherever it was found. Thus, the practice of *relic* worship had its **origin in the execution and dismemberment of Nimrod**, as each bone or body piece would be worshipped as holy, and all manner of religious relics would come to be viewed as having some sort of spiritual power. Babylonian and Egyptian relic worship spread to become an integral part of Buddhism and Greek paganism. We find it in one form or another all around the world, but, since the birth of Christ, it has been most widely developed and preserved in the practices of the ancient and medieval Roman Catholic Church and its Eastern off-shoots. Supposed (and perhaps some genuine) bones and body parts of apostles, "saints," and martyrs were popular objects of veneration and often said to perform miracles of healing. (Hislop, 175-81)

According to the 1st-Century A.D. Greek historian Plutarch who recorded the Egyptian version of Nimrod's death, Semiramis (Isis) found every body piece but one, the phallus. This member was consecrated as holy and she "'instituted a solemn festival to its memory.'" (Hislop, 179) **Phallic worship** did become another integral part of the paganism which spread around the world, as illustrated by the abundance of male-organ monuments still to be found in New England. (Fell, America, 219) Of course, this is also interpreted as basic fertility worship, which it is. However, the original inspiration for this practice may well have been Nimrod's execution and the resulting actions of Semiramis.

Reincarnation vs. Resurrection

We shall soon find that, through his death, **Nimrod became the false Messiah**, slain as the sacrifice for the sin of his followers, worshipped as "the great object of love and adoration, as the god through whom 'goodness and truth were revealed to mankind.'" (Hislop, 72, 181) The "sacrifice" would be **celebrated as "voluntary"** for the sake of the people, though Nimrod was **involuntarily executed** by men who took his life at their will. The false Messiah was **cut into pieces**, separating bone from bone, and his body was scattered. In order to return to his people as their savior, he had to be incarnated (made flesh) in **another body**. Thus, the **DOCTRINE OF SPIRITUAL REINCARNATION** was born by the false pretensions of Satan himself, and thus, ever since, people have believed, in total futility, that they had been, and would be again, reincarnated until they broke the sinful cycle and became one with the spiritual Whole. According to this doctrine, the physical body is no longer necessary or useful and so it is **CREMATED**, being that the spirit will either be incarnated into another body or will transcend the physical world altogether.

In complete contrast, the **true Messiah** took on flesh (incarnated Himself), and allowed Himself to be **executed, voluntarily** giving up His Spirit (as no man could actually take His life). As was prophesied in the sacrifice of the Passover lamb (Ex. 12:46) and the songs of King David (Ps. 34:20), *not a bone of Him was broken* (Jn. 19:36), and His physical body was hastily **buried** in a tomb, without time for any kind of bodily preparation or embalming because of the High Sabbath. This is why the women returned to the tomb on Sunday morning with their spices and ointments, in order to "treat" the body. However, He **rose from the dead** in that **very same but drastically altered and glorified body**, leaving an empty tomb and neatly folded linen wrappings with no bodily relics to be found anywhere.

Thus, the long-promised **DOCTRINE OF PHYSICAL RESURRECTION** was fulfilled and powerfully demonstrated, proving that the spirits of Christian believers will also be reunited with their own physically resurrected bodies.

Each human spirit is a unique creation of God, **incarnated only once** in **one specific body**, a body important enough to God that He purposes to resurrect it and transform it for an eternal habitation for the spirit. (John 10:17-18; Luke 24:3, 6, 12, 27, 39; Gen. 5:24; Job 19:25-6; Ps. 17:15; Isa. 26:19; Dan. 12:2; Luke 14:14; I Cor. 15; I Thess. 4) As further proof, the "first fruits" of resurrection were harvested as "the graves were opened; and many bodies of the saints that slept were raised, and came out of the graves after his resurrection, and went into the holy city, and appeared unto many." (Matt. 27:52-53, KJV) No wonder the truth at that time could not be suppressed or twisted. There was too much physical evidence and too many eye witnesses!

This is why Christians practice **BURIAL** and not cremation, as burial of the physical body **witnesses** to and **anticipates** the **resurrection and transformation** of that very same body. (Note Luke 24:31, 39) If a believer's body is destroyed in some manner, it is certainly within God's power to regather every molecule He deems necessary for resurrection (perhaps every particle that contains our unique code, our DNA), but it is biblically proper for Christians to bury their dead whenever possible and not to cremate, as cremation is strictly a pagan practice.

Paganism: Good is Bad and Bad is Good

Nimrod's trial and execution, led by Shem, is a central theme of paganism and can be seen in the myths and practices of pagan peoples everywhere. The name **"Shem,"** as does the name **"Seth,"** means *"the appointed one."* Before the Flood, Seth was appointed to father the godly, Messianic line. After the Flood, Shem was the one appointed by God to carry on the Noahic Covenant and patriarchal authority as well as to father the chosen Jewish race and, eventually, the Messiah Himself. But the **pagans** regarded **Shem as evil** and **Nimrod as good**, and the battle between these two is pictured throughout the nations.

In Egypt, **Shem** became the *primitive* or *ancient Hercules*. (The later Assyrian and Grecian Hercules was Nimrod.) Another name for this **Hercules** was "Sem." The Egyptians recorded that their Hercules defeated the "giants" by the power of the gods. (Shem defeated Nimrod, the giant, by the power of the Holy Spirit.) Fine chains of gold and amber are shown stretching from the ears of the people to the mouth of the **Egyptian Hercules**, illustrating that he overcame by way of **persuasion**, while the **Grecian Hercules** would be known for his **physical strength** in battle. (Hislop, 63, 66)

Egyptian paganism also came to refer to Shem as *"Seth"* or *"Set,"* and as *"Typho"* or **"Typhon."** The Egyptian story of Nimrod's execution is told in the myth of the death of *Osiris* (Nimrod), who was executed and dismembered by Set who also became *Typho, the "Evil One."* (Hislop, 65)

Probably the most prominent names used for the **Egyptian trinity** were *Osiris, Isis, and Horus*. It is interesting that, according to tradition, these gods came to Egypt **from the north**. Osiris was the slain "divine man," represented by the **"grain"** which was buried only to resurrect in the form of crops, an annual agricultural rite. [Remember that the truths which Jesus Christ revealed about Himself as the grain of wheat which would be killed, buried, and resurrected as the "first fruit" were known very early to the patriarchs (even before the Flood) as prophecies of the Messiah and the doctrine of bodily resurrection. (Gen. 3:15; Lev. 2, 23; John 12:24; Heb. 11; Jude 14) Remember also that all of *paganism is merely perverted truth.*]

Osiris was the king of Egypt (Nimrod was the world's first king) who was killed by his brother **Set** (Seth or Typho). Set and certain conspirators tricked Osiris into climbing into a box which Set then weighted and threw into the Nile River. The box was recovered by **Isis** on the coast of Syria and returned to Egypt. There, Set tore the dead body into **14 pieces** and scattered the pieces throughout the land. Isis then found every piece, except for the phallus, and, in one version of the story, reunited the pieces, embalmed the body, and magically brought Osiris back to life. Other stories say she buried Nimrod's pieces. (Hislop, 179; Dict. of Myst., 185, 202, 235-6; EB, 1972, 16:1138; 12:662-3) The significance of the lost phallus, of course, has to do with **"the Seed."** There is another Egyptian story which says that Set (Seth) lost his own testicles in his fight with Horus.

(Jairazbhoy, Ancient Egypt., 33) The true Seed of the woman is **Christ** while the seed of the serpent is the **Antichrist** (Gen. 3:15). The theme of history from the Garden to the Cross is Satan's determination to destroy the Seed (child) of the woman. From the beginning of paganism, this theme would lead humans into "child devouring" or **child sacrifice**. (Rev. 12:4; Ezek. 16:21, 23:37)

Note that the **Egyptians** did not cremate their dead, but *mummified* them with a process that, at its peak, achieved a remarkable state of preservation. The stories of Osiris show their **belief in resurrection** and the importance of the body to the afterlife. Their obsession with **mummification** demonstrates a *perversion of the truth of bodily resurrection*. Remember that the truth of resurrection was stronger in ancient paganism before the truth was progressively perverted and changed to reincarnation by later pagans. (Dict. of Myst., 185, 202, 235-6; EB, 1972, 16:1138; 12:662-3) We shall also see that the ancients of both **Mexico** and **Peru** were adept at mummification when we examine the pervasive evidence of Egyptian culture in the Americas.

Isis had magically become **pregnant** by former **King Osiris** (who became the god of the dead) when she recovered his body in the box, and so she gave birth to their son *Horus* (also Nimrod) who grew up to slay Set and avenge his father's death. (Dict. of Myst., 122, 236; EB, 1972, 16:1138; 12:662-3) **Horus** was pictured as *piercing the serpent/dragon Typho* (Set) with a spear (Gen. 3:15), as was his Greek counterpart, **Apollo**, shown battling the serpent **Pytho**. To the pagans, the evil serpent/dragon was no longer Satan, but Shem, the executor of the pagan Messiah, Nimrod. At one time, the Egyptian god Set was worshipped as Baal (meaning "Lord," actually Nimrod). He was also apparently good before he became evil, as Set himself was shown standing in the prow of the sun god's boat, stabbing the evil dragon Apophis with a lance. We shall see later that an ancient **Mexican** stone carving illustrates the same story. (Hislop, 151; EB, 1972, 20:263; Dict. of Myst., 13; Jairazbhoy, Ancient Egypt, 51)

The Greek **Plutarch**, who was **initiated** into the **Osirian mysteries** and who recorded much of these legends, wrote that another version of the story had Horus himself cut into pieces. As

Horus was also Nimrod, this would underscore the truth of Nimrod's execution. Though often suppressed, elements of Apollo's myth tell of his violent death, slain by the serpent. **Apollo** is also identified by some as the inventor of hunting and war, another proof of his identity with Nimrod. (Hislop, 151-2)

In reality, Shem was not Nimrod's brother (as Osiris and Set were brothers), but was his great-uncle. Shem outlived both Nimrod and Semiramis, but it is easy to see why the pagans imagined Nimrod's death revenged, by Nimrod's own reincarnation. [Though the Egyptians believed in a version of resurrection, it was Nimrod's (Osiris's) spirit that was in Horus, as the two gods represented the same person. Thus, the story is actually one of **reincarnation** of a spirit into another body.] In the story, Isis was the sister as well as the wife of Osiris. In reality, Semiramis may very well have been a sister or half-sister to Nimrod, just as Sarah was a half-sister to Abraham. It would become common practice for many cultures to enthrone married rulers who were brother and sister, with one or both parents being a god.

So, to the pagans, **Shem became the Destroyer**, or the devil himself. (Hislop, 63-6) Typho(n) the serpent/dragon was also Teitan (Titan) or Sheitan, which is the name for Satan used by the devil worshippers of Kurdistan in northern Iraq. (Hislop, 276) The giants (**Titans**) were originally Nimrod and his followers, the giants who rebelled against God. However, through the maze of paganism, *Nimrod and the bad guys became the good guys, while Shem and the good guys became the bad guys.* Shem became the evil serpent/dragon while the patriarchs, the "first race" or first rulers, became the "evil" giants or Titans. (Dict. of Myst., 257) Remember also that the people who lived for the first few hundred years after the Flood indeed were "giants" in both physical size and life span, in comparison to the later generations who developed this maze of myths. (Hislop, 232, 3rd note)

Weeping for Tammuz

We have seen Nimrod identified as Ninus, the Son; as Bel, the author of confusion and builder of Babylon; as Baal, the Lord; as Molech, the king; and as both Osiris and Horus, the father-god and son-god. But the name that is most closely associated with his death is *Tammuz*. We must remember that it was after Nimrod's death that he was elevated from the first and foremost priest of Baal and the rites of paganism which he initiated, to become Baal himself and the pagan version of the promised Messiah or Seed of the woman. (Hislop, 62, 229)

The word **Tammuz** is derived from *tam*, "to make perfect," and *muz*, "fire," thus meaning the purifying or **perfecting fire**. (Hislop, 245) We have already seen that, in his lifetime, **Nimrod** was seen as the great **Enlightener** and the great **Protector** of mankind. As the promised god-man, he would be seen as the great **Purifier**, *giving men not only knowledge and protection from both earthly and heavenly terrors, but also purification from sin.* We will examine the horrible impact of **fire worship** in connection with Nimrod's identities as Molech (Moloch), Zoroaster, and Vulcan as well as Tammuz, but first we will look at the pagan signs of *mourning and weeping for the dead Nimrod*.

The Babylonian god Tammuz was also known as the **god of agriculture**, experiencing death each winter and rebirth each spring, just as Osiris was believed to do. When Nimrod was Tammuz, Semiramis was *Ishtar*, the Babylonian goddess of love and fertility, later known in Egypt as **Isis**, Rome as **Venus**, Greece as **Aphrodite**, Phoenicia as **Astarte**, and Israel as **Ashtoreth**. (Dict. of Myst., 250)

The legend of the death of the god Tammuz was recorded by the medieval Spanish/Jewish doctor and philosopher, **Maimonides**, who lived in Egypt and who, according to Hislop, was "deeply read in all the learning of the Chaldeans." (Hislop, 62; *Webster's*) Maimonides calls Tammuz a "false prophet" who advocated the worship of the seven stars (the **Pleiades**) and the **12 signs of the zodiac** in the court of a "certain king." That king (obviously Shem) had **Tammuz executed** in a horrible way. On that night, all of the **"images"** (demons) from around the world came to the **temple at Babylon** to hear the news from the "great golden image of the Sun." The images *wept all night long* and then flew away back to their own temples. Thus, says Maimonides, began the practice of weeping for Tammuz on the first day of the month that came to be called Tammuz. (Hislop, 62) Tammuz is the fourth month of the Hebrew religious calendar and the 10th month of the Hebrew civil calendar, corresponding to mid-June/July on our modernized Roman calendar. In the vision of Ezekiel 8, the prophet is shown the temple at Jerusalem where **idolatrous Jewish women sat weeping for Tammuz**. (Eze. 8:14; *New Scofield Reference Bible*, Lev. 23, Note 2)

While the **Chaldean**, **Assyrian**, **Phoenician**, and idolatrous **Jewish** women wept for **Tammuz**, the **Egyptian women wept for Osiris**, the **Greeks for *Adonis***, and the **Romans for *Bacchus***. "Bakhah" means "to weep," and so Bacchus means "the lamented one." (Hislop, 56, 21, 46) *Nimrod was the great lamented one of pagan mankind*, whose weepings "can be traced not merely in the annals of classical antiquity, but in the literature of the world from Ultima Thule to Japan." (Hislop, 57) [Among the ancients, Ultima Thule was the "farthest Thule," or the northernmost region of the Earth. (*Webster's*)] In **Iceland and Scandinavia**, they wept for the slain god **Balder**, the son of Odin and Frigga, and in **China**, for the young Mandarin, **Wat-yune**. (Hislop, 57-8)

Odin, Frigga, and Balder are the Scandinavian version of Osiris, Isis, and Horus. Balder probably comes from Baal-der or Baal-zer, which means "seed of Baal." (Hislop, 312) The Scandinavian **Odin** apparently comes from the Germanic **Wodan** or Woden, from whom we get our **Wednesday** or Woden's Day. The Norwegian noble whose petroglyphs describe his ancient voyage to the copper-mining settlements on the Canadian side of Lake Superior (about 1700 B.C.) was named Woden-lithi, or "servant of Woden." (Fell, Bronze, 105-6) Hislop connects the Odin of Scandinavia to the Woden of England and northern Germany, to the **Wodan of Mexico**, and to the **Adon of Babylon**. (EB, 1972, 16:864; Dict. of Myst., 198; Hislop, 133-4) We shall see how this Babylonian/Germanic/English/Scandinavian version of Nimrod made his way to both North and Central America.

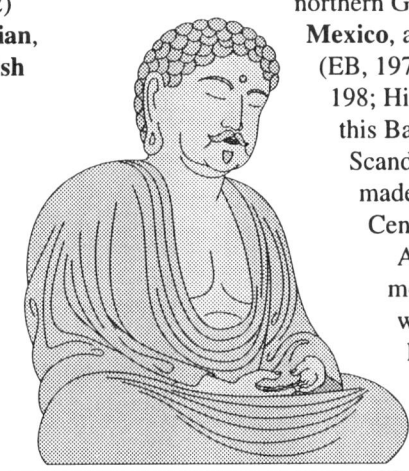

"Buddha" is much older than India's Siddhartha Gautama of the 500s B.C. Japan has a three-headed (Trinity) Buddha. India's Gautama shaved his head like the Egyptian priests of Osiris. The shaved head was a hidden symbol of "the mutilated Prince." Most Buddha images have a shaved head. Throughout Asia, Buddhists were obligated to collect and bury the bones or limbs of Buddha which had been scattered around the world. In other words, Buddha is just another NIMROD. (Dict. Myst., 34; Hislop, 18, 178-9, 193, 221-2)

Another result of the pagan mourning of Nimrod's death was the **weeping god**, particularly the **weeping sun god of Egypt** which also had a widespread presence in *Central and South America*. Ra, Osiris, Horus, Baal, and Apollo were all sun gods. At **Tiahuanaco**, the great stone ruins on Lake Titicaca in **Peru**, is a door on which is carved the weeping sun god of Egypt and Central America. (Jairazbhoy, Ancient Egypt, 65, 94) The Field Museum in Chicago houses a weeping god pottery sculpture from ancient **Alabama** and the mound builders of the **Central Mississippi Valley** in the U.S. It is also most interesting that many of the Catholic "miracles" through the centuries (and recently) involve a weeping statue of **Mary**. ✆

BIBLIOGRAPHY

Drury, Nevill, *Dictionary of Mysticism*, Bib. Chap. 2, p. 37.

Encyclopaedia Britannica (EB), Bib. Chap. 3, p. 51.

Fell, Barry, *America B.C.* New York: Pocket Books, 1989. (Revised and updated from 1976.)

Fell, Barry, *Bronze Age America*. Boston: Little Brown & Co., 1982.

Gallant, Roy A., *The Constellations*, Bib. Chap. 3, p. 51.

Hislop, Alexander, *The Two Babylons*, Bib. Chap. 4, p. 65.

Jairazbhoy, R. A., *Ancient Egyptians and Chinese in America*. Totawa, N.J.: Rowman & Littlefield, 1974.

New Scofield Reference Bible (KJV). New York: Oxford University Press, 1967

Pritchard, James B. (ed.), *The Ancient Near East*, Bib. Chap. 5, p. 80.

Strong's Exhaustive Concordance of the Bible, Bib. Chap. 3, p. 51.

Webster's New World Dictionary, Bib. Chap. 2, p. 38.

Young's Literal Translation of the Bible, Bib. Chap. 4, p. 66.

PROJECTS

CLASSICAL MYTHOLOGY: Books about Greek, Roman, and Egyptian mythology are plentiful and easy to find in most libraries. Look up the mythical characters who we noted are actually representatives of Cush, Nimrod, Noah, Adam, and Semiramis. While taking a cautious approach, see what information you might glean about the historical figures whose lives have become legend, hidden in the "mythology" of the Mystery System. You might also consult standard encyclopedias as well as occult dictionaries. Note the pervasive stories of "half-god/half-humans," and "old gods" versus "young gods." Note also the connection of many "gods" with the planets and the constellations of the zodiac. We will learn in Chapters 7 and 8 that "mythology" was originally a secret or hidden code developed by the priests and/or initiates of the Mystery System, the foundations of which were laid by Nimrod and Semiramis. The bodies of the heavens, intended to display the glory of the Creator, were given corrupted identities and eventually worshipped outright by the pagans.

MUSEUMS: Look for Buddha figures from various Eastern countries and notice the similarities and differences, the shaved heads, the rosary beads. Look also for figures of "weeping gods" which will have some sort of dots in lines below the eyes, and for pictures or statues of the "mother and son." Search for these items in Eastern, European, African, and especially *American* (North, Central, and South) cultural exhibits. ✔

WRITING NOTES

COMPARE & CONTRAST: Do some of your own research on such figures as Osiris, Zeus, Jupiter, Hermes, Bacchus, Tammuz, etc. (pick the ones who interest you most) and write a paper using the technique of "compare and/or contrast" to demonstrate similarities and/or differences between the figures to one another and to the historical person called Nimrod. Do the same for the goddesses who represent Semiramis, such as Diana, Venus, Rhea, Isis, etc. Two themes that run throughout mythology worldwide are the mother/son cult and the trinity, both of which are perversions of biblical truth. Compare/contrast one or both of these themes from country to country. Be organized and methodical in your comparisons. Do your research, prepare an outline, then write your paper. ✎

Chapter 7
The Legacy of Nimrod & Semiramis: The Mystery System

Power in Secrecy

After Nimrod's execution, **two very significant things happened**, orchestrated by Semiramis and the pagan priests. *First,* Nimrod's beautiful, licentious, and ambitious widow decided that she would present herself to the world as the **"virgin" mother** of the well-known, ancient prophecy which was later recorded by Moses in Gen. 3:15. **Nimrod** himself was **deified** both as the **father god**, and as the promised seed or **Messiah son**, *reincarnated* in a new form after his hideous death. This Satanic, copycat doctrine would be embraced, in one form or another, by every culture throughout the world. (Hislop, 58-9) *The unholy trinity was born.*

Second, Semiramis and her priests decided that **secrecy** was now necessary and so paganism was set up as the secret Mystery system into which people had to be **initiated**. One doctrine was established for the initiated and another for the **"profane vulgar"** [meaning the uninitiated, uncleansed commoners]. (Hislop, 7, 59, 62) Why was this done? For one reason, Shem, the godly executor of Nimrod, was still alive. For another, the consciences of the people had been severely pricked by the execution and the distribution of the body parts of the "great rebel.". Care had to be taken and Satanic power stealthily restored.

This secret pagan system, *set up by a woman*, is characterized as a woman in the Book of The **Revelation**. In fact, the woman is called the great harlot, with the name of **"Mystery, Babylon the Great."** This harlot, who rides on a beast, is identified as the *mother of all harlots and abominations* in the Earth. This woman is also called **"that great city"** which reigns over all of the kings of the Earth, a city home to demons and every foul spirit. (Rev. 17:5, 18; 18:2)

We need a general understanding of the Mystery system for three reasons:

Reason 1) As we study history, we shall see how this Mystery system *intoxicates every nation and empire,* every king and leader, including the United States, *up through today,* causing them to commit "fornication" with this false, demonic religion. [Only the nation of Israel has a special relationship to God as *wife*; so, these nations commit "fornication," while Israel, when unfaithful, commits "adultery." (Jer. 3)] The same Bible chapter in Revelation also speaks of **merchants**, the "great men of the Earth," who gain vast wealth through the power of this system, enticed by its demonic "sorceries." The system of Semiramis was, and still is, backed by evil spirit powers.

Reason 2) Both Nimrod and Semiramis would be given a host of names and identifications by the pagan system as it spread from Babylon to Egypt, to India and China and Polynesia, to Europe and Scandinavia and the **Americas**, and to Greece and Rome. *Paganism would take its unholy trinity and its mother/son worship to the ends of the Earth.* The doctrines and deities of paganism serve as excellent **signposts in tracing the dispersal of mankind**. A summary knowledge of the pagan names and practices will help us as we try to reconstruct the ancient history of the Americas.

Reason 3) We can *cautiously* decode *some* of the mind-boggling maze of the Mystery system and, in doing so, can gain important information concerning **ancient historical and cosmological events**. Clues from the Mystery system throw some light on the question of a geocentric universe as well as on scattered evidence that God may have involved certain planets and other heavenly bodies in executing various judgements on Earth. Once again, remember that the ancients were intelligent and capable, and even as they began to "deteriorate" over the centuries, these peoples kept knowledgeable, scrupulous, and accurate accounts of the movements of the heavenly bodies. The Mysteries were a CODED mythology that masked a historical cosmology.

Initiates — The Ultimate Insiders

The term **esoteric** refers to facts, plans, or ideas that are intended to be known, or able to be understood, only by a chosen few. (Webster's) **Arcane** is another word that refers to things hidden or secret. The Babylonian **priests** were the original **initiates**. They derived the foundation of their doctrines from Satanic sources — **fallen angels** — who were (and are) the original "masters of the universe." Human initiates fully enlightened in the Mysteries, whose souls are controlled and/or literally possessed by demonic beings, are "enlightened masters," "ascended masters," or "adepts." (Brooke, When, 55-7) Throughout history, priests have had great power because, in the mysteries, only they are supposed to have the *necessary knowledge for salvation.* [Under God's Mosaic Law, priests had specific, sacrosanct duties and position. However, they never came between believers and God in the matters of confession or prayer, as illustrated by Hannah, David, and Simeon. (I Sam., Psalms, Luke 2:25-35) Jesus Christ is the personal high priest of all believers while, under the New Covenant, all believers are themselves priests. (Hebrews, I Pet. 2:5)]

The priests disseminated their knowledge only through **levels of ritual initiation**. What was hidden, esoteric doctrine to the initiated was merely a moral code to the "commoners." This was the wisdom of a ruling class. (Hall, Secret, 23; De Santillana, Hamlet's, 8) According to Manley P. Hall, who published *The Secret Teachings of All Ages* in 1928 on the Masonic, Hermetic, Cabalistic, and Rosicrucian Symbolic Philosophy, *everyone would eventually be "saved," though some would have to return to Earth many times to learn the necessary lessons.* From this basic tenet came the doctrines of transmigration and reincarnation of the soul, and a purgatorial "hell," a "half-way house" where souls suffer to rid themselves of sin so they may gain entrance to "heaven." The Druids of ancient England and Europe, so often connected with Stonehenge, perpetuated these doctrines. (Hall, Secret, 23)

The Egyptians had **Lesser and Greater Mysteries**. Even the heir to Egypt's throne was not allowed initiation into the Greater Mysteries until he was actually crowned Pharaoh. (Hall, Secret, 27) This would mean that Moses must have been an initiate into the Lesser Mysteries, as he was heir to the throne and "learned in all the wisdom of the Egyptians, and was mighty in words and in deeds." (Acts 7:22, KJV)

Initiates, then and now, represent a **hierarchy of membership and accomplishment**. High-level initiates were given, or taught to develop, **special powers and faculties**. As Hall explains, masters taught secret practices and disciplines by which "properly qualified disciples could develop potent abilities latent" within their soul and "come into conscious communication with spiritual realities." (Hall, Secret, Foreword; Hislop, 5, 11, 18, 22; Bailey, Autobiography, 245-304) We see this today in "channelers" and those who have **"spirit guides."**

Theosophist Alice Bailey (1880-1949) was first visited by "adept" and "Master of Wisdom" Koot Hoomi (Master K.H.) in 1895 and she thought at first that this being was Jesus Christ. The "Tibetan," also called Master Djwhal Khul, is explained to be a disciple of K.H., and both are stated to be members of (note this) **"the Hierarchy."** The Tibetan is credited with dictating the books written and published by Alice Bailey and her husband Foster Bailey. Foster writes that "D.K." worked with the great disciple whom we know as H. P. B." He is referring to Helena Petrovna Blavatsky (1831-1891) who founded the Theosophical Society in 1875. D.K. sought Alice Bailey to transcribe the "next expanded teaching" following Blavatsky's works because Bailey was a "consecrated and daring disciple, available on the physical plane...." Blavatsky's and Bailey's writings are the foundation of the

New Age movement. (Bailey, Unfinished, 297-9; Dict. of Myst., 24, 30, 144)

In Exodus, we see the "wise men and the sorcerers" turning rods into serpents and water into blood, and calling forth frogs, but there the contest with Moses and Aaron ended. The magicians could not turn dust into lice and they were totally debilitated by the boils God brought upon every Egyptian. (Ex. 7:11-12, 22; 8:7, 18; 9:11) Even today, Johanna Michaelsen speaks of the miraculous healings she witnessed in *The Beautiful Side of Evil*, and Tal Brooke writes about astral projection (out-of-the-body travel) and forms of mind reading performed by *advaitin*, India's spiritual elite. "We were just discovering spiritual realities that Indian sages had exhausted millennia ago," says Brooke. "We were exulting over novel toys that the ancients had abandoned as tokens of spiritual infancy." (Brooke, When, 55)

An initiate was called **"Twice Born"** in honor of their "second birth" from the womb of the Mysteries. (Hall, Secret, Foreword) This was a perverse imitation of the true second, or spiritual, birth required by God. Also, Noah was celebrated as *Diphues* ("twice born"), the two-headed god with one old and one young face, Noah having been "reborn" into a second world after the Flood. (Hislop, 134)

Of course, to be "twice born," or "born anew," one had to be **cleansed of sin and purified**, once again a deceptive, copycat doctrine. Water baptism has always been God's symbol of identification. However, the first pagans, familiar with the symbol, perverted its meaning and instituted the pagan practice of **baptismal regeneration**, meaning that the actual act of water immersion or sprinkling had *efficacy in and of itself*, for spiritual cleansing and/or rebirth. As noted above, the practice was inspired by the judgement of the Flood and Noah's successful "rebirth" into a new world.

Water purification/rebirth was practiced by Babylonians, Egyptians, Hindus, Persians, Greeks, Anglo-Saxons, and Scandinavians. Infants were sprinkled or plunged into lakes or rivers. (Hislop, 129-144) Baptismal regeneration became a central doctrine of the Roman Catholics, and **infant baptism** became a heatedly divisive issue of the Reformation and 17th-Century America, pitting Puritans against Anabaptists. In 1654, Henry Dunster was forced to resign as the first president of Harvard College when he rejected the doctrine of infant baptism. (EB, 1972, 7:767)

Initiation into the Babylonian Mysteries required immersion in water. This dunking must have been rather rigorous as the initiate was admitted only if he "survived" the purification by water and other penances. (Hislop, 132) In later times, suspected witches were tied up and dunked in water to show their guilt or innocence. The belief was that a witch, having rejected her "Christian" infant baptism, would be repelled by the water and float. The innocent would sink and, thus, often drown. Witch testing did not have the best of options! (EB, 1972, 23:605; Dict. of Myst., 121) Nevill Drury's *Dictionary of Mysticism and the Occult* defines baptism as "Ritual immersion in water, based on the ancient concept that water is a source of life." He also says that baptism "was parodied in **medieval witchcraft**, where children and toads were allegedly baptized on behalf of the Devil during the witches' sabbath." (Dict. of Myst., 24-5)

Secrecy requires trust, and trust requires either undying devotion or a fear of "leverage" — blackmail, if you will. **Secret confession** to the pagan priest was a necessary part of the initiation into the Babylonian Mystery system, a practice that is easily traceable to the Greeks. In his *Des Sciences Occultes*, Eusèbe Salverté writes that all of the Greeks from Delphi to Thermopylae were initiated into the Delphic mysteries. They were sworn to secrecy and threatened with severe penalties if they ever broke their oath. However, continues Salverté, the initiates were also required to **confess their sins** to the priest, causing the initiates to *fear the priest's indiscretion far more than the priest feared a breach of oath* by the initiate. (Hislop, 9-11) The Roman Catholic Church adopted and perpetuated the ancient practice of priests who require secret confession to allow converts access to rituals necessary for salvation.

In his 5th-Century B.C. description of the feast of Isis, Greek historian Herodotus states that he was not at liberty to disclose in whose honor the worshippers scourged themselves. Herodotus was "not at liberty" because he was an initiate. (Hislop, 151) Secret initiation into levels of esoteric knowledge is still required of Masons, Mormons, all manner of occultists, and even such secret societies as Yale University's

Order of Skull and Bones, of which former U.S. President George Bush and his father, Prescott S. Bush, are members. (Sutton, Amer. Secret, 22, 38)

Herodotus mentioned worshippers who "scourged" themselves. A common practice of Babylonian paganism was **self-mutilation**. Scourging (whipping) oneself or cutting oneself was instituted as symbolic of the execution and mutilation of Nimrod. It became part of Egyptian, Hindu, Greek, and Roman religion. We will find it in the cultures of the Aztecs and Mayas and various North American Indian tribes. Modern-day Roman Catholic pilgrims in Europe and Latin America often crawl long distances on bloodied knees over rough stones to procure blessings from God. (Hislop, 151-4) Cutting oneself is also a well-known Satanic practice, and even the violent 1970s/80s fad of slam-dancing, head-banging punk rock harks back to aspects of the Babylonian Mysteries.

Control for the "Good" of Mankind

Control is exercised best by the "knowledgeable few" over the "ignorant masses." What is confusing to many is that, throughout history, more often than not these "knowledgeable few" have thought they were doing the right thing and working for the greater good. We have seen that, from a certain human point of view, Nimrod was a hero, a benefactor, and an enlightener of mankind. Manley Hall explains that the doctrines of the "ageless" Mysteries "lead to the **good of mankind**," and that secret societies are the custodians of the **highest cultural concepts**. The "adept-philosophers," writes Hall, were "truly **evolved** human beings" who emphasized **scholarship** and who are credited with the invention or introduction of most of the **arts and sciences** of the modern world. **Opposition** drove the enlightened ones underground, to secrecy, but this necessity brought no "decline" in the *"plan or purpose"* of the initiates, who have always been dedicated to, and appealed to, the "**rational soul** of the world." (Hall, Secret, Foreword)

This is the most **deceptive**, seductive, and elusive aspect of the Mysteries, the high ideals and good intentions of so many of its proponents. This is why the Masons, Mormons, and the New Age movement can be so **attractive**, particularly on the surface. And this is why it can get very **confusing** to sort out solid, uncompromising Bible doctrine from teachings of "love" and "spirituality" and bringing all peoples and all religions of the world together in peace and harmony without being "judgemental," "divisive," and "intolerant." Johanna Michaelsen had thought that her spirit guide, guru, and counselor was actually Jesus Christ who was merely the chief or highest *avatar* (incarnation of deity) until she discovered the *real* Jesus Christ and actually became a Bible-believing, born-again Christian. Alice Bailey was raised a "Christian," and at first thought the spirit being Koot Hoomi was Jesus until she found that he was a "'Master who is very close to Christ....and an exponent of the love-wisdom of which Christ is the full expression.'" (Michaelsen, Beautiful, 138-9, 148; Dict. of Myst., 144) Bailey was obviously never a real Christian.

Isn't it interesting that the **"intelligence" community** of our modern Western civilization is based on vitally important information kept (usually forever) hidden ("classified") from the citizenry and available only to initiates of varying levels of power on a "need-to-know" basis. All basic rules of morality and legality are totally suspended in the intelligence realm in the name of "national security." The end justifies the means in every case, and individuals are routinely sacrificed to the good of the group and the "good" of the country.

Medieval Europe saw the development of the **Roman Catholic system** which basically applied many of the practices of the Mysteries to the "new" Christianity to effectively gain control of Europe, culminating in the **Holy Roman Empire**. Priests (initiates) doled out salvation through secret confession and works oriented rituals regularly restored the faithful to good graces. The **Scriptures** were kept from the people, printed only in Latin and interpreted only by the Pope and the priests. By translating the Scripture into the languages of the people, men like John Wycliffe (1324?-1384) broke the stranglehold of the ruling elite but were martyred for their efforts.

The Code of Mythology

Most **mythologies of classical nations,** instructs Hall, are **originally the rituals of secret societies**. It is a "mistake," he continues, "to assume that earlier cultures accepted as literal the elaborate theology and legendry found in their traditions." (Hall, Secret, Foreword) The historical, cosmological (scientific), and philosophical truths were **hidden beneath a complex surface of fantasies, symbols, and code**s. Researchers and authors of *Hamlet's Mill*, Drs. Giorgio de Santillana and Hertha von Dechend state that this **"international initiatic language"** was purposefully devised to be misunderstood by both "suspicious authorities and the ignorant crowd." "Myth," they explain, "can be used as a vehicle for handing down solid knowledge independently from the degree of insight of the people who do the actual telling of stories, fables, etc. In ancient times, moreover, it allowed the member of the **archaic 'brain trust'** to 'talk shop' unaffected by the presence of laymen: the danger of giving something away was practically nil." (De Santillana, Hamlet's, 312, 347)

The Labyrinth symbolizes the maze of Mystery code as well as the region of the underworld.

As the code was developed and passed down, the pagans added **"levels of truth"** as another method of hiding their real beliefs from the general public and low-level initiates. A modern-day example of this is found in Alice Bailey's Arcane School which presents the **"great primary truths"** to their students as "foundational truths of all the world religions." The student accepts these because he either sees them as having "no sane opposition" or acknowledges them as fact "owing to his point in evolution." The **"second category of truths,"** writes Bailey, is "offered simply for consideration" because they "are more frankly controversial," though they "are held as beliefs by millions of people." (Bailey, Unfinished, 296) In other words, only the "truly evolved" get into the really weird stuff!

It is difficult and probably impossible to know how much the initiates through the ages understood of all the doctrines and information passed down to them and just how much has been lost. In the 300s B.C., Aristotle defined an esoteric doctrine as "one which is learned long before being understood." (De Santillana, Hamlet's, 118) **Drs. De Santillana and Von Dechend** contend that **"true myth"** is not **historical** at all but only **cosmological** — a code for complex, accurate, astronomical data that was the source of ancient concepts of time and cycles of existence. Though "mavericks" among their evolutionist colleagues (see Chap. 9), these seemingly indefatigable researchers dismiss the Bible as "that most unscientific of records" and flatly conclude that the "fable" of the biblical Flood and such other tales as the ancient Babylonian Creation Epic (*Enuma Elish*) and the Epic of Gilgamesh (which "mythologizes" Noah and the Flood) only symbolize heavenly and not earthly events. In other words, the "Great Flood" is not a flood on Earth but a symbol of the vernal equinox moving to another sign of the zodiac. (see Chap. 8; De Santillana, Hamlet's, 47-50, 323) We very much appreciate the amazingly detailed and thorough work of these fine professors, and we heartily agree that a great deal of the mythology is indeed astronomical in character. (see Chap. 8) However, we must point out, as we have already shown, that the foundation for the Mystery code is the historical events surrounding the Flood, Babel, Shem, Nimrod, the spiritual war in heaven, and the resulting pagan rebellion on Earth, as well as a worship of the pre-Flood world.

Another learned researcher who left us with an awesomely detailed reference work, the **Rev. Alexander Hislop**, reminds us that the heroes and events of the *pre*-Flood and *post*-Flood worlds are "commemorated in the secret system of Babylon with a minuteness and particularity of detail of which the ordinary student of antiquity can have little conception." Each pagan name, he says, was "skillfully selected" so as to have many twists and turns in its diverse meanings. This is the key to "the unraveling of the labyrinthine subject of Pagan mythology," a "mighty" but well-planned maze. (Hislop, viii-ix) *Thus, we have two keys to pagan mythology and the Mystery system code: 1) the heroes and events of the pre-Flood and early post-Flood world, and 2) the ancients' knowledge of the heavens.*

The Hidden Lord of Paganism

In past chapters, we have already examined a number of Nimrod's coded identities. However, one that particularly reveals the deceptive nature of the Mystery system is **Saturn,** which means the **"hidden one."** (Hislop, 32, 294-6) Evil is usually done in hiding. **Satan,** the Hidden Lord of Hell, hid himself in the body of the serpent in order to destroy all of mankind. **Adam** hid himself from God after eating the forbidden fruit. **Noah** was hidden by God from the terrible judgement of the Flood in the Ark. **Nimrod is hidden in the complex mysteries of paganism.** The hidden god of hell or the underworld, *Pluto,* is another identity of Nimrod, or Satan himself. (Hislop, 96)

Saturn is a Chaldean word. In Chaldee, the word has only four letters—*stur*—which add up in the mathematics of the Chaldean language to be **666**, as S=60, T=400, U=6, and R=200. (Hislop, 269) Of course, this is the famous, beastly number of the man in Rev. 13:18.

Saturnia was the ancient name of **Rome**, as recorded by Ovid, Pliny, and Aurelius Victor. A city and temple dedicated to Saturn was established by a Babylonian representative of Nimrod long before the traditional founding of Rome in the 700s B.C. The ruins of the original Italian kingdom are referenced in Virgil's *Aeneid*, as some revolution destroyed the pagan city. (Hislop, 239, 270)

As the Egyptian Osiris was the seed of grain, buried and resurrected as the annual harvest, so Saturn became the Roman god of agriculture. The feast of the harvest, or the *Saturnalia*, was held at the **winter solstice**, (see Chap. 8) which would have been **December 25** in the days of the Empire. This was a time of revelry and drunkenness, as was the Bacchanalia of Babylon. Slaves were temporarily "emancipated" and elevated over their masters, just as Nimrod had "emancipated" pagan man from God and "elevated" pagan man to be "as god." (Hislop, 96-7; Dict. of Myst., 232)

The date of the Roman feast, just as the name of the Roman god, had ancient roots. The winter solstice was the Mysteries' date for the **birth of the Sun god**. *Adonis* (Adon, Tammuz, Nimrod) was born, according to paganism, at midnight of December 24, or the winter solstice during the Roman Republic and Empire days. (Our winter solstice today has "precessed" to December 21/22.) Adonis was said to have been gored to death by a wild boar sent by Mars (the war god) in the month of Tammuz. Amidst great lamentation, he was **"resurrected" on March 25**, which would have been the **vernal equinox** of that time. (Our vernal equinox has "precessed" to March 20/21.) (Hall, Secret, 23, 35) This is why, even today, the modern Western world, as a result of the Roman Catholic system, celebrates Christmas (Christ's Mass) on December 25. *It is a pagan date commemorating Nimrod, not Jesus Christ.*

At any rate, the connections between Adonis, Tammuz, Saturn, and Nimrod are obvious. This is a perfect example of the coded maze of paganism. In *The Secret Teaching of All Ages*, Manley P. Hall states that the "supreme **allegory of the dying god** is the key to both universal and individual redemption and regeneration." (Hall, Secret, 36) This shows that indeed the ancients did understand the prophecy of Gen. 3:15 from the beginning, that a Messiah (or the pagans' "Miraculous Child") would be born of a virgin to suffer and die for mankind, to be the first fruits of resurrection, and to effect final judgement upon the Evil One. Job is believed to be the oldest book in the Bible and we believe that Job probably lived in the days before Abraham's sojourn in Canaan, though many contend that he was contemporary with Isaac or Jacob. Job said this to his friends: "For I know that my redeemer liveth, and that he shall stand at the latter day upon the earth; And though after my skin worms destroy this body, yet *in my flesh shall I see God,....*" (Job 19:25-6, KJV, New Scofield, italics added)

It is interesting that *Huang-ti*, the "mythical" **Yellow Emperor** of **China**, is identified as Saturn, and also as a Chinese version of the **Craftsman God** (the blacksmith of the heavens, the Creator, the demiurge who made and runs the Mill of Heaven, see Chap. 8). The **yellow** stands for the *element of the Earth which belongs to Saturn*, and Huang-ti is believed by the Chinese to have established the order of the Sun, Moon, and stars. [This indicates the double identity of **Nimrod/Satan**, as the Earth "belongs" to Satan until Christ officially takes it from him. (see Chap. 1, p. 5-6)] *Ptah* of Egypt is also Saturn, as is *Ea* of the Babylonians and *Enki* of the Sumerians. Both the Egyptians and the Persians (Iranians) celebrated their royal jubilee festivals every 30 years, the length of the planet Saturn's revolution around the Sun, showing how the *ancients connected heavenly movements with earthly history.* (De Santillana, Hamlet's, 129, 133-135)

Saturn also has a double identity as the "First King" (Nimrod), and as the **ruler of the Golden Age** (pre-Flood world). This could be a veiled reference to Noah, Adam, or even Satan himself. It could also show some degeneration, confusion, and/or wishful thinking in the Mystery code. It also shows the deceptive reference to the true (Jesus) and false (Nimrod) Messiahs, as Saturn is the **Lord of the Golden Age** and the **Once and Future King**. These are double references to the pre-Flood world and the Millennial Kingdom. The Golden Age is the time when there was *no war, no bloody sacrifices, and no inequality of classes.* (De Santillana, Hamlet's, 2, 135, 146-7) The pre-Flood world meets two out of the three while the Garden of Eden meets all three, as there was no sacrifice or killing of any kind before the Fall of man.

The identity (or identities) of Saturn gets even more confusing and intriguing when we see that **Zeus**, the leader of the "younger gods" against the "older gods" (or the gods against the Titans), knocked his father Saturn off the royal chariot, banished the creator deity to a peaceful island where he sleeps, "wrapped in funerary linen, until his time, say some, shall come to awaken again, and he will be *reborn to us as a child."* (De Santillana, Hamlet's, 148, italics added) This seems to refer to the battle between Shem and Nimrod, and the identity of Nimrod as both the father and son of the unholy trinity, and his role as the false Messiah or "Miraculous Child."

The Craftsman God

Tomoye-Symbol of Revolution of the Universe.

According to an Orphic fragment (written doctrines of Orpheus who was a mythical Greek poet) and to Dionysius of Halicarnassus, Saturn **lived and ruled openly among men on Earth**. In the Egyptian texts, Ptah also returns repeatedly as an earthly king. This "well-intentioned" ruler could refer to God walking with Adam in Eden (De Santillana, Hamlet's, 222), as well as to Nimrod, the benefactor and organizer of mankind. It is prophetic of the true Messiah either through understanding of the Gen. 3:15 judgement/promise given by God to Adam and the Serpent, or through understanding gained in later times from the Old Testament Millennial prophecies of the Jews.

Kronos, Zoroaster, and the Son

The Greek **Kronos** (Cronos or Cronus) and his wife **Rhea** correspond to the Roman Saturn and his wife Ops. As Nimrod is Saturn, so he is also Kronos, and his wife Semiramis is both Ops and Rhea. As Kronos and Rhea, Nimrod and Semiramis are recognized as the **"father and mother" of all the gods and men**, being the *first humans to be deified*. Kronos and Rhea are also the mythological parents of **Zeus** (Jupiter), who is seen as the ruler of heaven and Earth, (the supreme god) and also the "father of the gods." Remember, this confusion is caused by the fact that Nimrod is both the father and the son, both Kronos and Zeus. (Dict. of Myst., 280; Hislop, 32, 72)

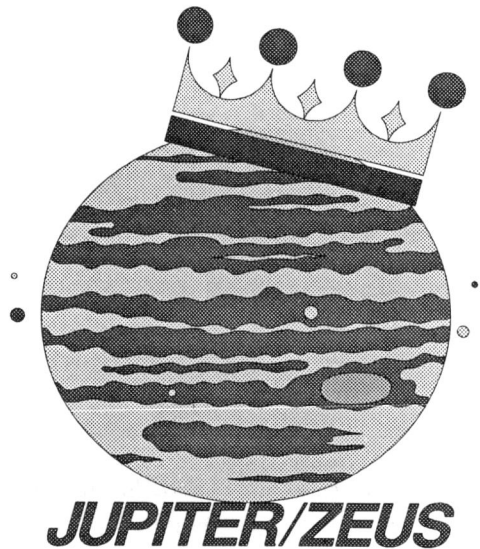

JUPITER/ZEUS

Kronos is recorded to be the offspring of **Ouranos** and **Gaia** (or Gaea). (De Santillana, Hamlet's, 133) The Greek word *ouranos* is the word used throughout the New Testament for heaven (heavens, sky, space, etc.) as the Hebrew word *shamayim* is used in the Old Testament. Hislop demonstrates that Ouranos is one of the oldest gods and is translated "The Enlightener." Though pagan, Ouranos is also "at bottom the 'God of Heaven,' the living and true God," says Hislop. (Hislop, 193-4) Gaia is the Earth goddess and the name most invoked by today's New Age goddess and Mother Earth worshippers. Ouranos and Gaia are the parents of the **Titans**, including Kronos who fathered the gods, including Zeus. Gaia is also known as the mother of the **Cyclops**, another identity of Kronos. (Dict. of Myst., 96)

The Cyclops, according to the writings of ancient Rome's Pliny, invented **tower building**. Remember that Nimrod helped his father Cush with the first tower (Babel), and then gained renown for building the first *fortified* cities. What is interesting is that the Cyclops as the **"god of fortifications"** (or "fortresses" or "strongholds") is referred to in Dan. 11:38. This is a double prophecy about **Antiochus Epiphanes of Syria** in the 100s B.C., a historical king who was also a "type" of the Antichrist to come during the "end-times" Tribulation. Verse 36 begins talking about

God of Fortifications

"the willful king" who is actually the **latter-day Antichrist**, who will exalt himself as "God", but who will also, in his office or palace, *"honor the god of fortresses,"* or **Nimrod** (who is Kronos who is the Cyclops). This fortress god is the same as the "god of war," **Mars** or Ares, two more identifications of Nimrod, the inventor of war. (Hislop, 30-2; Dan. 11:36-9, KJV and *Young's Literal*) *Thus, dead or alive, Nimrod embodies the "spirit of Antichrist" from the Tower of Babel until the Battle of Armageddon.*

Nimrod was also known to the Babylonians as **Zoroaster**. In Chaldee, **zero** was **a circle** standing for both the concept of zero and for a "seed" or child. *"Zero-ashta"* meant **"seed of the woman"** or "seed of **Astarte**," the Babylonian goddess form of Semiramis. This original, Babylonian/ Assyrian Zoroaster instituted the Magi and initiated **worship of the sacred and eternal fire**, according to

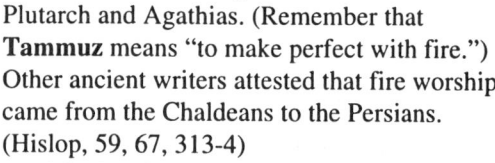

Plutarch and Agathias. (Remember that **Tammuz** means "to make perfect with fire.") Other ancient writers attested that fire worship came from the Chaldeans to the Persians. (Hislop, 59, 67, 313-4)

The Persian (Iranian) **Zoroaster of the 600s-500s B.C.** took the original name and revived the ancient religion which had existed before 1500 B.C. (At some point, the Persians rejected goddess worship and changed Zoroaster to Zarathushtra, which means "delivering seed.") This new Zoroaster claimed that the one creator god was Ahura Mazda, and that, at the beginning of creation, the god's twin spirit sons chose their paths, one picking good and the other evil. This set *good and evil on an equal basis* in the world, creating a **"duality."** We see this revived in the *Star Wars* movie series in the godlike spirit or **"Force"** that has both an evil and good side. (EB, 1972, 23:1011-12)

Events in the Heavens?

Kronos emasculated his father Ouranos (a reference to Shem and Nimrod) and then Zeus knocked *his* father Kronos off the Sun chariot and threw him into Tartaros (underworld). (De Santillana, Hamlet's, 134-5, 266) Could this second father/son altercation, which involves Time (Kronos or Chronos), the Sun, and Jupiter (Zeus), actually **"mythologize" a real heavenly event?** *Is it possible that God illustrated His anger with the pagans at the time of Nimrod's execution by altering the movements of certain heavenly bodies so as to, for example,* **change the calendar?** We know that the calendar changed at some point from 360 days to 365.25 days per year and that the Moon's orbit most likely changed from 30-day orbits to a "monthly" journey of from about 27.3 to 29.5 days, depending on the reference (whether stars or Sun). (Webster's) This type of spectacular judgement would have struck at the heart of pagan knowledge and worship. (see Deut. 4:19, II Kings 23:5, and Chaps. 8 & 10)

Notice that Kronos (Chronos) means "time," that Kronos is also Saturn, and that Zeus is equivalent to Jupiter. Saturn and Jupiter are Roman rather than Greek names, and since our civilization and country was born out of the extended Roman Empire, we are more familiar with Roman terminology. A Greek Orphic fragment credits Kronos/Saturn with the **"'division of beings'"** and with giving to Zeus **"'all the measures of the whole creation.'"** (De Santillana, Hamlet's, 134-5) This is probably a veiled reference to the **Babel judgement** and to Noah and/or Ham or Cush who gave the New World the **Old World's knowledge** of astronomy, mathematics, and measurement. However, it also refers directly to the heavenly bodies, their movements and interactions, such as the conjunctions of the planets Jupiter and Saturn, the possible "birth" of the planet Venus, and the measurement (division) of time and the ages by the **trackable movements of the heavens**. (De Santillana, Hamlet's, 134-5; see Chaps. 8, 10)

The ironic aspect of De Santillana's and Von Dechend's valuable research is the fact that they have defied traditional thinking and helped the archaeoastronomers document the intellect of the ancients regarding astronomy, particularly the ancients' obsession with the **precession of the equinoxes** (the "slippage" of the vernal equinox to a new sign of the zodiac about every 2100 or so years — see Chap. 8). However, because they are **spiritually blind**, they miss the very spiritual warfare and corresponding earthly events of pagan rebellion (which are indeed reflected in astronomical lore and real heavenly events) that lay the foundation for the Mystery code! In genuinely decoding part of the Mysteries, these researchers are still deceived by the Mysteries. *The code works!*

The Goddess

According to Syncellus, **Semiramis** outlived her husband by 42 years, dying, by our calculations, in 1942 B.C., or somewhere around the time that Abram left Ur of the Chaldeans (Babylon) for the city of Haran, on his way to Canaan. (Hislop, 6) [The *Timetables of History* lists the time of Abram's (Abraham's) departure as approximately 2100 B.C.] Hislop states that it was **after the death of Semiramis** that she was actually **deified**, becoming not just the "virgin" mother of the god Nimrod, the Seed or Son, but also the *mother of mankind* (identified with Eve) and the *mother of all of the gods* (deified

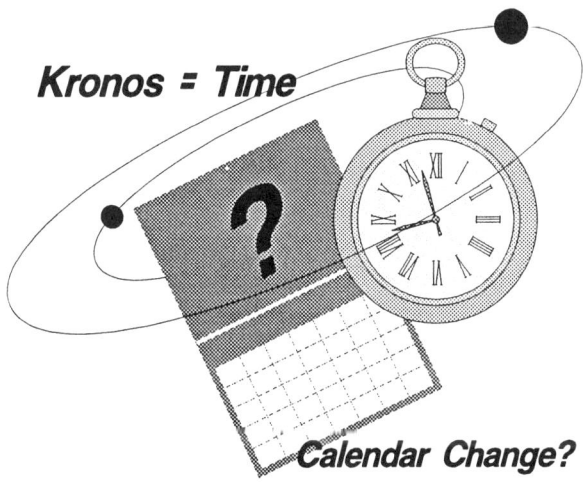

Kronos = Time

Calendar Change?

mortals). This would identify her as the mythological **Rhea**.

We have already noted that the **pagans** purposefully and progressively **rebelled against God whom they knew**. They were anything but ignorant. They knew the truth of the Flood. They understood sin and judgement and salvation. *Despite the ever-growing maze of pagan deities, there remained a universal belief in a "'sole and omnipotent Deity, who created all things,'" "'to whom all things were submissive and obedient.'"* Hislop cites specific evidence of this from Babylon, Egypt, Europe, Hindostan (India), and Iceland. (Hislop, 14, 15)

The pagans understood the trinity. However, they substituted their own creator/sun god for the Father, their own reincarnated Messiah (Nimrod) for the Son, and Semiramis, the "goddess mother," as the **female version of the Holy Spirit**. Called *Astarte*, Semiramis was deified as the **dove**, the symbol of the Holy Spirit. The pagans made her the incarnation of the Holy Spirit, knowing that no one could be a child of God without being born of the Holy Spirit. Thus, in the **pagan trinity**, *one becomes a child of "god" by being born of the "goddess," or the female "Holy Spirit."* This perverted doctrine of the trinity was **universal** among the ancient nations of the world, just as was the belief in one, sovereign, creator God. (Hislop, 16-19, 303, 307-309) Today, we can identify this same pagan trinity as consisting of **1)** *Satan,* **2)** the *Antichrist,* and **3)** the *mother goddess.* Pagan goddess worship is the origin of the term "Mother Earth." We see many of today's modern, radical environmentalists and abortionists practicing goddess worship and referring to the *"Earth mother."* We've seen a revival of all types of goddess-worshipping witchcraft in the U.S. and Europe (the West), and a strong movement in many church seminaries and denominations to refer to God in female terms. (*Wall Street Journal*, April 27, 1992)

This female "Holy Spirit" also became the **"Mediatrix"** or female mediator between God and sinful man. As the goddess of love and beauty (Ishtar, Venus, Aphrodite), and as the gentle and fluttering dove, she was merciful and tolerant of sin. The dove would also become symbolic of **Venus** (Aphrodite) as its generalized "surface" meaning of peace, love, and tranquility spread with the diffusion of paganism. Many would forget the dove's identification with the Holy Spirit (Jn. 1:32) and would point to the dove that returned to Noah's Ark with the olive leaf in its beak. (Dict. of Mysticism, 66-7, 229; Gen 8:11)

Semiramis as "the goddess mother" would also be given, as time went on, the *same basic characteristics and powers possessed by her "son,"* the counterfeit Messiah or Seed. She was deified and worshipped as the miraculous **virgin mother**. She was shown holding a serpent without a head, as a distortion of Gen. 3:15. She was made a mediator between sinful man and "God" and called the "hope of the world." As Nimrod, or Baal/Bel, was the Sun-god and Lord of Heaven, she was the Moon-goddess and **Queen of Heaven**. She was determined to be pure and undefiled with the power to wash away sin. She was killed with a sword by one of her sons who then carried her bodily to heaven. (Hislop, 75-6, 264-5, 310)

Note how similar much of this is to the attributes and powers of the **Virgin Mary** of the Roman Catholic Church, who, in Rome in December 1854, was declared to have had an *"immaculate conception,"* born without sin, which is the equivalent of *deification*. (Hislop, 266-8) How many "Hail Mary" supplications and other prayers are directed to the "great Mediatrix" who is known as the "Queen of Heaven?" Early in Roman Church history, she was declared to be a perpetual virgin, meaning that she remained a virgin her entire life, despite the biblical presence of the brothers and sisters of

Jesus, fathered by Joseph. Much later, a 19th-Century movement to decree her to have been directly *"assumed,"* body and soul, into heaven, was made official by Pope Pious XII in 1950. This meant that her body, according to the Roman Catholics, did not suffer decay as Jesus did not suffer decay (Ps. 16:10). But the new doctrine left unanswered the "question" of her physical death. Roman Catholic theologians also refer to Mary as the "Co-creator" and "Co-redemptrix" of mankind. Whole volumes are dedicated to Mariology. (EB, 1972, 14:991-2; Pictorial Bible Dict., 515)

We must remember that it was the real and true prophecy of the virgin birth, eventually fulfilled by Mary, that led Semiramis some 1980 years earlier to invent the counterfeit pagan "virgin" who became the deified "goddess mother." Hence, it was very easy to **paganize the real Mary** more than two millennia later. Hislop's research led him to the opinion that the "image of the beast" in Rev. 13 would be a form of the "goddess," as she has been given the same basic characteristics of the real and counterfeit Messiah, making her an "image" of the Son. (Hislop, 263-9) This conclusion may or may not be correct, but it is certainly interesting in the light of the amazing revival and spread of goddess worship in our modern, western world.

In a 1992 *New York Times* review of a new book called *The Myth of the Goddess*, the reviewer (a religion teacher at Williams College) attests to the "widespread interest and lively debate" surrounding **goddess figures**. "New Age devotees, psychologists, sociologists, anthropologists, feminists, writers, philosophers, theologians and critics of patriarchal societies" argue, he says, "that long-ignored traditions of goddess worship provide rich resources for social and cultural renewal." The two female authors of the book "write with a sense of impending ecological disaster, which, they believe," says the reviewer, "results from the **repression by Western cultures of the mother goddess** and her vision of 'the universe as an organic, alive and sacred whole.'" The authors trace the traditions of the **"great mother goddess who gives birth to a cosmos that is a part of her divine substance."** In other words, the goddess is the *creator of the world*, the *life-giver* who gives birth to the universe. Or, in short, the **goddess is God.** According to these authors (and standard feminist dogma), Western cultures and fundamentalist religions (Judaism, Christianity, Islam) repress both the goddess and women in general and exploit the earth for monetary gain, meaning that they actually exploit "Mother Earth" or the goddess herself (Mother Nature). This is the real foundation for the **modern feminist and environmental movements**. The authors' solution, says the reviewer, is that "we must become fully conscious of the goddess that lurks within us all." (Taylor, *The New York Times* Book Review, June 28, 1992) Note that these New Age feminists look not for the *god* in you, but for the *goddess* in you. What is intriguing is that worship of the goddess and the idea of birth goes hand in hand with the **abortion movement**. Once again, Satan does not make sense.

The name **Astarte** (also *Ash-turit*, and *Ashtoreth*) actually means "the woman who made the encompassing wall." Remember that Nimrod is the "god of fortresses" and Semiramis is credited with completing the fortress walls of Babylon, as gleaned from the writings of the Roman poet Ovid. (Hislop, 30) We have already noted that the Mediterranean goddesses **Diana**, **Rhea**, and **Cybele** all have turreted crowns on their heads, as if they are wearing a miniature fort, showing their origin in Semiramis. Diana (Artemis) is also the Moon goddess and the goddess of hunting. This points back to the reputation of Semiramis hunting at the side of Nimrod, the mighty hunter before the Lord, as well as to the fact that Nimrod became the Sun god and Semiramis became the Moon goddess. Rhea (Cybele) is a fertility goddess and the "mother of all the gods," also pointing back to Semiramis.

The **Jews** in Jeremiah's time, men, women, and children, were involved in making cakes for, burning incense to, and pouring out drink offerings to the **"queen of heaven,"** arguing that as long as they did this, they had plenty to eat, good health, and safety. (Jer. 7:18; 44:17-23) Much earlier, in Deuteronomy, Moses warned the Jews not to plant a grove of trees or set up any image near the altar of the Lord God. (Deut. 16:21-2) **Groves of trees** are seen as part of goddess worship throughout history among witches, the Greeks and Romans, the English Druids, and even today's New Agers. Even before the Old Testament was written, the ancients knew that one of the names of the Messiah, Jesus Christ, was the **Branch**. (Isa. 4:2; Jer. 23:5; Zech. 3:8, 6:12) This refers to "the Son." The pagans then made the goddess the *"tree" that gave birth to the "branch,"* or the pagan Messiah. In England, the **Yule log**, symbolizing the dead Nimrod, is put on the fire on Christmas Eve (Mother-night) and so is cremated. "Yule" in Chaldee means "infant" or "little child." Nimrod is then reincarnated into the **Christmas tree** which appears the next morning. (Hislop, 48, 93, 97) This is also associated with the **Tree of Knowledge of Good and Evil** which enlightened man and "freed" man from his subjection to God so that man could "be as a god."

The Branch

In their idolatry, the **Jews** turned to **Baal and Ashtoreth**, and to **Molech and Ashtoreth**. Baal and Molech are both the deified Nimrod. (Jud. 2:13, 3:7; I Kgs. 11:5, 33; II Kgs. 23:13) In Acts 19, Paul ran up against the worship of **Artemis (Diana) in Ephesus**, a source of great wealth for the local craftsmen who made silver shrines of the goddess. The locals claimed that Diana was worshipped throughout Asia Minor and the world and that the *image had fallen down from Zeus (Jupiter)*. We have already seen that Diana (Artemis) is the goddess of the Moon and hunting and is actually the deified Semiramis. A very interesting passage in Ezekiel 13:16-23 talks of Jewish women who made magic charms and veils for the rich and who "hunted their souls." (Nimrod was the mighty hunter of souls and Semiramis was the huntress.) These women were **sorceresses** who ensnared people with their false and evil practices and prophecies for money, as astrologists and palm readers do today.

The theme of **mother/son worship**, originated by Semiramis who twisted the truth of the ancient Gen. 3:15 prophecy, *pervades all of paganism*. In Babylon and Assyria, the mother and son were Ishtar and Tammuz, and Rhea and Nin (Ninus). In Egypt, the pair was Isis and Horus. In India, we find the worship of the goddess Kali and the god Siva who, as each story goes, was both Kali's husband and child.

Yule Log & Tree

Even today in India we find Isi and Iswara, as well as the child Crishna (Krishna), who is shown with classic Negroid or Cushite features like Osiris, sucking the breast of his mother, the goddess Devaki. (Hislop, 20 69, 159, 238) Note that both the Indian Krishna and the Greek Achilles had one vulnerable spot, the heel, showing their derivation from Gen. 3:15. (Dict. of Myst., 145; Hislop, 61)

In Rome, the mother and son were represented by Venus and Cupid, who was armed with a bow and arrows as was his counterpart, Nimrod. The same theme was carried on by Fortuna and Jupiter-puer, meaning "Jupiter, the boy." In Greece, the pagans worshipped Irene and the boy Plutus, or Ceres and the babe, while in China, they honored Shing Moo, the Holy Mother, who carried a babe and posed amidst some sort of surrounding "glory" or halo. (Hislop, 20-1) Finally, the perverted theme of Gen. 3:15 came to be embodied in the Roman Catholic Madonna and child.

Images of Good and Evil

The devil began as **Lucifer**, the angel of light, before he fell to become the evil Satan. Even so, **Nimrod and Semiramis** are represented throughout paganism with **both "good" (attractive) and evil (frightening) aspects**, a Satanic phenomenon experienced by former New Ager Johanna Michaelsen who wrote *The Beautiful Side of Evil*. Living in Mexico, she was drawn deeply and powerfully into the occult through psychic (shamanistic) healing, yoga, and mind control. She sincerely thought she was seeking God and spiritual peace. However, the healing, though often supernatural, was inconsistent, as was the peace. Intermittent with the power and the "peace" were horrifying experiences of hatred, ugliness, and evil. After a terrible spiritual battle, she became a Christian through the ministry of Dr. Francis Schaeffer's L'Abri in Switzerland.

On one hand, Nimrod was the pagans' **enlightener, deliverer, and Messiah**. As a deity, he was the giver of life and savior, with power to purge from sin and impart eternal happiness, while simultaneously encouraging debauchery and hedonism. On the other hand, Nimrod was the **horrible, bloody, Molech** (Moloch) who demanded **self-mutilation** and **child sacrifice**. In Lev. 20:6, Moses warned the 12 tribes of Israel that anyone who followed after wizards or "channelers" of familiar spirits (demons) would be ostracized — cast out from Israel. But in verses 1-5, he warned that anyone who gave a child to Molech should be stoned to death. The key phrase associated with Molech was *"passing through the fire."* In Jer. 32:35, God says that the Jews "built the high places of Baal...to cause their sons and their daughters to pass through the fire unto Molech...." (KJV) In looking at Jer. 7:31, Ezek. 16:21, 23:37-39, we find that "passing through the fire" means that the children were slain and offered to "the reigning one," Molech (or Moloch, Milcom, or Malcam). In some cases, the image of Molech was heated and the bodies of the sacrificed children laid in the arms of the demonic idol. (Pict. Bible Dict., 550) Hislop quotes 17th-Century English poet John Milton who referenced the worship of Molech (Moloch) in his famous work, *Paradise Lost*:

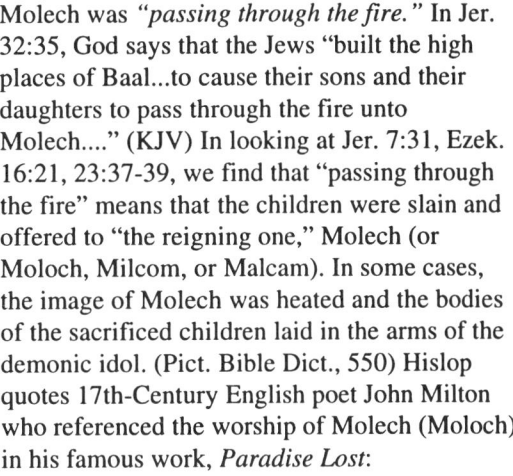

Cupid/Nimrod
The Child of Goddess Venus
The hunter with the bow

"First Moloch, horrid king, besmeared with blood
Of human sacrifice, and parents' tears,
Though, for the noise of drums and timbrels loud,
Their children's cries unheard, that passed through fire
To his grim idol." (Hislop, 151)

As Satan is the devourer of man (I Pet. 5:8), and the unsuccessful devourer of the Christ child (Rev. 12:4), so his earthly representative (Nimrod as Molech) became a **devourer of human children**. In pagan mythology, **Kronos/Saturn** devoured his children. In turn, the Phoenicians, Carthaginians, and the Rhodians offered their children to Kronos/Saturn (who was the same as Nimrod/Molech). The Druids of the British Isles offered their children to the fires of Baal. Before becoming Baal, Nimrod was *Bol-khan*, the priest of Baal, as "cahn" (khan) meant priest. Hence, the Roman fire god was none other than Vulcan. As "cahn" meant priest, "cahna" meant *"the priest."* Thus, *"cahna-baal"* meant *"the priest of Baal."* And, as priests are to partake of the sacrifices on the altars (as did the Hebrew priests under the Mosaic Law), the priests of Baal ate the flesh of the sacrificed children, making a "cannibal" an eater of human flesh. (Hislop, 229-232)

Totally deluded, the pagans offered their children to the **"purifying fire"** in order that the children would be "perfected" and thus sinless and qualified for eternity. The fire worship

The Mystery System

required that the children be passed *through* the fire and then burned *in* the fire. For the same reason, the history of India shows Hindu widows, seeking **eternal purification** and a blessed state, throwing themselves onto the funeral pyres built to cremate their dead husbands. (Hislop, 120-1, 315) Militant, modern-day pro-abortion feminists (a number of whom are also goddess worshippers) are driven by the same evil spirits that directed the sacrifices for Molech. **Abortion** today is a very profitable enterprise for its gory practitioners and obsessive promoters, just as idol worship was profitable for the idol makers in Ephesus and every idolatrous land (Acts 19:24-7). Taxpayer-supplied government support multiplies those profits.

The **month of Tammuz** begins at the **summer solstice** (longest day of the year), which is called the beginning of summer in the United States but *Midsummer* day in the British Isles. The Roman Catholic **Feast of the Nativity of St. John** marks **Midsummer in Europe**. Today, the summer solstice arrives about June 21, though in the early years of Roman Catholic history, the solstice came about June 24/25. As the day in the Middle East always begins in the evening, so this European festival begins on St. John's Eve when the Midsummer fires are lighted. Particularly in Ireland, the custom of passing through the fire (without actual sacrifice) and throwing children across the embers has remained at least into the 19th Century. (Hislop, 113-121)

As Nimrod developed **two aspects**, attractive and evil, so often did **Semiramis**. As Ishtar, she is gentle and loving as well as warlike and aggressive. (Dict. of Myst., 132) The mother goddess Shakti in India is both beautiful and evil. Her evil manifestation is as a giantess with black skin, a huge red tongue, and tusks like a bull. (Nimrod has often been symbolized as a bull. Horns are symbols of power or strength.) Shakti also wears a necklace of human skulls. (EB, 1972, 11:510)

Additional Pagan Signposts

The spread of predominantly pagan **mankind across the oceans to the Americas can be traced** using a number of specific tools, including written languages, petroglyphs, pottery, coinage, architecture, and maps. A people's social and intellectual culture, and especially their religion, also gives strong clues as to the people's origin. We can follow the various identities of Nimrod and Semiramis, perverted stories of the patriarchs, legends of the pre-Flood world, and different versions of mother/son worship from people to people, around the world. Note the following three additional symbolic signposts.

One interesting item that we will find in Central America is the **rosary**, the necklace of beads, shells, or stones that is used to count repetitions of rote prayers or devotions. The rosary, documents Hislop, is an **ancient pagan** religious article, found among the **Hindus** and **Buddhists** of India, China, and Tibet, as well as Greece and Rome. **Diana of the Ephesians** is shown wearing a large rosary. (Hislop, 187-8) 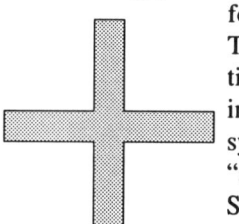 A jade Buddhist "saint" in the Ancient China exhibit of the Chicago Field Museum (1991) holds a string of rosary beads.

A popular symbol seen throughout paganism in a number of variations is the **cross** mark. Originally it was the **mystic Tau** of the Babylonians and Egyptians, the letter "T" which stood for the name of the god, Tammuz (Nimrod). Sometimes it was joined to, or inserted in, a **circle** which symbolized the Sun (and the "son"). We know that the Sun was considered the "giver of life" and was used to symbolize Nimrod, the pagan Messiah. As paganism developed, the Sun itself became an object of worship. The god **Bacchus** is shown wearing a headband covered with cross marks. **Buddhist crosses** symbolize the *tree of knowledge in the "terrestrial paradise."* This tree is also seen by Buddhists as the tree of life and the tree of the gods, and not as the tree whose fruit was the object of Adam's sin. (Hislop, 197-200) The *Dictionary of Mysticism and the Occult* defines the cross as an "ancient **pre-Christian** symbol interpreted by some occultists as uniting the male phallus (vertical bar) and the female vagina (horizontal bar). It is also a symbol of the four directions and a powerful weapon against evil." (Dict. of Myst., 51)

Only since World War II (almost a century after Hislop) have Westerners become sensitized to the special version of the cross we call a **swastika**. Once again turning to the *Dictionary of Mysticism*, we find that the swastika made so infamous by Adolf Hitler is a "**universal mythic symbol**" which adds four "arms" to a simple cross so that the figure appears to rotate. The swastika is really a **"Sun-wheel"** designed to represent "eternal movement and spiritual renewal." The *"counter-clockwise"* **Nazi** swastika is supposed to symbolize movement "away from the Godhead," while the *"clockwise"* swastika represents "movement towards God and suggests a cosmic rhythm in tune with the universe." (Dict. of Myst., 248-9) In Chicago's Field Museum (1991), in the **Ancient China** exhibit, is a **Taoist swastika**. In the Indians (American) Before Columbus exhibit (1991) are a number of copper swastikas found among the artifacts of the **ancient Ohio Hopewell** moundbuilders. *Webster's New World Dictionary* shows both the clockwise and counterclockwise swastikas, the one Hindu (India) and the other Nazi, defining the design as a mystic symbol of ancient origin found in both the Old World and the New World. (Webster's) In fact, the only places the swastika has not been found are the islands of the Pacific and Australia. (Hutchings, Europe, 23) The use of the swastika is only one indication of Hitler's occultic roots.

Mystery Babylon

It is amazing that, almost 4,000 years after Nimrod, in the **1990s**, political leaders ("kings" of nations) and international bankers and global corporate leaders (merchants) are putting together a **New World Order**. These leaders are members of secret societies and occultic New Age organizations. The most disturbing thing about **Rev. 18** is the fact that **"that great city, Babylon"** will be destroyed in one hour while the world's merchants and ship captains stand far off and greatly bewail the destruction. Since a *system* cannot be "utterly burned with fire," in one hour, while people actually view the "smoke" of the destruction from far off (certainly sounds like nuclear destruction), *it would seem that a place or nation or empire must embody the Babylonian pagan system at the time of this Tribulation judgement.*

Some prophecy teachers believe that **Babylon itself** will be restored and will once again be the capital of civilization and center of world commerce that it once was. One reporter recently described Babylon as "the most important city in the world" "for almost two millennia." Excavation among the ruins of the "great city" began in **Iraq** in the 1950s, but the restoration project accelerated in earnest in 1978, as ordered by **Saddam Hussein** who has held three annual **International Babylon Festivals**. The latest was during the autumnal equinox of 1989. By February 1990, the thousands of workers had used 60 million bricks and expected to finish in 1994. However, the Gulf War of 1990/91 may have served as a significant disruption. (Caballero, "Rebuilding Babylon," World Press Review, 37:74, Feb. 1990; Dyer, Babylon, 25-8, 209; Facts on File, 848:F1, 1989)

Some other teachers submit that modern-day Babylon is embodied by the **United States**. We do host the headquarters of the **United Nations** and we are universally recognized as the richest and most powerful nation in the history of the world. Perhaps if New York City or Washington, D.C. becomes the capital of the New World Order, that city will be destroyed by nuclear bombs. Rev. 17:12-18 says that the ten kings who receive power with the beast, or Antichrist, will be the "tool" God uses to destroy the woman, or "that great city." The ten kings are often identified as the **revived Roman Empire** in the form of the **new European Community** which is desperately trying to solidify even as we write. Will Europe under the Antichrist destroy all or part of the United States with nuclear weapons? Rev. 18:4 quotes a voice from heaven as saying "Come out of her, my people," indicating that God is warning the Jews to leave "that great city." At present, there are few if any Jews in Iraq, while the United States (particularly New York City) has more Jewish residents than the state of Israel.

However, *the world is in a period of fast and dramatic political change*. Political and economic power is already shifting away from the U.S. to Europe and the Far East. The U.S. is plagued with unprecedented debt and immorality. If pre-Millennium, pre-Tribulation dispensationalists are correct, the **Rapture** will occur prior to the Tribulation, taking perhaps some 28 million Christians from the United States. (Dyer, Babylon, 168) [That number may be on the high side.] The Rapture will disrupt the entire world and take people from every nation, but it will most likely affect the U.S. more than any other country. In today's world, the prophecy of Rev. 17 and 18 (and Jer. 50, 51; Isa. 13, 14) sounds like it is describing the United States. But this **complete annihilation by some type of fire** (or nuclear explosion) is scheduled to take place **toward the end of the Tribulation**, judging from its placement in Revelation and the use of terms like "in those days" (Jer. 50:4) and "latter days" (Jer. 48:47, 49:39) and "day of the Lord" (Isa. 13). *By the end of the Tribulation, the United States may be a second- or third-rate nation and the King of Babylon (Iraq) may rule all of the Middle East and control most of the world's oil.* People from many nations may work there and Jews may dwell there. Will the beast and his 10-nation, revived Roman Empire destroy a rebuilt Babylon? Perhaps the answer will become clearer as we study history.

BIBLIOGRAPHY

Bailey, Alice A., *The Unfinished Autobiography.* New York: Lucis Publishing Co., 1951.

Brooke, Tal, *When the World Will Be As One*, Bib. Chap. 1, p. 19.

Caballero, Antonio, "Rebuilding Babylon," *World Press Review,* Feb. 1990, 37:74.

De Santillana, Giorgio, and **Von Dechend,** Hertha, *Hamlet's Mill.* Boston: David R. Godine, Publisher, Inc., 1977.

Drury, Nevill, *Dictionary of Mysticism*, Bib. Chap. 2, p. 37.

Dyer, Charles H., *The Rise of Babylon,* Bib. Chap. 5, p. 80.

Encyclopaedia Britannica (EB), Bib. Chap. 3, p. 51.

Facts on File, 1989, 848:F1.

Grun, Bernard, *The Timetables of History*. New York: Touchstone (Simon & Schuster), 1982.

Hall, Manley P., *The Secret Teachings of All Ages*. Los Angeles: Philosophical Research Society, 1975 [original dated 1928].

Hislop, Alexander, *The Two Babylons*, Bib. Chap. 4, p. 65.

Hutchings, Noah W. (ed.), *Europe is Rising!*, Bib. Chap. 5, p. 80.

Michaelsen, Johanna, *The Beautiful Side of Evil*, Bib. Chap. 5, p. 80.

New Scofield Reference Bible (KJV). New York: Oxford University Press, 1967.

Sutton, Antony C., *America's Secret Establishment*. Billings, Montana: Liberty House Press, 1986.

Taylor, Mark C., "Ye Shall Be as Goddesses," *The New York Times Book Review*, June 28, 1992, p. 25.

Webster's New World Dictionary, Bib. Chap. 2, p. 38.

Young's Literal Translation of the Bible, Bib. Chap. 4, p. 66.

Zondervan Pictorial Bible Dictionary, Bib. Chap. 4, p.66.

PROJECTS

Christianity vs. Paganism: Make your own chart comparing the doctrines, characteristics, rituals, leadership, etc. of biblical Christianity with paganism. For example, compare the hidden "truths" of paganism with the handling of truth by Christianity. Compare the priesthoods of both. Use biblical references to support your comparisons/contrasts, such as I Pet. 2:5, 9 and Rev. 1:6 regarding priesthood.

Secret Organizations: Do your own research into the Masons and the Mormons and the secrecy behind which they operate. There are quite a few good books on both subjects by knowledgeable researchers and by high-ranking ex-Masons and ex-Mormons.

Write an essay on the power of secrecy and examine how it is used in government, in business, in the military, in special organizations or clubs, etc.

Goddess Worship: Use the Readers' Guide at your local library and see how many articles have been featured in the mainstream press on modern-day goddess worship. Note its strong connection with the feminist movement.

Chapter 8
Why Astronomy is the Telescope to Find the Ancient World

Why is Astronomy So Important?

Noah was *post-Flood* mankind's main resource of *pre-Flood* knowledge. (Noah's family and demonic angels were other sources.) Drawing from his ancient sources, the Jewish historian **Josephus** records that the **sons of Seth** were known as "the **inventors** of that peculiar sort of wisdom which is concerned with the heavenly bodies, and their order." (Josephus, I.ii.3) If Josephus and his ancient sources are correct, it was the *godly* line of men — the fathers of Noah, the line of Seth and not Cain — who became the **first astronomers**. Ancient secular Persian and Arabian traditions also attribute the invention of astronomy to Adam, Seth, and Enoch. (Bullinger, Witness, 10) *Thus, man has been concerned with astronomy since his very beginning, and the pursuit was a godly one, providing man with a **Bible in the heavens**.*

God plainly states in Gen. 1:14 that the heavenly bodies are to serve as **timekeepers** and **calendars** for man. Because of this, the stars and planets are often referred to as "governing bodies," providing a **sense of order**. *If time is not kept, crops cannot be managed, feasts cannot be observed, and prophecies cannot be tracked. Astronomy is necessary and practical.*

God also says, (actually first in the list) "let them be for **signs**," meaning divine demonstrations of power and warnings for mankind, even direct agents of judgement. Those who know and worship God are not to be disturbed by heavenly signs or events, though these portents cause the pagans much dismay. (Jer. 10:2) *Man's obsession with astronomy aids us in tracking the spread of mankind (diffusion) throughout the world and provides records of when certain things occurred. Astronomical knowledge is vital to the investigation of ancient America!*

We know from the Bible that **God** created all the stars (and planets), numbers them, calls them by name, and commands their movements and alters their composition at will. (Job 9:7-9; 38:31-3; Ps. 8:3; 147:4; Isa. 40:26; Jer. 31:35) God must have instructed **Adam** in the ways of the stars, so that Adam's godly sons through Seth learned to track the movements of the appointed timekeepers, duly recording the days, months, and years. This required mathematical as well as astronomical knowledge. Drawing from this pre-Flood knowledge, the early Babylonians (Nimrod's gang) tracked planets, predicted eclipses, studied sunspots, and reported comets, using mathematical calculations. (Bullinger, Witness, 12) Harvard's Dr. Barry Fell, a "maverick" evolutionist, concludes that the constellations of the Zodiac were drawn and named by the Babylonians about 2000 B.C. (Fell, Bronze, 130), a conclusion that fits well with our own **Flood** date of **2345 B.C.** It also supports our contention that the pagans revised the divine Zodiac for their own purposes not long after the Flood. *Astronomical records and sites are solid evidence of the sophistication and inventiveness of ancient man, even as he devolved over time from the degenerating effects of sin and the Curse.*

Times & Seasons
Seasons = Cycles of Time

Structure and Movements of the Heavens

Because of the **photomultiplying effect** of the pre-Flood, **crystalline firmament**, the stars appeared in color and three times brighter than we see them today. They also were visible in the daytime, providing the "sons of Seth" with a very good astronomical observatory. (Baugh, Panorama, 60-1) Josephus makes an interesting statement concerning these first astronomers. He explains that Noah and his pre-Flood ancestors lived such **long lives** not just because of the quality of their food and their virtue, but because *they made important astronomical and geometrical discoveries.* They had to live at least 600 years, he says, in order to observe the completion of the **Great Year** according to the stars. (Josephus, I.iii.9)

Now, what does Josephus mean by Great Year? At this point, we need to define some terms and acquire a basic understanding of constellations, the zodiac, the ecliptic, equinoxes, solstices, heliacal risings, and the precession of the equinoxes.

Constellations and the Zodiac

As the first astronomers looked at the night skies, they saw what appeared to be clusters of stars that could be grouped into "dot patterns" for **imaginary images** of animals, people, or things. The actual stars may have been many light-years apart, one **light-year** being the distance traveled (in a vacuum) by light (at 186,000 miles per second) during one year, or about **six trillion miles**. (Gallant, 173) But actual distances were not important. Appearances were all that mattered, and the **star pictures** made for much easier tracking. These pictures are called **CONSTELLATIONS**. **Modern astronomers** around the world have agreed to recognize **88 constellations**. (Gallant, 191)

This is the standard explanation for the existence of constellations, which are probably best known around the world in the stories of ancient mythologies and as the forecasting tools of pagan astrologers who believe that the stars influence the character and life of each person, as well as predict the future. (Dictionary of Mysticism, 19) However, men like **E. W. Bullinger** (1837-1913) have shown that the original constellations were truly a **Bible in the heavens**, and thus, these **star pictures** must have come **directly from God,** who instructed Adam and Seth in their proper construction, order, and interpretation. Using the meanings of the ancient star names, many of which have been preserved through the millennia, as well as Scripture references and traditional stories, Bullinger points out the **primitive biblical truth** *still clearly visible through the haze of time and pagan perversions.*

Bullinger points out something that has always puzzled this writer, that the *patterns of the stars themselves often have little to do with the picture shapes*. In other words, the stars that make up the constellation **Virgo** do not in any way suggest the form of a human, much less a woman. The same fact applies to **Pisces the Fishes, Aries the Ram,** and **Cancer the Crab,** as well as a number of other constellations. It is a little easier to see the horns of **Taurus the Bull** and the sword belt of **Orion the Hunter.** The **Southern Cross** is obvious, and once the stars of **Aquarius the Water Carrier** and **Draco the Dragon** are identified and connected, their shapes make some sense. But, if you look up at the night sky and see nothing identifiable but the two famous **Dippers**, don't feel alone.

However, each constellation figure carries its own ancient, traditional meaning, preserved over the millennia, which is affirmed by the meanings of the names of the stars which are grouped into the figure. (Bullinger, Witness, 17-24) Who named each star? God did. Who placed each of these carefully named stars in its position in the Universe? God did. This, more than anything else, confirms the fact that the constellations are truly **creations of God**, as **physical stars** and as **doctrinal symbols** which illustrate specific personages and events.

As Bullinger explains, 37 **new constellations** were added by Hevelius and Halley in the 1600s and 1700s in order to group important stars not included in the original ancient constellations. If identification were the sole reason for contrived star pictures, writes Bullinger, all of the stars would have been included in the first place by the expert pre-Flood astronomers. However, continues Bullinger, "only certain stars were used for the purpose of helping *to identify the pictures!*" (Bullinger, Witness, 43) *In other words, the pictures don't identify the stars, the stars identify the pictures.* Below, under the heading "Heavenly Gospel," we will examine both the Christian and the pagan versions of the constellations.

The best-known of the constellations are those 12 which make up the **ZODIAC**. The word zodiac comes from the Greek *zoion,* which means animal or a collection of animals. (Hutchings, God's Bible, 11; Webster's) Zodiac means **girdle or circle of animals**. It is defined as the **12 constellations** found in the **16°-wide** "highway" which circles the Earth with the ecliptic as its center stripe.

The **ECLIPTIC** is defined as the *yearly path that we see the Sun take across our sky and, thus, around the Earth.* This path is usually pictured as tilted at an angle of 23½° to the **celestial equator**, which is merely Earth's equator extended into space. The Moon and the planets of our so-called solar system (except Pluto) also move across our sky in the 16°-wide path of the Zodiac, generally following the ecliptic. (Gallant, 13-15, 174-5) This is why astrologers refer to the Sun, Moon, or one of the planets as being "in" a certain constellation. Though the Zodiac is called the circle of animals, only seven of the 12 constellations represent animals, six real (lion, crab, scorpion, fish, bull, ram) and one mythological (goat/fish). Three are human characters, one is a pair of scales (or possibly originally an altar), and one is a mythological creature, half human and half horse, called a centaur. We will find variations in constellation interpretations among ancient peoples of the world, but **what is most amazing is the consistency of the basic knowledge of the Zodiac worldwide and its durability throughout history.** See *Secrets of the Great Pyramid* by Peter Tompkins for excellent illustrations and commentary regarding the famous and controversial **Dendera Zodiac** from the Temple of Hathor at Dendera in Egypt. The 12 signs of the Zodiac are easily recognizable.

Standard diagram of Copernican view of Earth's tilted axis and the ecliptic

Pole of the Ecliptic
23½°
16°
N
Zodiac
Ecliptic
Earth's Equator
S
Celestial Equator
Celestial Sphere

Astronomy – Telescope To Find the Ancient World

Job calls God the Maker of the constellations, specifically **Orion, Pleiades**, and what is commonly believed to be a reference to the **Great Bear** (the Big Dipper), all of which are in the northern skies. Job adds that God also made the "chambers," or constellations, of the south. (Job 9:9, 38:32) An interesting observation is that Orion, Pleiades (the seven stars or "seven sisters"), and the Bear must have been important constellations to the Hebrews, as they are the only ones mentioned by name in the Bible, other that the "crooked serpent" which is **Draco the Dragon**. (Job 9:9, 26:13, 38:31-2; Amos 5:8) The Pleiades was a very important constellation to ancient peoples **all over** the world. However, *none of these constellations are members of the Zodiac.*

God asks Job if Job could possibly control the movements and "influences" of these constellations, or if he could "bring forth **Mazzaroth** in its season." (Job 38:31-2; see both KJV and NIV) Mazzaroth is generally recognized to be the Zodiac, though there is quite a bit of debate as to the precise Hebrew word translated as Mazzaroth. Bullinger states that *oth* means "sign," while *Strong's Concordance* says that *mazzarah* is a plural for something distinctive or set apart. As the word is always used in the context of constellations, it would seem that it does mean a collection of distinctive constellations, separate from Orion, Pleiades, the Bear, and Draco, which we noted above are not members of the Zodiac. God states that He brings forth this group of constellations "in its season," or, as Rev. Walter Lang says, "in his season." Could this be another indication that God named His Zodiac and gave it personality and a personal message as well as a connection with the seasons of the year? (Bullinger, Witness, 17; Lang, Job, 459-462; Strong's)

Bullinger thinks that the **twelve tribes of Israel** each claimed a sign of the Zodiac and points to Joseph's dream (Gen. 37:9) in which the Sun, Moon, and "the eleven stars" (his eleven brothers) bowed down to him. Each tribe, notes Bullinger, had a banner which carried the ensign of their father's house. (Num. 2:2) It is interesting that there are 12 signs in the Zodiac (and 12 months in the year), and that **the number 12** is so pivotal to Israel as well as to the New Jerusalem. The number 12 stands for the **perfection of government or rule**. The signs of the Zodiac thus represent God's order in the heavens and the stars that "govern" time on Earth. (Bullinger, Witness, 17-19; Bullinger, Number, 253-5) God asks if Job knows the **statutes of heaven** and if Job can appoint **heaven's dominion (government) in the Earth**. (Job 38:33)

Equinoxes, Solstices, Tropics, and Heliacal Risings

Before we can understand the *precession* of the equinoxes, we need to define *equinox* and discover just exactly what it is that precesses, and to do that, we must understand the **movements of the Sun**. If you kept careful track of the Sun's movements for a year, you would notice that its daily arc across the sky moves slowly, day by day and month by month, from closer to the horizon to high in the sky and then back toward the horizon. This movement is what gives us our regular **change in seasons** — winter, spring, summer, fall. In other words, if you live somewhere between 30° and 50° North latitude (in the United States, for example), the noon Sun would be closest to the horizon in December and highest in the sky in June.

Remember that this arc (the ecliptic) runs generally through the 16°-wide belt of the 12 constellations of the Zodiac. During the time that worldwide geography was being established after the Flood and Babel, around the 1900s B.C., the constellation **Aries** "housed" the Sun at the beginning of the year. [This lasted, says astronomer Roy Gallant, from about 1953 B.C. to about A.D. 220.] The **ancients**, *except for the Jews*, **began their year in the spring**, or during the time we now call March/April. [The *civil*, or *physical*, **Jewish calendar** related to the Earth began in the *fall*. The *religious*, or *spiritual*, Jewish calendar began at the Exodus with the new year in the *spring*.] During the **Age of Aries** (in the Northern Hemisphere), the *longest day of the year* occurred when the Sun was "housed" in the constellation of **Cancer**, while the *shortest day of the year* occurred when the Sun was "housed" in the constellation of **Capricorn**.

Now, look at a map or a globe. A globe is preferable. [If you don't have a big globe at home, the new map stores sell small globes with a diameter of about 4.5 inches. They are affordable and easy to handle.] Notice the line about 23½° above the equator. It is called the **Tropic of Cancer**. Next, notice the line about 23½°

below the equator. It is called the **Tropic of Capricorn**. Now you know what these lines mean and how they got their names. These lines mark the outside boundaries of the ecliptic, the path of the Sun, from the longest day of the year to the shortest day of the year. These days are called the **SUMMER SOLSTICE** and the **WINTER SOLSTICE**.

In **1993** in the Northern Hemisphere, the longest day and shortest night (summer solstice) occurs on **June 21**. The shortest day and longest night (winter solstice) occurs on **December 21**. Across the equator in the Southern Hemisphere, it is just the opposite, with summer in December and winter in June.

So the paths of the Sun, the Moon, the planets, and the constellations of the Zodiac stay within the 47°-wide belt around the equator between the two Tropics. That's why, if you're between those two lines, we say that you're in the **Tropics**, and the heat will daily remind you of that fact unless a high altitude changes the temperature. (Gallant, Constellations, 12-15, 174-7; Webster's; The Miller Planisphere; 1993 CEDCO calendar; Good, Rosh, 51-2)

An **EQUINOX** occurs **twice each year** when the Sun crosses the equator, making *day and night equal in length.* Equinox actually means **"equal-night."** Today, in **1993** in the Northern Hemisphere, the **AUTUMNAL EQUINOX** (fall) occurs on **September 22** while the **VERNAL EQUINOX** (spring) occurs on **March 20**. (Gallant, Constellations, 15, 175-8; Hutchings, God's Bible, 13; Webster's; E.B. 1972, 18:442) The vernal equinox was the **"New Year"** of all ancient pagan people. (Fell, Bronze, 123) In the course of our studies, particularly in Volume II, we shall see just how obsessed the ancients were with marking the vernal equinox each year, as well as the winter solstice, for religious as well as agricultural reasons.

Actually, these **dates slowly change** as the equinoxes precess, or occur earlier each year. In **45 B.C.**, the spring equinox occurred on **March 25**. Some four or five centuries after that, it fell on March 24, and so on. (Fell, America, 210-11) At the time the Roman Catholic Church set the date of Christ's birth, the winter solstice was about **December 25**. Remember from Chapter 7 (p. 98) that the winter solstice was the Mystery system's date for the **birth of the Sun god** Adonis (Adon, Tammuz, Nimrod). This makes sense because the winter solstice marks the time of the longest night and the beginning of the daily lengthening of daylight, or the "death" and "resurrection" of the Sun. Also, Tammuz was supposedly "resurrected" or "reincarnated" on the vernal equinox. (Hall, Secret, 23, 35)

The ancients observed the **HELIACAL RISINGS** and **SETTINGS** of the constellations to determine the Sun's position in the Zodiac. *Helios* refers to the Sun. Observers noted the constellation that rose on the horizon **prior to the sunrise** (heliacal rising). The Sun then rose with the next constellation behind it ("in" that constellation), the blinding sunlight naturally obscuring that constellation from view. Observers later noted the constellation on the horizon **after the sunset** (heliacal setting). The constellation that "housed" the Sun that month was the

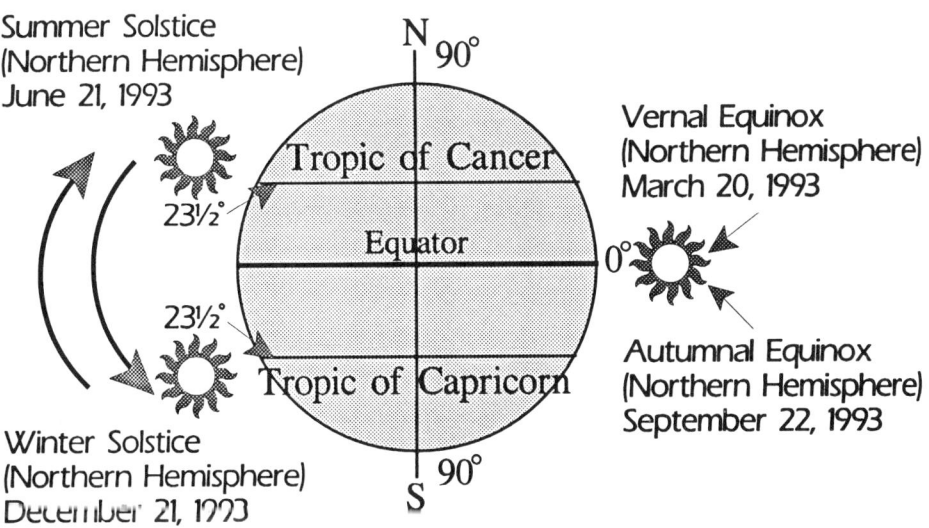

temporarily invisible constellation in between the other two. The heliacal rising of a certain star (the Egyptians closely tracked the star Sirius) refers to its first appearance above the horizon following its period of being obscured by the Sun. (Krupp, In Search, 32; Gallant, Constellations, 12; Webster's)

Precession of the Equinoxes and the Pole Star

The *normally accepted explanation* for the "precession of the equinoxes" is **gravitational forces** of the Sun and Moon acting on an Earth that has a slight bulge at its equator and an **axis** that is at quite a **tilt, inclined 23½°** to the plane formed by the Sun's equator. As it spins on its axis, the Earth wobbles like a top, the axis scribing a cone shape, so that the Sun changes one degree in relation to the Zodiac just over every 71 years (360 degrees x 71 = 25,560). This is a very, very, slow wobble. Because of this, the Sun, at the time of the **vernal equinox**, passes from one zodiacal sign to the next about every 2,170 years. This movement is in the *opposite direction* from the Sun's yearly journey, month by month, through the Zodiac. (Gallant, Constellations, 177-9)

Dr. Livio Catullo Stecchini uses slightly different calculations of 72 years, or a westward movement of 50" per year. [Circle=360°, each degree=60 minutes ('), and each minute=60 seconds (")] This gives a *Great Year*, or the time it takes to complete the circle, of **25,920 years** (360° x 72). (Tompkins, Secrets, 165, 381) **Sir Isaac Newton** (A.D. 1642-1727) first *postulated* this explanation. The movements can be tracked, but the explanation cannot be proven, only postulated. In reality, the **rate of the precession actually changes** and is currently slowly increasing. The figures here, then, are an attempt to compute an average rate of movement. Stecchini also points out that the angle of the ecliptic has changed over the millennia, moving the Tropic of Cancer south almost one-half degree. (Tompkins, Secrets, 112-3, 146, 180-1, 295-6)

According to Gallant, the vernal equinox (the ancient New Year) was in **Taurus the Bull** from about 4000 B.C. to 1953 B.C. Then it precessed into **Aries the Ram** from 1953 B.C. to A.D. 220. From A.D. 220 to about A.D. 2375, it occurs in **Pisces the Fishes**, and then it will move into **Aquarius the Water Carrier**. (Gallant, Constellations, 177-9) Now you understand why New Agers speak of the coming *Age of Aquarius*, though astrologers and New Agers tend to round the numbers off to fit the millennia — 4000 to 2000, 2000 to 1, 1 to 2000, etc. — so that the coming of the year 2000 is seen as a momentous event. But then, the entrance into a new millennium (even a new century) has always been marked with great attention and feelings of both hope and fear.

Now that we understand something about the Zodiac and the precession of the equinoxes, we need to examine a closely related and historically significant astronomical phenomenon — the location and movement of the **POLE STAR**. What is commonly referred to as the **celestial equator** is merely the extension into space (an imaginary celestial dome) of the *Earth's geographical equator*. This means that we consider "true north" and "true south" to be the celestial poles (as opposed to the *magnetic*

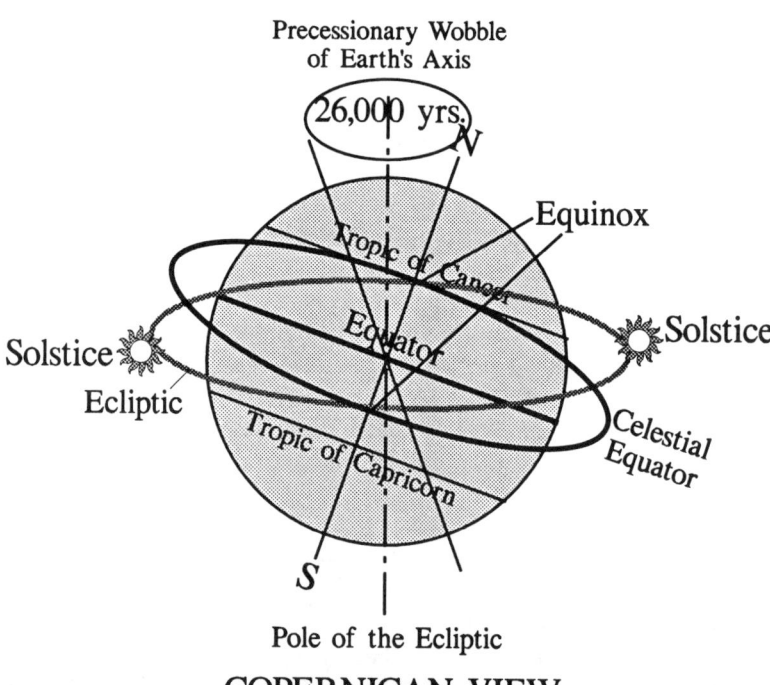

COPERNICAN VIEW

poles). The Pole Star in the Northern Hemisphere is an easily visible star that happens to appear to be positioned close to the **celestial North Pole**. Locating a Pole Star is important for navigational reasons, though there happens to be no pole star in today's southern sky. (Gallant, 28)

Take a quick look at a world map or a globe and you can readily see why world history is oriented to the **Northern Hemisphere** and the North Pole. All biblical events took place north of the equator. All of the world's *major* civilizations, ancient and modern, are found in the Northern Hemisphere. Only the Incas and pre-Incas represent what could be called a major, organized civilization or empire south of the equator. Historically, the **Southern Hemisphere** has been viewed as a region for exploration and high adventure.

For at least some 3,000 years, **Polaris**, the end star and brightest-appearing star of the **Little Dipper** (*Ursa Minor*), has been the North Star or Pole Star. At present, it appears to us on Earth to be located one degree from the celestial North Pole and is calculated to pass closest to true north (a distance of about 27 feet) in the year A.D. 2102. (Gallant, 27; EB 1972, 18:151) The Pole Star is always visible, (except for clouds) every night, all year, as it and the constellations around it *never set below the horizon*, and everything else appears to revolve around it. Because of its **navigational significance**, Polaris has been called the Lodestar, the Steering Star, and the Ship Star. From China to Scandinavia, ancient cultures have seen it as some sort of **World Spike** or **Golden Peg** around which the stars of the northern sky revolve. (Gallant, 24) It is also called the **North Nail**. (De Santillana, Hamlet's, 232)

However, because of precessional motion, the northern Pole Star *has not always been Polaris*, and, going by astronomical calculations based on the absence of any unusual celestial occurrence, there are long periods of time when there is no Pole Star. (Gallant, 28) When the **Great Pyramid** of Pharoah Khufu (Cheops) was built at Gizeh (or Giza) in Egypt, the North Pole Star was **Thuban** (Draconis), a tail star in the constellation **Draco the Dragon**. Thuban means *"the subtle"* in Hebrew, according to E. W. Bullinger, as in Gen. 3:1. Job refers to the crooked serpent which God formed in the heavens. This is universally recognized by Biblicists and pagans alike as Draco the Dragon, that Old Serpent, the Devil, the serpent of that central prophecy of Gen. 3:15. (Job 26:13; Bullinger, Witness, 71-3)

It has been determined that the Great Pyramid was actually planned and built around the location of this ancient Pole Star. The descending passage of the pyramid aligns with true north and Thuban was visible day and night from the bottom of this shaft. (Gallant, 38) *Whoever designed and built the pyramid knew where to find true north.* Today, after some 4200 or more years, the *pyramid's orientation to north* is off only three minutes (3/60) of a degree, while the modern-day Paris Observatory is six minutes of a degree off of true north. (Capt, Great, 11; see Chap. 10)

Astronomer Roy Gallant estimates the construction of the Great Pyramid, aligned with Thuban as Pole Star, took place about 3000 B.C. (Gallant, 38) Archaeologist and pyramidologist E. Raymond Capt gives the ground-breaking date as 2623 B.C. (Capt, Great, 5) Obviously, according to our dating calculations, these dates would place the building of the pyramid before the Flood, and, even though some ancient sources (including Josephus) attribute the edifice to Enoch or Seth, it is difficult to imagine even the Great Pyramid surviving the Flood.

However, Capt also says that, in 1840, **Sir John Herschel**, the famous Astronomer Royal of England, calculated the 2100s B.C. as the only time that Thuban, the ancient Pole Star, shined directly down the descending passageway. In fact, Sir John also found that the **Pleiades** were aligned with the peculiar scored lines found on the wall of the descending passageway about 40 feet from the entrance. He further calculated that the **Pleiades and Thuban** *were in the precise locations indicated by the pyramid* at the **vernal equinox of 2141** B.C. (Capt, Great, 75) This last date would place the pyramid's construction in the *latter days of Peleg*. This seems most reasonable as it would have to have been built after the Tower of Babel dispersion and we approximate the **Babel** judgement to have taken place **around 2174** B.C.

So, according to these astronomers, Thuban was the Pole Star for perhaps 1,000 or 1,500 years after the Flood. The **Greeks realized by 320 B.C.** that Polaris did not mark the pole precisely and that the Pole Star changes over the centuries. The Egyptians, or whoever built the Great Pyramid, probably realized this long before the Greeks wrote about it, and the sons of Seth and the Babylonians probably knew about it from the beginning (unless the precessionary wobble did not begin until after the Flood). Dr. Stecchini argues that the ancient Egyptians did indeed understand and track the precession, while astronomer Sir Norman Lockyer's writings state that the ancient Babylonians distinguished the pole of the equator from the pole of the ecliptic. Thus, the Greek Hipparchus only *re*discovered this phenomenon in 127 B.C. (Tompkins, Secrets, 174; De Santillana, Hamlet's, 66, 142)

It is interesting, if all of this is correct, that the first 1,000 or 1,500 years of history after the Flood involved the *removal of the Pole Star from the Dragon*, or, perhaps, a **symbol of the removal of Satan's domain over the Earth.** The ancient semitic name of Polaris is *Al Ruccaba*, which means *the turned* or *ridden on*. Bullinger believes that this name is far more ancient than Polaris's actual position as Pole Star, and he is correct if this is the name originally given the star by God. (Bullinger, Witness, 152)

Dr. Immanuel Velikovsky notes that 1st-Century Roman philosopher **Seneca** wrote that the Pole Star was once in the constellation of the **Great Bear** (includes the Big Dipper) before it moved to the Lesser Bear (Little Dipper). **Hindu** astronomical tablets from before the 500s B.C. gave the Great Bear as the location of the Pole Star, and the **Egyptians** are known to have used a Pole Star located in the Great Bear (or the Ox's Leg). (Velikovsky, Worlds, 312-14)

Dr. Velikovsky's works suggest that one or more catastrophic events involving comets and planets caused changes in the Earth's pole positions that are not accounted for by the precession of equinoxes or any other accepted astronomical phenomenon. In other words, he presents evidence that the Earth may have tipped over sideways, or over completely, perhaps more than once, and that the apparent paths of the Sun and stars have changed several times due to cosmic influences. We considered this evidence carefully — and there are a number of scientists and philosophers, both Christian and secular, who promote **pole-shift** and **axis-tilt theories** — but we believe the Bible offers a better explanation which we will examine below under the heading "Heliocentricity vs. Geocentricity." However, Dr. Velikovsky certainly understood catastrophism and we agree in general that there is evidence to show that there have been changes in the heavens.

Unhinging the Universe?

Remember from the introduction to this section on star movements the interesting statement made by Josephus concerning the length of the Great Year? The **Great Year** is the time it takes to complete one **full precession of the equinoxes**, which is calculated today as taking anywhere from **25,560** to **25,920** years. How could Josephus say that it took only some **600** years and thus could be accomplished within one pre-Flood lifetime? We have determined that the Earth was drastically different before the Flood. What about the heavens? Is Josephus's statement accurate? Was there indeed a minor pre-Flood precession that only took 600 years to accomplish? *Was there actually any precession at all?* We know from the Bible that heaven (the entire Creation) travails under the Curse. (Rom. 8:19-23; Job 15:15, 25:5) We know from science that the other planets in our solar system are hellish witnesses to cosmic violence and meteorological extremes. Are exploding stars, asteroids, and comets the debris of an on-going spiritual war in heaven? Did God involve His heavens in the judgements at Lucifer's Fall, Man's Fall, the Flood, Babel, the Exodus? (Judges 5:20)

From their extensive research of ancient mythology worldwide, **Drs. Giorgio de Santillana and Hertha von Dechend** determined that the roots of **mythology** are actually a very real, accurate, and sophisticated cosmology — **a record of the heavens**. We agree. Where we disagree is in the areas of theology and history. While we believe the Bible, they don't. And we believe that mythology is also **a record of the Mysteries**, and a veiled and often perverted version of biblical, historical truth. They see only the heavens and the ancients' concept of time.

De Santillana and Von Dechend discovered that their explorations revolved around the **precession of the equinoxes**, a phenomenon that the ancients universally connected with the disturbance of an existing harmony, "a kind of cosmogonic 'original sin,'" which involved the "unhinging" of the equator from the ecliptic, introducing *cycles of change*. There was once a **Golden Age**, a paradise, ruled by Titans, headed by the Craftsman God (Demi-urge, Lord of the Golden Age, Once and Future King), who turned the Mill of Heaven which ground out gold, peace, and plenty. Then the Titans overstepped their bounds and the **Golden Lord (Saturn, Kronos)** separated the "parents of the world" (equator and ecliptic) and "Time" (Ages) came into being. Or, as **Marduk** says in the Babylonian *Era-Epos* tablets, *"'When I stood up from my seat and let the flood break in, then the judgement of Earth and Heaven went out of joint...The gods, which trembled, the stars of heaven — their position changed, and I did not bring them back.'"* (De Santillana, Hamlet's, 2-5, 152-3, 323-5)

Marduk was king of the younger gods (Pritchard, Ancient, 31), and we have identified him as **Nimrod**, leading the rebels against the "older gods" (Titans), Noah and Shem. We have also identified Nimrod with Saturn and Kronos. The Golden Age refers to the pre-Flood world, and perhaps also to the pre-Fall world in Eden. The *Titans overstepping their bounds* may refer to: **1)** Satan's angels cohabiting with pre-Flood women, **2)** to pre-Flood Cainites and/or angelic/human half-breeds rebelling against God, **3)** to post-Flood patriarchs trying to assert *godly* authority, and **4)** to the orbits of planets like Venus, Mars, Saturn, and Jupiter which God may have used in His orchestration of judgement. [Remember that Mystery mythology is a deliberate maze, layered with meanings, and so a historical Nimrod, for example, can be pictured as post-Flood and pre-Flood, father and son, victim and victor. That is why there are probably multiple meanings associated with the above reference to the Titans.]

The point is that the ancients saw the precession as having a beginning, as an upsetting event that "unhinged" the Mill of Heaven, as an event connected with judgement. The Mill fell to the bottom of the ocean and ground out **salt**, making the sea salty. (Did the ocean become salty only during and after the Flood?) The **Mill's axle taken out of its peg** — and the axle is also associated with a **World Tree** reaching from Earth to Heaven which was chopped down — opens the "navel of the world" and lets the Flood waters out upon the Earth. This unplugging of the hole or navel (or chopping of the tree) produces the **whirlpool** (the *Maelstrom*), which is associated with both the sea and the heavens. This whirlpool also represents the connection of the worlds of the living and the dead. Now the Mill lies at the bottom of the ocean grinding out rocks and sand. (De Santillana, Hamlet's, 5, 90-1, 214, 412)

Does the tree refer to the **Tree of Life** guarded against man after the Fall and removed from Earth before the Flood? (Gen. 3:24) De Santillana thinks the World Tree is actually the **Earth's axis**. (De Santillana, Hamlet's, 232) Hislop reminds us that, as the **true Messiah** is called the **Branch** (Jer. 23:5; Zech. 3:8), so **Nimrod as the false Messiah** is also identified with a branch, log, or tree. He was chopped down (and chopped up) and became a "dead stump," but is supposed to "come again" in a new incarnation as the divine child on the **winter solstice**. He is the "sacrificed" Yule log on "Mother-night" and "born of the fire" on winter-solstice morning (Dec. 25 in Roman days) as the "Tree that brings all divine gifts to men." (Hislop, 97-8)

It seems that the movement of the heavens which we observe as the precession of the equinoxes may have come about as a result, or even a cause, of the Flood. Did God partially "unhinge" His heavens in executing His judgement? Was this part of the war in heaven? It also seems that the pagans connected the judgement of the Flood with the judgement upon Nimrod.

The cutting down of the tree may also refer

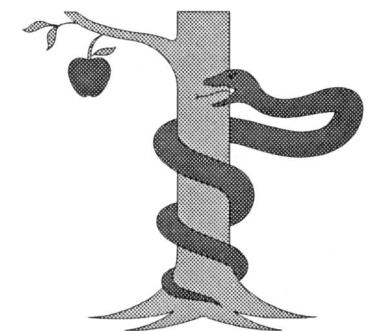

The Serpent (Satan) is often shown in both ancient and modern illustrations as wrapped around a tree or stump, symbolizing Nimrod.

to Eve eating the fruit of the **Tree of Knowledge of Good and Evil**. [Remember that Christians see the Tree of Life as the way to heaven, whereas pagans see the Tree of Knowledge as the way to heaven.] De Santillana and Von Dechend relate the *creation story* of the **Ackawois people of British Guiana** (now Guyana in South America). The great spirit's son is sent to rule over the Earth. One wonderful tree contains all of the plant life now cultivated on Earth, and the son decides to cut the tree down in order to spread this bounty all over the world. Once the tree is cut down, the son finds that the tree's stump is hollow and full of water and every kind of freshwater fish. However, the stump begins to overflow and so the son stops it by covering it with a basket. A mischievous monkey, thinking there would be something good to eat under the basket, lifts it and releases the Flood. (De Santillana, Hamlet's, 217-8)

Many more such stories exist around the world telling of **"a plug whose removal causes the flood,"** write De Santillana and Von Dechend. The **Agaria tribe of Central India** say that the breaking of an iron nail [the North Pole is the North Nail] caused their Golden Age city to be flooded. The **Mongolians** believe that the movements of heaven depend on the stability of the pillar of the Pole Star. This star is also a stone which, if unplugged, lets out water which submerges the Earth. (De Santillana, Hamlet's, 219)

In applying his pioneering work on the decay of the speed of light to chronology, Barry Setterfield cites a study by **George F. Dodwell**, the late Government Astronomer of South Australia. Dodwell compiled **66 ancient astronomical observations** having to do with the **path of the ecliptic** in relation to the Earth's equator. When charted on a graph, the observations plot a curve that indicates the equator and ecliptic came "unhinged" in **2345 B.C.**, which happens to be *precisely our date for the Flood*. [Setterfield's own date for the Flood is 3536 B.C. He believes that 2345 B.C. would have been in the days of Terah, Abraham's father.]

The *accepted explanation* is that the **Earth's axis tilted** at this time. According to the chart, it looks to have been "pushed over" about 26½°. Then, like a top or gyroscope, it returned to a new position of balance and gradually stabilized, writes Setterfield, at the present 23½° angle. This conclusion is said to be verified geologically, archaeologically, and climatically by Dr. M.M. Mandelkehr of the United States who collated worldwide data which points to the same "unhinging" in 2300 B.C. (Setterfield, Geological, 8, 11, 16)

Certain creationists, including retired Air Force Colonel, Dr. Walter T. Brown, Jr. (Center for Scientific Creation, Phoenix, AZ), believe that Earth's axis tilt was caused by the Flood. (Setterfield, Geological, 12) **Actually, however, from mere observation of the ecliptic path, we cannot tell if: 1)** the Earth's axis tilted, or **2)** the star dome or Universe tilted on its own axis and took on a slight wobble. All we know is that something to this effect happened, seemingly caused by the Flood, and greatly upset the ancients.

If the path of the Sun — the ecliptic — was not angled or tilted or "out of joint" before the Flood, the only way the pagans could have known that fact is from Noah and his family. And, if the World Tree — the Earth's axis — was verticle in relationship to the plane of the Sun's equator (not tilted), then the **ecliptic would have been steady at right angles to the axis**, parallel to the equator. Before the Flood, the crystallized hydrogen canopy diffused the Sun's heat and light. Thus, though there must have been some sort of growing and harvesting cycle before the Flood, there were not the **harsh seasonal changes** that we know today, so that Noah and his sons were required to adapt their knowledge of astronomy and related mathemat-

---

Star Pictures

Star charts, planispheres, and drawings of the Zodiac signs are easy to find in public libraries and usually very reasonably priced in secular book stores, specialty shops and planetariums. Christian books on the divine meanings of the heavenly configurations are also relatively easy to obtain through Christian book stores or catalogs. A simple set of binoculars and a star chart can greatly enhance your knowledge of God's handiwork.

ics to the "new heavens" of the post-Flood world. Anticipating the new seasons would be crucial to agriculture in the "New World." What is intriguing is that the **Mayas of Central America** represent the ecliptic with a double-headed serpent that crosses the World Tree at right angles on the night of Creation. Some archaeoastronomers think the Mayan World Tree is the Milky Way. (Wertime, "Written," *Archaeology*, July/August 1993, 30) However, if it is actually the Earth's axis, were the Maya saying that the ecliptic was perpendicular to the axis at Creation? Does that show remnants of pre-Flood knowledge taught by Noah, diffused to the Americas?

The Heavens and Measurement

The Bible clearly teaches us that accurate (and honest) measurement is **important to God**. Divine and human construction are closely linked by the same symbols. Read Job 38 and note that God laid the **Earth's foundations and its measures** and stretched a line upon it, just as the Egyptians did in their own construction projects. Isaiah 40:12 tells us that God measured the waters in the hollow of His hand, **measured out heaven** with the span [4 fingers=1 hand; 3 hands=1 span (Scofield KJV, note II Chron. 2:10)], put the dust of the Earth in a measure, and weighed the mountains and hills on scales. We know that God numbers the stars (Ps. 147:4) and the hairs on our heads (Matt. 10:30). The Ark, Tabernacle, Ark of the Covenant, Solomon's Temple, and the New Jerusalem are all carefully built to measure (Gen. 5; Ex. 36-38; I Kgs. 6, 7; Rev. 21), and **every number has meaning and purpose**. (See Bullinger's *Number in Scripture*) We noted in Chapter 2 how God carefully numbered the ages of the patriarchs in the Genesis genealogies. The numbering of **days and years** is very important to God, as is shown in Gen. 1:14, in the Flood account of Gen. 7 and 8, in the observance of the feasts listed in Leviticus 23, and in the many prophecies such as is given in Dan. 9. The Bible is written in Hebrew and Greek, both of which are numerical languages, meaning each letter has a number, each word and sentence have a value, and each number, once again, has a meaning. (See Jerry Lucas's *Theomatics*, the work of Ivan Panin, and many other studies on this subject.)

Time, construction (masonry), astronomy, and music are all based on mathematics, and though godly pursuits, they have always been obsessions of the pagans. Remember that **Cush** was **Hermes**, Her-mes meaning *son of Ham*. Hermes and Mercury were the same, and Plato credits Mercury with "inventing" arithmetic, calculation, geometry, astronomy, dice games, and the written language. Cush was connected with language because of the Tower of Babel and, as the son of Ham, most likely played a pivotal role in disseminating pre-Flood knowledge. Cush's son **Nimrod** was **Saturn** (and Enki/Ea and Ptah) who was the **Lord of Measures**. (De Santillana, Hamlet's, 135, 271) Nimrod was also connected with **Kronos** and Jupiter. Kronos means time. Saturn is also the heavenly *plumb line*. The pagans carefully tracked the **conjunctions of Jupiter and Saturn** as an aid in following the precession. (De Santillana, Hamlet's, 268-272)

Just as God is the true Measurer, **Marduk/Jupiter/Zeus**, the king of the young gods (Nimrod the Rebel), went forth in the **Babylonian Creation Epic** called the *Enuma Elish* to measure the New World. [Instead of original Creation, this actually would have been the New World after the Flood, or a mythological mixing of both Creation and the post-Flood world.] He crosses and surveys the heavens, "squares *Apsu's* quarter" and measures its dimensions, and assigns stations to the constellations and the Zodiac (*Ea* represents Capricorn the Goat/Fish and *Enlil* is Cancer the Crab or Sacred Beetle). He designates the new "zones" of the Tropics (Ea and Enlil), caused by the new precession, defines the days of the year by the heavenly bodies, and assigns three constellations to each of the 12 months, each of which has a sign of the Zodiac. These **36** *decans* were adopted by the Egyptians. (Pritchard, Ancient, 31-6; De Santillana, Hamlet's, 430-1)

As long as anyone can tell, **circles have been divided into 360°**. The 12 designated constellations just happen to be placed more or less evenly along the 360-degree circle of the Zodiac at *roughly* 30-degree intervals. The Babylonians, the Egyptians, the Chinese, the Hebrews—in fact, *all* the ancients—originally had **calendars of 360-day years**, and all of them eventually changed their calendars to match the "solar year" of roughly **365¼ days** (actually

365.242). (Timetables, 2-3; Capt, 72) We just saw how the Babylonian Marduk established 12 months for the year. They must have kept the same **30-day month** used in Genesis before the Flood because the Egyptians assigned 10 days to each of the three decans in each month. The 12 months and 36 decans are illustrated on the Dendera Zodiac.

The first logical conclusion is that the **number 360** was a major mathematical foundation of the original heavens and Earth. In the Bible, the **number 12** stands for *governmental perfection*. Just a few examples of its usage are the 12 tribes of Israel, the 12 apostles, and, in Revelation, the 24 elders (2 x 12), the 144,000 sealed Jews (12 x 12,000), and the 12,000 furlongs of the New Jerusalem. Twelve months of 30 days equals a 360-day year. The number 360 is also divisible by **40**, another biblically significant number relating to periods of *trial and probation*. The **number 10** stands for the *perfection of Divine order*, as in the Ten Commandments, and the **number 30** is a number of *maturity*. (Bullinger, Numbers, 243, 253, 265-6) The second logical conclusion is that, at sometime in Earth's history, something drastic happened to change the length of the solar year from 360 days to 365.242.

In Chapters 10 and 11 we will examine the significance and ramifications of the ancients' sophisticated abilities in mathematics, astronomy, and measurement, as well as the question of the calendar change.

The Cardinal Directions

With an excellent knowledge of astronomy and mathematics, post-Babel man certainly understood the **cardinal** (principal or major) **directions** of *north, south, east,* and *west*. It is interesting that, immediately after Creation, God planted **Eden "in the east."** (Gen. 2:8, KJV) East of what? There was no western world, no Egypt, no Israel. We know that Genesis was actually written by Moses sometime during the journey between Egypt and Canaan, which we would date in the 40 years after 1488 B.C., when there indeed *was* an Egypt and a Canaan. But Genesis gives us the impression that "the east" was always "the east," from the beginning.

As there is no time with God, it may be safe to assume that, even before its existence, **Jerusalem** was the **center of the world**, meaning that Eden was east of the future site of Jerusalem. (According to the Bible, no matter where a person is, he goes *up* to Jerusalem.) In Hebrew, the word for **"east"** actually means **"ancient,"** or that which went before, or "the forepart," that which comes or goes before, or is

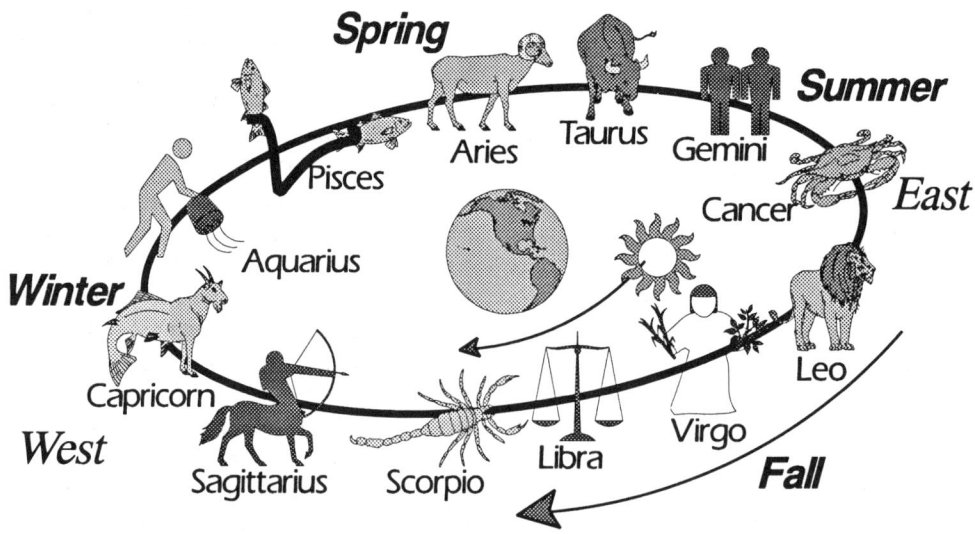

What We See in the Sky: Stars and Sun go around Earth ONCE A DAY. Because the Sun's orbit speed is faster than that of the stars (perhaps because it is closer to Earth and has less distance to travel), the Sun moves through the Zodiac ONCE A YEAR. (About one sign per month.) However, each *year*, the Sun "loses" about 50 seconds of a degree in its orbit time compared to the stars, edging slightly "backwards" so that the vernal equinox moves about every 2,100 years from Taurus to Aries to Pisces to Aquarius.

located in front. (Strong's) Now, this definition is particularly interesting considering our discussion in Chap. 1 (p. 6) of Ezek. 28 and the statement that Lucifer was in a jeweled Eden, the Garden of God, before he sinned.

As early as Gen. 13:14, God tells Abraham (Abram) to look north, south, east, and west. According to historical records, the **ancient Semitic** peoples regarded **east** in the same way that we Westerners today regard north, as our **directional standard of reference** and our main map direction. (Fell, Bronze, 125) The *Mishna*, the first part of the *Talmud* written by Jewish rabbis, records that the entrance of **Herod's Temple**, the Beautiful Gate, was directly opposite the **Eastern Gate** of the city of Jerusalem. (Jeffrey, Armageddon, 125, 127) Most probably, the entrance of **Solomon's Temple** also faced east, as did the gate of its prototype, the **Tabernacle**. (Ex. 38:13-14) In the wilderness, the assigned position of the tribe of Judah was on the east side of the Hebrew camp, (Num. 2:3) and Ezekiel witnessed the glory of the Lord leaving Solomon's Temple by the east gate. (Eze. 10:19, 11:23)

Chapters 43 and 44 of Ezekiel explain that the Lord will return to a rebuilt **Millennial Temple** through a future eastern gate. Dr. Charles Dyer points out that the dimensions of Ezekiel's east gate differ from the Eastern Gate (or Golden Gate) of Herod's Temple. **Herod's Eastern Gate was sealed** and remains so today, despite the fact that **King Hussein** of Jordan in **1967** ordered the gate opened to provide access to a planned Arab luxury hotel. A crane and air hammers were brought to the site and work was to begin on June 7. On June 6, the Israelis captured Jerusalem in the famous **Six-Day War**, reuniting Jerusalem under Jewish control for the first time in nearly 2,000 years. Due to the fact that Herod's Eastern Gate was sealed, and to such events as this miraculous Jewish victory which saved the gate only hours before its "desecration," many believe that Christ will enter Jerusalem (the city, not the new Temple) through this very Eastern Gate following His victory at Armageddon and His return to the Mount of Olives. Perhaps this is true, since Ezekiel's east gate to which Dyer refers belongs to the new Temple proper, which may not be completed until after the Millennium begins. (Church, Hidden, 183; Dyer, BKC, "Ezekiel," 1309)

Since the ancient Semites (Mesopotamians or Babylonians) regarded east as their direction of reference (and, later, reverence), they would face east in order to name the other cardinal points. Naturally, **east** was most often referred to as the direction of the **sunrise** and **west** as the direction of the **sunset**. **South** then became the **"right-hand"** direction and **north**, the **"left-hand"** direction. We will find that this same method was carried by the post-Babel migrants rather quickly into ancient **Scandinavia**, where south was referred to as "to the right" and east was the only direction with a proper name. (Fell, Bronze, 125-6) We will also find that the sacredness of the four cardinal directions is a fundamental belief among most Native Americans (Amerindians). (Hadingham, Early, 94)

However, De Santillana and Von Dechend write that the **Egyptians** considered east *as* the **face of the world** and so actually **looked west** when naming north as right and south as left. The Egyptian lament sung for Cronus (Nimrod/ Tammuz) honored him who was born in the regions on the left (south) and was "terminated" in the regions on the right (north). Nimrod was executed by Shem, God's representative, and north is God's direction. (De Santillana, Hamlet's, 283) Egypt's Sphinx of Giza faces due east. East being the direction of sunrise makes it important to any culture which worships the Sun.

According to the famous calendar stone found among the **Aztecs** of ancient Mexico City, **south** was the major and sacred direction of that people and perhaps their ancestors, just as it was with the ancient **Chinese** and pagan sunworshippers in general who believed that south was the principal pole and the divine location. (Johnston, Phoenicians, 86-7; Berlitz, Mysteries, 37) The fallen Lord of the Golden Age supposedly sleeps at the South Pole, often in the star Canopus. (De Santillana, Hamlet's, 265) According to legend, the Chinese emperor in what is conventionally dated as 2634 B.C. crushed a rebellion, directing his troops through fog with a chariot that carried a human figure with an outstretched arm that always pointed south. (EB, 1972, 6:225; see Chap. 12 for further discussion of the early compass)

What is interesting is that the **Bible** regards **north** as **God's direction**, indicating that Mount Zion, the mount of the congregation, and God's throne are in "the sides of the north." (Isa. 14:13; Ps. 48:2) The Hebrew word for north means "hidden," "dark," or "unknown." (Strong's) *Do these verses imply that the Universe itself has directions, and that "north" is more than just one end of Earth's axis?*

Dr. Emil Gaverluk has written an intriguing discourse on the discovery of the **supercluster of galaxies** around the **constellation Virgo**. At the heart of the cluster is galaxy **M87** which emits about one million times more energy than a typical spiral galaxy. Ezekiel describes the throne of God as amber in color. M87 is described in the May 1987 issue of *Astronomy* magazine as amber in color. Dr. Gaverluk believes that M87 may be the location of God's throne in this Universe. (Gaverluk, Rapture, 191-9, 284-5) Others believe that God's throne is in the "third heaven" spoken of by Paul in II Cor. 12:1-4, the "first heaven" being Earth's atmosphere and the "second heaven" the stars, or what we would call the Universe or "space." (Scofield notes, II Cor. 12:1-4; Hanson, "The Bible and Geocentricity," Bib. Astro. I:56, pp. 28-32 and Bib. Astro. I:55) Since creatures cannot exist outside of Creation, the Creator must have some place *within* Creation that would allow His creatures to appear before Him *en masse*, as in Job or in Revelation.

We will examine some informative applications of directions and orientation in Chapters 10, 11, and 12, as well as in our discussion below of Heliocentricity vs. Geocentricity.

Heliocentricity vs. Geocentricity

Any educated person today knows that the **Earth rotates on its axis** and **orbits around the Sun** and that the movements of the Sun and the stars across the sky are merely *apparent* due to the Earth's movement. Thus, when the Bible states that the Sun rises and sets, it is merely using the *"everyday"* language we all use in daily life to describe what we observe. The idea that the **Earth does not move** and the **Sun goes around it** is *intuitive*, meaning it's what our senses tell us is happening. We see the Sun rise and set. We don't feel the Earth move. In fact, we sheepishly accept the explanation that some force called gravity holds us to the Earth which is spinning beneath us at roughly 740 miles per hour at 45° latitude (that's about *1,085 feet per second* at the latitude of Portland, Oregon, or southern France), and speeding around the Sun at about 67,000 miles per hour (while who knows what all carries us with our Solar System and our Milky Way Galaxy hurtling through space) and *we don't feel a thing!* (Hanson, "History and Geocentricity," Bib. Astron. I:58, p. 7) But, obviously, the space program has proved Copernicus correct and our senses are wrong. Right? Guess again!

For almost 3,600 years, men firmly believed that the Earth was the center of the Universe, that the Earth was immovable, and that everything they observed in the sky circled around the Earth. This model of the Universe is called *geocentricity*.

Then **about 450 B.C.**, a Greek philosopher and student of Pythagorus called **Philolaus** proposed that the Earth, the Sun, and the five visible planets (Mercury, Venus, Mars, Saturn, and Jupiter) move around a central lake of fire, that the Sun is a giant mirror that merely reflects the lake of fire, that the Earth rotates on its axis, and that the Earth is too bad a place and not worthy to be located at the center of the heavens. This is the **first recorded step in the direction that 1) the Earth moves, and 2) the Earth is not special and is not central in Creation.**

In the 300s B.C., **Heracleides Ponticus** pointed out that *Mercury and Venus are never seen to venture too far from the Sun*, meaning that they probably revolve around the Sun while the Sun orbits the Earth. Over the next few centuries, most Greeks, including Plato and Aristotle, remained geocentrists, while Pythagoreans and others such as Aristarchus and Seleucus promoted *heliocentricity*, saying that the Earth orbits the Sun. However, **Claudius Ptolemy's** (A.D. 100s) geocentric model would hold official sway for another 1,500 years. (Asimov, Chronology, 44-5, 62; Hanson, "History and Geocentricity," Bib. Astron. I:59)

Ptolemy modeled a series of concentric spheres with the Earth at the center, then the Moon, Mercury, Venus, the Sun, Mars, Saturn, Jupiter, and the star dome. However, the movements of the heavens are complicated to explain, and so Ptolemy devised a method of mathematical computation (*Fourier, or harmonic, analysis*) using combinations of circles (*epicyclic motion*) which, despite much modern Ptolemy bashing, is still used today to assign an orbit to observed data. (Hanson, "History," Bib. Astron. I:59)

The Copernican Revolution

But Polish astronomer and canon (clergyman) **Nicolaus Copernicus** (1473-1543) decided things would be simpler if he revived the basic idea of Aristarchus and put the Sun at the center of the heavens. This, he believed, would make it easier to explain the abiding proximity of Venus and Mercury to the Sun, as well as the fact that the planets grow brighter and dimmer as they travel across the sky and occasionally appear to move backwards. Called retrograde motion, this observed behavior is merely the planets appearing to our eyes to move backwards for a time against the background of the stars which are also in motion. Copernicans have a much more difficult time accounting for this phenomenon than do geocentrists. (See the geocentricity series by James N. Hanson in the *Biblical Astronomer*, Fall 1990 to Summer 1992 for an excellent analysis of geocentricity and Copernicus's work.)

Educated in medieval Roman Catholic universities at Cracow, Poland, and Padua, Italy, with a doctorate in canon law (EB, 1972), Copernicus well knew that the Roman Catholic Church and the new Protestant reformers would seriously object to his work. Copernicus did not agree to make public his basically heliocentric theory until just before he died, when his book was complete. The main reason for the furious and widespread objections in 1543 was not that the theory flew in the face of experience, or that it overturned thousands of years of ancient wisdom, but that it *contradicted the then universally recognized fact that the Bible teaches geocentricity.*

One of the major points we want to make in this discussion, second only to the fact that the Bible is geocentrist, is the foundational, belief-shaping effect, clearly acknowledged by anti-biblicists, that Copernicus slowly but surely had on all of mankind. World-famous science and science-fiction writer Isaac Asimov explains that Copernicus totally overturned Greek astronomy, though it took 50 years for the heliocentric model to convince the majority of astronomers to reject Ptolemy. Copernicus's book, writes Asimov, "marked the birth of what came to be called the *Scientific Revolution*. With it came final proof that the ancients did *not* know it all and that moderns might strike out on their own in new directions and reach new heights — and they certainly did." (Asimov, Chronology, 109, italics as in original)

PLEASE CAREFULLY NOTE WHAT ASIMOV SAYS:

FIRST, this highly venerated, rarely-if-ever challenged expert tells you, without reservation, that there is *final proof* for the Copernican model. **There never has been any proof.** Copernicus had no proof at the time. Today, even the United States National Aeronautics and Space Administration **(NASA)** has no proof. That may be a shock, but that is indeed the case, and any honest physicist will admit that all observed phenomena are explainable by either model. In fact, non-mechanical experiments using light (Michelson-Morley), designed to prove Copernicus correct, continue to demonstrate a non-moving Earth. (Henry, "Geocentrism," Proceedings, 28; Hall, "Symbiotic," Proceedings, 16; Bouw, "Geocentricity" and "Foucault," Bulletin reprints) It may also be a shock to know that, while preaching a *moving* Earth, all **applied sciences** such as practical astronomy, navigation, rocketry, oceanography, and gyroscopy use the model of a *fixed* Earth. A 1989 government letter from the National Oceanic and Atmospheric Administration (NOAA) to researcher and author Marshall Hall documents that adjustments to geostationary satellites are planned and executed on the basis of a fixed Earth. (Goldberg, "Earth," Jewish Tribune, Jan. 11, 1990; Hall, The Earth, 261)

Absolute proof of what is and what is not moving in the Universe can only be determined by either **1)** establishing a **reference point** *inside* **the system** (the Universe) certain to be at absolute rest and/or **2)** observing moving bodies from a **vantage point** *outside* **the system** (Universe). Sir Isaac Newton speculated that there very well might be no object at rest in the system and merely *assumed* something called the "inertial field" as his absolute reference frame for his gravitational mathematics. Thus developed what is called **Newtonian Relativity**. What Newton speculated, Albert Einstein arbitrarily ordained into two theories that became **Einsteinian Relativity**. (More about this below.) As for number two above (looking into the system from outside), we know that there is only One capable of *that* field trip, and He is a geocentrist! (Henry, "Geocentrism," Proceedings, 22-5; Van der Kamp, Cosmos, 11)

SECOND, Asimov exults in "demonstrating" that the "ancients did *not* (his italics) know it all...." The two major points of *this* book (*They Came From Babel*) are **1)** that the Bible is divine, literal, infallible, and a reliable source of historical and scientific knowledge, supported by genuine secular discoveries, and **2)** that the ***ancients,*** in the realm of divinely imparted *human* knowledge, **did indeed *know it all.*** *Please note that Asimov points to Copernicus, not Darwin, as the seminal source of the Scientific Revolution and the emancipation of the moderns from the ancients.*

The Tychonic Model

For a while, the most famous astronomer in Europe was a young man from Denmark named **Tycho Brahe (1546-1601)** who gained his fame from his careful, 485-day-long observations of the supernova of 1572-4. He also gathered data on the movement of Mars that led his German assistant, **Johannes Kepler (1571-1630)** to reject Ptolemy's *circular* orbits and postulate *elliptical* ones. It is interesting that, in his book *The Earth is not Moving*, Marshall Hall reproduces a time-exposure photograph of stars moving through the sky around the Pole Star. The photo is a mass of concentric *circles*. Brahe died before the discovery (*re*discovery?) of the telescope, pleading from his deathbed for Kepler not to use Brahe's data to support Copernicanism. Hall makes the case that Kepler poisoned Brahe in order to do just that. (Hall, Earth, 42-53)

The modern discovery of the **telescope in 1608** was the result of a happy accident. An unnamed apprentice (talk about not getting credit!), playing with two lenses, looked through them at the scenery outside the office window of Dutch optometrist **Hans Lippershey (c. 1570-1619)**. Astonished, the apprentice reported that the bigger, closer, upside-down image he saw was actually a distant church steeple. Lippershey realized the implications, mounted the lenses in a tube, and *voilà!*, the telescope.

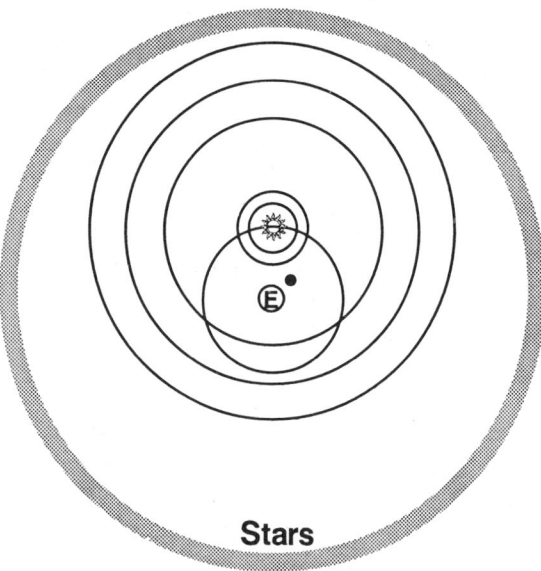 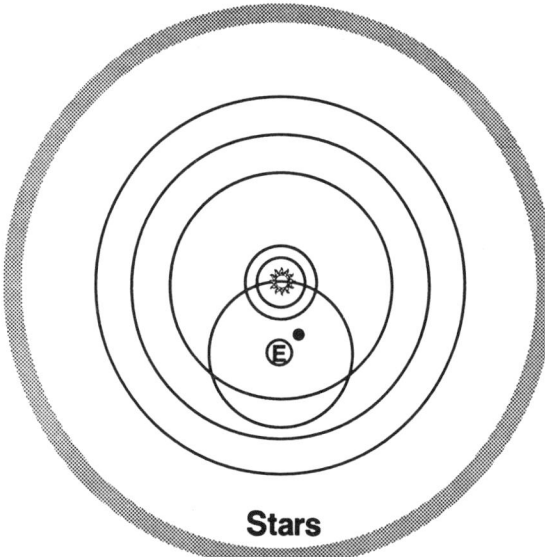

Tychonic Model   **Modified Tychonic Model**

Tycho Brahe modeled the Universe with the Earth at the center, the Sun revolving around the Earth, and the planets around the Sun, with the stars revolving around it all. In the above diagrams, the black spot is the Moon. The Sun is orbited by Mercury, Venus, Mars, Saturn, and Jupiter. In the modified model, the Sun is placed at the center. According to Dr. Bouw, the Sun and the stars revolve east to west (clockwise, looking down at N Pole) around Earth *daily*, while the entire Universe *oscillates counter-clockwise* around Earth *yearly*. (Bib. Astron., No. 58, p. 15) Ptolemy's earlier model centered Sun, stars, and *planets* around Earth.

Italian astronomer **Galileo Galilei (1564-1642)** *improved* the telescope and offered a *public* argument, in Italian (not scholarly Latin), for the basic heliocentric model (Earth and all the planets moving around the Sun). Galileo gained fame for his sarcastic writing and his 1633 trial before the Catholic Inquisition. Threatened with torture, the 70-year-old Galileo recanted. He lost the battle, so to speak, but won the war. Heliocentricity continued to gain favor. (Asimov, Chronology, 117, 130-3, 141) We are forced to admit that the inquisitors realized the foundational and pivotal effect of the Copernican Revolution. Whether or not their motives were purely to protect the Bible or were tainted with the desire to protect their own positions, Galileo's Bible-bashing heresy was serious business indeed.

"Our **present picture of the Solar System**," writes Asimov, "remains essentially that worked out by **Kepler**. No substantial change is expected in the future." (Asimov, Chronology, 131) However, the model of the Universe constructed by Kepler's mentor, Tycho Brahe, is the basis for the *modern geocentric movement* (thus, the **Tychonian Society**). Tycho, as he is referred to, agreed that the planets orbit the Sun, but maintained that the Sun and all the planets revolve around the Earth, which is the fixed, unmoving, center of the Universe. (Van der Kamp, Cosmos, 8, back cover) In other words, the planets center on the Sun, but the Moon, the Sun, and the stars of heaven all center on the Earth. This is called the Tychonian model.

Most, but not all, of today's geocentrists are **creationists**. As you can well imagine, geocentrists are few and far between, even though their ranks include highly credentialed experts in a variety of scientific fields, including astronomy. **Geocentric creationists are a small group** among their own fellow creationists who mostly look askance at such a "crackpot" and "primitive" notion. Regrettably, instead of being a topic of healthy, fruitful, and friendly discussion and exploration, geocentricity is a **subject of extreme controversy and heated debate**. Rocking boats, crossing grains, and questioning traditions is never popular, no matter one's background, philosophical group, motive, or evidence.

On the one hand, many creationists have the same reaction as evolutionists when geocentricity is mentioned — "Oh, right, let's go back to the Flat Earth Society." (It was this writer's initial personal reaction.) If we stop and think about it, that very common reaction demonstrates how thoroughly we have been "Copernicanized." And any good Berean should always stop and *think*.

On the other hand, a number of prominent creationists might be willing to consider, or even admit to, the geocentric viewpoint, but genuinely, and somewhat understandably, fear that 10, 20, or 30 years of uphill battles to gain a mere measure of professional respect in the evolution/creation debate would be destroyed by such a controversial stand. Isn't it interesting that such intuitively foreign concepts as order from disorder, reversible time, relative time, and parallel universes should entertain serious discussion and even acceptance, while the simple idea that possibly — just possibly — what we observe in the sky is actually what is occurring is branded as bizarre and quackish?

Geocentrists themselves are not in total agreement. However, many have adopted a **modified Tychonic model** in which the Sun is in the "midst of heaven" (Josh. 10:13), with the *stars* as well as the planets centered on the *Sun*, while the Moon and the Sun center on the Earth. [Perhaps they have other reasons for this model, but that particular verse seems to say merely that the Sun stopped and stayed in the middle of the sky for "about a whole day."] Geocentrist, creationist, and computer scientist James Hanson rejects both the Tychonic and modified Tychonic models because he believes that the Bible teaches a **strict geocentric model**, "whereby the [E]arth is the center of *all* celestial motions." (Hanson, "History," Bib. Astron., I:58, 10)

Experiments and Observations

Subjects that are the stuff of Geocentricity 101 are: the Michelson-Morley and related experiments, geosynchronous (or geostationary) satellites, the Foucault pendulum, and stellar parallax and/or aberration, just to barely scratch the surface. Here, we will briefly introduce these subjects and some reference works by those who are qualified to deal with them. [**We can't even begin to deal adequately with geocentricity in this book,** but we do plan (Lord willing) to put together a book totally separate from this

American history series which will describe this debate in much more detail, along with the work of certain creationists on classical physics and an electromagnetic theory of the Universe versus relativity, quantum physics, and chaos theory.]

MICHELSON-MORLEY: English mathematician and natural philosopher **Sir Isaac Newton (1642-1727)** voiced what had been known by Copernicus and Galileo, that *mechanical experiments* (observation of physical objects) cannot determine a reference point of absolute rest in an isolated system. In other words, you can only detect that your car is moving because you know for certain that the scenery around you and the road beneath you is *not* moving. Have you ever been caught off guard and noticed something moving beside you (like a big truck or another car) and slammed on your brakes automatically because, for an instant, you could not tell whethere you or the other object were in motion? Not until you frantically looked around for a known, stationary reference point could you regain your sensory perspective.

*And **neither can astronauts nor satellites nor space probes determine** whether or not the Earth is moving relative to the Moon, the Sun, the stars, or a satellite* without having an already determined, proven reference point of absolute rest. For a biblical geocentrist, that reference point is the fixed, stationary, motionless Earth. For the Copernican, there is no proven reference point and so mechanical experiments are useless.

Newton was very "religious" and apparently believed in a divine Creator. However, **Newton was not a Christian**. His views were anti-Trinitarian and, according to a London-published biography, he considered the worship of Christ as God to be idolatry and the fundamental sin. John Maynard Keynes calls Newton "'a **Judaic monotheist** of the school of Maimonides.'" (Hall, Earth, 88-9; EB, 1972, 16:421) Newton basically cast his lot with the Copernicans. He took the ideas of a universal gravitational force, the Moon's supposed effect on the tides, and the concept of inertia *from Kepler* and then developed differential calculus to support his "laws" of motion. (Hall, Earth, 86-7; EB, 1972, 16:420-1) Because he needed a fixed reference point, he chose what he called the *inertial field*. "Newton himself never figured out what his assumed-to-be-fixed inertial field consisted of or how it worked. He just took it to be his 'absolute space' to which he related his mass and motion. In other words, the physical cause of the 'F' in F=ma was never identified." (Elmendorf, "More on Geostationary," Bib. Astron. No. 63, p. 7)

What came to be called **Newtonian Relativity** (or Galilean Relativity) applies only to observers *within* the system, allowing that an observer *outside* the system could determine by mechanical means what was moving and what was at rest. It also allows for the possibility of determining a body at absolute rest within the system by way of *non-mechanical experiments* using electromagnetic radiation, or light. German-born U.S. physicist **Albert Einstein (1879-1955)** is said to have "rescued" Copernicanism because his theories of relativity are designed to show that absolute rest is *totally*

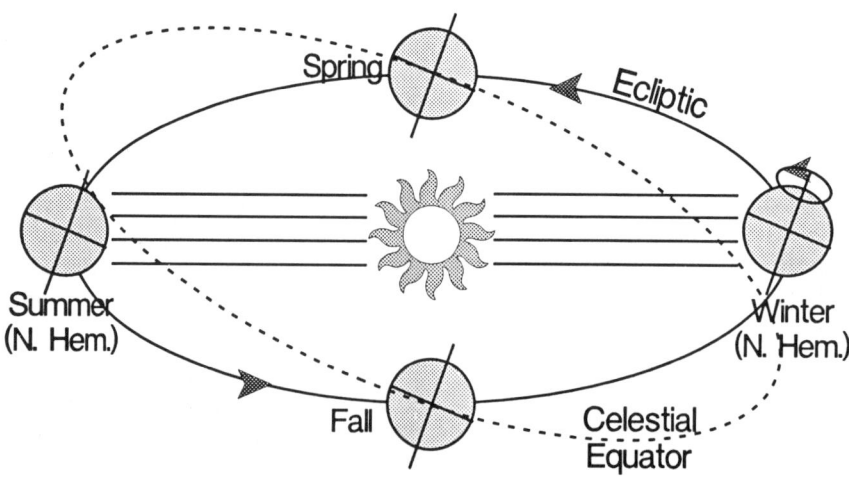

Copernican explanation of the seasons and Sun's yearly path across the sky

undetectable by any means. This is **Einsteinian Relativity**. (Henry, "Geocentrism," Proceedings, 21-3; Van der Kamp, Cosmos, 18-19, 53-4; Webster's) [The results of non-mechanical speed-of-light experiments depend, of course, on the movement or motionlessness of the light-carrying medium (aether). This is complicated stuff, but all Jonathan Henry is trying to establish here is the difference between Newtonian and Einsteinian viewpoints.]

Why did Einstein have to "rescue" Copernicus? One of the main reasons occurred in the 1880s. No one, including Newton, had provided any real proof by mechanical observation that the Earth moves. So German-born U.S. physicist **Albert Abraham Michelson (1852-1931)** decided to prove that the Earth was in motion using *non-mechanical* means, or light. Michelson took the ancient, and still valid, stance that the Universe is an integrated entity, an "aether," a "medium," a "fabric," through which light (which is a wave only and not a particle) moves. [A wave must have a medium through which to move. There can be no wave motion unless there is something to wave. (Barnes, Space, foreword)] Michelson reasoned that if the Earth is moving in respect to this aether, at roughly 67,000 miles per hour around the Sun, that he should be able to measure a **difference in the speed of light** moving **parallel to**, and **perpendicular to**, the **direction of Earth's motion**. So, in 1881, and in 1887 joined by Morley, and then many times thereafter, Michelson split a light beam so that one half traveled parallel to Earth's motion and the other half perpendicular to it. If Earth moves, the two halves **should have recombined out of phase**, showing up on the interferometer as an interference pattern or a "fringe shift." (Henry, "Geocentrism," Proceedings, 28-9; Van der Kamp, Cosmos, 14-15; Hanson, geocentricity series, Bib. Astron. I:58, 7)

"However," writes Dr. Jonathan Henry, **"no fringe shift was seen or ever has been seen** in any subsequent M-M [Michelson-Morley] type of experiment done on the [E]arth." (Henry, "Geocentrism," Proceedings, 28) "The Michelson-Morley experiment and its descendants have all measured the [E]arth's velocity to be zero," writes Professor Hanson. "Physicists hide this fact by referring to the measured results as *null results*," he continues. "This 'intolerable' situaltion precipitated by the Michelson-Morley experiment gave rise (after about 25 years of groping) to the mathematical metaphysical mystification called Einsteinian Relativity. In this way physicists tried to get the [E]arth moving again; albeit merely mathematically. The Michelson-Morley experiments have been performed yearly with ever-increasing precision since the 1880s and all with the same result: zero. **The [E]arth just won't move.**" (Hanson, geocentricity series, Bib. Astron. I:58, 7-8)

And so this is why in 1905 Einstein had to *declare* (not prove) that **1)** there is no light-carrying aether and thus **2)** space is basically a vacuum through which light, which is a particle, moves at an absolute constant speed,

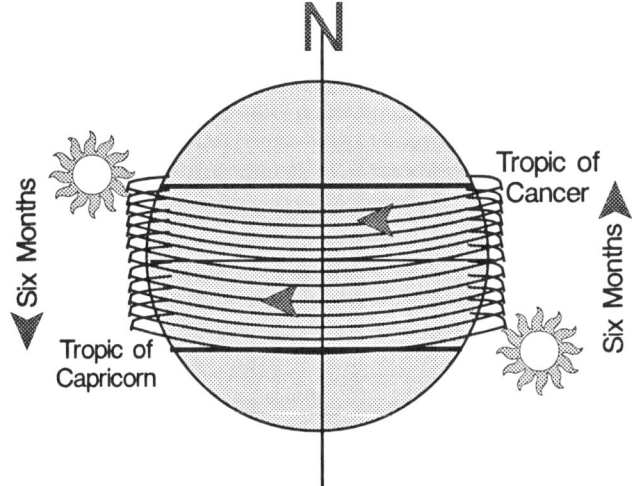

Geocentric explanation of the change in seasons.

This is a very rough illustation of the Sun orbiting east to west around the Earth in a fine-pitch, recursive spiral (double helical) path that moves from one Tropic to the other every six months. According to mechanical engineer Richard Elmendorf, the Moon "follows a similar recursive spiral path, but with a monthly rather than a yearly period. (Elmendorf, letter, 1993) Further details of the geocentric model must await more research and a book dedicated to the subject.

and 3) that "the speed of light in a vacuum is hence constant for all observers *regardless of the motion of the source or observer.*" (Van der Kamp, Cosmos, 18-19, italics added) And that's how Einstein "rescued" Copernicus. The work of creationist physicists Dr. Charles Lucas, Dr. Thomas Barnes, and Dr. Harold Slusher refutes the theories of Einsteinian Relativity. (see Chap. 9)

GEOSYNCHRONOUS (GEOSTATIONARY) SATELLITES: Now, what about geosynchronous satellites? These are satellites placed in **geosynchronous alley** about **23,300 miles** above Earth's equator. The standard *heliocentric* explanation is that, at this height, the angular velocity of the satellite is such that it moves with the Earth's rotation (and orbit), maintaining a constant position in regard to the Earth's surface (with the aid of periodic station-keeping maneuvers using wheels and jets due to unexplained anomalies), offsetting Earth's gravity with centrifugal force. (Elmendorf, "More on Geostationary," Bib. Astron., No. 63)

The *geocentric* explantion, based on a non-orbiting, non-rotating, non-moving Earth, takes into account all of the attendant forces produced by THE MASS AND MOVEMENT OF THE REST OF THE UNIVERSE, a Universe that is an integrated entity and space that is truly a wave-propagating medium. At 22,300 miles, the velocity of the satellite and its mass balances against the gravitational forces and velocity of the Universe and the gravity of the Earth. As mechanical engineer Richard G. Elmendorf writes, "whatever the satellite is doing, it is doing it with **respect to the inertial frame in which it [is] launched**. This is the key to the whole matter of geosynchronous satellites, and of gyroscopes and Foucault pendulums as well." (Elmendorf, "Geosynchonous," Bulletin of Tychonian Soc., No. 50)

The rotational, light-splitting Sagnac experiment (1913) was designed to measure the rotation of the aether about the Earth. Physicists can detect a rotational speed of 740 miles per hour at 45° latitude, but that, writes Hanson, is the speed of the aether (the Universe) rather than the speed of the Earth. (Hanson, geocentricity series, Bib. Astron. I:58, 7; Barnes, Space, 159-61. Note that Barnes discusses Sagnac with regard to the aether, not to geocentricity.)

FOUCAULT PENDULUM: French physicist **Jean Bernard Léon Foucault (1819-1868)** originally performed his pendulum experiments in 1851, supposedly "proving" that the Earth rotates on its axis. A long cable with a bob or weight on the end is suspended from a structure (like a cathedral ceiling) theoretically over the North Pole and put in motion. From a *heliocentric* viewpoint, the **inertial frame of the "fixed" Universe holds the pendulum while the Earth rotates beneath it.** The observed phenomenon is that the direction of the swinging pendulum changes so that the bob or weight travels around a complete circle in one 24-hour period. (Elmendorf, "Heliocentric Hocus-Pocus," paper, Feb. 12, 1993; Webster's)

However, in 1976, Dr. David Park, professor of physics at Thompsonville Physical Laboratory, Williamstown, Massachusetts, wrote that "**You don't have to explain it that way.** The laws of nature that you would use if you were interested in doing mathematical physics while assuming the [E]arth to be at rest would contain a velocity-dependent force that would act upon the pendulum in such a way as to produce the observed rotation." (As quoted by Bouw, "Foucault," reprint, Tychonian Society) In other words, as Austrian atheist physicist **Ernst Mach (1838-1916)** wrote in 1912, consider the cumulative effect of the inertia of the ROU – the rest of the Universe! **Stars whirling around a stationary Earth every 24 hours would account for the reported bulge of the Earth's equator and would drag the pendulum bob around like a leaf in a whirlpool.** This was also explained by a German physicist named Gerber in 1898. (Bouw, "Foucault," reprint, Tychonian Society; Webster's)

A famous example of the Foucault pendulum hangs in the **United Nations** building in New York City, a most appropriate location for a purported demonstration that the Earth rotates and the Bible is wrong. R.G. Elmendorf, currently pursuing his own pendulum investigations and experiments, notes that "various devices are used to make foucault pendulums operate correctly and do what they are supposed to do." (Elmendorf, "Heliocentric Hocus-Pocus," paper, Feb. 12, 1993)

STELLAR ABERRATION/PARALLAX: Editor of *The Biblical Astronomer* and a Ph.D. in astronomy, Gerardus D. Bouw, writes that *parallax* "is best illustrated by holding one's finger in front of one's face, closing one's left eye and noting against which point in the background the finger appears and then opening the left eye and closing the right eye. The finger will appear to have jumped against the background." (Bouw, "How Big," Bib. Astron. No. 64, p. 13)

Now, pick a post on your porch or a tree trunk in your yard or something similar. Note something such as a house or other object in the background some distance behind your post or tree. Now back up a short distance away from the post and then move several steps, first to one side, then the other. Note how the post *appears* to move relative to the house or object in the background. From experience, you know that the post is not moving and the house (background object) is not moving, so your brain tells you that *you* must be moving. Now move directly toward the post. It does not appear to move. Once again, this is called *parallax*, and involves only your motion *perpendicular* to the line from the post to the background object.

If you believe that Earth is merely another planet ("wanderer") and revolves around the Sun once a year, while the stars are relatively fixed (not revolving around the Earth), then you would expect a star closer to the Earth to exhibit the same parallax against more distant stars from the vantage point of Earth moving along in its orbit. This is precisely what British astronomer **James Bradley** and **Samuel Molyneux** expected to find in December of 1725 when they mounted a telescope to Molyneux's chimney. They picked a star in Draco the Dragon, very close to the North Pole, and observed it presumably over a year's time. Bradley did indeed find that the star, Gamma Draconis, "appeared" to move in a small circle with a radius of 20.5" (seconds) of arc. The problem was that Gamma Draconis did not move relative to the stars around and "behind" it. The rest of the stars joined in the motion and so, "consequently," writes Walter van der Kamp, "would all have to be situated at about the same distance from the Earth. In other words: to accept the phenomenon as a parallax would mean to reintroduce the discarded medieval image of a **Stellatum**, a gigantic 'shell' of stars...." which revolves, in some manner, around the Earth. (Van der Kamp, Airy's, unpublished paper)

Bradley pondered his dilemma until 1729 when he declared the phenomenon to be the *aberration* of starlight. Because the Earth is moving, he explained, a telescope must be tilted at a precise angle "ahead" of a star in the direction of the Earth's movement so that the star's light will travel unheeded down the tube of a telescope. This is likened to holding a pipe verticle in a calm rain so that a raindrop falls directly through the pipe. If you begin to move, you have to tilt the pipe at the proper angle in the direction of your movement for the drop to fall undisturbed through the pipe.

However, this phenomenon does not prove whether it is the Earth or the star that is moving. **Jesuit R.G. Boscovich** realized this in the late 1700s and suggested that a telescope filled with water would decide the matter. The water would slow the light and, if the Earth were indeed the mover, the tilt of the telescope would have to be increased (a greater angle of aberration). If there were no change, the Earth would then be at rest and the star would be the mover.

No one saw fit to try this experiment until 1871 when British astronomer **George B. Airy** performed it and, to everyone's consternation, measured equal results — no change in aberration. The experiment became known as **"Airy's Failure,"** though Fresnel's postulate of a dragging coefficient and eventually Einstein's relativity were trotted out to "solve" the problem and put the Earth back in motion. (Van der Kamp, Airy's, unpublished paper and Cosmos, 12-13; Hanson, "History," Bib. Astron. No. 64, 34-5)

> **Capital E in Earth**
> We decided to capitalize Earth for several reasons:
> 1) Earth is a proper name
> 2) Astronomy magazine capitalizes Earth, the names of the planets, our Sun, and our Moon (and we have followed suit)
> 3) The capital emphasizes our biblical belief that Earth is unique, central, special, and not "just another evolved planet."

Is God A Geocentrist?

In the beginning, says Gen. 1:1, God created the heavens and the Earth. This verse seems to indicate *all* of Creation, and so in all of Creation, God singles out only one body — Earth. That can only mean that, from the beginning, Earth is indeed special, singular, central. In Chapter 1, we discussed evidence to believe that the Universe may very well be home to dominions and kingdoms of powerful *spiritual* beings and that Earth was originally — and still is for a time — the dominion of Lucifer (now Satan). It was a different Earth, with a jeweled Garden of Eden. There were no physical beings and so no need for an atmosphere or even a Sun or Moon. But, whether or not Earth was central to God's activity *before* man, it is certainly central to His activity *with* man. Jesus was born here, died here, rose here, and will reign here. Revelation prophesies, once again, a **new heavens and a new *Earth***, with a New Jerusalem located on Earth.

Now we can say that, "Of course, Earth is central, because we humans know nothing but Earth and humans wrote the Bible and the Bible is centered around God's activity with us, from our viewpoint." *That is a grave error* in thinking. **The Bible is God's Word, from God's viewpoint.** *And the fact that the theory of a Sun-centered Universe could lead us to abandon an obvious biblical teaching, and further lead us into a humanistic, "scientific revolution" in a Universe with no center, no absolutes, and no Creator, should stop us in our intellectual tracks and force us to reexamine the origin, the veracity, and the implications of Copernicanism* — don't you think?

The Bible makes it clear that the Earth is special, but it also repeatedly tells us that the Earth has a **place** (Job 9:6; Isa. 13:13), that it **hangs on nothing** (Job 26:7), that it has **fastened foundations** [sockets] (Job 38:4-6; Ps. 102:25, 104:5; Prov. 8:29; Isa. 48:13; Mic. 6:2), and that it is **God's footstool** while heaven is God's throne (Isa. 66:1; Mt. 5:34-5; Acts 7:49). The Temple is also God's footstool and the Temple is at Jerusalem, on Earth (I Chron. 28:2; Ps. 99:5, 132:7). God says that the Earth, His footstool, **cannot be moved** (I Chron. 16:30; Ps. 93:1) **unless He moves it** (Isa. 24:18-23) in judgement.

Thus, *Earth is not a planet!* The word planet means "wanderer" and so applies only to those bodies that wander across our skies, and only, interestingly enough, to those peculiar round bodies that are not stars. By the way, are you aware that there have been **no other "planets" discovered** to date anywhere else in the Universe other than our own "solar" (actually Earth) system? "Though astronomers have long thought that planets should be common in our Galaxy," writes *Astronomy* magazine, "they have never seen any beyond our solar system." (Astronomy, April 1993, 18; Webster's)

Professor James Hanson points out that commentators exult over the literal science taught in verses four, six, and seven of Ecclesiastes 1 while verse five (which says that the Sun rises and sets and hastens back to the place where it rose) must be pulled out of this literal context and interpreted ***phenomenologically***. (Hanson, Geocentricity series, Bib. Astron., I: 54-61, 1991-92) This means that suddenly the Bible uses language that describes what we observe rather than what is actually true. *The Bible could easily say that the Sun appears to rise and set as the Earth turns, but humanist evolutionists want us to buy the idea that "primitive" man of 1500 B.C. to A.D. 1500 could not comprehend such "advanced" knowledge — and we have bought it!* They also want us to lose confidence in the reality of our observations because this is the only way anyone can accept the many bizarre teachings of modern science. (See Chapter 9)

The Bible teaches, then, that the Earth remains stationary while the Sun, Moon, and stars move. (Eccl. 1:5, Job 38:32, Josh. 10:12-14) In trying to deal with **Joshua's Long Day**, this writer doubted the logic (not the ability) of God's stopping a rotating Earth, with all the disturbing and mind-boggling implications thereof, and so examined the theories of axis tilts and complete flips of the Earth's axis, which

---

> **PSALM 19**
> *The heavens declare the glory of God, and the firmament showeth his handiwork.*
>
> *Day unto day uttereth speech, and night unto night showeth knowledge.*
>
> *There is no speech nor language, where their voice is not heard.*
> (Scofield, KJV, Ps. 19:1-3)

also imply similar problems. However, stopping the Earth would still require that God stop the Moon, as the Moon's orbit is independent of Earth, and stopping the Earth does not stop the Moon.

Turning the Earth upside down or tilting its axis would not cause the Sun and Moon to *stop* for almost a day in the middle of the sky. The Sun and Moon would merely begin to "move" backwards. An eclipse certainly does not lengthen the day, as was Joshua's intention, nor does it even begin to fit the description. However, geocentricity provides logic, order, and a literal interpretation to this passage. (Hanson, Geocentricity series, Bib. Astron I:54)

The BOTTOM LINE is this: if we can be arbitrarily selective of the Bible's literalness, how can we be absolutely certain that a verse is literal or phenomenological or symbolic? Jesus made it absolutely clear when He was using parables or similes or metaphors and when he wasn't (Luke 8:9-11). The Bible makes it clear when someone has a vision or dream and what the interpretation of it is (Dan. 2 & 7, Ezekiel 1, Revelation 4), if an interpretation is given. Obviously, we would really like to have a lot more detailed information about the visions of Ezekiel and John, though much of Daniel's prophetic history has been specifically documented.

But, if Noah did not build an Ark, if the whole world did not flood, if a large sea monster did not swallow Jonah, then how can we be sure that Christ literally rose from the dead? If we cannot believe that the Sun, Moon, and stars move as the Bible teaches, and that Earth is special, as the Bible teaches, then how can we be sure that we can be forgiven and saved and resurrected — as the Bible teaches?

Heavenly Gospel

The Bible is full of references to the heavens, stars, Sun, Moon, and even some constellations, but **Psalm 19** gives us the clearest picture of the heavens as a starry gospel. To this point, the psalm is analyzed most ably by **E. W. Bullinger (1837-1913)** in *The Witness of the Stars*. An Anglican clergyman, Bullinger descended from Swiss Reformer J. Heinrich Bullinger. A major resource for his extensive research was the mass of information collected by **Frances Rolleston of Keswick** (England) who "performed the drudgery of collecting the facts presented by Albumazer, the Arab astronomer to the Caliphs of Grenada, A.D. 850; and the Tables drawn up by Ulugh Beigh, the Tartar prince and astronomer, about A.D. 1450, who gives the **Arabian astronomy** as it had come down from the earliest times." **Dr. Joseph A. Seiss** of Philadelphia, known for his work *The Gospel in the Stars*, made Rolleston's work popular on the American side of the Atlantic. (Bullinger, Witness, v)

Bullinger points out that Psalm 19 has **two parts** which celebrate the *two great Revelations*, God's **works**, and God's **Word**. One is written in the sky, while the other is written "in the Earth," on parchment or paper.

The first explains that the "heavens declare the glory of God, and the firmament showeth his handiwork." (Ps. 19:1, KJV) Using his knowledge of the original language, Bullinger demonstrates by word study that this declaration is the equivalent of an **engraved, written message** that is unveiled to *all* the Earth, day after day, and night after night (as in continually *adding* precept upon precept). Verse 3 makes it clear that, no matter the language or dialect, translation is not even a factor. In this Revelation, the **Sun is the type of Christ**. Note that the *Sun travels a circuit* which reaches from one end of the heavens to the other, an unequivocally **geocentric** statement. The somewhat vague, general, and plural Hebrew word *shamayim* is the only word used for heaven or heavens in Psalm 19, the same word used throughout Genesis and in all but a few cases in the Old Testament. [The New Testament almost always uses the Greek word *ouranos*.] The terms used in this part are basically *astronomical* in nature.

The second part of Psalm 19 praises the law, testimony, statutes, commandment, and ordinances of God. The terms are *literary* in nature and "thy servant" **David is the type of Christ**. This Revelation does require translation into languages and dialects. This Revelation involves man in both its production and preservation, while the first is produced and preserved by God alone. (Bullinger, Witness, 1-6)

The point is that both Revelations are from God and their original meanings are divine. The Evil One has viciously attacked the meanings and integrity of both.

The Starry Story

The Sun moves through the Zodiac and its attendant decans. But where, Bullinger asks, do we break into the circle? The only intelligent biblical approach, he says, is to begin with **Virgo** and end with **Leo**, or the basic outline of Gen. 3:15. The **Sphinx**, so famous in Egypt, is an ancient symbol that means *to bind closely together*. It is often pictured as a female head with a lion's body. The Zodiac on the ceiling of the Portico of the Temple Esneh pictures a sphinx between the signs of Virgo and Leo, binding together the two ends of the Zodiac. (Bullinger, Witness, 19-22)

VIRGO: Gen. 3:15, issued by God immediately after the Fall of man, promises a Messiah Who will be born of a *virgin*, the seed of a woman. Virgo the virgin is pictured holding two things, a *branch* and *ears of corn*. We have seen in earlier chapters that Christ is the Branch (Jer. 23:5). The ear of corn (the seed) also represents the Messiah. Pagans later gave Nimrod the symbol of the branch. The Mayans worshipped a maize (corn) god. The Hebrew, Arabic, and Latin names of many of the stars in the constellation mean virgin, branch, or corn. In some cases, the ears of corn became a sheaf of wheat which carries the same Messianic significance. In the pagan Mystery system, as Nimrod became the Branch, Semiramis became the "virgin" and so Virgo has also been associated over the millennia with the numerous and varied versions of the Earth goddess.

The three decans are 1) **Coma**, the *desired or longed for*. The *ancient* zodiacs show this constellation as a young virgin holding an infant boy. The divine mother/child symbol is found throughout paganism around the world. However, modern zodiacs show it as *Berenice's Hair*. Bullinger attributes this to Egyptian politics in the 200s B.C. Berenice, wife of King Ptolemy III, dedicated her long hair to the goddess Venus to insure her husband's safe return from an expedition. When the hair was stolen from the temple, Alexandrian astronomer Conan declared that Jupiter had made it a constellation. 2) **Centaurus**, the *despised sin offering*. A two-natured being, the Centaur is half male warrior and half horse. Christ's two natures as God and Man are often pictured by some double figure. The Southern Cross lies beneath the body of the horse. 3) **Boötes**, the *Coming One* or the *Herdsman*. In this constellation is the bright star *Arcturus*, meaning *He comes*, and the constellation may have originally been called Arcturus (and may be the one referred to in Job rather than the Bear). He carries a sickle which represents harvest. To see both the confusion and the consistency of the Zodiac over the millennia, note that the illustration of the sickle-wielding figure is drawn with the star Arcturus in the knee in Bullinger (p. 43) and near the head in Gallant (p. 152), a 180° difference in position. In other words, the basic figure is the same, but the way it is drawn over the stars varies.

Both Bullinger and Gallant note that Boötes, or Arcturus, was also known as the guard or watcher of the Great Bear. In the famous **Egyptian Zodiac of Dendera**, what we call the Bear (the Big Dipper) is what the Egyptians saw as the *Ox's Leg*. The Little Bear is a *Jackal*, and Boötes seems to be combined with Draco the Dragon to form a large figure normally identified as the *Hippopotamus*, though it actually looks much more like a bear on its hind legs draped with an animal skin. See Peter Tompkins's book on the Great Pyramid to see how the Dendera Zodiac shows the *pole of the ecliptic* located in the breast of the Hippopotamus and the *pole of the equator* in the Jackal (Polaris). All of the figures march in one direction, east to west. Virgo reaches toward Coma. Coma, the infant boy, seems to be holding onto Leo's tail while Leo treads or rides on the back of a snake — the picture of Gen. 3:15. (Bullinger, Witness, 29-44; Hutchings, God's Bible, 13-14; Gallant, Constellations, 154-161, 151-4; Tompkins, Secrets, 172-4; De Santillana, Hamlet's, 216-17)

LIBRA: Bullinger presents both linguistic and pictorial evidence that the constellation known as the *Scales* is an ancient Egyptian corruption of the original *Circular Altar* embraced by the claws of the Scorpion. The scales, reasons Bullinger, may be an Egyptian introduction of human merit (weighing the works and sins) rather than the pure grace of God (unmerited favor). This can be seen in the

Dendera Zodiac. With Libra as the Altar, we have a picture of the virgin birth, the Sacrifice, and the Enemy together in the first three zodiacal signs. For some ancients, Libra became the *Claws*, and then later, the Scales.

The three decans are 1) **Crux**, the *cross endured*. The Southern Cross was just visible in the skies of Jerusalem at the time of Christ's birth, but soon after sank below the equator to become the modern-day symbol of both Australia and New Zealand. What does this say about the movement of the Universe of stars? Is this due to a wobble? We have already discussed the cross or the Tau as an ancient symbol and the fact that Nimrod is called Tammuz. Bullinger points out that *Tau* is the last letter of the Hebrew alphabet, "anciently made in the form of a cross," and used as a boundary mark to denote the *limit* or the *finish*. 2) **Lupus** or **Victima**, the victim slain. On the Cross, Christ became the sinner, the sacrifice for the sinner, and the priest who slew the sacrifice. 3) **Corona**, the crown bestowed. At His First Coming, Christ endured the Cross, while at His Second Coming, He will wear the Crown. (Bullinger, Witness, 45-53)

SCORPIO: Certain star names in this constellation translate as the *wounding* and *war*. The scorpion is another symbol for Satan, the dragon or serpent. Pagans almost universally regard it as evil, though New Zealanders see it as a magic jawbone used by the god Maui as a fishhook to pull New Zealand from beneath the sea. (Bullinger, Witness, 54-6; Gallant, Constellations, 83-5)

The three decans are 1) **Ophiuchus**, the *serpent holder*, and 2) **Serpens**, the *serpent*. Ophiuchus has his foot on the heart (near the head) of the scorpion while the tail of the scorpion reaches to wound the heel of Ophiuchus. The serpent the Man wrestles with stretches its head for Corona, the Crown. This is the struggle for dominion prophesied by Gen. 3:15. At the Cross, Christ is wounded in the heel, but through the Resurrection, Second Coming, and Final Judgement, He gains final and complete victory over Satan. 3) **Hercules**, the mighty vanquisher. Wearing a lion skin and weilding a club, Hercules kneels with one foot held up as if wounded while the other foot treads on the head of Draco the Dragon. (Bullinger, Witness, 56-62)

SAGITTARIUS: Once again, the two-natured Centaur, half horse and half man, represents the two-natured Christ. Known as the Archer, the bow-wielding Sagittarius aims his arrow at the heart of the Scorpion.

The three decans are 1) **Lyra**, the *harp*, also perhaps an *eagle*, symbolizing praise soaring to heaven. 2) **Ara**, the *altar of consuming fire*. This is a fire of judgement, pointing down towards the abyss. 3) **Draco the Dragon**, that *old serpent, the Devil, cast down from heaven*. The star *Thuban* means the *subtle*. The name Draco comes from a Hebrew word meaning *to tread*, or *trodden on*. (Bullinger, Witness, 62-73) In pagan mythology, Nimrod is the Centaur, the hunter who trained the horse for riding.

CAPRICORNUS: The two-natured, part goat, part fish is certainly not a natural animal. It represents the Atoning Sacrifice (the scapegoat) and the people on whose behalf the sacrifice is made. As Bullinger states, the "living fish proceeds from the dying goat, and yet they form only one body." (Bullinger, Witness, 76) In Mystery language, the goat/fish represented the two fathers of the two worlds, Adam (Pan, meaning all) and Noah.

The three decans are 1) **Sagitta**, the *arrow of God*. 2) **Aquila**, the *eagle, the smitten One falling*. 3) **Delphinus**, the *dolphin, the dead One rising again*. The fish is upright, while the eagle points down. (Bullinger, Witness, 74-84)

AQUARIUS: The famous water bearer pours living water from an urn into the mouth of a large fish. Individual star names attest to the water pourer's identity. *Here, Bullinger makes one of his most interesting points, showing himself to be a **true** **dispensationalist**.* (See Chap. 1) Signs are not for the Church, but for Israel. The Church is the Mystery not revealed until the New Testament.

Isaiah 32:1-2 speaks of the King, the Man, Who will be like rivers of water in a dry place. In Isaiah 44:1-6, God tells the **believing remnant of Israel** that He, (Jesus) as the King of Israel, will revive them, pour water upon him who is thirsty and pour His Spirit upon Israel's seed. Aquarius is the picture of the **Millennial King**, reviving the Earth from the Curse, reviving Israel from judgement. (Bullinger, Witness, 84-8) It is interesting that the much heralded Golden **Age of Aquarius**, the pagan's version of the Millennium, begins theoretically in A.D. 2000, literally about A.D. 2100. The Greeks once associated Aquarius with Zeus and also with a Flood myth. Deucalion and Pyrrha survived in a great boat that landed after nine days and nights on Mount Parnassus. By throwing stones over their shoulders, they created a new race of men and women. (Gallant, Constellations, 110-11)

The three decans are 1) **Piscis Australis**, the *Southern Fish, the blessings restored*. The large fish receiving the blessings is most probably Israel. 2) **Pegasus**, the *Winged Horse, the swift blessings*, brought by He Who goes and returns, according to the name of the star Scheat, part of the square of Pegasus. 3) **Cygnus**, the *Swan, the returning Blesser*. The star Deneb means *the judge*. (Bullinger, Witness, 88-92)

PISCES: This well-known sign is made up of **two fish**, one perpendicular to the circle of the Zodiac and one parallel to the circle, tied together by a band fastened to each tail. Both Christians and New Agers usually identify the fish as the sign of **Christianity**, or the Church. The Greek word for fish is (spelled in English) *ichthus*. The first letters of the Greek words for *Jesus Christ, God's Son, Savior*, are the same letters in the word fish. (Zondervan Parallel New Testament in Greek and English) Another reason for this identification is that the vernal equinox entered the sign of Pisces fairly soon after the birth of Christ, actually about A.D. 220 according to astronomer Roy Gallant. Many consider it to have moved into the sign at the time of the actual birth. Thus, the Age of Christianity is also the **Age of Pisces**. The two fish could possibly represent the binding together of **Jew and Gentile** into the Church. However, Bullinger sees this also as a **Jewish sign**, with the perpendicular fish picturing the Israelites (Old Testament saints) who looked for the heavenly blessings, and the parallel fish picturing the Israelites who are satisfied with the earthly blessings.

Gallant relates one pagan Greek myth in which the evil and monstrous god Typhon tried to overthrow Zeus and chased all the gods who followed Zeus into exile in Egypt. Zeus remained to battle and eventually defeat Typhon. Goddess Aphrodite and her son Eros (Cupid) both plunged into a river and became fish to escape Typhon. The two fish of Pisces are actually Aphrodite and Eros. We recognize the "evil" Typhon to be the godly Seth while Zeus is Nimrod. Seth did in fact have Nimrod tried and executed, but the pagan story has a different ending. Since Nimrod is both the father and son, he is also Eros. Aphrodite is Semiramis. (Bullinger, Witness, 92-9; Hutchings, God's Bible, 24-5; Gallant, The Constellations, 106-8, 177)

The three decans are 1) the **Band**, the *bound redeemed awaiting redemption*. 2) **Andromeda**, the *Chained Woman, Israel bound*. 3) **Cepheus**, the *Crowned King, the redeemer*. Cepheus is coming quickly to redeem his chosen ones from the bondage. (Bullinger, Witness, 100-4)

ARIES: This is the famous Ram or Lamb. Prominent star names translate as the *slain, wounded*, and *bound*. The **Age of Aries**, according to Gallant, lasted from 1953 B.C. to A.D. 220. This means that the vernal equinox was in Aries at the time of the Exodus and, at the time of Christ's birth, in the major stars of the Ram's head whose meanings are given above. (Bullinger, Witness, 104-7; Gallant, Constellations, 177)

The three decans are 1) **Cassiopeia**, the *Enthroned Woman*, the *Queen* or the *Lady in the Chair*. This is the woman freed and exalted. The Woman in the Bible is Israel (Rev. 12) and Bullinger, holding to his strict dispensationalism, regards Israel as the Bride of Christ rather than the Church. The Church, he says, is the Body of Christ and so part of the Husband. It is an interesting argument as most dispensational evangelicals regard Israel as the Wife of God and the Church as the Bride of Christ. 2) **Cetus**, the *Sea Monster or the great enemy bound*. Bullinger sees Cetus as Satan, while others see him as the Whale who swallowed Jonah. 3) **Perseus**, the *Breaker, or the warrior*. A picture of Christ the Subduer, he carries a sword and the head of the adversary. Bullinger says that, by perversion, this became the head of Medusa. Some have seen him as David with the head of Goliath. Gallant relates the Greek myth of Andromeda, the beautiful daughter of King Cepheus and Queen Cassiopeia. Because of Cassiopeia's pride in her daughter's beauty, Cetus was sent by Poseidon to ravage the coast of the Queen's land. The only way to stop the killing was to sacrifice Andromeda. She was chained to rocks by the sea to be eaten by Cetus, an armored Sea Monster that sounds a lot like Leviathan. Perseus, a son of Zeus and killer of the snake-headed Medusa, slew Cetus and rescued Andromeda. (Bullinger, Witness, 107-18; Gallant, Constellations, 39-43, 125-6)

TAURUS: The great Bull, the coming Judge, has horns which are an ancient symbol of power. (Rev. 13; Hab. 3 — note verses 3, 4, and 11) A symbol of Christ, it became the symbol for Nimrod. The vernal equinox was in Taurus before it moved into Aries, supposedly from about 4000 B.C. to 1953 B.C., according to Gallant. Of course, if the precession did not begin until the time of the Flood, we don't know what the situation was prior to this Earth-shaking judgement. According to Tompkins, the cult of the Bull preceded the cult of the Ram in Egypt. Bulls adorn the Ishtar Gate of Babylon and human-headed, winged bulls were common carvings in Assyria, while Egyptians worshipped the Apis bull. In North America, the bullish-bodied, horned bison (buffalo) served as an acceptable substitute. (Bullinger, Witness, 120-4; Gallant, Constellations, 126, 177; Tompkins, Secrets, 169; Dyer, Rise, photos)

The three decans are 1) **Orion**, the *Coming Prince, or the Hunter*. He holds a club and a lion and has a sword in his famous three-star belt. He is associated with light. A symbol of the conquering Christ, he became the Sun god of the Egyptians and Phoenicians and was considered to be Nimrod, even by later Jews who called him the Giant. 2) **Eridanus**, the *River of the Judge*. It seems to issue forth from the foot of Orion. 3) **Auriga**, the *Shepherd*. The bright star in the right foot translates as wounded or slain. This is the Messiah Who gathers His flock. (Isa. 40:11) (Bullinger, Witness, 124-137; Gallant, Constellations, 121-3)

GEMINI: The twins are another double figure which the Romans named Castor and Pollux. The Hebrew name means *united*. They were patron saints of navigation (Acts 28:11) and both Greeks and Romans commonly swore by them. Even today in America, "By Gemini!" became "By Jimminy!" (sp?) Once again, we have the two-fold nature of Christ as God and Man.

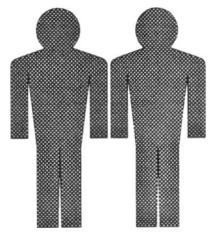

The three decans are 1) **Lepus**, the *Hare or Enemy*. In ancient Persia this was a serpent. In Egypt, it was an unclean bird standing on a serpent under the foot of Orion. 2) **Canis Major**, the *Big Dog or Sirius*. Its original meaning has to do with the coming of the Prince. *Sirius means Prince*, says Bullinger, and is the *brightest star in the sky*. It was highly important to the Egyptians and its heliacal rising signaled their New Year's Day. 3) **Canis Minor**, the *Little Dog or Redeemer*. The meaning of Redeemer comes from the bright star Procyon, one of the sky's brightest. (Bullinger, Witness, 137-146; Gallant, Constellations, 142)

CANCER: The Crab (or Sacred Beetle of Egypt) is the namesake of the Tropic of Cancer. It's original meaning is mysterious, though Bullinger finds linguistic evidence to show that it refers to a hiding place for the congregation of the Redeemed.

The three decans are 1) **Ursa Minor**, the *Little Bear or the Lessor Sheepfold*. Bullinger points out that no bear was ever seen in the ancient zodiacs and no bear ever had a long tail. 2) **Ursa Major**, the *Big Bear or Greater Sheepfold*. Its brightest star is called *Dubheh* which means *herd of animals*. A related Hebrew word means *fold*. Thus, Bullinger sees the Lessor Sheepfold as those Old Testament (Jewish) saints who sought the heavenly blessings, and the Greater Sheepfold as the Israelites who will inherit the Kingdom on Earth. Once again, one might stretch it to cover all believers or to symbolize the Jew and Gentile of the Church, or Israel and the Church. Bullinger also points out that the Hebrew word for *bear* is very close to that for *fold*. 3) **Argo**, the *Ship*. In Greek myth, Argo carried Jason and the Argonauts to redeem the lost treasure of the golden fleece from the serpent. This speaks of Christ the Redeemer of His sheep from the Evil One. Bullinger says that the meaning of *Canopus*, Argo's brightest star, is the *possession of Him who comes*.

LEO: The royal Lion ends the story, just as Christ the Lion of Judah will return to defeat the Antichrist, crush the serpent's head, and establish His Kingdom on Earth.

The three decans are 1) **Hydra**, the *Serpent*, who writhes beneath the feet of Leo. 2) **Crater**, the *Cup* of divine wrath poured out. 3) **Corvus**, the *Raven*, the bird of prey devouring the serpent.

Pagan Astrology

"**Astrology** is a fundamental and most necessary science," according to the **Tibetan**, one of the "Masters" of the universe (actually a demonic angel), as quoted by occultist **Alice Bailey**. However, "orthodox astrology," or "modern ordinary astrology," deals only with the fate and destiny of the personality and the physical concerns of the incarnated soul, say Alice Bailey and her "Master." What we know as astrology today, handed down from ancient Babylon, will "be gradually superseded" by esoteric astrology, the "new and future astrology" which "endeavours to give the key to the horoscope of the soul...." (Bailey, Education, 71; Bailey, Autobiography, 247-8; note British spelling of endeavors) This is the **plan of the New Agers** and their *"Masters,"* the demonic angelic beings, led, of course, by Satan. *If you are truly wise, you will never put your body or your soul in the hands or minds of these occultic New Agers. However, if we are to understand the history of the world and of the Americas, we must understand something of both astronomy and astrology.*

Earlier in this chapter, we defined the precession of the equinoxes and the "Ages" associated with the location of the vernal equinox in a certain sign of the Zodiac for some 2,000 or so years. Even if the precession only began at the Flood, it must have started in the latter part of the **sign of Taurus**, moving into Aries within 300 to 400 years.

However, probably because the kingdoms of Ham's sons were powerfully established by this time and paganism was taking on new and more ominous forms after the execution of Nimrod, **Aries**, not Taurus, is considered by pagans to be the **first sign of the zodiac**. The vernal equinox, when the Sun crosses the equator, is still called the **First Point of Aries** today, even though that "point" has moved across Aries and into another constellation.

We have seen that, to the *Christian*, Aries is the ram found in the bushes by Abraham to substitute for Isaac, the slain lamb of the passover in Egypt, the slain Lamb on the Cross at passover in Jerusalem, and the victorious Lamb of the Second Coming. At the time of the first passover and the Exodus, the vernal equinox was in Aries (Age of Aries), and the Sun in the course of its *yearly* journey was in Aries on the 14th day of the Jewish month, Nisan, the date of that first passover. (Hutchings, God's Bible, 26)

It is very interesting that modern-day, New Age writer **Alice Bailey** calls the **Age of Aries** "the start of the **Jewish dispensation**," explaining in *The Reappearance of the Christ* that "Christ came to bring an end to the Jewish dispensation which should have climaxed and passed away as a religion with the movement of the Sun out of Aries into Pisces." She goes on to say that the Jews rejected Christ as the Messiah, thus remaining "symbolically and practically" in the sign of Aries, the Scapegoat. She indicates that the Jews must change their attitudes and move, "symbolically," into the sign of Pisces so that they can recognize their Messiah "when He comes again in the sign Aquarius." (Cumbey, Hidden Dangers, 106) This is just one example of the closeness of Satan's copycat technique.

Of course, the "Christ" Alice Bailey is referring to is actually the **New Age Christ**, or **Maitreya**, or the **Antichrist**, for whom Jesus seems to have been some sort of precursor. Jesus, say the New Agers, is only a "fourth-level initiate," as opposed to the Lord Maitreya who is supposedly a "seventh-level initiate." [Remember the Mystery system and initiation?] Bailey also refers to "the difficulty of the Jew," which is that they have "little desire to change." This comment should be a warning to both Christians and Jews of the intentions of New Agers as we approach the year A.D. 2000 (Cumbey, Hidden Dangers, 96-7, 106)

The **astrological tables** that are used today and that are published in almost every modern daily newspaper, were developed at this time, when the Sun was in Aries. So, using the First Point of Aries, and the modern date for the vernal equinox, astrologers say that anyone born from March 21 to April 20 is born under the sign of Aries, and anyone born from April 21 to May 20 is born under the sign of Taurus, and so on. Whether astrologers use March 25 from the time of Christ or March 21 from today, the vernal equinox is no longer in Aries, but in Pisces, and so **astrologers ignore the actual movements of the stars** and cling to the **original pagan guidelines** set down by the Babylonians. This means, of course, that people walking around today thinking they are "an Aries" are actually "a Pisces" and so forth. (Gallant, 175-8) What many of them also do not realize is that, if they truly believe in the influences of the stars and direct their lives by the advice of astrologers or psychics, they are also a Babylonian pagan.

About A.D. 220, the Sun at vernal equinox moved into **Pisces**, the Two Fishes. Thus, we today, are still in the **Age of Pisces**. The modern-day pagans called "New Agers" see the Piscean Age as **"a dark, violent age."** (Ferguson, Aquarian, 19) It is also called **"the Christian Age,"** by pagans and Christians alike, as the sign of the fish is considered by many to be a Christian sign and the age itself corresponds roughly to the Church Age. (Matrisciana, Gods, 17; Bailey, Education, 121; Dictionary of Mysticism, 14) The New Agers see the Piscean Age as an ultimately undesirable but necessary rung in the evolutionary ladder, according to **Alice Bailey**, "transcriber" of *Education in the New Age,* which was dictated to her by a spiritual being called "The Tibetan." From 1919 to 1949, Mrs. Bailey transcribed from demonic dictation "a series of books presenting the next phase in the continuity of the Ancient Wisdom teaching for the present and the immediate future." (Bailey, Autobiography, back cover) This series of books comprises a major part of the "blue prints" for the New Age. According to Christian writer and New Age exposer, Constance Cumbey, the *New Agers follow Alice Bailey like a recipe.* (Cumbey, Hidden Dangers, 90, 194)

The **Piscean Age** is an authoritarian or paternalistic age in which people are told what to think by "unenlightened" authorities who promote *divisiveness* in government, religion, education, and society. By "divisiveness," the New Agers mean such "ideas" as the sovereignty of nations, doctrinal differences between religions and denominations, the sanctity of each human life, individual property rights, and fact/reality based education. According to New Agers, the true hierarchical structure of the social order has been terribly distorted, misused, and undermined, leading to the wrong kind of racism, hatred, and separateness. However, the New Agers acknowledge that this age has also seen much "kindly paternalism of the privileged classes, seeking to ameliorate the condition of their dependents...." (Bailey, Eduation, 105, 120)

The Bible and Equinoxes

Remember that the observance of the SOLAR equinoxes and solstices was more than accurate astronomical timekeeping. It was a PAGAN religious obsession. Though the Jews noted these occurrences, as would any good astronomer/timekeeper, God's chosen and set-apart nation was concerned first and foremost with the LUNAR calendar and with the totally independent day count of SABBATHS, or every seventh day. In 1993, the vernal equinox occurred on March 20, while Nisan 1 (first day of first month of religious calendar) fell on March 24, right after the new Moon, and Nisan 14 (Passover) fell on April 6 at the full Moon. The Jewish New Year and traditional date of Creation did not begin with the vernal equinox but came in the fall on Tishri 1, at the new Moon which, in 1993, fell one week before the equinox. In other words, don't apply pagan or secular traditions to biblical events.

[Remember, don't expect ancient pagans or modern-day New Agers to be consistent or to make sense. They don't. They are contradictory, convoluted, and elusive. Satan doesn't make sense.]

During this age, "the Guides of the race have emphasized the idea of the virtues of sorrow and the educational value of pain." For example, the two World Wars [which are considered to be "one war" lasting from 1914 to 1945] are viewed as a painful but necessary "surgical operation." (Bailey, Education, 45, 111) The problem, according to New Agers, is that "lesser teachers" have overdone the lessons in sorrow and pain, causing people to develop a "feeble hope" in some sort of material reward after this life, such as heaven. (Bailey, Education, 120)

Most important, though, is the fact that the Piscean Age emphasizes **materialism**, **possession**, **commercial expansion** and **production**, and the "aggressive taking of that which is desired....Aggression in order to possess has been the keynote of our civilisation during the past fifteen hundred years," explains the Tibetan. (Bailey, Education, 121; note British spelling of civilization, using "s" instead of "z") The "three foundational ideas" taught to youth in the Piscean Age are material ambition, social ambition, and a deeply rooted sense of individual inferiority which results from the teaching that man has a sin nature or a "natural inclination to do wrong". (Bailey, Education, 104-5) Thus, the New Agers view the Piscean Age as dark and violent, an age of self, separateness, greed, ambition, cruelty, and pride, but a necessary predecessor to the coming enlightened age.

The Sun is slowly passing out of Pisces into **Aquarius**, and will move into Aquarius, according to astronomical calculations, in A.D. **2375**. (Gallant, 178) This precession of the equinox technically should usher in the Age of Aquarius. However, astrological calculations must differ, as the *Dictionary of Mysticism and the Occult* gives the date as 2740. "Each epoch," says the *Dictionary*, "lasts approximately 2000 years...." (Dictionary of Mysticism, 14) This is an interesting statement, considering the Jewish belief in 2000-year epochs. Despite the actual date of the precession into the new zodiacal sign, the **year 2000** is viewed as a significant date:

*The year 2000 looms before humanity as a **gigantic milestone** which marks both an ending and a beginning. It marks the **end of a volatile millennium** which has seen enormous progress and change, particularly in the fields of science, technology, education and government. But more importantly, the year 2000 stands as a **symbolic portal** through which humanity can pass into a **New Age of true peace**, cooperation and creativity — if it so chooses.* (Quoted from the Lucis Trust *World Goodwill Newsletter* of July, August, September, 1982, in Cumbey, Hidden Dangers, 227; note that it should read "more important" — see Writing Notes at end of chapter)

The reason the modern-day Babylonian pagans are called **New Agers** is that they are actively working to bring in the New Age, which is the **Age of Aquarius**. Meanwhile, they tell us that we are in a transition stage. Even though the year 2000 does not represent the technical movement of the equinox into the sign of Aquarius, it is viewed as the beginning of a new, enlightened and peaceful millennium (1,000 years) and the ending of a dark and violent millennium.

Alice Bailey, writing for the Tibetan, calls it the **most difficult transitional period** the world has ever seen. (Bailey, Education, 99) Her husband, Foster Bailey, says that, "Humanity is passing through the greatest spiritual crisis of its long history on this planet. The implications are too deep for our understanding." (Bailey, Autobiography, 302) Samuel Beckett, in the *World Goodwill Newsletter*, says that we are "'transiting from the present 'Age of Authority' into the 'Age of Experience,'" an age in which we will "'discover the true authority of our divine inner Self. *Fundamentally*,'" emphasizes Beckett, "'*we must believe in*

Age of Aquarius?
YEAR 2000
? Tribulation?
Millennium?

the divinity of humanity.'" (Cumbey, Hidden Dangers, 238)

We have seen that the zodiac sign of **Aquarius** is a young man pouring out a bucket of water, called the Water Carrier or Water Bearer. To the New Ager, he is a sign of man carrying his own load, taking control of himself and his own destiny. The **Aquarian man** — the *enlightened superman* — will **save himself and mankind through his own knowledge**, "liberating himself from all the powers of this old world and the world of his body." (Matrisciana, Gods, 17-18) This means liberation from God, and liberation from the restraints of the physical, or the "outer form."

The New Agers plan to "liberate" some two to four billion of us from our bodies by the year 2000, in the name of "zero population growth" and the cause of **overpopulation**. The **Global 2000 report** was the result of a meeting in 1984 of 3,000 delegates from 156 countries. The world's population was estimated at 4.7 billion in 1983, with a projected total of 6.2 billion by the year 2000. This New Age report aims instead to **reduce the Earth's population to only two billion by 2000**, by way of abortion, euthanasia, suicide, homosexuality, and who knows what else that is not mentioned. That is an awful lot of "liberation"! (Webber, Gospel, Dec. 1985, 2-3; Cumbey, Hidden Dangers, 152)

The **New Age movement** actually begins with the Satan-possessed **serpent in the Garden of Eden**, promising man that, **1)** he would have knowledge, **2)** he would not die, and **3)** he would be like God, or actually, would be a god. After the cataclysmic judgement of the Flood, the New Age movement revived under Cush and Nimrod, who promised to liberate mankind from God, while offering mankind the opportunity of achieving immortality and holiness through knowledge and effort. The exact same doctrines continue today as New Agers seek, **1)** enlightenment, **2)** progression up the ladder of repeated incarnations to the eternal, spiritual union with the Whole, and **3)** the god within each of them. In other words, *unregenerate man has always sought knowledge, immortality, and godhood.*

To the *Christian*, **Aquarius the Water Bearer** pictures the **returning Jesus Christ**, the true Messiah. As Rev. Noah Hutchings states in *God's Bible in the Heavens*, the "coming of the promised Messiah as a water bringer to Earth is prophesied in far too many scriptures to mention." (Hutchings, God's Bible, 23) The prophecy from Peor in Numbers says that, "He shall pour the water out of his buckets, and his seed shall be in many waters, and his king [Jesus Christ] shall be higher than Agag, and his kingdom [the biblical Millennium] shall be exalted." (Num. 24:7, KJV)

So, that is what is meant by the **Age of Aquarius**. It is merely mankind once again uniting to get God off their backs, just as they attempted to do under Cush at the **Tower of Babel**. It is interesting that the pagan New Agers' expectations for a New Age and an enlightened, peaceful millennium roughly correspond with the belief of many Christians that the year 2000 may welcome the return of Jesus Christ and the establishment of His 1000-year Kingdom rule on Earth.

Cush's movement and insurgency lasted a mere 200 or so years. Nimrod revived and propelled the movement, but it has taken some 4,000 years to approach culmination. One must clearly understand the Bible and the biblical plan of God, as well as the copycat, Satanic plan of the Babylonian pagans, in order to understand the history of the world and the history of the Americas.

WRITING NOTES

Over the past five or ten years, you may have noticed a steady increase in the use of *"***more important***,"* or rather, "more important*ly*." The word *importantly* is an adverb, meaning "done in an important manner," though it is rarely used because it sounds awkward and strange to the ear. However, it has become faddish in both writing and speaking to emphasize a point by starting a sentence or paragraph with "More important*ly*, this is so or that is so." What the writer or speaker is actually saying is the "understood" phrase, "What is more important is the point that...," or "Even more important is the fact that...." The quote at the top of column two on page 30 is actually saying, *"But what is more important is the fact that the year 2000 stands as a symbolic portal...."* This fact, then, is more important than the previous points, and so "important" is an *adjective* in this usage and not an *adverb*. Actually, the most important point should be stated *first* and not last. Follow that rule and "more important" won't be a problem.

BIBLIOGRAPHY

Asimov, Isaac, *Chronology of Science and Discovery*. New York: Harper & Row, 1989.

Bailey, Alice, *Education in the New Age*, Bib. Chap. 5, p. 80.

Bailey, Alice, *The Unfinished Autobiography*, Bib. Chap. 7, p. 108.

Barnes, Thomas G., *Space Medium*, Bib. Chap. 1, p. 19.

Baugh, Carl E., *Panorama of Creation*, Bib. Chap. 2, p. 37.

Berlitz, Charles, *Mysteries From Forgotten Worlds*. New York: Doubleday & Co., 1972.

Bouw, Gerardus D., "Geocentricity: Does the Earth Move?" *Bulletin of the Tychonian Society*, revised reprint, available from The Biblical Astronomer.

_____, "The Foucault Pendulum Question," *Bulletin of the Tychonian Society* reprint, available from The Biblical Astronomer.

_____, "How Big is the Universe?" The Biblical Astronomer, Vol. 3, No. 64, Spring 1993, 10-22.

Bullinger, E.W., *Number in Scripture*, Bib. Chap. 2, p. 37.

Bullinger, E.W., *The Witness of the Stars*. Grand Rapids: Kregal Publications, 1967. [Reprint of 1893 edition]

Capt, E. Raymond, *The Great Pyramid Decoded* (rev. ed.). Artisan Sales, 1978. [Dr. Gene Scott teaches on this subject: The University Network, P.O. Box 1, Los Ang., CA 90053]

Church, J.R., *Hidden Prophecies in the Psalms*. Oklahoma City: Prophecy Publications, 1986.

Cumbey, Constance, *The Hidden Dangers of the Rainbow*, Bib. Chap. 1, p. 19.

De Santillana, Giorgio, and Von Dechend, Hertha, *Hamlet's Mill*, Bib. Chap. 7, p. 108.

Drury, Nevill, *Dictionary of Mysticism and the Occult*, Bib. Chap. 2, p. 37.

Dyer, Charles H., "Ezekiel," *The Bible Knowledge Commentary, Old Testament (I)*, Bib. Chap. 4, p. 65.

Dyer, Charles H., *The Rise of Babylon*, Bib. Chap. 5, p. 80.

Elmendorf, Richard, "More on Geostationary Satellites," *The Biblical Astronomer*, Vol. 3, No. 63, Winter 1993, 3-8.

_____, personal correspondence, 1993.

_____, "Heliocentric Hocus-Pocus," unpublished paper, February 1993.

Encyclopaedia Britannica (EB), Bib. Chap. 3, p. 51.

Fell, Barry, *America B.C.*, Bib. Chap. 6, p. 91.

_____, *Bronze Age America*, Bib. Chap. 6, p. 91.

Ferguson, Marilyn, *The Aquarian Conspiracy*. Los Angeles: J.P. Tarcher, Inc., 1980.

Gallant, Roy A., *The Constellations*, Bib. Chap. 3, p. 51.

Gaverluk, Emil, *The Rapture Before the Russian Invasion of Israel*, Bib. Chap. 1, p. 19.

Goldberg, Amnon, "The Earth is established–It cannot be moved," *Jewish Tribune*, Thursday, January 11, 1990.

Good, Joseph, *Rosh HaShanah and the Messianic Kingdom to Come*, Bib. Chap. 2, p. 37.

Hadingham, Evan, *Early Man and the Cosmos*. New York: Walker and Co., 1984.

Hall, Manley P., *The Secret Teachings of All Ages*, Bib. Chap. 7, p. 108.

Hall, Marshall, "The Symbiotic Relationship...," *Proceedings...*, Bib. Chap. 9, p. 160

_____, *The Earth is not Moving*, 1992. Fair Education Foundation, Inc., P.O. Box 866, Cornelia, GA, 30531.

Hanson, James N., "The Bible and Geocentricity" (Series), *Bulletin of the Tychonian Society*, No. 54, Fall 1990. [Becomes *Biblical Astronomer*]

_____, "The Testimony of God's Cosmic Geometry," (same series), *The Biblical Astronomer*, Vol. 1, No. 55, Winter 1991.

_____, "The Testimony of Cosmology in the Bible," (same series), *The Biblical Astronomer*, Vol. 1, No. 56, Spring 1991.

_____, "The Biblical Testimony of Geocentricity From Chronology, Time and Place," (same series), *The Biblical Astronomer*, Vol. 1, No. 57, Summer 1991.

_____, "History and Geocentricity," (same series), *The Biblical Astronomer*, Vol. 1, No. 58, Fall 1991.

_____, "Pre-Christian Descriptions of Celestial Motions," (same series), *The Biblical Astronomer*, Vol. 2, No. 59, Winter 1992.

_____, "Copernicus' Philosophical Reasons For the Earth's Motions," (same series), *The Biblical Astronomer*, Vol. 2, No. 60, Spring 1992.

_____, "Copernicus' Physical Evidences For the Earth's Motions," (sames series), *The Biblical Astronomer*, Vol. 2, No. 61, Summer 1992.

[**The Biblical Astronomer**, 4527 Wetzel

Ave., Cleveland, OH 44109; Hanson's series continues in 1993]

Henry, Jonathan F., "Geocentrism and Heliocentrism," *Proceedings...*, Bib. Chap. 1, p. 19.

Hislop, Alexander, *The Two Babylons*, Bib. Chap. 4, p. 65.

"Hubble Discovers Protoplanetary Disks in Orion Nebula," AstroNews, *Astronomy*, April 1993, 18.

Hutchings, Noah W., *God's Bible in the Heavens*. Oklahoma City: Southwest Radio Church, 1985. [Southwest Radio Church, P.O. Box 1144, Oklahoma City, OK 73101]

Jeffrey, Grant R., *Armageddon*, Bib. Chap. 2, p. 37.

Johnston, Thomas Crawford, *Did the Phoenicians Discover America?* London: James Nisbet & Co., Ltd., 1913. (Original: 1892, San Francisco)

Josephus, Bib. Chap. 2, pp. 37-8.

Krupp, E.C. (ed.), *In Search of Ancient Astronomies*. New York: Doubleday & Co., 1977.

Lang, Walter, *Job and Science* (Second edition). Richfield, MN.: Genesis Institute, 1992. [Genesis Institute, 7232 Morgan Ave. S., Richfield, MN 55423-2940]

Matrisciana, Caryl, *Gods of the New Age*. Eugene, Oregon: Harvest House Publishers, 1985.

Miller, Robert D., *The Miller Planisphere*. Addison, Illinois: Datalizer Slide Charts, Inc., 1988.

Pritchard, James B. (ed.), *The Ancient Near East*, Bib. Chap. 5, p. 80.

Scofield, C.I. (ed.), *The New Scofield Reference Bible*, Bib. Chap. 2, p. 38.

Setterfield, Barry, *Geological Time and Scriptural Chronology*, Bib. Chap. 2, p. 38.

Strong's Exhaustive Concordance, Bib. Chap. 3, p. 51.

Timetables of History (Grun), Bib. Chap. 7, p. 108.

Tompkins, Peter, *Secrets of the Great Pyramids* (paperback). New York: Harper & Row, 1978. [Appendix by Livio Catullo Stecchini]

Van der Kamp, Walter, *The Cosmos, Einstein and Truth*. Walter van der Kamp, 3687-1507 Queensbury Ave., Victoria, British Columbia, Canada, V8P 5M5, January 1993.

_____, *Airy's Failure Reconsidered*, unpublished manuscript.

Velikovsky, Immanuel, *Worlds in Collision*, Bib. Chap. 5, p. 80.

Webster's New World Dictionary, Bib. Chap. 2, p. 38.

Wertime, Richard A., and Schuster, Angela M.H., "Written in the Stars," *Archaeology*, July/August 1993, 26-32.

PROJECT & ESSAY IDEAS

Learning the Sky: Visits to planetariums are fun and fascinating, even if usually "evolutionary" in presentation. Planetarium gift shops and mall specialty shops offer sky maps and posters and inexpensive "planispheres" which will help you learn the night sky where you live. Of course, the best views are from the highest elevations farthest from the lights. If you have the resources and the desire, you might want to purchase your own telescope. It's amazing how much mere binoculars enhance your ability to see the Moon, planets, and brighter stars. Learning to identify only a few constellations will greatly increase your appreciation for the skill of the ancient skywatchers who could read the stars like a book and track their movements with incredible precision.

Essay and Research Topics: Do further research on figures at the center of the ancient geocentric/heliocentric debate, men such as Tycho Brahe, Johannes Kepler, Copernicus, and Galileo. Examine the secular and religious forces at work in this debate and what effect it has had on all of modern science. The research topics suggested by this chapter are plentiful, including geostationary satellites, the Foucault pendulum, the Michelson-Morley experiment, and the New Age's zero-population-growth movement. Is the world *really* overcrowded?

For essay topics, consider such questions as whether or not the Bible teaches geocentricity, whether Copernicus or Darwin began the scientific revolution, and what effect, if any, the study of geocentricity has had on your own point of view and faith.

Chapter 9
Sifting for Truth Through a Variety of Scholarly Views

Conflicting Camps

Though we dealt with major world views in our first chapter, there are within these broad views a number of specific scholarly positions which we need to define and understand. This will greatly enhance our ability to carefully and properly evaluate the research and teachings of both secular and religious historians and scientists.

First, we will briefly review the major **antibiblical** intellectual movements that have provided the basis for 20th-Century thinking in science, history, and philosophy.

Second, we will define and examine **diffusionism** and **autochthonism**.

Third, we will look at the findings and beliefs of two camps of evolutionist geneticists and anthropologists called **1) the Noah's Ark theorists** and **2) the multi-regional theorists**.

Fourth, we will consider several prominent dogmatic teachings of **traditional historians**, every one of which we find faulty.

Fifth, we will discuss three **"maverick" evolutionist groups** whose research often unintentionally supports the biblical viewpoint, and we will also see how *traditional evolutionists* fight *maverick evolutionists* as vehemently as they all together attack *Biblicists*.

Sixth, we will mention that group of **non-traditional researchers** who pursue the mysterious and often unexplainable elements of history and archaeology. This group consists of both the religious and the secular and includes, of course, many New Agers. Discoveries are most often interpreted as evidence of UFO activity or the remains of legendary Atlantis. However, this group has some useful, valid, and thought-provoking findings to offer the careful Biblicist. One problem we note among certain (not all) in this "category" is poor, or no, documentation, a problem that is much too often a failing of Christian writers.

Pro-Bible/Anti-Bible

Essentially every thought and act of mankind from the day Adam was created can be explained as either willing submission to God or as willing rebellion against God. Disobedience was introduced by the very first man and woman, while rebellion began with the very first human to be born on Earth — Cain. We have also seen just how quickly organized rebellion arose after the miraculous event of the Flood. As accessibility to the Scriptures increased, particularly in medieval Europe (A.D. 500s to 1500s), people became more aware that **intellectual movements** either supported or challenged the Bible, and/or the Catholic Church which dominated Europe.

In the words of theoretical physicist Dr. Charles Lucas, "**man has deliberately developed a world view whose main purpose is to deny God** as [C]reator and sustainer of the [U]niverse and [J]udge of all mankind. This view now dominates world thought." (Lucas, Soli, preface) We will now attempt to trace the shaping and placement of the basic building stones in the construction of this world view. We will see how physics affects biology, affects history, affects religion, and so on.

Building Anti-Bible Scientific Theories

The main point of this exercise is not that you understand all of the science to which we refer, but that you grasp the insidious "brick-upon-brick" process of building this scientific "Tower of Babel."

Atomistic World View

According to theoretical physicist Dr. Charles Lucas, the major anti-biblical intellectual movement of the modern world is called the **atomistic world view**, of which secular humanism and communism are actually subsets. [Carrots are a *subset* of vegetables which are a *subset* of food.] This view was promoted by the 1st-Century B.C. Roman poet and Epicurean philosopher **Lucretius** who wished, *like Nimrod*, to deliver mankind from the bondage of religion while freeing man to pursue physical pleasure and happiness with a clear conscience. Just like the originators of the "sky stories" of the ancients (Chaps. 5, 6) Lucretius saw man prostrate on the Earth, weighed down by heaven (God). (Lucas, Soli, preface)

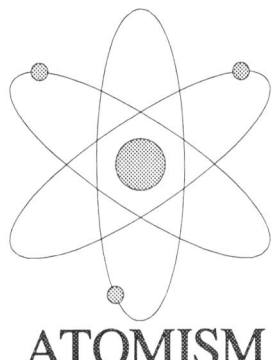

ATOMISM

Though popularized by Lucretius, **atomism** was developed by the **Hellenistic Greeks** of the 300s to 100s B.C. (after the death of Alexander the Great in 323 B.C.). The Hellenists taught that *matter is eternal* and consists of units called **atoms** which are *absolutely indivisible and indestructible*. This teaching that matter is eternal (only God is eternal, not the things He creates) flew in the face of Creation and established a **materialistic world view**. It also attempted to explain all psychological and emotional phenomena (the soul) as purely physical. Harvard historian of science Stephen Mason concludes that atomism was invented with more than the purpose of escaping burdensome religion. Atomists intended to "'**combat religion** even to the detriment of extending man's understanding and control of nature.'" (Lucas, Soli, preface, Lucas,

"Renewed Call," Soli, 10-11

Copernican Revolution

Another major development in the anti-biblical intellectual movement arose some 1600 years later — **the Copernican Revolution.** The Bible repeatedly refers to the **fixed foundations of the Earth** (Job 38:4, 6; Ps. 104:5) and always describes the Sun and the Moon as orbiting around the Earth (rising and setting). From Lucifer's connection with the Earth (see Chap. 1) to man's creation, Christ's crucifixion, and the Millennial Kingdom, the Earth is presented as the *center of God's focus in the Universe.* Thus, whether for God's sake or man's sake, the Greeks, Romans, and Europeans held firmly to the belief that the Earth is the center of the Universe and that everything we observe orbits around it.

Based on the work of Hipparchus, **Ptolemy's** order of the Universe (2nd-Century A.D.) modeled concentric spheres with the Earth at the center. The Moon and planets each occupied a sphere, with the Sun as the fourth from the Earth, ending with Saturn. The sphere of the stars was much further away than the planets. *Ptolemy argued effectively for the fact that the Earth is immovable*, while later Europeans saw **geocentrism** as a central teaching of the Bible and the Church. (EB, 1972, 18:813) Unlike today, true secularists were comparatively rare in medieval Europe, but even they held the general intellectual world view of that time which put the Earth at the center of Creation. For well over a thousand years this pro-biblical belief held sway in the minds of most men.

In 1543, the highly controversial work of Polish astronomer **Nicolaus Copernicus** (A.D. 1473-1543, Webster's) was published, presenting the world with a **heliocentric** model of the known solar system, putting the Sun at the center of concentric orbits occupied by Mercury, Venus, Earth, Mars, Jupiter, and Saturn, in that order. As we saw in Chapter 8, there was absolutely *no real proof* for this model, and there never has been! Walter van der Kamp quotes

famous naturalist Alexander von Humbolt (1769-1859) as saying, "'I have known too, for a long time that we have *no arguments for the Copernican system*, but I shall never dare to be the first to attack it.'" Van der Kamp also quotes well-known atheist philosopher **Bertrand Russell** (1872-1970) as commenting that it does not matter whether the Earth "'rotates once a day from west to east as Copernicus taught, or the heavens revolve once a day from east to west, as his predecessors believed, the observable phenomena will be *exactly the same*.'" (Van der Kamp, "Does Space," Proceedings, 86-90, italics added) As we also noted in Chapter 8, astronomer and computer scientist **Dr. Gerardus Bouw** explains that he was certainly not originally a geocentrist, but that he knew enough physics to realize, even before his own step-by-step conversion to Christianity, creationism, and geocentricity, that *both the geocentric and heliocentric models account for the same observed movements.* (Bouw, Geocentricity lecture, Feb. 12, 1990)

The point is that this **unproven hypothesis** became the **next false cornerstone** of an **eventual institution of humanism**. The German poet **Goethe** (1779-1832) was very pleased that "'Among all the discoveries and convictions, probably not a single fact has had a *deeper influence on the human spirit* than the teaching of Copernicus....'" Later in life, Goethe remarked on the incredible stress applied to the "understanding" (beliefs, knowledge) of man when required by Copernicus "'to renounce the immense privilege of the world to be the centre of the [U]niverse.'" Referring to the "cosmic quest" initiated by Copernicus, **Arthur Koestler** states that it "'*transformed the European landscape*, society, culture, habits, and general outlook, as thoroughly as if a new species had arisen on this planet.'" (Van der Kamp, "How Long," Proceedings, 98, 105, italics added)

It is interesting that the heavenly body put at the center of the Copernican Universe has always been the major symbol of God and specifically of the Messiah, (more often the false Messiah), as well as an object itself of pagan worship.

Copernicanism continued to cut deeper at biblical teachings and laid the foundation for the Earth, and for man, to become just another speck in an expanding or even "infinite" Universe of "eternal and indestructible" matter.

Darwinism

Of course, the next cornerstone was the **Darwinian Revolution**. Since matter is eternal and not created (atomism), and the Earth no longer the center of the Universe and merely another "orbiting body" (Copericanism), then man is logically nothing more than another "evolved product of the Universe" and certainly not the object of the saving love of an omnipotent Creator.

The famous French writer and philosopher Voltaire (1694-1778, Webster's) was a Copernican, as was English naturalist and physician Erasmus Darwin (1731-1802, Webster's). Both of these influential men "were developing 'ape-man' theories in the 1700s." (Hall, "Symbiotic," Proceedings, 18) In the 1850s, **Charles Lyell** and **Charles Darwin** (grandson of Erasmus) began to publish their own works on **uniformity** and **evolution** and the **antiquity of man**, and *ever since, almost all works of history, philosophy, and science are based on the premises that the Universe and its creatures somehow randomly evolved from chaos to order and from simple to complex.* Thus, the study of ancient knowledge and technology view all of its findings within an evolutionary framework, from **stone,** to **bronze,** to **iron,** or basically from primitive to modern.

Every skeleton, every artifact, every record, and every structure found by archaeologists or historians or anthropologists is dated and analyzed according to these false assumptions. The only real exceptions are those few explorations conducted by strongly biblical Christians, of which Dr. Carl Baugh is a leading example. This overwhelmingly dominant, evolutionist viewpoint insists that man is merely a higher form of animal, that man and Universe continue to evolve to higher forms, that no worldwide

catastrophes have drastically altered the Earth's condition, and thus the past can be extrapolated based on the observations of the present. Point by point, evolutionary humanism and biblical Christianity are totally antagonistic.

This is why most of the past that is reconstructed by archaeologists, anthropologists, and geologists ranges from faulty to false, particularly the histories of Egypt and the Americas. We single out Egypt because world history in general is measured against an incorrect and incredibly inflated Egyptian time line. (see Chap. 5, p. 79)

One of the most recent products of Darwinism is the Steven Spielberg/Michael Crichton **movie *Jurassic Park*,** a popular novel and blockbuster film geared for the masses. This hard-preaching flick drives home, from beginning to end, these points:

1) that **dinosaurs and man** are of *two different eras,* millions of years apart, and so do not belong together. The dinosaurs were naturally selected for extinction. In the movie, viciously carnivorous dinosaurs naturally select man for dinner. This denies the biblical teaching that we examined in Chap. 3 as well as ignores and attempts to discredit the evidence found by Dr. Baugh and others that dinosaurs and man were **alive together,** that dinosaurs could only be supported for any length of time at their original size in a **canopied environment,** and that dinosaurs (and man) before the Flood were **herbivorous,** except for a few possible "clean-up crew" omnivores.

2) that dinosaurs were **not cold-blooded** reptiles but **warm-blooded** creatures and the **ancestors of** (believe it or not) **birds.** Evolutionists are vigorously pushing this idea because they **need this "link" in their evolutionary chain.** As always, evolutionists groom their facts to fit their agenda.

Relativity

Copernican scientists desperately wanted to prove that the Earth was indeed moving and orbiting the Sun, but since no absolute reference could be established, they could not. *Mechanical* experiments performed inside a system (inside the Universe) cannot detect what is really moving. The only way to establish the truth is from *outside* a system (outside the Universe) which is, of course, impossible for man. Thus, in 1881, physicist **A. A. Michelson** first decided *to prove Copernicanism* with an *electromagnetic* experiment which split a beam of light, sent the two half-beams in different directions, then recombined them. If the Earth moves, the two halves should recombine *out of phase* with one another. Michelson repeated the experiment with **E. W. Morley** in 1887, then many times afterward in various places and conditions. It became known as the **Michelson-Morley experiment**. However, *the light halves always recombined in phase, indicating that the Earth is at rest!* (Henry, "Geocentrism," Proceedings, 22-3, 28-9; EB, 1972, 19:96-7)

This "failure" was one of the main motivations for **Albert Einstein** to construct his **Special Theory of Relativity** which was published in 1905. Because "common-sense, classical, three-dimensional science could not straightforwardly prove what it wanted to prove..., a special effect for this case alone had to be invoked for the salvation of the heliocentric theory." (Van der Kamp, "Does Space," Proceedings, 91) In order to attempt to discredit the "null" result of Michelson-Morley, Einstein had to *theorize* that the **speed of light** is *constant* regardless of the motion of the source or the observer. He also had to declare that all motion is relative and that there is no "center," no frame of reference, only movements relative to one another or relative to an observer. (Henry, "Geocentrism," Proceedings, 28-9) What most people don't understand is that it is all *nothing more than theory!* And bad theory at that. Lucas states that "the speed of light is **not a constant** in the **real world** but only in a vacuum." (Lucas, "Renewed Call," Soli, 22)

The first step to declaring all motion relative was Einstein's **denial of a "medium"** or "aether" (ether) in space. "The *rational* approach to physics leads one to the conclusion that there is *a medium for propagating electromagnetic waves,"* explains physicist Dr. Thomas Barnes. "It is axiomatic: If one is to have waves, *something* must wave." (Barnes, Space, 35, italics added) **Classical physics** presents an *electrodynamic Universe* in which there is electromagnetic interaction among all the *real* particles of the Universe (as opposed to the idealized "point" particles of modern particle physics). Gravity, for example, is an electromagnetic force. (Lucas, "Revision of Electrodynamics," Soli, 9; Lucas, "Electrodynamic Model," Soli, 22)

When Einstein denied an electrodynamic medium, he "unhinged" the particles in the Universe from one another. Everything became relative and, though our Sun had been moved to the center of the Universe by the Copernican solar system, it would soon become, thanks to the foundation laid by Einstein, merely one more "sun" in an expanding and possibly *infinite* Universe with no center of reference and no unifying force.

Motion wasn't the only thing that became relative under Einstein's theories. So did **time**, which Einstein decided was *elastic*, "stretched and shrunk by motion." Time became the *fourth dimension* of space, so that we no longer had space and time, but the **spacetime continuum**. Time became stoppable, and reversible! Past, present, and future became meaningless because, according to relativity, there is no universal present. (Davies, God, 120-4) *In direct contrast, the real world of Classical physics sees space as three-dimensional and time as absolute, independent, and universal.* (Barnes, Space, foreword)

In 1916, Einstein generalized his Special Theory to explain the force of **gravity**. It was this **General Theory of Relativity** that actually created the spacetime continuum concept and demanded the **curvature of geometrical space**, which, since space included time, meant the **curvature of spacetime**. (Davies, God, 13) Some claim that Einstein developed this concept *"in part to avoid the conclusion that the [U]niverse must be finite."* (Henry, "Geocentrism," Proceedings, 35, italics added) Whether or not Einstein himself ever believed in the possibility of a Universe **infinite** in either size or age, his "concepts" certainly freed physicists from reality and from the confining notion of special creation by an infinite Creator.

Actually, Einstein used his curved spacetime idea to propose that the Universe could be **finite in volume,** but **"unbounded."** From this came the example of the theoretical astronaut who always points his spaceship in one direction but who eventually arrives at his starting point. And, from the idea of an *infinitely shrunk Universe* (a **"singularity"** of infinite density), comes the **"Big Bang"** in which some scientists postulate that *spacetime was created out of nothing.* (Davies, God, 16-19) Dr. Gerardus Bouw says that the **Big Bang is in trouble** and will soon be replaced by the **Inflation** theory. (Bouw, Geocentricity lecture, Feb. 12, 1990) The Big Bang depends on a **homogenous, uniformly expanding Universe**, a claim which is called "wishful thinking" and "deliberately inaccurate" by physicist Dr. Jonathan Henry. Ongoing discoveries continue to *defy the assumption of a smoothly expanding, uniform Universe.* (Henry, "Red Shift," Proceedings, 44-5)

Einstein's elastic spacetime has given rise to the idea that our Universe might be nothing more than a "disconnected fragment of spacetime" and only one of a **possibly infinite number of universes**, all physically inaccessible to one another! This is an easy way to dismiss God. (Davies, God, 42)

The **convenience of an infinite Universe** is to have "no fear of statistics." If the Universe is infinite, then *"anything* that is possible *must* happen somewhere by pure chance." (Davies, God, 70, 168) How's that for allowing evolution free rein? *Infinite size, age, and even number* provide evolutionists, in their own minds, with the "possibility" of anything and everything. Remember that atomism says that matter is eternal? If matter is eternal, why shouldn't the Universe be infinite? Thus, the Creation becomes God, and so 20th-Century science worships and serves the creation more than the Creator. (Rom. 1:25)

Dr. Emil Gaverluk provides us an example of a scientist and Bible-believing Christian who makes the *mistake of compromising generally doctrinally sound biblical beliefs with unbiblical science*. In a fascinating and often brilliant work called *The Rapture Before the Russian Invasion of Israel*, Dr. Gaverluk writes that, because our God is infinite, He must have created an **infinite number of perfect universes**. At first, this idea is intriguing and even attractive, in that it shows how limitless our God is and how we humans tend to limit Him in our own finite minds. But further examination shows us that the foundation of this science is unbiblical and faulty -- mere theory -- and deeper thought reminds us that only God is infinite, not His Creation, and that an infinite number of universes is idealistically meaningless and certainly belittling to the Universe in which Christ died.

Dr. Gaverluk cites a 1986 article in Science (AAAS) by Professor K.Y. Lo of the University of Illinois at Urbana that references Einstein and other scientists, *theorizing* that **black holes** are time **tunnels which lead to an infinite number of universes**. A black hole is believed to be a huge, dying star that has shrunk or imploded to an infinitesimal point (a *singularity*), where gravity, spacetime, and matter become "infinite," a mass of absolute density that sucks everything within a certain perimeter into itself.

For example, at the center of our own Milky Way Galaxy, scientists claim to have found a very dense object that is four million times the mass of our Sun, surrounded by a cavity 60 trillion miles wide. (Gaverluk, Rapture, 218, 235, 242, 248-9, 255)

Dr. Gaverluk also cites an article by two professors named Birrell and Davies of Kings College in England which states that the quantum effects on energy present in the intense **gravitational field of a black hole** distorts the field, "'effectively twisting the neck of the **space-time bridge** and *preventing any connection with another universe,'*" and that these quantum effects "'operate on a black hole, whether or not it is sweeping up matter from the surrounding space.'" (Gaverluk, Rapture, 218, 250, italics added) Dr. Gaverluk explains this apparent contradiction between scientists in this way: the black holes are indeed time tunnels to other universes, but have been closed off by God in order to prevent any contamination of these universes by our own sin-scarred and cursed Universe. *Our Universe, he says, is sealed off to keep Satan and his evil angels from the other perfect universes.* (Gaverluk, Rapture, 255) Though we at first found this conclusion to be intriguingly attractive, we have had to reject it as unsound both scientifically and biblically.

We can see from our research above how these "weird" concepts are **constructed upon one false assumption after another**, each leading us further and further from reality and from the Bible. Frankly, we have determined from what little research we have done to be **extremely skeptical** of most of what modern science teaches. Obviously the *whole concept of black holes is false*, based as it is on the unreal ideas of elastic spacetime. It would be very interesting to be able to know exactly what the astronomers **really do observe** and not just their own wild and wooly **interpretations** of what they observe. Einstein, a Jew — a descendant of the chosen people — often referred to God as Creator, (Davies, God, 25, 222) but he certainly left us an unbiblical legacy!

Atomism, Copernicanism, and Darwinism all involve **"idealizations of nature"** which do not exist in the real world. Dr. Charles Lucas explains that scientists and philosophers, because of the complexity of physical Creation, "have tried to grossly simplify scientific analysis through the use of certain idealized notions," which are "chosen in such a way as to distill the essence of nature and allow scientists to **more easily perform scientific analysis.**" He adds that scientists are always careful to see that these "notions" comply with the current prevailing world view. (Lucas, "Renewed Call," Soli, 8)

Such a notion that developed from atomism is the **point-particle idealization**. This notion assumes that particles are "point like." This certainly is an "idealized," even silly-sounding concept which Nobel-prize-winning (1961) physicist **Robert Hofstadter** says is **not true**. Lucas quotes Hofstadter's Nobel lecture which proclaims that "'newer and more powerful studies ... show that the 'elementary particles' [point particles] have a structure themselves'" which "'may be quite complex....'" Hofstadter concludes that the "'elegant idea of [point particles] **must be abandoned**.'" (Lucas, "Renewed Call," Soli, 15, 21)

These point particles are also supposed to move around in **"empty space"** (denial of the "medium") which is assumed to be *absolutely uniform* everywhere. Even a layman would have to question the absolute uniformity of space, and we have already seen that astronomical observations defy the idea. In addition, these point particles are not affected by gravity or any other "forces," because all of the **intrinsic properties** (shape, spin, electrical charge) of each particle are assumed to be **"inherent, fixed, and independent** of interactions with the rest of the [U]niverse." (Lucas, "Renewed Call," Soli, 19)

The brilliant Scottish physicist who developed the electromagnetic theory of light, **James Maxwell** (1831-1879, Webster's), translated the empirical laws of electrodynamics (laws of Faraday, Ampere, Gauss) into differential equations. However, in doing so, Maxwell *used the point-particle idealization.* These equations "worked well for a time," but were found inadequate to describe newly discovered phenomena. Instead of ridding Maxwell's equations of the point-particle idealization, explains Lucas, **Einstein invented Special Relativity to "patch up the inadequacies of Maxwell's equations."** (Lucas, "Renewed Call," Soli, 11)

BLACK HOLES
Reality or Just Theory?

Thus, Einstein's Special and General Theories of Relativity were devised to rescue Copernicus; to deny an electromagnetic medium and thus a sensible, biblical, unified explanation of Creation; and to advance the point-particle idealization.

Quantum Theory

The hypotheses (they don't really qualify for the status of theory) of atomism, Copernicanism, Darwinism, and relativity laid the foundation for the weirdest of all imaginary constructions of "an **Alice-in-Wonderland world** that cuts right across the traditional framework of religion." (Davies, God, 99) That's what famed British theoretical physicist Paul Davies calls the quantum theory.

This 1920s physics revolution purports to demonstrate that the nature of **physical reality** is dependent upon **consciousness**, and *not necessarily human* consciousness. In other words, the precise nature of reality (what is really there or what is truly happening) cannot be determined without the participation of a conscious observer — a human, an animal, perhaps a computer. Or, to put it another way, things (and we suppose people) and events aren't real until they are observed. Quantum theorists even talk about **retroactive causation**, or reality that is created by an observer that comes along after the fact, so to speak, and **self-observing systems**, such as a Universe that focuses itself into concrete reality by looking at its earlier self. (Davies, God, 100, 107, 111) Yes, grown men and women actually talk seriously about such things. But, wait! That's only the beginning.

Quantum theory **denies cause and effect**, saying that there are effects that have no cause. It says that an atom can have location (place) or a definite motion (speed), but it can't have both. "This," explains Davies, "is the celebrated **uncertainty principle** of Heisenberg, one of the founders of the theory." (Davies, God, 102-3) A Universe "governed" by randomness has no use for God.

In the bizarre world of modern particle physics, all manner of "potential" particles consist of however many **"ghosts"** until one of the ghosts is observed or measured into concrete reality, at which point the other ghosts disappear. Quantum theory also defines light as both a wave and a particle, which Davies calls a **"wave-particle duality."** But "the **quantum wave**," continues Davies, "is not like any other sort of wave anybody has ever encountered." It is **not physical** or made of the "atom" itself. It is the **information** about the atom or particle. And this so-called wave is only an **unpredictable probability**. (Davies, God, 104-8) *Classical physics defines light as a massless electromagnetic wave, not a particle.* (Barnes, Space, 129-36)

The random unpredictability, ghosts, and observer-created reality of quantum theory leads us where? Why, to the **parallel universe theory**, of course, which was invented by Hugh Everett in 1957 and later promoted by Bryce De Witt of the University of Texas at Austin. As each possibility arises, a new universe branches off, resulting in the **simultaneous existence of all possible universes**. You may not

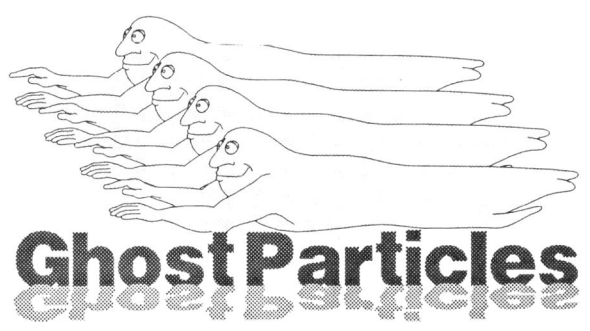

Ghost Particles

realize it, but, since the beginning of your existence, a copy of you exists in each of the equally real but totally inaccessible universes that has branched off every time a new possibility has arisen. "Countless times each second," says Davies, "the [U]niverse is replicated." (Davies, God, 116-18) Consider that all of this "scientific" nonsense is supported by your, or your family's, tax dollars. Think about that, and then multiply it by all your universes.

Why is this ridiculous mess called the **quantum** theory? Apparently the wave-particle duality of light began with **Max Planck** about 1900. Light, he said, consists of **"indivisible lumps or packets"** which Einstein later defined as **photons**. Hence, a quantum (or quantity) of light is one of those "lumps." In the 1920s, Danish physicist **Niels Bohr** led the charge *against* Einstein, championing the uncertainty principle and the hybrid realities of ghosts and so on. Einstein argued that every effect did indeed have a cause, that there were no ghosts, and that "'God does not play dice.'" (Davies, God, 108-9, 102)

Lucas writes that the packaging of light (energy) accounted for certain observable phenomena, but that Einstein's *photon* was an *incorrect explanation* of the packaging. Optics expert **Herbert Ives** of Bell Labs rejected the photon as did **H. A. Lorentz** in 1910. (Lucas, "Renewed Call," Soli, 26-7) Barnes writes that Einstein "made no attempt to arrive at a physical concept of a photon." Instead, Einstein merely "proposed" and "assumed" a nonphysical concept. (Barnes, Space, 130)

In the 1930s, **Paul Dirac** combined electrodynamics (using the point-particle idealization), relativity theory, and quantum theory to develop **quantum mechanics** and an equation which produced the current theory of the

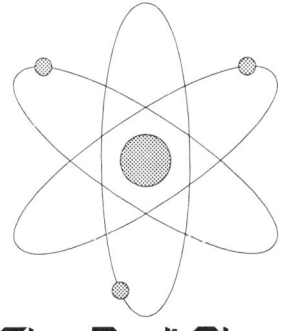

The Pauli Atom Electron Levels

Sifting for Truth Through Scholarly Views   Page 149

atom. More concerned with what physicists call "elegance" than with reality, Dirac wrote that it "'is more important to have beauty in one's equations than to have them fit experiment....'" (Lucas, "Renewed Call," Soli, 27; Davies, God, 27, 220) Austrian physicist **Wolfgang Pauli** contributed the **Pauli exclusion principle** which limits the number of electrons in each energy level ("orbit") around a nucleus. (Lucas, "Renewed Call," Soli, 28; Webster's)

Chaos Theory

Actor Jeff Goldblum in the movie *Jurassic Park* plays the part of a mathematician who is a chaos theorist who has been hired as a business consultant. He rattles off "quickie" references to the Butterfly Effect, randomness, predictability, strange attractors, and loops in phase space.

In the financial business weekly publication called *Barron's* on March 22, 1993 appeared an article with the title "A Quantum Vision: Chaotic Organization Must Replace Newtonian Bureaucracy." A scientific article? No, an article written by Margaret J. Wheatley, a business consultant and associate professor of management at Brigham Young University, adapted from her book *Leadership and the New Science*. Wheatley contends that the creation and management of organizations should be grounded in the **science of our times** and no longer in the **organized, predictable, 17th-Century world of Isaac Newton**. Managers have been confusing control with order, she writes, and it is suicidal (businesswise) to impose control through *permanent* structures when we are dealing with *process* structures.

It seems that the latest fad in the "new science" is chaos theory and, instead of becoming one more specialty, it is not only bringing together specialists from every scientific discipline, but it is also pervading every other manner of discipline, including the business world. Your government, the Pentagon, the CIA, foundations, universities, etc. are pouring millions of dollars (mostly your tax dollars) into research on chaos theory. Chaos "believers" like Ms. Wheatley above are promoting chaos theory in the board room, the business school, and the manager's office, which is not nearly as disconcerting as chaos on the battlefield.

What is chaos theory? It has something to do with structure and pattern within incomprehensible **complexity**, with "orderly **randomness**" and patterns in chaotic **fluid processes**, and with the idea that order comes from disorder — that there is **order *from* chaos**, and **order *in* chaos**. If that sounds fuzzy to you, that's because it is. "Where chaos begins, classical science stops," writes James Gleick, author of the national best-seller *Chaos: Making of a New Science*. Chaos is a **"holistic"** science, a science of the "global nature of systems."

Gleick quotes one physicist as saying that "'**Relativity** eliminated the *Newtonian illusion* of absolute space and time; **quantum theory** eliminated the *Newtonian dream* of a controllable measurement process; and **chaos** eliminated the *Laplacian fantasy* of deterministic predictability.'" (Gleick, Chaos, 6, 299, 3-5) The first two subjects we have discussed enough to have some understanding of what this physicist means, but what is the meaning of the third? What is the Laplacian fantasy of **deterministic predictability**?

Pierre de Laplace (1749-1827) was a French mathematician and astronomer who interpreted **Newton's laws of mechanics** (motion and gravity) to mean that the Universe is a giant machine — like a clock — consisting of particles (atoms) that are governed by forces that in turn are determined by other particles, and all according to specific laws and a "rigid network of cause and effect." In other words, "Newtonian mechanics permits, in principle, the accurate prediction of everything that will ever

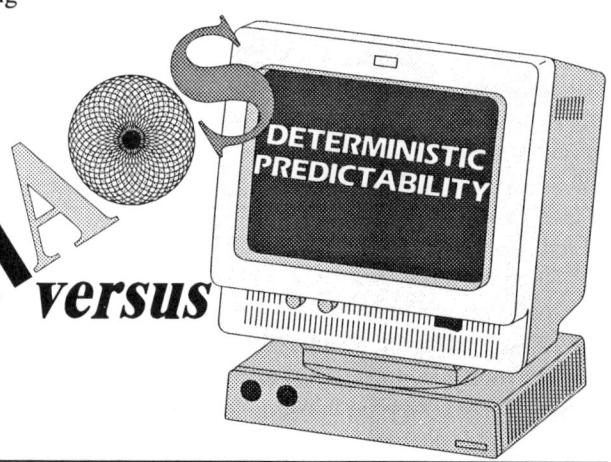

happen on the basis of what can be known at one instant." (Gleick, God, 135-6; Webster's) This led Laplace, who was far from alone in this belief, to state that **"if a being knew at one instant the positions and motions of every particle in the [U]niverse he would have at his disposal all the information necessary to compute the entire past and future history of the [U]niverse."** (Gleick, God, 136)

So, if we can devise a computer big enough, powerful enough, and fast enough to catalog every particle in the Universe and then apply to each the physicals laws of motion and cause and effect, we can predict the future and then reverse the process to reconstruct the past. This is **omniscience without God**, the atheistic version of foreknowledge. Not only does this **remove God** from His rightful role as Creator, Designer, Planner, and Sovereign Controller, but it removes Him from existence altogether. It also removes the human soul and **reduces humanity** to nothing more than a highly evolved, high-level complex of organic molecules.

Then, since chaos theory supposedly *eliminates* deterministic predictability, does that mean that it restores God? Of course not. What it *does seem* to do — and we say this with much caution and admitted ignorance — is to recog-

REDUCTIONISM

nize some very logical, practical, obvious, and yet awesomely incomprehensible aspects of **the complexity of Creation, but without God.** *And without God, an astoundingly planned and controlled complexity becomes chaos to the limited, finite, natural human mind.*

It does make one wonder if **Satan** is "pushing" supercomputer development because he thinks that he might be able to **approach omniscience himself**. Top-secret computer research is rumored to be beyond our imagination. Most likely, a computer will issue and track the Antichrist's mark of the beast.

Chaos theory (based on all of the other theories we have discussed) is also loosely seen as a "holistic" counter to **reductionism**. The last three centuries of Western scientific thinking, says Davies, have been reductionist in nature, meaning that science developed ever-increasing levels of specialists who took things apart to find answers instead of putting the pieces together to find a "whole" with "a higher level of structure than the individual pieces." (Davies, God, 61; Gleick, Chaos, 5)

"Reductionists assert that consciousness is

VITALISM

a product of brain chemistry," summarizes Phillip E. Johnson in a review of Steven Weinberg's *Dreams of a Final Theory*. DNA governs life and DNA is "reducible to the laws governing the physics and chemistry of lifeless matter...." All life is merely the purposeless, mechanical product of the Big Bang and impersonal laws. Reductionism is also a "world view aimed at producing a **rational society**." Johnson finds Weinberg to be incredibly intolerant, unwilling to accept any dissent as rational. (Johnson, "Science Without God," WSJ, May 10, 1993)

However, as we noted above, chaos theory may in some ways reverse reductionism, but it does not reverse the godlessness of any of modern science. Davies readily recognizes that the holistic movement in science is "in tune with **oriental philosophy and mysticism**." A "holistic perspective," he states, "removes the need for a **life-force**." The so-called life-force is the nearest these scientists come to mentioning God. Johnson comments that "any biologist who invokes some mystical element in the life processes that is not derived from chemistry or physics is deemed guilty of **'vitalism,'** which in contemporary science is a thought-crime only marginally less reprehensible than outright creationism." Davies calls vitalism an ancient doctrine that life cannot come from non-life and so requires a life-force, a spiritual essence ultimately of God. (Davies, God, 64, 60; Johnson, "Science Without God, WSJ, May 10, 1993)

We hope that you can now see just how far things can get away from God and from basic reality when the first step is made. Brick by brick, this modern Tower of Babel has been built with human reasoning. Notice **how many**

countries are represented in the formation of these sciences, even in our scant list of participants: America, France, Denmark, Italy, Greece, Poland, England, Scotland, and Austria, all nations that emerged from the Greek and Roman world.

Not only is today's physics divorced from reality, but it is expressible only through **abstract, advanced mathematics.** In today's science, math is God. While De Santillana and Von Dechend search for the identity of the Demiurge, the Craftsman God, who runs the heavens, physicists search for the **Grand Unified Theory,** the *master formula for the Universe,* the "single, simple breathtakingly elegant mathematical principle" which runs the heavens. (Davies, God, 158-62) "Mathematics has come to run away with and misguide the whole scientific effort," writes Dr. Harold Slusher. (Barnes, Space, 7) Indeed, to modern physicists, math is God and God is math.

Classical Physics

However, **certain physicists who insist on a real world** are progressing nicely on a new Unified Theory based on **revised (classical) electrodynamics,** an electromagnetic theory of physical Creation. [God is light, I Jn. 1:5] Dr. Lucas names these four groups as **1)** Prof. Joseph **Barredo,** representing Spanish Roman Catholics working in America since 1935, **2)** John **Kenny** of Bradley University starting about 1975, **3)** Dr. Thomas **Barnes** and Dr. Harold **Slusher** (both creationists) of the Geo/Space Research Foundation, University of Texas at El Paso, starting about 1976, and **4)** Dr. Charles **Lucas** (creationist) of Temple Hills, Maryland, starting in 1977. (Lucas, "Renewed Call," Soli, 38-40)

Revised Classical Electromagnetism

Classical physics upholds absolute and independent space and time, cause and effect, real physical evidence, an electromagnetic Universe, and the common experience of the observable world.

Of course, the **"world view" of this book** is forthrightly based on the unashamed belief that the **Bible is infallible truth** revealed to man by the only and almighty Creator God. This means, according to the world, that this book is fanatical, right wing, cultish, closed minded, narrow, intolerant, mean spirited, ignorant, anti-intellectual, radical, irrational, and just plain wrong. But that's all right because the Bible tells us not to marvel at the hatred of the world, and Jesus Christ made it clear that, as the world hated Him, so it would hate anyone who dared follow Him. It comes with the territory. (John 15:18-19; I John 3:13)

Our purpose here is not to call the world "wrong" merely to shout back at the world. **We are seeking for truth,** as much of it as we can find. In the process, if we find evidence that the world is clearly wrong about something, we will say so. And, if we find that the world seems to be correct about something, we will certainly and gratefully acknowledge that fact and make use of their findings. Remember the points of our world view as you review the following scholarly camps.

Diffusionism vs. Autochthonism

In *Skywatchers of Ancient Mexico,* archaeoastronomer Anthony Aveni refers to the "age-old debate between diffusionism and autochthonism." (Aveni, Skywatchers, 199) What in the world does that mean? You need to know, because this book is "dirty diffusionist" to the core. The *diffusionist* generally believes that man diffused, or dispersed, across the Earth from the *cradle of civilization,* which requires that he somehow crossed the oceans at various ancient times to settle the continents and islands.

The **cradle of civilization** is most often considered the Euphrates/Tigris River Valley of Mesopotamia, though some researchers point to the Indus River Valley of West Pakistan and some to Africa. There are **variations among the diffusionists,** from "Babel-believing" Christians like us to evolutionists who recognize the amazing abilities of ancient man some 4,000 years ago. Such a "diffusionist evolutionist" would believe that apes evolved into man in one location and man subsequently evolved to a much higher stage than is admitted by most other evolutionists sometime between 10,000 to

4000 B.C. *Diffusionists agree that there were pre-Columbian (before Columbus) voyages to America and advocate that human contact was responsible for the abundant, obvious cultural parallels between the Middle East, Europe, the Americas, and many Pacific Islands.*

"Autochthon" is a Greek word that means *"sprung from the land itself."* It refers to a native, original, or earliest-known inhabitant. (Webster's) The *autochthonist* is an evolutionist who may believe that man evolved in more than one location and that there is **no specific cradle of civilization**. Most believe that the Americas were populated 70,000 to 40,000 years ago by Monguls (Asians; see Chap. 2:14, 5:68) who migrated to the Americas across the Bering Strait (Russia to Alaska) **land bridge** and that independent evolution on both sides of the oceans led to the observed cultural parallels. These early migrants were, of course, primitive food gatherers and hunters.

The admitted problem with **man developing from apes in the Americas** is that *apes apparently did not reach the Americas until they were imported by Europeans after Columbus!* [Actually, we find that quite amusing.] So, the autochthonists, or "isolationists," had to find some explanation for man in America, and the *Bering Strait became the traditional, accepted answer.* Autochthonists/isolationists believe that the oceans effectively isolated the Americas from the rest of the world, except for the period during the so-called Ice Age when ice formation and low ocean levels conveniently formed the land bridge. (Heyerdahl, Early Man, 30, 59-64)

One *genuine* autochthonist who does not subscribe to the land-bridge theory is adventurer and archaeologist **Gene Savoy**, a specialist on ancient South America, who believes that the aboriginal Americans are older than migrating Mongollans and independently evolved, truly "sprung from the land itself." "Land-bridge theories serve only to make American aborigines dependent on the Old World," writes Savoy. He claims adamantly that white, Aryan-type Chachapoya Peruvian Indians, as well as Negroid sculptures and Nordic elements among the Olmecs all belong to peoples "proven" by excavations to be American Indians and not European transplants. **"Americans were simply here,"** he says, "possibly before the continents began to drift apart." He pursues the various Viracocha culture-hero legends of the wise white "god" from across the ocean but thinks the hero was actually home grown. However, he crosses tradition by advancing the maritime capabilities of the Mayas and the west-coast South Americans, and he admits that a "degree of transoceanic migration was probable, but certainly whole cultures did not cross the seas." (Savoy, Feathered, 9-11, 17-19) Savoy's view is that diffusionism degrades the Amerindians. He is a true, theoretical evolutionist, apes or no apes.

Cradle of Evolution
Cradle of Civilization

An excellent demonstration of the amazing stubbornness and blindness of **traditional autochthonists** is a paper by J.H. Rowe called "Diffusionism and Archaeology" published in *American Antiquity* in 1966. The paper lists **some 60 cultural parallels** between peoples of the ancient Mediterranean and the ancient Andes Mountains (Peru), including hide or coiled rope sandals that show "'very specific resemblances in design and manufacture.'" Naturally, one would think that such a paper would conclude decisively (and diffusively!) that such evidence demands human contact between the two remote cultures, that one culture came from the other, was influenced by the other, or at least traded with the other. But, no, that is not the case. This died-in-the-Andean-wool autochthonist *concludes that the evidence examined obviously supports* **parallel evolution!**

According to this paper, "'**science fiction, doctrinaire diffusionism**'" is "'a menace to sound archaeological theory.'" (Heyerdahl, Early Man, 64-5) Whenever arguing with a traditionalist, remember what you are up against! And...glean the truth where you may, even from an autochthonist!

The Cradle of Evolution

We should note that the autochthonist/diffusionist debate seems to center around more "modern" history of 1,000 to 10,000 years ago. And perhaps we should also note a difference between a **"cradle of civilization"** and a **"cradle of evolution."**

In today's *anthropological* circles (study of man), there are *paleontologists* who study bones and *geneticists* who study genes, such as DNA. What is quite interesting is that geneticists believe they have discovered a *common female ancestor* to all of the 5+ billion people now living on earth. They call her (what else?) **Eve**. She lived, they say, between 140,000 and 290,000 years ago. They don't believe she was the first of all women. They believe that the world was already covered with an "archaic" human-type species (sub-human, pre-human), but that a fully human Eve mothered the species of *modern* man. Her superior descendants fanned out (diffused), settling the whole world and replacing the previous species by virtue of more highly evolved genes. Called the **"Noah's Ark" theorists**, these evolutionists say that the races of modern man thus had a single, fully human, "recent" common ancestor who gave birth to humanity in Africa some 200,000 years ago. (Tierney, *Newsweek*, "The Search for Adam and Eve," Jan. 11, 1988, 46-52; *World Press Review*, "The Mother of Us All," November 1988, 54-5)

This "discovery" led to the conclusion that "modern humans didn't slowly and inexorably evolve in different parts of the world, as many anthropologists believed." The geneticists' findings challenged the paleontologists' long-held belief, as expressed by Richard Leakey in 1977, that there "'is no single center where modern man was born.'" (Tierney, *Newsweek*, Jan. 11, 1988, 47)

Many of the geneticists' *opponents* hold to a **"multi-regional" theory** that believes the separate races diverged *before* "man" was fully human, and then evolved into fully human man independently in various parts of the world (autochthony). This would make our most recent common ancestor less than human and living perhaps 500,000 or more years ago. This is also called the "candelabra hypothesis," with the separate evolution of the races represented by the parallel candles of a candelabra. (*World Press Review*, 54; *Newsweek*, 51-2)

So, the "Noah's Ark" geneticists now say that there was a single "cradle of evolution" for modern man, as well as a common ancestor. Does this make them diffusionists? As the term is generally applied to more modern history, it doesn't, and they would probably be horrified at such a thought. If you think this is confusing, you're right, but then evolutionist theories are generally confusing.

The other upsetting part of the geneticists' findings involves time, since most anthropologists thought that the divergence of man from chimpanzee began about 15 million years ago while the geneticists now say 5 to 7 million years. Apparently, Eve's dating of about 200,000 years ago is also considered very "recent," prompting Harvard paleontologist Stephen Jay Gould to say that it "'makes us realize that all human beings, despite differences in external appearance, are really members of a **single entity that's had a very recent origin in one place.'"** (Tierney, *Newsweek*, 47) Of course, Bible scholars have known all along that mankind came from a "single entity," very recently, in one place.

The evolutionists still argue over the location of the "cradle of evolution," with most pointing to Africa, but others to Asia, and even China. However, as states one paleontologist,

Diffusion
versus
Autochthony

"'If you look at the fossils, the good evidence on Africa can be placed in the palm of your hand.'" (*Newsweek*, 52) Most people don't realize that massive pillars of evolutionist theories, usually taught in public schools as fact, are built on the foundation of skeletal bits and pieces that would literally fit in the palm of your hand. Meanwhile, the geneticists continue to look for "Adam."

Prominent Traditional Dogmas

If you were famous or well-respected as an expert on some subject, wouldn't you have a hard time listening to someone not so respected who questioned your expertise? If you had spent your entire career writing widely accepted papers and books on a subject, would you be happy if someone told you everything you had written was wrong? If you had a well-paying job as a renowned professor, researcher, or museum curator, would you want to be discredited as presenting falsehoods and possibly lose your job and reputation?

Those are just some of the reasons that people don't just throw up their hands with glee and pounce on "new truth" or "wonderful discoveries." Anything that is established is just that—difficult if not impossible to budge. That's why we call it the **"establishment."** Human nature is human nature, and, in most cases, *people will go to great lengths to protect their turf,* their positions, their income, writings, teachings, egos, reputations, power, and influence before they will ever let the truth prove them wrong. This applies to the study of science and history as well as to politics.

We have already seen that **traditionalists in American history** hold that the Americas were populated by way of the **Bering Strait** 70,000 to 40,000 years ago. Another traditionalist dogma states that **migration across the Pacific was done by Asians from west to east,** a belief seriously challenged by famous Norwegian scholar and seafarer, Dr. Thor Heyerdahl. Another is that **ancient peoples were primitive** and could not possibly have had any type of sophisticated technology or knowledge. Real scientific discoveries, say traditionalists, were begun by the **Greeks** and continued later by enlightened Renaissance Europeans (about A.D.1300 to 1600).

Columbus Was First

Probably the most well-known bastion of traditionalism is the teaching that **Columbus was the first** to "discover" America and that no ocean crossings were made before his in 1492. In many public-school textbooks, Columbus also supposedly proved to a skeptical Europe that the **world was not flat**. The revered American historian **Samuel Eliot Morison**, a truly wonderful writer of history, published a biography of Christopher Columbus in 1942 and, though Morison mentions the Vinland stories of Leif Ericsson, his work became the central, unmovable pillar of authority that no European had come to America before Columbus. (Fell, Saga, 49; Morison, Admiral, 25-6)

Morison also presents the story of the "Unknown Pilot," a captain of a Spanish ship said to have been blown across the Atlantic to islands where he saw naked people. According to the story, first published in 1535, the captain

barely survived his return to Spain, only to die in Columbus's care. Columbus supposedly kept the information "secret." Both the initial publisher and Morison doubt the story in relation to Columbus, and with good reason. But Morison emphasizes the impossibility of a vessel being blown across the North Atlantic from east to west, that currents were not charted until the 1800s, and that the early Portuguese sailors met strong westerly winds and rough seas that prevented their venturing too far into the Atlantic. He says that there is no hint in

Columbus's Journal that the adventurer knew anything about the zone of the northeast trade winds and credits Columbus's path to luck. He also states that Englishman John Cabot "was the first mariner to cross the Atlantic by the short northern route," and that only after two of Columbus' voyages. (Morison, Admiral, 59, 62, 157)

In other words, Morison's work cemented the belief that, until the amazing vision and luck of Columbus, the **Atlantic was a virtually impassible barrier** between Europe and the Americas. Why did he and others think that no one in earlier times might have ridden the northeast trade winds to the Americas? The "Columbus route" is so easy, with "very gentle climatic conditions and extremely favorable currents and winds," that in "our days," (1970s) "there is an **annual regatta** of single-handed navigators, men and women, **following precisely the Columbus route** from the Canary Islands to the Caribbean," says Dr. Thor Heyerdahl. "Beginners who boast of never having sailed before go across in tiny **open rowboats, dinghies, canoes, and rafts of all kinds."** Heyerdahl's reed ships of ancient design, the *Ra I* and *Ra II*, led the way in 1969 and 1970 along the same route. (Heyerdahl, Early Man, 51-2)

When Morison published *The Oxford History of the American People* in 1965, he introduced America as having been visited by **Norsemen from Greenland** about A.D. 1000 and possibly even earlier by "an **unknown Irishman**," but still had no thought of ancient Atlantic crossings. However, he does confirm that the Greeks and the medieval theologians (Middle Ages c. A.D. 600 to 1500) taught that the world was not flat and that "Columbus never had to argue for it." (Morison, Oxford, 17-19) This was something he had emphasized in his earlier *Admiral of the Ocean Sea*, that "of all the vulgar errors connected with Columbus, the most persistent and the most absurd is that he had to convince people 'the world was round.' **Every educated man in his day believed the world to be a sphere**, every European university so taught geography, and seamen...knew perfectly well from seeing ships 'hull-down' and 'raising' mountains as they approached, that the surface of the globe was curved." (Morison, Admiral, 33)

Many traditionalists had to be dragged kicking and screaming into admitting that Norse Vikings and even possibly some Irishman had landed on the North American continent several centuries prior to Columbus. But, writes **Dr. Barry Fell**, during "the past hundred years the belief that no European settled America before Leif Eriksson or Columbus has grown from an hypothesis into a firmly rooted dogma." (Fell, America, 9) In the words of **Dr. Thor Heyerdahl**, there "is something amusing about the desperate desire of so many historians and anthropologists to reserve the first possible crossings of the Atlantic to the Spaniards and the Vikings." (Heyerdahl, Tigris, 280)

For a well-written but standard anti-diffusionist summary of early American history (and prehistory), see the first two chapters of Morison's *Oxford History*. He presents the popular Bering Strait explanation for man in America, then defends the ability of the "American Indians" to develop their own civilization, upholding the position of parallel evolution, but only after the Monguls had migrated. He cites the accepted line that important navigational, astronomical, and geographical advancements originated with the Greeks, and that the first effective European contact with the Americas was made by the Spaniards. (Morison, Oxford, 3-33) Despite these problems, the many important works of Samuel Eliot Morison are delightful and absolutely "must" reading for anyone seriously interested in American history.

Mavericks Among The Evolutionists

Evolutionist Harvard professor **Dr. Barry Fell**, author of *America B.C., Saga America,* and *Bronze Age America,* has been called, most disdainfully, a diffusionist. Dr. Fell is a marine biologist who specializes in studying "the ancient voyages of peoples who left inscriptions on remote islands which, of course, could only have been approached by sea." He tries to determine how the dispersal of man, plants, and animals has been affected by ocean currents and winds. Of necessity, he also became an *epigrapher*, epigraphy being "the art of reading ancient inscriptions engraved or otherwise imprinted on stone or other durable materials." (Fell, America, 19-20, 13)

As his early work was confined to inscriptions of the Old World, he was amazed when he discovered the existence, long known by some, of so many **ancient European, African, and Asian inscriptions from sites all over the Americas.** This highly educated Harvard professor states that he "had never seen such materials mentioned or illustrated in books on the archeology of the Americas and indeed was

ΕΠΙΥΡΑΦΕ

oblivious of their existence." (Fell, America, 19)

In **defying accepted tradition,** Dr. Fell has suffered much persecution from his own "establishment" colleagues. In the 1989 Epilogue of the latest edition of *America B.C.*, Dr. Fell shares that his book has been labeled "rubbish" and that he has been subjected to ridicule and even personal abuse. Generally, students are warned not to read Fell (you'd think he was a radical Christian and not a Harvard evolutionist) and are punished if they cite Fell in exam papers or theses. This treatment has also extended to respected Emeritus Professor of Engineering Science, **Alexander Thom,** of Oxford University in England, whose work on ancient observatories was, for years, refused publication because traditional archaeologists do not accept that ancient man was advanced enough to design and build such an observatory. (Fell, America, 331-2, 323)

The mavericks among the archaeologists who do quote Professor Thom are called *archaeoastronomers,* generally humanistic evolutionists who combine the scientific disciplines of archaeology and astronomy. Though traditional in their basic evolutionist, scientific approach, they have forged a new path in discovering and documenting the **amazing astronomical abilities of ancient peoples** as well as the uncanny **similarities of this knowledge from continent to continent**. They have rewritten a good deal of history but continue to force it into a broader evolutionist framework, **pushing man's "intellectual development" up in scale and back in time.** They recognize much of **mythology to be cosmology,** showing that seemingly childish doodles are accurate astronomical observations and that mysterious stone monuments are actually astronomical observatories.

These archaeoastronomers have taken a tremendous amount of **flak from traditionalists** for steering history in an unconventional direction, similar to the experience of Dr. Fell and Professor Thom. Dr. Fell, who uses archaeoastronomy in his own work, quotes Oxford University archaeology professor Dr. Catherine Hills who explains that professional archaeologists are "'very suspicious of astronomical interpretations, equating an interest in the moon with lunacy.' Advocates of ancient astronomy are usually astronomers and mathematicians," Fell adds, "and their writings appear obscure to innumerate archeologists who think that whatever they cannot understand must likewise have been incomprehensible to stone-age people." (Fell, America, 331) Of course, we "Babel-believing" diffusionists know that Adam, Cain, Seth, Noah, Shem, and Nimrod were anything but "stone age" in their knowledge and abilities.

However, archaeoastronomers close ranks with those same traditional archaeologists to knock the "clearly absurd claims of this new breed of diffusionists...." In the book *Archaeoastronomy in the Americas*, editor Ray Williamson

archaeoastronomy

thus **attacks the work of Dr. Fell,** who we just quoted as defending archaeoastronomy. Williamson goes on to say that "the data which Fell and his adherents present as evidence of such visits [to America by ancient Europeans, etc.] are poorly documented and of generally doubtful quality. In addition, the arguments they follow are composed largely of leaps of faith interspersed with unimpressive visual comparisons of New England and European similarities." (Williamson, Archaeoastronomy, 79)

So, "mainstream" archaeoastronomers are not diffusionists but autochthonists. However, they recognize that it is time to "kick" the traditional archaeologists' established idea that astronomical knowledge was gained after agriculture developed. (Williamson, Archaeoastronomy, Foreword) What is interesting is that the studies of archaeoastronomers are quite helpful to us Christian diffusionists.

Another important maverick among the evolutionists is **Dr. Thor Heyerdahl** who received his degrees in zoology and geography from the University of Oslo, Norway. A field expedition to the South Pacific in 1937-8 changed his interest to the origin of cultures in the Pacific Islands, and so he returned to Norway for a Ph.D. in archaeology. Heyerdahl is cer-

Ancient Ocean Craft

tainly **a diffusionist of sorts,** though he makes it perfectly clear that he never claimed that Maori-Polynesians descended from Peruvian Incas, or that Incas, Mayas, or Aztecs descended from Egyptians.

What Heyerdahl is uniquely famous for are his gutsy and adventurous voyages in ancient craft across both the Pacific and Atlantic Oceans as well as the gulfs and sea between Mesopotamia and Africa. He scolded both autochthonists and diffusionists for ignoring the winds and currents of the oceans, the former for viewing the oceans as total barriers and the latter for considering them as "skating rinks," which could be crossed anywhere in any direction.

Heyerdahl **exploded the "west-to-east" theory of Pacific Island settlement** by pointing out that the middle latitude winds and currents all move strongly east to west. He then demonstrated by sailing a South American **balsa-log raft** called the *Kon-Tiki* (see Chap. 12) of ancient design 4,300 miles from Peru to Raroia atoll in the Tuamotu Islands, Polynesia, in 1947. In the 1960s, he made one almost-successful and one successful Atlantic crossing in a **reed boat of ancient Egyptian design**, sailing over 3000 miles from Morocco in Africa to Barbados in the Caribbean. In 1977-8, he sailed another reed boat 4,200 miles from Iraq to Ethiopia. He strongly supports the idea of European and Eastern colonization in the West and points out that there is no evidence of gradual evolution anywhere in America. Civilizations appeared suddenly, as if imposed on primitive peoples. (Heyerdahl, Early, preface, 3, 14-15, 60-5, 216)

Even much more supportive of **cultural diffusion** are **Drs. Giorgio de Santillana and Hertha von Dechend**, authors of a "maverick" work called *Hamlet's Mill*. These professors present an intimidating mound of research to counter the "ruling opinions" that ancient mythology consists merely of the fantasies of primitive and superstitious peoples. **Myth**, they say, is an elitist **code** for extensive **astronomical knowledge**, centered around the world ages dictated by the precession of the equinoxes. The authors openly acknowledge the "formidable difficulties" they faced in disagreeing with "modern, current scholarship..., a wall, a veritable Berlin Wall, made of indifference, ignorance, and hostility. Humboldt, that wise master, said it long ago: First, people will deny a thing; then they will belittle it; then they will decide that it had been known long ago.'" However, De Santillana and Von Dechend were determined to "rescue those intellects of the past, distant and recent, from oblivion." (De Santillana, Hamlet's, ix, xii)

Through their research, De Santillana and Von Dechend were forced to the opinion that the body of astronomical "myth" was **common doctrine among the ancients** "all over the belt of high civilizations around our globe." This "cumulative thought" demonstrates a "coincidence of details" of an intensity and richness that demands a **single origin** and that must be, they conclude, in the **Near East**. "It is evident," they

Cosmological Myth

write, "that this indicates a **diffusion of ideas** to an extent hardly countenanced by current anthropology." The "complex of uncommon images" that they discovered in China, in Babylon, in Polynesia — indeed, around the world — "nobody could claim had risen independently by spontaneous generation." Von

Dechend first unlocked the key of astronomical code after spending more than a year examining 10,000-plus pages of Polynesian myths. The Polynesians, she concluded, could not have invented this code by themselves. (De Santillana, Hamlet's, 3, 7, x)

The professors despair of "science" derived from "preconceived convictions" and the "steady decline of scientific ethics." They **call "evolution" a "lazy word"** which has "blinded us to the real complexities of the past," a stupefying doctrine of gradualness "which is at best a platitude, only good for pacifying the mind, since no one is willing to imagine that *civilization appeared in a thunderclap.*" It is fascinating that De Santillana and Von Dechend are indeed evolutionist but on a vastly different time scale, pointing to the Earth sciences as the origin of the concepts of uniformity and gradualness with "a precise meaning." Transferred from geology to biology, these terms became "less precise in meaning, though still acceptable." They talk of natural law and natural selection and state that "events are determined by the rolling of the dice over long ages." They say that the "overall historical hypothesis" of biological evolution is supported by "sufficient data — and *by the lack of any alternative,*" [!!] but the details, they readily admit, raise "an appalling number of questions to which we have no answer." (De Santillana, Hamlet's, 67-70, italics added)

The writers contend that **"evolutionism"** has been applied to man and civilization "with all scale lost" and recognize the **destruction it has wreaked on cultural history**. They raise the case of Rudolf Virchow who warned of an **evil "'monkey wind'"** and pointed out repeatedly to his colleagues the **"unchanged quantity of brain"** *in all of the so-called "prehistoric" skulls of "Homo sapiens."* The starting assumption of De Santillana and Von Dechend, not "preconceived" but based in fact, is that **"our ancestors of the high and far-off times were endowed with minds wholly comparable to ours, and were capable of rational processes — always given the means at hand.** It is enough to say," they add, "that this flies in the face of a custom which has become already a second nature." (De Santillana, Hamlet's, 68-71, italics added) Though these authors would probably accuse us of having preconceived notions unfounded in fact (holding up the Bible as literal, revealed truth), they offer us much with which we can profoundly agree and much which lends support to our conclusions. The sheer weight of their research has demanded that they see some truth, despite their spiritual blindness.

"Open-Minded" Researchers

Mixed among the "serious scientists" of ancient history are a number of writers whose research is often fascinating but also usually poorly documented, if documented at all. Sadly, many Christian writers and publishers **neglect to properly document** their work, a fact which weakens their claims and, in some cases, perpetuates wrong information. Some clear *exceptions* to this problem include Christians who are scientists such as Dr. Carl Baugh and Dr. Henry Morris. In response to totally unfounded criticism due to the controversy of his findings, Dr. Baugh has employed exponentially meticulous documentation.

Included in our "open-minded" group are those who are looking for the lost continent or world of **Atlantis** and a race of super-humans, and those who believe in earthly visits by higher evolved beings from other parts of the galaxy or universe. This group can vary from psychics to astrophysicists and, frankly, for a non-Christian, the **UFO phenomenon** offers some plausible explanations. We Bible-believing Christians realize that there are indeed "extraterrestrials," but that they are spirit beings created by God and not evolved products of the universe. A number of the writers we lump in this "open-minded" group can be classified as New Agers, or are declared Theosophists, or have some other connection with what we would term the occult, though they would probably vehemently deny any "occult" label.

Especially in the study of something like the **Great Pyramid of Egypt,** the claims of various schools of scientists, Christians, and New Agers sometimes clash and sometimes cross over, which often is the cause of much confusion. We can glean viable information from some surprising sources, but we do need to be cautious as we sift for truth among such varied works, especially those with inadequate documentation.

BIBLIOGRAPHY

Aveni, Anthony F., *Skywatchers of Ancient Mexico*. Austin: University of Texas Press, 1980.

Barnes, Thomas G., *Space Medium*, Bib. Chap. 1, p. 19.

Bouw, Gerardus D., "Geocentricity," lecture delivered Feb. 12, 1990, Bloomington, Minnesota. [Association for Biblical Astronomy, 4527 Wetzel Avenue, Cleveland, OH 44109; or The Genesis Institute, 7232 Morgan Ave. S., Richfield, MN 55423]

Davies, Paul, *God and the New Physics*, Bib. Chap. 1, p. 19.

De Santillana, Giorgio, and Von Dechend, Hertha, *Hamlet's Mill*. Boston: David R. Godine, Publisher, Inc., 1977.

Encyclopaedia Britannica (EB), Bib. Chap. 3, p. 51.

Fell, Barry, *Saga America*. New York: Times Books, 1983.

_____, *America B.C.*, Bib. Chap. 6, p. 91.

Gaverluk, Emil, *The Rapture Before the Russian Invasion of Israel*, Bib. Chap. 1, p. 19.

Gleick, James, *Chaos*, Bib. Chap. 1, p. 19.

Hall, Marshall, "The Symbiotic Relationship Between Copernicanism and Darwinism," *Proceedings of the Second Conference on Absolutes*, July 28-29, 1992, edited by Gerardus D. Bouw. Cleveland, Ohio: Association for Biblical Astronomy, 1992. [4527 Wetzel Avenue, Cleveland, OH 44109; or The Genesis Institute, 7232 Morgan Ave. S., Richfield, MN 55423]

Henry, Jonathan F., "Geocentrism and Heliocentrism: A Comparison of Two Models of Our Planetary System," *Proceedings of the Second Conference on Absolutes*, July 28-29, 1992.

_____, "What Does the Red Shift Really Mean?" *Proceedings of the Second Conference on Absolutes*, July 28-29, 1992.

Heyerdahl, Thor, *Early Man and the Ocean*, A Search for the Beginnings of Navigation and Seaborne Civilizations. New York: Doubleday & Co., 1979.

_____, *The Tigris Expedition*, In Search of Our Beginnings. New York: Doubleday & Co., 1981.

Johnson, Phillip E., "Science Without God, *The Wall Street Journal*, May 10, 1993, op-ed section.

Lucas, Charles W., "Preface," *Soli Deo Gloria*. Temple Hills, Maryland: Church Computer Services, 1985.

_____, "A Renewed Call for Reformation," May 1985, *Soli Deo Gloria*.

_____, "A Revision of Electrodynamics for Real Particles," January 1978, *Soli Deo Gloria*.

_____, "An Electrodynamic Model for Charged Elementary Particles," September 1979, *Soli Deo Gloria*.

Morison, Samuel Eliot, *Admiral of the Ocean Sea*. New York: Little, Brown & Co., 1942.

_____, *The Oxford History of the American People*. New York: Oxford University Press, 1965.

Savoy, Gene, *On the Trail of the Feathered Serpent*. New York: The Bobbs-Merrill Co., Inc., 1974.

"The Mother of Us All," (from *The Economist*), *World Press Review*, November 1988, 54-5.

Tierney, John, "The Search for Adam and Eve," *Newsweek*, January 11:1988, 46-52.

Van der Kamp, Walter, "Does Space Know Place and Movement Rest?" *Proceedings of the Second Conference on Absolutes*, July 28-29, 1992.

_____, "How Long Halt Ye Between Two Opinions?" *Proceedings of the Second Conference on Absolutes*, July 28-29, 1992.

Webster's New World Dictionary, Bib. Chap. 2, p. 38.

Wheatley, Margaret J., "A Quantum Vision: Chaotic Organization Must Replace Newtonian Bureaucracy," *Barron's*, March 22, 1993, p. 12.

Williamson, Ray A., *Archaeoastronomy in the Americas*. Los Altos, California: Ballena Press, 1981.

NOTE: For some brief but enlightening reading concerning current thinking on **science and religion**, look up the Letters to the Editor in the June 16, 1993 *Wall Street Journal* (A13). It will probably be on microfilm in your local library. If not, talk to your librarian about having another library photostat the section (it might take two pages) and send it to you through your local library. The charge should be minimal. Note in particular the letter from the Ph.D. assistant professor from St. Martin's College. This subject should inspire a number of **essay topics**.

Chapter 10
Ancient Technology for Worldwide Dispersal

Advanced Ancient Geography?

There was no need for world maps, boats, or navigational techniques before the Babel judgment. The world's land was one mass before the Flood, and for a time thereafter, not truly "canaled by water" until Babel and the days of Peleg (2174 B.C.?). Mankind remained in the same general vicinity until Babel, when God created nations and enforced dispersion. *Now*, there were other lands to occupy and oceans to cross and various nations with whom to compete for land, resources, and trade.

The Bible says that God scattered the ancients across the face of *all* the Earth. We've seen that ancient man was highly intelligent, capable of sophisticated mathematics and astronomy. *Do we have any clues as to what the ancients knew about Earth's geography and how they diffused to all of the new continents?* Yes, we have some rather fascinating pieces of the ancient puzzle, pieces which we will examine in these next three chapters.

Remember that, in this book, when we refer to **"the ancients"**, *we* mean those people who lived from the time of the *Flood to about the 900s B.C.* (The term also includes those ancients who lived before the Flood, but we are most concerned in this book with post-Flood events.) In common usage, the term *ancient* is often connected with the **classical** period of Greece and Rome, roughly from the 800s B.C. to the fall of Rome in A.D. 476. The Middle Ages (**medieval**) generally refer to those years between A.D. 476 and about 1450. The European **Renaissance** usually designates the 1400s, 1500s, and 1600s as a transition phase from the "dark" and religious medieval era to the "enlightened" secularism and rationalism of the modern age. The **Enlightenment** refers specifically to the 1700s, while the term **modern** encompasses the years from about 1450 to the present. (Webster's) In this book, we use "modern" in this general sense, and also to refer specifically to the late 1800s to the present, when Darwin laid the popular foundation for the advancement of the evolutionist mindset. The meaning of **"traditional"** is relative, but we use it in this book to indicate the entrenched evolutionist teachings found in the modern textbooks of the late 1800s and the 1900s.

Did The Ancients Know the World Was Round?

Traditional wisdom wonders why the ancient Babylonians and Egyptians did not realize from their astronomical studies and other simple observations that the world was a sphere. The answer is, of course, that they *did* realize it. "But," insist traditionalists, "the significance of these phenomena dawned on mankind only slowly." The Greek poet **Homer** (800s B.C.), it is said, believed **Earth was a convex disk** while other Greeks of his time apparently thought the **"plate" of the Earth** balanced on four elephants standing on a *turtle*. (EB 1972, 10:132) This so-called "long-lived" belief seems to have varied from a convex disk to a flat disk, surrounded by an ocean stream and covered by a dome of sky, or sometimes floating free in a spherical sky. (EB 1972, 14:827; Timetables, 11) Thus explaineth the traditionalists.

← Ancients		Classical Ancients		Middle Ages	MODERN			
					Renaissance	Enlightenment		
2345 B.C.	800s B.C.		A.D. 476	1450	1700s		1800s	1900s

Ancient Technology For Dispersal

Page 161

However, remember the **Mystery code**? The research of De Santillana and Von Dechend strongly indicates that traditionalists have been led far astray by their **uninitiated interpretations** of mythical code. *Hamlet's Mill* reproduces a number of ancient illustrations from Egypt, India, Africa, and the Americas (including the Maya) which show the **turtle** as the fixed base upon which the mighty **churn of heaven** was turned in the **"Battle of the Gods."** The older and younger gods use a long *serpent* as the "golden rope" to churn or drill the heavens. This symbolizes the **precession of the equinoxes** and the separation of the "parents of the world," the ecliptic and the celestial equator. The battle may represent both the spiritual battle in the Garden of Eden as well as the spiritual battle between Noah and Cush, and between Shem and Nimrod. Apparently, the "victory" of the younger gods (Satan at the Fall; pagans under Nimrod) set the precession moving inexorably in one direction. (De Santillana, Hamlet's, 152-163, 369, 435)

The point is this: traditionalists interpret ancient mystical symbolism as literal, naturally concluding that ignorant, unevolved ancients had primitive ideas of a flat Earth. However, evidence shows that those same illustrations represent *ancient understanding of complex astronomical movements and a very real spiritual conflict.*

Another traditional teaching is that Greek mathematician **Pythagoras** (500s B.C.) was "perhaps the first" to determine that Earth is indeed a sphere, (EB 1972, 10:132; Morison, Oxford, 17) and the traditional belief since medieval times has been that "exact science" began with the later Greeks of the 500s B.C. This would only show a fast degeneration of knowledge among certain peoples, considering what we have determined to be true about the an-

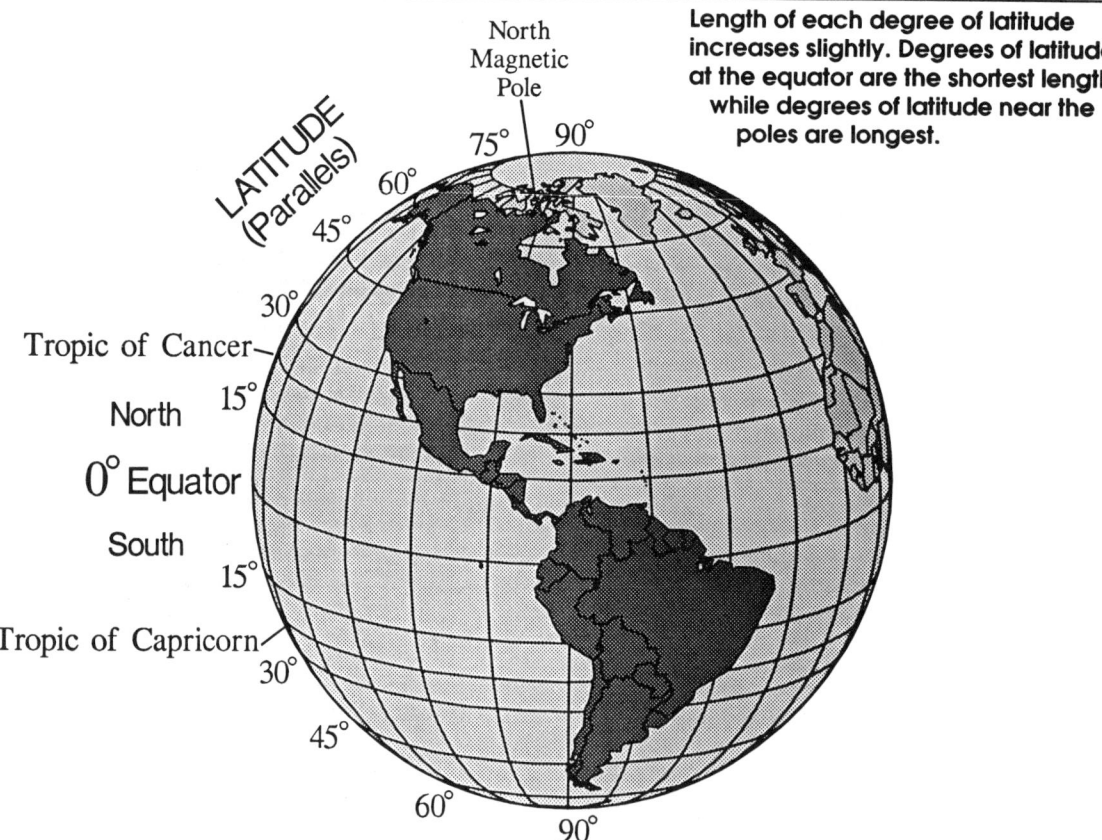

LATITUDE measures your location north or south of the equator. There are 180° from pole to pole, and 90° from the equator to each pole. The only parallel that equals 360° is the equator. There is a PARALLEL of latitude for each degree, but maps normally mark the parallels at 15° intervals (15 x 6 = 90). Each degree is divided into 60 minutes (60') and each minute into 60 seconds (60"). The Tropic of Cancer (northern boundary of the Sun's path) today is at 23° 27', but was at 23° 51' when Egypt was first mapped.

cients. Traditionalists also point out that a large number of medieval maps (A.D. 1000 to 1500) "appear to show the world as a flat disk." (EB 1972, 14:830) However, the same maps can be easily interpreted as illustrations of a round world on a flat surface, and Samuel Eliot Morison makes it quite clear that the "spherical globe was taught to every lad who attended a medieval university." (Morison, Oxford, 17)

Did They Know Earth's Circumference?

The Greek **Eratosthenes (200s B.C.)**, who presided over the library/museum at Alexandria, Egypt, is said to be the first to measure the circumference of the Earth, "assuming" Earth to be a sphere. He used, according to one writer in the *Encyclopædia Britannica* (EB), angles of sunlight at two Egyptian cities and the estimated distance between those cities, to determine the length of a meridian (or great circle) to be 250,000 *stadia*. The question is, did he use the Attic (Greek) *stade* (or "stadium") which is said to be very close to 185 meters in length (or 600 Greek feet or 606.75 US feet), or a stadium of a different length? Using a Greek stadium of 185 meters, the estimate of Eratosthenes would equal about 28,739 miles, or **15% to 16% too large**. [Mean circumference is 24,800 miles while equatorial is about 24,903 miles.] (EB, 1972, 10:132-3; Webster's; Hapgood, Maps, 33; Tompkins, Secrets, 45-6, 206) However, another writer in EB states that Eratosthenes overestimated by only "a few hundred miles." (EB, 1972, 14:828)

Charles Hapgood gives 252,000 stadia as the estimate of Eratosthenes, using a stadium of 547 US feet, determining that Eratosthenes **overestimated by only 4½%**. (Hapgood, Maps, 32-3) So, depending on the source, Eratosthenes overestimated the circumference of the Earth by anywhere from "a few hundred miles" to some 1,100 miles to over 3,800 miles. However, this is *still considered a pretty close guess*, since he is *traditionally* chronicled as the "first" to apply an "astrogeodetic" method to this question. (EB,

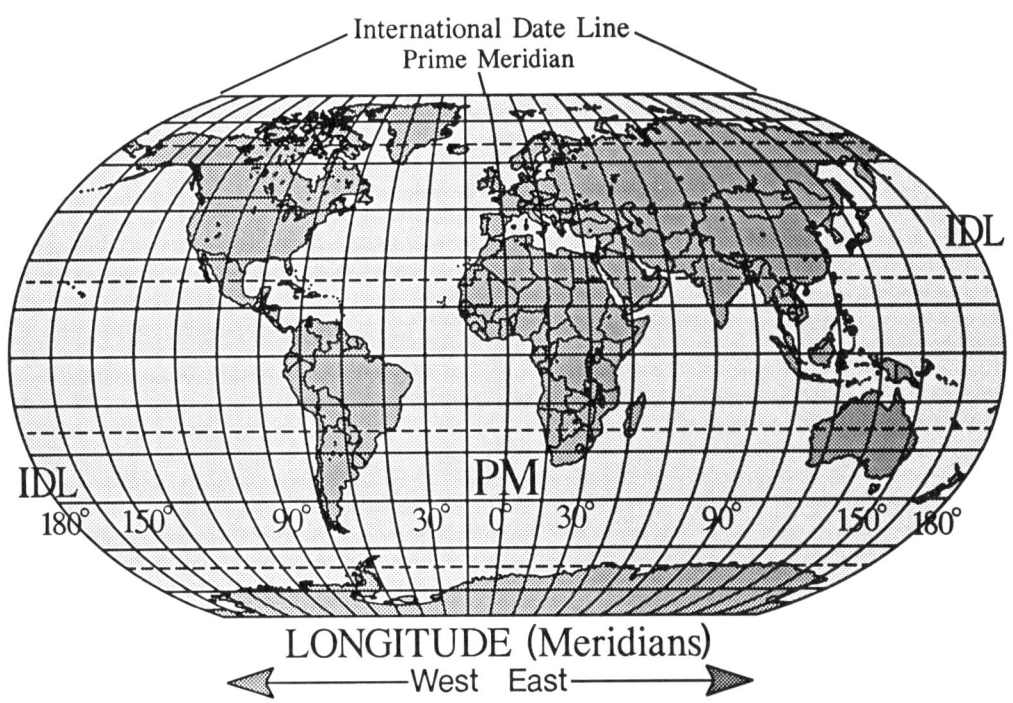

LONGITUDE marks your position east or west of the **Prime Meridian** which runs through Greenwich, England. **Meridians** are *not* parallel, as they meet at each pole. Thus, a degree of longitude is measured at the equator. Every meridian is one half of a **GREAT CIRCLE** around the Earth. A great circle is the intersection of Earth's surface and a plane which passes through Earth's center. The shortest distance between Dallas, Texas, and Tokyo, Japan, is along the great circle which runs through Canada and southern Alaska, not across the Pacific Ocean. Get a globe and look!

Ancient Technology For Dispersal

1972, 10:13203)

Dr. Livio Catullo Stecchini is a specialist in ancient measurement and quantitative science with a Ph.D. from Harvard University. Having taught at major universities in Rome and Chicago, at Massachusetts Institute of Technology (MIT) in Cambridge, and at Rutgers in New Jersey, he is called "a Copernicus of the 20th Century" by Professor Giorgio de Santillana of MIT. Stecchini's research shows that *Eratosthenes relied on ancient Egyptian data which he did not truly understand*, not realizing that the Tropic of Cancer had shifted by his lifetime, due to the precession. Eratosthenes made several errors, including using the Babylonian "great cubit." Instead of 250,000 stadia, his estimate should have been a much closer figure between 216,000 and 217,000 stadia. (Tompkins, Secrets, ix, 176, 287-8, 215-16, 209)

According to one writer in EB, the Greek Stoic philosopher and historian, **Poseidonius (100s B.C.)**, arrived at a circumference about 11% too long. (EB, 1972, 10:133) However, according to another writer in EB, Poseidonius recalculated Earth's circumference to be much shorter than the overestimate of Eratosthenes. Then, in the **A.D. 100s**, the Greek mathematician and astronomer **Ptolemy**, who lived in Alexandria, Egypt, promoted this shorter estimate as the most correct. (EB, 1972, 14:829) Peter Tompkins gives Ptolemy's estimate as **18,000 miles**, or almost 7,000 miles off the mark. (Tompkins, Secrets, 6)

One way to estimate the size of the Earth is to measure one degree of *latitude*. In the A.D. **800s, Arab Islamic conquerers of Egypt** used astronomical observations and overland measurement to determine the length of 1° of latitude on the plain of Palmyra, north of the Euphrates River. (Actually, to calculate the most accurate estimate of the Earth's equatorial circumference, a surveyor needs to know the length of 1° of *longitude* at the equator. However, latitude is much easier to measure.) According to Peter Tompkins, the astronomers of **Abdullah Al Mamun** calculated Earth's circumference to be equal to **23,180** of our miles, or some 1,700 miles short. Actually, this measurement represents a **north/south "great circle"** as opposed to the actual equatorial circumference because the poles are slightly flattened. (Tompkins, Secrets, 5-6)

[Heliocentrists claim that Earth's rotation gives the equator a bulge. Geocentrists counter that the rotation of the rest of the Universe could also account for a bulge. However, there is controversy as to whether there is a bulge, or very much of a bulge. The Earth looks very round from space. (Hall, Earth, 194-7)]

However, another writer in EB states that the **same Arabs** arrived at a figure of about **25,741 miles**, or only **about 3.6% too long**. (EB, 1972, 10:133) *It would be interesting to research why all the disagreement about who estimated what*, but the main point here is that **Ptolemy's preference and influence prevailed**, regardless of his source. His much-too-short estimate of 18,000 miles distorted maps into the 1700s, encouraged Christopher Columbus to sail west, and helped to delay publication of Sir Isaac Newton's theory of gravitation, a theory dependent upon an accurate knowledge of Earth's circumference and the reason for Newton's interest in measuring the Great Pyramid. (Tompkins, Secrets, 31-2, 362)

All of these estimates, long or short, also demonstrate a **deterioration of knowledge by the 200s B.C**. As we shall soon see, the *ancients had very accurate knowledge of Earth's geography*.

Ancient Knowledge Lost

In the early 1500s, **Girolamo Cardano**, an "astonishing Milanese" [from Milan, Italy] physician and mathematician and close friend to Leonardo da Vinci, decided that there must have been **a knowledge of "exact science"** *hundreds or even thousands of years before the time of the Greeks,* that this knowledge included the **true length of a degree of longitude**, and that the place to find this knowledge would be **Egypt!** Supposedly, **Pythagoras** himself, the Greek mathematician (500s B.C.), wrote that the "measures of antiquity" were based on Egyptian standards, and that these measurements were based on the **unchanging and natural dimensions of the Earth**. Having lost the ancient knowledge, man continued his search for "an imperishable standard of linear measure." (Tompkins, Secrets, 22)

Though traditional wisdom continues to point to the Greeks of the 500s B.C. to the A.D. 200s as the fathers of modern science, Dr. Stecchini contends that these Greeks were for the most part "handling and mishandling" an ancient knowledge which they only partially understood. Peter Tompkins reports that Stecchini has become convinced that people living several millennia before the Greeks were quite advanced in mathematics and astronomy. (Tompkins, Secrets, 215-16)

Another bucker of traditional wisdom, in the same spirit as Cardano, Pythagorus, and Stecchini, is **A.E. Nordenskiöld**, the great 19th-Century Swedish explorer and cartographer. After compiling an **atlas of medieval maps**, he concluded that, **1)** the maps he gathered were **too accurate** to have come from medieval sailors, **2)** there was **no development** in the maps from the A.D. 1300s to 1500s, **3)** the maps all seemed to have come from a *single, ancient source,* and **4)** the apparent ancient source had to be drawn by **higher technology** than that available in medieval or classical (Greek/Roman) times, or, in other words, a technology that preceded the Greeks! (Hapgood, Maps, 9-11) In addition, several maps dated from the 1300s to the 1500s have been found to show an **almost ice-free Antarctica** or a **partially ice-free Antarctica** (a continent that wasn't "discovered" until 1818) as well as **Greenland** (probably several islands) with **no ice cap**. These same maps incorporate a highly sophisticated method of **spherical projection**. (Hapgood, Maps, 72; 99;116-17; 149-154, 224-5) So much for "flat-Earth" ancients!

From where did this knowledge come? *How soon after the Babel judgment was man able to map the radically changed Earth?* Did the pre-Flood and post-Flood patriarchs know the accurate circumference of the Earth? Though an evolutionist, **Professor Charles H. Hapgood** concluded from his extensive geographical studies that "the evident knowledge of longitude [shown in the medieval maps] implies a **people unknown to us**, a nation of seafarers, with instruments for finding longitude undreamed of by the Greeks, and, so far as we know, not possessed by the Phoenicians, either." (Hapgood, Maps, 49) These ancient geographers knew the exact circumference of the Earth, and thus "had a more accurate knowledge of the [Earth's circumference] than Eratosthenes or the astronomers of the Renaissance." (Mallery, Rediscovery, 244)

Hapgood goes on to say that the evidence points to an ancient, advanced civilization with knowledge and abilities of the A.D. 1700s and beyond. This civilization was either a **worldwide culture** or one with **worldwide navigation**, thus *destroying the theory of the steadily progressive, linear development of society.* He also suggests that ancient Egyptian, Hindu, and Buddhist writings indicate that mankind once had a **single language**. (Hapgood, Maps, 193-206) In order to reconcile these "amazing" discoveries with his evolutionist beliefs, including the accepted Ice Age theories, Professor Hapgood places this ancient civilization many thousands of years ago. However, he has also had to abandon certain evolutionist dogmas. Isn't it interesting that we Bible believers already knew that mankind had one language, that ancient man possessed superior intelligence, and that there was indeed a single, ancient, advanced civilization prior to Babel that later dispersed around the world?

Mysterious Monument of Ancient Knowledge

Ten miles west of modern Cairo, Egypt, on a plateau meticulously leveled to within a fraction of an inch by human construction workers, stands an ancient edifice consisting of 201 stepped tiers of stone blocks which reach the height of a 40-story building. The number of these blocks has been estimated from 2.3 million to 2.5+ million, each weighing from two to 70 tons, or about 4,000 to 140,000 pounds. (Tompkins, Secrets, 1) Greek historian **Herodotus** (400s B.C.) writes that it took a force of 100,000 men 10 years of preparation and 20 years of construction to build this edifice that was one of the **Seven Wonders of the Ancient World**. If Herodotus is correct, that would require, at the very least, the laying of more than 300 massive stones per day, every day for 20 years! (Capt, Great, 6)

The Ancients' Superior Masonry

In the late 1800s, **Sir William Flinders Petrie** measured a distance of 350 feet along a certain passageway in this mighty Egyptian structure and found the passageway walls to be within 1/4th inch of being absolutely straight! The stone blocks, he said, were cut with a "staggering accuracy" that "was equivalent to the most modern optician's straight edges." Carving so many mammoth stones with such fineness is almost unbelievable, but the fact that mortar the average thickness of 1/50th of an inch was placed between the stones, and then the stones perfectly fitted together, is almost beyond comprehension. "'It is to be compared to the **finest opticians' work on a scale of acres,'"** wrote Petrie. In addition, the cement between the casing stones was so finely textured that after some 4,000 years of exposure, the stones chip before the cement gives. (Tompkins, Secrets, 105)

Until at least the 1st Century A.D., the structure was covered with massive but perfectly cut and polished limestone blocks that were angled and fitted to produce a face so smooth that the joints were hardly visible. Marble erodes with time and exposure, but limestone only becomes harder and more polished. The feat of erecting this ancient monument, in just pure magnitude of masonry, was not equalled until the building of Boulder (Hoover) Dam near Las Vegas, Nevada, in 1936. And even today, engineers continue to marvel at and argue over the construction methods used to accomplish such an enormous and yet exquisitely precise architectural triumph. (Tompkins, Secrets, 1-3)

Ancient Controversial Mystery

The structure, if you haven't already guessed, is called the **Great Pyramid**, and it has boggled men's minds for almost four millennia. Several **Christian** explorers and researchers have worked out elaborate systems of biblical prophecy based on this pyramid's measurements. The **occultists** claim it as the ancient temple for initiation into the pagan Mysteries. Certain **maverick evolutionists** see it as an ancient storehouse of knowledge possessed by a highly evolved, advanced civilization that disappeared several (or more) thousand years ago.

Archaeoastronomers generally acknowledge certain "astronomical interpretations" and alignments of the Great Pyramid, but dismiss the more "extreme" claims made by "pyramid enthusiasts," claims such as the use of *pi* (mathematical value of 3.14159....) in the design. The Greek letter pi is used to symbolize the *mathematical relationship of the circumference of a circle to its diameter*, or as Tompkins puts it, the "unchanging value which links a **straight** diameter to a **curved** circumference." (Tompkins, Secrets, 196) A circle's **circumference** equals πd (pi times the diameter), which is the same as $2\pi r$ (pi times twice the radius), while the **area** of a circle equals πr^2. Traditionalists and many archaeoastronomers scoff at the use of pi in the Great Pyramid because, according to *accepted* history, π was not correctly worked out to four decimal places until the A.D. 500s by the Hindu sage Arya-Bhata. (Modern computers have run it out to 10,000 decimal places, with no end in sight!) Tompkins records that the oldest Egyptian document showing a value of π is dated about 1700 B.C. and was found in mummy wrappings by a Scotsman named Rhind. The value given is a rough 3.16. (Tompkins, Secrets, 71-2)

However, using his research and the writings of Agatharchides, Dr. Stecchini demonstrates how the Egyptians who designed the Great Pyramid calculated pi to at least 3.1416. (Tompkins, Secrets, 373-4) Archaeologist **R. A. Schwaller de Lubicz** found an illustration in the tomb of Rameses IX (1080s B.C.?) that shows a royal mummy as the hypotenuse (side c) of the sacred, 3-4-5, Pythagorean right-angled triangle ($a^2 + b^2 = c^2$). A snake forms the right angle and sides a and b. The king's body is 5 cubits long while his outstretched arm adds a 6th cubit for a ratio of 6/5 which equals **1.2**. The body is also divided, says Schwaller, into a phi + 1 proportion. (See phi below.) **Phi (ϕ)** equals 1.618. Phi plus one (2.618) is the same as phi times itself, or ϕ^2. (Tompkins, Secrets, 145, 194)

$$\phi^2 = \phi + 1$$
$$1.618 \times 1.618 = 2.6179 \ (2.618)$$
$$1.618 + 1 = 2.618$$

It so happens that $\phi^2 \times 1.2 = \pi$ accurate to four places.

$$2.618 \times 1.2 = \mathbf{3.1416}$$

The use of pi in the construction of the

Great Pyramid, says archaeoastronomer James Cornell, was "probably" accomplished as a happenstance by-product of laying out the foundation by rolling a barrel on the ground. (A barrel is circular.) "'In this way,'" he quotes Kurt Mendelssohn, "'they would have arrived at the transcendental number, 3.141...without trying and without knowing.'" (Cornell, First, 106; Krupp, In Search, 232-3) What we have just seen, plus our study of the incredible precision, sophistication, and artistry of the Great Pyramid, as well as our study of the ancients in general, makes this attempted explanation sound silly.

The First World Map?

Actually, the Great Pyramid, among other things, both biblical and occultic, astronomical and mathematical, is a MAP — **a sophisticated reference map of the Earth's Northern Hemisphere**, a fact that is "indicated repeatedly in the ancient texts." The writings of **Agatharchides of Cnidus**, a Greek of the 100s B.C. who was a guardian of the king of Egypt, *quote ancient Egyptian sources* as saying that one side of the **base** of the Great Pyramid is equal to 1/8th of a minute of a degree of latitude at the *equator*, and the **apothem** (the slant height, perpendicular from the middle of one base to the tip of the pyramid) is equal to 1/10th of a minute of a degree of latitude at the parallel of the *Great Pyramid*.

So, what does this "degree of latitude" signify? Agatharchides refers to the degrees, minutes, and seconds which are used to measure **latitude** and **longitude** to establish location and distance on the face of the Earth. Since the Earth is basically a sphere, it is measured on a standard of **360°** with each degree consisting of **sixty minutes** and each minute of **sixty seconds**. From where did the numerical system of 60s and the 360° division of a circle come? The system came from (where else?) the **Babylonians**, and is considered to be the most ancient of measurements. Using math and astronomy, the first Egyptians were able to measure *accurately* the length of degrees of latitude and to achieve almost the same precision in measuring longitude, which gave them an *accurate figure for the circumference of the Earth*. (Tompkins, Secrets,

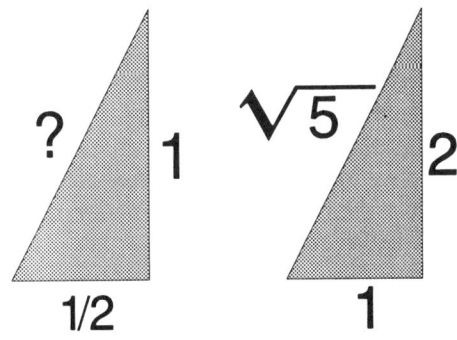

The triangle formed in the square has a base (a) equal to 1/2 and a side (b) equal to 1. To find the length of the hypotenuse, we would have to square a fraction. So, let's take the base to equal 1. We know then that the side is twice the base, or 2. Thus:

$$a^2 + b^2 = c^2$$
$$1^2 + 2^2 = c^2$$
$$1 + 4 = 5$$
$$c^2 = 5$$
$$c = \sqrt{5}$$

Since we multiplied by 2 with the second triangle, the hypotenuse of the first triangle equals $\sqrt{5}/2$ which equals **1.118**. Note that the squares tell us that:

0.5 + 0.618 = 1.118
0.5 + 1.118 = **1.618**

Note that this can also be written as

$$1/2 + \sqrt{5}/2 = 1.618 = \text{phi}$$

Two equal squares together have a length-to-width ratio of 1 to 2. **Phi** is found easily by halving one square and creating two triangles. The hypotenuse equals 1/2 + 0.618. The **Golden Section** proportion is thus demonstrated as: AB/AC = AC/CB
AB is to AC as AC is to CB.

Ancient Technology For Dispersal

201, 206, 209, 364)

Pi, Phi, and Spherical Projection

Stecchini and other researchers document, both historically and mathematically, that the Great Pyramid was indeed designed using not only *pi* (3.1416), but *phi* (1.618) as well.

Phi (φ) was called the **Golden Section** of architecture and design by **Leonardo da Vinci**, and the proportional equation was used in the composition of many Renaissance masterpieces. Plato considered the eye-pleasing proportion to be the "most binding of all mathematical relations" and "the key to the physics of the cosmos." This proportion is also called the "golden mean" and has been found in the mathematical measurements of the growth patterns of spiral sea shells. "With the incorporation of the Golden Section," writes Tompkins, "the Great Pyramid provides an effective system for *translating* **spherical** *areas into* **flat** *ones*." (Tompkins, Secrets, 190-3; Mysteries, 262)

The measurements of the Great Pyramid were approached in two ways:
1) an **ideal** as well as **practical plan** of rounded numbers illustrating **mathematical principles**
2) a plan of **exact and complex measurements** showing **geographical precision**.
First, let's see how pi and phi are practically illustrated by the rounded-off dimensions of the GP.

The GP is measured in **royal cubits** as opposed to geographic cubits or Egyptian cubits. The royal or sacred cubit is a *septenary* system

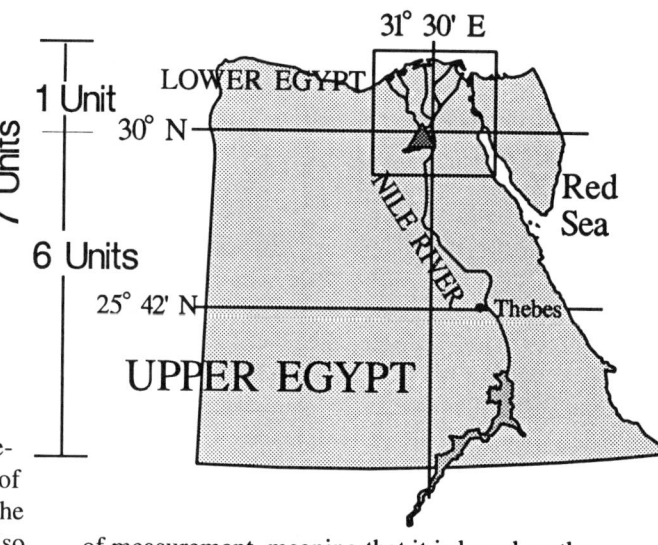

of measurement, meaning that it is based on the **sacred number 7**. It consists of **7 hands**, or 28 fingers. Don't let the terms *hand* and *finger* fool you. These units represent exact measurement standards and not the bumbling efforts of primitive men using the body parts of royalty or commoners to rough out a distance. (Tompkins, Secrets, 305)

A **cubit** equals 1½ feet. An **Egyptian foot** is 300 millimeters (mm) and an **Egyptian cubit** equals 450 mm. A **geographic foot** is about 307.8 mm (308) while a **geographic cubit** equals 461.69 mm (462). The geographic foot (and cubit), writes Stecchini, was the *standard of the ancient world*, except for Egypt, where the royal cubit became the standard. Both the Egyptian and geographic cubit are **6 hands**. Egyptians saw Upper Egypt (South) as 6 units and Lower Egypt (Delta) as 1 unit, and Egypt as the perfect 7 units. (Tompkins, Secrets, 300,

GREAT PYRAMID

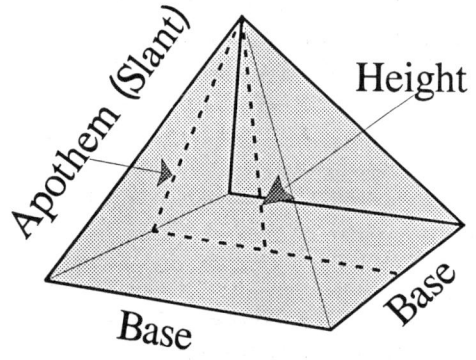
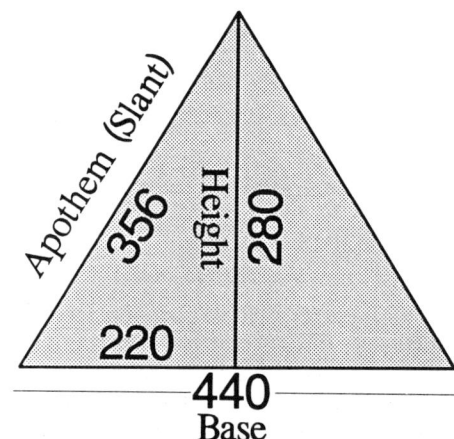

The Great Pyramid is measured in ROYAL CUBITS. Shown is the *ideal* plan based on a *septenary* pi value of **22/7** and rounded numbers.

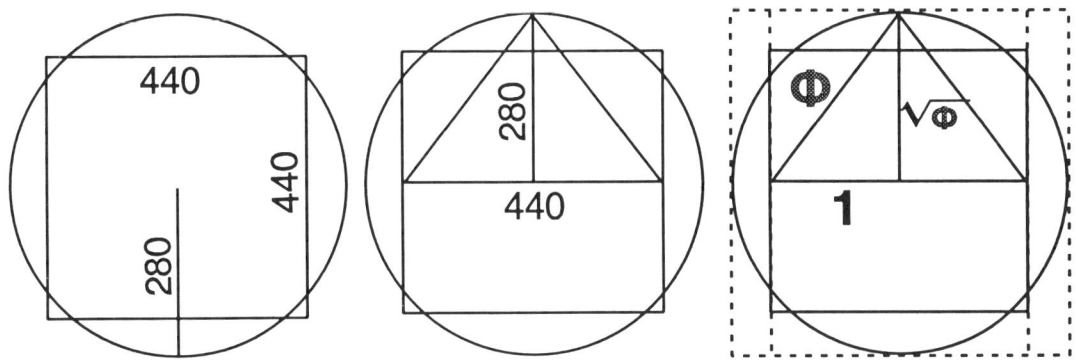

The *square* is the **perimeter** of the **base** of the Great Pyramid: 440 x 4 = **1,760**. The *circle* has a **radius** equal to the **height** of the Great Pyramid. Thus, its **circumference** is also 1,760.
c = 2πr   π = 22/7
2 x 22/7 x 280 = 12,320/7 = **1,760**

The triangle is a cross-section of the Great Pyramid. If the **meridian triangle of the GP** is given a base of 1, then the side equals the square root of phi and the hypotenuse equals phi: $a^2 + b^2 = c^2$ and $1 + \phi = \phi^2$. Thus, the height of the GP and the radius of the circle becomes the **square root of phi**.

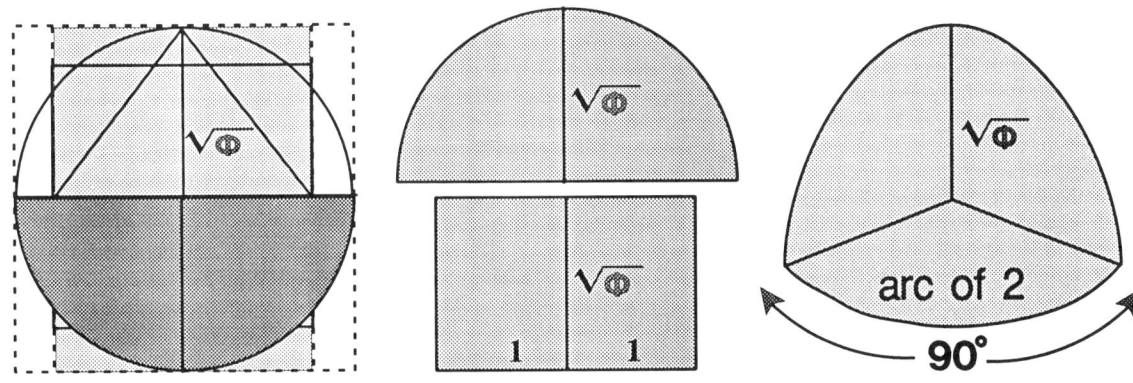

By making the square a rectangle with the same width of 440 and a new height of 2 x 280, its area equals the area of the circle.
Rectangle: L x W = A
280 x 2 x 440 = **246,400**
Circle: πr^2 = A
22/7 x (280 x 280) = 22/7 x 78,400 = **246,399.99**
Rectangle: 2√φ x 2 = 4√φ
Circle: $r^2 = \phi$ and so $\pi r^2 = \pi\phi$
π basically = 4/√φ
4/√φ x φ = 4√φ

Since the whole rectangle equals the whole circle, then half the rectangle equals half the circle. Half a flat circle is essentially equal in area to a spherical quadrant of the same radius. And so a rectangle of the same height and a base of 1 + 1 or 2, virtually represents the same area as a sphere of that height and an arc of 2.
Rectangle Area = 2 √φ
Sphere Area = 2 √φ
This is called **spherical projection**.

311-314, 320)

Tompkins points out that the **geographic foot**, the most common ancient measurement, found by Stecchini in the oldest Babylonian temples, was measured *astronomically*, and so its *exact length varies slightly from nation to nation* because of the minor increase in length of a degree of *latitude* from the equator to the pole. A geographic foot is intended to represent **1/100th of a second of a degree of latitude**. Thus, at the equator, a geographic foot equals 307.15 mm. At the mean latitude of Egypt which is 27° 45' N, a geographic foot equals 307.795 mm. **At the latitude of the Great Pyramid** (30°N), it equals 307.9 mm. At this latitude, a geographic cubit (1½ feet) equals 461.8 mm, or 6 hands. (Tompkins, Secrets, 206, 373)

However, remember once again that, according to Stecchini, the GP is measured in *royal* cubits of 7 hands. The basic plan of the GP is this: a **base** of 440 royal cubits, a **height** of 280 royal cubits, and an **apothem** (slope) of 356 royal cubits. It is impossible to construct such a right triangle, according to the Pythagorean theorem, but these numbers allow practical solutions to geometrical problems involving irrational numbers like pi and phi.

With a base of 440, the GP has a **perimeter** of 1,760 (440 x 4). Now, let's look at a **circle** with a circumference equal to the GP perimenter (1,760) and a radius equal to the GP height (280). Since the circumference of the circle equals pi times twice the radius (c = 2rπ), then we can substitute these values such that

$$1,760 = 2 \times 280 \times \pi$$
$$1,760 = 560\pi$$
$$1,760/560 = \pi$$
$$\mathbf{3.1428 = \pi}$$

A more precise value for pi is 3.14159... or 3.1416. However, the often-used *practical* value of pi is **22/7** which is septenary (based on the sacred 7) and is equal to **3.1428**. Half the GP base is 220, which serves as the base of the **meridian triangle** of the GP. Its height is 280. The ratio of pi over 4 is expressed as:

$$22/7 \times 1/4 = \mathbf{22/28}$$

Thus, the GP meridian triangle base equals π/4 of the GP height. [3.1428/4 = 0.7857 and 0.7857 x 280 = 219.996 or basically 220] And the height of the GP (280) bears the same relationship to its perimeter (1,760) as a circle's radius does to its circumference (2πr). [2 x 3.1428 x 280 = 1,759.968, or 1,760] Note also that the apothem (slope) of 356 divided by 220 equals phi, or **1.618**. (Tompkins, Secrets, 197, 306-7, 368-9)

It also so happens that if we designate the base of the meridian triangle (or any right triangle) as a unit of 1, we can assign the value of the square root of phi to the height, and the value of phi to the hypotenuse. Note from the diagram that the **area of a rectangle** with a width equal to the base of the GP (1 + 1) and a height equal to twice the height of the GP (2) is the same as the **area of the circle** with a circumference equal to the perimeter of the GP and a radius equal to the height of the GP. Then note that half the circle is equal to half the rectangle. Half a flat circle is essentially equal to a **spherical 90° quadrant** of the same dimensions. These are the basic mathematics behind the projection of a sphere onto a flat surface, or **spherical projection**. As Tompkins writes, in the plan of the Great Pyramid, "the ancient Egyptians had not only squared the circle but

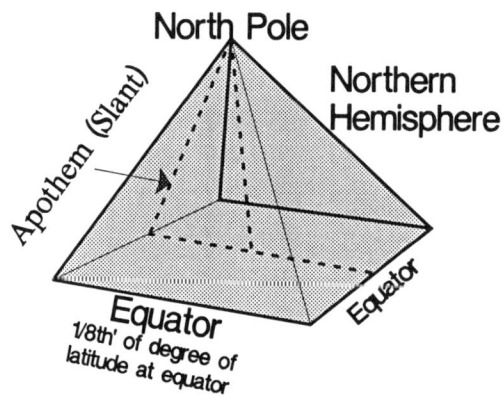

GREAT PYRAMID

Base = average of 439.5 royal cubits
  = 1/8th minute of °lat. at equator
Perimeter = exactly 921.453 meters
  = 1/2 minute of °lat. at eq.
2 x Per. = 1 minute of °lat. at eq.
2 x 921.453 meters = **1,842.906 meters**
International Spheroid measures
  1 minute of °lat. at eq. = **1,842.925 meters**

effectively cubed the sphere." (Tompkins, Secrets, 189, 197-200)

Now let's look at measurements **exact** within millimeters. Following theoretical principles, Dr. Stecchini *estimates* that, if the north face of the GP is calculated by φ and the west face by π, then the perimeter should equal 921,452.72 mm. In the late 1920s, engineer and surveyor **J.H. Cole** measured the GP's perimeter to be **921,453 mm**, or 921.453 meters. That is equal to 1,758 royal cubits (as opposed to 1,760), giving the GP an actual average base of 439.5 royal cubits, as opposed to the rounded number of 440. If each **base** is supposed to represent *1/8th minute of a degree of latitude at the equator*, then the **perimeter** would represent *1/2 minute of a degree of equatorial latitude*. Twice Cole's actual measurement, or *one full minute*, equals 921.453 x 2 or **1,842.906 meters**. According to the **International Spheroid** (the Earth measured by an American named Hayford in 1910, and "the calculation most usually considered authoritative by scholars"), a minute of a degree of latitude at the equator is **1,842.925 meters**. (Tompkins, Secrets, 202-3, 327, 359, 364-6) Thus, according to the exacting measurements of a surveyor, *the Egyptians knew the size of the Earth almost to the millimeter!*

But, if the base of the GP represents the equator and Earth's circumference, why does the base not equal a portion of a degree of *longitude* rather than latitude? This makes a difference if the poles are indeed slightly flattened and/or the Earth's "beltline" slightly bulged. Dr. Stecchini explains that the builders were concerned with the length of the *arc of meridian* (distances between parallels of latitude) because of their obsession with the Nile and the geographic proportions of Egypt. (Tompkins, Secrets, 373, 291-303) In fact, Stecchini's work shows that the Egyptians understood the change in degrees of latitude from the equator to the pole, and reflected this knowledge in the **apothem** of the GP.

The Great Pyramid does not have a capstone as do the other Giza pyramids. Christians point to the fact that only a pyramid has a **chief cornerstone** (four at the corners and one at the apex) and that Christ, the chief cornerstone, was rejected by the builders. (Eph. 2:20-22; I Pet. 2:6-8) However, the GP is supposed to have had a *pyramidion*, perhaps made of some precious metal or polished black granite. According to Agatharchides, the pyramidion was four cubits high and was either included in, or excluded from, calculations, depending on the problem at hand.

The subtraction of a 4-cubit pyramidion leaves an apothem of 352 royal cubits as opposed to the ideal rounded number of 356. An apothem of precisely 351.6 royal cubits of 524.1483 mm results in the 184.29 meters that equal 1/10th of a minute of degree of latitude at the **equator**. An apothem of 352.5 royal cubits of 524.1483 mm results in 184.76 meters, which is within 1/100th meter of the 184.75 meters of the 1/10th minute of degree at **30° latitude** (location of GP). An apothem of 354.24 royal cubits equals the 185.67-meter length of 1/10th minute of degree at **60° latitude**. And an apothem of 355.17 of the same royal cubits equals the 186.16-meter length of 1/10th minute of degree at **90°** (the pole). (Tompkins, Secrets, 206, 328-30, 373) Thus, the ancient Egyptians understood that degrees of latitude increase slightly from equator to pole, knew how to measure this increase accurately, and incorporated this knowledge into the design of the Great Pyramid. The actual total variance for 90° is less than a mile, indicating the degree of precision attained by the Egyptians. Today, for practical purposes of navigation, aboard a modern-day jet

ANCIENT MEASURES

Ancient measures of length depended upon latitude at which they were used, or latitude important to that nation. For example, the mean latitude of Egypt; the latitude of Athens, Greece; the latitude of Babylon, etc.

Roman foot (short)	295.9454 mm
Roman foot (long)	297.1734 mm
Egyptian foot	300.000 mm
English foot	304.79974 mm
English inch	25.4 mm
Geographic foot	307.7957 mm
Greek foot	308.27 mm
Egyptian foot	4 hands
Egyptian cubit	6 hands (1.5 feet)
Geographic cubit	6 hands
Royal cubit	7 hands
Egyptian cubit	450 mm
Geographic cubit	**461.6935 mm**
Royal cubit #1	**524.1483 mm (GP)**
Royal cubit #2	525 mm (2nd Pyr.)
Royal cubit #3	526.3231 (coffers)

Stadium = 600 geo.ft. = 400 geo.cub.
= 1/600th° lat. = 1/10th' = 6"
= 351.6 royal cub.
600 Stadia = 360,000 geo.ft. = **1° lat.**
= 110,806.5 meters (at 27° 45'N lat. Egypt)
500 Stadia = 300,000 geo.ft. = **1° long.**
= 92,339 meters (between 34° - 35° lat.)

Pyramid Inch	1.001 British inches
25 Pyramid Inches	1 Sacred Cubit
Sacred Cubit	635.6 mm
	25.025 British "
1' lat. at eq.	1,842.9 meters
1' lat. at 27° 45'	1,847.38 meters
1' lat. at pole	1,861.65 meters

24 hours = 1,440 minutes of time
1,440 minutes/ 360° = 4 minutes
1° of distance = 4 minutes of time
1 U.S. mile = 5,280 U.S. ft. = 1,609.3 meters
1 U.S. ft. = .3048 meters or 304.8 mm
Equator = 24,902.45 U.S. miles
(Ref. Peter Tompkins, *Secrets of the Great Pyramid*)

Ancient Technology For Dispersal

airplane for example, a degree of latitude remains constant worldwide at an average length of 60 nautical miles (69.047 statute miles).

So, due to its mathematical proportions and the exactness of its measurements, **each face** of the GP represents a **90° spherical section of the Northern Hemisphere mathematically projected onto a flat, undistorted triangle**. (Tompkins, Secrets, 200) The base of the GP is the equator and the apex is the North Pole.

Astronomical Observatory

The ancients linked *time* with their measures of length, weight, and volume, which means that their measuring systems were directly related to both the heavens and the Earth. Well-known 19th-Century British astronomer **Richard A. Proctor** discovered a reference in the writings of the Roman philosopher **Proclus** that the GP had been used as an astronomical observatory *before* the pyramid was completed. Proctor determined that the **Descending Passageway** and the **Grand Gallery** of the GP provided an excellent system for accurately measuring the movements of the stars. The Grand Gallery slopes upward, ending at the center line of the pyramid. It runs precisely north/south so that it is bisected by a true longitudinal meridian. Its roof stones are removable and its high walls include 7 progressively overhung (corbeled) levels. As construction proceeded, the Gallery would have formed an observation slot much like the huge observatory slots that modern telescopes are aimed through.

The Descending Passageway is also aimed at the **North Star**. A reflecting pool at the temporarily plugged intersection of the passageways would have allowed the North Star to be seen from the Grand Gallery. It would also have allowed split-second timings of star transits by sighting down the Descending Passageway into the pool of reflective water. The evidence goes on, but the point is that Proctor believed that "'the Great Pyramid thus constructed would have been the greatest observatory and the most perfect till the art of the telescope could reveal a way to more exact observation without the need for such a massive structure.'" (Tompkins, Secrets, 152-6; Capt, 33-6)

The Egyptians (and Babylonians) knew that a **second of time** in the motion of the **stars of heaven** corresponds to a **definite distance on Earth.** They observed the speed of rotation to be about 1,000 *geographic* cubits per second of time. (Using the precise numbers determined by Stecchini, it would be closer to 1,004 per second.) There are 86,400 seconds in 24 hours. These calculations give a circumference for the Earth that is only about 47 miles short of modern measurements. They also give nice round numbers like 129,600,000 geographical feet or 86,400,000 geographical cubits in the Earth's circumference and a GP base of 500 geographic cubits or 750 geographic feet (actually about 1.5 cubits too long) and a GP apothem of 600 geographic feet. (Tompkins, Secrets, 208-9, 291, 317, 348, 378)

Ziggurat Maps in Babylon & America

A degree of *longitude* varies significantly in length from equator to pole because meridians of longitude grow ever closer as they meet at each pole. The ancients understood this also, and displayed their knowledge in somewhat less sophisticated **stepped pyramids** called *ziggurats*. Just like the GP, the ziggurat presents four roughly triangular faces which each represent a 90° quadrant of the Northern Hemisphere. The base is once again the equator and the apex the pole. However, the **height of each step** marks a **significant parallel of latitude** while the proportionally diminishing length of each step allows for the fact that a degree of longitude grows progressively smaller from the

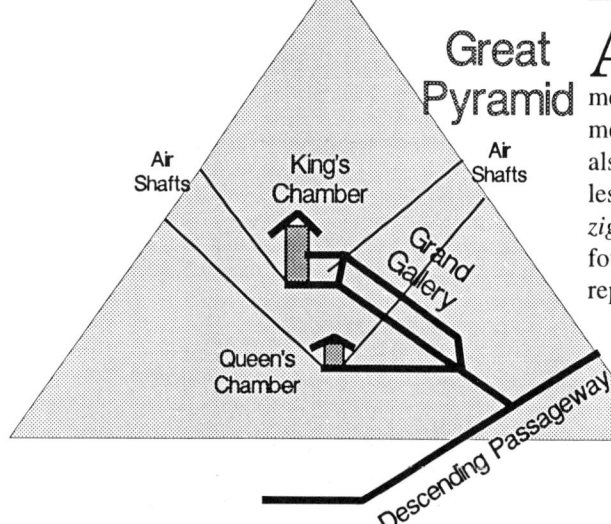

equator to the pole. Today, this is called a **Mercator projection**, a type of spherical projection often used on modern maps. (Tompkins, Mysteries, 248-9)

Not the Tower of Babel?

A cuneiform tablet found by George Smith, F.R.G.S. (Fellow of the Royal Geographic Society) has allowed Dr. Stecchini and others to reconstruct the **Temple of Jupiter Belus** ziggurat in Babylon. It had seven steps or "belts" (the Greeks named them "zones") which marked parallels of latitude. With the base as the equator, or 0° lat., the top of the first step was usually intended to mark the 30th parallel (30° lat. N) which is the parallel that runs through the Great Pyramid in Egypt. [Actually, the GP's position deviates barely over a minute south of 30°, but there are several explanations that the deviation is either intentional to compensate for the Earth's shape, or due to movement of latitude over the years.] However, the Babylonians raised the first step of this ziggurat to match the **latitude of Babylon** which is 33° lat. N. The top of the sixth step marked 75° lat. N, or the **magnetic pole**, while the top reached 90°. The Smith tablet indicates that the ziggurat was designed on a basis of 360, with the base 3600 inches by 3600 inches and a total height of 3600 inches, or 300 geographic feet. According to a number of cuneiform tablets, the **area of each level** corresponded to some **standard unit of land measure**. (Tompkins, Secrets, 86, 184-188; Tompkins, Mysteries, 248-9)

Does this geodetic design of the ziggurats indicate that the Tower of Babel was indeed something other than a standard ziggurat and that it was destroyed by God? Travel and trade did not require international standards until *after* the dispersion judgment. (We shall soon see that the Great Pyramid was also a storehouse of standards for weights and volume measures, needed for trade goods and the exchange of gold and silver between nations.) The Mesopotamian ziggurats were obviously built after Babel, and this particular function of their design seems to be further evidence that the actual Tower of Babel was not one of these ziggurats. According to Josephus, the Tower was "overthrown" by supernatural forces. (Josephus, Ant., I.iv.3) And,

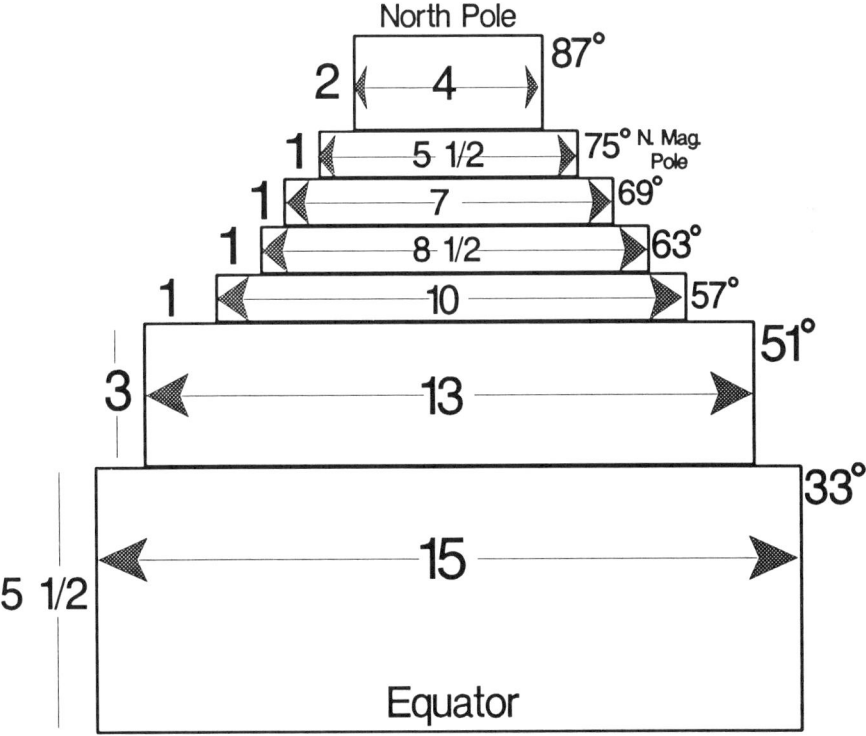

Temple of Jupiter Belus: base is 3600" x 3600". In relative proportions, a unit equals 6°. The first step of the **7-step** pyramid is raised to equal the *latitude of Babylon*. Decreasing width of steps represents **decreasing longitude** from equator to pole. This is basically a modern Mercator projection.

according to the Bible, the people of Cush and Nimrod were frightened of being scattered upon the Earth. They had no interest in long-distance travel and only wished to solidify their unity. Also, remember, the original Tower of Babel may have had more to do with the heavens and fallen angels than with the Earth.

The American Connection

It is believed that ziggurat-style stepped pyramids were the first pyramids built in Egypt, before the unique Great Pyramid and the many other "classic-style" pyramids for which Egypt is famous. The Babylonian-style pyramids also spread to the Orient and to the Americas, becoming the most obvious piece of disputed evidence in the diffusionist/autochthonist debate. And evidence indicates that at least some of the **Mesoamerican ziggurats** served the **same mapping function as their Babylonian prototype**.

The **Pyramid of Quetzalcoatl** is part of a pyramid complex in the ancient city of **Teotihuacán** near modern-day Mexico City. In 1972, an American engineer named **Hugh Harleston, Jr.** established a basic **unit of measurement** for the pyramids through a system of proportions of large measurements made throughout the complex. The unit he discovered turned out to be the 12th root of 2, or **1.059 meters**, which is also equivalent to **1/12 millionth part of the polar diameter**, making it an Earth-commensurate measurement like the ancient geographic foot (a unit of measure based on the dimensions of the Earth). Using this unit, Harleston obtained lengths of buildings, walls, and platforms that were round numbers divisible by **6**, a number favored by both ancient Mexicans and Mesopotamians. The base of the Quetzalcoatl Pyramid measured 3600 x 3600 units or 12,960,000 units, which is equal to 43,482 English square feet or virtually an English acre. This also compares with the Mesopotamian land measure of 60 double cubits. (Tompkins, Mysteries, 242-5, 248)

Boundary markers along the Way of the Dead in the Teotihuacán complex measured 378 units of 1.059 meters, and 378 x 1.059 x 100,000= **40,030,200 meters** which is *very close* to the modern-day estimate of the **circumference of the Earth**, between **40,075,000** and **40,076,000 meters**, or an error of about 30 miles. The base of the Quetzalcoatl Pyramid measured 60 units of 1.059 meters, which, if multiplied by 100,000, gives the polar radius of the Earth. Harleston's reconstructed measurements of the pyramid indicate that it also is a scale model of the Northern Hemisphere, with **7 tiers** marking significant latitudes and using the decreasing-step-length, **Mercator-type projection**. "The first step produced a result of 23.449 degrees, which corresponds to the latitude of the Tropic of Cancer. Other steps gave the latitude of the Arctic Circle, and the magnetic pole." [The magnetic pole is offset from the geographic pole.] It appears to be the same system used by the Mesopotamians. (Tompkins, Mysteries, 247-250)

Even more interesting is the fact that Harleston's measurements of the complex come very close to significant even numbers when based on the ancient Egyptian and Mesopotamian geographic foot and cubit, often giving results of, or related to, 1,296, 360, or 864. Late 19th-Century archaeologist **Dr. Daniel G. Brinton** of the University of Pennsylvania was convinced that the *Aztecs, Mayas, and Cakchiquels of Mesoamerica used the foot, cubit, palm and finger as basic units just as did the ancient Middle Easterners.* According to Dr. Brinton, the Aztecs officially defined and protected their measures and severely punished any falsification thereof, just as did the Hebrews. Author/researcher Peter Tompkins asks: "Is it a coincidence that a circle [with an area] of 1,296,000 units has a radius of 206,265 units and that 20.6264 [inches] is the length of both an English and Egyptian [royal] cubit, that the Hebrew shekel weighs 129.6 grams, and the English guinea 129.6 grains, and the measure of the Most Holy in Solomon's Temple is 1,296 inches?" (Tompkins, Mysteries, 253-6)

Ancient Standard of Weights & Measures

The **Great Pyramid** apparently also served as a standard for **weights** and **volume measures** which were crucial to the **trade of goods** and to **payments in gold and silver**. The two air vents which run through the solid stone in opposite directions from the **King's Chamber** to the outside, when kept clear, keep the King's Chamber at a constant 68°, no matter what the weather or season. A *constant temperature* is necessary to preserve standards of measurement. Dr. Stecchini writes that all the measures of *length, volume, and weight* of the *ancient world* were part of a *rational and interrelated system* which can be *reconstructed beginning with a fundamental unit of length*. (Tompkins, Secrets, 67, 304)

Inside the King's Chamber is the mysterious **coffer** which has never held a body. It has no lid, but there is a groove around the inner top edges which indicates it may have been designed to receive a sliding lid, though there is no evidence it has ever had one. The coffer is not inscribed or decorated, and neither is the pyramid. These facts and the presence of the air shafts reinforce the writings of Herodotus and Diodorus Siculus that say the Great Pyramid was **never used as a tomb**, that Pharaoh Cheops (Khufu) was buried elsewhere. Due to its size and the design of the GP, the coffer had to be placed in the King's Chamber *before* the chamber was sealed and the pyramid finished. (Capt, Great, 45)

Dr. Stecchini maintains that, though the King's Chamber was designed according to the royal cubit of 524.148 millimeters which was used for geographical distances, the **coffer** was designed according to **another royal cubit** of **526.3231 millimeters** which was used to calculate fundamental units of volume and weight. Thus, Stecchini concludes that the contents or volume of the coffer equals **8 cubic royal cubits**, or **40 artabas** which equal 1166.40 liters. By modern measure, 1166.4 liters equals 33.099 bushels which, according to U.S. standards, translates to *about 1,986 pounds of wheat*, just shy of a ton. The volume of the thick walls of the coffer is actually twice the inside volume, or 16 cubic royal cubits = 80 artabas. Tompkins adds that research conducted by **Professor José Alvarez Lopez** of Argentina claims to demonstrate that the GP's coffer embodies the various *astronomical* constants of what's known as our solar system. (Tompkins, Secrets, 322-6, 266) The capacity of the coffer is also said to equal that of the **Ark of the Covenant**. (Capt, Great, 47; Tompkins, Secrets, 278)

British/American Measures Preserve Ancient Originals

Have you ever wondered why the **United States** has a measurement system based on the number **6**, using inches, feet, yards, and miles? We inherited our measurement system from the **British**, and we have seen that *British measurements are related to the Egyptian royal cubit, the Hebrew shekel, and the base of a Mesoamerican stepped pyramid*. The **sacred cubit** is equal to **25 x 1.00101 British inches** and is based directly on the *polar radius* of the earth.

Is the British (U.S.) inch actually an ancient unit of measure which has lost a thousandth part as it has been handed down from generation to generation? Remember, **6 and 7** were the favorite counting numbers of ancient Babylon and Egypt, and the two counting systems originally established by God (360-day years and 7-day weeks). Engineer and architect **Algernon E. Berriman** published *Historical Metrology* in 1953, saying that the **English acre** is "'the most intriguing of ancient measures'" as it virtually equals a geodetic acre (based on the size of the Earth) based on the sacred cubit. One side of a British acre equals 100 sacred cubits of (about) 25 British inches. The slightly larger Scottish and Irish acres, he says, "are related to each other and to the basic English acre as a square to an inscribed circle." (Tompkins, Secrets, 74)

Dr. Stecchini ridicules the **traditional primitive explanations** given for the origin of British measures, such as the foot and the arm of the king. He points out that the English foot was also the basic measure of **Russia** from the first available records to the Soviet revolution. The law of King Athelstan (A.D. 924-940) defined the **British foot**, a length which Stecchini believes to equal 1/18,250th of 3 minutes of a degree of latitude, using the length of degree of latitude as it measures at towns like Winchester, England. Though his research is not yet complete, *Dr. Stecchini believes that the measures of pre-Columbian America are actually those of the Old World*. Until the adoption of the **French metric system**, European measures were basically the ancient ones, or modifications introduced for specific reasons.

Thus, in preserving British measurement standards, the U.S. unintentionally preserves the standards of ancient measures. For example, the 16-ounce pound of 453.8 grams was used in Mesopotamia in the third millenium B.C. Stecchini also says that "there are well known Greek temples which have been planned in English feet, and that archeologists of English and American nationality have studied them without realizing what they had before their eyes." (Tompkins, Secrets, 305, 343-5)

New Age Metric System

The *metric system* now adopted by the British originated as a result of the pagan or "New Age" character of the **French Revolution** which began in **1789. Napoleon** was a **Free Mason** and Masonry is based on the ancient pagan Mysteries. The French revolutionaries threw out and executed the French remnants of Holy Roman Empire royalty, banned Roman Catholicism, and elevated humanism, reason, and nature as well as "the Supreme Being," replacing all of the old holy days and changing the biblical seven-day week to the ancient Egyptian 10-day week. A metric system of tens had been suggested as early as the 1600s, but the revolutionaries took the occasion now to complete their humanist "cleansing" by introducing the **French metric system** based on a new measurement of the arc of the meridian from Dunkirk at the northern tip of France to Perpignan, almost the southern tip of France. The meridian runs through Paris, the French capital. They computed the meter to be 1/10 millionth of this longitudinal meridian from pole to equator and based the system on **units of 10.**

This **remeasurement** turned out to be in **error,** making the *meter 0.0002 too short.* In addition, Britain's leading astronomer, **Sir John Herschel,** criticized the system as erratic and variable from place to place due to the nonuniformity of the Earth's shape. Herschel discovered that the **British inch** only needed to be lengthened by 1/1000th to be a truly Earth-commensurate unit equal to 1/500 millionth of the Earth's *polar* axis, which is the theoretical line running straight through the Earth from pole to pole. A cubit of 25 such inches (1.00101 of a regular British inch) equals **25.025 British inches.** The polar *radius* (half the axis) was measured by satellites in the International Geophysical Year (IGY) of 1957-58 as 3,949.89 miles or 250, 265, 020 inches, proving that a *cubit of 25.025 inches is indeed equal to 1/10 millionth of the polar radius.* [250,265,020 divided by 10,000,000 = 25.0265020]

In addition, 3,949.89 miles is equal to 6,356,557.9 meters. The cubit of 25.025 British inches equals 0.6356 meters or, once again, exactly 1/10 millionth of the Earth's polar radius. (Tompkins, Secrets, 38, 71-5; Timetables, 366-70) **This is further evidence that the British (and U.S.) system has closely preserved ancient standards based on accurate measurements of the Earth.**

The French metric system represents a New Age attempt to support the theory of evolution and to abolish ancient knowledge that is now considered pagan but was originally given by God's patriarchs. When the French revolutionary government put the metric system into law, the United States Congress considered adopting the system, but **Thomas Jefferson** opposed it on the grounds that the system was inadequate and did not relate measurement to time. (Tompkins, Secrets, 316) Isn't it interesting that the modern-day European Community has moved to the metric system and is pressuring the U.S. to do the same?

The Sacred Cubit & Pyramid Inch

We have seen that the measurement of **25.025 British inches** called the *sacred* cubit is indeed based on the polar radius of the Earth and is an ancient measurement preserved in the British/American system. The "rediscovery" of the sacred cubit actually originated with **Sir Isaac Newton (1642-1727)** who studied the data gathered in 1638 by Oxford trained astronomer/mathematician **John Greaves** and Venetian **Tito Livio Burattini.** From their measurements of the **King's Chamber,** Newton concluded that the Great Pyramid had been built on the basis of two cubits, one "profane" (equal to the royal cubit), and the other "sacred," equal to between 24.8 and 25.02 English inches. (It has since been established as 25.02614 English inches.) Newton derived this cubit from the measurements of the pillars of **Solomon's Temple** given by Josephus, their circumference being 12 cubits. (Webster's; Tompkins, Secrets, 21, 30-1, 74; Josephus, Antiquities, VIII.iii.4.; I Kings 7:15, KJV) Divide a sacred cubit by 25 and the result is a *"pyramid inch,"* which, we have seen, is nothing more than the English inch lenthened by a little over 1/1000th.

The 19th-Century British amateur mathematician, astronomer and devout Christian, **John Taylor,** used these units and the reports of several explorers to measure models of the Great Pyramid and laid the foundation for later systems of astronomy and **biblical prophecy** according to the measurements of the Great Pyramid in **"pyramid inches."** (Tompkins, Secrets, 70-2; Capt, Great, 8) Though this inch is definitely derived from the Earth's polar radius, it does not fit the precise measurements of the GP base made by **J.H. Cole**, the surveyor, in the 1920s.

Pyramidologists, as they are called, claim that the perimeter of the base of the GP equals 36,524,235 pyramid inches, demonstrating, they say, that the Egyptians knew the precise length of the solar year. However, according to the survey by Cole, the GP perimeter actually equals 36,241,435 pyramid inches. (Cole's figure for the perimeter of the GP base is 921,453 millimeters and a pyramid inch equals 25.4254 mm.) Instead of producing recurring figures of the length of the **solar year** (365.24235 days) and the length of the **sidereal year** (365.25636 days) as claimed by most pyramidologists, the precise measurements of the GP produce figures related to 362.4. We have seen that Cole's measurements of the GP base are minutely accurate in regard to the Earth's circumference and lengths of degrees of latitude/longitude. *We do not argue that the Egyptians were not capable of accurately measuring the solar and sidereal years, but we do wonder at the precise length of those years at the time the GP was built.* [Note section below called "Calendar Change?"]

The sacred cubit and pyramid inch may have been used in the **King's Chamber** and other inner measurements, but there are no specific, detailed inside measurements in our sources in order that we might confirm this. However, there is a raised **"Boss"** or seal in a horseshoe shape on a granite leaf of the **Ante-Chamber** of the King's Chamber which is said to measure exactlyly **five pyramid inches** across its face, or 1/5th of a sacred cubit. The Boss is a pyramid inch thick and is also said to be located precisely a sacred cubit from the eastern end of the leaf. (Capt, Great, 39) Pyramidologists who see Bible prophecy in every measurement of the GP also see the numbers for the solar year (365.242) in many measurements other than the perimeter of the base. Actually, **Bible prophecy** is based on the **360-day Jewish year**, as we shall see, and it is impossible at this point, with the sources at hand, to know for certain whether or not our present solar year was incorporated in the GP

Calendar Change?

One of the important questions we need to ask concerning the question of the length of the year and a possible calendar change is whether or not the **Great Pyramid** was constructed on the basis of the solar year of 365.242 days. The pyramidologists base their claims on this point. But, there is both biblical and historical evidence to indicate that the ancients were on a calendar of 360 days per year for some period before they were forced to change to 365.25 days per year.

If the Great Pyramid *does* incorporate the length of the solar year in its design, is that a *prophetic* inclusion, or evidence that the calendar changed just before the GP was built? Would that then validate the claims of the pyramidologists–that the GP is a monument to biblical prophecy and a coded timeline of history? However, if the GP does *not* include the solar year figure, does that then *invalidate* the biblical claims of the pyramidologists? And does that further indicate that the GP is, as the pagans claim, an occultic structure as well as a testament to human knowledge and skill, aided by "enlightened masters" who are actually fallen angels? Or, would the absence of figures related to 365.25 merely mean that the calendar changed *after* the construction of the GP?

The First 360-Day Calendars

We know that the **Babylonians** are generally credited by all groups as originating the **360° circle**, counting by 6 and 60, and the 12-sign Zodiac. The Babylonians seem to be the most logical source of our 24-hour day with 60-minute hours and 60-second minutes. It is also logical to assume that they derived their 360° circle from a **360-day year**.

The Bible clearly indicates that God Himself established timekeeping and counting and gave this knowledge to Adam. He set up two concurrent systems, one based on 6 and one based on 7. Thus, knowing that both God's

Creation and His biblical revelation insistently proclaim order, beauty, symmetry, numerical complexity, and numerical symbolism, should we conclude that God originally established a **360** heavenly time clock that is "out of kilter" with uneven, fractional numbers for both solar and lunar cycles? Or should we consider that this clock now labors under the Curse and the effects of several major judgments?

After more than 2,000 years, we in the U.S. still use a 12-month calendar, with months that are "about" 30 days each, and a 360° circle, all standards which dominate the world. *The Timetables of History* list: **1)** an **Egyptian** calendar of **360 days** with 12 months of 30 days each as dating between 5000 and 4000 B.C., **2)** an ancient **Chinese** lunar year of **360 days** that predated 2500 B.C., and **3)** an **Indian** (India) lunar year of **360 days** which predated 1000 B.C. (Timetables, 3-7) Prominent archaeoastronomer **E.C. Krupp** agrees that Egypt had a lunar calendar in the "earliest days," while the *Encyclopædia Britannica* states that the nation counted three seasons, each with four 30-day months, or a 360-day year. Over the years, the solar discrepancy was noted and an extra five days added to form the civil year. The Egyptians also copied the Babylonian 12-sign Zodiac, adding 36 decans (other star signs), one for every 10-day week in a 30-day month. (Krupp, In Search, 206-9; EB 1972, 5:723)

Massachusetts Institute of Technology (MIT) Classics professor **Harald A.T. Reiche** confirms that the **Egyptians** explained the differing solar and lunar years as the result of **"the deliberate departure from an original 360-day cycle** of twelve 30-day lunar months," caused by the actions of the planet **Mercury**. In a game of dice, Mercury won five days from the lunar year and gave them to the solar year, resulting in 355 days and 365 days. (Brecher, Astronomy, 155) One creationist science writer, **Donald W. Patten**, believes that God used Mercury to interact with Earth to trigger the Flood. (Patten, *The Biblical Flood and the Ice Epoch*)

Could the actions of the planet Mercury, commanded by God, have had anything to do with these orbital changes, whenever they took place? Or, is this a coded Mystery reference to the earthly Mercury/Hermes who we have identified as Cush, the son of Ham? If so, does this connect the calendar change with the Tower of Babel rebellion and judgment?

From the prophetic numbers given in Daniel 9 & 12 and in Revelation 11, 12, & 13, Bible scholars teach that the **Jewish calendar** was based on a lunar year of 360 days with 12 months of 30 days each. (Pentecost, BKC, OT, 1365) **Grant Jeffrey** writes that this interpretation is detailed in the *Chronography* written about A.D. 240 by a Christian named **Sextus Julius Africanus**. According to Jeffrey's research, **Abraham** brought the 360-day year with him from Babylonia (Ur of the Chaldees) and continued to use it in Canaan. The Genesis account of the **Flood** indicates that God used a 360-day-year count before and during the Flood, counting five months (out of 12) of 150 days. Jeffrey also quotes **Sir Isaac Newton** as writing that all nations used a 360-day year until, according to Newton, the correct solar length of 365.25 days became known. (Gen. 7:11, 24; 8:3-4, KJV; Jeffrey, Armageddon, 27, 221-4; Ross, BKC, OT, 39)

$$6 + 7 = 13$$
$$13 \times 4 = 52$$
$$7 \times 52 = 364$$
$$12 \times 30 = 360$$

Even in the Americas

Across the ocean in Mesoamerica, the **Mayas** preserved the tradition of an earlier, 360-day calendar. They had a **360**-day year (based on 6), a **364**-day computing year (7 x 52 = 364; 52/4 = 13 = 6+7), and a **365**-day "Vague Year" to which they applied a year-drift correction formula to compensate for the extra quarter-day. The **Maya Dresden Codex** of eclipse tabulations includes the number 360 to count days. The Mayas also had a **260**-day cycle of 13 months of 20 days each, and a similar 18-month

365.25

year count of 360 days to which they added five days at the end to adjust to the "Vague Year" of 365 days. (Hadingham, Early, 200-1; Brecher [Aveni], Astronomy, 79-80; Aveni [Gibbs], Native, 22-24; Williamson [Carlson], Archaeoastronomy, 211) The *Encyclopædia Britannica* explains that, in the viewpoint of the lowland Maya, the year consisted of one *tun* (360 days) *plus five days* which were considered very *unlucky* and during which life was in a state of suspension. (EB 1972, 5:729) This would seem to connect the forced addition of these extra days to some sort of frightening or destructive event.

In South America, the **Incan Huari Textile** shows a pattern of three vertical columns of 10 circles for each of 12 human figures, which has been interpreted as 12 lunar months of 30 days each in a 360-day year. **R.T. Zuidema** believes the Incas had a complex calendrical system of four different month counts, including a 364-day and 365-day year. (Aveni [Zuidema], Native, 229-59)

So, from the Babylonians, Egytians, Hebrews, Indians, and Chinese, to the Mayas and Incas, it seems that the major ancient civilizations of the world counted with a 6-system, a 7-system, and an additional "solar" system which was connected with annoyance, consternation, and even fear.

When Did the Change Occur?

All of this evidence from both biblical and secular sources certainly supports the idea that the original orbits of the Sun and Moon were such that the year was indeed 360 days long and the lunar month 30 days long instead of the modern 29.5+ days. The same sources record a **series of calendar changes and adjustments**, with the **Egyptians** supposedly adopting a 365-day year about 3000 B.C. or the early 2000s B.C., though they kept the division of 12 months of 30 days, merely adding on an extra five days at the end of the year. (Cornell, First, 92; Timetables, 3) This date, as most Egyptian dates, is obviously too old and so this probably happened in the 1000s B.C. or possibly even later.

The **Chinese** lunar calendar is said to have changed to a variable Sun/Moon cycle after 2500 B.C. (another "extended" date), the **Indian** calendar adjustment to the solar year is dated in the 900s B.C., and new calendars are confirmed in **Babylon** in the 700s B.C. and in **China** in 721 B.C., because, says **Dr. Velikovsky**, *the order of the heavens had changed.* Velikovsky also records that a new calendar was introduced in **Japan** in 660 B.C. (Timetables, 3-7, Velikovsky, Worlds, 358) According to the three writers of *The Long Day of Joshua*, the Greek mathematician **Thales** (c. 624-546 B.C.) wrestled with a new number of days in the calendar, a new latitude for Greece, a new solar path, and a new lunar period. It is difficult to gauge the reliability of this statement, as most of what is known about Thales is tradition and hearsay from later writers. (Patten, Long Day, 10)

Dr. Velikovsky quotes the writings of the secretary to the Spanish viceroy, **Fernando Montesinos** (A.D. 1500s), as saying that the **Inca Capac Yupanqui** (c. A.D. 1300s) ordered new calculations to be made and the Incan 360-day calendar changed to 365 days, 6 hours. The **Incas** of South America apparently computed time from the "last cataclysm." This would imply more than one cataclysm in the history of South Americans. This was also a very late date for such a change compared with the other nations of the world. (Velikovsky, Worlds, 357-8; EB 1972, 1:890))

Was It the Flood or Babel?

Were the orbital patterns somehow altered, changing the 360-day year to 365.25 days, destroying a former synchronous movement of the Sun and Moon around the Earth? And, if so, *when* did this change take place? It would be

Solar Year   365.24235 (Sun)
Sidereal Year   365.25636 (Stars)

easy to conclude that the **catastrophe of the Flood**, which may or may not have involved the interactions of other bodies in the Earth-based solar system, would cause the orbital changes and mark the new solar year. In earlier chapters, we examined evidence that the polar axis of the Earth tilted at the time of the Flood (though geocentrists would interpret that rather as a movement of the cosmos).

The **Babel judgment** occurred some 170 to maybe 300 years after the Flood and, according to our research, involved major geophysical changes. *However, the nations that formed after the Babel judgment all used 360-day calendars and the practice continued long enough to leave evidence of its use in the Americas.* The Chaldeans and Abraham continued to use a 360-day year at least into the 1900s-1800s B.C.

Indeed, if Grant Jeffrey is correct that the 180-day feast of Xerxes mentioned in Esther 1:4 is equal to six months, then perhaps the same 360-day reckoning was still used by Chaldeans and Jews alike as late as the 400s B.C. (Jeffrey, Armageddon, 224)

The 360-Day Prophetic Year

In fact, the Jews have always been on a 360-day year prophetic calendar and God's covenant promises and prophecies for Israel are based on a 360-day-year count. The **7-year Tribulation** period (Daniel's 70th week) references in Rev. 11:2, 3 and Rev. 12:6, 14 and Rev. 13:5 make it clear that 3.5 years = 42 months = **1,260 days**, numbers which require a 30-day month and a 360-day year. [Note once again a combination of the 7-system and 6-system.]

The prophecy in **Daniel 9** of the 69 weeks of years from the order to rebuild Jerusalem until the execution of the Messiah has been calculated by numerous prophecy scholars who all use the **360-day year** and who all agree on a total of **173,880 days**, which is the exact time period, to the day, between the decree to rebuild Jerusalem in Nehemiah 2:1-6 and Palm Sunday. The scholars do disagree on the corresponding astronomically and historically computed Western calendar dates, with certain prominent men picking March 14, 445 B.C. and some March 5, 444 B.C. as the date of the decree of King Artaxerxes. This means Christ rode into Jerusalem either on April 6, A.D. 32 or March 30, A.D. 33, both of which match dates for the examination day of the Lamb four days before Passover. The point is that the period of time and the 360-day basis for counting is obviously correct. (Jeffrey, Armageddon, 28-31; see Sir Robert Anderson's *The Coming Prince* and Dr. J. Dwight Pentecost's *The Words and Works of Jesus Christ*)

Another point which should be made is the matter of the **7-day week**, the foundation for which is established in **Genesis** during creation (6+1=7). However, the sabbath, or day of rest, is not mentioned in connection with man until it is given to Israel as part of the **Law at Sinai**, after the Exodus. A 7-day week does not fit mathematically with either 360 or 365.25. It is a system that **runs parallel to**, and in conjunction with, the 360-day prophetic calendar and the modern-day solar calendar. For example, the sabbath will be observed in Israel during the Tribulation period (Matt. 24: 20-24), a time we have already established as being based on 360-day years. The number 7 is used in sabbath days, sabbath weeks, and years of Jubilee in Exodus and Leviticus, "weeks" of years in Daniel, the number of feasts, and examples too numerous to mention. According to **E.W. Bullinger**, the use of **6 and 7** together combines and contrasts what is human and what is spiritual, as **6** is the number for **man** and **7** is the number of **spiritual perfection.** (Bullinger, Numbers, 150, 158) This makes the fact that the Egyptians used both a 6-hand geographic cubit and a 7-hand royal cubit that much more interesting! [Also note that the ancient game of **dice** is based on two 6-sided dice, each die with a high number of 6 for a highest total of 12, but the highest number of combinations possible equal to 7. The ancient game of **cards** is based on 6+7=13 x 4 = 52.]

At some point in time, the **Jews** began adding the leap-year month of Second Adar every second or third year in a 19-year cycle to adjust their lunar, 360-day calendar with the solar, 365.25-day calendar. (Pict. Dict., 140) **Calendar changes** seem to preoccupy the wise men of most nations after the time of the Exodus and particularly around the 700s B.C. and later. *Thus, the evidence certainly points to an event some years after the Flood, long enough after the Flood to give the peoples of the world time to build a tradition of an accurate, 360-day calendar as well as a geography and geometry of 360°.*

Two Catastrophic Periods 1500s/1400s & 700s B.C.

Or is it more plausible to look to the period of the **Exodus**, when God judged Egypt and freed Israel? We know that it was a time of significant judgment, catastrophe, and miraculous events. *Our* date (in this book) for the Exodus is **1488 B.C. Dr. John D. Hannah** of Dallas Theological Seminary writes that some biblical scholars put the Exodus in what is believed to be the reign of the Egyptian

Pharaoh **Rameses II**, or about **1290 B.C.** Others, including Dr. Hannah, date the world-changing event in the year **1446 B.C.**, or during what is said to be the reign of Pharaoh **Amenhotep II**. (Hannah, BKC I, 104) The writers of *The Long Day of Joshua* date it on March 20/21 (vernal equinox) of 1447 B.C. **Dr. Immanuel Velikovsky** believes the Exodus took place in the 15th Century B.C. (1400s).

The significance of these dates lies in what else was taking place in the world at this time. Professor and archaeologist **Claude Schaeffer** published a 1000-page study in 1948 of explorations at Troy and other sites in Asia Minor, in Palestine, Egypt, Persia, Cyprus, and lower Russia. He concluded that the **entire ancient Middle East** suffered from **periodic catastrophes** that destroyed walls and buildings, left large common graves of victims and layers of dust and ashes yards thick, and extinguished cultures and empires. He found evidence of climate change and population migration, but the most devastating of the many disasters, in Schaeffer's opinion, seems to have occurred in the **15th Century B.C.**, an opinion bolstered by the work of **Arthur Evans** on Crete. (Velikovsky, Earth, 188-193)

It seems that *about the time of the Exodus*, that the Middle Kingdom of the **Egyptians**, the highly advanced **Minoan** culture centered at Crete, and the sophisticated, fortified civilization of the **Indus River** Valley in the West Pakistan/India region *all ended abruptly*. Whether by "nature" or by invader, this was a time of upheaval, instability, and disaster. On the Mediterranean island of Crete, the remains of successive "periods" of Minoan civilization seem to be punctuated by earthquakes or some other destructive force, as archaeological investigations indicate that the Minoan Middle II period ended in catastrophe, with even worse destruction left after the Late I period. However, the Late II period ended with unequaled devastation and suddenness. The ancient Minoan Cretan city of Knossos once had a harbor but the site is now greatly elevated.

About the same time period (1500s-1400s), the **ocean level dropped**, according to Harvard Professor R. Daly and Professor P.H. Kuenen of the Netherlands. Participants in the **International Geological Congress** in Stockholm in 1910 presented findings that **climatic plunges** occurred about the **1500s B.C.** and again about the **700s B.C.**, the climate suddenly becoming so unstable as to be catastrophic in character. The **Rhone Glacier** in the Alps started melting about the 700s-500s B.C. European lake dwellings in Scandinavia, Switzerland, Germany, and Italy were found to have been swept away by flood at both times, and the phenomena seem to have been accompanied by strong tectonic movements. (Velikovsky, Earth, 173-183, 188-199, 201)

The **first time period (anywhere from 1490s to 1270s)** seems to connect with the **Exodus** and the conquest of **Canaan** which includes the long day of Joshua. The **second time period** recalls a century of upheaval which included two terrible plague/famines in **Assyria (765 and 759 B.C.)**, a total eclipse of the Sun in the Middle East (June 15, 763 B.C.), the repentance of the great Assyrian city of Ninevah (759 or 756 B.C.), the great earthquake in the reign of Judean King Uzziah (between 790-739 B.C., maybe 756 or 747 B.C.), the **Assyrian captivity** of the northern 10 tribes of Israel (722 B.C.), God's supernatural **destruction of the Assyrian army** which tried to capture the southern tribes of Judah and Benjamin (701 B.C.), and the sign to Israel's King Hezekiah as God moved the shadow of the sundial backwards 10 degrees, or the equivalent of 40 minutes. (Hannah, BKC I, 1462; Sunukjian, BKC I, 1425-7; Patten, Long Day, 208; Velikovsky, Worlds, 210; Amos 1:1, I Kings 17-20) We can only speculate at this point on the connection, but the coincidence is certainly worth examining.

The oldest **Great Sequoias** (giant redwood trees) of California are dated after 1300 B.C. and their rings indicate a series of climatic disturbances about the 700s to 680s B.C. Did worldwide destruction occur about the time of the Exodus? Was the period of the Assyrian captivity and judgment one that affected the world? Tests performed and then reported in 1907 by P.L. Mercanton and G. Folgheraiter on ancient Etruscan (Italy) vases show that the Earth's magnetic field reversed, at least in the Central Mediterranean area, in the 8th Century (700s) B.C. Rock and lava samples show **geomagnetic changes** have taken place. Rocks showing reversed magnetism register magnetic force from 10 to 100 times that of normal rocks, a fact Velikovsky says is considered "astonishing."

(Velikovsky, Earth, 144, 175; Hapgood, Path) It is also interesting to note that the **north magnetic pole** is offset 15° of latitude from the north geographic pole. (Look at a globe.) What do these magnetic reversals or variations mean? There are many hypotheses but, after reviewing much of the literature on the subject, it is difficult to say.

[Note: The erroneous myth of the so-called **"lost ten tribes"** of Israel comes from the **Assyrian captivity** of the bulk of the people of the Northern Kingdom. The **Southern Kingdom** consisted of the two tribes of *Judah* and *Benjamin* and was known as **Judah**. The **Northern Kingdom** of the other 10 tribes was known as **Israel**. Over the years, a number of members of all 10 tribes repudiated the rebellious Northern Kingdom and allied themselves with the house of David in the Southern Kingdom, so that "Judah" represented all 12 tribes. **Remnants of all 12 tribes** returned to Jerusalem following the Babylonian captivity and, even after thousands of years of worldwide dispersion, it is amazing how many Jews know who they are and to what tribe they belong. Witness the return to Israel of Jews from all over the world (even Ethiopia) since 1948.]

Volcano of Santorini (Thera)

A **Minoan Cretan** colony is buried beneath volcanic ash on the Greek island of **Thera (Santorini)**, north of Crete. Though the island has suffered repeated eruptions and earthquakes, the tremendous volcanic explosion that buried the Minoan colony is dated in the **early 15th Century B.C.** It is believed that the tidal wave from Thera's volcano destroyed the coast of Crete and finally put an end to the long-dominant Minoan culture. In fact, this particular eruption was so devastatingly significant that it is used by many scholars to explain the legends of **Atlantis**, a tradition which we, of course, connect with the Flood. (EB, 1972, 21:1001)

Archaeologist and seafarer **Thor Heyerdahl** writes that, either about **1400 B.C.** or **1200 B.C.**, there was a **universal Mediterranean catastrophe**. Actually, he leans toward the 1200 B.C. date, as does archaeologist **L. Pomerance**, who believes that the eruption of Santorini (Thera) should be dated at this time as the cause of massive tidal waves that wrecked the coastal civilizations of Egypt and the Hittites as well as the Minoans. The Mediterranean region experienced a dramatic depopulation during this period in which famines haunted the entire Middle East. (A famine drove Jacob and his family to Egypt.) The mysterious "**Sea Peoples**" began their raids of Asia Minor and Egypt about this time, and the **Phoenicians** began widespread colonization effort on the Atlantic coasts of Spain and Africa and probably the Americas, especially considering that the advanced **Olmec** culture sprang up out of nowhere in Mesoamerica just about this time. (Heyerdahl, Early, 82, 358-9, 370-1)

In eulogizing the Exodus, Psalms 114 and 77 recall the parting of the Red Sea and the parting of the Jordan River. They also say that the Earth trembled and shook and the mountains and hills skipped, which could only refer to some sort of earthquake or earthshaking event. (Ps. 114; Ps. 77:15-20, KJV) Perhaps the period of the **10 plagues of Exodus**, and **Joshua's Long Day** some 42 or 43 years later, have a connection with the disastrous events that befell the Mediterranean and Middle East about the same time. And perhaps the Earth was shaken such that heavenly orbits and the calendar year were changed. Also, consider how long it must have taken for Egypt to accomplish even partial recovery after the judgment of the Exodus, which included massive destruction of crops and livestock as well as the loss of the entire army (it never says for sure whether or not Pharaoh himself ventured into the Red Sea though he was leading the army), and the death of every firstborn, man and animal.

Velikovsky's Extraordinary Comet

The writings of the highly educated and very controversial **Dr. Immanuel Velikovsky** present the thesis that the **Universe** was **highly unstable until after the 700s B.C.**, and that **Venus** was originally a **comet** whose orbit disturbed the Earth about every 50 years, especially as the **Aztecs** and **Mayas** were so intent on tracking Venus and so afraid that the

Earth would end every 52 years. (Velikovsky, Worlds, 154, 157, 197; see Chap. 8 on "Stars") Velikovsky's thesis uses the comet Venus to explain all of the judgments and events of the Exodus, with the comet dragging its tail across Earth and colliding with **Mars**. When the comet collided with Mars again in the 700s, Venus stabilized as a planet and Mars became the universal threat, disturbing the Earth every 15 years. (Velikovsky, Worlds, 48-65, 154, 244, 259)

Dr. Velikovsky earned the respect of **Albert Einstein** through his derided but accurate predictions of the surface temperature and rotational direction of Venus, the craters on Mars, the radio noises of Jupiter, and the electromagnetism of the Universe. He actually proved Einstein wrong on several points. So, the man was not a kook, though he suffered tremendous professional persecution. However, this gifted and intelligent **Russian Jew** viewed the Bible as history and tradition and not as the accurate Word of God. His theories combine science with extensive research into the cosmologies of ancient peoples around the world. It may be that Venus was indeed originally a comet and God may have used various bodies of His Universe as tools to accomplish certain of His works. [In mythology, Venus sprung full grown from the head of Zeus/Jupiter.] We know that the ancients were anything but stupid and there is much evidence to show that they were seriously concerned with carefully tracking certain planets and star groups. But Velikovsky replaces God and the miracles of the Exodus with a "system" or "model" of planetary action and his thesis is obviously strained. (Berlitz, Mysteries, 202; White, Pole, 112-116)

Joshua's Long Day and the Fearsome Mars

The Bible-believing writers of *The Long Day of Joshua* (one is a physicist, one a Ph.D. in aeronautics) present a "model" that says the **orbit of Mars**, from the time of the Flood to the Assyrian destruction in 701 B.C., intersected the Earth's orbit in two places (they are *not* geocentrists), lapping the Earth every two years but coming very close to Earth about every 52 or so years. They use Mars to explain the string of biblical catastrophes of this period. They rely on much of Velikovsky's work, and they believe that the **calendar change** from 360 days to 365.25 days **occurred as a result of the 701 B.C. "fly-by" of Mars** which was the divine agent of the Assyrian's destruction. (Patten, Long Day; Gaverluck, Rapture, 228) Once again, Mars may indeed have been used by God in more than one instance, especially as it plays such a prominant place in the cosmologies of so many nations. However, the **"model" is strained** and the authors stretch the Bible to fit their model. They also interpret prophetic Tribulation passages as past history. But there seems to be significant truth to be gleaned from the research and observations of both Velikovsky and the "Long Day" writers.

By calculating according to Deuteronomy 1:3 and 2:14, with Joshua 14:7-10, it appears that about 42 or 43 years passed from the Exodus to the long day of Joshua, when the "sun stood still and the moon stayed," and the "sun stood still in the midst of heaven, and hastened not to go down about a whole day." (Joshua 10:13-14, KJV) This was certainly a unique event in the Earth/solar system, "no day like that before it or after it," which surely affected the entire Earth and not just the land of Canaan. (See Chapter 8) Was this the occasion of the orbital and calendrical changes? Was this the event that inspired the ancestors of the Aztecs and Mayas to build the tradition of possible catastrophe every 52 years?

The 52-Year Cycle of Mesoamerica

The **Aztecs** measured the end of each 52-year cycle by the date that the constellation **Pleiades** crossed the highest point in the sky (culmination or zenith) at midnight. A feast was held and the Aztecs awaited this sign that the world would not end but would continue for another 52 years. As did many other nationalities, they offered **human sacrifices**. The special victim was positioned and a fire started over his heart. Wood was added so that the fire reached its peak the moment Pleiades "culminated." If the sacrifice was done correctly, the world would continue. As the world *did* continue, it seemed to provide proof for the efficacy of the sacrifice. This culmination was observed by the Egyptians, ancient Britains, Mesoamericans, Chinese, Japanese, and others, all who looked upon the occasion as one of human sacrifice, death, and the appeasing of evil gods, spirits, and witches. It was also a time when the spirits of the dead left Earth for the Underworld, flying through the sky at midnight.

In the Northern Hemisphere, the culmination of Pleiades occurs in November, or around the time of our **"Halloween"** or the **Feast of All Souls Day**. The ancient pagan feast of **All Hallows' Eve** on October 31 marks the change from autumn to winter, a symbol of death. At this time, the spirits of the dead are said to come back to visit their former homes. The Catholic Church celebrates All Saints' Day on November 1 and All Souls' Day on November 2, during which they first feast in honor of the saints, then hold services and prayers for the dead (Gallant, 130-1; Dict. of Myst., 8; Webster's)

Pleiades had been carefully tracked in the Americas long before the Aztecs, according to the alignments of the temples, and was an important constellation to nations all over the ancient world. Called the "Seven Sisters" by Westerners, Egyptians, Greeks, and Hindus, the Pleiades were called *Tianquiztle* (marketplace) by the Aztecs and *Tzab* (the snake's rattle) by the Mayas. The 52 years equaled four sections of 13 years, the first connected with the favored direction of **east**, the second with the underworld direction of **north**, the third with the evil sunset direction of **west**, and the last with the neutral direction of **south**.

Yearly calendars of both Maya and Aztec, going back to the Olmecs, involved twenty 13-day weeks which equaled an important **260-day period**. They also counted 18 months of 20 days for a 360-day calendar. Five "useless days" were later added to make a "Vague Year" of 365 days. A **"Calendar Round"** equaled **52 Vague Years** or 18,980 days. Two 52-year cycles or 104 years was considered "One Old Age." Five periods of 52 equal 260. *The 52-year cycle and the number 52 was important in all Mesoamerica.* The carefully tracked, much feared, and highly worshipped planet **Venus** was also connected with the Calendar Round and Old Age cycles.(Krupp, In Search, 31; [Aveni] 174; Aveni, Skywatchers, 30, 151, 192; Durán, 388-411)

Did one of God's frightening judgments occur connected with or marked by the Pleiades and/or Venus that would cause the ancient Mesoamericans to fear the reoccurrence of that celestial position? Some archaeoastronomers believe they have found a **Mars table**, indicating that nervous Mesoamericans also tracked Mars. (Aveni, Skywatchers, 198) The Mesoamericans were also quite afraid of **darkness** (the modern Aztecs still are). Most archaeologists and anthropologists connect this with primitive and ignorant fear of eclipses, but these people actually predicted eclipses and were highly sophisticated astronomers. Most likely their fear of darkness was caused by one or more of the judgments performed by God. **Joshua's Long Day** would have *extended the night in Mesoamerica*. The thick darkness over Egypt before the Exodus may have been local, but the darkness connected with the cross was probably worldwide. Also, Jewish prophecy, some of which was most likely transported to the Americas by someone before the era of the Spaniards, predicts the blackening of the Sun and darkness as signs of the coming Great Tribulation judgments.

Who Built the Great Pyramid and When?

It certainly does not seem that entombing a pharaoh was the purpose of the designer(s) of the Great Pyramid. In fact, there is no reliable report of a mummified body found in *any* of the pyramids. "Even the 'unplundered' tomb of Cheops' mother," says Peter Tompkins, possessed an empty "sarcophagus," though the tomb appeared untouched. (Tompkins, Secrets, 236)

Our research has penetrated certain of the mists of mystery that surround the world's most fascinating structure, revealing something about *why* it was built, but the questions of *who* and *when* remain shrouded in a number of possibilities.

A Pre-Flood Construction?

Evolutionist archaeoastronomers generally agree that the GP was constructed about **2650 B.C.**, a date which is about 500 years earlier than what we might guess, but then traditional chronologies push Egypt's Pre-Dynastic period back to at least 5000 B.C. (Hadingham, Early, 22; Krupp, In Search, 235) The **prophetic** system of pyramid inches gives a start date of **2623 B.C.**

and a completion date of 2141 B.C., for a construction period of 482 years. (Capt, Great, 76) What then would *we* guess?

Some Christians propose that the GP was actually built **before** the Flood, which would mean that the structure would have had to survive that mind-boggling catastrophe in perfect shape, with no water damage or residue in the interior. (It has open air shafts.) Why do they think this? Once again, it is connected with the belief that the base and other dimensions of the GP, when measured in pyramid inches, demonstrate the numbers 365.242, or the solar year. This connects, they contend, with the fact that **Enoch**, "the seventh from Adam," was raptured in his **365th year**, and the fact that certain ancient writers apparently refer to the GP as the **"Pillar of Enoch."** Some go so far as to say that Enoch was taken by God when he was precisely 365 years, 88 days, and 9 hours old. (Krupp, In Search, 235; Hadingham, Early, 22; Capt, 73-4; Webber, New Light, 18)

The pre-Flood construction is not merely a Christian idea but a long-standing **Arab legend**. A premonition of the Flood is credited to an antediluvian king named Saurid as well as to the occultic figure of **Hermes Trismegistos**. The Giza Complex would then have been erected to preserve pre-Flood knowledge. (Tompkins, Secrets, 217-18)

The Jewish historian **Josephus** records that, since **Seth's descendants** were "the inventors of that peculiar sort of wisdom which is concerned with the heavenly bodies," they intended to preserve their knowledge from the *two worldwide destructions*, one by **fire** and one by **water**, prophesied by Adam. Thus, they inscribed their discoveries on **two pillars**, one of **brick** and the other of **stone**, in case the brick pillar was destroyed by the water, the stone pillar would survive. Aside from exhibiting the scientific knowledge to mankind, the stone pillar would record that the brick pillar had also been erected. "Now this [stone pillar] remains in the land of Siriad to this day," affirms Josephus. (Josephus, Antiquities, I.ii.3)

"To this day" means sometime between A.D. 70 and the early 100s. The land of **Siriad** refers to Egypt and that nation's attentiveness to the star **Sirius**. As to the solar year, we have yet to substantiate the measurement and we have strong evidence that the 360-day orbital system was not altered until later. Enoch and the other sons of Seth could certainly have *planned* the GP, but there again the **geographic alignments** and **measurements** would have to be *prophetic*. Perhaps the "Pillar of Enoch" either refers to Enoch as the original father of the mathematical and astronomical knowledge that went into building the GP, indicates another Enoch, or preserves a meaningless tradition.

As for Josephus, he is very valuable but far from infallible. Seth and his progeny were probably the recipients, preservers, and developers of knowledge given by God, probably through Adam. We have already established that these "Titans," as the pagan world calls them, were superior to us both intellectually and physically. It is also quite possible that Adam did prophesy the Earth's destruction by water and fire just as Enoch prophesied the return of Christ. (Jude 14) However, the GP is *not inscribed* and there is *no record of a brick pillar*.

One of the premises of this book is that traditions usually become traditions because they preserve kernels of truth, perhaps distorted or embellished over time. It is obvious that this pre-Flood tradition is strong, coming as it does from a number of sources. It is also interesting that these same traditions agree that the Giza complex is connected with the preservation of sophisticated ancient knowledge. *Could the pre-Flood construction possibly be true?*

A Steadfast Witness of the New Geography

We don't believe that a pre-Flood construction date is a reasonable possibility. The **major objections** to a **pre-Flood construction** involve **1)** the survival of the structure, **2)** the positioning and design of the structure, and **3)** the fact that Noah would have known of the structure and yet mankind "ignored" it.

After what we have studied about the mechanics and hydrology of the Flood, we would conclude that only the most illogical miracle would preserve anything on Earth except the Ark atop the waters and certain of the animal inhabitants of the waters. We do not question God's ability, merely the *probability*.

Then we have to consider that **Earth** underwent **drastic geographical changes** following both the Flood and the Babel judgment. The heavens were also affected. The GP aligns to the **cardinal directions** and to certain **star positions**. It also maps the latitude and longitude of the Northern Hemisphere, a feat which involves heavenly movements. The GP could not have been built until the NEW GEOGRAPHY of the world was established and heavenly adjustments stabilized. [The "heavens were of old," and "the heavens and the earth which are now." II Pet. 3:4-7]

Tompkins states that the GP is so closely aligned with the **cardinal directions** (north, south, east, west) that *compasses are adjusted to the GP*. The west face, which in Stecchini's opinion is the first face drawn, is agreed to be 2' 30" west of true north. Stecchini explains this very slight deviation from true north as "the result of the precession of the equinoxes." Says Stecchini, "If there had passed exactly three years from the drawing of the plan to the ceremony of the 'stretching of the cord,' the clustering of stars, which gave the exact north of the moment of the drawing of the plan, would give an orientation 2' 30" west of north, because of the precession of the equinoxes, which displaces the star taken as the polar star in practical calculations to the west at a rate of about 50" a year." (Tompkins, Secrets, xiv, 380-1) The east face shows the largest discrepency of 5' 30" west of north which Cornell explains as the result of continental drift. (Cornell, First, 103)

Tompkins states that this still **surpasses in accuracy any human construction to date**, including what Capt calls modern man's best effort, the Paris Observatory, which is 6' off true north. (Tompkins, Secrets, 100; Capt, Great, 11) The point is that the GP had to be designed and built after the Flood and after Babel in order to maintain these alignments. This **steadfast orientation** also seems to preclude certain hypotheses of polar axis movements. (See Chap. 8)

There were no kings or rulers or Egypt until after Babel. And there were no **earthquakes** until during and after the Flood, and the GP is intentionally designed to withstand Earth movement and earthquakes. Only the GP has its four baseline cornerstones laid into **five special sockets** which are perfectly leveled. Some experts say these sockets held anchorage stones which "were so placed as to allow a space between the sides of the mortises and the corner stones, thus allowing expansion caused by changes of temperature or earthquakes, serving the purpose of ball and socket joints." (Capt, Great, 23) But others dismiss this contention because of the shallowness of the northeast and southwest sockets, saying they were merely for positioning or measurement. (Tompkins, 106) But why are they so perfectly level and so peculiarly designed? The complex, multi-layered, limestone and granite roof structure over the King's Chamber is generally agreed to be designed to cushion shocks and subsidence, as well as to hold the great weight above it. (Tompkins, Secrets, 248-9; Capt, 41-2)

A massive earthquake of the A.D. 1200s cracked the smooth, limestone face of the GP and dislodged some of its limestone casing stones. As a result, the Arabs began using the limestone blocks to build new structures. The Mosque of Sultun Hasan in Cairo was erected in 1356 almost entirely from GP casing stones. The stripping of the GP continued until almost every one of the some 144,000 (22 acres) casing stones were part of another structure. (Tompkins, Secrets, 18; Capt, Great, 17-18)

How Soon After Babel?

It seems fairly obvious that the GP was not only *constructed* after Babel, but *designed* after Babel as a **"pillar" of the new geography** and a tool to address the brand new concerns of **international travel and trade.** It may also be a witness to the **stability of the Earth's orientation** in space and the **position of the continents** since the time of the GP. A clue to the actual construction date may be found in the astronomical alignments of the air shafts and Descending Passageway.

Our date for the **Flood** is **2345 B.C.** and our best guess for **Babel** is **2174 B.C.**, or the 70th year of Peleg's life. Egypt was founded by Ham's son **Mizraim** and his family immediately after Babel. Did the building of the GP involve the supernatural abilities of **fallen angels**? Or was it totally a manmade project?

And, if so, did the superior intellect and even strength of these early **post-Flood humans** account for their mastery in **masonry**, an ability we see demonstrated from Egypt to Babylon, to the Orient, to Europe, to the Americas, to Easter Island, and elsewhere? Was this truly the incredibly labor-intensive job that most experts depict?

Herodotus, to whom the GP was as ancient as Herodotus is to us, saw the GP about 440 B.C. and his writings tell us that the project took 10 years of preparation and 20 years of construction by teams of 100,000 men. (Capt, Great, 6; Tompkins, Secrets, 2, 227) Was the project only possible after Egypt and possibly the surrounding nations had grown to this size? With their intelligence, most likely they were able to fashion simple but ingenious machines for lifting heavy stones. (Tompkins, Secrets, 226) If the project was indeed designed by God as a pillar of divinely revealed knowledge and/or biblical prophecy, it certainly would not have involved fallen angels. If it did involve fallen angels, then it certainly wasn't a pillar to divine glory. As for the workforce, we don't know how many people Mizraim led into Egypt but it does seem that the nation progressed rapidly.

Star Alignments

In the early 1800s, a Genoese (Genoa, Italy) merchant ship captain named **G.B. Caviglia** settled in Egypt to study the GP. After clearing the **Descending Passageway** of the rubble left by the Arabs in the A.D. 800s, he noticed one night that as he looked up the passageway toward the sky, the **North Star** (Polaris in the Little Dipper or Little Bear) appeared in the small, 1°-square opening. This observation was told to the next explorer, **Col. Richard Howard-Vyse** of the British Guards, who in turn asked eminent British astronomer **Sir John Herschel** if the passage could indeed be aligned with the Pole Star. The problem, explained Herschel, was that the *precession of the equinoxes*, especially over such a long period, would point the North Pole toward a different part of the sky. However, he said that the star *alpha Draconis* (Thuban) would have been near the pole position and, though not as bright as Polaris, could have been seen from the bottom of the passage when at its lower culmination or lowest point in the sky. (Tompkins, Secrets, 56, 59 72, 86-87; Gallant, 34; see Chap. 8 on Stars)

According to archaeoastronomer **E.C. Krupp**, Thuban could have been sighted through the Descending Passage in 3440 B.C. and in 2160 B.C., but he subscribes to the 2600 B.C. era date for the construction of the GP so he dismisses Thuban as the possible alignment. Astronomy professor and planetarium director **Roy Gallant** believes that the GP as well as other Egyptian pyramids were designed to align with Thuban, but at dates "around 3000 B.C." Apparently **C. Piazzi Smyth**, the Astronomer Royal for Scotland, calculated in the late 1860s that the angle of the Descending Passage was 3° 43' and that Thuban would have been 3° 43' from the pole at its lower culmination in 3440 B.C. and in 2123 B.C. British astronomer **Richard Anthony Proctor** calculated the latter date to be 2160 instead of 2123 B.C.

In addition, Smyth determined that, at the autumnal equinox of 2170 B.C., the passage would have aligned sufficiently with **Thuban** while the star *Alcyone* of the **Pleiades** was crossing its zenith at midnight directly above the high point of the GP's **Grand Gallery** and the top of the GP. Smyth considered this an important occurrence which could have marked a design or construction date for the GP. Writer E.R. Capt says that Sir John Herschel found that the Pleiades aligned with unusual **scored lines** found 482 pyramid inches down the Descending Passage from the GP's entrance. At the vernal equinox of 2141 B.C., says

Capt, the Pleiades aligned with the scored lines while Thuban aligned with the passage. This date of 2141 B.C. is used as the foundation for a well-known biblical prophecy map of the GP. (Krupp, In Search, 235; Tompkins, Secrets, 78, 86-88, 149; Gallant, 34, 38, 105; Capt, Great, 75-77; also see work of Robert Menzies and Adam Rutherford for biblical prophecy)

We have already seen that the midnight upper culmination of **Pleiades** at the autumnal equinox was an important and fearsome event for pagans, inspiring human sacrifice among many peoples at different periods of history. But all heavenly movements and the seasonal markers are originally of God and we have wondered if this position of Pleiades possibly marked a judgment by God that frightened pagans and thus became a historical marker of occultic fear. Also, Thuban is in **Draco the Dragon**, the constellation which represents the "Old Serpent" or Satan. The Persians saw Draco as a Dragon while the early Hindus considered him to be an alligator. (Gallant, 38)

The question for the GP is whether or not the alignments with Thuban and the possible alignment with the Pleiades were **pagan**, or **merely a geographical measure of true north**. The two **air shafts** that extend north and south, respectively, from the King's Chamber align with important stars, the one to the north with the upper culmination of Thuban and the one to the south with the stars of Orion's belt, **Orion** being the constellation which represents both Christ and Nimrod. The only constellations mentioned by name in the Bible are Orion, the Pleiades, the Crooked Serpent (Draco), and the Great Bear, and they are called God's creations to be ordered about at His will. (Job 9:9, 38:31-2; Amos 5:8) In fact, the Pleiades is said to have "sweet influences" by the King James Version (Job 38:31), a translation that is supported by *Strong's Concordance*. (See Chap. 8)

If we consider our own approximate date for Babel is 2174 B.C. (and could be later), then the later dates for the astronomical alignment, especially with true north, make sense. In addition, we know that the GP's alignment with true north was important to its geographical function, that the GP could not have been built and probably not designed before the Flood, and that it must have been constructed soon after Babel. Thus, a date in the **2100s B.C.** is logical.

What About the Enigmatic Sphinx?

The most *accepted* thinking about the GP and its close neighbor, the Sphinx, is that the GP was built by **Pharaoh Khufu (Cheops)** who is supposedly the second king of the Fourth Dynasty, and the Sphinx by his son **Khafre (Chephren or Kephren)** who is said to have been the fourth king of the Fourth Dynasty. Dates given for their reigns vary from the 2600s to the 2500s B.C. (EB 1972, 13:323, 336; Webster's) The **only original heiroglyphics or markings** to be found on the GP are in red paint (not inscribed in the stone) on stones above the King's Chamber. These paint markings have been translated as quarry marks and include what is said to be the "cartouche" of Pharaoh Khufu. These stones, say translators, were laid in the 17th year of the reign of Khufu. (Capt, Great, 43) This may be the main reason for the opinion that the GP was built about 2650 or 2600 B.C.

The **Sphinx** is carved from a **single limestone knoll** and has the **body** of a **lion** with the **head** of either a **man** or a **woman**. The traditional view is that the head is female and represents the constellation **Virgo** while the body represents **Leo**. However, most archaeologists now believe the head is that of **Chephren** who is also credited with building the **Second Pyramid of Giza** which is part of the Giza complex of five pyramids and the Sphinx. Now this belief is being challenged by facial analysis techniques which indicate that the Sphinx head is not that of the proto-European Chephren (whose carving is in the Cairo Museum) but possibly that of a black African. Looking at photographs of the Sphinx and Chephren's bust in the *Reader's Digest* publication *The World's Last Mysteries*, and the drawings and old photos in the Tompkins book, it is difficult to judge the eroded features of the Sphinx. Chephren has a straight nose, thin lips, and a thin face with prominent cheek bones.

Another challenge to the Chephren claim is the fact that **Sir Flinders Petrie** found depictions of the Sphinx which he dated from the First Dynasty or earlier. From Sumerian cuneiform tablets and cylinder seal markings, **Zecharia Sitchin** maintains the entire complex dates to 9000 B.C. (*New York Times*, op-ed/letters, 7/18/92; World's Last, 200-1; Tompkins, Secrets, 22, 33, 57, 76, 109, 141) Sitchin is a Jewish writer and researcher who is famous for his command of cuneiform but whose books reveal his strong New Age beliefs. He was often referred to at a recent UFO seminar in Dallas, Texas.

An Obelisk and More Heavenly Alignments

If our own research is correct, we know that the Sphinx was built after Babel. What connection does it have with the Great Pyramid of Giza? It lies only 1,200 feet southeast of the GP. It is 240 feet long, 66 feet high, and 13 feet, 8 inches at its widest point. It may originally have been plaster coated and brightly painted. Its first European explorers had to excavate it from the sand as only its head was uncovered. When the sand was cleared from its base, a setting for a now-missing, **six-tiered obelisk** was revealed between its paws! (Tompkins, Secrets, 33, 142)

An obelisk is a slender, four-sided stone pillar with a pyramid-shaped top. To compute Earth's **polar circumference**, the Egyptians measured "the distance between two obelisks a few miles apart and the difference in the length of the shadows of the obelisks." For the **equatorial circumference**, "an observer at the base of an obelisk at the thirtieth parallel [where the Sphinx is located] could signal the appearance on the eastern horizon [the Sphinx faces east] of a zenith star to an observer at a measured distance in the western desert where the tip of the obelisk [or the Sphinx?] would be on the horizon." By using the time it took for the second observer to sight the same star on his horizon and the fact that the Earth rotates 360° in 24 hours, they could calculate the circumference at the 30th parallel of latitude, which varies from the equatorial circumference by the cosine value of 30°, which is the square root of 3/2. (Tompkins, Secrets, 33, 57, 210-11)

At the turn of the 20th Century, **Moses B. Cotsworth** examined the Sphinx and decided that it was indeed a sighting device. A priest standing on its rump could sight the rising Sun "in a direct line to the horizon marked by the point of the asp [snake] on the crown on the Sphinx." There were also, Cotsworth discovered, a series of ancient lines which fanned out toward the east from the neck of the Sphinx, lines which could have marked the sunrise [or certain star risings] at different points of the year including the solstices and equinoxes. Cotsworth believed that the obelisk was used for sighting the noon Sun. (Tompkins, Secrets, 121, 142)

Grassland Turns to Desert

Every time the base of the Sphinx has been cleared, windstorms have quickly refilled it with sand. The obvious observation is that the **Sahara was not desert** when the Sphinx and the Great Pyramid were built. (Tompkins, Secrets, 142) **Thomas J. Crowley**, an expert in climate history from Texas A&M University, has found geological evidence to indicate a "wet-to-dry transition in northeast Africa around 2500 B.C." Evidence indicates, he says, that such transitions could have lasted decades to a century. (*New York Times*, op-ed/letters, 7/18/92) **Dr. Henry Morris** says that most of the world's large deserts, including those in the U.S. and Africa, were once covered with large lakes and all of the deserts were once well watered. (Morris, Gen. Flood, 314-17)

There is ample archaeological/anthropological as well as geological evidence of a once-green Sahara. **Thor Heyerdahl** writes of the **petroglyphs** on the canyon walls of the now bone-dry Wadi Abu Subeira in Upper Egypt (southern Egypt) over 100 miles from the Red Sea and the **rock paintings** in the Tassili desert of southern Algeria, 1,000 miles from the Mediterranean Sea. These petroglyphs and rock paintings show **reed boats**, like the ones Heyerdahl used to cross the Atlantic and sail the Persian Gulf, as well as *crocodiles, hippos, water buffalos, giraffes, deer, lions, gazelle, elephants, antelopes, ostriches, domesticated cattle*, and other river and forest animals where there is nothing now but sand or barren land. The desert continues today to encroach on fertile jungle and pastures, he says, at a rate measurable in miles per year. (Heyerdahl, Early, 355; World's Last, 205-19)

Velikovsky also mentions this evidence, saying that the Sahara was once a great grassland with herds and people. He cites the presence of polished stone implements, weapons, and vessels. The drawings show extinct animals and Egyptian motifs. The **ancient lake** has been named **Triton**. (Velikovsky, Earth, 93-4) Also found are numerous bone harpoons, fishing-net weights, fishbones, and freshwater mussel shells. And there seems to be several waves of cultures, from bow-carrying hunters to herdsmen to horse-owning, chariot-driving people. The **camel** does not appear one time in any of the many drawings, showing that it came to the area later after the climate change. It is first mentioned in writing in 46 B.C. However, the Sahara was **desert at least by 430 B.C.** because **Herodotus** describes it as such. (World's Last, 205-19, 308-9)

So, the GP, the Sphinx, and the entire Giza complex were built probably fairly soon after Babel, with a date range of **2170 to 2120 B.C. likely for the GP** because of the angle and alignment of the Descending Passage and other possible alignments. Only 350 to 400 years after the Flood, what we now call North Africa was not desert but grassland with one or more large lakes. This was probably also true for the entire Middle East and Arabia. The Dead Sea was higher and, at the time of Abraham and Lot, 100 to 200 years later, the cities at the south end of the Dead Sea were thriving in a richly fertile Jordan River Valley. The world was covered with large post-Flood lakes that the new rainfall patterns were not able to maintain. Hence, they eventually dried up. (Morris, Gen. Flood, 314-23) Today's deserts may be due in part to the longterm consequences of the New World atmosphere and weather, and in part to specific divine judgments. If this book's timeline is even close to correct, the climate transition recognized by Texas A&M climate expert Thomas J. Crowley took place some 500 to 600 years later than 2500 B.C. Even then, as Crowley says himself, it was a transition that took place over a period of "decades to a century." (*New York Times*, op-ed/letters, 7/18/92)

Is the Sphinx Prophetic?

The Sphinx is **markedly eroded**, more so than surrounding monuments, leading some to think that it is much older than the GP. This is unlikely according to our research. Two factors which may affect the weathering are the relatively delicate **features** of the Sphinx and the **composition** of the knoll from which it is carved.

The **earliest European explorers** saw the Sphinx in a less eroded state and their impression was that the **face was female**. The French drawings shown in the Tompkins book are decidedly feminine in character. The **Greek sphinx** was generally **female**. (EB 1972, 21:16) Astronomer Roy Gallant refers to the "famous Egyptian Sphinx" as "that creature with a woman's head and a lion's body" and speculates that it might represent the two constellations of **Virgo** and **Leo**. (Gallant, 165) Side by side in the Zodiac, these two constellations represent the virgin birth and Christ, the Lion of Judah, to the **Christians**. To the **pagans**, Virgo is Semiramis, the pagan counterfeit of the virgin mother, the mother goddess, while Leo is either Nimrod, the mighty hunter and Sun god (the summer solstice occurred in Leo in 2000+ B.C.), or the "evil" Shem (a type of Christ) who executed Nimrod.

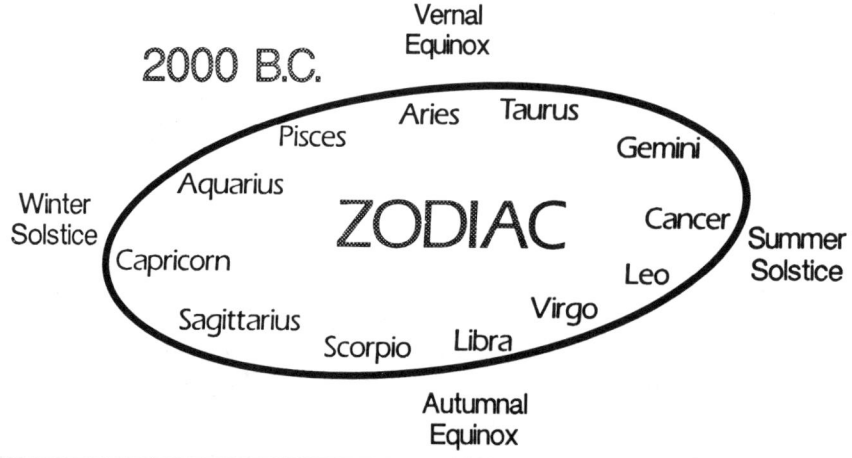

The constellation of Orion the hunter, who represents both Christ and Nimrod, holds up a lion as his kill. (Gallant, 154-167, 121-3)

In the course of a year, the Sun journeys through the entire **Zodiac**. If we start with the Sun in Virgo, we will travel through each constellation until we end with Leo. However, for gentile nations, the beginning of the year is generally recognized as spring, and the first constellation of the Zodiac has always been the constellation in which falls the **vernal equinox**, when night and day are equal.

Immediately after the Flood, the vernal equinox was in **Taurus**, and thus the importance of the bull, its association with Nimrod, and the cult of bull worship in Egypt. Then, about 1953 B.C. according to astronomer Roy Gallant, the Sun at vernal equinox moved into **Aries**, and so for the greatest period of the ancient world, Aries was the "first constellation." This is why both astronomers and astrologers still refer to the **First Point of Aries**. (Gallant, 126-8, 175-8; see Chap. 8)

If the Sphinx is indeed intended to begin with Virgo and end with Leo, this combination may mark some interesting dates. First of all, the promise of Christ's incarnation began with the prophecy of the **virgin birth** in Gen. 3:15 (not long after 4000 B.C.), then matured with the actual virgin birth almost 4000 years later. Christ did not come the first time as the conquering **Lion of Judah**, but will return in triumph to fulfill that role, perhaps about A.D. 2000. Extrapolating backwards and disregarding what astronomical changes may have occurred at the Flood, the summer solstice would have been in Virgo about 4000 B.C. The summer solstice moved to Leo by about 2000 B.C.

But the conjunction of Virgo and Leo marks one interesting event in almost 26,000 years and that is the **autumnal equinox** at the time we are now living, the late 1900s. **Rosh Hashana**, the fifth Jewish feast and the feast of ingathering, is only a week before or after the autumnal equinox in the early 1990s, and there are some believers, both Jewish and gentile Christians, who think that the Rapture may possibly occur at this time, given that Christ so carefully fulfilled the first four Jewish feasts with His death, burial, resurrection, and giving of the Holy Spirit. This is only pure speculation, but could the Sphinx be a prophetic marker for the era of the Rapture, Tribulation, and Second Coming of Christ?

A Pagan or Godly Builder?

We have already wondered whether or not the Great Pyramid (and the Sphinx) is a pillar of and to God, or a monument to the intelligence and accomplishments of pagan man, with possible outside help from fallen angels. There are many theories and traditions and modern teachings as to who built the GP, as this astonishing structure is claimed as their own by both ancient and modern Christians, Jews, pagans, Arabs, and humanists alike.

We have already seen that the standard, scholarly humanist teaching presents Pharaoh Khufu (called Cheops by the Greeks) as the power behind the construction of the GP and his son Chephren as the builder of the Second Pyramid and the Sphinx. Actually, these conclusions are derived from a series of assumptions based on minimal evidence. (Tompkins, Secrets, 64-5) We have also seen that there is some new controversy over this generally accepted view, evidence which only pushes the GP farther into

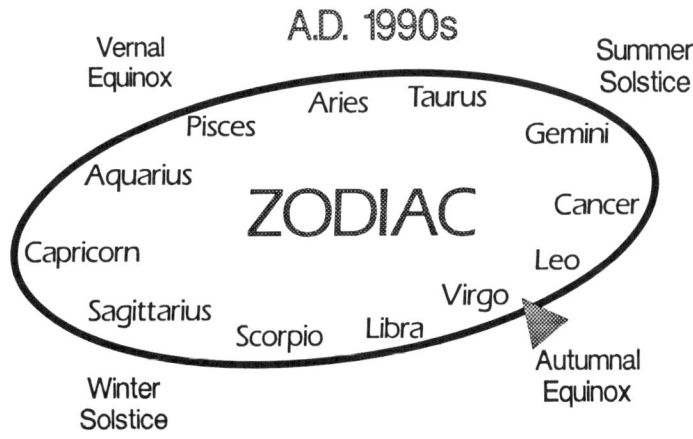

the mists of the ancient world. We have seen that Arab, Jewish, and Christian traditions attribute the GP to a pre-Flood king, an occult figure, or a patriarch (Enoch).

Besides Enoch, there are other biblical figures named as possible architects of the GP. One is **Almodad**, the first of the 13 sons of Joktan listed in Gen. 10:26-29. Joktan was the son of Eber, the brother of Peleg. According to Capt, Almodad is described in the Chaldean "*Paraphrase of Jonathan*" as "the Inventor of Geometry and the Measurer of the Earth." Of course, it was in the lifetime of his uncle that the Earth was divided. Some apparently interpret this as when the Earth was *measured* instead of actually geographically canaled by water. This explanation does harmonize with the geographical purposes of the GP. (Capt, Great, 71)

Could He Be Job?

The other biblical figure referred to by Capt is Job. Capt calls Job (the patriarch of the Bible book called Job) the "youngest brother of Joktan," equating the patriarch Job with **Jobab** listed in Gen. 10:29. This reference does fit the logical timeframe, between the Tower of Babel and the life of Abraham, around the 2100s B.C. Dr. Roy Zuck of Dallas Theological Seminary points out that **Job's life span** is indicated to be **210 years** (70 when Satan attacked him and 140 years after Job's testing), that Mosaic Law was not in force, that he had massive wealth in livestock as did Abraham, and that names and words point to immediate relatives of Abraham or the time of Jacob. (Zuck, BKC I, 716-17)

In the Book of Job, God refers to him as His servant, perfect and upright, and absolutely unique in all the land. (Job 2:3) This seems to indicate that possibly he lived before Abraham, as the names involved were probably common over centuries. We also know from Job 40-41 that Job was contemporaneous with **dinosaurs** who had not yet become extinct following the Flood. Capt notes the peculiar introduction in **God's speech to Job** (Job 38:1-6) in which God asks Job where Job was when God "constructed" the Earth, laying its foundations, measuring it, and stretching a line or cord upon it. ("Stretching the cord" was a prominent and well-known Egyptian ceremony.) It seems as though God is addressing an **experienced engineer** who understands these terms. In fact, in *Young's Literal* translation, God asks "On what have its *sockets* been sunk? Or who hath cast its cornerstone?" This is most intriguing, considering the GP is unique in its sockets. (Capt, Great, 23, 71-2) Could Job have been the unique servant of God assigned to build this wondrous structure?

The Strange Outsiders

Traditions abound that the GP was built by "outsiders" who came from the east. The Greek historian **Herodotus** states that "'strangers to Egypt' supervised the building of the Great Pyramid." (Capt, Great, 5) Indeed, the surviving fragments of the writings of the Egyptian priest **Manetho** tell us that **Shepherd Kings (Hyksos)** came from the east and conquered Egypt without a battle, men of "an ignoble race" who subdued Egypt with their power and caused all of the pagan temples to be closed. Some believe that it was during their reign that the GP was built. (Capt, Great, 5) Others believe that the Hyksos ruled Egypt at the time of **Joseph** and thus explain the favor shown the Jewish shepherds and the hatred restored when a nationalistic Egyptian rebellion raised up a Pharaoh "who knew not Joseph." (Pict. Dict., 367)

We find in Gen. 46-47 that Joseph's Pharaoh had cattle and asked that any able shepherds among Joseph's relatives be put in charge of his herds. (47:6) Joseph in verse 1 tells Pharaoh that his family has brought not only herds but flocks, indicating both sheep and cattle, and that the entire entourage is in the land of Goshen. Joseph wanted them near to him (45:10, 11) in order to take care of them during the five remaining years of famine. Another reason Joseph wanted them in the land of Goshen was the fact that **"every shepherd is an abomination unto the Egyptians."** (v. 34) Perhaps they would be away from most of the Egyptians in Goshen. Dr. Allen Ross thinks that Joseph told them to emphasize cattle over sheep to Pharaoh (v. 33-4) as the Egyptians hated sheep, but it seems clear that Joseph told Pharaoh they brought "flocks." And how could they hide the fact very long? (Ross, BKC I, 97) If the Hyksos Kings did rule at the time of Joseph, then they were probably not the "outsiders" who built the GP.

Egypt was originally **Hamitic** and there is strong tradition that the GP builder was **Semitic**. Egypt would have been pagan from the beginning, considering Ham's son Mizraim founded it following his separation from Cush and Nimrod and the rebellious people of Babel. Thus, if any of the godly followers of Shem, such as Job, came to construct the GP, they would certainly be considered strange outsiders. Could outsiders also apply to fallen angels?

A Witness to Masonry?

Freemasonry is a *secret society* which openly points to its roots in the **ancient Mysteries** and considers itself to embrace the guardians of ancient wisdom, custodians of the highest cultural concepts and the "doctrines that lead to the good of mankind." (Howard, Occult, 1-3; Hall, Secret, foreword) To advance in Freemasonry, Masons must pass a series of initiations, gaining evermore **esoteric** knowledge. They claim **geometry** and the art of **building in stone** as their own. It is indeed interesting that we find often massive, mysterious stone structures throughout the world that persist in boggling the minds of modern man.

Two centrally important structures revered by the Masons are the **Great Pyramid** and **Solomon's Temple**, both claimed to be built by **Master Masons** who left the mark of the Master Mason on both. (Clark, Masonic, 52-3; Howard, Occult, 5-6) Of course we know that Solomon's Temple was designed by God Himself, though Satan seems to have claimed it as his own through the traditions of the Masons. Occultists believe that the Great Pyramid was dedicated to **Hermes Trismegistus**, an occult figure they equate with the biblical **Enoch** who they call the "Second Messenger of God" who was the supposed author of the Masonic (Mystery) rituals and the *one responsible for increasing the year from 360 days to 365 days*. The Great Pyramid, they claim, was not only a **repository for the secret wisdom** which is the foundation of all the arts and sciences, but was also used for **initiation rites**. The Sphinx, they believe, was a secret entrance to the GP, connected by a network of underground tunnels and priests' quarters that are yet to be found. (Hall, Secret, 37, 44; Tompkins, Secrets, 284, 256-9; 270)

A Witness to God?

What evidence do we have to show that the GP was perhaps originally a monument of and to the God of the Bible? We have not been able to draw any satisfactory conclusions concerning the prophetic "map" based on the **pyramid inch**, though much of the material offered by those such as **Adam Rutherford** appears to be amazing in its chronology. We have noted that Bible prophecy is based on a 360-day year, not a 365.25-day year to which the pyramid inch is directly connected. We have also shown that, if Cole's figures for the base are correct, the math offered by the pyramid prophets does not add up to 365.242 but to 362.4. Also, there are inconsistencies in the claims of the pyramid prophets, several having established dates for the return of Christ that have come and gone. In addition, the Egyptian *Book of the Dead* has its own interpretive "map" of the GP's interior. (Tompkins, Secrets, 116)

In **Isaiah's prophecy** concerning Egypt at the time of the Assyrian and Babylonian captivities, Isaiah predicts judgment to come upon Egypt (this is long after the Exodus) as well as a day of redemption which will come in the prophetic **"in that day"** or at the time of the Tribulation and Millennium. *"In that day there is an altar to Jehovah, In the midst of the land of Egypt, And a standing pillar near its border to Jehovah, And it hath been for a sign and for a testimony, To Jehovah of Hosts in the land of Egypt, For they cry unto Jehovah from the face of oppressors, And He sendeth to them a saviour, Even a great one, and hath delivered them."* (Young's Literal, **Isa. 19:19-20**; Martin, BKC I, 1067) This translation from *Young's Literal* uses the present and past tense in reference to the "pillar" while the New American Standard and the King James Scofield use the future tense in both cases.

Dr. John Martin says that this restoration will indeed come at the time of the Millennium and that this **"pillar"** will be built then. However, the Great Pyramid is in the midst of Egypt and it does sit on the ancient border between Upper and Lower Egypt (at the base of the Nile Delta). Thus, this verse is not a perfectly clear reference.

Another verse used by Christians is **Jer. 32:20** which, in the KJV, says "Who hast *set* signs and wonders in the land of Egypt, even unto this day...." But *Young's Literal* translates this as *"done* signs and wonders," a translation upheld by the context of the Exodus. Once again, we Christians seem to be pushing the point.

The most intriguing biblical references are to Christ as the **"chief cornerstone."** It is true that only a pyramid can have a "chief" cornerstone, with four corners and the tip, making a total of five cornerstones, the "chief" one being at the top. (Isa. 28:16, I Pet. 2:6, Zech. 4:7, Eph. 2:20-1) He is also the stone which the builders rejected as well as the "head of the corner." (Matt. 21:42, Ps. 118:22-23, Luke 20:17-18) The GP has never had, that we know of, a **capstone**. **Agatharchides of Cnidus** apparently indicates that there was once a "pyramidion" of four cubits. From descriptions of other pyramids, researchers have assumed that this was of gold or silver metal and this assumption is recorded in most occult literature as well as some scholarly literature. (Tompkins, Secrets, 203, 372, 366-7) Stecchini notes that the apex of the GP is off center due to the intentional widening of certain of the base angles and his belief that the north face was calculated by *phi* while the west face was calculated by *pi*, giving the two sides different slopes. The north/south axis is off center. (Tompkins, Secrets, 366-8)

Would this **intentional, off-center design** cause the capstone not to fit and the builders to reject it? Or was the capstone merely removed with the rest of the limestone casing blocks? Or was it indeed a removable metal pyramidion? Of course, such a pyramidion would not be a *stone*. An occultic illustration of the uncapped Great Pyramid appears on the **U.S. one-dollar bill** as part of The Great Seal of the United States, with the occultic "all-seeing eye" serving as a detached pyramidion.

If "enlightened," occultic humanists can lay claim to God's own Temple, designed by God through David and built by Solomon, then the same claims should not in themselves disqualify the Great Pyramid as a divinely inspired monument. However, the evidence we have does seem to weigh in favor of the pagans. What do *you* think?

BIBLIOGRAPHY

Aveni, Anthony F., *Skywatchers of Ancient Mexico*, Bib. Chap. 9, p. 160

Berlitz, Charles, *Mysteries From Forgotten Worlds*. New York: Doubleday & Co., 1972.

Brecher, Kenneth, *Astronomy of the Ancients*. Cambridge: MIT Press, 1979.

Bullinger, E.W., *Number in Scripture*, Bib. Chap. 2, p. 37.

Capt, E. Raymond, *The Great Pyramid Decoded*, Bib. Chap. 8, p. 139.

Carlson, John B., "Numerology and the Astronomy of the Maya," *Archaeoastronomy in the Americas* (edited by Ray A. Williamson). Los Altos, California: Ballena Press, 1981.

Clark, Col. H.H.H., *A Masonic Digest*, Bib. Chap. 1, p. 19.

Cornell, James, *The First Stargazers*. Boston: Charles Scribner & Sons, 1981.

Cumbey, Constance, *The Hidden Dangers of the Rainbow*, Bib. Chap. 1, p. 19.

De Santillana, Giorgio, and **Von Dechend**, Hertha, *Hamlet's Mill*, Bib. Chap. 7, p. 108.

Drury, Nevill, *Dictionary of Mysticism and the Occult*, Bib. Chap. 2, p. 37.

Durán, Fray Diego, *Book of the Gods and Rites* and *The Ancient Calendar*. Norman: University of Oklahoma Press, 1971. (Translated and edited by Fernando Horcasitas and Doris Heyden.)

Encyclopaedia Britannica (EB), Bib. Chap. 3, p. 51.

Gallant, Roy A., *The Constellations*, Bib. Chap. 3, p. 51.

Gaverluk, Emil, *The Rapture Before the Russian Invasion of Israel*, Bib. Chap. 1, p. 19.

Gibbs, Sharon L., "Mesoamerican Calendrics as Evidence of Astronomical Activity," *Native American Astronomy* (edited by Anthony F. Aveni). Austin: Univ. of Texas Press, 1977.

Hadingham, Evan, *Early Man and the Cosmos*. New York: Walker and Co., 1984.

Hall, Manley P., *The Secret Teachings of All Ages,* Bib. Chap. 7, p. 108.

Hall, Marshall, *The Earth is not Moving*, Bib. Chap. 8, p. 139.

Hannah, John D., "Exodus," *The Bible Knowledge Commentary, Old Testament (I)*. Wheaton: Victor Books, 1985.

Hapgood, Charles H., *Maps of the Ancient Sea Kings*. Philadelphia: Chilton Company, 1966. Revised edition, New York: E. P. Dutton, 1979.

_____, *The Path of the Pole*. Philadelphia: Chilton Book Co., 1970.

Heyerdahl, Thor, *Early Man and the Ocean*, Bib. Chap. 9, p. 160

Howard, Michael, *The Occult Conspiracy*. Rochester, Vermont: Destiny Books, 1989.

Jeffrey, Grant R., *Armageddon*, Bib. Chap. 2, p. 37.

Josephus, *Antiquities*, Bib. Chap. 2, pp. 37-8.

Krupp, E.C. (ed.), *In Search of Ancient Astronomies*. New York: Doubleday & Co., 1977.

Mallery, Arlington, and Harrison, Mary Roberts, *The Rediscovery of Lost America*. New York: E. P. Dutton, 1979.

Martin, John A., "Isaiah," *The Bible Knowledge Commentary, Old Testament (I)*. Wheaton: Victor Books, 1985.

Morison, Samuel Eliot, *The Oxford History of the American People*. New York: Oxford University Press, 1965.

Morris, Henry M., *The Genesis Flood*, Bib. Chap. 2, p. 38, see **Whitcomb**.

Patten, Donald W., Hatch, Ronald R., and Steinhauer, Loren C., *The Long Day of Joshua and Six Other Catastrophes*. Seattle: Pacific Meridian Publishing Co., 1973.

Pentecost, J. Dwight, "Daniel," *The Bible Knowledge Commentary, Old Testament (I)*. Wheaton: Victor Books, 1985.

Ross, Allen P., "Genesis," *The Bible Knowledge Commentary, Old Testament (I)*, Bib. Chap. 2, p. 38.

Sunukjian, Donald R., "Amos," *The Bible Knowledge Commentary, Old Testament (I)*. Wheaton: Victor Books, 1985.

Timetables of History (Grun), Bib. Chap. 7, p. 108.

Tompkins, Peter, *Secrets of the Great Pyramid*, Bib. Chap. 8, p. 140

_____, *Mysteries of the Mexican Pyramids* (paperback). New York: Harper & Row, 1987.

Velikovsky, Immanuel, *Worlds in Collision*, Bib. Chap. 5, p. 80.

_____, *Earth in Upheaval*, Bib. Chap. 3, p. 51.

Webber, David, and Hutchings, N.W., New Light on the Great Pyramid. Oklahoma City: Southwest Radio Church, 1985. [P.O. Box 1144, OKC, OK 73101]

Webster's New World Dictionary, Bib. Chap. 2, p. 38.

White, John, *Pole Shift*. Garden City, NY: Doubleday & Co., Inc., 1980.

World's Last Mysteries, The. Pleasantville, New York: The Reader's Digest Assoc., 1982

Young's Literal Translation of the Holy Bible, Bib. Chap. 4, p. 66

Zondervan Pictorial Bible Dictionary. Nashville: The Southwestern Company, 1972.

Zuck, Roy, "Job," *The Bible Knowledge Commentary, Old Testament (I)*. Wheaton: Victor Books, 1985.

Zuidema, R.T., "The Inca Calendar," *Native American Astronomy* (edited by Anthony F. **Aveni**). Austin: Univ. of Texas Press, 1977.

Chapter 11
Ancient World Maps *Before* the Ice Caps

From the Earth to the Sky

We have discovered that the post-Babel ancients were excellent astronomers, knew the size and shape of the Earth, accurately calculated both latitude and longitude, could find true north with or without a pole star, and understood the advanced mathematics required to convert spherical surfaces to flat maps. In this chapter, we will consider evidence that the ancients applied this knowledge to **map the entire world**. This same evidence **sinks** the widely accepted **Ice Age theories** and indicates that the ice caps and glaciers we see today formed in **very recent** times.

First, we will examine hieroglyphic evidence that reiterates the important, ancient, technical connection between the heavens and the Earth. *Then* we will identify a number of events that led to a progressive loss of ancient knowledge, and review the legacy of the transitional scientific center of Alexandria, Egypt, which flourished during Greek and Roman rule. *Last*, we will define a few important map projections and study several medieval maps which reveal some of the astounding accomplishments of the ancients as well as surprising characteristics of ancient and medieval world geography.

Stylized representation of Dendera Zodiac figure

The Square of Pegasus

In Chapter 10, we saw from the research of Dr. Livio Stecchini and the study compiled by Peter Tompkins the cartographic (mapping) functions of the Great Pyramid and the Babylonian ziggurats. Apparently the early **Egyptians** were concerned about carefully *mapping their own country*, using the knowledge of the heavens that they brought from Babylon and specifically the **Square of Pegasus**, the Egyptian **hieroglyph** for which was a rectangle, sometimes empty, sometimes filled with water or fish.

"In," or directly above, the Zodiacal sign of **Pisces** is the constellation named after the mythological winged horse called **Pegasus**. Pegasus contains four bright stars, each about 15° apart, which make up a square. The square's parallel lines run along the **parallels of celestial latitude** and its vertical lines run basically along the **celestial longitudinal meridians**, almost matching their diverging angles. [Lines of celestial latitude and longitude are merely Earth's grid lines projected upon an imaginary heavenly sphere that surrounds the Earth.] The heavenly square thus roughly represents the most common *grid section of Earth*, as latitudinal and longitudinal lines are normally marked on maps at 15° intervals. Thus, any great circle of 15° segments times 24 hours equals 15° per one hour or 360° per day.

The four stars are called *Markab, Al Genib, Scheat,* and *Al Pheratz* (or Sirrah). (Bullinger, Witness, 88; Map of the Sky poster) According to Stecchini, the ancients used the Square of Pegasus as their **reference point to map the heavens**. In the same way on **Earth**, they began a map with a basic surveying square or a **unit of land surface**, and measured out from it in a **checkerboard pattern**. The fundamental field measure of the **Sumerians** equals about 3,600 square meters, according to *Hamlet's Mill*. [A U.S. acre = 4,046.72 sq. mt.] From reading cuneiform tablets, Stecchini notes that the ancient Babylonian or Chaldean word *iku* was

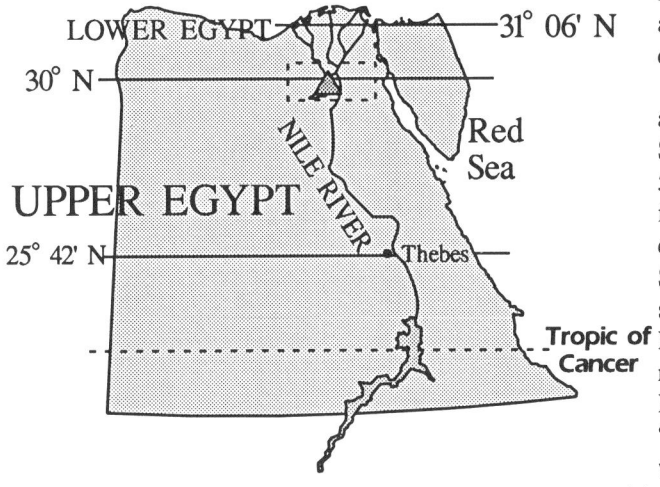

applied to these earthly square units as well as to the heavenly Square of Pegasus itself. (DeSantillana, Hamlet's Mill, 435; Tompkins, Secrets, 297)

In Babylon, the "Iku-star" was called "the image of heaven and [E]arth." In the Babylonian Flood epic of *Gilgamesh*, Utnapishtim's ark has a floor space of one iku. James B. Pritchard translates iku as "acre" with equal dimensions of *ten dozen cubits*. A cube measuring 120 cubits in each direction would equal four units of 3,600 square cubits each. (DeSantillana, Hamlet's, 435; Pritchard, Ancient, 66-7) Using the geographic cubit of 0.462 meters, a square cubit equals 0.2134 square meters, and 3,600 square cubits then equals 768.24 square meters. Four of these units total 3,072.96 square meters. Did they use a longer cubit, if the above measure of "about 3,600 square meters" is correct?

The *l-iku* appears on the Dendera zodiacs of **Roman Egypt** as a checkerboard pattern in a square between the two fishes of Pisces. Pictured in *Hamlet's Mill*, one board has 29 dots while the other has 30. (Could this is any way relate to days of the month?) On the Guinea Coast of **Africa**, the illustration becomes two intersecting turtles or lizards with a common, crosshatched back. In **Sumatra**, the square looks like turtle heads and feet protruding from one square back marked by nine circles. From the **Americas** comes a turtle with two fish tails marked by an 11 x 13 square checkerboard. (DeSantillana, Hamlet's, 420, 430-5) Note once again an ancient measure and illustration that crossed the oceans.

The **Egyptians** marked such a "square" as a **special district** between their Southern and Northern regions, from 29° 51' to 30° 06' N latitude. The hieroglyph for this district was a rectangle, sometimes containing water or fish, the sign for the Square of Pegasus, the water or fish showing the position of Pegasus "in" Pisces. Stecchini asserts that this was the reference unit from which the ancient Egyptians mapped their country. Their "narrow" or geodetic southern boundary was marked by three corresponding positions of the **Tropic of Cancer**, at 23° 51', at 24°, and at 24° 06' N, also the location of the first waterfall (Little Cataract) of the Nile River. The southern boundary in the "broad" sense, the one you see on a modern map, is located at the second waterfall (Great Cataract). The ancient geodetic northern boundary was established at 31° 06' N, the point at which a degree of longitude is 6/7ths of a degree of longitude at the equator. It is interesting that the **Great Pyramid** sits basically in the center of the reference rectangle (the special district), barely below the "perfect" 30° parallel. (Tompkins, Secrets, 181, 295-7)

Loss of Ancient Knowledge

Charles Berlitz estimates that we **possess today less than 10%** of the body of ancient records. Charles Hapgood states that the most advanced cultures are the easiest to destroy, leaving the least evidence of their accomplishments. Progress in technology, adds Hapgood, is always matched by "progress" in the means of destruction. For example, the ancients' massive walls of defense (invented by Nimrod) were soon effectively challenged by ladders, catapults, and battering rams. Today's high-tech cities face the possibility of nuclear attack. Professor Cyrus Gordon also comments on the speed with which a culture can be lost, in one or two generations. (Berlitz,

Mysteries, 35; Hapgood, Maps, 194; Gordon, Before, 37)

Catastrophes of weather, geophysical disturbances (volcanos, earthquakes, etc.), disease, and war can wreak decisive and immediate cultural annihilation, not forgetting extraordinary events in the heavens or divine judgments. Consider the search for Sodom and Gomorrah. People are killed, monuments and records are destroyed, and knowledge is lost. Social and political factors are generally slower, but can achieve the same end. *Let's quickly examine some of the events, structures, and ideas that have obscured the past.*

The **Genesis Flood** certainly wiped more than 1,600 years of advanced civilization from the surface of the Earth in a matter of months. The forced dispersion at the **Tower of Babel** divided mankind physically and linguistically, with the explicit purpose that humans should not be able to achieve what was in their rebellious imaginations. Language, terrain, and distance became barriers while new locations required new beginnings. The traditional belief that the **Great Pyramid** was designed as a time capsule of ancient knowledge was, and is, very widespread among prominent people throughout history. Such strong tradition cannot be ignored, and centuries of modern research have proved fruitful in understanding the technology embodied by the GP. However, in many ways, the Great Pyramid still remains stubbornly enigmatic and controversial, its perfect form ravaged over the centuries by vandals and exploiters.

The execution of Nimrod, which we estimate occurred in 1984 B.C., spurred the beginning of the **Mysteries**, an enduring method by which the highest cultural and scientific knowledge, as well as powerful political and religious knowledge, has been reserved for the *initiated few*. The Mystery system spread quickly throughout the ancient world and has endured in medieval and modern times through such organizations as the Masons, the Knights Templar, the Rosicrucians, the Illuminati, the Thule Society, the Theosophical Society, the Mormons, European secret societies from which sprung Yale University's Skull & Bones, the Club of Rome, the Bilderbergers, the elite of the New Age Movement, and every manner of order of priests, brotherhoods, shamans, witches, gurus and the like.

The ancient Mystery concept, as we have studied in earlier chapters, is **esoteric knowledge**, knowledge that is kept from the masses, knowledge that is carefully guarded and passed down to loyal initiates. Professor Gordon states that this even applied to the **complex systems of writing** in Mesopotamia, Egypt, and China, systems which kept literacy from the common people. (Gordon, Before, 100) Dr Barry Fell explains that the term *runes* applies to any *Nordic* (language group of Norse or West Scandinavian which includes Iceland, Germanic, English, and Gothic peoples) script because it comes from the Old Norse word *runar* which means **"secret writing."** Original Nordic scribes were *wizards* who carefully guarded the meanings of the Nordic letters (runes) from the uninitiated common people. (Fell, Bronze, 297-8; Webster's) The term **wizard** is derived from the Old English (Nordic language group) word *wis* meaning "wise." A wizard was an *adept*, an initiated one, a magician, sorcerer or warlock (male witch). (Dict. of Myst., 270, 274) The strict use of **Latin** by the Roman Church during the **Middle Ages** effectively kept the Bible from everyone but a few scholars and the Roman Catholic priesthood. In fact, the Roman Catholic Inquisition of A.D. 1229 in Toulouse, France, forbid all laymen to read the Bible. (Timetables, 168)

The first catastrophic divine judgment after the Flood and Babel, of which we are told, is the destruction of **Sodom and Gomorrah** which we estimate to have occurred in 1894 B.C. Only regional, it did however destroy a prominent portion of that era's society, and not even modern excavational technology has been able to find the pieces. Hundreds of years later, possibly 1488 B.C., the renowned Egyptian civilization was seriously damaged by the judgments connected with the **Exodus**. During this same era, we also have widespread evidence of what seems to be a series of catastrophic happenings that affected the **entire Mediterranean and Middle East**, from the eruption of **Santini** and the destruction of the **Minoans**, possibly accompanied by drastic changes in sea level, to the sudden demise of the **Indus Valley** civilization, and the invasions of the **Sea Peoples**.

After the disappearance of the highly advanced, Crete-centered Minoan culture, the **Mycenaean** civilization of mainland Greece and coastal Asia Minor rose to prominence. It lasted into the 1100s B.C. when, one by one, all of its important cities, including Troy, were **"sacked and left in ruins."** (Chadwick, Linear B, 7; Hapgood, Maps, 194-7) Who knows how much ancient knowledge was lost as the Mediterranean suffered from divine judgments, earthquakes, volcanoes, tidal waves, barbarian invasions, and wars.

In the 500s B.C., the **Medo-Persians** conquered the Babylonians. In the 300s B.C., the Macedonian **Alexander the Great** subdued the Greeks and led them on to conquer Asia Minor, Egypt, the famous Phoenician port city of Tyre, the Middle East, and, briefly, part of India, all of which constituted the Medo-Persian Empire. [See Daniel 7 & 8] We shall see later that the Phoenicians were world travelers and colonizers and, thus, the world's best seamen. **Tyre** was the center of the Phoenician world. The famous ancient cartographer Marinus (A.D. 100s) was from a rebuilt Tyre. However, ancient Tyre, and probably much valuable geographical and navigational knowledge, was first destroyed by Nebuchadnezzar's Babylonians in the 500s B.C. Some of the Phoenicians escaped to an island just off the coast and built a new Tyre. Then, in the 300s B.C., Alexander used the remains of the ancient city to build a causeway to the island city and overthrew it, thus fulfilling Ezekiel 26. (Scofield Bible notes, Ezek. 26:14)

Alexander also plundered and partly destroyed the Persian capital, **Persepolis**, burning the palace of Xerxes in revenge for the destruction of the great temple of Babylon. (Berlitz, Mysteries, 35; Tarn, Alexander, 54) Compare this with the instant demolition during **World War II** by American bombers of the **Abbey of Monte Cassino**, an 11th-Century Italian monastery and the oldest such structure in the West. (Hapgood, Maps, 195) Such monasteries were the main preservers of knowledge through the Middle Ages.

However, Alexander offset some of the effects of his military campaign by building a number of cities, the most notable being **Alexandria, Egypt**, where all the remaining knowledge of the ancient world was gathered into its great library and museum where Eratosthenes, Hipparchus, and Ptolemy would work and study. The **Romans** under Julius Caesar conquered Alexandria in the 40s B.C. and, in the battle, the **library** suffered its first burning, being about one-third destroyed. The Romans had already destroyed the reputed 500,000-volume library at **Carthage** in 146 B.C., along with some 450,000 of the 500,000 Carthaginians. Carthage was another important Phoenician seaport and center of trade, navigation, and world colonization, and so, once again, invaluable and irreplaceable Phoenician records of world history and geography were destroyed. Greece had come under Roman control in 147 B.C. and Rome would soon be history's greatest empire. (Timetables, 22; Hapgood, Maps, 194-6; Berlitz, Mysteries, 35)

The **Alexandrian library** was restored and expanded after the Roman conquest, but fell victim to further destruction by a **Christian mob** inflamed by a fanatical bishop's warning that the library was a dangerous center of heathen teachings and thus a threat to Christianity. Just how genuinely and biblically Christian that mob was is certainly difficult for us to judge. The final destruction occurred in the 600s as the fanatical warriors of **Islam** swept across northern Africa and portions of Europe. One story credits this burning to religious zeal, and the other to a need for fuel to heat water for the Roman baths. (Hapgood, Maps, 195-6) Whatever the reason, Alexandria was lost and the Western Roman Empire had finally been completely conquered by Asian and European **barbarian tribes** in A.D. 476. **Rome was sacked** and **Constantinople** would become the new center of surviving records of ancient culture.

Meanwhile over in **China**, the Emperor Shih Huang Ti of the Chin Dynasty decided that all history should begin with his own rule in the 200s B.C. He ordered all previous records destroyed, exempting only works on medicine, agriculture, and necromancy (black magic, contacting the dead). (Berlitz, Mysteries, 35) And back in **Israel**, we cannot forget the terrible tragedy of the destruction of Jerusalem and Herod's Temple in **A.D. 70**. Jerusalem had been burned and Solomon's Temple destroyed in the 500s B.C. by the Babylonians. How many biblical manuscripts and historical records were lost or hidden at the time of the **Babylonian Captivity**?

Even before that, following the **Assyrian Captivity** of the Northern Kingdom in the 600s B.C., the high priest *found* a copy of the books of Moses (Torah) in the neglected Temple. (II Kings 22:8) Does that mean only one copy of the

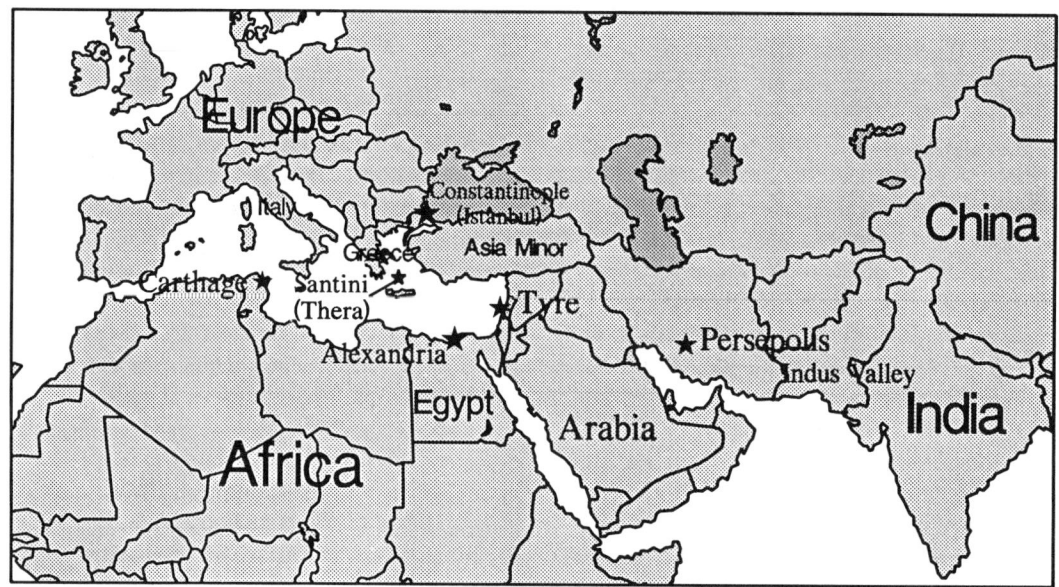

Law still existed at that time? What about manuscripts of the other biblical "books" written by that time? We know much was hidden before the Roman army came in A.D. 70, as was demonstrated by the discovery of the first **Dead Sea Scrolls** in 1947. Scholars still argue over the actual site of the Jewish Temples and over the possible location of the **Ark of the Covenant**. Some show evidence to believe that the Ark is hidden below the Temple Mound, while others present believable evidence that it is secretly guarded in Ethiopia. So much has been lost!

After the defeat of the Western Roman Empire and the conquests of the Islamic Arabs in the 600s, Western Civilization descended into what is known as the **Dark Ages**. Wars continued, the **Holy Roman Empire** was established in A.D. 800, and the **monasteries** of the Roman Catholic Church became the preservers and recorders of ancient and current history. The **Catholic Crusaders** fought the Byzantines and the Turks in the 1100s and 1200s over Constantinople and the Holy Land, but ultimately failed. The **Black Plague** began in India and, in only four years, from 1347 to 1351, *killed 75 million people*, including *one-third* of the population of England. (Timetables, 191) The Eastern Roman Empire (Byzantium) with its capital at Constantinople continued until the Islamic Turks conquered the city and the empire in 1453.

Scientific scholars bemoan the religious and literary emphasis of the Middle Ages, as apparently religious/literary works were considered most important to mass produce as **Gutenberg's printing press** changed the world in the 1450s. Science was neglected, say scholars, and again knowledge was lost. (Timetables) Of course, in the long run, this invention became the worldwide instrument of the preservation and dissemination of knowledge.

The religious mindset of the Middle Ages also led the Catholic Church into several periods of what is known as the **Inquisition**, or an attempt to purge the population of doctrinal heretics, Jews, Muslims, or Protestants, by civil penalty, torture, or execution. Begun in the 1200s and continued, especially in Spain, in the 1500s to early 1800s, it resulted in the deaths of thousands. According to 19th-Century historian William Prescott, the Inquisition "did more to stay the march of improvement than any other scheme ever devised by human cunning." (Prescott, Mexico, 51) However, the Inquisition itself requires a detailed examination for a fair hearing because we saw in Chapter 8 that Inquisitors properly upheld biblical truth when they opposed Copernicanism.

Meanwhile, highly advanced **civilizations rose and fell** in the **Americas**, from the Great Lakes Copper Culture of the 2000s to 1700s B.C., to a North African colonial community begun about 300 B.C. in western North America that thrived for some 1200 years, then suddenly vanished. (Fell America, vi; Fell, Saga, 247-8, 283-4) A fortified, iron-working culture of Ohio and Virginia also disappeared by A.D. 1450, a victim, believes Captain Arlington Mallery, of the Black Plague which crossed into America in the late 1300s or early 1400s. (Mallory, Rediscovery, 160-7) Many of the sites of early North American peoples were destroyed by **dam, lake, and flood-control projects**. Early New Englanders used the slabs of ancient stone observatories for their own buildings, having no idea what they were "vandalizing." (Mallery, Rediscovery, 30; Fell, America, 83-4)

In Central America, the ancient and highly cultured **Olmec** civilization suddenly began as early as 1200 B.C. but **disappeared** in the 400s B.C. or later. The **Toltecs** appeared possibly around the 600s A.D. but their great capital, Tula, was in ruins and the stuff of **Atlantis-type legends** by the time the Mexicas and other tribes became the brutal Aztec Empire in the 1300s and 1400s. The **Mayan** civilization began anywhere from 2700 B.C. to the A.D. 200s, depending on the source. But all agree that they mysteriously began to **decline and disperse** in the A.D. 800s to 1000. Even the advanced and incredibly organized **Incas** of South America looked back to greater ancestors. (Jairazbhoy, Egyptians, 7; Prescott, Mexico, 13; Bierhorst, Mexico, 19-22; Williamson, Archaeoastronomy [Collea], 228; Aveni, Skywatchers, 12; Heyerdahl, Early, 67, 104-5, 382; McKern, Exploring, 70-3)

Much knowledge had already been lost or obscured by legend by the time the **Spaniards** arrived in the 1500s. Of course, few people are unaware of the human and material destruction wreaked by the **conquistadors** throughout the Caribbean, Central, and South America. The **Catholic priests or Jesuits** who accompanied the Spanish military burned most of the carefully kept records of the Aztecs and Mayas, while the oral histories collected by a few far-sighted clerics were tainted by both fear of the Spaniards and an eagerness to please the conquering invaders. (Krupp, In Search [Aveni], 167) It is, however, to a small group of determined and dedicated **Spanish Catholic missionary/ scholars** that researchers turn for the bulk of our knowledge concerning the histories of ancient Latin American civilizations.

In 1630, a fire in the cathedral of Skalholt, **Iceland**, deprived us of the archives stored there, (Mallery, Rediscovery, 147) and possibly of

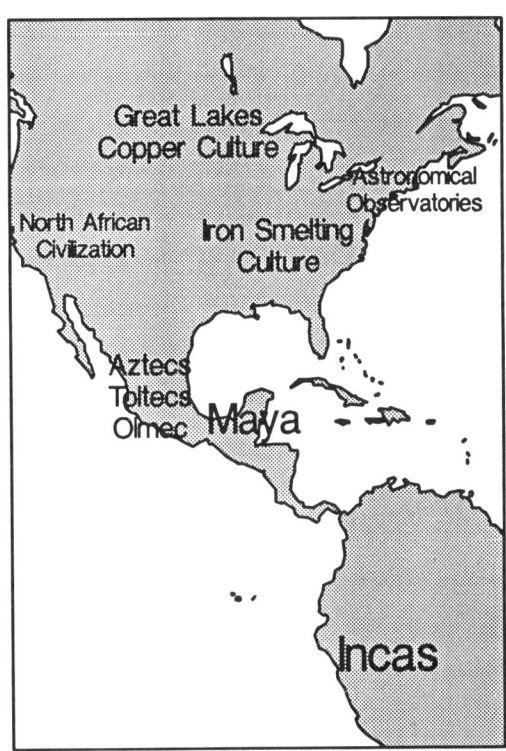

additional chronicled accounts of the North American explorations of the Vikings in the A.D. 900s and 1000s and/or records of settlement and climate changes in the North Atlantic. We can only speculate.

After the **American Revolution** in the late 1700s, the resulting **split between the scholars of Great Britain and America** stymied, until only recently, the realization that ancient European language inscriptions abound in the Americas. American archaeologists had no interest in ancient European or African scripts and labeled the markings that they found as the result of "creative" plows and tree roots. Fell writes that these scholars "have never explained how it is that plows in Pennsylvania usually write in Basque or Iberian Punic, whereas those of New England are apt to ascend the walls of stone buildings to write Celtic Ogam upside down on the ceiling." (Fell, America, 12-3)

Probably the *very worst enemy* of ancient history reared its ugly head in the 1860s when Darwin and others sold the basic idea of universal **evolution** to the Western world. The belief that the more ancient a man, the more primitive he must be, infected the minds of scholars and eventually invaded the schoolrooms and churches of the civilized world. It is very difficult, even for a biblically educated Christian, to strip the mind of the idea that all earthly, heavenly, and human development is always simple to complex, inferior to superior, primitive to advanced. Combined with the ideas of ages and cycles, evolution is nothing more than Hinduistic or Eastern paganism. *If it were not for the Bible, we could not even begin to reconstruct what has really occurred on this planet.*

Greek Cartography of Alexandria

In the 330s and 320s B.C., **Alexander the Great**, son of Philip of Macedonia, conquered Greece and the entire **Medo-Persian Empire**, making **Greece** the *third major world power* as prophesied by Daniel. (Dan. 7 & 8) Thus, the Greeks ruled **Egypt** until Rome finally conquered all of Greece in 147 B.C. (Timetables, 22) Alexander founded the port city of **Alexandria, Egypt**, in **332** B.C. With its famous library, Alexandria became the *world's center for culture and science*, and the major repository of ancient documents.

The Greek scientist **Eratosthenes** (200s B.C.) was put in charge of the **library/museum** at Alexandria. As we studied in Chapter 10, his estimate of the circumference of the Earth was one of the closest of his time, depending on the historical source. However, we have seen that, long before Eratosthenes and the Greeks of Alexandria, whoever designed the Great Pyramid knew the precise circumference, and that the geography of the Egyptians was accurate and sophisticated. We must then conclude that much knowledge was lost along the journey from 2000 B.C. to the 300s B.C.

Hipparchus (100s B.C.) was another Greek scientist who is traditionally credited with the "discovery" of plane and spherical trigonometry and the precession of the equinoxes. (Chaps. 8 & 10) He is also acknowledged as the first to locate points on the Earth by longitude and latitude. What we know of him comes almost exclusively from the writings of **Strabo** (c. A.D. 20) and **Ptolemy** (A.D. 100s) He probably did some of his work at Alexandria. He criticized Eratosthenes for not using a mathematical approach to his geography. Hapgood asks why, if Hipparchus "discovered" the math, did he criticize someone who lived 100 years before him for not using it. Of course, we know from our research that trigonometry was ancient knowledge, as was the precession of the equinoxes and latitude and longitude. The **Alexandrian Greeks** only **revived** and **rediscovered** knowledge that was almost lost over the years. (Hapgood, Maps, 31-33, 51, 181; EB, 1972, 11:516-17)

Hipparchus does deserve credit for **rejecting** the teachings of early **heliocentrists**. Revolutionary at the time, the idea that the Earth and the five known planets revolve around the Sun was argued as early as the 270s B.C. by **Aristarchus of Samos**. However, Hipparchus and most other scholars of his day held fast to the ancient belief that Earth was the center of the Universe. As we saw in Chapter 8, they taught that the Moon, then Mercury, Venus, the Sun, Mars, Jupiter, and Saturn all revolve around Earth, in that order. (EB, 1972, 11:516-17)

Ptolemy (A.D. 100s), a Greek scientist who did much of his work in Alexandria, would have the *greatest influence on the medieval world.* He relied heavily on the writings of Hipparchus and thus adopted the view that the Earth was the center of the known universe. This aspect of his influence was good, as geocentrism would dominate Europe until Copernicus (A.D. 1400s/1500s). But apparently Ptolemy rejected the findings of Eratosthenes and claimed **Earth's circumference** to be the equivalent of **18,000 miles**, almost 7,000 miles too short, a figure attributed by some to Poseidonius.

Ptolemy also recalculated the rate of precession arrived at by Hipparchus who had figured the rate of change to be 45 or 46 seconds (45" or 46") of a degree per year. Ptolemy calculated it to be only 36" per year. The actual rate today is about 50.26", though the rate is not uniform and is, in modern times, increasing. (EB, 1972, 18:812-4; Bullinger, Witness, 14; Tompkins, Secrets, 5-6, 112-3)

What does all this mean? Ptolemy's seven-volume *Guide to Geography* profoundly influenced the medieval world and map making for 1,500 years. However, Ptolemy's circumference was far too short and he placed the equator too far north. (EB, 1972, 18:813-4) In Alexandria, **accurate ancient source maps** were gathered and compiled by Ptolemy and the other Alexandrian Greeks into **world maps**. Though some of the Greek cartographers used Eratosthenes's estimate of Earth's circumference, as evidenced in the medieval *Piri Re'is* map, *Ptolemy's estimate would eventually dominate.* Because of the degeneration of knowledge, these Alexandrian Greeks did not understand how the ancient maps had been constructed and so often made **disastrous "corrections"** or **pieced maps together inaccurately**, using faulty projection methods.

The Alexandrian Era maps that survived the destruction of the Alexandrian library and the coming centuries of political and religious upheaval eventually passed into the hands of medieval cartographers who possessed even less knowledge than the Greeks. More additions, corrections, compilations, and new projections were made, further *obscuring the accurate worldwide geographical knowledge of the post-Babel ancients.*

Thus, though Ptolemy had access to the **surviving ancient geographical literature and maps**, as well as maps drawn from the great, seafaring Phoenician tradition by the geographer, **Marinus of Tyre** (A.D. 100s), he obscured a lot of these ancient sources and then himself became an inaccurate source for later medieval cartographers. However, we shall see that he also preserved some very intriguing bits and pieces of ancient maps which raise interesting questions regarding changes in Earth's geography. (Hapgood, Maps, 180)

Ancient, Alexandrian, and Medieval Maps

In order to examine some of these maps, we need to establish working definitions of several types of map projections. We'll look at the Mercator, Portolan, and Azimuthal projections. If you have a world atlas and/or encyclopedia with maps, look through them and note the different types of projections used, as each map should be labeled as to its construction.

Mercator Projection

A European named **Gerhard Kremer** (1512-1594) was the most prominent geographer of his time and the father of modern cartography. He used the Latin translation of his name, **Gerardus Mercator**, and he **rejected Ptolemy's methods**. For example, he did *not* apply a mean length of latitude throughout a map, as did Ptolemy. *Even traditionalists realize that Mercator was not the inventor of what is now known as the Mercator Projection.* Of course, we have seen that the ancients used this method of spherical projection in the **ziggurats**. Ptolemy attributed a similar projection to the Phoenician geographer, **Marinus of Tyre** (A.D. 100s)

Mercator was the first in the modern world to apply this projection scientifically to a *navigation chart for seamen.* His famous **world map of 1569** was drawn on a Mercator projection, and his **massive atlas** was divided into sections of *ancient maps, Ptolemaic maps,* and *modern maps.* However, he still had the *Ptolemaic misconception of the size of the Earth* and so did not understand the comparatively accurate distances he found on surviving fragments of ancient maps. Thus, his distances were not nearly as accurate as those of the ancients. An interesting aside is that Mercator became a **Protestant** during the **Reformation** which Martin Luther officially began in 1517. An arrest for heresy in 1544 and the threat of further religious persecution led to Mercator's acceptance of a Protestant nobleman's invitation to move his family to the German Rhineland in 1552. (EB, 1972, 15:176-7; Hapgood, Maps, 17-18, 102-7, 226-7, 235-6)

Remember from the section on the pyramids that the Mercator projection makes the *longitudinal meridians* **straight and parallel** while it places the *parallels of latitude* **ever further apart from the equator to the pole.** This placing of latitudinal lines is calculated using spherical trigonometry to maintain the *correct ratio of longitude to latitude* and so compensate as much as possible for the distortion of a flat map with meridians that are straight and parallel rather than curved to meet at the poles. This projection is in widespread use today. It is interesting, in light of our discoveries concerning the ziggurats and Great Pyramid, that Mercator journeyed to see the Great Pyramid in 1563, carving his name among the other European graffiti. (Tompkins, Secrets, 38, 285)

Portolan Charts

The term *portolan* or *portolano* refers to **"port to port"** as these were practical, **navigational charts** used by medieval sailors, as opposed to world or regional maps drawn by academicians (scholars). These amazingly accurate portolanos charted the Mediterranean and the Black Sea on a technical level far beyond the capabilities of medieval sailors and cartographers, the very fact which caused Swedish cartographer **A.E. Nordenskiöld** (1800s) to suspect a common ancient source map, possibly Phoenician. (Hapgood, Maps, 9-11)

The portolan system was apparently used in medieval times as an *excellent method of constructing or copying maps*. It is unclear exactly when the method was devised, but it may have come from the Alexandrian Greek era. Because portolan cartographers were copying copies of copies of one or more ancient source maps, their sea charts were much more accurate than Ptolemy's maps, for example. Certain world maps of the 1300s to 1500s tacked Ptolemaic and portolan maps together with other source material to create intriguing combinations of accuracy and inaccuracy. These composite world maps individually provide evidence for accurate ancient mappings of Europe, parts of Asia, Africa, the North Atlantic, North and South America, and Antarctica.

Hapgood discovered that the portolanos were based on a **flat projection** which incorporated **plane trigonometry**, a fact unrecognized by "expert opinion". (Hapgood also found that the original, ancient sources were based on spherical trigonometry, as we saw in the pyramids.) Portolan distortion was compensated for with the use of a **different north for each section of the map**. Hapgood speculates that a medieval map maker ignorant of spherical projection would naturally treat an ancient map fragment as a series of flat planes, and so devise a method of giving each grid or section its own north to compensate for the distortion in longitude. (Hapgood, Maps, 4-9, 17-22, 49, 53-4, 98, 145)

Portolan charts were constructed using a *polar projection*, polar meaning **"circular"** and not necessarily involving the North or South Pole. The map would have **one or more center points**, each of which was the center of a circle which was divided into 8, 16, or 32 sections like a pie. The lines radiated from each center like spokes in a wheel, also resembling compass points. From the center point and the radiating

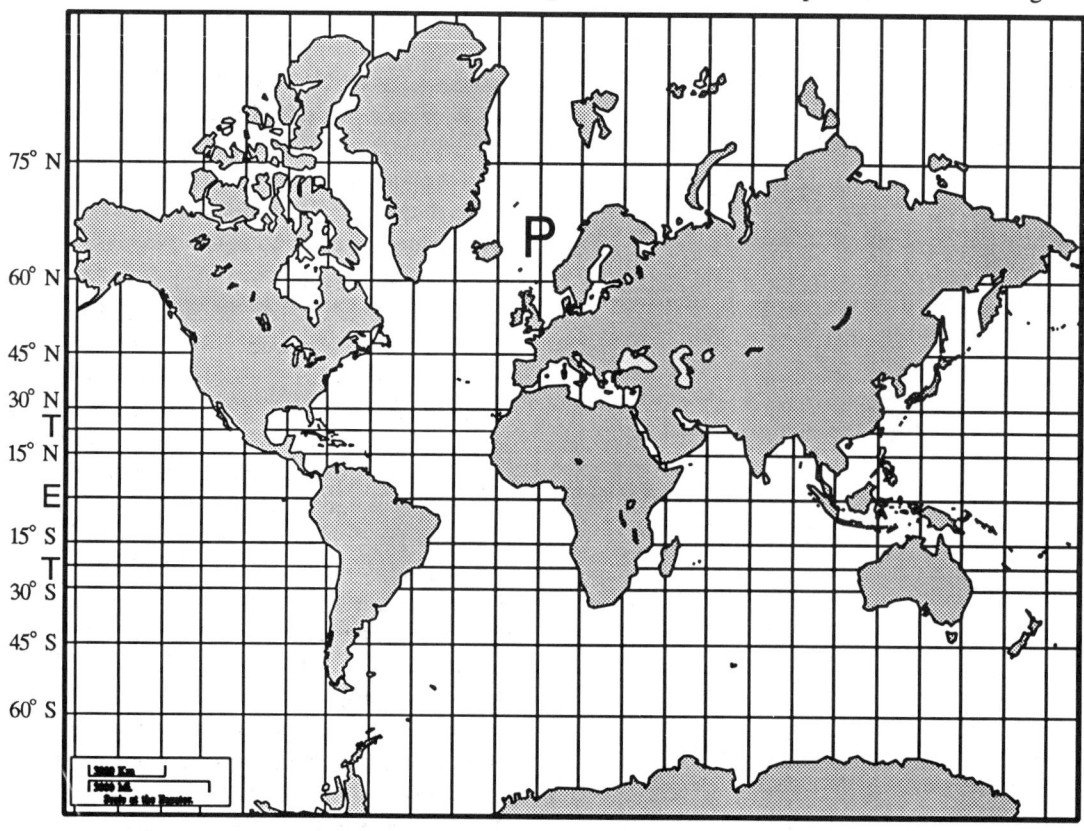

MERCATOR PROJECTION

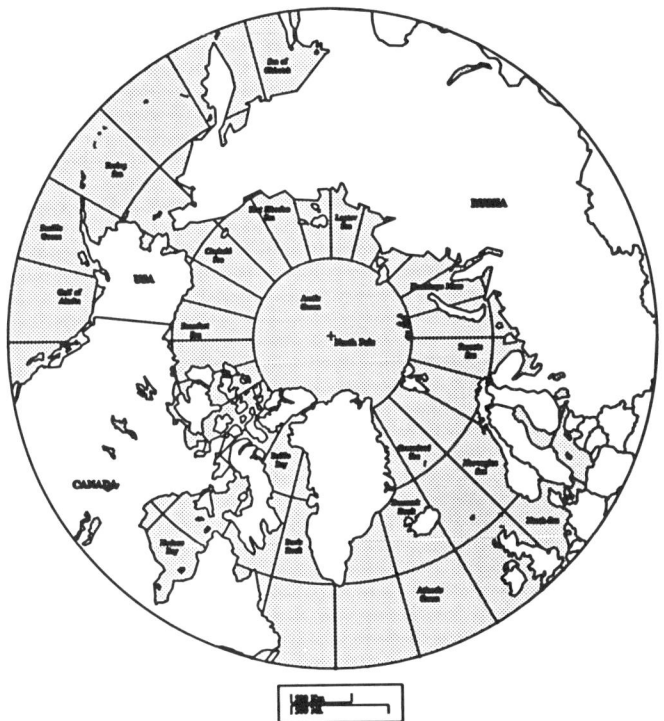

AZIMUTHAL PROJECTION

lines of each circle, a grid could be drawn to represent lines of longitude and latitude. Each grid might have a different north. See Hapgood's reproductions of the *Piri Re'is* map, the *Zeno* map, and the *Bonne* projection maps for excellent illustrations of variously oriented grids. (Hapgood, Maps, 32-3, 52-3, 129, 224-5)

Using trigonometry, Hapgood demonstrated that the experts were wrong in believing that the portolanos were not mathematical in design. He also found that many medieval portolanos were oriented to **magnetic north**, a common practice in medieval and Renaissance years. However, the *Piri Re'is* map and the African portion of the *De Canerio* map orient to true north, showing that their common ancient source map(s) was designed by someone who could find true north. (Hapgood, Maps, 14-17, 99)

Azimuthal Projection

Take a piece of paper (a flat plane) and, keeping the paper flat, hold it against a globe (or a ball of some kind) so that the North Pole is the only point touching the paper. Thus, the flat plane is **"tangent"** to the globe at the pole. Imagine then that the Northern Hemisphere (above the equator) is "projected" onto the flat piece of paper. Now hold the paper tangent to the globe at some point on the equator. The *tangent point can be any point on the globe*, depending on what part you want to map.

There are different types of azimuthal projections defined in Note 5 of Hapgood's book (first version), but the modern Air Force world map (Bonne projection) in Hapgood's third chapter vividly illustrates an **azimuthal equidistant projection**. Hapgood then very effectively relates the Air Force map to the polar portolan projection of the Piri Re'is map and its use of different norths. The *tangent point* of the *azimuthal* Air Force map is Cairo, Egypt, while the main *center point* of the *polar* Piri Re'is map is the intersection of the longitudinal meridian of Alexandria, Egypt, with the Tropic of Cancer. (Hapgood, Maps, 31, 52-3, 225-6)

The Piri Re'is Map: *Mallery*

First a pirate, then a captain and later an admiral in the Imperial Ottoman Fleet, the **Turkish seaman** called **Piri Re'is** authored a detailed, **16th-Century geography** of the Mediterranean Sea and compiled a **world map dated 1513**. In his notes, Piri Re'is explains that he used some 20 charts and world maps from the Alexandrian Greek era, a number of Arab maps, four maps drawn by Portuguese explorers, and a map drawn by Columbus. The map languished in the Topkapi Palace Library of the Imperial Palace of Istanbul (Constantinople) until either **1929 or 1931** (two dates are given) when it was "discovered" by the **director of Turkish National Museums** and reproduced in a London newspaper. Drawn on a gazelle skin, only about half of it survives. (Mallery, Rediscovery, 201; Hapgood, Maps, preface, foreword, 209-10)

Secretary of State Henry Stimson, highly interested in finding the "lost map of Columbus," had the American ambassador to Turkey obtain copies for the Library of Congress. The map *did not conform to the ideas of scholars* at the time who *ignored its unique aspects* and rejected its claim of the Columbus source map, and so the world lost interest. Once again the old map lay unnoticed until a visiting **Turkish naval officer** brought a copy to the U. S. Navy Hydrographic Office in **1953**, unaware that copies were catalogued in Washington, D.C. and other large American libraries. This time, however, it fell into the hands of the right man at the right time. (Hapgood, Maps, 1-3, 207; White, Pole Shift, 38)

Captain Arlington H. Mallery had worked with the Navy cartographers, particularly M.I. Walters, since shortly after World War II researching **ancient Viking sailing charts and maps** that show Greenland *before it was covered with ice!* Mallery was a seaman, an engineer, and a navigator. During World War II, he was First Officer under a Captain Myrdal of Scandinavian descent, a man who traced his family back to Bergen, Norway, in A.D. 985. Captain Myrdal came from a long line of sea captains. This fact was fascinating to Mallery who had already begun his pursuit of Nordic navigational history years before the war.

The Vikings of Iceland and Greenland were Norsemen, and Mallery was an avid studier of ancient Icelandic documents and navigational charts. A seaman himself, Mallery realized that seamen had to have accurate charts for the sake of their ships, their crew, and their own lives. Thus, he worked with the ancient portolanos until he discovered that they were "accurate plats of the Arctic coastline" drawn using "a projection system unknown in modern times." (White, Pole Shift, 38-40; Mallery, Rediscovery, 54-5)

An engineer and bridgebuilder, Mallory noticed that bridgeworkers on a Canadian project looked **Norse**. He discovered they were all **Iroquois**. An experienced mason, Mallery examined the ancient masonry structures (actually astronomical observatories) found all over New England and concluded that what he saw was the work of expert technicians of an advanced society. Mallory also studied the round, **stone, church tower** in **Newport, Rhode Island**, which has a base of open arches and several small windows (openings) and looks like a very small fort. It is popularly attributed to Governor Benedict Arnold, grandfather of the infamous traitor and three-time governor of Rhode Island in the last half of the 1600s.

However, the tower is noted on the much earlier **1524 map** of Italian explorer **Giovanni da Verrazzano** who called it the **"Norman villa"** and who reported encountering fair-skinned, civilized natives who knew nothing of how the tower was built. It is also mentioned during the reign of England's Queen Elizabeth I (1558-1603) in plans to colonize the "new" land. The tower was a ready refuge, reasoned the planners, for English troops should they be attacked. The English sent several explorers to the general area but their first colony was established instead on the coast of modern-day Virginia (Jamestown, 1607).

Thus, the *tower has to be much older than the late 1600s.* **Dr. Barry Fell** of Harvard credits it to the Vikings about A.D. 1124 (or perhaps the 1300s), identifying is as a Norse church building influenced by Byzantine style, probably with an original outer shell of timber. Mallery determined that it was not Viking but Celtic, due to the masonry structure. The Norse *Sagas of the Vinland Voyages* record that the Celts crossed the Atlantic centuries before the Vikings and had established some settlements. What is interesting is that Dr. Fell documents Celtic visits to, and settlements in, America by 800 B.C. and probably as early as 1700 to 2000 B.C. (Mallery, Rediscovery, 3, 55-6; Fell, America, 233, 330-1, vi-viii; Fell, Saga, 362-3, 373; Webster's)

Mallery recognized the sophistication of the **Great Lakes Copper Culture** as early as the 1940s. He carried out tests on copper tools excavated in the modern Great Lakes region of the U.S., proving that the tools were not hammered into shape by "Stone Age" Amerindians, as believed by the traditionalists, but were expertly cast by "metallurgists of an **advanced civilization**." Skilled foundrymen agreed. Particularly in *Bronze Age America*, as well as in *America B.C.*, Dr. Fell describes the trans-Atlantic trade carried on by this thriving mining region which dates to 2000 B.C., and specifically the 1700 B.C. trading visit made by Norseman Woden-lithi. (Mallery, Rediscovery, 3, 4, 223-4; Fell, America, vi, 302-8)

At the bottom of a fortified hill in **Ross County, Ohio**, lie the remains of a city that had houses with cellars, stone foundations, and streets laid out in regular squares. Mallery researched this **iron-smelting culture of the Ohio and Virginia region**, with its fortified remains and ancient furnaces which revealed the skill of the early "Americans" in the *powder metallurgy* of the Egyptians and Incas, and the Americans' knowledge of the process called *cladding* which provides superior strength to the metal. Though traditional archaeologists firmly believed the Egyptians never made iron, the British Museum invited tests which proved them wrong, discovering that the powder metallurgy connected with the atomic, jet, and space ages was practiced long before Christ (and probably before the Flood). Mallery states that modern-day Americans thought they "discovered" the powder-metallurgy process which made the atom bomb possible, not realizing that *much* earlier Americans had practiced it. (Mallery, Rediscovery, 2-3, 20-24; White, Pole Shift, 45-6; EB, 1972, 15:237, 241)

In 1951, Mallery published a book called *Lost America*, documenting his research. When the Turkish naval officer brought the Piri Re'is map to the Navy cartographers in 1953, they knew whom to call. The chief engineer, a Mr. Medina, briefed Mallery on the history of the map and asked him to examine it. Mallery first noticed the **correct positional relationship of the coasts of Africa and South America,** and then the **general longitudinal accuracy of the map**, a feat which should not have been possible in 1513, certainly not until the 1700s.

Not long prior to this, Mallery had read an article in *Journal of Geography* which contained **seismic sounding maps of both Greenland and Antarctica**. He had already researched the accuracy of other ancient maps with Walters of the Hydrographic Office, discovering that the maps indeed showed the landforms of Greenland before it was covered by its now incredibly thick ice cap. But what caught his attention on the Piri Re'is map was the **outline of Antarctica**. The frozen continent was not officially discovered until 1818, and the medieval map before him not only displayed it, but showed the Palmer Peninsula and the Queen Maud sections of Antarctica *free of ice!* With further investigation aided by the Naval cartographers, the men actually found the seismic soundings to prove the *ancient map correct in several places where the modern maps were in error!* (Mallery, Rediscovery, 199-206; White, Pole Shift, 38-45)

Mallery could only conclude that **a scientifically and technologically advanced civilization** had possessed the ships, the seamanship, the organized governmental leadership, the manpower, the economic resources, and the knowledge in math, astronomy, hydrography, geography, and surveying to *accurately map such a vast area* of the globe. Indeed, the accomplishment staggers the mind, considering that our modern-day mapping is done by aerial and satellite photography, aided by infrared, radar, seismic, and computer technology. The idea was so mind boggling that he even allowed himself to wonder if they might have been **aviators!**

[Actually, there are a few scattered, strange indications that this might possibly not be so far fetched. Mallery mentions the tradition of the **Greeks** and the **airplane**. Charles Berlitz quotes the most astounding directions for building a **Hindu flying machine** called a *vimana* from India's ancient *Mahabharata*. Berlitz also pictures a **gold artifact** from a tomb in **Columbia, South America**, dated about 1,000 years ago, that is designed like (and looks like) a **delta-wing, jet fighter** sporting modern, aerodynamic details. Then there are the incredibly mysterious, mammoth Nazca-plains drawings, the illustrations of Leonardo da Vinci, and the possible involvement of fallen angels, which includes the modern-day UFO "phenomenon." Who knows?] (Mallery, Rediscovery, 206; White, Pole Shift, 41-43; Berlitz, Mysteries, 30, 32, 212-3)

Certainly a **maverick**, but still an **evolutionist**, Mallery also reasoned that this civilization had to exist, at the very least, **hundreds of thousands of years ago**, if the Ice Age theorists were correct. *If maps and other knowledge have a difficult time surviving a few thousand or even a few hundred years, how could they survive a few hundred thousand or million years?* However, a study carried out in 1949 and the early 1950s gave Mallery an **alternative**. Sediment cores from the bottom of Antarctica's Ross Sea were dated by atomic-energy scientists using radiometric methods. (Of course, we know that these methods are flawed due to several reasons, particularly the Flood. See Chaps. 1 & 3) These researchers determined several ice-free periods in Antarctica "during the last million years," with the **most recent 9,000-year period** ending only **6,000 years ago**. This is still off base, but a lot closer to our way of thinking than traditional evolutionism. Thus, Mallery decided that such ice activity just might be relatively recent. (Mallery, Rediscovery, 206-7)

Mallery's factual conclusions concerning the maps (not necessarily his interpretations) were confirmed by the research of the Hydrographic Office of the Navy, the seismic soundings of the Norwegian-British-Swedish Expedition to Antarctica in 1949, the Antarctic seismic expeditional experience of Reverend Daniel L. Linehan, S. J. (Society of the Jesuits), director of Boston College's Weston Observatory, and the Reverand Francis Heyden, S.J., director of the Georgetown University Observatory in Washington, D.C. On August 26, 1956, Mallery, Linehan, and Walters (Hydrographic Office) were interviewed on radio by Matthew Warren of the Georgetown University Forum. The transcript appears in White's *Pole Shift*. At the time, a copy of the transcript was given to **Charles H. Hapgood,** F.R.G.S. (Fellow of the Royal Geographical Society) and a professor at Keene State College of the University of New Hampshire. Once again, the right information fell into the hands of the right man at the right time. (Mallery, Rediscovery, 199-206; White, Pole Shift, 38-45; Hapgood, Maps, 2, 3)

Piri Re'is Map: *Hapgood*

Hapgood first published *Maps of the Ancient Sea Kings* in 1966. Following Captain Mallery's death, Mary Roberts Harrison edited his additional research and published *Rediscovery of Lost America* in 1979. Hapgood also published a revised edition of his own work in 1979.

Inspired by Mallery's work, Hapgood and his geography students began with the 1513 Piri Re'is map and, with help from an M.I.T. mathematician, discovered the "secrets" of the portolan projection. They determined that the **ancient source maps** were incredibly accurate, while the **medieval compilation** demonstrated the *decline in knowledge* from ancient to classical and then to medieval times. Hapgood also found that the original source maps must have been based not just on plane trigonometry, but on spherical trigonometry and an accurate knowledge of the circumference of the Earth. (Hapgood, Maps, 9, 35)

The **Andes Mountains** ("unknown" in 1513) seem to be indicated on the Piri Re'is map, as well as the **Falkland Islands** (officially discovered in 1592) which are shown in correct relative latitude but with a small error in longitude due to the mismatched compilation. The outline of the **Atrato River,** which empties into the Caribbean from Colombia, is correct, which means that its full length must have been explored prior to this time, a trip for which there is no known record. Columbus touched only briefly at Panama in 1502/03 but was run off, while Balboa didn't see the Pacific until 1513, not even then knowing on what he gazed. (Hapgood, Maps {revised ed.}, 52, 59, 62; Morison, Oxford, 31-2) All of these features indicate that *some ancient cartographer knew far more about both coasts of South America than anyone in classical or medieval times.*

The outline of **Cuba** shows only its eastern half, according to Hapgood, and the **Azores Islands** appear much larger on the Piri Re'is map than they are today. This, plus the presence of a mysterious, large, **unknown Atlantic island**, indicate *considerable land subsidence* and/or a *lower sea level* at the time the original source maps were drawn. The Azores and the mysterious island all sit atop what modern undersea mapping has identified as the **Mid-Atlantic Ridge**, a long, north/south undersea mountain range roughly equidistant from Africa and South America that practically copies the outline of the two coasts, and that may very well have formed during the Flood and then sunk at the time of Babel and the "canaling" of the continents. **Sediments from the ridge** examined by Belgian scientist **Dr. René Malaise** show the presence of **"recent" fresh-water species**, evidence that the land that makes up this ridge was *formerly above sea level*, and/or below fresh water. [See Chap. 8. Was the ocean fresh before the Flood and salty after?] The islands of the Azores match the mountain tops of the ridge, lying on either side of the earthquake epicenter line which runs down the middle of the ridge. (Hapgood, Maps {revised ed.}, 50, 55-59, 66-8)

In other words, *when the ancient source maps were drawn*, the Mid-Atlantic Ridge mountain tops that form the present-day Azore Islands stuck further above the water, and another mountain top may have formed the mysterious, now-missing island featured by Piri Re'is. In addition, the western half of Cuba may have been under water, only to rise later.

The Oronteus Finaeus Map of 1531

Knowing what Mallery found concerning the outline of an ice-free Antarctica, Hapgood broadened his research to other maps to find corroboration. After solving a scale problem, Hapgood and his students discovered that the map by Oronteus Finacus featured a *compilation of a*"**truly authentic map of the real Antarctica,**" showing the correct size of the continent and indicating that the original cartographers also had a *correct idea of the size of the Earth.* Oronteus Finaeus used a type of *cordiform* projection in which the **meridians of longitude fan out in curves from the pole**. The **concentric circles** of **latitude** are marked **every 10°** but are actually spaced ever further apart to maintain proper degree ratios as in the Mercator projection. Hapgood points out that this use of 10° intervals and a 360° circle (which originated in Babylon) was not supposedly used on maps until the Renaissance.

By this time, Hapgood had access to the **subglacial soundings** produced by the **International Geophysical Year (IGY) polar team of 1958**. He concludes that this map may indicate *glaciation on the western part of the Antarctic continent* and the *deep interior*, judging by the rivers shown. The OF map *excludes* the upper part of the **Palmer "Peninsula,"** but for a reason, since the IGY results show that there is, indeed, *no such peninsula beneath the ice!* This map shows the **Ross Sea** and its coastline *free of ice*, an area that now lies under an *ice cap a mile thick*, with a floating ice shelf on the sea several hundred feet thick. Hapgood explains that the minor error in locating the South Pole could be due to a number of logical reasons, and that the original source maps may have been drawn at different times. (Hapgood, Maps {revised ed.}, 69-71, 75-6, 78-9, 83-4, 212-3)

The Hadji Ahmed World Map of 1559

Whereas the Eastern Hemisphere pictured on this Turkish map is probably Ptolemaic, the **Western Hemisphere** must hark back to the **portolanos** based on accurate ancient maps because, not only does the western half have a remarkably **modern look**, but it also indicates a sophisticated **spherical projection.** In addition, it suggests a broad **landbridge from Alaska to Siberia**, once again pointing to the possibility of a difference in sea level. Of course, the landbridge is the evolutionists' sole explanation for the settlement of the Americas. It certainly may have been one of the routes used by the ancients, though we shall discover in our study that the oceans were no barrier to ancient travel.

The map is drawn in two halves on a slightly heart-shaped globe with every meridian curved out from the North Pole except for the prime meridian which runs straight north and south just off the coast of Europe and Africa. This projection was probably imposed, says Hapgood, upon **older originals** drawn with a **different projection**. (Hapgood, Maps {revised ed.}, 84-7)

Zeno Map of 1380

Two **Zeno brothers** named Niccolo and Antonio voyaged to Greenland and Iceland (and maybe Nova Scotia) in the 1300s. They are credited with drawing this map, though evidence shows that it *existed long before 1380.* In addition to **Greenland** and **Iceland**, it shows **Norway, Scotland**, and **Denmark**. A descendant found the map in the family archives in 1588 (which were later destroyed in 1630), and published it, along with related family letters. **Captain Mallery** realized that the map showed *Greenland with no ice cap*, with *rivers* and *detailed mountain ranges* and a *central plateau.* He interpreted it to show Greenland as **three islands**, and used the **seismic soundings** of Frenchman Paul-Emile Victor's late-1940s polar expedition as confirmation. (Mallery, Rediscovery, 196-8; White, Pole Shift, 45; Hapgood, Maps {revised ed.}, 124)

After much research, **Hapgood** discovered that the map was **incorrectly compiled** from **four different originals** that each had its own grid and north. A **more recent seismic map of Greenland** published by National Geographic showed a **large inland sea** which cuts well into the middle of Greenland, instead of a strait completely across Greenland which was indicated in the French findings used by Mallery. On the Zeno map, the western coast of Greenland extends only as far as the inland sea and stops.

Hapgood agrees with Mallery that the map

certainly shows Greenland prior to the ice cap, but he disagrees with Mallery about a large island, with other islands to its north, shown off Greenland's east coast. Mallery believed this to be **Gunnbiorn's Skerries**, islands reported in medieval times, that are now underwater and partially under the ice cap. Hapgood determined that it was actually Iceland before significant land subsidence and uplift. He cites Mallery's several authoritative sources that say a series of severe **volcanic eruptions** caused several provinces of **Iceland** to be submerged *between 1340 and 1380*, with more subsidence continuing into the 1400s. This would be further evidence that the Zeno brothers of 1380 did not draw the map and that it is much older than 1380. Hapgood also found the latitudes and longitudes to be amazingly accurate in what he determined to be the four ancient source maps. (Hapgood, Maps {revised ed.}, 124-133)

Hamy-King Chart of 1502/1504

This is another **Ptolemaic/portolan compilation** with contemporary discoveries added by an early explorer, possibly Amerigo Vespucci. It clearly shows the polar (circular) portolan projection used by Piri Re'is, with a central circle having a radius from the equator to the poles, and subsidiary center points prominently marked with compass-like drawings around the perimeter of the main circle. Grids are formed from the intersection of all the lines which run through the center points.

The **European section** is *exceptionally accurate*, was originally oriented toward magnetic north, and probably represents the *original portolano referred to by Nordenskiöld*. This map, says Hapgood, shows **Egypt's "original Suez canal,"** which was actually a freshwater canal from the Nile Delta to a point on the Red Sea close to present-day Suez, thus allowing ancient shipping to sail from the Mediterranean to the Red Sea and into the Indian Ocean. Dated as far back as the **1900s B.C.**, such a canal was neglected and restored throughout Egypt's history. The conquering Persians completed one restoration about 500 B.C. Used on and off over the centuries, it was repaired by Arabs in the A.D. 600s and then finally permanently shut down by Arabs in the 700s. The **modern-day Suez canal** is dug through the isthmus and directly connects the Mediterranean to the Port of Suez on the Red Sea. It was first opened as an international waterway in 1869. (EB, 1972, 21:366-8)

Thus, the presence of the canal only says that the *map was drawn sometime after perhaps the 1900s B.C.* Actually, if the mark on the map which according to Hapgood is indeed supposed to be the canal (a grid line runs across it and it is difficult to tell with merely a printed reproduction), then the mark is closer to the modern-day canal, as it runs from the oversized Red Sea straight to the Mediterranean, instead of over to the Nile Delta.

The map also shows the **island-city of Tyre** at almost exactly the correct coordinates. Hapgood claims the map shows the **causeway** to the island and dates the causeway back to 2800 B.C. However, the mainland city would have to date, according to our calculations, from no earlier than the 2100s B.C. It is said to be mentioned in Egypt's *Tell-el-Amarna* letters dated in the 1400s B.C. Founded on the mainland, it expanded to the adjacent island and featured two harbors. It was beseiged in the 700s B.C. by the Assyrians and in the 500s by the Babylonians, but the causeway did not exist until Alexander the Great built it with the ruins of the ancient mainland city that he conquered and destroyed in 332 B.C. Even with his causeway, Alexander had to mount a long and complicated seige to prevail over the island city. (EB, 1972, 22:452; see Ezek. 26) The prominence and the accuracy of the island on the map may well indicate that the European section dates from before 332 B.C. However, if the causeway is indeed there (the map does seem to show a peninsula rather than an island), it would merely date the compilation after Alexander's conquest. [The point? Don't take everything even a good, valuable source says for granted.]

The map shows a **partial and recognizable outline of South America** and Hapgood believes its relative accuracy indicates an ancient source map. In the **African interior**, at correct latitude and a longitude correct relative to the coastlines, we find **Lake Victoria** and other lake sources of the Nile, geographical features which lay "undiscovered" until the 1800s. **Southern India** is shown as a *large island*, which corresponds to an ancient tradition about **"Dravidia"** which is recorded in the

Vedas. **Ptolemy's world map**, part of which was incorporated into the Hamy-King map, also draws the bottom two-thirds of India as an island, and labels **rivers** flowing from mountains and **lakes** in what is now **Northern Africa's Sahara Desert**. We know from other abundant evidence regarding the Sahara that, for sometime after the Flood, that was indeed the case. In the Hamy-King map, **Southeast Asia** is shown as *one, extended land mass,* but there are native traditions that say this was true only a few thousand years ago, while evolutionist **Alfred Russel Wallace** believed there was much evidence for a landbridge connecting Java, Borneo, and Sumatra with either the mainland or Australia. (Hapgood, Maps {revised ed.}, 11, 151-173, 179)

Hapgood's Conclusions

Hapgood reviews a **number of other medieval maps** that offer additional evidence of ancient sources which were originally drawn using spherical trigonometry and a knowledge of true north, and so demonstrate a decline of scientific knowledge from ancient to classical to medieval times. A **Chinese map** carved in stone dated A.D. **1137** seems to originate from the *same ancient sources* as the European portolanos. One map dated 1508 seems to show an **ice cap on Scandinavia,** while another portolano gives possible evidence of **glaciers in central Ireland and England**. This last map, the portolano of **Ibn Ben Zara of Alexandria**, also shows more and bigger islands in the **Aegean Sea**, especially Thera (Santini), once again indicating *possible significant changes in sea level,* perhaps following the great volcanic explosion of Santini. (Hapgood, Maps {revised ed.}, 95-98, 104, 119-120, 140, 144-150)

Like Mallery, Hapgood is a **maverick among traditionalists**, and a **catastrophist**, but still an **evolutionist**. After studying the various magnetic orientations of sedimentary and volcanic rock samples from around the world, Hapgood believes that the Earth's magnetic field (and thus the magnetic poles) has shifted position rather drastically many times. Also believing that the magnetic poles always stay within a certain radius of the geographic poles, Hapgood then concludes that the **positions of the North and South geographical poles have also shifted at least 200 times** throughout "geological history," in accordance with the magnetic reversals shown in the rock samples. The mechanism for this, Hapgood explains, is the **shifting of Earth's entire outer shell** across the deep, soft layers of magma underneath it.

This is how Hapgood explains the worldwide evidence of a warm climate, of "glacier marks," and the other geological phenomena which are supposedly the results of millions of years of the kind of geological action we see today and a number of Ice Ages. So, as the Earth's shell has shifted back and forth around the inner magma, says Hapgood's theory, it has brought different continents into the cold polar regions while moving others into tropical regions. The most recent upheaval must have taken place, according to the evidence on the maps, about 1400 B.C., forcing land lower and the sea higher in the Aegean, western Mediterranean, North Atlantic, equatorial Atlantic, and Indonesia, while uplifting the land and lowering the sea level in Siberia, India, the southwestern United States, the Caribbean, and the west coast of South America.

Hapgood also agrees with Mallery (and others) that there must have been an **ancient, scientifically and technologically advanced, worldwide civilization** capable of the cartographical feats demonstrated in the maps we have examined. Thus, says Hapgood, the "idea of the simple linear development of society from the culture of the paleolithic (Old Stone Age) through the successive stages of the neolithic (New Stone Age), Bronze, and Iron Ages must be given up." He admits that man can indeed go from advanced to primitive, and that "ancient" certainly does not automatically imply primitive, as is believed by the traditionalists.

Our Conclusions

First of all, we realize that Hapgood is trying to explain away the conditions of the canopied, pre-Flood world and the effects of the Flood by some means other than the canopy or the Flood. (See Chaps. 1 & 3) And, of course, we date the existence of created (not evolved) man from only some 6,000 years ago, and the existence of present-day geological and meteorological forces from only 2345 B.C. However, we agree that the Earth has undergone several periods of dramatic, **worldwide change and upheaval**, the most catastrophic being the

Genesis creation (or restoration), the Flood, and the Babel judgment. Dr. Henry Morris states that the geologically disruptive effects of the Flood (and probably Babel) would have continued for a period after the major event was over.

We also agree that indeed there was an **ancient, scientifically and technologically advanced civilization**. We identify them as living before the Flood, beginning with Adam, and continuing after the Flood with Noah. However, because of sin and the curse which affects the entire Universe, the "progression" of man and Earth is toward greater deterioration, physically, mentally, and spiritually. The only two offsetting factors are 1) spiritual salvation, and 2) the technological boom of the 20th Century, prophesied in Daniel 12:4. The entire Universe and we Christians must await the Rapture and the Millennium for "physical" salvation. (Rom. 8:18-23) Instead of living almost 1,000 years or several hundred years, we now depend on drugs and surgery to get us through to 70 or 80 years. Sophisticated urban comforts are offset by rising crime and immorality. The spread of the Gospel throughout the world is "countered" by the prophesied rebellion of the majority of mankind. (Ps. 2; John 14:17, 15:18-25)

What we do see in Mallery's and Hapgood's research is **evidence to support our belief that man was created with superior mental and physical faculties**, that the entire Earth was populated soon after Babel by men still advanced in their abilities, all descended from Noah's family, and all **diffused from Babylon** and the general area around Ararat. We see confirmation that the Earth continued to undergo **drastic physical changes** and, it seems, judgments. Some of the most interesting specifics are:

1) *Post-Babel mankind managed to map essentially the entire globe*, perhaps by the time of the Exodus, perhaps earlier, but certainly well before the time of Alexander the Great. We earlier concluded that, between the Flood and Babel, the land was split and altered but still remained in one basic mass. The "canaling" of the land by water did not occur until the days of Peleg and the judgment of Babel, thus the mapping had to be done after the "new geography" was reasonably stable. The maps strongly indicate that the Earth continued to undergo certain changes for probably quite some time after Babel, as we would expect, considering the mind-boggling alteration in the world's geography from one land mass to separated continents.

The mapping was done with amazing accuracy, using sophisticated mathematics and a correct understanding of astronomy. We speculate that, through the colonization efforts of major Mediterranean cultures, regional maps found their way into major libraries and were eventually centralized and compiled due to international trade as well as to the political consolidation accomplished by one nation conquering another. Navigators and traders exchanged maps, scholars gathered and compiled them, and the builders of empires collected documents in certain major cities. Knowing that ancient pre-Flood, post-Flood, and post-Babel man trafficked with the fallen angels, we can only wonder if the spiritual realm had any hand in the amazing feat of mapping the world.

2) *The ice that now covers the Arctic, the Antarctic, Greenland, and portions of Iceland is of very recent origin, even by our own timeline.* We know that the evidence of a mild, worldwide climate is due to the pre-Flood canopy. We have also concluded that our present continental geography was not completed until after Babel, requiring our ancestors to map a "New World" as they were forced by God to disperse. The maps we have studied indicate that the **present polar conditions were not immediate results of the Flood or of Babel**, but came about after the ancients had the opportunity to map these areas when they were ice free. Other maps seem to indicate mapping that was done as ice was forming and glaciers were advancing. In further studies, we will see that Greenland was not given its name as a joke and that northern Iceland was able to support agriculture as recently as A.D. 1200 but, by 1400, even southern Iceland was no longer warm enough to grow grain. (Mallery, Rediscovery, 157) Perhaps the well-preserved Arctic mammoths that were buried immediately by the Flood were only "refrigerated" for a time before they were finally frozen by the effects of the colder conditions that brought advancing ice.

In the 19th Century, a president of Boston College, **Dr. William F. Warren**, published a book which presented evidence from a wide study of ancient languages and literature to show that the "cradle of civilization" was actually the North Pole, not the Middle East. In the early 20th Century, a Vedic scholar of India (the *Vedas* are ancient Hindu sacred books) named **B.G. Tilak** was inspired by Warren's work and found in the *Vedas* **accurate descriptions of polar conditions** and the **lengths of polar nights and days**. Because there is no record of polar expeditions by Indian Hindus, Tilak decided that the Vedic people must have lived at the North Pole before moving to India to escape the beginning of the last ice age. However, there is **presently no land at the North Pole**. Hapgood speculates that people living instead at the **South Pole** on the continent of Antarctica fled advancing ice and sailed across the ocean straight north to southern India. We could certainly agree with Hapgood's basic idea, though not with Hapgood's evolutionist dates.

3) *The time of the Exodus may indeed have been a period of judgment upon the entire Mediterranean and Middle Eastern area.* It is certainly interesting that so many scholars from a number of scientific disciplines point to the many disasters that seem to have befallen this region around the 1400s B.C. In his theory, Hapgood names this date as the time of the last major adjustment of the Earth's outer shell, using this as his explanation of the physically catastrophic happenings that are evidenced. The maps indicate changes in the Mediterranean sea level and land subsidence in the Aegean where the massive volcanic explosion of Santini (Thera) took place.

BIBLIOGRAPHY

Aveni, Anthony F., *Skywatchers of Ancient Mexico*, Bib. Chap. 9, p. 160

Berlitz, Charles, *Mysteries From Forgotten Worlds*. New York: Doubleday & Co., 1972.

Bierhorst, John, *The Mythology of Mexico and Central America*. New York: William Morrow and Co., Inc., 1990.

Bullinger, E.W., *The Witness of the Stars*, Bib. Chap. 8, p. 139.

Chadwick, John, *The Decipherment of Linear B*. London: Cambridge University Press, 1970.

Collea, Beth A., "The Celestial Bands in Maya Hieroglyphic Writing," *Archaeoastronomy in the Americas* (edited by Ray A. Williamson), Bib. Chap. 9, p. 160

De Santillana, Giorgio, and **Von Dechend,** Hertha, *Hamlet's Mill*, Bib. Chap. 7, p. 108.

Drury, Nevill, *Dictionary of Mysticism and the Occult,* Bib. Chap. 2, p. 37.

Encyclopaedia Britannica (EB), Bib. Chap. 3, p. 51.

Fell, Barry, *America B.C.*, Bib. Chap. 6, p. 91.

_____, *Bronze Age America*, Bib. Chap. 6, p. 91.

_____, *Saga America*, Bib. Chap. 9, p. 160

Gordon, Cyrus H., *Before Columbus*, Bib. Chap. 4, p. 65.

Hapgood, Charles H., *Maps of the Ancient Sea Kings*. Philadelphia: Chilton Company, 1966. Revised edition, New York: E. P. Dutton, 1979.

_____, *The Path of the Pole*. Philadelphia: Chilton Book Co., 1970.

Heyerdahl, Thor, *Early Man and the Ocean*, Bib. Chap. 9, p. 160

Jairazbhoy, R.A., *Ancient Egyptians and Chinese in America*, Bib. Chap. 6, p. 91.

Krupp, E.C. (ed.), *In Search of Ancient Astronomies*. New York: Doubleday & Co., 1977.

Mallery, Arlington, and Harrison, Mary Roberts, *The Rediscovery of Lost America*. New York: E. P. Dutton, 1979.

McKern, Sharon S., *Exploring the Unknown*, Bib. Chap. 2, p. 37.

Morison, Samuel Eliot, *The Oxford History of the American People*. New York: Oxford University Press, 1965.

Prescott, William H., *History of the Conquest of Mexico*. New York: Random House, 1936.

Pritchard, James B. (ed.), *The Ancient Near East*, Bib. Chap. 5, p. 80.

Scofield, C. I. (ed.), *The New Scofield Reference Bible*, Bib. Chap. 2, p. 38.

Tarn, W.W., *Alexander the Great* (paperback). Boston: Beacon Press, 1956.

Timetables of History (Grun), Bib. Chap. 7, p. 108.

Tompkins, Peter, *Secrets of the Great Pyramid,* Bib. Chap. 8, p. 140

Webster's New World Dictionary, Bib. Chap. 2, p. 38.

White, John, *Pole Shift*. Garden City, NY: Doubleday & Co., Inc., 1980.

Chapter 12
Ancient Ocean Vessels and Global Navigation

Modern Misconceptions of the Ancient Mariner

"They that go down to the sea in ships," says the psalmist, "that do business in great waters, These see the works of the Lord, and his wonders in the deep." (Ps. 107:23-4, KJV) *When was man first able to challenge ocean waves in a boat?* How long has man carried cargo across "great waters"? Dr. Thor Heyerdahl writes that in the 1700s, when "sail still ruled the sea," it was generally assumed that ancient civilized people were "capable of almost unlimited movement." (Heyerdahl, Ocean, 3)

However, in the last 125 or so years, that once-dominant opinion has changed considerably. The **standard teaching** of our **modern traditionalists** is that the oceans were uncrossable barriers for the "primitive" ancients whose knowledge of boat building and navigation began, they conclude, with simply straddling a floating log on a stream or lake and then slowly evolved to fashioning simple rafts, dugout canoes, bundled reeds, light frames covered with skins, and finally to constructing wooden-plank ships with keels and ribs. First they poled, then paddled, then pulled a sail to the top of a mast and learned to let the wind do the work. In "great waters" like the Mediterranean Sea, Red Sea, or Persian Gulf, they hugged coastlines both for safety from open water and knowledge of where they were. (Casson, Mariners, 1-3; Heyerdahl, Ocean, 64)

Pacific historian **J. C. Beaglehole** states that long voyages of any sort were not possible until the "Portuguese invented the three-masted ocean-going ship, in place of the medieval oared galley or one-masted vessel" which, he says, could only sail along the coast. He cites **scurvy** as the *most formidable obstacle to long-distance sailing*, "human or technical." Scurvy was a debilitating and soon fatal disease unless remedied by decent food and vitamin C. Limes were the British answer to scurvy (probably also an ancient answer) and thus why British sailors became known as "limeys." (Beaglehole, Pacific, 10-12)

Of course, for many reasons, we now know that most of this, especially for the ancients, is hogwash. The **coastline**, says Heyerdahl, was the *fear* of the ancient mariner. With its reefs and swell patterns, currents, tides, and waves, the coastline is always the most dangerous of waters, while **open water** is the safest. Also, **distance** alone, he adds, has never been any real factor in ocean travel, but, instead, the combination of **wind** and **current**.

Wind, Current, and Climate

In the millennia of sail power, wind and current were the darlings or demons which turned the sea into mistress or monster. Wind and current not only could destroy a water-proofed, hulled vessel, but also could becalm or trap one in a situation which led to mutiny, starvation, and/or dehydration. The pattern of prevailing winds and currents actually creates *"highways" in the seas* that greatly help or hinder ocean travel along specific routes in certain directions, literally increasing or decreasing the distance a ship has to travel over moving water. This is much like the effect of tail, head, or crosswinds on an aircraft, except that an aircraft has powerful engines independent of nature, while ancient watercraft had to rely on the skill of the navigator with sail, rudder, and centerboard, aided only by human muscle power applied to an oar. The consideration of the effect these highways had on ancient migration and trade is only one of the significant contributions made to the study of the past by **Dr. Thor**

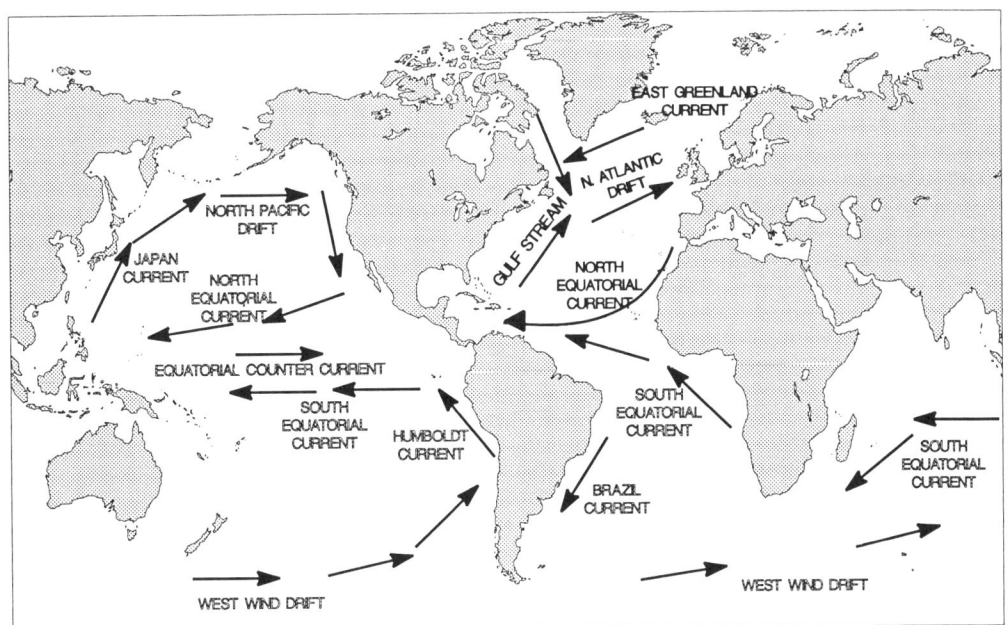

Source: Encyclopaedia Britannica, 1972

Ocean Currents

Heyerdahl, Norwegian zoologist, archaeologist, seafarer, and adventurer. (Heyerdahl, Ocean, 32-3, 37)

The major equatorial currents run *east to west*, leading Heyerdahl to believe that major migration patterns were in that direction. Heyerdahl partially demonstrated his point with two journeys from Africa to the Caribbean, each in a sail-powered, bundled reed boat along the **North Equatorial Current** which is known as the **Columbus route**. The **South Equatorial Current** begins down the east coast of Africa, and continues around the Cape of Good Hope and up the Brazilian coast, also entering the Caribbean. These east-to-west combinations of winds and currents are such that Heyerdahl compares them to **conveyor belts**.

After it became a somewhat regular event for lone individuals to cross the Atlantic east to west on the Columbus Route from the Mediterranean to the Caribbean in tiny open boats, even a rowboat, and even to circumnavigate the world from east to west alone in a small craft, Harvard's duly renowned maritime historian, **Admiral Samuel Eliot Morison,** grudgingly acknowledged that such an ancient crossing was possible. His writings maintain, though, that ancient craft were not capable of a return trip, west to east, and that it was a thoroughly different matter to set forth into the unknown, with no Coast Guard, radios, or airplanes, but with an "unruly, timid, and suspicious crew" to keep fed, healthy, and obedient. (Morison, European North, x, 8)

Morison's points are well taken for *medieval* sailing, though we know from our biblical and secular research that the *ancients* dispersed from Babel, mapped the world before the ice caps, and calculated accurate readings of both longitude and latitude. True, the only *west-to-east* "free ride" across the Atlantic is the warm **Gulf Stream** which runs from the Gulf of Mexico up the east coast of the United States, then turns east at Newfoundland and heads toward northern Europe through the **cold North Atlantic**. This severe temperature change would certainly have been a challenge (if not a danger) to ancient people acclimated to warmer climes. (Heyerdahl, Ocean, 50, 52; Webster's) However, remember that the *climate remained much warmer worldwide* for a long time after the Flood, and that Earth's icecaps and floes are a relatively recent development.

In Volume II of this series, we will examine a reasonable portion of the ample supply of European, African, and Asian inscriptions and artifacts found all over the Americas, finds that can no longer be denied, even though Morison remained dogmatic that the ones he saw were nothing more than natural grooves and scratches or fakes. There is "no evidence from classic writers," adds the stubborn traditionalist, "to justify any assumption that the ancients communicated with America." (Morison, European North, 9, 11)

Heyerdahl had emphasized his east-to-west migration theory years earlier in the **Pacific** by sailing a South American balsa-log raft from Ecuador to Tahiti. Traditionalists maintained that the Pacific was settled from west to east. Heyerdahl argued that even the "advanced" **Spaniards** in their comparatively big, three-masted wooden ships could not sail successfully east from Asia across the Pacific unless they went to the far north, by Japan, or to the far south, below Australia. They made all of their Pacific island discoveries following the winds and currents west from the Americas. Thus, they did not discover Guam until 1521, Melanesia until 1567 to the 1600s, Micronesia until 1595 to the 1600s, Easter Island until 1722, and Tahiti until 1767. (Heyerdahl, Ocean, 37-9)

However, Heyerdahl discovered, through both experience and research, that South American as well as South Pacific watercraft **could literally go anywhere** in the ocean, **in any direction**, over long distances. The key factors were **navigating skill** and **centerboards** which allowed experienced sailors to tack against the wind. Heyerdahl concluded that, because of the difficulty of negotiating adverse winds and currents (or the problem of no wind) without modern engine power, that such trips must have required *advance knowledge of destinations.*

Of course, though a maverick, Heyerdahl still thinks like an evolutionist. But consider that, on a modern map, the land area of the Pacific islands (not counting New Zealand) comprises less area than one half of New York State, while the Pacific Ocean's expanse of water could accommodate the surface area of all the Earth's continents and other oceans combined! Yet the "primitive" ancients found and settled all these islands, long, long before the Europeans. The **Peruvians** (Incas) gave the Spaniards *specific* **directions to Easter Island**, a speck of land halfway between South America and Polynesia and, at that time, "the loneliest inhabited land in the world." (Heyerdahl, Ocean, 55, 228, 151, 185-7, 290) Perhaps, at the time of initial settlement after Babel, certain islands were bigger and others were parts of peninsulas, as indicated by ancient maps and other evidence of significant geological changes. It's a fascinating question to ponder.

The writers of *Hamlet's Mill* readily acknowledge the superior navigating skills of the **Polynesians** "to whom," they write, "our much praised discoverers from Magellan to Captain Cook confided the steering of their ships more than once." Remember from Chapter 8 that Dr. Hertha von Dechend determined that the Pacific Islanders were also skilled astronomers after she realized that two "cult centers" are located precisely on the Tropics of Cancer and Capricorn. (DeSantillana, Hamlet's, ix-x)

Navigational Tools

Another traditional argument against ancient ocean navigation, raised by Beaglehole, is that **navigational tools** were **primitive** until the 18th Century and that the "problem of longitude remained, seemingly, insoluble." (Beaglehole, Pacific, 10-12) We have seen what the ancients did with both latitude and longitude, and even Admiral Morison, a seaman himself in the great New England tradition, affirms that a true mariner can find his way without a compass. The Polynesians, he writes, plied the vast Pacific expertly without a compass, as did the Norse in the Atlantic. (Morison, European North, 34-5)

Conventional, evolutionary history teaches that man did not have the **compass** until the era of **Medieval Europe**. Some historians believe that the compass may have come a little earlier from **China**, but the first acknowledged, written record of compass use was made by an **Englishman** in A.D. **1180**. (EB, 1972, 16:140) However, the compass may be much older than is commonly thought.

Noah, under the pagan name *Oannes*, was glorified as having come from the sea, providing ancient man with superior knowledge and technology. The writings of Phoenician historian **Sanchuniathon** tell us that, "'It was the god **Ouranos** who devised **Baithulia**, contriving *stones that moved as having life*.'" (Italics added) The name Ouranos means "the Shiner," or "the Enlightener." Alexander Hislop shows that Ouranos actually represented God Himself, as well as the false pagan Messiah, Nimrod. As Noah was the original enlightener of post-Flood civilization, he is most likely also represented by Ouranos, meaning that Noah may well have been the "inventor" of the compass, actually preserving the knowledge from the pre-Flood world. (Hislop, 193-4, 300; Johnston, Phoenicians, 90-1)

We have seen from the Great Pyramid that the ancients were capable of finding true north, and **Dr. Barry Fell** is convinced that ancient navigators knew how to find true north and true south, even when there was no pole star to act as a guide. (Fell, America, 110) Tracking star movements using simple cross-sticks is a common motif in **Mayan** hierographic literature, with the **cross-sticks** often pictured as having an eye or a heavenly body centered in the top of the X. (See illustrations, Cornell, First, 136-7; Krupp, In Search, 170-1) Measuring the **elevation** of a heavenly body from the horizon is as simple as using a **staff with a sliding cross-piece**. From this information, the ancients, who knew the heavens far better than most of us know our own neighborhoods, could calculate time and latitude. (EB, 1972, 16:141)

Fell's book *America B.C.* shows models of a cross-staff, **astrolabe**, variable latitude **sundial** and mechanical planetary **motion calculator**, all from 2nd and 3rd Centuries B.C. North Africa. It also pictures an **analog computing device** (a slide rule is an analog computing device) which used a system of bronze gear wheels, much like a mechanical clock, to compute latitude, time of day, and star positions. Fell dates the device, found on the seabed off the Mediterranean Island of Crete in 1900, at about 150 B.C., while British archaeoastronomer **Evan Hadingham** dates it at about 87 B.C. The miniature planetarium is marked with inscriptions and directional indicators which required many years of research to interpret. (Fell, America, 118-9; Hadingham, Early, 18-19)

Archaeological investigator **Dr. Derek de Solla Price** concludes, as quoted by Charles Berlitz, that the computing device is probably "'part of a *large corpus of knowledge that has since been lost to us* but was known to the Arabs...developed and transmitted by them to medieval Europe, where it became the foundation of the whole range of subsequent invention in the field of clockwork....'" (Berlitz, Mysteries, 32-3, italics added) Remember that this era from about the 400s B.C. to A.D. 100s was a time of scientific revival following a long, slow intellectual decline. The Alexandrian Greeks and the Arabs delved into remnants of a body of ancient knowledge which they did not completely understand.

Though much progress has been made in penetrating the fog surrounding the history of ocean navigation, the capabilities and activities of the truly ancient mariner are still suspect in the arena of modern traditionalism. "Even today," writes Sharon McKern, "the greatest obstacle to acceptance of the theory of prehistoric transoceanic contact remains the improbability that any Old World group possessed the means or the motivation to undertake such a perilous voyage." (McKern, Exploring, 111) The **"means"** we will examine in this chapter. The **"motivation"** of trade, colonization, political persecution, wars, and/or religious beliefs we will examine in Volume II.

The First Ocean Cruise

Before the Flood, we know there was construction of cities, tilling of fields, manufacturing in bronze and iron, nomadic shepherding of sheep and cattle, and cultural entertainment with musical instruments. (Gen. 4) With *one land mass*, there was no need for ocean navigation, though pre-Flood man may have floated cargo and passengers up and down rivers. However, when God called for the building of a

three-story boat the size and proportions of a **modern-day ocean liner** or battleship, **Noah and his sons were up to the task!** Of course, everything about Noah and his Ark flies full in the face of evolutionist thinking.

Bible translators are neither certain nor agreed as to the exact **materials** used for the Ark. **1)** The King James and New American Standard versions say that the boat was built of *"gopher wood,"* divided into rooms, and covered inside and out with *"pitch."* Pitch is a naturally occurring, carbon-based, tar-like substance related to coal or petroleum. **2)** *Young's Literal* translates the passage as describing an Ark of gopher wood, covered within and without with *cypress*. **3)** The New English Bible interprets the passage to mean an ark with *ribs* of cypress, covered with *reeds*, and coated inside and out with pitch. (Gen. 6:14-16)

The word translated "gopher" is unknown elsewhere in Hebrew or other related languages. Some say it was pine, cedar, or cypress. Some say it could have meant **reeds**. Tradition and reported eye-witness accounts agree that the boat was made of wood, and it does seem more feasible, especially to our Western minds, that a three-story boat loaded with Noah and his cargo for a year was most likely covered by **heavy, wood planks**. However, pre-Flood reeds most likely would have been massive in size and formidable in strength. The **Marsh Arabs of Mesopotamia** still use wood-ribbed, reed-covered boats to float and sail on the Tigris and Euphrates Rivers, and Thor Heyerdahl (as we shall see) has proved the seaworthiness of properly built, *un*coated, bundled reed boats.

Reed hull coverings were often **pitched inside and out**, just as the vessel prepared for the baby Moses (Ex. 2:3) and the river vessels of the Mesopotamian Marsh Arabs. [1993 note: Iraq's Marsh Arabs are part of the population the U. S. and its Western allies are trying to protect from Saddam Hussein with the "no-fly zone" over southern Iraq.] However, wood also has a history of being "pitched." According to Samuel Eliot Morison, medieval English and French boat builders coated the outside of their wooden ships below the waterline with pitch to "discourage the growth of weed and barnacles." And, says Heyerdahl, pitch was a common waterproofing for ancient hulled vessels. Medieval Arabs, though, used concoctions of fish oil, lime juice, and vegetable oil on the wood planks and coconut-husk rope in their vessels. (Morison, European North, 116; Heyerdahl, Ocean, 20; Severin, Sindbad, 40-1, 68)

Is it possible that the Ark could have had a wooden frame, perhaps wooden partitions for rooms, but a pitched reed covering? Perhaps it was easier for four men to cover a vessel the size of the Ark with reeds rather than with wood planks, even though they had the better part of a century to complete the job. The Ark was merely to act as a **cork on the water** and reed, properly cut and handled, is certainly suited for that. Plus, we must reiterate that the reed available to Noah was giant-size, canopy-grown, pre-Flood reed. However, if the *Young's Literal* translation is correct, the Ark had a wooden frame with a covering inside and out of cypress wood. (Pict. Dict.)

Heyerdahl points out that **wood** is superior for speed and durability, whereas **reeds** are safer and can carry more (probably meant in the context of a size-to-buoyancy ratio). Wood may be ultimately superior for speed, but two biblical references to reed (bulrushes or papyrus) boats refer to their swiftness. (*Young's Literal* and NIV, Job 9:25-6; KJV and NIV, Isa. 18:2) South American explorer Gene Savoy states that an "Indian with a paddle could propel a reed boat at an amazing speed, fast enough to overcome any current." Noah did not need speed and only needed the boat for one year. He did need safety and maximum cargo-carrying capability. However, the safety to which Heyerdahl refers may apply to the virtually unsinkable, *un*coated, wash-through, bundled reed boat, while the Ark was a ribbed, waterproofed, displacement vessel. (Heyerdahl, Ocean, 20-1; Savoy, Feathered, 20)

Whether wood or reed, cyprus or cedar, the Ark was the world's first ocean-going vessel. Suffice it to say that ancient man could build with wood or reeds and that, **before the Flood**, God taught Noah something about **ribbed frames, displacement hulls**, and the **proper proportions of large boats**. An interesting aside to consider is the fact that we can put men on the Moon and photograph the galaxy, but *we cannot get to the Ark*. It seems that, by way of national hostilities as well as forbidding terrain and weather, the Lord has purposely prevented access to the Ark, probably for a number of reasons including the demands of faith and the abuse of relics.

Thus, we date man's first ocean cruise in the year **2345 B.C.** Noah had no itinerary so he had no need for means of power or guidance. God shut him in the Ark and then brought him down on Ararat. The Ark was designed to be merely a **massive, seaworthy, floating crate**. Between the Flood and Babel, there was still no reason for ocean travel, and it seems from Genesis 11 that rebellious man was determined that no reason should develop. However, God foiled that plot and introduced His own New World Order, complete with new languages and new geography. Suddenly, man faced the *necessity* for travel, then soon realized the *opportunities* that travel created for trade and colonization!

Between the Flood and Babel, man had time to study the mysterious **new wind and weather** conditions that came with the post-Flood world. Man also had time to study the **new Zodiac** of constellations along an **altered ecliptic** which seems to have resulted from the awesome Flood judgment. *After Babel*, man had to apply this knowledge to the **new oceans and seas** that now separated the pieces of the broken-up land mass. *A floating crate would not do.* Man needed devices for **propulsion** and **steering**. Whether man accomplished this solely with his own God-given intelligence, or whether he was aided by further divine or angelic input, we do not know.

Records and Remains of Ancient Shipping

The **ever-growing evidence** for the ancient mariner has finally convinced certain of the humanistic evolutionists that early man could indeed cross formidable bodies of water. "The existence of seagoing craft during the Ice Age," states Hadingham, "is now widely accepted, since we know that Australia was settled by at least 30,000 B.C." (Hadingham, Early, 90) We'll dismiss the Ice Age and the far-reaching date and focus on the evidence for ancient seagoing craft.

We know that Nimrod's Babylonians (or Sumerians) made up Earth's first "kingdom," followed by Mizraim's Egyptians. Studies indicate that these earliest Babylonians first wrote with **hieroglyphs** (picture symbols) before they changed to **cuneiform** (wedge-shaped) characters. Whether reed or wood, ancient ships almost all show the same *sickle-shaped*, high-prowed, high-sterned profile. The oldest known Babylonian (or Sumerian) hieroglyph for "ship" was a little picture of a **sickle-shaped reed boat** with cross lashings and what looks like unique, S-shaped ornaments on the bow and stern. The same hieroglyph meant "marine" in ancient Egypt. (Heyerdahl, Ocean, 9) Perhaps these reed boats, the same type that carried Thor Heyerdahl's crews across the Atlantic Ocean in 1969 and 1970, were the first vessels used by the New World's earliest cultures.

Sickle Shape

The culturally advanced **Indus River Valley** civilization must also have developed about the same time as Egypt, or soon after. Both Heyerdahl and Cyrus Gordon date the culture from about 2500 B.C. We would put the date closer to the 2100s B.C. Archaeologists have discovered much evidence for active **trade** on what we now call the **Persian Gulf** and **Arabian Sea** between the Babylonians (and/or Sumerians) and the Indus Valley people, while remains show that the islands of **Bahrain** served as a central marketplace. If certain tablet translations are correct, some people who fled Babel may have returned later from an "eastern land" called *Dilmun* (or **Telmun**) to found Sumer on the Tigris and Euphrates Rivers below Babylon. Dilmun is generally thought to have been Bahrain, though this little trading center only a short distance to the south of Sumer does not seem to fit the reference to an "eastern land." That sort of language makes more sense in terms of India, Indonesia, or even the Americas.

At any rate, these **cuneiform tablets** apparently talk of **seagoing kings** and **merchants**, imports and exports, **ships** and **shipwrecks**. One recorded transaction, if accurately translated, is dated between 2000 and 1750 B.C. and speaks of a merchant from Ur named **Ea-nasir** who was involved in the delivery of a shipment of copper from Telmun to Mesopotamia. Something about the shipment was very unsatisfactory because the buyer (or a secretary) grabbed a wooden stick and a clay tablet and "wedged" the following objection:

"'Who am I that you treat me in this manner and offend me? That this could happen between gentlemen as we both are! Who is there among the traders of Telmun who has ever acted this way?'" (Casson, Mariners, 9)

As Solomon says, there is nothing new under the Sun! (Eccl. 1:9) Ethics in business and customer satisfaction are hardly new concerns. Whether or not Dilmun (or Telmun) was actually Bahrain or truly an "eastern land," seaworthy cargo ships plied the seas and oceans of the Middle East and probably Far East amazingly soon after the Babel dispersion. The **ancient ships of Babylon and Ur** are recorded to have been 50-ton to almost 100-ton cargo vessels. (Gordon, Before, civ. chart; Heyerdahl, Ocean, 9; Tigris, 4-5)

The Timetables of History notes that **Cretan ships** (from the Mediterranean island of Crete) were predominant in the Mediterranean Sea at the time of the early Sumerian and Egyptian cultures which the book dates between 4000 and 3500 B.C. Another source dates the invention of sails about 3500 to 3400 B.C. Shipping between **Egypt** and **Phoenicia** (Lebanon) and Crete is dated from 2650 B.C. Mesopotamians sailed the Indian Ocean to southern India and Ceylon (Sri Lanka) as early, say some evolutionists, as 2500 B.C. (Timetables, 3; Casson, Mariners, 247, 8-9) We disagree a little with the dates but concur that *ancient man learned the art of sailing open water very quickly.*

Ancient Boat and Raft Construction

Thor Heyerdahl explains that there are **two types of buoyancy: 1)** a *wash-through* vessel made of such buoyant materials as reeds or balsa logs, *not* coated with pitch so that water washes through the buoyant bundled reeds or lashed logs, and **2)** a *displacement* vessel with a watertight hull, which floats because the boat weighs less than the amount of water it displaces. The first, if properly built, is unsinkable by mere waves and can survive a fair amount of damage. The second will sink if turned over or filled with water from high waves or damage to the hull.

Heyerdahl believes that the wash-through vessels were developed first, in both the Eastern and Western Hemispheres, followed by hulls of wood ribs covered with pitched reeds, and then ribbed, wood, displacement hulls. The first wood displacement hulls, adds Heyerdahl, were *sewn*-plank ships held together with rope and cordage, a design based on the bundled-reed boat. Pins, nails, ribs, and keels came next. (Heyerdahl, Ocean, 4, 11-13, 20-1)

Lionel Casson presents a more traditional evolutionist interpretation of ancient ship design, viewing certain engineering elements as unique to the Egyptians. He flatly states that in "almost all times and places people have, in building ships, used a framework of keel and ribs." He ignores the reed boats and states that, when Egyptians used wood to build Nile River boats, they did indeed use no keel and only a few, light wooden ribs, but "pinned" (not sewed or lashed) the planks to one another. (Casson, Mariners, 12-16)

However, we have seen that the **Ark** was a displacement vessel and that it had wooden ribs, and so we can conclude, unequivocally, that **displacement** and **ribbed construction** were both known **from the beginning.** *Why, then, would wash-through, bundled-reed boats be the first ocean-going vessels of the "New World"?*

The Reed Boat and Balsa Raft

W*ash-through*, bundled-reed boats were exceedingly *safe* and *forgiving* for ocean travel. Heyerdahl crossed the Atlantic twice in such a boat with a number of *inexperienced crew members*, a feat which could not be done in other types of marine craft. Both **Mesopotamia** and **Egypt** had an abundant supply of reeds. We have noted that the earliest symbol for "ship" was identical in both of these, the world's first kingdoms, and that it was a sickle-shaped reed boat.

Besides safety, ease of handling, and availability of raw material, the reed boat had the additional advantage over wood of *greater size* and *cargo-carrying capacity* (once again, we assume in a size-to-buoyancy relationship). Heyerdahl states that wooden vessels cannot get too large or they risk a break-up in heavy seas. However, **reed vessels** could be built **as large as a modern ocean liner**, if an owner had the time and manpower. (Heyerdahl, Ocean, 25, 22-3)

This is an interesting statement considering that there have been some **massive wooden ships** constructed, in ancient times to carry soldiers and in medieval times to carry cargo of 500 and even 780 tuns, a *tun* being an English or French *double-hogshead* barrel of wine. From the tun evolved the modern *maritime ton* of 40 cubic feet. Practical European seamen and explorers such as Columbus did prefer smaller ships under 100 tuns, writes Samuel Eliot Morison, probably for reasons of both safety and handling. (Morison, European North, 114, 270) Heyerdahl must be speaking in terms of safety, construction, and buoyancy.

Also, though evolutionist primitive-to-modern, simple-to-complex thinking is generally invalid, it does apply to specific technical developments over certain time periods in certain regions or under certain conditions.

The Eastern World

Archaeological finds show that **reed boats** were used **all over the Mediterranean**, from Israel, Syria, and Lebanon, to Cypress, Crete, and Italy, and the North African coast as far west as Morocco. A Phoenician jar showing reed boats, complete with Sun symbol, has been recovered off the Atlantic coast of Spain. Rock carvings in the **Nubian Desert**, between the Nile and the Red Sea, show reed boats with crews of up to 50 men, forty oars, fore and aft cabins, a mast and rigging, and a cargo of cattle dwarfed by the size of the ship. (Heyerdahl, Ocean, 6-8)

The same type of Nubian reed-boat illustrations were found by **Henri Lhote** in the Tassili N'Ajjer desert region of southeastern Algeria, part of the massive **Sahara Desert**. The ancient residents tended herds of cattle and drew pictures of giraffes, elephants, rhinos, gazelle, ostriches, and buffalo, along with large, spotted, long-horned cattle and not one camel! They hunted the hippopotamus from reed boats. The similarity in reed-boat design led the evolutionist Lhote to propose a connection between the earliest cultures of Egypt and Algeria. (To us, that's no surprise!)

What is additionally intriguing is the fact that, at that early time after the Flood, the Sahara was **green and fertile** and, according to Lhote, the area's mountain peaks "enjoyed a **Mediterranean climate**, and analyses of ancient pollens have shown that the Aleppo pine grew there, together with cypresses, cedars, ash trees, evergreen oaks, nettle trees, walnuts, alders, myrtle, limes and olives." This means that both wood and animal skins were available to these ancients for boat, raft, or canoe building, but they used reed from the valley rivers and marshes instead. (Heyerdahl, Ocean, 8; Lhote, in World's Last, 212, 204, 206, 209, 214)

The Americas

Regarding the western side of the Atlantic, post-Darwin history has taught us to think of nothing more than the use of skin- or bark-covered canoes or dugouts in North America, long canoes with outriggers and large catamarans in the South Pacific, and some type of canoe or primitive fishing boat on the Amazon River of South America. As we already noted, even staunch traditionalist Samuel Eliot Morison agrees that the early peoples of the South Pacific were accomplished mariners who could find their way across the world's broadest ocean without a compass, but *how many people think of the ancient South Americans as seafarers?* (Morison, European North, 34)

Ancient pottery designs from South America's **Chicama Valley** in **Peru** (pre-Inca) show **bundled-reed boats** with the typical, ocean-going, Middle Eastern sickle shape, lashed with cord. A lower deck houses a cargo of pottery while an upper, bamboo-cane deck supports a priestly-looking man. The stern shows two upturned bundles, suggesting a multi-hulled craft, while the deck is lashed across, catamaran style. Brightly striped **centerboards** indicate that these are **seagoing sailing vessels**, even though no sail or mast is shown in this pottery decoration. (Centerboards are used like an adjustable keel in concert with sails to navigate against wind and current.) This hybrid version of a bundled-reed boat and a catamaran "raft" is commonly called a *balsa*, even though no balsa wood is involved in this craft. (Savoy, Feathered, 42)

Explorer and South American ancient history expert **Gene Savoy** agrees with Dr. Heyerdahl that the reed boat is the most ancient of watercraft. "It was and still is the predominant watercraft of the Indians," says Savoy. Central and South Americans used (and still use) native *totora* reed which has the same buoyancy characteristics as **papyrus**. The **cultural-hero legends** common to the Central and South American peoples (Viracocha, Con, Quetzalcoatl, Kukulkan) often involve a reed boat or a fleet of reed sailing ships, or balsa rafts. Sickle-shaped reed boats were common at Lakes Chapala and Tlaxcala in **Mexico** and all along the coast to **California**. Even the Amerindians of Pyramid Lake in **Nevada** bundled bulrushes into crafts with curved-up prows. (Savoy, Feathered, 14, 20-1; Heyerdahl, Ocean, 122, 192-3)

Noting that ample artifacts exist to demonstrate that the **earliest American natives** built **seagoing, cargo-carrying rafts and boats** of reeds and balsa logs, Heyerdahl also points out that these same early Americans never progressed to the ribbed hull (except for a light-framed canoe) or wood-planked ships. They were still expertly plying the Pacific in unribbed reed or lashed balsa-log wash-through vessels when the Europeans arrived in the 1500s. Either, he thinks, the same type of Middle Eastern, deep-sea navigation "developed independently" in the Americas, or ancients ignorant of the ribbed hull transferred their influence across the Atlantic. (Heyerdahl, Ocean, 5-6, 188-9; Savoy, Feathered, 18)

We have noted that knowledge of the ribbed, displacement hull began with the Ark. Was it indeed lost by those post-Babel groups who dispersed to the Americas, or did they simply prefer their quite adequate reed or balsa craft? In our next volume, we will examine the evidence for the virtually uninterrupted *parade of traffic* from the Middle East, Europe, Africa, and Asia to the Americas, dating from the 2000s B.C. to the A.D. 1000s, a fact which *precludes any supposition of initial American ignorance of ribbed, displacement-type vessels.*

Unique Construction

Ocean-going reed boats had several specific and ingenious design points. Mesopotamian reeds were cut in August, because at that time, the reeds produced an inner substance that served as a natural waterproofer. Two large **cylinders of bundled reeds** were tightly roped together, with a small cylinder squeezed in between, to form a **double-cylinder hull**. The ends were curved up high to form the characteristic **sickle shape**, the high-prow, high-stern curve that can be seen on almost all ancient vessels, from the Egyptians to the Phoenicians, Celts, and Vikings. Heyerdahl's three boats ranged from 39 to 60 feet in length. Many ancient reed boats were much larger. One ancient Egyptian boat, probably a sewn, wood-plank adaptation of reed-boat design, was 180 feet long and 60 feet wide.

Because of the double-bundle construction, the ancients used an "A-frame," **bipod mast** which straddled the deck, one foot on each bundle. Because waves and swells create uneven support for a boat hull, the rigging was the special ingredient that literally held the boat together in rough seas. This applied particularly, as Heyerdahl discovered the hard way, to the **harp string** which ran from the upper tip of the curved stern to the rear deck. These reed boats were built in Mesopotamia, Egypt, coastal and central North Africa (Lake Chad and southern Algeria which is now desert), all over the Mediterranean, the Americas, and Easter Island (South Pacific).

An Art Almost Lost

In fact, the Marsh Arabs of Mesopotamia and Africans from Lake Chad can construct reed boats adequate for lakes or rivers, but only the **South American Indians of Lake Titicaca** (Peru and Bolivia) remember the art of building an ocean-going reed boat! The art has been lost in Egypt and Sumeria. What is even more intriguing is the fact that these South Americans come from the **Quechua**, **Aymara**, and **Uru** tribes, and that *Amara and Ur are two of the most important names in the region of the Iraqi marshes!* The South Americans of Lake Titicaca, the world's highest lake at an altitude of some 12,500 feet, use the native totora reeds to build boats, houses, and floating reed islands, just as do the Mesopotamians half a world away. (Heyerdahl, Ocean, 14-16, 25, 95, 303, 328, 355; Tigris, 26, 43-7, 89; Casson, Mariners, 11, 15)

An interesting aside concerns Egypt, where the once-plentiful and world-famous **papyrus reeds** of the Nile were used for boat construction as well as for paper. Dr. Heyerdahl comments that botanists have no idea why the papyrus plant **disappeared** entirely from the northern (lower) Nile and, today, is extinct throughout Egypt, apart from a modern plantation in Cairo which produces tourist souvenirs. Heyerdahl had to go to Ethiopia and the source of the Blue Nile River to obtain papyrus for his two Egyptian boats. (Heyerdahl, Ocean, 22)

The great majestic and Messianic prophet, **Isaiah**, addresses Ethiopia (founded by Cush) as "Ho, land shadowed with wings, that is beyond the rivers of Cush," (*Young's Literal*, Isa. 18:1) a nation "that sendeth ambassadors by the *sea, even in vessels of bulrushes* upon the *waters*, saying, Go, ye swift messengers...." (KJV, Isa. 18:2, italics added) In the next chapter, Isaiah addresses Egypt, prophesying judgment, predicting civil war, subjection, and drought, when "the *paper reeds* by the brooks, by the mouth of the brooks, and every thing sown by the brooks, shall wither, be driven away, and *be no more*." (KJV, Isa. 19:7, italics added) Thus, the disappearance of the papyrus was a **divine judgment**, prophesied in the Bible. Perhaps this judgment was a major factor in the abandonment of reed-boat building in Egypt.

The **Bible** attests to the **ancient origin of the reed ship**. We have discussed the age of Job, dating him as living probably around the 2200s to 2000s B.C. In the midst of his suffering, Job describes the swiftness with which the days of his life pass, comparing it to the swiftness of "ships of reed." Then, in the 1400s B.C., the mother of Moses put her baby son into an "ark of bulrushes" which she daubed with slime and pitch. (KJV, Ex. 2:3; *Young's Literal*, Job 9:25-6)

The *Ra* and *Tigris* Voyages of Heyerdahl

Dr. Thor Heyerdahl sought to demonstrate the seaworthiness of ancient reed boats and the fact that ancient man could have easily **crossed the Atlantic** from Africa to the Americas in such a craft. *Ra I* was constructed in Egypt, in the shadow of the Great Pyramid, directed by reed-boat builders from Lake Chad. It was 50 feet in length and carried an international crew.

The voyage began on **May 25, 1969** and nearly reached Barbados in the Caribbean. The Chad builders did not realize the importance of the stern "harp string," the rope from the tip of the curled stern to the aft deck which acted as a spring to support the rear section of the boat in the uneven environment of waves and troughs. Still the improperly rigged craft kept the crew safe and traveled more than 3,000 miles from Safi, Morocco to American waters before abandonment became necessary on July 18.

Realizing his mistake, Heyerdahl returned to Egypt and built the 39-foot *Ra II* with the help and guidance of **Aymara Indians** from **South America's Lake Titicaca** and the enigmatic Bolivian city of Tiahuanaco, almost 13,000 feet high in the Andes. Of all the cultures in the world, these people from the world's highest navigable lake, half a world away from Mesopotamia and Egypt, are the only ones known to remember the almost-lost art of properly constructing an *ocean*-going reed boat. This time the boat was perfectly designed and rigged, so Heyerdahl and his eight-man crew launched a second voyage from **Morocco** in **May of 1970**. Five of the eight were inexperienced sailors, one an inland African who did not discover that sea water is salty until the trip was underway. They reached **Barbados in July** without loss or damage to a single papyrus stem, covering **3,270 miles** of ocean in only **57 days**, for an average speed of over 57 miles per day. (Heyerdahl, Ra; Tigris, 26, 43, 52, 89; Ocean, 14-15)

Not content with proving the ability of ancient reed boats to make safe crossings of the Atlantic from east to west, Heyerdahl began construction of another reed boat in the ancient marshes of **Mesopotamia in August 1977**. Once again, he brought his Aymara Amerindian friends from South America to supervise the boat design. Heyerdahl noted that these **Lake Titicaca natives** demonstrated an immediate, instinctive, and intriguing reverence for what the **Iraqis** had marked as Adam's Tree in the Garden of Eden. He also realized that the "Aymara" and "Uru" tribal names of Bolivia's ancient Tiahuanaco region were very close to "Amara" and "Ur," two of the most prominent names of the lower Tigris-Euphrates region.

Built with Mesopotamian *berdi* reeds, the *Tigris* was 60 feet long and carried an 11-man crew from **Mesopotamia** through the Persian Gulf to the **Indus Valley,** and on through the Arabian Sea and the Gulf of Aden to the port of **Djibouti**. The voyage began in November 1977 and ended five months and **4,200 miles** later on the African coast. From the Mesopotamians, Heyerdahl learned, after he had already crossed the Atlantic twice in two different reed boats, that reeds should be cut in August to obtain the longest period of natural buoyancy — an additional secret of reed-boat building, forgotten by some peoples, remembered by others. (Heyerdahl, Tigris, 1-4, 26, 43-4, 89, 336-7; Ocean, 24)

South American Balsa Rafts

Actually, Dr. Heyerdahl astounded the world long before his *Ra* and *Tigris* trips. He pointed out that the Spaniards and other 16th- and 17th-Century Europeans could not fight the winds and currents to sail from **west to east**– from Asia–into or across the Pacific. If so, he reasoned, how could the Pacific be populated by ancient Asians sailing or paddling from west to east? **Traditionalists** maintained that the **South Pacific** islands were populated by Asians in a **general west-to-east migration**, and that South Americans did not possess the vessels nor the skill to cross the ocean to Polynesia. (Heyerdahl, Ocean, ix [see quote from Sir Peter Buck], 37) Heyerdahl set out to demonstrate that historians and anthropologists must consider the role of **ocean currents and prevailing winds** in the history of mankind as well as the fact that **ancient South Americans** were quite **capable of sailing** to Polynesia and beyond.

When the Spaniards came to Peru, they noted the ease with which the natives sailed their balsa rafts up and down the South American coast, navigating to islands and fishing 15 to 20-plus miles out to sea. Since ancient times, these Peruvians had designed **balsa-log rafts** with large sails which could carry as many as **50 men** and **30 tons of cargo**. Spanish naval officers observed that these "primitive" natives could *sail their balsa rafts in any wind* as well as the Spanish could sail their three-masted, keeled wooden ships. We realize today, says Heyerdahl, that the South Americans had adequate vessels and navigating skill to sail theoretically *anywhere in the Pacific*, using their centerboard and sail system to navigate in any wind or current. (Heyerdahl, Ocean, 207-10, 228)

The Challenge of *Kon-Tiki*

On **April 28, 1947**, more than 20 years before the *Ra* trips, Thor Heyerdahl and five other crew members defied conventional wisdom and launched the *Kon-Tiki* outside the harbor of **Callao, Peru**. They set out into the Pacific Ocean where the Humboldt Current that flows north along the coasts of Chile and Peru swings west into the South Equatorial Current conveyor belt which runs east to west through Polynesia and all the way to Melanesia. The soon-to-be world-famous *Kon-Tiki* was made of nine balsa-wood logs that were two feet thick and 30 to 45 feet long. These logs were lashed to crossbeams supporting a bamboo deck and an open hut. Like Heyerdahl's later reed boats, this raft had a bipod, "A-frame" mast. It also had a square sail, five centerboards, and a steering oar.

Contrary to unbelieving critics, the green, sap-filled balsa wood proved wonderfully water resistant. (Dry balsa is not.) The outer parts of the logs turned spongy which prevented chafing of the ropes which lashed the raft together, and the craft itself rose magnificently on every wave, sending what water that did hit the deck right between the logs in the same wash-through fashion as a bundled-reed boat. This native design wasn't primitive, it was brilliant!

By 93 days, the *Kon-Tiki* passed the first island sighted in Polynesia. On **day 101**, after traveling **4,300 miles**, the raft was swept onto a Raroia Atoll reef in the Tuamotu Islands near **Tahiti**. The crew had experimented with tacking into the wind using the centerboards but lacked skill and experience. (They tried the tacking experiment again in 1953 with guidance and were quite successful.) (Heyerdahl, Kon-Tiki; Ocean, 216-17, 226)

In the wake of the pioneering *Kon-Tiki*, from **1954 to 1973**, **nine other balsa rafts** and **one rubber raft** have adventured into the South Equatorial Current from **South America to Polynesia**, with five reaching **Melanesia** or as far as **Australia**. Two additional rafts went too far north to the Galapagos Islands and then into the Equatorial Counter Current where they were unable to sail either direction and had to be rescued. On an innocent map, this "current" looks as if it would carry a craft from Asia east to Equador, but it is in reality a deceiving, narrow band of swells and whirls in the doldrums between the strong, westward flowing North and South Equatorial Currents. These two "unsuccessful" trips further supported Heyerdahl's point that only **extremely skilled navigators** with **advance knowledge** could *sail both east and west* in the Pacific, and that even the Europeans could manage to sail only west for the 500 years between the 1270s to the 1770s.

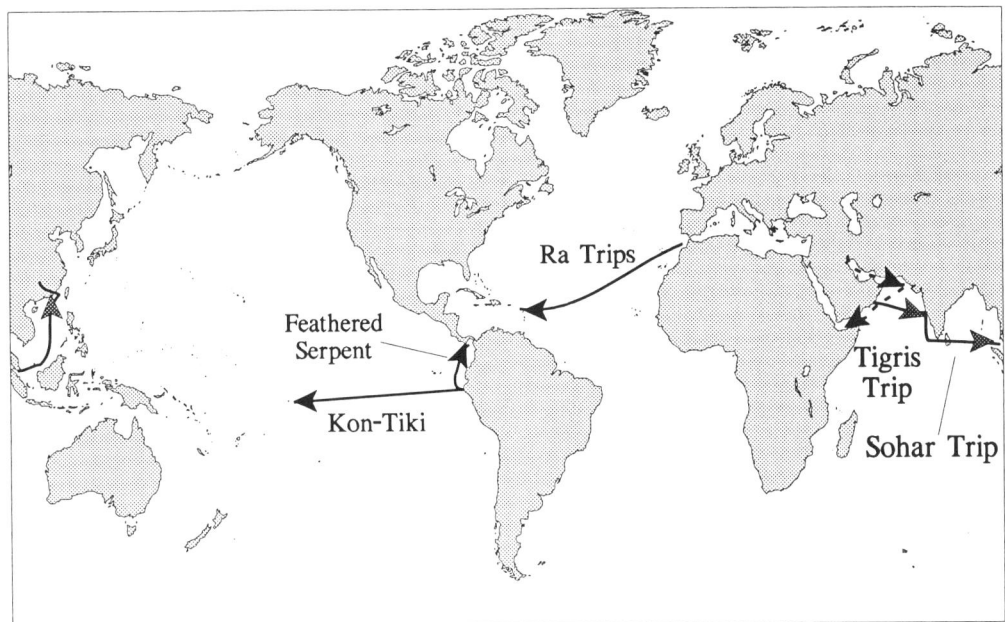

(Heyerdahl, Ocean, 38-40)

Isn't it interesting that, in modern times, the *Kon-Tiki* trip was considered pioneering and dangerous, if not completely crazy? Such trips had been made successfully countless times by ancients throughout the millennia. But to a modern man unfamiliar with an ancient craft, and challenged by the unequivocal opinion of experts that the feat had never been done and couldn't be done, the trip was something akin to an early space launch. It serves as a dramatic illustration of how out of touch we "moderns" are with our ancient past.

Savoy's *Feathered Serpent*

Another adventurer and South American ancient history expert, **Gene Savoy**, determined to prove that the ancient South Americans could and did navigate through the difficult currents along the coast between **Central America and Peru**, carrying on an active and vital trade between the cultures. It is interesting, though, that after all of the above-mentioned trips, Savoy believes that the Amerindians were limited by "primitive nautical technology" to only 15 or 20 miles off the coast. Savoy is an adamant believer that *American peoples evolved independently*, producing the same variety of skin colors and features that are evident in the Eastern Hemisphere. Though an **autochthonist**, he agrees that a certain "degree of transoceanic migration was probable," and believes in the underlying truth of the **cultural hero legends** that pervade Central and South America. Those legends all involve a foreign, white teacher of superior intellect, morals, and culture who came from over the sea, enriched the people with knowledge, then left by way of the sea. However, any ancient sea trade that linked cultures across the oceans only came "at a relatively late date," Savoy contends. As for the origin of American man, Savoy says that the "Americans were simply here, possibly before the continents began to drift apart." (Savoy, Feathered, 10, 11, 17)

Savoy built a type of "raft" that is called a *balsa*, though it is made of bundled-reed hulls in a catamaran style with a lashed cane deck, bipod mast, and square sail, but no balsa wood. The deck of the balsa measured roughly 13.5 by 18 feet. Christened the *Feathered Serpent*, Savoy's craft defied predicted failure and carried its three-man crew from **Salaverry, Peru, to Panama** in **64 days**, from mid-April to **July 17, 1969**. (Savoy, Feathered, 19-21, 61-9, 213)

From Reed to Sewn Wooden Ships

Dr. Heyerdahl points to an impressive array of archaeological evidence to support his opinion that the first real open-water navigation was done in sickle-shaped, bundled-reed vessels. The second major development in watercraft, he argues, was a displacement-hull boat constructed with cedar planks sewn together with cordage, but copying the same basic design as the original bundled-reed craft. This began to happen, says Heyerdahl, around 3000 B.C. (we would date it closer to 2200 to 2000 B.C.) when the **Canaanites** decided to start substituting **Lebanon cedar** for the reeds they were importing from Egypt, and the Egyptians began to import cedar for their own boats. [Gen. 10:15 tells us that Canaan was the ancestor of the Phoenicians and the Hittites.]

The Cedars of Lebanon

Some hieroglyphics found in Egypt have been translated to describe six years of the reign of a **Pharaoh** called **Snefru** (or Snofru or Sneferu) who is conventionally dated during the 4th Dynasty or about 2650 or 2600 B.C. Once again, we would have to bring the date forward 400 or 500 years at least. Apparently, the Pharaoh ordered **40 ship loads** of **cedar logs** from the port of Byblos in **Phoenicia** (Lebanon). Were these Phoenician ships or Egyptian ships? Were they reed or wood? If wood, were they sewn or pegged, with or without ribs? Whatever they were, they were big enough to carry cedar logs and sturdy enough to sail the Mediterranean. Snefru is listed as the pharaoh who ruled right before **Cheops** (Khufu) who is credited with the building of the Great Pyramid. We shall see in a moment that these cedar logs were indeed used for royal Nile River boats, planked and sewn. (EB, 1972, 8:34; Heyerdahl, Ocean, 11; Casson, Mariners, 4; Landström, Voyages, 10)

Cedar wood is first mentioned in the Bible in Leviticus while the cedars of Lebanon are first mentioned in the book of Judges. However, Job is often considered to be the oldest book of the Scriptures, and Job describes the great behemoth (brontosaurus-type dinosaur) as moving his tail like a cedar. (Job 40:17) Such a comparison must refer to the world-renowned cedar trees of Lebanon. These trees had several hundred years to grow following the Flood until the nations formed after Babel. They remained strong and famous at least to the time of Solomon's Temple.

The first sewn, wood-plank boats carefully *imitated the exact lines of the papyrus vessels*, including the high curves of bow and stern which came so naturally to the flexible reeds, complete with the symbolic papyrus-flower shape that crowned one or both curves. Heyerdahl calls them **"papyriform"** ships. These boats had **no keel** and only a **few, light ribs** and were literally **sewn** together with cordage or rope. Though they had the proper shape for an ocean-going vessel, they were not built to sail on anything but the Nile. The ancient boat builders continued to use the "A-frame" bipod mast designed to straddle the double-bundle hull of a reed boat, even though this was not a necessary design point for the wood ships. The best and most ancient example of this type of shipbuilding was exquisitely preserved for us in an underground vault right next to —where else — the Great Pyramid. (Heyerdahl, Ocean, 11-13, 20; Casson, Mariners, 14-16)

A Great Pyramid Surprise

It isn't surprising that the Great Pyramid itself has something important to offer on the subject of ancient ships. In 1954, in a deep vault on the south side of the massive wonder, excavators revealed what they thought was the **"solar boat"** intended to carry the soul of Pharaoh Cheops to paradise. The **cedarwood ship** was found in an astounding state of preservation, but unassembled in 1,224 pieces. When uncovered, the boat's cedar planking demonstrated an original color that was warm and light and polished to the point of reflection. One scientist described it to be as hard and new as if it had been buried only a year. (Webber, New Light, 105-7, quoting Nancy Jenkins, *The Boat Beneath the Pyramid*)

As of 1982, the "solar boat" sits, complete with oars and rigging, in its own glass-and-concrete museum atop the vault. At present, it is the largest and best preserved specimen of the ancient shipbuilder's art, dated by archaeologists as being built anywhere from 2500 to 2700 B.C., or about the time they date the construction of the Great Pyramid. [We would date it as sometime soon after 2300 to 2100 B.C.] The boat has an overall length of 143 feet and a width of about 12 feet. When unearthed, the wood still smelled like cedar and only five percent was unusable. The rope used for the rigging and to tie the planks together was in fairly good condition, though new rope was used to reassemble the boat.

Dr. Heyerdahl notes the wear on the original

ropes and concludes that this boat was not a mere religious exercise, but an **active Nile River boat**, designed for and used in royal ceremonies, a perfect specimen of the **sewn, wood-plank, papyriform boat** described above. This also shows us that, according to our own dating, this wood design was added to the reed design very quickly. (Webber, New Light, 105-7; *Dallas Morning News*, "Journey across the ages," 11/22/92, p. 23A; Heyerdahl, Ocean, 10-12)

Another similar boat in yet another pit next to the Great Pyramid has been discovered, also unassembled but made, they think, of sycamore instead of cedar. It is not in good condition and the Waseda University of Tokyo has joined the Egyptian Antiquities Organization in an effort to rescue the ancient artifact. (AP report, *Dallas Morning News*, 11/22/92, 23A)

Ocean-Going, Sewn Wood Ships

The same papyriform boat design can be readily seen in **ancient petroglyphs** (rock pictures) of a fleet of seagoing vessels carved in rock in **Bohuslän, Sweden**, while ancient rock carvings in **Norway** show ships with the same basic high-prowed, high-sterned profile displayed by Egyptian boats. The sickle-shaped Norwegian ships are shown with crew and cargo, docked next to four-wheeled carts and what looks like draft animals. (EB, 1972, 16:648)

Across the sea in **North America**, the same type ships are carved in rock at **Peterborough, Ontario**, Canada. One Canadian glyph, says Dr. Fell, represents the solar boat carrying the Sun symbol, which is pervasive in ancient mythology from Egypt to Norway to Central and South America, while the other glyphs show actual, sickle-shaped, **wooden Norse trading boats** that plied the Atlantic between Scandinavia and Canada, about the year **1700 B.C.**! We will investigate Norwegian trade in ancient America in Volume II, but right now we are interested in the *very early and almost worldwide dissemination of the bundled-reed and papyriform wood boats*. (Fell, America, 303-7)

These ancient Scandinavian drawings probably represent sewn-plank ships that, unlike Pharaoh's river craft, were *reinforced to negotiate the open ocean*. Dr. Fell mentions the discovery of an **ancient Norwegian ship** 13 meters long (over 42.6 feet) made from adzed, wood planks that were sewn together. (Fell, Bronze, 249) He may or may not be referring to the same boat described by Roger Charles Anderson which, as of 1972, was the oldest recovered specimen of a northern boat. Found in Als, **Denmark**, this specimen is dated about **300 B.C.** and is built from adzed wood planks which overlap and which are sewn together. Anderson records this boat as being 45 feet long (14 meters) and makes the traditionalist claim that it must have descended from a dugout. (EB, 1972, 20:401) By the way, a boat or ship made with **overlapping planks** is called *clinker built*, while one with a smooth hull where the planks are fitted together **edge to edge** is called *carvel built*. (Webster's)

Anderson mentions several other finds of northern European boats, dated from 200 B.C. to A.D. 900 Some are clinker built and some carvel built. The earlier ones are sewn while some later ones are partly nailed and partly sewn. Like the Egyptian boats, they had no true keel. Apparently by about **A.D. 1000**, **Viking boats** were built on a **true keel**. (EB, 1972, 20:401) Heyerdahl points out that the Vikings of the A.D. 700s to 1100s built their ocean-going wood ships with lines very similar to the classic, Middle-Eastern **sickle-shaped profile**, the same profile that Dr. Fell documents was used by their Norse ancestors of 1700 B.C. Dr. Fell also notes that the later Scandinavian boats (and obviously, from the drawings, also the ancient ones), were flat bottomed, either without a keel or with some sort of flat keel. (Heyerdahl, Ocean, 11-12; Fell, America, 115)

On the other side of the world, the ancient **Polynesians** also used cordage to **sew** together **adzed wood planks** to make raft-like boats in which, according to records, they sailed 3,000 miles from Tahiti to New Zealand, covering 100 miles a day. It took medieval sailors a long time to "catch up" to that level of skilled navigation. (Fell, Bronze, 249) We continue to see the *early, widespread dissemination of the sickle-shaped lines and keelless, sewn-plank ship construction*, methods which perhaps were designed to retain the grace, maneuverability, and flexibility of the bundled-reed craft.

Meanwhile, back in Egypt, did the Egyptians retain their bundled-reed vessels for ocean travel? *Could keelless, sewn, wood ships be made seaworthy?* After ancient pharaohs began to build with wood and had need to venture into or across ocean water, they merely **adapted their wooden river boats** using some basic design ideas inspired by the reed boats. Lacking a strong, wooden skeleton of keel and ribs, the wood-boat hulls needed the same type of support that proper rigging had provided for the reed hull.

This was accomplished with the use of a **large rope (hawser)** which **wrapped around the prow**, threaded through supports above the center of the deck, then **wrapped around the stern**. A stout piece of wood stuck through the strands of the rope was twisted to provide the tension needed to support the ship and hold it together. These details are illustrated on the walls of a pyramid attributed to **Pharaoh Sahure** whose reign is dated anywhere from 2550 to the 2400s B.C. These dates are too early for our thinking, but do confirm the ancient time period. The Pharaoh built a **fleet** of these ships, designed for both sail and oar power, to transport his troops to fight somewhere in Asia, according to Casson who gives a detailed description of the carvings. (Casson, Mariners, 14-15, 27; EB, 1972, 8:38)

Artist and maritime historian **Björn Landström** says that Sahure sent a large fleet to the **Land of Punt** and that the ships returned bearing 80,000 measures of myrrh, 6,000 weights of electrum (alloy of silver and gold), and 2,600 logs of expensive wood which Landström assumes to be mostly ebony, as ebony was a product of the area. It is not clear whether these are different accounts of the same trip, or two separate trips. Due to the detail and knowledge offered by both men, we assume they describe two trips, one military and one commercial, which only further demonstrates the ocean-going activity of wooden, Egyptian ships at a very early date. Landström adds that a steersman named **Khnemhotep** of the next dynasty (6th) left an inscription on his tomb that he made **11 trips to Punt**. (Landström, Voyages, 10; EB, 1972, 8:38)

Usually dated sometime between 1504 and 1468 B.C., **Queen Hatshepsut** of Egypt reigned as part of the Thutmose/Amenhotep (18th) dynasty which is said to have restored Egypt to power after the nation was conquered and ruled by foreign Hyksos kings (15th & 16th Dynasties) and after a period of civil war and political fragmentation. In the midst of family intrigue, Hatshepsut, who was a legitimate heiress but obviously not a male, seized power and had herself declared "king," even posing in the kingly attire. It was the year of the woman in Egypt! (Casson, Mariners, 11-13; Finegan, Light, 97)

Hatshepsut's grandfather and father had reunited their nation and the new queen was apparently strong enough to retain rule over both Lower and Upper Egypt, though she presided from **Thebes** in Upper Egypt, as did the entire dynastic line. Apparently her religious zeal for Amon-Ra inspired her to *reestablish direct, maritime trade* with the **Land of Punt**, trade that had been discontinued for some 300 years, so long that the *sea route had been forgotten!* Punt was the land of **sacred spices** and incense which was also called the **Land of the Gods**. It seems fairly certain that Punt was basically the ancient land of **Somalia** where myrrh trees still grow and monkeys still play, though it may have stretched as far south as the isle of **Zanzibar** off Tanzania, or even **Mozambique**.

The direct shipping of goods from Punt by water to Egypt avoided overland trade that passed through the exceedingly expensive hands of many middlemen. To avoid this, Hatshepsut raised a **fleet of ships** and may well have redredged Pharaoh Senusret's (Sesostris or Senusert) **old 1900's B.C. canal** from the eastern Nile estuary above Memphis to the Red Sea. This canal was abandoned and revived numerous times in Egypt's history.

The canal would have allowed her to sail the 440 miles north on the Nile from Thebes to Memphis, then enter the Red Sea through the canal and turn south. Would she have done that? It would have avoided a hard trek across the desert from Thebes to the coast. Even if she, instead, ordered the cedar and other materials brought to the coast off Thebes to build the ships there, the canal would have allowed cedar from Lebanon to sail directly from the Mediterranean to the Red Sea, and so the canal would have helped either way.

Some 500 or 600 years *earlier*, **11th Dynasty Pharaoh Mentuhotep III**, dated about 2100 to 2000 B.C. (if these dates are correct), sent his minister **Henu** with **3,000 men** and building materials directly across the *waterless desert country between Thebes and the Red Sea* in order to get myrrh from Punt. Henu had to dig **12 wells** to supply the men with water along the eight-day trek. They built the ship on the coast and sent it south to Punt. However, that was before the canal existed. Note that they only sent *one* ship, while Hatshepsut would send a fleet.

The Hyksos, Hatshepsut, and the Exodus

Since we are currently immersed in Egyptian history, this is as good a point as any to consider the date of the Exodus, the reign of the Hyksos Kings, and the reign of Hatshepsut.

The **Hyksos pharaohs** of Egypt (**15th & 16th Dynasties**) were not Egyptian, but **Semitic** Canaanites known as the **"Shepherd Kings."** They are said to have introduced the Egyptians to the **horse and chariot**, something we know from the book of Exodus that the Egyptians had adopted for themselves by the time of Moses. Genesis 46 & 47 informs us that the *Egyptians vehemently hated shepherds* when **Jacob** and his family came to Egypt. This has led many to conclude that Jacob came to Egypt *after* the Hyksos, or possibly even *during* the Hyksos reign, when a Hyksos pharaoh might be friendly to Joseph and welcome his non-Egyptian, Semitic shepherding family.

A very odd piece to the Egyptian puzzle is a **papyrus** stored in Leiden, Holland, called *The Admonitions of Ipuwer*. The papyrus contains the **lamentations of an Egyptian sage** who voices a type of Messianic hope for an **ideal, shepherd-like king** to rule Egypt. Ipuwer explains that the social order of Egypt is basically turned upside-down, that barbarians have entered [Hyksos? Hebrews?], and that a few irresponsible men have despoiled the kingship. But the ideal king, he says, shall bring "'coolness [peace?] upon the heart. Men shall say: 'He is the herdsman of all men. Evil is not in his heart. Though his herds may be small, still he has spent the day caring for them.' "' (Finegan, Light, 89-90; White, Pole, 113)

To us, this description certainly sounds very biblical and very much like the "Good Shepherd" (Jesus). This Egyptian certainly does not abhor shepherds. He is dated between 2200 and 1991 B.C., long before the Hyksos, but his lamentations are considered by some to parallel the Exodus, mentioning the same plagues. (White, Pole, 113) But the dating is certainly too early for the Exodus. Is the dating of this papyrus way off the mark? Why did this Egyptian look for a "Good Shepherd"? Who were the barbarians? Another writer, supposedly of the same time period as Ipuwer, wrote "'Death is in my eyes today....'" and so on, in a death-wish poem that certainly makes one think of the plagues of the Exodus. (Finegan, Light, 90) Learn from this that **Egyptian history is by no means a settled chronology**. Like much of science, it is guesswork built upon guesswork and presented to you as fact.

Some say that Jacob came to Egypt *before* the Hyksos, during the so-called **12th Dynasty** which is dated between **1990 and 1780 B.C.** This same line of thinking casts **Hatshepsut** (**18th Dynasty**) as the pharaoh's daughter who adopts Moses. The standard dates of her reign are given anywhere from **1504** or **1501 to 1480**, to between **1486** and **1468 B.C.** (Landström, Voyages, 12; Finegan, Light, 97) The reign of Hatshepsut's father **Thutmose I** is dated about 1526 to 1512 B.C.

Thutmose III, who may have executed Hatshepsut, is considered to be one of the greatest pharaohs, a great builder and warrior who *used Asiatic captives as slaves*. His reign is said to have ended about 1436 B.C., which would make him, according to this scenario, the **pharaoh of the Exodus**. Thutmose III was an illegitimate son by a harem girl. A first-born son would have died in the last of the 10 plagues. Did the pharaoh who pursued the fleeing Israelites lead his chariots into the parted waters? If so, he died in the Red Sea. The Bible seems to indicate that he did, though it does not make a clear statement to that effect. (Hannah, BKH I,

The story does not say whether they hauled reeds or cedar logs overland to build this ship. Whatever it was, it took 3,000 men to do it.

Another point of interest in this story is the fact that a ship had to be specially constructed for this expedition, meaning *no ocean-going vessel remained* to sail south. Perhaps there were some ocean-going ships left on the Mediterranean. How much time had actually elapsed between 5th Dynasty Sahure and 11th Dynasty Mentuhotep III? Our own dating, plus other evidence, seriously questions the accuracy of the dynastic list and we *cannot agree to some 400 or more years between the two pharaohs.* Even so, **Sahure's fleet was gone**. It may have been destroyed or just rotted with age and use. It is

When did the Hyksos reign? Did Hatshepsut adopt Moses?

106-7; EB, 1972, 8:38-9; Pict. Dict., 367, 705, 851; Landström, Voyages, 12-14; Finegan, Light, 117-8)

In *this* book, we date the *entry of Jacob* in **1703 B.C.**, the *birth of Moses* in **1568 B.C.**, and the *Exodus* in **1488**. It is possible that the above personalities could fit into our own chronology.

However, the above line of thought requires that the *Hyksos kings ruled during the time that the Israelites were slaves.* There is no indication in the Bible that Egypt was conquered by outsiders while Joseph was there, and it does not seem sensible that Semitic Hyksos would be part of the long oppression of fellow Semites. (Gen. 15:13) Then again, Semite nations certainly fought among themselves. Since we have concluded that the Manetho Dynasty list and its dates are unreliable, could we assume that **Joseph**, and later **Jacob**, both entered Egypt **toward the end of Hyksos rule?** Consider these points:

1) The Egyptians hated shepherds, Gen. 46:34, most probably because the Hyksos had come in and taken over without striking a blow.
2) The Hyksos knew about the Hebrews because the Hyksos were also Semites from the Fertile Crescent region.
3) The Hyksos worshipped their own Syrian god, and it was for this reason, perhaps, that Pharaoh was disposed to recognize that the Spirit of the Hebrew God was in Joseph, Gen. 41:38. (Of course, no matter who it is, if God wants a person to recognize His Spirit, that person will indeed do so. Also remember that the ancients certainly knew who was the real Creator God, whether or not they chose to worship Him. Consider the Pharaoh and Abram in Gen. 12.)
4) Why is Gen. 39:1 so careful to specifically designate Potiphar, the captain of Pharaoh's guard, as an Egyptian? And why does his wife tell the men of her house that her husband purposefully brought a Hebrew into their house to mock them all? (Gen. 39:14)
5) Was it a Hyksos Pharaoh who allowed the Hebrew shepherds to dwell separately from the Egyptians in the northeast delta land of Goshen and allowed Jacob to bless him? (Gen. 47:1-11)
6) The Hyksos kings ruled from the delta area rather than from Thebes, and the Hebrews would live in the delta. When the Hyksos took over, Egyptian royalty probably retreated to Thebes in Upper Egypt. [EB, 1972, 8:35] Hatshepsut's dynasty ruled from Thebes.

The Pharaoh who arose "who knew not Joseph" may have been **Ahmose** of the **Amenhotep/Thutmose line**, the great-grandfather of Hatshepsut. This group ruled mainly from Thebes, far away from the delta, but conquered Palestine and Syria during their reigns. It would make sense that this conquering of Palestine happened while Israel was in Egypt. **Amenhotep III**, two pharaohs after Thutmose III, was called **"the Magnificent,"** indicating Egypt's continued power and success during this period. The Israelites were in Egypt 135 years before Moses was born, according to our reckoning. Note the Thutmose and Rameses names. **Thutmose** is also **Thothmes**. *Mes* (or "mose" or "meses") means "to draw forth" and also "son of." Thus Thothmes is "the son of Thoth" and Rameses is "the son of Ra." Note that pharaoh's daughter named the Hebrew baby "Moses" because she drew him out of the water (Exo. 2:10; Scofield Bible note 2, p. 72; Hislop, note, 25; Finegan, Light, 134)

Now, what about the **Rameses pharaohs**? The land of **Goshen** where the Jews dwelled was called the *land of Rameses* and the Jews were eventually enslaved to build a **treasure city called Rameses**. A stone **stele** of **Pharaoh Rameses II** claims that he built the city of Rameses with *Asiatic Semitic (meaning Hebrew)* obvious from this story that the fleet was not replenished in the years following Sahure.

Like Sahure, Hatshepsut left a beautifully carved record of her official expedition to Punt on the walls of her temple to Amon-Ra in the valley of Thebes, the uniquely designed temple of Deir-el-Bahari. Our main interest lies with the design and construction of the ships she used and the time period involved. Casson remarks that Hatshepsut's **many-oared wooden ships** now had a **single-pole mast**, more **graceful lines**, and a much **broader sail** than similar earlier craft, but retained the **keeless construction** that required the same **hawser contraption** used by Sahure to survive the waves of the Gulf of Aden and the Indian Ocean. (Finegan, Light, 90-1, 97;

Who was the pharaoh of the Exodus? When did Hatshepsut reign?

slaves. (Gen. 47:11, Ex. 1:8-11, 12:37-41; Pict. Dict., 705) But the Rameses pharaohs are dated much later in history as the **19th Dynasty**, ruling from about **1320 to 1200 B.C.** (EB, 1972, 8:38) These pharaohs ruled from the delta and concentrated their efforts in the delta, where the Jews lived and toiled. (Finegan, Light, 119; Ps. 78:12, 43)

Merneptah, the son of Rameses II, carved a victory message on a large, **black, granite stele**, dated about **1220 B.C.**, that talks about his plundering and/or pacification of Palestine, Syria, and Libya. One line reads, "'**Israel** is laid waste, his seed is not.'" *This is the only use of the name Israel that has been found (as of 1959) in Egyptian inscriptions.* According to the Bible and generally accepted Jewish history, the Israelites dealt with Midianites and Philistines and Canaanites, but not with the Egyptians, from the time of the Exodus even into the time of Saul and David. Thus, either the dating is wrong, the translation is wrong, Merneptah is lying, or the Jews are wandering in Sinai and Merneptah thinks they are as good as dead. (Finegan, Light, 116; Judges through I Sam.)

Once again, if **Rameses II** was the pharaoh of the Exodus, rather than Thutmose III, we have the questions of his being a first-born son and of his drowning in the Red Sea. Both Rameses III and IV, dated in the 1100s B.C. list *'Apiru* among their labor forces. This word may well have referred to Semites in general and not merely the Hebrews. (Finegan, Light, 120) However, if it did specifically reference the Hebrews, then *possibly the Exodus pharaoh was a later Rameses and the dating of the Rameses dynasty is really off.* Joseph was referred to as a Hebrew (*'Ibriy*) in Genesis by Potiphar's wife (Gen. 39:14), by himself (Gen. 40:15), and by Pharaoh's chief butler (Gen. 41:12), indicating that Abraham's descendants already had a well-known identity.

If we decide that the Jews spent a **full 430 years in Egypt** rather than the 215 in our chronology, we arrive at a very late Exodus date of **1273 B.C.** This date fits the standard dates of Rameses II (c. 1290-1224 B.C.). It also fits the 1200s time period given for the establishment of Edom and Moab west of the Jordan, the kingdoms with whom Israel had to deal on its way to Canaan. As Finegan says, "the situation presupposed in Numbers 20:14-17 did not exist before the thirteenth century B.C. [1200s] but did prevail from that time on exactly as reflected in the Bible." (Finegan, Light, 153, 120) But this date pushes Solomon's beginning of the **Temple from 966 B.C. to 796 B.C.** The 900s dates for Solomon are very well accepted by the best, conservative Bible scholars, and it is difficult to cram all of biblical history into this shortened time period.

Another piece of evidence that points the Exodus to the **Rameses dynasty** is that *Egyptian power declined during and after their reigns.* What truly is strange is that **clear records** of an event of the magnitude of the Exodus, which was known of in Palestine, are not extant. Perhaps they were expunged on purpose by a proud Egyptian, or were lost or nonexistent due to what must have been complete chaos and devastation following the 10 plagues of divine judgment.

To return to **Hatshepsut**, we have seen that there is some evidence to indicate that she may have been the adoptive mother of Moses. On the other hand, if the Rameses pharaohs were actually reigning in the 1400s instead of the 1200s, it would push Hatshepsut to an earlier reign, merely showing the true ancientness of Egyptian ocean-going navigation,

Casson, Mariners, 10-11, 14-16; Landström, Voyages, 10-13) Is it possible that one reason for continuing the keelless construction originally inspired by the reed boats was the ability of these ships to negotiate the canal and the river as well as the ocean?

Hatshepsut's ships were **papyriform** in their traditional sickle-shape and the prominent papyrus-flower ornamentation of the stern that curved up and back over the deck, just like the bundled-reed boat. Her carved illustration is reproduced by Casson, but displayed most vividly in Landström's book. Not only did these ships (and Sahure's ships) successfully handle the Indian Ocean, but they and their crews mastered the Red Sea which, as Casson and Landström both remind us, is "unfriendly" and "tricky" to navigate "at all seasons." Difficulties included coral reefs (perhaps another reason for keelless construction), heat, sandstorms, contrary winds and currents, not much in the way of harbors or shelter, and pirates. (Casson, Mariners, 10, 12; Landström, Voyages, 2-3, 11)

Perhaps about 100 years after Hatshepsut (according to conventional dating), **Pharaoh Amenhotep III**, who is listed by some as reigning from 1417-1379 B.C., was visited by **Semitic ships** which were probably Syrian or Phoenician. Shown riding very high in the water, these boats are even more traditionally sickle-shaped than Hatshepsut's, though without the papyrus flower. Casson calls the artist a "landlubber" for drawing the ships with so little hull in the water, but other ancient illustrations of reed or papyriform boats reproduced by Heyerdahl show those boats the same way. Either those boats really did float like little corks or it was, for some reason, very important to emphasize the sickle shape.

The Semitic ships have a single-pole mast and show no oars except for the steering board off the right side (hence, *starboard* for "right side" on a ship, to this day [Morison, European North, 35]). The illustration, carved on the tomb of Kenamon, a commerce official of the pharaoh, shows the ends of cross planks sticking through the sides of the boats, indicating that they are indeed wood. And the ships are *without* the **hawser contraption**, apparently unnecessary on the **sturdier Phoenician ships**. (Casson, Mariners, 17-19; Heyerdahl, Ocean, 13)

Several hundred years later, between **1100 and 1000 B.C.**, when Egypt was in decline and divided into small states, an official of the Temple of Amon at Karnak took a ship to Byblos in Phoenicia to procure cedar logs to build "the great and august barque of Amon-Re, King of the Gods...." The papyrus record of **Wen-Amon's journey** mentions an argument over a cedar ship, as to whether or not the ship is Phoenician or Egyptian. It talks about loading cedar logs for Egypt, hewn timbers, a bow post and stern post, and a "*keel*," though the word keel is in italics which indicates a doubtful translation. Thus, we cannot rely on this manuscript for indication of a change in building technique in Egypt. (Pritchard, Ancient, 16-24)

More on Keelless and Flat-Keel Sailing

We have seen that Egypt's papyriform Nile River boats had no keel, and that the Egyptians successfully adapted keelless papyriform boats to negotiate ocean voyages, transporting large cargos or whole armies. We have seen that ancient Scandinavians sailed across the ocean in papyriform boats, and that their descendants continued to build sewn-plank and partly sewn boats with no true keel up until about A.D. 900. Later Scandinavian boats had a flat keel. Polynesians mastered keelless sailing, even using craft of adzed and sewn wood planks.

In **55 B.C.**, **Julius Caesar** wrote about the ships of the **Gallic (French)** and **British Celts**, with whom he was engaged in his most challenging sea battle. The *triremes* of Julius Caesar each carried 200 soldier/sailors to fight and to man the three banks of oars on either side of the Roman warship. However, writes Caesar, the **Celtic warships** from Britain were **much larger and sturdier** with tall masts and leather sails and stronger beams tied with iron chains instead of ropes. These great ships had no oars, but were capable of sailing the "'vast open sea'" through storms, even *sailing into the wind*, adds the astounded Caesar, though the Celtic ships had **flat keels**. The **Roman galleys had deep keels**. Thus, the Celts were able to maneuver in shallow water, a definite advantage over the Romans, though Roman military genius and becalming weather won the day for Julius Caesar. (Fell, America, 110, 116)

Of course, we have seen that the ancients certainly understood the concept of a keel to aid navigation. Dr. Heyerdahl explains that the ability of **South Americans** and **Polynesians** to navigate against wind and current was accomplished with the use of *guaras*, a somewhat complex **centerboard system** used in conjunction with sails on reed boats, double canoes, and balsa rafts. A number of centerboards could each be adjusted in differing patterns to tack against the wind and/or current. Through personal experimentation, Heyerdahl determined that centerboard navigation was an art that required skill and experience, but worked as well as a keel. This was also attested to by Spanish naval officers who observed firsthand the skill of the Peruvian balsa-raft sailors and who tried, unsuccessfully, to introduce the centerboard system into Europe in 1748. Centerboards were not tried in Europe or the United States until about 1870. A single centerboard is a common feature of many modern yachts. (Fell, America, 110, 112-6; Heyerdahl, Ocean, 55, 207-8, 224-8)

Sewn-Plank Ships in Medieval and Modern Times
Severin, Sindbad, and the "Sohar"

In case you still have trouble believing in the existence and/or seaworthiness of wooden ships that are sewn together, consider that a version of the ancient Middle Eastern sewn-plank ship survived to carry expert **Arab navigators** from **Arabia to Hong Kong** in the **A.D. 600s to 1000s.** This is the same time period during which the Irish and Norse were sailing the North Atlantic.

Looking past the fanciful embellishments of the tale of Sindbad the Sailor in Arabia's famous *The Thousand and One Nights*, **Tim Severin** recognized underlying truth and so decided to duplicate a medieval Arabian vessel and retrace Sindbad's celebrated journey. Though he resides in the ancient, seafaring land of Ireland, Severin is an Englishman with extensive sailing experience and a degree in medieval Asian exploration from Oxford University.

A major difference between the Arab boats and the Egyptian boats is that the Arab boats were built on a keel, and the **keel** of Severin's *Sohar* was **52 feet long** and 12" by 15" in thickness. It was carved absolutely straight from a massive, single tree trunk and, because it was **flat**, the ship could maneuver in fairly shallow water and could literally be drug up on the beach to have the hull scraped. The ship was built from *aini* wood which grows in India and is a cousin to the breadfruit. This wood is actually more durable in water than teak and contains lime which makes the wood difficult to paint but helps protect it from deadly **teredo (boring) worms**. Aini also happens to cost half the price of teak. *However, the wood splits when nailed, so the ship must be sewn!* (Severin, Sindbad, 15-6, 35, 38)

Like the old reed boats, the medieval Arab ship was **pointed at both ends** (compare with the later European ships), and carried a huge, **triangular sail** with spars so long that the sail is "delicate and dangerous" to handle. The *Sohar* required **400 miles** of **coconut-husk rope**, specially prepared in sea water. Construction was difficult and exacting because the planks had to be sewn to the keel and to each other before the ribs were stitched into the boat. Planks as long as 80 feet had to be accurately cut and fitted to better than 1/64th of an inch variance along the entire plank! The builders drilled some 20,000 holes for the cordage. The outside of the boat was treated with a mixture of fish oil and lime to foil the infamous teredo worms, while the inside stitching was painted with vegetable oil, a process which, if done every four to six months, guaranteed the boat to last 60 to 100 years. (Severin, Sindbad, 19-21, 40-1, 55, 68)

Famous 13th-Century Venetian explorer **Marco Polo** wrote that these sewn boats were risky and inferior and that many were lost in the stormy Indian Ocean. Other writers said that the boats were **flexible**. Sewn-plank boats are **still built today** in the **East Indies**. (EB, 1972, 20:399) With experience from a previous voyage in a replica of an ancient Irish boat, Severin ignored the modern experts and even Marco Polo and **trusted the ancient texts** on the subjects of materials and construction. (Severin, Sindbad, 19-21)

Told that such craftsmen no longer existed, Severin explored **Oman** (Arabia) and the **Malabar Coast** of India. He found the *shasha* on the beaches of Oman, a half-raft, half-boat type of bundled-reed craft built from the central spines of date palm leaves cut at a particular season, another modern-day survivor of ancient boat design. And in nearly every fishing village on both coasts, he found the *bedan*, a sewn and

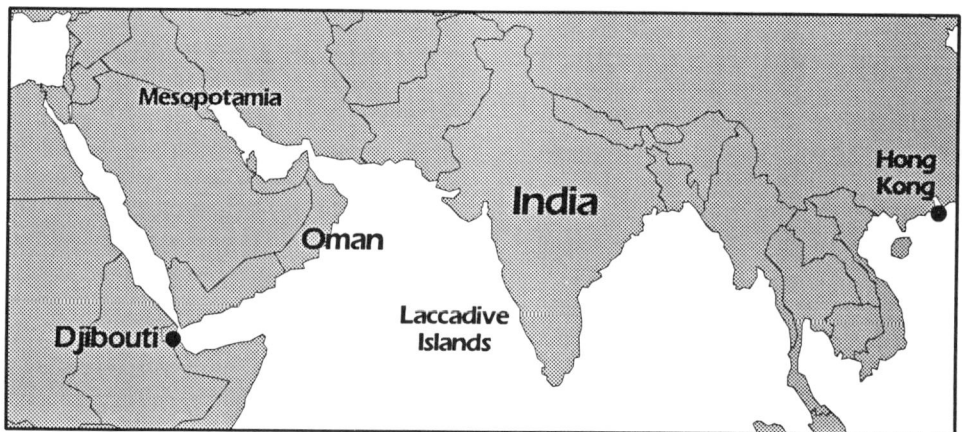

stitched wood boat about 30 feet long with a high, upward-curved stern and a pointed bow. However, he had to go to the **Laccadive Islands** off India's Malabar Coast to find the only **craftsmen** who remembered how to construct a large, ocean-going, sewn-plank ship. Severin was told that it would take 16 months to three years to build the 80-foot *Sohar*, but the task was completed in only **165 days**. (Severin, Sindbad, 22-3, 34, 45, 72, 235)

The crew of 20 set off from Oman on **November 23, 1980**. They began with a speed of about four to five knots or 70 to 80 miles per day. Their best speed for the trip was eight or nine knots but a month trapped in the doldrums south of Sri Lanka, where they almost ran out of drinking water, gave them a trip-long average speed of two knots. (Remember the discussion of the dangers of ocean travel in unfavorable winds and currents without modern power?) They sailed from Oman to Calicut, India, to Sri Lanka, to Sumatra, and through the Malacca Strait to Singapore. They survived very heavy weather in the South China Sea and avoided that area's some 15,000 pirates to arrive in **Hong Kong** harbor **6,000 miles** and **7½ months** later, on **June 28, 1981**. The ship was in excellent condition and had no damage from teredo worms, proving that the ancients knew how to solve such problems. The crew sailed up the Pearl River to Canton for an official reception. In the archives of the **University of Canton**, Severin found a **record** dated from the **A.D. 700s** of a **ship in the Canton harbor** described by a Chinese official as having **no nails**. It was sewn, read the report, with coconut fiber! (Severin, Sindbad, 86, 102, 141, 217, 220, 229, 238)

Through his research and voyage, Severin discovered that the Arabs navigated only by the stars and did not take readings on the Sun. Severin himself learned to take accurate latitude readings using the ancient Arab "tools" of a thin piece of wood about 3" square with a hole in the middle and a string with a knot. The Arabs had what Severin calls an encyclopedic knowledge of the constellations and the movement of the stars and did not need the Pole Star to calculate latitude. The best Arab captains could navigate out of sight of land but they could not calculate longitude as could their ancient forebears. (Severin, Sindbad, 91-4)

The Ancient Irish Oxhide Boat

The Arab ocean voyages to Asia were the result of the founding of **Islam** in the early **A.D. 600s**. and its **conquering spirit** which drove the new converts to win lands and trade routes from Morocco and Spain, to the Middle East and Central Asia, to Zanzibar, India, Indonesia, and Hong Kong. (Severin, Sindbad, 15-16) These zealous campaigns would lead both to the further **destruction and loss of many ancient records**, as well as to the **continuance and preservation of certain portions of ancient knowledge**. Meanwhile, in Europe, a century or so earlier, Irish Catholic monks are said to have voyaged throughout the North Atlantic, not in wooden ships but in oxhide-covered *curraghs*.

St. Brendan and the Irish Monks

In the **A.D. 700s and 800s**, as the Norsemen ventured out to find the Faroe, Shetland, and

Orkney Islands and Iceland, in each place they found the **Irish** there before them! Christianity reached Ireland in the 400s, but apocryphal doctrines of extremism such as celibacy, denial of the flesh, the innate evil of the material world, enforced poverty and isolation, and even self abuse inspired a number of people to become **monks**, whether alone or in a monastery. Sailing the sea provided a naturally ascetic, physically taxing way of avoiding fleshly temptations while fulfilling the Irish love for the sea. *Settling on newly discovered and remote islands in the North Atlantic* also provided opportunity for self-denial as well as escape from the long arm of the Roman popes who, in the middle 400s, began to assert their absolute authority over all Christians, including the independent-minded Irish. In the 600s to 800s, the steady encroachment of **hostile, marauding Vikings** offered another incentive for farther-flung Irish voyages. (Roberts, Generations, 71-78; Morison, European North, 13-14, 25; Landström, Voyages, 70-1; Pyle, Remains, 65)

Irish monastic records and the journal of **St. Brendan**, called *Navigatio Sancti. Brendani Abbatis*, provided medieval Europe with its most popular and fanciful tale of religion and adventure, the seven-year voyage of St. Brendan and 18 fellow monks (one died to leave 17). Their little **curragh** took them to an isle of huge white sheep, the Paradise of Birds, the Isle of Grapes, and other locations where they encountered an array of biblical and mythical personalities, including Jasconius the whale which they took to be a treeless, black island upon which they landed. They saw fire-hurtling demons and a floating crystal palace (volcano and iceberg?).

St. Brendan was inspired to undertake his journey by the testimony of the **Abbot Barinth** who said that his son **Mernoc** had sailed westward and found a "delicious island" full of Irish monks and the "Promised Land of the Saints," a floral paradise. The Abbot accompanied his son on a repeat journey which included the 40-day return from the **"Promised Land."** Brendan and his crew also reached the Promised Land, but were told to leave and return home because it would not be opened until all peoples were converted.

St. Brendan was indeed a historical figure, dating perhaps from **484 to 577** (or maybe 490 to 583). and many scholars now firmly believe that he made more than one voyage, that he did reach **Newfoundland**, that he may well have been preceded by others, and was obviously followed by other Irishmen who have left evidence of their settlements from Newfoundland to **West Virginia**. Harvard's Dr. Barry Fell notes the Irish monastic records which tell of **two voyages** made by St. Brendan during the reign of **Pope Pelagius (555-561)** on which he *discovered a land far to the west*. In 1983, Fell translated a number of ancient **Irish Ogam** inscriptions found in West Virginia. (Pyle, Remains, 60-67; Morison, European North, 13-28; Landström, Voyages,

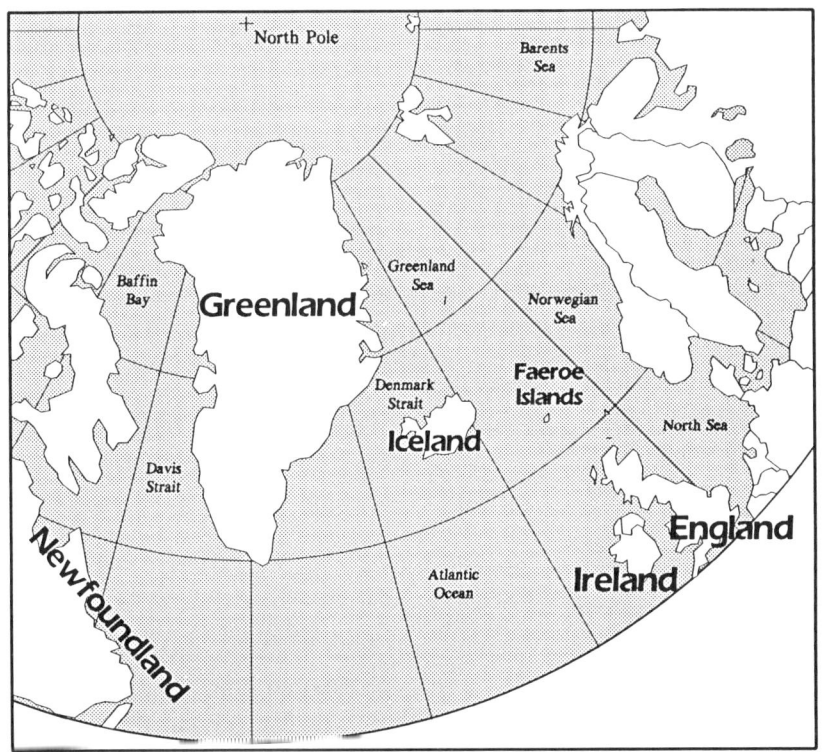

Ancient Ocean Vessels and Global Navigation

70-3)"

The same inscriptions have also been authenticated by **Dr. Robert T. Meyer**, professor of Celtic studies at the Catholic University of America, Washington, D.C. Dr. Meyer identified the **petroglyphs** as "very archaic Old Irish" Ogam which he dated to be from the 500s to 600s. "'This for Celtic scholars,'" said Dr. Meyer in a West Virginia Public Television interview, "'is probably at least as important as the discovery of the Dead Sea scrolls, I think. Because it shows that Irish monks, I suppose, came here — I would say, about 1500 years ago.'" "'Do you feel very certain about that?'" asked the interviewer. "'Yes,'" replied the professor, because "'this gives us examples of complete sentences disclosing the use of a regular Celtic-type syntax'" and "'really archaic forms as, for example, that phrase, *oin Dia*, which means 'one God.' This is even older and more antique archaic than classical Latin, which would have read *unus Deus*.'" (Pyle, Remains, 63-4, italics added; Fell, America, 338)

In *America B.C.*, which he originally published in 1976, Dr. Fell describes the **Irish oxhide curragh** (or "coracle") as a fragile vessel which could only have made channel crossings in calm weather and could never have carried anyone safely across the stormy North Atlantic. He considers St. Brendan merely a tradition, but believes instead that the 7th-Century Irish must have acquired a fleet of ships and hired sailors and looked to the western ocean "as their [Celtiberian] ancestors had done a thousand years before, as a possible means of access to lands more peaceful than ravaged Europe."

But, on the other hand, Fell admits that the manuscripts of early and late medieval Ireland show only small and large versions of the oxhide curragh. Though seemingly puzzled by this, Dr. Fell points to an **Ogam inscription** discovered in **Newfoundland** by **Dr. Robert McGhee**, professor of archaeology at Memorial University, and concludes that future finds may evidence a "later phase of Celtic seamanship," meaning Atlantic crossings by early medieval Irish (500s to 800s). Dr. Fell updated his 1976 book for a new 1989 release in which he cited his 1983 translation of the West Virginia medieval Irish Ogam inscriptions. Perhaps after Tim Severin's 1976-77 voyage and the 1980s medieval Ogam finds, Dr. Fell has a different view of the Irish and their curraghs. (Fell, America, 113, 121, 338)

Professor Morison came to agree that there is ample evidence to conclude that St. Brendan and other Irishmen sailed to the North Atlantic isles, including Iceland and possibly as far south and west as the Azores, but he remained adamant that no Irish had reached American shores because, as he wrote in 1970, "As yet, not one early Irish artifact has been found in North America." (Morison, European North, 28) The **Admiral died in 1976**, the year of the initial publication of another Harvard professor, Dr. Barry Fell's *America B.C.*, and too soon to know of Tim Severin's successful duplication of St. Brendan's trip in an ancient Irish oxhide boat, or the medieval Irish Ogam finds of the 1980s. Perhaps with another few years, the staunchly traditionalist historian would have finally been convinced. [Read as much of Morison as you can. He was a renowned historian, marvelous writer, and knowledgeable seaman. Just be ever cognizant of his non-Bible-believing bias and resulting limitations. One of the main purposes of *this* book is to provide a biblical context with which to approach worthwhile secular or semi-secular historians.]

In our next volume, we will examine the Celtic artifacts and Ogam inscriptions left in America by the ancient Celts and early medieval Irish monks, as well as the Norse sagas that indicate the presence of Irish people in Newfoundland from the 800s to 1200s. We will consider the Icelandic saga of the 1200s which says that "'Ari was driven out to sea to Hvitramannaland which many call Great Ireland. It lies to the west in the sea near **Vinland the Good**.'" (Landström, Voyages, 73; Pyle, Remains, 65-6) However, at present, we are interested in the boat used by the Irish, its construction and its seaworthiness.

Severin and the Voyage of *Brendan*

St. Brendan himself wrote that the monks constructed "'a very light little vessel, ribbed and sided with wood, but ... covered with oak-tanned oxhides and caulked with ox-tallow.'" The Irish made do with what they had, explains Professor Morison, in a land where timber was scarce and cattle were plentiful. (Morison, European North, 16) **Tim Severin**, the English sailor and expert in medieval Asian exploration, is an Irish resident. Both he and his wife *saw reality through the miraculous haze of the St. Brendan legend* and Severin determined to replicate the **ancient Irish, oxhide curragh** and duplicate the **voyage** of St. Brendan from **Ireland to Newfoundland**.

As he would be in his later Arab adventure, Severin was **discouraged by the "experts"** who believed that a leather boat would disintegrate. Modern curraghs used for fishing are covered with tarred canvas, though Severin discovered firsthand with the sailors of County Kerry that they "are true sea boats, not merely inshore skiffs." (Severin, Brendan, NG, 772-5) What is interesting is that this is *another type of lashed and stitched boat!* The wooden frame is a light lattice work of straight-grained ash laths. For the **36-foot by 8-foot** *Brendan*, Severin and a variety of *real* experts used two miles of alum-tanned thongs to bind the hull's framework. Forty-nine oxhides were tanned in oak bark and formed into a hull by some 20,000 stitches of hand-rolled, 14-strand flax thread. The wood and leather were coated with wool grease which provided a waterproof environment with a "stench no human body could equal." (Severin, Brendan, NG, 774-7)

The **five-man crew** were all experienced as this was **no forgiving craft** like the ancient wash-through, bundled-reed boats. One misstep could take a crewman overboard and, because it drew only one foot of water, the curragh could *not* tack into the wind. (Severin, Brendan, NG, 776, 783) Long-ago monks had relied on a larger crew of **rowers**. The ancient craft of the warmer waters in the Mediterranean and the oceans between the Tropics of Cancer and Capricorn were capable of sophisticated navigation as well as carrying impressive loads of cargo. Was the Irish oxhide curragh representative of a deterioration in maritime knowledge, or merely a specific adaptation to the limitations of available materials and forbidding weather? *The Irishmen and their curraghs were obviously able to negotiate their way back to Ireland, as St. Brendan did, even though their craft could not sail upwind.*

Over the course of the trip, Severin and his fellow sailors discovered more of the **wisdom of the ancients** in the sense that modern **tools and materials** made from plastic and metal were not able to withstand the elements as were "primitive" materials like wood, flax, and leather. The crew also abandoned their modern artificial-fiber outerwear for "old-fashioned woolen clothes with their insulation of natural oils." Also, mistakenly, they began with leather sails which became waterlogged and so they switched to sails woven out of Irish flax. (Severin, Brendan, NG, 777, 783)

The voyage began on **May 17, 1976** from southwest **Ireland**, where Brendan himself is reputed to have launched. There were stops in the Scottish Islands and in the Faroes. The *Brendan* arrived in **Iceland** on **July 17** and the boat **wintered** there until early **May 1977** when the crew continued on the famous "stepping-stone" route, "the shortest way between the Old World and the New. It is the route followed today by transatlantic jets, in the past by the Vikings, and almost surely by any Irish monks." (Severin, Brendan, NG, 775, 778, 787)

They rounded the southern tip of **Greenland** on **May 29** and, after some rather harrowing adventures through which the *Brendan* proved the genius of its flexible, waterproof construction, the crew arrived at **Peckford Island, Newfoundland** in late **June, 1977**. The boat had been six weeks on the sea and traveled over **3,500 miles** of ocean without losing one lashing or one stitch. The boat was still seaworthy in 1983 and is kept at Craggaunowen, Ireland. (Severin, Brendan, NG, 774, 787-90; Pyle, Remains, 67)

Knowledge of Ancient Boats and Boat Size

There is really **so much we don't know about** ancient boats and ships and maritime trading and transportation. "Maverick" researchers such as Heyerdahl, Severin, Fell, Savoy, and Landström have made singular and significant contributions to the study of truly ancient shipping. **Roger Charles Anderson** admits that "comparatively little is known of the ships of the Cretans," or of the Phoenicians, and that the multi-banked galleys of the Mediterranean are "still to be satisfactorily explained." Much controversy remains, adds Anderson, who states that it is still unknown from where or how the Greeks and their predecessors "evolved" their "advanced" methods of ship construction. Greek ships, he says, were very much like modern carvel-built ships, with a frame of keel, stem, sternpost, and ribs and a smooth hull attached plank by plank to the frame. It is "guessed" that the stern rudder was first introduced in northern European ships in the late 1100s. (EB, 1972, 20:401)

Even much about medieval and Renaissance European shipping remains a mystery. Morison writes that the task of detailing the ships of the European explorers "with any degree of accuracy" is "difficult if not impossible." **Scarcely any records** exist that describe English ships of the late 1400s, though a little more is known of French and Venetian (Venice, Italy) vessels. Morison points out that **artists' drawings** of the time, on which much of our knowledge rests, are often not accurate, and that illustrations are rare of northern boats of the 15th Century. (Morison, European North, 112, 118-9)

Landström, an artist as well as author and researcher, complains that 15th- and 16th-Century illustrators and artists portrayed the ships, clothes, and backgrounds of earlier explorers much as they did their paintings of Christ, putting their subjects into the time period in which they themselves painted. Even when painting or drawing their own era, these artists knew generally what a ship looked like, but were not concerned with depicting the details of individual ships. (Landström, Voyages, 9; Morison, European North, 118-9) As for how early European explorers handled their ships in storms or contrary seas and how the ships performed, there is almost nothing in the way of data, says Morison. (Morison, European North, 124)

An interesting newsbrief in the July/August 1993 issue of *Archaeology* magazine notes the discovery of a Greek cargo ship off the Aegean Sea isle of Alonisos. It is believed that the ship sank between 400 and 380 B.C. and that the ship was as long as 85 feet and as wide as 35 feet. "Until now," writes the publication's managing editor, "it was believed that ships this large had not been built until the first century B.C." ("Vintage Wreck," in "Newsbriefs," *Archaeology*, July/August 1993, p. 21)

However, as Dr. Fell points out, we have seen that the ancients were capable of building ships as long as 180 feet, not to mention the Ark. Comparing ancient with medieval times, Fell notes that, in 1492, Columbus needed three ships, two of which were only 50 feet long, to carry only 88 men. In Egypt around 1200 B.C., says Fell, the Rameses pharaohs could ship 10,000 miners across the Indian Ocean to southern Africa or to Sumatra, Indonesia. (Fell, America, 110) But Columbus did not have small ships because the Europeans were suddenly unable to build anything bigger.

The **Europeans**, perhaps the Portuguese, took ships from one mast to three in a major shipbuilding leap in the early 1400s. Anderson says that there was a brief two-masted stage, but by about 1435, the three-master was the standard. In 1419, Henry V built a ship that was 186 feet long and 46 feet wide. The *Grace Dieu* of 1418 was even bigger, so that the Europeans were certainly **capable of building large ships**. However, **ship size decreased for a time** after these first "monsters," probably due to matters of money, labor, and seaworthiness. The early explorers were not given the best ships. They were exploring and not carrying cargo, and they found that the smaller ships were better for handling and safety. Heyerdahl affirms that, with "aboriginal watercraft," it is also true that safety does not increase according to the size of the boat or ship and that, up to a point, smaller is better. Thus, the Irish curraghs, papyriform boats, and Egyptian reed boats of 30 feet or less were safer in many ways than the Spanish caravels. (EB, 1972, 20:402-3; Morison, European North, 114; Heyerdahl, Ocean, 32)

Isles of the Gentiles

Sing to the Lord a new song, his praise from the ends of the [E]arth, you who go down to the sea, and all that is in it, you **islands**, and all who live in them," enjoins Isaiah the prophet. (Isa. 42:10, NIV) The editors of the New Scofield version substitute the word *coasts* for the *isles* used in the King James.

In this Millennial section of Isaiah, the prophet refers a number of times to the "isles" (KJV) or "coasts" (NIV) that wait upon the Lord, that fear and obey the Lord, in the context of the **"ends of the Earth."** (Isa. 41:5, 9; 51:5; 66:19) The word translated as isles, coasts, or coastlands comes from a Hebrew root signifying *desirable*, as in a *desirable habitation or country*. These "isles," says **J. Vernon McGee**, are "all the **continents** which are inhabited by the human family," referring to all mankind. (McGee, Thru, III:307, 403)

The "isles of the Gentiles" in the KJV of Genesis 10:5 is changed in the Scofield to "the borders of the nations." In Jeremiah 25:22-26, the "kings of the **coastlands across the sea**" (NIV) are referred to in the context of **all the kingdoms of the world**, upon the face of all the Earth. Jeremiah 31:10 speaks of the "distant coastlands" (isles). In his study of Ezekiel, **Dr. Charles Dye**r writes that the "coastlands" mentioned in God's judgment upon Tyre (Chaps. 26 & 27) imply the farthest reaches of the known world. (Dyer, "Ezekiel," BKC I, 1301)

Professor Cyrus Gordon notes that, in a work titled *Meropis*, **Theopompus of Chios** (300s B.C.) wrote of a continent beyond Africa and islands of the ocean that had cities. The "Old Mediterranean people," explains Gordon, "used the term 'island' to mean **any land mass that can be reached by sea**–even huge **continents**–as is natural for mariners who, on reaching some shore, cannot tell whether they have come to a large island or a whole continent." (Gordon, Before, 38, 193)

Thus, the Bible *does* refer to the Americas and to all of the world's continents, even as the post-Babel gentiles dispersed across the face of the Earth. And, it continues to refer to these continents in the prophecies of the Old Testament. In our next volume, we will follow the new nations with their new tongues, as they came from Babel and crossed the oceans, bringing their knowledge, beliefs, and technology to the new "isles" of the Americas.

BIBLIOGRAPHY

Beaglehole, J.C., *The Exploration of the Pacific.* Stanford: Stanford Univ. Press, 1966.

Berlitz, Charles, *Mysteries From Forgotten Worlds.* New York: Doubleday & Co., 1972.

Casson, Lionel, *The Ancient Mariners.* New York: The Macmillan Company, 1959.

Cornell, James, *The First Stargazers*, Bib. Chap. 10, p. 194.

De Santillana, Giorgio, and **Von Dechend,** Hertha, *Hamlet's Mill*, Bib. Chap. 7, p. 108.

Drury, Nevill, *Dictionary of Mysticism and the Occult,* Bib. Chap. 2, p. 37.

Dyer, Charles H., "Ezekiel," *The Bible Knowledge Commentary, Old Testament (I)*, Bib. Chap. 4, p. 65.

Encyclopaedia Britannica (EB), Bib. Chap. 3, p. 51.

Fell, Barry, *America B.C.*, Bib. Chap. 6, p. 91.

_____, *Bronze Age America*, Bib. Chap. 6, p. 91.

Finegan, Jack, *Light From the Ancient Past*, Vol. I (paperback). Princeton: Princeton Univ. Press, 1969.

Gordon, Cyrus H., *Before Columbus*, Bib. Chap. 4, p. 65.

Hadingham, Evan, *Early Man and the Cosmos*, Bib. Chap. 10, p. 194

Hapgood, Charles H., *Maps of the Ancient Sea Kings*. Philadelphia: Chilton Company, 1966. *Revised edition*, New York: E. P. Dutton, 1979.

Heyerdahl, Thor, *Early Man and the Ocean*, Bib. Chap. 9, p. 160.

_____, *The Tigris Expedition*. New York: Doubleday & Co., 1981.

_____, *The Ra Expeditions*. New York: Doubleday & Co., 1971.

_____, *Kon-Tiki*. Rand, 1960.

Hislop, Alexander, *The Two Babylons*, Bib. Chap. 4, p. 65.

Jairazbhoy, R.A., *Ancient Egyptians and Chinese in America*, Bib. Chap. 6, p. 91.

Johnston, Thomas Crawford, *Did the Phoenicians Discover America?*, Bib. Chap. 8, 140.

Krupp, E.C. (ed.), *In Search of Ancient Astronomies*. New York: Doubleday & Co., 1977.

Landström, Björn, *Bold Voyages and Great Explorers*. New York: Doubleday & Co., Inc., 1964.

Mallery, Arlington, and Harrison, Mary Roberts, *The Rediscovery of Lost America*. New York: E. P. Dutton, 1979.

McGee, J. Vernon, *Thru the Bible*, Bib. Chap. 4, p. 66.

McKern, Sharon S., *Exploring the Unknown*, Bib. Chap. 2, p. 37.

Morison, Samuel Eliot, *The European Discovery of America, The Northern Voyages.* New York: Oxford Univ. Press, 1971.

Pritchard, James B. (ed.), *The Ancient Near East*, Bib. Chap. 5, p. 80.

Pyle, Robert L., *All That Remains.* Charleston, WV: Cannon Graphics, Inc., 1991. [418 Lehigh Terrace, Charleston, WV 25302.

Roberts, Frank C., *To All Generations, A Study of Church History.* Grand Rapids: Bible Way, 1981. [Christian Reformed Church]

Savoy, Gene, *On the Trail of the Feathered Serpent.* New York: The Bobbs-Merrill Co., Inc., 1974.

Scofield, C. I. (ed.), *The New Scofield Reference Bible*, Bib. Chap. 2, p. 38.

Severin, Tim, *The Sindbad Voyage.* New York: G.P. Putnam's Sons, 1983.

_____, Timothy, "The Voyage of 'Brendan,'" *National Geographic*, December 1977, pp. 769-797

Timetables of History (Grun), Bib. Chap. 7, p. 108.

Tompkins, Peter, *Secrets of the Great Pyramid*, Bib. Chap. 8, p. 140

Webber, David, and Hutchings, N.W., *New Light on the Great Pyramid*, Bib. Chap. 10, p. 195.

Webster's New World Dictionary, Bib. Chap. 2, p. 38.

White, John, *Pole Shift.* Garden City, NY: Doubleday & Co., Inc., 1980.

World's Last Mysteries, The, Bib. Chap. 10, p. 195.

Young's Literal Translation of the Holy Bible, Bib. Chap. 4, p. 66.

Zondervan Pictorial Bible Dictionary, Bib. Chap. 4, p. 66.

Be a Berean!

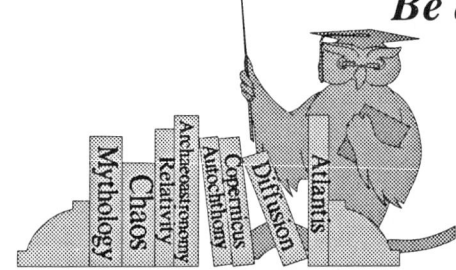

We encourage you to pursue your own studies in the many subjects examined in this book. And we urge you to look up in the library, or to purchase, many of the sources used in our study.

Peter Tompkins books on the Middle Eastern and American pyramids are marvelously illustrated and packed with interesting stories and facts. Both are available in paperback. Thor Heyerdahl's books are easy, entertaining, and educational to read. So are the works by Tim Severin and Gene Savoy. All have plenty of fascinating photographs. It's so much more interesting to read high adventure stories that are true.

Björn Landström's book on ancient ships is beautifully illustrated. Dr. Fell's America B.C. is available in paperback and well worth owning.

If you are interested, become a subscriber to the Biblical Astronomer (see the Bibliographies for the address). The works by E.W. Bullinger and by Alexander Hislop can be found at, or ordered through, your local Christian bookstore.

We would be greatly excited to have you share with us the results of your own research efforts, or your own thoughts on any of the questions we raise.

May this work further strengthen your confidence in the absolute infallibility and comprehensive teachings of the Bible, and may your biblical glasses improve your focus on the amazing plan of our Great God.

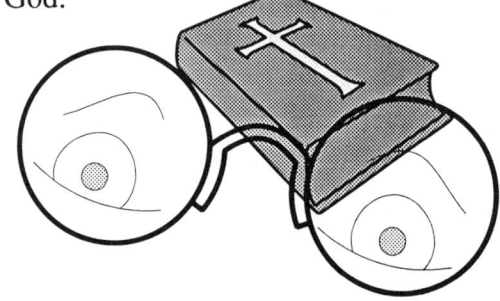

INDEX

A

Abraham 6, 23, 30, 57, 83, 179
Adam 3-5, 7-8, 22, 33, 36, 40, 56, 71, 74-75, 98-99, 109, 133, 142
Adonis 91, 98, 113
Ages 144, 211
  Bronze 33
  Iron 33
  Stone 33, 56, 206
Airplane 207
Alexander the Great 199, 202
Alexandria, Egypt 199, 202
Angels
  Fallen 4, 34-35, 71, 76, 94, 109, 117, 186, 193
  stars 5
  Unfallen 4
Antarctica 207, 209
Antichrist. *See* Messiah: False
Aphrodite 134
Apollo 89
Aquarian 73
Aquarius 18, 111, 114, 134, 136, 138
Archaeoastronomy 157, 166, 172, 187, 217
Aries 111, 112, 114, 134, 136, 191
Aryan 73
Ashtoreth 104
Astarte 102, 103
Astronomy 109
Atlantis (pre-Flood world) 71-73, 99, 117, 182, 201
Atlas 76, 84
Atomism 143
Autochthonism 21, 153, 225
Aztecs 11, 121, 174, 183, 201

B

Baal 70, 84
Babylon 64, 70, 73, 76, 81, 90, 93, 107, 109, 136, 167, 173, 197, 199, 212, 220
Bacchus 82, 91, 106
Bailey, Alice 73, 94, 96, 97, 136, 137, 138
Balder 91
Balsa raft 224, 225
Bel 70
Belus 82
Big Bang theory 146
Birth of Christ. *See* Messiah: True: birth
Black holes 8, 147
Black Plague 13, 200
Blavatsky, Helena 73, 94
Brahe, Tycho 124, 125

C

Calendar change 10, 29, 34, 101, 119, 177, 179, 182
Canaan 61, 62, 79
Cancer 119
Canopy. *See* Earth: canopy
Capricorn 74, 119, 133
Catastrophism 4, 9, 10, 41, 48, 116, 211
Chaos theory 12, 14, 150
Christmas 98, 104, 113, 117
Church
  Bride of Christ 4
  mystery 4
Classical physics 152
Climate
  post-Flood 8, 45, 52, 56, 58, 181, 189, 211, 221
  pre-Flood 7, 42
Columbus, Christopher 155, 221, 239
Compass 217
Constellations 44, 110
Continents 63, 77, 239
  separation 9, 40, 48, 60, 65, 77
Copernican Revolution 143
Copernicus 15, 122, 123, 143, 202
Craftsman God 99, 117
Currents, Ocean 156, 158, 214, 224
Cush 61-62, 68-70, 72, 78, 81, 119, 162
Cyclops 100

D

Dagon 75
Darwin, Charles 144
Darwinian Revolution 144, 201
Diana 82, 103, 106
Diffusionism 37, 119, 152, 158, 212
Dinosaurs 7, 8, 43, 57, 145, 192
Diphues 95

Dippers
  Big   112, 132, 135, 188
  Little   115, 135
Draco the Dragon   84, 111-112, 115, 130-133, 188
Druids   94

E

Earth
  age   1, 4, 21, 22, 24, 28, 29, 30
  and Lucifer   4, 6, 143
  axis   44, 48, 114, 116-119, 131, 176, 211
  canopy   6-7, 42, 44, 48, 50, 56, 110, 145
  capitalization   2
  circumference   163, 167, 170, 174, 189, 202
  cursed   4, 6-8
  geocentricity   10, 15, 44, 122, 143, 164, 202
  new heavens and Earth   9, 130
  reformed   6
  round   156, 161
Ecliptic   44, 111, 113, 117-118, 132, 162
Eden   6, 33, 40, 65, 99, 120, 139, 162
Egyptian bondage   29, 30, 229
Einstein   12, 15, 28, 124, 126, 145, 183
Enoch   109, 115, 185, 192, 193
Enuma Elish   84, 97, 119
Equinox   98, 101, 113-115, 136, 188, 191
Eratosthenes   163, 199, 202
Eve, common ancestor   55, 154
Evolution   15
Exodus   10, 180, 182, 198, 213, 229

F

Fell, Barry   156
Frigga   91

G

Gaia   100
Galileo   125
Genealogies, Biblical   22, 32
Gilgamesh Epic   97, 197

H

Ham   61, 63, 68-72, 79
Hapgood, Charles   208
Hatshepsut   228-231
Heliocentricity   122, 143, 202
Hercules   88

Hermes   70, 119
Heyerdahl, Thor   156, 158, 182, 189, 215, 223
Historical periods   161
Horus   89
Humanism   12
Hyksos   192, 229

I

Ice ages   21, 45, 48-49, 165, 208, 211-212
Inca   47, 179, 201
Indus Valley   10, 181, 198, 219, 223
Infant baptism   95
Ishtar   104
Isis   89, 104
Isles   239. *See also* Continents

J

Janus   70, 75
Japheth   61, 62, 63
Job   57, 99, 112, 192
Joshua's "Long Day"   10, 29, 42, 131, 181-184
Judgment or Gap Theory   7
Jupiter   117

K

Kepler, Johannes   124
Kon-Tiki   158, 216, 224
Kronos   99, 117, 119

L

Land bridge   21, 41, 153, 155
Leo   136, 188, 190
Light, speed   15, 22, 28, 118, 146
Lucifer (Satan)   4-7, 16-17, 34-35, 58, 71, 73, 83, 93, 98, 105, 115-116, 130, 136, 139, 151

M

Mach, Ernst   129
Mallery, Arlington   201, 206, 209
Mammoths   8, 42, 45, 59
Man
  cursed   10, 12, 71, 85
  intelligence   32, 36, 212, 216, 238
  life span   8, 9, 24, 56, 57, 64, 85, 110
Manetho   79
Maps, ancient   165, 202
  Greenland   50, 165, 206, 207, 209

Hadji Ahmed   209
Hamy-King chart   210
Iceland   50, 209
lat/long   164, 167, 169, 171-172, 196, 203, 210
Oronteus Finaeus   209
Piri Re'is   202, 205, 208
Portolan charts   203, 210
Zeno map   209
Marduk   84, 117, 119, 120
Mars   8, 10, 34-35, 77, 98, 100, 117, 183-184
Masonry   16, 17, 74, 94, 95, 176, 193
Maya   119, 132, 174, 178, 183-184, 201, 217
Menes   78, 79
Mercator   173-174, 203
Mercury   70
Messiah
  False   72, 74-75, 82, 86, 88, 93, 98-99, 104, 117, 132, 136
  True   27, 86, 88, 104, 117, 132, 139, 190
    birth   24, 25, 29, 113
    Child   4, 34, 83
Millennium   3, 9, 25, 27, 87, 99, 121, 134, 139, 212
Mizraim   61, 62, 78, 79, 193, 219
Molech   104, 105
Moloch   82
Morison, Samuel Eliot   155, 163, 215, 237
Mormonism   16
Mother goddess   103
Mystery system   16-17, 89, 93, 116, 158, 162, 166, 193, 198

N

Nazca   86
New Age   15, 17, 73, 95-96, 100, 114, 136, 139, 176
Newton, Sir Isaac   114, 123, 126, 150, 178
Nimrod   23, 69-70, 74, 76, 78, 79, 81, 85, 87, 93, 96, 113, 117, 119, 121, 132, 134-135, 162, 188, 191, 198, 217, 219
Ninus   70, 82
Noah   8, 23, 33, 36, 55, 60, 62, 64, 68, 72, 74-75, 95, 97, 109, 117, 133, 162, 217-218
  Ark   34, 55, 61, 218, 220, 239
North Pole   115, 118, 172, 209, 213
North Star   172, 187
Numbers, special

twelve   112, 120
52   183
seven   25, 28, 30, 168, 179, 180
six   25, 168, 179, 180

O

Oannes   74, 217
Occult   17, 34, 73, 95, 138, 166, 184, 194
Odin   91
Ogam   236, 237
Olmecs   182, 184, 201
Ops   100
Orion   111-112, 135, 188, 191
Osiris   89, 91
Ouranos   100, 101
Oxhide boat   237

P

Pan   74
Papyriform vessels   226, 232
Pegasus   134, 196
Peleg   9, 41, 74, 77, 115, 161, 192
Phi   166, 168
Phoroneus   82
Pi   166
Pisces   111, 114, 134, 136, 137, 196
Pleiades   90, 112, 115, 183, 187
Polaris   115
Precession of the equinoxes   11, 101, 112-117, 136, 162, 187, 197
Ptolemy   122, 124, 143, 164, 199, 202
Put   62, 79
Pyramids
  Great   115, 159, 165, 173-176, 184, 191, 197-198, 202-203, 217, 226
  Mars   35
  stepped   76, 78, 172, 174
Pythagoras   162, 164

Q

Quantum theory   12, 13, 16, 28, 74, 148
Quetzalcoatl   86, 174

R

Radiometric dating   8, 10, 14
Reasoning
  Deductive   2
  inductive   1
Reductionism   151

Index   Page 243

Reed boat   158, 189, 218-221, 225
Relativity   145
Renaissance   13
Rhea   99
Roman Empire   64

S

Sagittarius   81, 133
Saturn   98, 99, 117, 119
Savoy, Gene   153, 221, 225
Semiramis   82, 87, 93, 100-101, 104, 132, 191
Seth   68, 73, 83, 88, 109, 115, 134, 185
Severin, Tim   234, 237
Sewn Wood Ships   227, 233
Shem   23, 56-57, 61, 63, 68, 73, 78, 83, 87-88, 99, 117, 121, 162, 191
Shinar   65, 70, 72, 81
Sodom and Gomorrah   198
Solstice   98, 106, 113, 117, 191
South Pole   121
Sphinx   35, 121, 132, 188, 190, 193
St. Brendan   236-237
Stonehenge   94
Swastika   107

T

Tammuz   90, 98, 100, 106, 113, 121
Taurus   111, 114, 135-136, 191
Thermodynamics, First Law   11
Thermodynamics, Second Law   7, 11-12
Thuban   115, 187
Time   5, 11, 15, 101, 116, 146, 172
Titan   90, 99, 117, 185
Titicaca, Lake   47, 91, 223

Tower of Babel   9, 16, 23, 41, 60, 65, 69, 72, 74, 76, 78, 87, 139, 173, 179, 198
Tribulation   9, 25, 107, 191
Tropics   119, 216
   Cancer   112, 135, 174, 197, 205
   Capricorn   113
Typhon   89, 134
Tyre   199, 210

U

UFOs   7, 14, 72, 159, 189
Uniformism   4, 10, 14, 29, 41, 144, 159
Ussher, James   24, 29

V

Velikovsky, Immanuel   183
Venus   10, 36, 90, 101, 117, 123, 183-184
Vikings   155-156, 201, 206, 227, 236-237
Virgo   111, 122, 132, 188, 190
Vishnu   75
Vitalism   151

W

Wat-yune   91
Weeping sun god   91
Witchcraft   95
Wodan   91

Z

Zeus   84, 99, 100, 134
Zodiac   11, 44, 109-110, 119, 132, 191, 219
   Dendera   111, 120, 132, 197
Zoroaster   100

AUTHOR: The author earned a B.A. in Humanities and completed graduate course work in History. After a number of years as creative director for an advertising agency, she wrote and produced programming for cable television, edited a national trade journal, wrote for a national business publication, and worked for a publishing firm dedicated to political, historical, and demographic research and writing. She currently lives with her husband in Texas.

For information regarding this book, contact:

New Works Distribution Center
Box 637
Rockwall, Texas   75087-0637